THE SWEEP OF AMERICAN HISTORY

THE SWEEP
OF AMERICAN
HISTORY

Volume I

EDITED BY   Ivers

ROBERT R. JONES

University of Southwestern Louisiana

GUSTAV L. SELIGMANN, JR.

North Texas State University

JOHN WILEY & SONS, INC.

New York · London · Sydney · Toronto

TO

Our wives, Pat and Janelle,
and our children, Tricia,
Bobby, Tommy, and Amy

PREFACE

One of history's most valuable lessons is that events often do not follow human plans. Such is the case, in a sense, with this collection of readings. Several years ago, we began work on this collection simply to improve our basic American history survey courses and without the intention of producing a book. However, once the collection had been made, we concluded that, if published, it would meet a basic need in the teaching of United States history.

We do not claim that this is the best collection of readings in American history, nor that it is the most imaginative, nor the most entertaining. But, in our opinion, these two volumes are unique in this field. We believe strongly that they are more than simply collections of readings; they are, to us, histories of the United States (in an admittedly unusual form) from European beginnings to the present day.

Our purpose is to provide a selection of readings that gives a comprehensive coverage of United States history on a basic survey level. This volume contains 40 major topics, arranged in chronological order, with a single reading on each topic. This format provides approximately a topic per class period in a normal semester. An introductory essay to each reading links the topics, places the reading in proper historical perspective, and suggests key points, questions, and additional bibliography for the student's consideration. In selecting the readings, we consciously avoided the specialized and sophisticated studies that appear in professional historical and scholarly journals. Most of the selections were made from broad historical syntheses or from historical monographs. All of the readings, we believe, are suited to the level of students in college survey courses. A few of the readings are primarily descriptive and narrative, but most of them combine these elements with a broadly interpretive approach that should help make history understandable to the freshman and sophomore student. Although several selections have been made from old classics, most of them represent the most recent scholarship. Their authors are among the most talented writers in their profession.

This book is based on one educational premise: the use of material to supplement the text and/or the lecture is generally valuable in the learning experience. We do not claim that the material here constitutes the only material to use in this connection; we do not suggest that readings in primary source materials or readings from secondary sources, arranged in patterns, themes, or problems, are not useful. We do believe that the readings in these two volumes can be used quite effectively in the teaching of American history. They can be used (1) as a substitute for the lecture in a discussion-oriented class, (2) as a substitute for the text, or (3) simply as supplementary reading in a normal lecture class. They also can be used in the lecture-discussion group arrangement of many large colleges, with the weekly discussion based on several of the readings in a particular chronological period; or they might be used in conjunction with other types of supplementary readings (for example, documents or monographic literature). In any event, this collection will introduce the survey student to various approaches to and different interpretations of United States history, bringing him into contact with a great deal of the best history being written.

We thank Frank Shelton and Matt Hodgson for encouragement and advice in the early stages of our project. We are grateful to the administrations of our respective universities and, particularly, to the Faculty Research Committee of North Texas State University for a grant that aided us in the earlier stages of this project.

We are most appreciative of the cooperation and aid of our colleagues, Professors James H. Dormon, Henry C. Dethloff, and Donald K. Pickins, who read parts of the manuscripts and made helpful suggestions in specific areas. Special thanks are due to Professor R. Jackson Wilson of Smith College for his constructive critique of our project; Miss Patricia Hickman and Mrs. Laura Whitelaw of North Texas State University for their help in many of the more mundane tasks of coordinating our efforts; and William L. Gum and the staff at Wiley for guiding us firmly but gently through the various stages of publication. Finally, we thank all of the teachers and colleagues who may, perhaps in some unknown way, have helped to make these volumes a contribution to the teaching of history.

Robert R. Jones
G. L. Seligmann, Jr.

CONTENTS

THE SWEEP OF AMERICAN HISTORY

CHAPTER 1

THE EUROPEAN
BACKGROUND

Two of the most common questions that the historian asks of the past
are: How did an event happen? Why did an event happen? Of these
two questions the "How" of the past is generally the easier to answer.
If H. Trevor Roper had set out to answer the question "How was the
New World discovered?" he would have given us an account of the southern voyages of the Portuguese as they pushed back the frontiers of geographic knowledge; he would have followed this with the epic of Columbus's several voyages, and perhaps would have concluded with a
description of Magellan's voyage around the world. This account would
be rich in detail, stirring in excitement, and historically complex when
dealing with the values and motives involved in the decision-making
procedures of the several courts.

As enjoyable to read and as valuable to know as this might be, it is
not what the author set about doing. Hugh Trevor-Roper, instead, has
asked the question: "Why did Europe turn West?" This different question
creates a different kind of history. We now are led into a series of
complex variables such as the nature of public health, the conditions of
land tenure, the economic systems of the several countries, the political
institutions of the time, and a host of other factors. Moreover, these
factors are not only more complicated in and of themselves but also

1

interact with each other in varying degrees. It is not surprising that the most serious historical controversies involve "Why" questions.

In reading this essay, bear in mind the continuing relationship of Europe to the New World. Also ask: If the New World was discovered by the Norsemen in the eleventh century, why did the discovery not "take" until Columbus rediscovered it in the fifteenth century? Is the answer to this question to be found in the changes in the nature of European society? Or is there another explanation?

For more detailed descriptions of Western Europe on the eve of discovery, see Edward P. Cheyney, *The Dawn of a New Era, 1250–1453** (1936), and Myron P. Gilmore, *The World of Humanism, 1453–1517** (1952). For a comprehensive discussion of probable Norse discoveries, R. A. Skelton, Thomas E. Marston, and George D. Painter's book, *The Vinland Map and the Tartar Relation* (1965), is indispensable. *The Vinland Map* and several other works on the same topic are critically reviewed by J. H. Parry in *Perspectives in American History,** Vol. I (1967).

* Available in a paperback edition.

EUROPE TURNS WEST
HUGH TREVOR-ROPER

If we were to take a date to represent the highest point of the European Middle Ages, I suppose that date would be about 1250. Up to that date we see—from about 1050 onwards—only advance. There is growth of population, agricultural revolution, technological advance. The frontiers of Christendom are pushed forward in all directions; new worlds are discovered, and also old; there is a sophistication of manners, a revival of letters. New institutions are founded, both lay and spiritual: on the one hand towns and universities, on the other new orders of improving monks and missionary friars. And meanwhile, within Europe, art and literature are reviving: barbarian Europe has been captured by its more cultivated victims, just as barbarian Rome had been fourteen centuries ago.

However, as history constantly reminds us,

> 'everything that grows
> holds in perfection but a little moment',

and from about 1300 the decline is obvious. Already in the middle of the thirteenth century the territorial expansion had been halted. In 1242 the eastward advance of the Teutonic Knights had been held up by the ruler of the Russian Slavs, Alexander Nevsky. . . . Directly or indirectly, feudalism was yielding to finance. In 1311, nine years after the feudal knights of France had gone down before the Flemish townsmen at Courtrai, a generation before they would go down before the English bowmen at Crécy, the Frankish chivalry of Greece was mown down on the banks of the river Cephisus by the plebian foot-soldiers of the Catalan company. . . .

But if the fourteenth century saw the downfall of European chivalry, it was not easy going for the bankers either. Indeed, in the years from 1300 to 1350 the heavyweight horsemen of the financial world suffered

SOURCE. From *The Rise of Christian Europe* by Hugh Trevor-Roper, pp. 161–164, 166, 168–170, and 172–191. Copyright 1965 by Thames and Hudson. Reprinted by permission of Harcourt, Brace & World, Inc., Thames and Hudson International, Ltd., and the author.

their Courtrai, their Cephisus, their Crécy too. It was half a century of successive bankruptcies. . . .

The financial crisis of the fourteenth century, like that of the early seventeenth century, or that of the nineteen-twenties, was not self-contained. It was part of a general crisis, a crisis of society, and—like those later crises—it marked the end of an age: the great divide between the age of expansion and the age of contraction, the earlier and the later Middle Ages. Moreover, it was accompanied by another, even greater disaster. The year after the collapse of its feudal and financial pillars, Europe, already weakened by a series of famines, was visited by a more general calamity: the Black Death.

The Black Death was bubonic plague, carried by black rats—or rather, by a flea parasitic on black rats—and spread, in favourable circumstances, in crowded, dirty, medieval towns. Once before it had come to Europe. In the sixth century, in the reign of Justinian, corn-ships had brought it to Constantinople, causing, in Gibbon's words, 'a visible decrease of the human species, which has never been repaired in some of the fairest countries of the globe'. In the words of one great authority on the subject, this terrible plague of Justinian's time and the Black Death of the fourteenth century 'are the two greatest pestilences in recorded history; each has no parallel except in the other'. At least they had no parallel when those words were written, in 1890. The earlier plague had come from Egypt, from Pelusium, the great port of entry for the goods of Asia. Perhaps the plague had been brought from Asia too. The Black Death came from Crimean Tartary, and it was from the Genoese station of Caffa in the Crimea, which had suffered a three years' siege by the Tartars, that Genoese ships brought it to Genoa in the spring of 1347. It also came indirectly through Constantinople, which was similarly infected from the Crimea. . . .

The Black Death raged at its worst for three years; but even when the worst was over it still lingered in the soil of Europe. There were five severe secondary outbreaks before 1400. Nor did they end with the century. Though it gradually contracted into the great cities, the plague was domesticated in Europe till the mid-seventeenth century. The Great Plague of London in 1665 was its last English, the plague of Marseilles in 1720 its last European, eruption. After that, conditions changed. In 1727 came a new invasion from the Russian steppes. Brown rats swarmed over the Volga, displacing the black rat, with its parasites and its plague.

The immediate consequences of this terrible mortality, which carried off in some places half, in general perhaps a third, of the population, were enormous. Everywhere there was a shortage of labour. Everywhere the established classes, the beneficiaries of past expansion, sought to conserve their now threatened gains by a policy of artificial reaction. To do so they devised new legislation, new machinery, even new myths. And everywhere, equally, there was resistance. In the expanding world of the twelfth and thirteenth centuries there had been room for all and a certain unity of social classes could be preserved. Landlords had granted freedom to their serfs because the serfs had acquired money from agriculture and could buy it, or because, if it were not granted, they might run away to the freedom of the new cities. In the cities, society had been fluid: apprentices had risen to be masters and the city offices had passed from old families to new. But in the contracting world of the fourteenth and fifteenth centuries there was less room; and the lord and peasant in the country, great merchant and small—or merchant and craftsman—in the town fought, the one to retain, the other to acquire his share of the dwindling stock of wealth or power.

The struggles did not all go the same way. In England, immediately after the Black Death, the landlords passed the Statute of Labourers, designed to peg agricultural wages at or near the rates obtaining before the plague. In France, a royal ordinance did the same. In Spain, similar regulations were issued by the *cortes* or Estates for the various regions. But ultimately, in most of these western countries, the shortage of labour gave advantages to labour, and peasants were able to buy their freedom. In eastern Europe, on the other hand, the landlords enforced their will. In the face of Slav pressure, they found means, little by little, to reimpose serfdom, so that by the sixteenth century, when the free peasantry of England boasted of their superiority to the wooden shoes and canvas breeches of the less free peasants of France, the French peasants could look with equal disdain at the serfs of Germany, sent out to gather snails and strawberries for their despotic masters. In each country the same causes led to the same 'landlord reaction'; but the outcome was different. Even in Spain there were differences between Catalonia, where the new legislation was afterwards revoked, and Castile where it was not. The same causes do not necessarily produce the same results in history; or at least, to do so, they require the same social context. Failing that context, the results may even be opposite.

Meanwhile, the towns too were in crisis. In the late fourteenth and the fifteenth centuries nearly all the established towns of Europe suffered eclipse. With the decline of population and of trade, their wealth and confidence sagged, and within them there were new struggles for privilege and power. To resolve these struggles, different factions sometimes appealed to neighbouring princes, and so the civil struggles of the towns became involved—often disastrously involved—in the foreign wars of kings. Sometimes, in their despair, the towns cannibalized their neighbours, as Florence strengthened itself by swallowing up Arezzo and Pisa, and Augsburg by squeezing out Memmingen and Ulm. And many towns, in the precariousness of trade, turned themselves into landlords. Land might bring its troubles but they were often less than the troubles of foreign trade. So the towns too became investors in the 'landlord reaction'. We see it happening in Barcelona where the city merchants switch their capital from overseas commerce to agricultural improvement at home. We see it most clearly in Venice. While the great Venetian merchants clung to their dwindling commercial empire in the Aegean sea, the lesser, weaker merchants supported a policy of conquering a *terra ferma* on the mainland. In 1381 there was a general economic collapse of the merchant houses in Barcelona, followed, in the fifteenth century, by civil war. In the same fifteenth century Venice, which had hitherto looked seawards, to the gorgeous East, turned round and fought war after war to secure territory in Italy: territory in which, in the next century, Palladio would build and Veronese decorate the majestic villas of a once mercantile aristocracy which had gradually turned from commerce to office and from office to land.

Finally, what of the Church? In these years of depression it too turned in on itself. I have already remarked that any genuine, living counter-reformation, as distinct from mere reaction, must spring out of the same forces which have produced the original reformation. The friars had begun as revolutionary, not reactionary forces: they had canalized, in defence of the Church, some of the new radicalism of the twelfth-century heretics—the ideas of apostolic poverty and missionary evangelism. But in the fourteenth century this radicalism was effectively crushed out of the Church. The friars became an extra buttress of a bureaucratic property-owning Church deprived of spiritual authority first by the 'Babylonish captivity'—the migration of the papacy from Rome to Avignon—then by the 'Great Schism', when pope and antipope, from Rome and Avignon, hurled at each other their sizzling but ineffectual spiritual thunderbolts. In 1322 Pope John XXII, the risen cobbler's son who savoured the pleasures of wealth among the delicious, specially planted papal vineyards of Avignon, condemned as heretical the doctrine of the poverty of Christ and thereafter the early lives of St Francis were re-written to tone down the unfortunate views of the founder on that subject. The popular fame of the friars of the fourteenth and fifteenth centuries was less for their poverty and their preaching than for their wealth and the interesting new ways in which they built it up. The Franciscans were famous as the inventors or improvers of those 'mechanical' aids to religion which would provoke the Reformation: indulgences, fancy new devotions, new dogmas like the Immaculate Conception. The Dominicans built up their power as the formulators of orthodoxy, and as the manipulators of the Inquisition which would defend orthodoxy by crushing out every new idea.

As for the monks, if the new mendicant orders, which professed poverty, could boast so openly of their wealth, why should the old monasteries hold back? Everywhere the monasteries had extended their landed property. They too had invested in the 'landlord reaction'. The Black Death, in this respect, had been a positive benefit to them. In the years of desolation men had turned to religion and left their lands to the Church. And with land the monks also swallowed up the tithes of the parish churches. . . .

For of course this 'landlord reaction', this dull, reinforced, conservatism of the established classes, did not go unchallenged. It was challenged in the country: the fourteenth century was punctuated by desperate, sometimes terrible, peasant revolts. The peasants revolted in western Flanders from 1323 to 1328. In 1357 they revolted in France: it was the famous Jacquerie, which gave its name to all other purely peasant risings. In 1381 they revolted in England: it was the great Peasants' Revolt of Wat Tyler and Jack Straw whose names remained bogeys to alarm the gentry in the seventeenth century. In the towns, too, there were risings against the closed merchant oligarchies which controlled all economic life. Between 1348 and 1400 there was numerous 'strikes'—in Paris, in Speyer, in Siena, in Strassburg, in Constance. There were also some full-scale revolts. . . . It was called the rebellion of the Ciompi. 'It would be no exaggeration to say', wrote Henri Pirenne, that in those years 'on the banks of the Scheldt, as on those of the Arno, the revolutionaries sought to impose upon their adversaries the dictatorship of the proletariat.' And to sanction their revolt, peasants and craftsmen alike armed themselves against the Church of the rich with radical, heretical doctrines. In France and England the peasants attacked the great landowning abbeys and burnt their archives, the record of their own subjection; they listened to anarchical preachers of human equality like John Ball; and even unrevolutionary enemies of the Church, like Wyclif, found their doctrines turned into revolutionary slogans. Wyclif's heresies were preserved in England, especially by communities of weavers, and would survive to give substance to the Protestant Reformation of the sixteenth century. . . .

Finally, the fourteenth century saw another form of popular revolt: anti-semitism. Indebted peasants in the country, starving craftsmen in the towns, looked for scapegoats in their midst and found the Jews. The Jews were expelled from England in 1292. At the same time there were pogroms in the kingdom of Naples. In 1348–9, on the approach of the Black Death, the Jews were massacred throughout Switzerland and Germany. Popes, princes, bishops, great landlords, sought to protect them, for they found them useful; but in vain: in city after city the Jews were rounded up and burnt alive, until, as a German chronicler wrote, 'I would have believed that the last end of Jewry had come if the time prophesied by Elijah and Enoch had been completed; but since that is not so, some must survive, that the Scriptures may be fulfilled.' . . .

What was the cause of this general decline of the fourteenth century, this collapse of the vitality which had sustained Christendom in the two centuries of expansion? It was not only the Black Death. Population had already begun to fall before the plague had come, and it did not recover momentum until well after it was over. The abandonment of villages beyond the Elbe had also begun well before the Black Death; so had the agrarian and urban discontent in the West. In general a healthy society soon recovers from decimation by an epidemic. London would shrug off the terrible plagues of 1625 and 1665. It is feeble societies which are fatally damaged—and which then ascribe their weakness to that cause. We cannot therefore put all the blame on the Black Death. We have to ask why European society was already so enfeebled in the fourteenth century that the impact of the Black Death was so formidable. For one reason we must look once again outside Europe, to the source whence the Black Death and so much else had come: the East.

For these years of European reaction were years of spectacular change outside Europe; and once again, as in the days of the Huns and the Avars, the immediate cause of the change was one of those sudden, great confederations of the nomads of the steppe. This time it was the greatest of all such confederations: the Mongol confederation of Genghis Khan who, in the early thirteenth century, from his capital of Karakorum in Outer Mongolia, had created an empire of heathen conquest from the Pacific to the Volga. Under his sons and grandsons this empire was extended still farther. . . .

To the rulers of western Europe these convulsions of Islam were not unwelcome. Here was a powerful second front against Mamelukes and Turks; here also was a huge free-trade area from Budapest to Canton; and both could be exploited. Franciscan missionaries were sent to convert the heathen khans to Christianity and Italian merchants found their way, through Central Asia, into China, 'the head of the world and the beginning of the earth'. . . .These missionary efforts were a failure. . . .But the merchantile expeditions were more successful. The heathen khans needed foreign experts and preferred, in their immediate entourage, not to use either Moslems or Chinese. Genghis Khan liked Uighurs, those fascinating Turks of Sinkiang, who had once been Manichaeans and who now served their conquerors by reducing the Mongol language to writing. Under him the Uighurs became the court aristocracy of Karakorum, and he appointed an Uighur as tutor to his sons. But there were also Christians. Guillaume de Rubrouck found numbers of them in Karakorum in 1254; and when Kublai Khan established his power they began to flow to his courts at Cambalu and Peking. The first to come from Europe were two Venetian merchants, Niccòlo and Maffeo Polo, who set out from the Crimea via Bokhara to Peking. Ten years later Marco Polo, the son of Niccolò, would begin his fifteen years as a favoured officer of Kublai Khan, and by his famous book would inspire numerous other Italian merchants to find their way to China in the years 1300–50.

Thus, when the crusaders' way of imperialist colonization had failed, the alternative way of 'pure and friendly correspondence' succeeded, and in the century after the failure of the Crusades, Europe was still living, successfully, on the East. Indeed, it was living more successfully than ever. The great, orderly, tolerant Mongol Empire, crossed and re-crossed by continual caravans, provided one of the most effective means for the diffusion of culture and technology. It was in those years that some of the great Chinese inventions came to Europe. Gunpowder was first mentioned in Europe by Roger Bacon, the friend of that Guillaume de Rubrouck who had visited Karakorum. It was first used in the West, by both Christians and Moslems, in the early fourteenth century. Printing also reached Europe from China during the period of the Mongol peace. The first printed document in Europe is perhaps the stamped signature of the reply of Kayuk Khan to the pope, written in Uighur script, which Giovanni da Piano Carpini brought from Karakorum and which, long unknown, was discovered in the Vatican archives in 1920.

Such was the beneficient *Pax Mongolica* which coincided with the European prosperity of the thirteenth century, and brought Christendom, as never before, into touch with the great, old civilizations of the East. But in the middle of the fourteenth century, this Mongol peace came to an end in anarchy and civil war. In the Far East, a national revolt in China ultimately brought the native Ming dynasty to power, and Karakorum itself was burnt. In the Middle East, Mongol rule collapsed in

Persia; the great irrigation system of Mesopotamia, preserved for centuries, fell into ruin, and the anarchy was exploited by a new, temporary, destructive conqueror, Timur or Tamerlane. In the West, a new Turkish tribe, the Ottomans, displaced by the Mongol conquests, pushed into Europe, made their capital at Adrianople, and reduced the Greek emperor to vassalage. Thus the collapse of the Mongol Empire shook the fabric of society alike in China, in Islam, and in Europe. It was out of the anarchy in China, before the triumph of the Ming, that the Black Death came to Europe; it was during the anarchy of Islam that Ibn Khaldoun, in North Africa, elaborated his defeatist philosophy of history; and the convulsion of the Middle East, together with the collapse of the Mongol peace, dislocated the delicate mechanism of Europe's trade with the East. Indeed, the great caravan-route across Central Asia was finally broken: two centuries later, even its existence had been forgotten.

If the century from 1150 to 1250 can be seen as the highest point of medieval Europe, the century from 1350 to 1450 was, I suppose, the lowest. The old institutions had stiffened and a devitalized society could create no new, elastic institutions to replace them. In that period of contraction and reaction, of deadening clericalism and vain social revolt, intellectual life sank into formalism or took refuge from reality in satire, mysticism or myth. We have the good-humoured satire of Boccaccio and Chaucer, the bitter satire of *Piers Plowman*. We have the great medieval mystics, Suso and Tauler, Richard Rolle and Thomas à Kempis. Above all, we have the archaic myth of chivalry. Never was the spirit of feudalism so elaborate in literature as when it was dead in fact: when feudal bonds were rotted and feudal obligations ignored. . . .

If a philosopher, trained in modern theories of cyclical history, were to place himself in the early fifteenth century, what, I wonder, would he conclude? At that time, it must have seemed that the future was not with Europe, frozen in archaic postures and privileges, not with Islam, helpless before successive invaders, but with China. China had provided almost all the technical innovations of Europe, and now, under its new Ming dynasty, it seemed set on a new policy of expansion. In the years 1405–33 the Chinese court-eunuch Chêng-Ho—one of the really great eunuchs of history (Justinian's general Narses is the other)—led or sent a series of naval expeditions which brought the whole Indian Ocean under Chinese control. Thanks to his enterprise, the rulers of India and Ceylon, the commercial centres of Malacca and Calicut paid their tribute or sent their exotic wares to China. Chinese fleets visited the Red Sea and the coast of East Africa. Only a little continuity was necessary and perhaps Chinese fleets, half a century later, would have arrived in Lisbon and

London. Who would have supposed, at that time, that the reverse would happen: that instead, Portuguese fleets would arrive in Malacca and Calicut to divert the tribute of India and Ceylon westwards to Lisbon and Antwerp, and thereby initiate the new, half-millennial supremacy of Europe?

For this indeed is one of the apparent miracles of history. To explain it, Portuguese historians have discovered an almost fabulous character, Prince Henry of Portugal, 'the Navigator', the Chêng-Ho of the West (except that Prince Henry himself never went to sea), the solitary pioneer of European expansion, the founder of that trans-oceanic Portuguese Empire which was the first, and threatens to be the last, of European empires overseas. For some forty years, from about 1420 till his death in 1460, Prince Henry, we are told, sat at Sagres, on the Atlantic tip of southern Portugal, surrounded by his cartographers and scientists, devising ever new and longer journeys. What inspired him? A crusading zeal against the Moslems of Africa? A dream of India? An image of the legendary Christian king in the East, Prester John? We do not know. We only know that in those years fleet after fleet sailed out from Portugal into the Atlantic, down the coast of Africa, preparing the way for the great sudden voyages, at the end of the century, of Bartholomew Dias and Vasco da Gama, and for the new empire of Asia and Brazil.

The legend of Prince Henry reads well; but let us not be bowled over by it. True history is not made by single heroes. At most, such figures are catalysts, or leaders of forces already there, and the question we must ask is not who inspired those new Portuguese voyages, or with what motive, but why, in the fifteenth century, when the rest of Europe was apparently fixed in social sclerosis and economic decline, one corner of it was able to break the spell and set this new example. For it was an example of great importance. Thanks to the free competition between the monarchies of Europe, all the other maritime powers of Europe would soon turn aside to follow it; that imitation, and that competition, would give to Europe its long ascendancy over the rest of the world.

What was the particular character of Portuguese society in the fifteenth century? This is a large, factual question, to which nevertheless I shall offer a short general answer: an answer drawn not only from these particular circumstances but also from other comparable turning-points in history, when the centre of power has moved from one part to another of a continent or of the world.

For if history is to be seen, as I believe it should be seen, as a continuous process, then certain general conclusions always emerge. We find, for instance, that just as old institutions, unless they are continually adapted, will not serve new purposes, so new problems are rarely solved, in the first instance, by old societies. The reason can easily be guessed. Any society, so long as it is, or feels itself to be, a working society, tends to invest in itself: a military society tends to become more military, a bureaucratic society more bureaucratic, a commercial society more commercial, as the status and profits of war or office or commerce are enhanced by success, and institutions are framed to forward it. Therefore, when such a society is hit by a general crisis, it finds itself partly paralysed by the structural weight of increased social investment. The dominant military or official or commercial classes cannot easily change their orientation; and their social dominance, and the institutions through which it is exercised, prevent other classes from securing power or changing policy. If policy is to be changed to meet new circumstances we are more likely to find such a change, in the first instance, either in a complex elastic society—what today we would call a liberal society—in which different interests have separate, competing institutions, or in a less mature society: a society whose institutions have not been hardened and whose vested interests have not been deepened by past commitment. This general social truth, it seems to me, explains why it was not Ming China but fifteenth-century Europe, for all its temporary decline, which captured the next stage of history, and why, within fifteenth-century Europe, it was not Italy or Flanders or even France or England which showed the way, but a minuscule kingdom at the back end of eastward-looking Europe, Portugal.

We have seen, in the century from 1350, all Europe in crisis and the mature societies of Europe unable to create new institutions whereby to surmount that crisis. To say that they did nothing in that century would be an exaggeration. In numerous ways they responded to the challenge. Some new techniques were devised, some new forms of social organization were evolved. There was agricultural improvement: the landlord reaction had its brighter side. There was a revolution in cloth manufacture and in mining which made the fortune of new merchant cities in Germany. There was a development of gilds which, for a time, preserved a social balance in older cities. Princes, by extending their jurisdiction and absorbing new areas, sometimes increased their free-trade area and learned mercantile policies from the cities which they subjected. But, in general, what we see is over-emphasis on old forms; modification of old forms, perhaps, but not discovery of new. Landlords seek to preserve their power by reaction, not innovation. Capitalists, frustrated in trade, turn to banking or to land, or invest in taxes and offices. Even the gilds soon become restrictive and crush production in the cities in which they triumph: the economic decline of many a Swiss or German city was caused by this 'socialism' of the fifteenth century. In general, we may say that the existing structure of Europe, the structure acquired in the years of expansion, and strengthened by the passage of time and growth of interests, continues to absorb its energies, and by absorbing them, to use them up. Even the artistic Renaissance of the fifteenth century is not necessarily a sign of progress. Lavish patronage of the arts is perfectly compatible—as in the Baroque age—with economic decline. The new princes and their couriers are often merchants who have switched their investment from trade to politics. Instead of increasing wealth by industry or commerce, they are accumulating it by taxation and dissipating it, through lack of other outlet, in conspicuous waste.

In Ming China it is the same. For centuries the Chinese Empire had lived on its bureaucracy of scholar-gentry, with which no dynasty could dispense. Foreign rulers might conquer central power, but always, in the end, they had turned to the Chinese bureaucracy in order to rule. Even the Mongols, in the end, had succumbed to it. They might prefer Uighurs or Christians at court; but there were not enough of them to go round the empire. So Kublai Khan ended by restoring the old bureaucracy, recruited by examination. When the nationalist Ming replaced the Mongols, they naturally returned with enthusiasm to the national system. Outwardly it might appear that Chêng-Ho was dished by a court intrigue; fundamentally, Chinese society was absorbed by its ancient structure, its ancient institutions.

But if China was a uniform, centralized empire, Europe's good fortune had always lain in its variety. If all Europe, like all China, had been centrally ruled, how different our history would have been! But in fact it was not so. In fact, in 1400, while the economic life of older Europe was being brought under princely control, there were some countries in which feudal institutions had taken but slender root, and one of those countries, happily placed for the new age, was Portugal.

The kingdom of Portugal, we have seen, had only been founded during the Second Crusade. It was a creation of northern Europe, like the kingdom of Jerusalem; and its very narrowness—a mere strip along the Atlantic coast—had protected it from the general fate of other societies in the fourteenth century. If Portugal, like Andalusia, had been reconquered from Islam by Castile, and governed from Burgos or Toledo, much of its economic life would no doubt have been drained away into the Spanish monarchy—as indeed was to happen after it was united with Spain in 1580. But because of its independence, and its smallness, it was forced to live by its own economy; and that economy lay on the sea. Portugal in the fifteenth century was like Genoa or Venice in the twelfth century, or Holland in the seventeenth: a small state forced by geography to look outwards to the sea. In the narrow space allowed to it there was no Portuguese feudalism powerful enough to absorb the mercantile life of its

Atlantic coast; and in the great depression of the fourteenth century, when the mercantile cities of the Mediterranean turned away from commerce to land or banking—when Venice became a land-power and Genoa a finance-capital, and when Barcelona was swallowed up by the kingdom of Aragon—Lisbon retained its old character. It was still a capital of merchants and seamen, carrying salt to northern Europe, entering the internal markets of northern Europe, fishing and whaling in the Atlantic Ocean. It was now also a main port of the route from north to south Europe—the sea-route which was becoming more popular as the land-route suffered from the crisis of the times and the exactions of its rulers.

To Lisbon therefore, the new Venice, the new Genoa of the Atlantic, the heirs of the old Venice, the old Genoa of the Mediterranean would now turn. In the middle of the fourteenth century Italian merchants, squeezed out of Italy—the Bardi of Florence, the Lomellini of Genoa—converged on Lisbon, just as the *émigré* capitalists of Counter-Reformation Europe would converge on seventeenth-century Amsterdam. In 1391, when the Jews were slaughtered throughout Spain, the Jewish cartographers of Majorca—the best in Europe, the makers of the great medieval 'portulans' or sea-maps—fled to Portugal. The mercantile and scientific expertise of Italy, Flanders and of Catalonia was united, in Portugal, with the native shipbuilding industry; and the result was to make Portugal an economic and maritime force, as Venice and Genoa had been, as Amsterdam would be.

As such, Portugal was brought into the wars of Europe. In the Hundred Years' War, that struggle of feudal princes for land in France, it was enlisted as the essential sea ally of England. It was to celebrate the Anglo-Portuguese victory of Aljubarrota that the great abbey of Batalha, the Battle Abbey of Portugal, was built. But the effect of the war, and the victory, was far more decisive for Portugal than for England. For Portugal, those years of war, 1383–5, were also years of internal revolution, a revolution which in form was dynastic, but which in substance went far deeper. It was a political and economic revolution which was the reverse of the other revolutions in Europe at that time. For whereas in the rest of Europe, in those years of crisis, feudal or bureaucratic princes were absorbing the once free cities—the Medici would become despots of Florence and the Visconti of Milan and the Dukes of Burgundy would absorb the cities of Flanders—the city of Lisbon was, in effect, to absorb the new Anglo-Portuguese dynasty of Aviz. In Portugal, and only in Portugal, the 'feudal' nobility, with their 'feudal' fighting tastes, would accept, through the house of Aviz, the leadership of those maritime, mercantile forces which in the Mediterranean would be turning, under the seduction of a hardening social structure, from the sea to the land, from commerce to finance. The arts in Italy and Flanders would be bent to glorify the new princely state, and the myths of the Church which sustained it; but in Portugal even solid stone would soon be made to re-create, with its fantastic imagery of twisted cables and symbolic anchors, coral and shells and waves, the spirit of maritime journeys, commerce, and the distant seas.

The result was spectacular. With new leadership, new financial resources, new technical developments, the Portuguese mercantile state would send ever stouter ships out into the Atlantic in search of that African gold which, for so long, had been the motor of European commerce with the East. With the new growth of population in the fifteenth century, a new movement of expansion would be launched, comparable with that movement of which the Crusades had been a part; and this time it would be launched from Portugal. The pioneers were not necessarily Portuguese. Prince Henry's explorers who first reached the equator, Alvise de Cadamosto and Antoniotto Usodimare were, respectively, a Venetian and a Genoese. The techniques of colonization were not necessarily Portuguese: the wine- and the sugar-industries which the Portuguese and Spaniards would plant in the islands of the Atlantic were those which the Venetians and Genoese had first established in the islands of the Mediterranean. Chios and Crete were the models for Madeira and the Canaries: the wine of Madeira is Malmsey from Greece. But Portugal accepted the legacy of Italy, and passed it on. Columbus was a Genoese in the service of Spain; Magellan, a Portuguese, was also in the service of Spain; but the voyages of both, no less than those of Bartholomew Dias and Vasco da Gama, were technically prepared by Portugal. From that little corner of Europe, from that solitary revolution of 1383, in the period of European recession, Europe found the way to America, to India, and round the world.

With the discovery of those new worlds, the medieval history of Europe can be said to have come to an end. Thanks to those discoveries, and to the institutions which could exploit them (for once again, let me repeat, contact alone is nothing: it is the power to grasp and learn from contact which counts), as well as to the continued fragmentation and competition of the European states, Europe since 1500 has in fact dominated and transformed the world. Slowly, with difficulty, other powers followed the Portuguese lead. The 'feudal' monarchies of the West adapted themselves to the new opportunities; the 'feudal' chivalry which had wasted itself in European anarchy was turned once again, as in the eleventh century, outward; and a new age began.

CHAPTER 2

THE SPANISH
IN AMERICA

In eighteenth- and nineteenth-century Anglo-American historical writings, an interpretation of the Spanish conquest of the New World took root that portrayed the Spanish in unflattering terms—so unflattering that the interpretation is known to modern historians as *La Leyenda Negra*—The Black Legend. Although this interpretation is generally false, it is true that some of the Spanish were cruel, blood-thirsty, rapacious, and avaricious. However, they did not have a corner on these vices, nor were they all guilty of perpetuating atrocities. The sixteenth century was, by our standards, a cruel age, and the Spanish along with the English and the French were products of their age.

Moreover, as Professor Parry shows in the next selection, their policies toward the Indians in many respects were genuinely enlightened. Although it was a Spanish policy to use the Indian population as laborers and servants, this certainly compares favorably with the Anglo-American practice of forcible removal and ofttimes extinction of the Redman.

Parry also discusses the Spanish system of colonial government with its close ties of authority to the home court. How does this compare to the English system? Did different techniques of colonization affect the ways colonies developed and became independent nations? These questions are not answered in this selection but should be borne in mind as you read it and the later material bearing on the English colonizing experience.

17

There are a number of excellent works on the Spanish in the New World, of which perhaps the best are Clarence H. Haring, *The Spanish Empire in America** (1947), Lewis Hanke, *The Spanish Struggle for Justice in the Conquest of America** (1944), and the more recent synthesis by Charles Gibson, *Spain in America** (1966). For a recent summary of the literature dealing with *La Leyenda Negra,* see Lewis Hanke, "More Heat and Some Light on the Spanish Struggle for Justice in the Conquest of America," *Hispanic American Historical Review,* XLIV (August 1964). An excellent treatment of the Spanish Indian is found in Charles Gibson, *The Aztecs Under Spanish Rule: A History of the Indians of the Valley of Mexico* (1964).

* Available in a paperback edition.

THE SILVER EMPIRE
J. H. PARRY

THE SPANISH CONQUEST

If the first two decades of the sixteenth century may be called the age of the professional explorer, the next three decades from 1520 to 1550, were the age of the *conquistadore*—the professional conqueror. In those years a few thousand down-at-heel swordsmen, themselves the product of the tradition of the Moorish wars, possessed themselves of most of the settled areas of both Americas and established the first great European land empire overseas.

Before 1520 most of the larger islands of the West Indies had been explored and a considerable number of Spaniards had settled, especially in Hispaniola and Cuba. These settlers imported cattle and horses, and negroes to replace the dwindling native Arawaks, and set up as slave-owning ranchers. Their settlements were turbulent and unstable. Many of the settlers were soldiers who had served in Moorish or Italian campaigns; there was no congenial work for them in Spain, nor did they propose to work in the Indies. They would settle for a short time, and then desert their holdings to investigate a rumoured gold strike, or simply through boredom and restlessness.

Balboa's glimpse of the Pacific in 1513 encouraged some of these adventurers to join in the general search for a sea passage through Central America; at various points on the Gulf coast these explorers found gold and silver ornaments in use among the natives, and heard rumours of civilized city-dwellers living in the mountains inland. Scattered through tropical America, mainly in highland areas, there were in fact a number of distinct peoples, who, though lacking wheeled vehicles and beasts of burden, and using tools of wood or stone, had nevertheless achieved a remarkable skill in some of the arts, in sculpture and building, in agriculture and in handicraft industries, including the working of soft metals. Their principle settlements, adorned with stone or

SOURCE. J. H. Parry, "The Silver Empire," *The Establishment of the European Hegemony*, London: Hutchinson and Co., Ltd., 1949, pp. 60–75. Copyright 1949. Reprinted by permission of Hutchinson and Co., Ltd., and the author.

adobe temples and community-houses, were large enough to be called cities. In two centres at least—in Mexico and the central plateau of the Andes—warlike tribes had established themselves as overlords, exacting tribute and forced labour from subject peoples over a wide area; and had set up political organizations bearing a superficial resemblance to empires or kingdoms in the Old World sense. Among Spaniards, the wealth and power of these peoples lost nothing in the telling; and for pious Christians their religions had a horrible fascination, combining, as in some cases they did, messianic legends of strange beauty with revolting rites of human sacrifice and ritual cannibalism.

The speed with which the Spanish *conquistadores* seized the chief centres of American civilization compares with the speed of Portuguese commercial expansion in the East; but the Spanish conquest achieved far more enduring results and its success is even harder to explain satisfactorily. The possession of firearms was an important but probably not a decisive factor. A ship carries its armament wherever it goes; but on land cannon had to be dragged over mountains and through swamps by human strength. The army with which Cortés invaded Mexico possessed only a few small cannon and thirteen muskets. Horses were perhaps more important than guns; but the Indians soon lost their fear of horses and even learned to ride them. Cortés had sixteen horses when he landed. For the most part his men fought on foot with sword, pike and crossbow. They had the advantage of steel over stone; but they were not a well-equipped European army fighting a horde of helpless savages.

The Spaniards had unbounded courage and the discipline of necessity. . . . They were able to exploit some of the legends and superstitions of their adversaries in such a way as to paralyse opposition, at least temporarily. They had the help of large numbers of Indian allies who—having never heard of King Log and King Stork—gleefully attacked their former overlords or rivals. Finally the Spaniards had the advantage of their truculent missionary faith: the Indian believed that his religion required him to fight and if need be to die bravely; the Spaniard believed that his religion enabled him to win.

The expedition destined for the conquest of Mexico, promoted by the Governor of Cuba and commanded by Cortés, consisted of about six hundred men. Cortés landed near what is now Vera Cruz in 1519 and began operations by two symbolic acts: the burning of the ships which had brought him from Cuba, and the ceremonious founding of a municipality. To the magistrates of the 'town' of Vera Cruz Cortés resigned the commission he had received in Cuba; from them, as representatives of the Spanish Crown in Mexico, he received a new commission, and having thus legalized as best he could his assumption of an independent command, he led his army up the rugged climb from the steamy jungles of Vera Cruz to the high plateau of central Mexico. The outlying towns of the plateau, after some fighting, agreed to help him with food, with porters, and with fighting men; and by playing adriotly upon the superstitions of Montezuma, the Aztec war-chief, Cortés effected the peaceful entry of his army into Tenochtitlán, the capital city, build upon islands in the lake of Mexico. His peaceful occupation was short-lived; the zeal of the Spaniards in destroying heathen temples caused a rising in which Montezuma was killed, and Cortés had to fight his way out of the city along the causeways by night, losing in that one night a third of his men and most of his baggage. The auxiliary tribes remained loyal to the Spanish alliance, however, and Cortés was reinforced by another expedition from Cuba. He had boats built for fighting on the lake, and laid formal siege to the city, systematically looting and destroying it building by building as he advanced towards the centre, until in 1521 the surviving Aztecs surrendered. In the beautiful Spanish city which Cortés began to build on the site, there is hardly a trace of the former Indian buildings: the place was built over as completely as the Roman cities of Europe.

Cortés showed genius, not only in holding his own men together, but in securing at least the passive loyalty of the conquered Indians. He worked so wisely that there was never afterwards any serious trouble with the natives of the plateau region. His imitators in Central and South America were less fortunate or less adroit. The Maya territories in Central America were subdued with great brutality by Cortés's lieutenants. The Inca Empire, with its centre at Cuzco on the high plateau of the Peruvian Andes, was not discovered by Spaniards until 1530, after eight years of exploration, by land from Cartagena, by sea from Panama. The conquest of Peru was organized by a syndicate whose principal member was an obscure adventurer named Francisco Pizarro. Pizarro entered Peru with a smaller following even than that of Cortés. He was fortunate in finding a usurper on the Inca throne. In imitation of Cortés he contrived to seize the person of this reigning chief, Atahualpa, whom he afterwards executed. Like Cortés, also, Pizarro organized his conquests by founding municipalities with due legal pomp. Like Cortés, he sent his lieutenants exploring, south into Chile, and north to Quito and New Granada. But though he had all Cortés' generalship, Pizarro had little of the diplomacy and charm which Cortés displayed. His appointment as governor of the best part of the Inca dominions provoked fierce personal quarrels and eventually civil war among the conquerors. Francisco Pizarro, his brother Gonzalo, his partner and rival Almagro, and hundreds of their followers were killed. Their factions raged intermittently for nearly twenty years, and peace was restored with great difficulty by the intervention of the home government.

Naturally the surviving Indian rulers tried to turn the situation to their own advantage; but too late. Only in southern Chile did Indian arms prevail against the Spaniards. A major rebellion in western Mexico was crushed by the first viceroy, Antonio de Mendoza, in 1542. By 1550 all the chief centres of settled population in tropical America were in Spanish hands—but not in the hands of the great *conquistadores*. Private commanders like Cortés, Pizarro, Belalcázar and Nuño de Guzmán, who depended for their power upon their personal following, if they escaped the knives of their rivals, were displaced by royal nominees. Exploration and conquests went on in frontier regions, in northern Mexico and east of the Andes; and in the fifteen-sixties a well-planned, ably-led, and almost bloodless conquest added the Philippines to the Spanish empire. In most parts of the Americas, however, the great age of the *conquistadores* ended when the principal settled areas were secure. Forests and empty prairies were not to their taste. Cortés spent his last years in bored and litigious retirement. There was little left for him to conquer.

THE THEORY OF EMPIRE

The Spanish conquest in America was a genuine crusade, appealing alike to the missionary's zeal for souls and the soldier's desire for military glory and for plunder. Unlike earlier crusades, however, it brought in its train an immense task of imperial government. The *conquistadores* had gone to America at their own expense, endured great hardships, risked their lives and fortunes—such as they were—without help from the Spanish state. Most of them looked forward to a pensioned retirement; some living in Spain upon the proceeds of their plunder, but many more living in the Indies upon the labour and the tribute of the conquered races as the Incas and the Aztecs had done before them. Left to themselves, they would probably have settled in loose communities, employing the feudal forms which already were anachronisms in Spain, exploiting the Indians as the needs of the moment dictated, and according verbal homage but little else to the Spanish Crown. Many of the rebel leaders in Peru—in particular, Gonzalo Pizarro—contemplated just such a society, extravagantly loyal in sentiment but in practice virtually independent.

The rulers of Spain never for a moment thought of allowing such a state of affairs to persist. In the late fifteenth and early sixteenth centuries the Crown, with considerable bloodshed and expense, had successfully cut the claws of the great feudal houses, of the knightly orders and of the privileged local corporations. A growing royal absolutism could not tolerate the emergence of a new feudal aristocracy overseas. At the same time royal government was by no means a lawless or unbridled absolutism. The Church and the legal profession were its honoured partners and its most useful servants. The conquest of America touched not only the royal authority, but the royal conscience and the tradition of royal justice.

Discussion of the nature and duties of kingship, in both legal and theological terms, was a commonplace in sixteenth-century Spain. It was an age of vigorous and outspoken political thought, thought which was, for the most part, resolutely opposed to despotism and which placed the law of God and the laws and customs of free peoples above the will of kings. The conquest of a great and semi-barbarous empire obviously presented a difficult problem to the apologists for constitutional kingship. They all admitted—no Catholic could deny—that the bulls issued by Alexander VI in 1493 had given to the Spanish Crown the duty and the sole right of converting the American natives to the Christian faith. If the Indians resisted the preaching of the Gospel, they might lawfully be subdued by force of arms. The duty of civilizing a barbarous people and the fact that the Spaniards were the first Europeans to discover America were valid, though secondary reasons for the conquest. But if the Indians should be reduced by a just conquest, what legal and political rights remained to them? Should their rulers be deposed—if indeed they had legitimate rulers? Should they be 'converted' by force? Might they be enslaved, or deprived of land or property? Were they to be subject to Spanish courts of law, civil and ecclesiastical? What claims had the Spanish settlers upon the tribute and labour of the Indians?

Spanish writers differed profoundly in their answers to these questions, and the main ground of difference was the nature of the Indians themselves. The colonists naturally emphasized the apparent idleness of people accustomed to subsistence farming, and the treacherous resentment of a conquered race. They claimed unfettered local lordship based on forced labour and maintained, not without some plausibility, that a paternal feudalism would best serve the interests of the Indians themselves. Many missionaries, on the other hand—in particular the famous Dominican preacher Las Casas—insisted on the purely spiritual nature of the Spanish enterprise. Las Casas's theory of empire rested upon the belief

that the Indians, equally with the Spaniards, were the natural subjects
of the Spanish Crown, and enjoyed from the moment of entering into
the Spanish obedience all the guarantees of liberty and justice provided
by the laws of Castille. He maintained that they were capable intellectually of discharging the duties of Spanish subjects and of receiving the
faith. He contemplated an ideal empire in which the Indians would live
under their own headmen but subject to the authority of benevolent
royal officials who would instruct them in European customs and persuade
them to abandon barbarous practices. The Church would proceed peacefully with its work of conversion and spiritual ministration. If other
Europeans, as private persons, were allowed to reside in the Indies,
they would live apart from the Indians and support themselves by their
own labour.

Las Casas was no mere theorist, but a devoted missionary who had
himself pacified a large and savage tract of country in Central America.
In Spain he was a powerful and respected personality. He represented,
of course, an extreme view. The opposite view, that of the colonists,
also had its defenders, notably Juan Ginés de Sepúlveda, the distinguished
scholar and humanist and friend of Erasmus, one of the ablest apologists
of European imperialism. Between Sepúlveda and Las Casas, and between the schools and interests which they represented, there was fierce
and acrimonious debate. The importance of such controversies lay in
the public interest which they aroused, and in their effect on royal
policy. Spanish methods of government, as distinct from methods of conquest, were cautious, legalistic, slow, above all conscientious. They were
influenced both by reports of practical experience and by considerations
of abstract right. By the middle of the sixteenth century there emerged
from the dust of controversy an official policy and an official theory of
empire which, despite constant vacillations in matters of detail, were
maintained with very fair consistency for over two hundred years.

The Indies were kingdoms of the Crown of Castille, separate from the
kingdoms of Spain, and administered through a separate royal council.
The Indians were the direct subjects of the crown, not of the Spanish
state or of any individual Spaniards. They were free men, and might
not be enslaved unless taken in armed rebellion. Their land and property
were their own, and might not be taken from them. Their headmen
were to be confirmed in office and employed as minor officials. They
were to be subject to Spanish courts of law, and might sue Spaniards
and be sued by them; but their own laws were to be respected except
where they were clearly barbarous or repugnant to the Spanish laws of
the Indies.

The Indians were, of course, to be converted to Christianity as soon as possible and were to be admitted to all the sacraments of the Church. Their conversion was to be free and not forced, and their lapses into heresy were to be dealt with by the ordinary jurisdiction of the bishops, not by the Inquisition.

To meet the claims of the colonists, the Crown granted to deserving conquerors and settlers the right to draw the assessed tributes of specified villages, by way of pension. These grants of *encomienda* involved no jurisdiction or territorial lordship; nor, after the middle of the century, forced labour. They did involve, for the *encomendero,* the obligation of military service and the duty of paying the salaries of the parish clergy. Forced labour was permitted—was indeed found to be indispensable; but under the *mita* or *repartimiento* system, the compulsion was applied by public, not private authority, and official wage-rates were laid down for labour so recruited.

Of course, the decrees enjoining this policy were often obstructed and sometimes openly defied; but that does not detract from the merits of the policy, as a product of sixteenth-century thought and experience. The enforcement of the policy, moreover, though incomplete, was by no means as incompetent as the enemies of Spain pretended.

SOLDIERS, MISSIONARIES AND LAWYERS

The Spaniards who went to the New World were not settlers seeking an empty land, but soldiers, missionaries, administrators—a ruling class. They sought not to displace the native population, but to organize it, educate it, and live by its labour. They took over as a going concern the systems of tribute collection formerly organized by the dominant tribes in Mexico and Peru. Within a few years they created a number of deeply-rooted vested interests, which made the enforcement of a uniform official policy extremely difficult.

The most powerful group of interests was naturally that represented by the 'old conquerors' and their descendants. They formed a quarrelsome and disorderly society, whose good behaviour had to be bought with *encomiendas,* grants of land, and minor salaried offices. The one attempt made by the Crown to give legislative force to the proposals of Las Casas and to abolish the *encomienda,* in the 'new laws' of 1542, caused an armed revolt of the settlers of Peru, in which the viceroy was killed. The 'new laws' had to be amended; and the settlers constantly pressed for further concessions, in particular for the right to turn their *encomiendas* from terminable grants into entailed estates. There were never enough *encomiendas* or offices to go round, and almost from the beginning a 'poor white' class made its appearance, living among the Indians and giving endless trouble to the missionaries. Many settlers, rich and poor, took Indian wives, and so added a *mestizo* class to an already complex society. These people of mixed blood came in time to outnumber both pure Indians and pure Spaniards; and many of the Latin American peoples to-day are predominantly *mestizo*.

The Spanish settlers found their chief organs of expression in the town-councils, powerful and jealous of their privileges in the Indies as in Spain. There was nothing democratic about these bodies; they were local oligarchies. Councillors in the early days were appointed by military commanders or provincial governors, but in the second half of the sixteenth century the practice grew whereby they purchased their offices from the Crown for life. The councils elected municipal magistrates, and exercised wide administrative powers, not only within the town area, but over considerable tracts of surrounding country. They corresponded directly with the Crown and were always determined upholders of local Spanish interests. They rarely displayed much constructive vigour, however. They were neither responsible, nor in any exact sense representative institutions; and in the seventeenth century, as the power of the *corregidores* increased and the sale of offices became more nearly universal, the councils sank into decline.

The Spanish conquest, however, was a spiritual as well as a military conquest, and the principal local opposition to the rule of swordsmen came from the soldiers of the Church—the friars of the missionary Orders. All three Orders, but especially the Franciscans, in the early days sent picked men to the Indies, and the conversion they sought to achieve was more than a mere ourward conformity. The friars taught and preached, as soon as they were able, in the Indian languages. They established mission communities and made the mission Church the centre of the lives of many thousands of Indians. They made at least a beginning in the provision of both primary and secondary religious and literary education for the Indians—an ambitious undertaking designed, ultimately, to prepare selected Indians for the priesthood. It is true that this last undertaking was, in the main, a failure. The Church in the Indies never produced a numerous native priesthood, and its spiritual strength and hold upon its converts ultimately suffered as a consequence. The reasons for that failure are too complex for analysis here; what is certain, is that the policy of the Orders in the sixteenth century interfered with the lord-and-vassal relation which the settlers sought to establish with the Indians. The difference in attitude was not merely one of humanitarian sentiment; for the *encomienda* and *repartimiento* were not inherently cruel institutions, though they led to many abuses. The important differences were legal and spiritual.

On the whole, the Crown endorsed the views of the missionary Orders, but dared not enforce them in full. The friars also differed among themselves, and they, too, could be rebellious and impatient of control; not, of course, to the extent of armed revolt, but in many lesser acts of indiscipline. They challenged the power of the Crown indirectly on many occasions, by flouting the authority of the bishops whom the Crown appointed.

The differences among Spaniards were reflected by differences among the Indians themselves. For the most part the Indians showed a surprising docility and resignation. Their acquiescent nature, under the shock of conquest, often sank into apathetic melancholy, broken only by religious festivals and their accompanying drunken orgies. The settled Indians lost the material and spiritual culture of their ancestors, without fully acquiring that of the Spanish conquerors. They became strangers in their own land. Many tribes, however, remained unsubdued and dangerous throughout the colonial period, and even among the settled peoples wide differences persisted. Some Indian chiefs received *encomienda*s or became great landowners. Many others, if official reports are to be believed, willingly exploited their own people on behalf of the Spanish colonists. From the beginning, a considerable class of skilled workmen, household servants, and the like, threw in their lot with the Spanish community. In many parts of the Indies the old village life soon began to disintegrate, though not without protest. The Crown repeatedly insisted that Indian complaints should be freely heard, not only by the courts, but by the administrative authorities. The government even retained salaried advocates to present Indian pleas.

The royal insistence that all parties should have a hearing helps to explain one of the leading characteristics of Spanish colonial government —the great power and prestige of the professional judiciary. Ten *audiencias*—courts of appeal—were established in the Indies in the sixteenth century. The *audiencia* judges were always school-trained lawyers and always peninsular Spaniards. They were the only branch of the colonial service whom the Crown really trusted. Professional lawyers were the ideal agents of centralized government. They had no excessive family pride and no ambition, as a rule, for military glory. Their training gave them a deep respect for authority and a habit of careful attention to detail, while it discouraged any tendency towards rash or unauthorized action. Judges, moreover, representing the jurisdiction of the monarch, preserved a certain impersonality which helped them to control *conquis-tadores* who would have resented the authority of one of their own caste.

Every province had its governor and the governors of the two greatest provinces—Mexico and Peru—enjoyed the title and dignity of viceroys. Some of these governors were churchmen or lawyers; more were aris-tocratic soldiers; but under the suspicious Hapsburg kings, soldiers with-out armies. They were never trusted with the powers and temptations of independent command. Even a great administrator like Francisco de Toledo received inadequate support from home, and small thanks from Philip II for thirteen years of empire-building in Peru. Most viceroys served for much shorter terms, and all were carefully watched by their *audiencias*. The *audiencias* were much more than courts of appeal. They were cabinet councils empowered to advise the viceroys and gov-ernors in all administrative matters, to report on their conduct, and to hear appeals against their decisions. A viceroy might override his *aud-iencia* temporarily, but on appeal to Spain the judges were likely to be upheld; for the Council of the Indies was itself a predominantly legal body, to which colonial judges might hope to be promoted in due course of seniority.

This cumbrous system of checks and balances might make for im-partiality and respect for law—respect, at least, for the forms of law. It certainly did not make for administrative efficiency or speed of action. All important decisions, and many unimportant ones, were made in Spain. In the Indies, there was no decision which could not be reversed and on jurisdiction which could not be inhibited. Appeals and counter-appeals might hold up essential action for years, until the occasion for it were forgotten. 'Obey but not enforce' became the administrative watch-word of an empire whose legislation and basic policy were, in many respects, models of enlightment for their time.

ATLANTIC TRADE AND THE SILVER FLEETS

The characteristic occupation of the New World Spaniard was stock-farming. It was an occupation peculiarly well suited to the temperament of the *conquistadores,* an open-air life covering great areas of country, offering considerable excitement, calling for great skill in horsemanship and periodic outbursts of great energy, but for the most part requiring no steady or sustained effort. In Spain, the owners of flocks and herds were favoured socially and economically at the expense of the arable farmer; grazing rights tended to override all other kinds of land rights.

A similar situation soon arose in the temperate parts of Spanish America, where the work of arable farming was left mainly in the hands of the Indians. Horses, cattle and sheep were imported in great numbers and multiplied rapidly. As in all the economic activities of the Spaniards in the New World, the methods used were slovenly and wasteful. Leather commanded a high price in Europe in those turbulent times; for an ox-hide jerkin would turn a knife-thrust. Often the beasts were slaughtered for their hides alone, the carcases being left to rot on the ground. Nevertheless, the industry prospered. Great estates grew round the ranch-houses, where the Spanish ranchers lived in patriarchal state, surrounded by their poorer Spanish and *mestizo* dependents and their Indian *peones*.

In the tropical coast lands, where cattle could not thrive, the principal Spanish product was sugar, which had been introduced into the West Indies by Columbus and into Mexico by Cortés. Sugar was a crop which lent itself to large-scale production, since fairly elaborate equipment was needed for crushing the cane, extracting and refining the syrup, and crystallizing the final product. Sugar plantations were started by many Spaniards, particularly near the Caribbean and Gulf coasts. There was a steady demand for sugar—then an expensive luxury—in Europe, and the industry prospered reasonably in spite of wasteful methods and government interference. Both sugar and tobacco—a crop of great economic importance in the seventeenth century—were largely produced by slave labour, African negroes being imported for the purpose. Since negroes were the subjects of barbarous African kings and not of the king of Spain, there was no legal and little, if any, humanitarian objection to their purchase as slaves. They had to be obtained through Portuguese middlemen, and were extremely expensive in the Indies.

The animal and vegetable products of the Indies were almost insignificant to many Spaniards in comparison with the mineral products —the precious metals. Gold and silver mining in the early days of the conquest was a simple affair of prospecting and washing in likely streams; but about the middle of the sixteenth century, immensely productive silver veins were discovered at Zacatecas and Guanajuato in Mexico and Potosí in what is now Bolivia. Various forms of crude mass-production quickly took the place of the primitive washing process, and extensive plant—extensive for those days—was set up for extracting the silver from the ore, usually by a mercury amalgamation process. These developments produced lawless and exciting silver rushes, and special courts were hastily set up in the mining camps to register claims and settle disputes. Probably some Spaniards worked small claims by hand; but the typical silver miner was a capitalist and an employer of native labour, skilled and unskilled, on a fairly large scale.

The Crown claimed a share, usually one-fifth, of all metal produced. This was the income which aroused the envy and suspicion of all the other monarchs in Europe. In actual fact in most years it was probably not much more than ten or fifteen per cent of the total revenue of the Spanish Crown, and was pledged to German bankers long before it left America. The constant import of silver had disastrous effects on prices and on the economic structure of Spain as a whole—effects which contemporaries attributed to almost any cause but the right one. The economic theories of the time treated bullion as the most important and most valuable product of the Indies; the government sought by all possible means to encourage gold and silver mining, and to enforce payment of the bullion tax. A considerable body of officials was employed to weigh, test and stamp the silver ingots as they issued from the mines and to take out the royal share. Still further officials at the ports watched for attempts to smuggle unstamped silver. About the middle of the sixteenth century, a convoy system was devised for protecting the bullion cargoes on the Atlantic crossing. From 1564 two armed fleets were dispatched from Spain every year, one to Mexico and the Gulf ports, the other to the isthmus of Panama. Both fleets wintered in America and reassembled at Havana the following Spring for the return voyage. Each fleet consisted of from twenty to sixty sail, usually escorted by from two to six warships. It was forbidden for any ship to cross the Atlantic except in one of these convoys, unless special license had been granted. The sailings were sufficiently regular for privateers to lie in wait for them, and one or two ships were lost almost every year. The whole plan illustrated Philip II's excessive confidence in the power of combination and weight, and his inability to see the value of maneuvering and speed —the very mistake which led to the Armada disaster of 1588. Still, on the whole the convoys served their purpose; they maintained regular sailings for a century-and-a-half, and only three times during that period was a whole fleet intercepted and defeated, once by the English and twice by the Dutch. The cost of the convoys was borne by a heavy and complicated series of duties on all goods carried from or to America; so the safety of the fleets was dearly bought, and the whole arrangement added greatly to the delays in obtaining goods in the colonies, and to the price of the goods when they eventually arrived.

The trade to the colonies was a monopoly throughout most of the sixteenth and seventeenth centuries. The monopolist was not the Crown (as in Portugal), but the *consulado*—the merchant guild—of Seville, with its subsidiary organization at Cadiz. By an elaborate series of fictions, merchant houses all over Spain became members by proxy of the Seville guild, consigning their cargoes in the name of resident Seville merchants. Even foreign commercial firms, German, English and Flemish, adopted this device, so that the genuine members of the guild performed a vast commission business which came to over-shadow their own legitimate trade. Seville was the bottleneck of the Indies trade; a bottleneck still further narrowed by the licensing regulations of the royal House of Trade —licensing of emigrants, to prevent the emigration of Jews and heretics; licensing of ships, to ensure their sea-worthiness; of navigators, to ensure their competence. Some commodities might only be exported with special license—fire-arms and negro slaves, for instance. This regulation is understandable, since the Crown was always afraid of the possibility of a slave mutiny; but the whole system constituted a formidable obstacle to trade.

Apart from monopoly and regulation, there was a rigidity in the economic structure of Spain as a whole, which made a rapid expansion of export trade extremely difficult. Among the causes of this rigidity were the contempt widely felt for humdrum employment; the decline of handicrafts and agriculture, due to the Moorish wars and the expulsions of Jews and Moriscos; the privileges accorded to pastoral farming and the consequent damage to arable interests; the large proportion of people in unproductive occupations, especially the Church; heavy taxation and constant European war. Furthermore, the most flourishing commercial centres of Spain, in Cataluña and Aragon, were committed to their Mediterranean connections, and had no great interest in entering the Indies trade.

The whole of the Indies was an eager market for cloth, weapons, tools and hardware of all sorts, books, paper, wine, oil and slaves. Spanish producers could not, or would not, export these goods in sufficient quantities or at competitive prices. The Indies trade therefore was a standing temptation, not only to pirates and privateers, but to slavers, smugglers and illicit traders of all nations.

CHAPTER 3

ENGLAND ON THE
EVE OF COLONIZATION

American civilization is an outgrowth of European civilization, modified by the New World environment and experience. The United States, of course, is in particular a product of the English heritage. The thirteen original colonies were English before they were American, and because they were English their colonial experience, their institutions, and their patterns of life differed from those of the colonies of other European countries. Hence, if the student of United States history is to understand his country's colonial experience, he must begin by examining the mother country, England, in the period of European expansion and colonization.

In the next essay, the colonial historians, Max Savelle, of the University of Washington, and Robert Middlekauff, of the University of California at Berkeley, give a summary view of England on the eve of the English colonization of America—a view based solidly on recent scholarship on Elizabethan England. These authors perform two functions for the student of American history. First, they examine English economic, political, and religious institutions—institutions that were to play major roles in the establishment of the English colonies, and that were to be transferred to America and modified by the American experience. Secondly, they focus specifically on the factors and motives precipitating the migration of Englishmen to Virginia, New England, and the other English colonies.

In reading this and subsequent selections, explore the relationship between the political, economic, and religious conditions in England and the English colonial system that emerged in the New World. Did English institutions contribute to the success of the English colonial experiment? In light of the evidence presented by Professors Savelle and Middlekauff that the vast majority of English colonists were Anglicans who did *not* come to the colonies seeking "religious freedom," what were the motives that led thousands of Englishmen to pour into colonial America? Are these motives different from the motivations for Spanish settlement, examined in the previous selection?

Wallace Notestein, *The English People on the Eve of Colonization, 1603–1630** (1954), and Alfred L. Rowse, *The Elizabethans and America** (1959), are excellent studies of Elizabethan and Stuart England at the beginning of English colonization. William Haller, *The Rise of Puritanism** (1938), is indispensable.

* Available in a paperback edition.

ENGLAND ON THE EVE OF COLONIZATION
MAX SAVELLE AND ROBERT MIDDLEKAUFF

ENGLISH COMMERCIAL EXPANSION

Although most men in sixteenth-century England earned their living on the land, cultivating the soil or raising sheep and cattle, trade at home and abroad was growing. The wool trade with Flanders was the most important activity; the capital it provided financed other ventures organized and controlled by English merchants. Such control was a relatively new thing. Prior to the sixteenth century the English carrying trade had been monopolized by the Venetians on the one side and the Hanseatic League on the other. England was then the commercial outpost of Europe. But with the "discovery" of the Atlantic Ocean and the New World beyond, "the outpost of the Old World became the emporium for the new." For of all the modern nations of western Europe, England is the one most dependent upon commerce for progress, the one which is most clearly the result of, and the one whose history is most clearly determined by, the insularity of the country and its position at the crossroads of world trade. Englishmen were aware of the sudden expansion of British commerce and gloried in it. Richard Hakluyt gives expression to this enthusiasm for overseas commerce when he says:

> Which of the kings of this land before her majesty [Elizabeth], had their banners ever seen in the Caspian Sea? Which of them hath ever dealt with the Emperor of Persia, as her Majesty hath done, and attained for her merchants large and loving privileges? Who ever saw, before this regiment, an English Ligier in the stately porch of the Grand Signor at Constantinople? Who ever found English consuls and agents at Tripolis in Syria, at Aleppo, at Babylon, at Balsara, and, which is more, who ever heard of Englishmen at Goa before now? What English ships did heretofore ever anchor in the mighty river of Plate?

SOURCE. From *A History of Colonial America*, Revised Edition, by Max Savelle and Robert Middlekauff, pp. 48–57. Copyright 1942, © 1964 by Holt, Rinehart and Winston, Inc. Reprinted by permission of Holt, Rinehart and Winston, Inc. and the authors.

An important element in this budding commercial adolescence of the Elizabethans that the patriot Hakluyt overlooked, however, was the fact that many of these vigorous English merchants were, to all intents and purposes, pirates. It is quite possible that he had Sir John Hawkins in mind when he wrote of the English ships that were anchoring "in the mighty river of Plate," and Hawkins had, indeed, carried British trade into distant places. But Hawkins had gone to the slave coasts of Africa in defiance of the Portuguese, and he had taken his cargoes of human freight, in 1562–1563 and 1568, to the Spanish colonies in defiance of Spanish regulations excluding foreign traders, and he had sold his Negroes to the Spanish planters—at the point of a gun when they were slow to buy. Spain had protested, but to no avail.

Quite the contrary, indeed; for Hawkins was only one of the best-known of the daredevil, swashbuckling English sailors, the "Elizabethan sea dogs," who drew no sharp distinction between piracy and legitimate trade, and who drew a certain unctuous satisfaction from hoodwinking, robbing, or even murdering Spaniards—after all, were not the Spaniards Catholics, the disciples of the papal "anti-christ," and the sworn enemies of England? No faith need be kept with Spaniards.

The greatest of the Elizabethan sea dogs was Francis Drake, who became "Sir" Francis Drake after he had "singed the king of Spain's beard" on both sides of the Atlantic. Drake was with Hawkins at San Juan de Ulloa, in 1568, when the expedition was trapped in the harbor by the great Spanish admiral Pedro Mendez de Aviles. Mendez violated the truce arranged between them, with the result that Hawkins lost all but two of his ships, his own and the one commanded by Drake. From that time on Drake became a terror to Spanish shipping and the Spanish colonies. His depredations reached their culmination in 1577–1581 when he sailed boldly into the Pacific and robbed ship after ship of its gold and silver treasure, failed to find a passage back to England north of California (New Albion), and returned round the world in his own small ship, renamed the *Golden Hind,* having enriched himself and his queen with Spanish gold.

This was the more adventurous, more irresponsible side of Elizabethan expansion, and it was not without its significance for the founding of a British empire in America, for Humphrey Gilbert and Walter Raleigh were no less "Elizabethan sea dogs" than Hawkins and Drake, and these were the men who first colonized Newfoundland and Virginia for England.

But Elizabethan expansion had its more conservative, more methodical and businesslike side in the rapid and substantial growth of Britain's world-wide trade. In the course of this expansion of British commerce the merchants, in the interest of greater capital strength, devised several forms of commercial organization that had considerable effect upon the later establishment of the colonies. The first of these types was the so-called "regulated company." Such a company would customarily be organized for the purpose of exploiting some commercial market or undertaking some commercial enterprise, and it would be composed of members who operated independently of each other under their own capital but who cooperated to the extent of obeying such regulations as were laid down by the company. The second general type of trading company was the so-called "semi-joint-stock company" that was customarily organized for a short period of time and usually for the purposes of one enterprise only. Under this type of organization a group of merchants would contribute a certain amount of capital each for the conduct of one trading expedition, say, to the coast of Africa, and that expedition would be conducted as a unit by the company; but the company would dissolve after the return of the expedition and the division of the profits. The third type, which is the more important of the three, was the permanent joint-stock company. Ordinarily such a company was composed of a permanent group of stockholders and was governed by a president or "treasurer," a board of directors called "assistants," and an assembly of the stockholders meeting periodically, usually every three months. There were other types of commercial companies, but it is this third type which is most important for the history of the British colonies in America; for this was the form eventually adopted by the Virginia Company and this commercial way of government was taken over in large measure by certain of the colonies for political purposes.

The first great overseas company in England was the Muscovy Company, founded in 1553 and chartered in 1555 with a capital of six thousand pounds, for a monopoly of the trade with Russia. While it was of the regulated type, it was governed democratically by a governor, an elected council of twenty-eight, and an assembly of all the investors. In 1577 the Cathay Company was organized along similar lines to exploit the trade of China. This was the company whose object was to discover the northwest passage and which sent Martin Frobisher out to do so. In 1581, the Levant Company was organized to exploit the trade of Turkey and the eastern Mediterranean, and in 1588 another company called the African Company was organized to exploit the British trade on the coast of Guinea.

The classic example of these British trading and colonizing companies was the British East India Company, founded in the year 1600 to exploit the trade of the East Indies. The seizure of Portugal by Philip II of Spain in 1580 drove the English and Dutch merchants, who had hitherto bought

Far-Eastern goods at Lisbon or Cadiz, into a direct trade with the East. And the first English expedition to the East Indies sailed under the command of Sir James Lancaster in 1591. This trade proved to be so profitable that companies were formed both in Holland and in England to promote it. The English company was formed under the leadership of Sir Thomas Smythe, perhaps the greatest capitalist of his day. Under its charter, this great company was both a corporation and a body politic, for it was given not only a monopoly of all the English trade in the lands between the Cape of Good Hope and the Straits of Magellan, but it was also empowered to license others to trade in this area, to buy land for the establishment of posts, and to make laws for the government of its trade and its lands. It could even fine and imprison offenders against the law and could maintain soldiers and armed fleets for its own protection. Not only was it empowered to carry on commerce, but it was practically sovereign within the areas defined by its charter. This company was governed by a president, a council of twenty-four assistants, and a general assembly of all the stockholders meeting annually. Within a very short time of its organization the East India Company began to pay fabulous profits and it served as both the inspiration and the model for the men who were responsible for the establishment of the colony of Virginia. It is to be noted also that the government of this company was democratic, in the sense that each stockholder in it was considered to have the same voice in its affairs as all the others.

These were the men, and such were the companies, who furnished the capital and the original impulse toward the founding of English colonies in America in the seventeenth century. Had it not been for the accumulation of capital in the hands of these merchant princes, surplus wealth which they were willing to risk in colonial enterprise, the settlement of British America probably could not have taken place at that time.

ENGLISH POLITICAL INSTITUTIONS

Englishmen who came to America left behind a complex structure of government. Heading it was the monarch in whose name all laws were made, justice was given, and officials chosen. The monarch's formal authority and prestige were immense but knowledge and wisdom and character were essential if he was to exercise his power effectively. Elizabeth, though a woman in a society long accustomed to male dominance, usually got her way in most matters on her charm and brilliance. Her councillors and her Parliaments soon came to sense that in her the nation had a leader with unsurpassed gifts. Her subjects respected her and soon loved her, and Elizabeth loved them. Like her father Henry VIII, the queen made policy and saw to it that her councillors worked in Parliament to secure the laws she considered desirable.

Her successors, James I and his son Charles I, allowed the royal power to decline. In political skill they were inferior leaders; moreover they lacked both the respect of the English people and Elizabeth's understanding of English institutions. Their failure was not simply political; personally James was mean-spirited and Charles, though pious and well-meaning, was dull and stupid.

Though the monarch had much hard work to do—especially if he was to keep himself informed of the activities of his government—most of the administrative supervision of government was carried on by the Privy Council. This body of great officials and advisers varied in size from twelve to twenty under Elizabeth. The early Stuarts, James I and Charles I, increased its members to over forty. The Privy Council's functions ranged from making decisions on large questions of policy and administration to the consideration of the smallest details of government. It helped conduct foreign affairs; it instructed ambassadors; it prepared legislation for Parliament's consideration; it supervised business; it supervised justices of the peace. Poor relief was a matter of concern to it, as were, also, the number of alehouses in a country village and a thousand other petty local problems.

Not the least of the Privy Council's concerns was Parliament. As the legislative body in England, Parliament was composed of two houses, the House of Lords and the House of Commons. The landed aristocracy and the high church officials—"lords temporal and spiritual"—sat in the House of Lords. On the surface, as the seventeenth century opened, the House of Lords still appeared to be the more powerful of the two houses. After all, it sometimes, when consulted, advised the king on important matters of state. Its members were the privileged class; they could be tried only by juries of their peers; and they had the privilege of direct, personal audience with the sovereign. Moreover, the House of Lords constituted a high court for the trial of impeachments and a final court of appeal from the lower courts of the realm. These were formidable powers, but the House of Lords had begun to decline in importance—most seriously in the reign of Elizabeth's father, Henry VIII. Henry, in the interests of his reformation of the church, had changed its composition by creating more temporal peers. The spiritual peers of Henry's creation and the recently created lay peers lacked independence and the House of Lords consequently lost force.

Equally important in the decline of the Lords was the rise of the House of Commons. Though the Tudors were masters at leading Parliament and getting what they wanted while conceding only what they desired in return, the House of Commons was maturing. Composed of the country gentry, government officials and lawyers, who sat as representatives of counties and boroughs, the House of Commons attracted some of the ablest men in the nation. By Elizabeth's day it had become a self-conscious, proud, and powerful body. Elizabeth, by careful management, had held it in check, but under James I Commons broke the old bonds. It developed an elaborate committee system and began staking out the limits of royal authority. Before the end of James' reign it had won the right to initiate legislation; the king's failure to keep privy councillors in the House of Commons advanced the process. Thus organized, the Commons legislated on its own initiative; furthermore, it began to assume certain executive functions; for example, it forced James to cancel a large number of patents, as licenses to do exclusive business were called.

On the local level, officials remained agents of the Crown and not of the Commons. In the county, the most important unit of local government, justices of the peace conducted the government. They were of course judicial officers. Cases of serious crimes were referred to a higher court, but the justices kept busy trying misdemeanors. Drunkenness, gambling, idleness, and a host of other small crimes concerned the justices, who could order whippings or impose fines. Their most important duties were administrative rather than judicial. Often the justices received directions from the Privy Council; more often they decided for themselves what had to be done—a bridge built, constables supervised, roads mended, the poor housed and fed, and so on.

The sheriff, also a royal appointee, helped them though he had his own duties to perform. Selected for one year, the sheriff was the king's representative in the county. He called together the county court; he supervised elections; he arrested criminals; he collected dues owed the king; and at times when the king passed through the sheriff entertained him and his court. The sheriff's job was an unpopular one—expensive and arduous—but indispensable to the welfare of the county.

There were other local officers of course; in the village the constable performed many tasks. He enforced the law and collected taxes, the most difficult of all his jobs. He was not alone in his responsibilities; church wardens, elected by the parish (a governmental and ecclesiastical unit) managed church property, kept up the church building, and collected the parish rates, among other tasks.

THE ENGLISH PROTESTANTS

Long before the Jamestown expedition of 1607 the lines of religious conflict in England had been drawn. Henry VIII had achieved the separation of the English Catholic Church from Rome by about 1540, and the two decades following that date were in large measure taken up with a struggle to decide whether England was to be Catholic or Protestant. Gradually Lutheran and Calvinistic ideas crept into English religious life, and at the time of the accession of Queen Elizabeth in 1558 England had become predominantly Protestant. The adoption of the Thirty-nine Articles in 1563 established Anglican Protestantism in England, and this core of Anglican doctrine was reinforced by the adoption of a new prayer book, the re-enactment of the Act of Supremacy, and the passage of the Act of Uniformity, all between 1559 and 1563.

Anglican Protestantism, as established in England by the "Elizabethan settlement," was governed by a hierarchy of archbishops, bishops, priests, and deacons. The monarch was the supreme head of the church, but its active leader was the archbishop of Canterbury, who was appointed by the king. It preserved a large portion of the Roman Catholic ritual, retaining a belief in the apostolic succession, the wearing of vestments by the clergy, the use of holy water, the sign of the cross, and other ritualistic practices.

But there were many men in England who were not satisfied with what they considered only a partial reformation of the English church by the Elizabethan settlement. They continued to agitate for a further purification, and for dispensing with the hierarchial organization of the church, the use of holy water, the sign of the cross, and other vestiges of the "papish" ritual. These men had no quarrel with the doctrines of the church, but sought only to purify it of "popery." For this reason they were called "Puritans." The Puritans themselves, however, split into various groups; one group of the Puritans favored a central, presbyterian form of church government, and were called "Presbyterians." Another group rejected all hierarchial or coercive church government and insisted upon the independence or autonomy of every congregation of believers; they were the "Congregationalists." Two types of congregationalism developed: the "Separatists" version that rejected all ties to the Church of England, and nonseparating congregationalism that held that the Church of England was the true church although corrupt and polluted. The Separatists founded Plymouth Colony in New England; the nonseparating Congregationalists settled the Massachusetts Bay Colony.

As time went on, the Puritans came to differ more and more widely from the Anglicans in matters other than church practice. As a reaction against the gaiety and the worldliness of Elizabethan England, for example, and as a part of their effort to live the sort of life prescribed by the Bible, they followed a rigorous code of morals, and Puritanism came also to mean a moral domination of one's self. Similarly, whereas Anglicanism allowed for a wide play of human reason in interpreting the Bible and other expressions of God's interest in men, the Puritans considered the Bible to be the literal word of God, the only clear and definite expression of the divine mind with regard to men. Puritanism thus came to be marked by its literalism and its disciplinarianism, whereas Anglicanism, while placing more emphasis upon ritual, was much more latitudinarian with regard to individual believers. Both these bodies of belief were of profound importance in the formation of an American colonial culture.

By the time of the accession of James I there were three major groups of religious believers in England: there were still some Roman Catholics, following their religion more or less surreptitiously; there was the great body of Anglican believers; and there were the Puritans, united in a desire to purify the Church of England, though differing in their ideas of the scriptural ecclesiastical organization. In 1604 about one thousand pastors of the Puritan persuasion presented the so-called "millenary petition" to King James I asking that they be allowed to worship in their churches according to their own Puritan way instead of according to the way laid down by the Elizabethan settlement. James is said to have heard their arguments until his patience was exhausted, and then, putting on his hat as though to leave, to have said "they will conform themselves or I will harry them out of the land."

That was the beginning of a new wave of official and semi-official persecution of the Puritans and Separatists. Those persecutions were not severe under King James I but became increasingly troublesome after the accession of Charles I and after Bishop William Laud of London became Archbishop of Canterbury in 1633. Laud attempted to force the Puritans to conform to the Anglican way. He even leaned somewhat toward Catholicism. But he probably made more Puritans by his reforms that he saved to the Anglican church. Thus, beginning about 1625 or a little earlier, there took place an era of religious persecution that brought sincere Puritans face to face with the necessity for deciding whether they would give up their Puritanism in Anglican conformity or seek for a haven of religious freedom elsewhere. To the motives for emigration springing from economic and political conditions, then, was added the desire to escape from religious persecution. All three of these sets of motives were important in the movement of men and women out of England into America in the first four decades of the seventeenth century.

THE MOVE TO AMERICA

Popular interest in emigration was spurred in a number of ways. The exploits of Hawkins, Drake, and other Elizabethan adventurers interested people; moreover such colonial promoters as Humphrey Gilbert, Walter Raleigh, and Richard Hakluyt "advertised" the New World. Elizabethan literature, indeed, is shot through with reflections of a widespread popular interest in the New World and the adventures to be had there. "The world's mine oyster, which I with sword will open!" exclaims one of the characters in *The Merry Wives of Windsor,* and Shakespeare's plays are full of the jargon of the sea and tales of far-off countries. *The Tempest* is said to have been inspired by the shipwreck of the Somers expedition on Bermuda in 1610. One of the most popular plays of the time was *Eastward Ho,* a play upon the popular craze for sailing, commerce, and exploration.

It took more, however, than a merely literary interest in adventures overseas to send thousands of common men away from their native land into the dangers and uncertainties of colonization in a distant wilderness. By the end of the sixteenth century England seemed to be overrun by beggars, vagrants, criminals, and the indigent poor. England seemed to be overpopulated. This condition was probably due to the social maladjustment brought about by the practice of enclosing agricultural land for sheep-raising purposes, which forced many agricultural workers off the land. England's total population, as a matter of fact, was hardly more than three million persons—considerably less than half the present population of the City of London—but near the end of Elizabeth's reign English leaders began to look toward colonies in the New World as a possible receptacle for the overflow of the burdensome "surplus" of population in England itself.

The flow of Englishmen overseas began with the founding of Virginia in 1607, and the first two decades of the seventeenth century constituted a period of English experimentation in colonization, not only in Virginia, but also in Newfoundland, along the shores of New England, in the islands of the West Indies, and on the mainland of South America. By 1620, however, the feasibility of colonies had been demonstrated, and in the next two decades, that is to say, between 1620 and 1640, the stream of emigration from England to America reached its flood.

During this twenty-year period some 70,000 people left England for the New World. Of the total, some 12,000 went to Virginia, Bermuda, and the new colony of Maryland. About 18,000 went to New England, 14,000 of whom stopped in Massachusetts Bay, and about 37,000 went to the West Indies, where some 18,000 settled in Barbados, 4000 in Nevis, 12,000 in St. Christopher's, and some 3000 in the smaller English islands.

These people came for a variety of reasons. Most seemed to desire a new start, either at getting a living or in realizing their own vision of a religious society. The Puritans who settled in Massachusetts Bay, for example, were filled with a desire to create "a city upon a hill"—a holy society that would serve as a model for the still unreformed Europe. Of course, many plain people came to New England and the other colonies with the hope that earning a living might be easier in the New World. Others simply looked forward to political and religious tranquility. It must be remembered, of course, that the vast majority of the Englishmen who came to the colonies as settlers were Anglicans, who had no quarrel with the established church or with the crown. Whatever their reasons, these people poured into America, in the first of many such hopeful movements.

CHAPTER 4

THE COLONISTS
AND THE INDIANS

Like Ralph Ellison's Negro, the American Indian also has been an invisible man. Standard historical treatment of Indians often has been narrow and superficial, even if outwardly sympathetic. In the absence of well-founded knowledge about the Indian, stereotypes and myths have developed, ranging from the "noble Indian" concept of the eighteenth and nineteenth centuries to the war-bonneted, horse-riding Indian of motion pictures and television. In general, American Indians have been treated as one of the natural factors, like weather, great distances, and wild animals, impeding the westward march of civilization. In the words of Daniel J. Boorstin, "The Indians thus seem nothing more than sand in the smoothly oiled gears of American progress."[1]

The Indian occupies an important role in American history. He aided European settlement by imparting to the white man his knowledge of how to live—to hunt, to fish, and to grow crops in the wilderness. He named many of our lakes, mountains, and states; more important, he helped to stamp on the American character its frontier traits; he gave the world the potato, the tomato, and tobacco.

[1] From the Editor's Preface to William T. Hagan, *American Indians,* The University of Chicago Press, 1961, p. v.

45

In the following selection from his book, *American Indians,* William T. Hagan suggests that there was, and is, no "average" Indian, in view of the great variety and complexity of the hundreds of different Indian cultures in the present-day United States. Hagan's emphasis is not on these diverse cultures as such, but is on the relations between the Indians and the Europeans with whom they came into contact. Hence, the account often tells us as much about the white conqueror as about the exploited Indian. In a day when many Americans are questioning whether America is a racist society, such a perspective is particularly useful. The essay points up clearly that the current problems of human relations facing Americans are, at least partly, historical problems, faced by red men and white men (and black men) in the years after 1607.

Clark Wissler, *Indians of the United States** (1940), and John R. Alden, *Pioneer America* (1966), are excellent surveys of the Indian. White attitudes toward Indians are explored in Roy Harvey Pearce, *The Savages of America** (1963). A monograph on the archetypical Indian is Robert H. Lowie, *Indians of the Plains** (1954).

* Available in a paperback edition.

COLONIAL PREPARATION
WILLIAM T. HAGAN

Nambok the Unveracious, a product of Jack London's literary skill, was a native of the North Pacific Coast who returned unexpectedly to his people after a mysterious disappearance years earlier. After hearing him relate the fantastic ways of the whites with whom he had associated during his absence, the tribe concluded he was either a liar or a spirit returned from the dead and they drove him from their midst.

Shocked incredulity must have been the usual Indian reaction to their initial white contacts. The huge, wind-propelled craft bringing these strangers to their shores could have inspired it. And if the natives were able to master their awe at the size and style of these tremendous canoes, they were astounded by the sight of the great dog-like animals which carried the strangers and their equipment. If in fear of their lives the Indians attempted to drive the invaders back to their boats, they quickly learned to their dismay the superiority of firearms and metal armor over clubs, bows, lances, and leather shields. Subsequent contacts revealed additional miraculous objects to the natives: metal cooking vessels, wheeled transport, sheep, and swine.

The Indians readily learned to use copper kettles and ride horses and eat mutton. Their difficulty lay in their associations with the strangers who had thus enriched their lives. Before many years had passed there were tribes in the South that had encountered Spaniards, Frenchmen, and Englishmen. Along the North Atlantic Coast, Swedes and Dutch had arrived on the scene as well. The confusion of tongues and claims to sovereignty was compounded by the varieties of personality each nation seemed to represent. The Catholic and Protestant missionaries did not agree among themselves, as the Indians came to learn. They, however, clearly had different interests in the Indians than the traders who introduced them to the copper kettles and rum, or the official representatives of the Great Fathers across the waters. The officials talked con-

SOURCE. William T. Hagan, *American Indians,* Chicago: The University of Chicago Press, 1961, pp. 1–18 and 29–30. Copyright 1961 by the University of Chicago. Reprinted by permission of the University of Chicago Press and the author.

fusingly of permitting the Indian to occupy land which his tribe had claimed as far back as Indian memory ran, or which the Indian and his fellow warriors had conquered at the risk of their lives.

Over the years closer associations simply deepened the Indians' perplexity. Tenaciously they clung to their own way of life, although they lacked the numbers and disciplined organization to resist the intruders effectively. Over 600,000 Indians occupied the area covered today by the forty-eight states, but the physical and cultural variations were many. Red men came in as many different sizes and shapes and skin tones as the whites who were about to overwhelm them. The only features the Indians had in common were black hair, brown eyes, and some shade of brown skin. The Winnebagos were noted for their large heads; the Utes for their squat, powerful frames; the Crows for their height. These physical variations, coupled with the hundreds of different dialects spoken (although scholars have classified them in six major language groups) offer the best evidence that the migrations from Asia began perhaps 30,000 years ago and included many fragments of Asiatic peoples.

Certainly the white man who had encountered Indian tribes in various parts of the continent had more difficulty in arriving at an "average" Indian than has the producer of the western epics for Hollywood and television. The Chippewa rode in a birchbark canoe, the Chickasaw in a dugout; the Sac slept in a bark wigwam, the Kiowa in a skin tepee, and the Pueblo in a stone apartment house. The Seminole hunted with a blowgun, the Sioux with a bow. Did this average Indian take his foe's head for a trophy, or did he content himself with just the scalp, and did the scalp include the ears? Did he grow corn, or dig camas roots, or spear salmon? Was boiled puppy a delicacy or a last resort to stave off famine? The Papagos regarded war as a form of insanity, the Comanches gloried in it. The list of variations seemed infinite, and well it might when it is noted that perhaps as many as six hundred different cultures were involved.

Nor did the white man have to travel hundreds of miles to find these cultural variations. The Choctaws and Chickasaws lived side by side, yet the Choctaws were noted for their agricultural skills, the Chickasaws for their belligerency. The Sac and Fox tribes were even more closely allied, but the Sacs were more stable and dependable in political matters. Even within tribes these differences were apparent. Skidi Pawnees were reputed to be better warriors than those from other Pawnee bands, and the Mohollusha Choctaws were noted for their improvidence as contrasted with other Choctaws. Nor were national characteristics any more permanent among the Indians than among other peoples. A tribe conspicious for political stability and economic competency might degenerate into a mob of quarreling, drunken brutes within a span of two generations.

Degeneration did not automatically follow tribal associations with the whites. The acquisition of metal tools and utensils, firearms, horses, and sheep simplified life for the Indian. Totem poles and dugouts were more easily fashioned with metal tools, the women fleshed buffalo and deer hides less laboriously with metal scrapers, and they found copper kettles more durable than pottery or woven baskets. Warriors could chisel arrowheads from hoop iron in a fraction of the time required to chip them from flint. Although the early muskets were crude weapons compared with the modern rifle, their superiority over lances and bows and clubs was clearly recognized by the Indian, who cherished the musket which came his way.

Sheep made a new way of life for a few tribes such as the Navaho, but it was the horse which had the greatest impact. For those today classified as plains Indians it facilitated a genuine revolution. Some of them had been primitive agriculturists living on the edge of the plains in permanent villages. Others had been semi-nomadic, but inhibited by their poor transport—dogs carrying packs or dragging travois. As horses drifted north out of the Spanish settlements, being traded from tribe to tribe, or stolen, they produced a new culture for these tribesmen. When these people became mobile, they abandoned their garden patches to follow the buffalo herds. Tepees grew in size and camping equipment became more elaborate as horses were acquired to pull larger travois. An entirely new pattern of life developed, complete with a new religious orientation, new dances, and new games.

Tribes near the plains went through a similar transformation when horses became available to them. The Nez Percé typified those attracted by the new culture. Although some bands remained true to the old ways and subsisted by fishing, root digging, and hunting smaller animals, many Nez Percé now trailed the buffalo herds and borrowed freely from the plains tribes with whom they fought and socialized. They might well have joined the Navahos who denied any pre-horse history: "If there were no horses, there were no Navahos."

Among the eastern tribes, whose forest environment made the horse less valuable, the impact of white culture was still remarkable. With their newly acquired metal files, chisels, needles, knives, and firearms the Indians were able to support themselves with less effort, leaving more time for religious ceremonials, war, and recreation. The old crafts declined and some, like pottery making, became lost arts. But what warrior armed with a trade musket and tomahawk, resplendent in a silk turban and scarlet blanket and jingling silver ear bobs, would be perturbed at this obvious march of progress? Some Indian crafts such as totem pole carving and weaving, challenged by European designs and materials and facilitated by metal tools, achieved new levels of technical excellence. This flurry of creative effort stimulated by the new contacts occurred repeatedly as the white and Indian cultures came into contact.

But not all the tribes enjoyed this renaissance before degeneration set in. For some tribes their first contact with metal weapons came when traditional enemies suddenly appeared so armed and put them to flight. The first two centuries of Indian-white contact produced a prodigious shifting of tribes in response to such pressure. The Iroquois in the East, the Apaches in the Southwest, and the Crees in the Hudson's Bay area were among those Indians who early acquired metal weapons and used them with devastating effects on their neighbors, driving them from choice hunting grounds, seizing their property, enslaving and killing them. The relatively politically sophisticated Iroquois established an empire in New York, Pennsylvania, and the upper Ohio Valley. Crushing the Huron, the Iroquois drove them and other tribes as far west as Wisconsin. When Pawnees ventured east of the Mississippi to raid tribes subject to the Iroquois, these liege lords dispatched war parties nearly a thousand miles to teach the Pawnees a lesson.

As the tribesmen increased their holdings of firearms, metal traps, blankets, and other trade items, they became dependent upon the whites. La Salle recognized this relationship when he commented, "The savages take better care of us French than of their own children; from us only can they get guns and goods." A delay in the arrival of traders with gunpowder and muskets could put the Indians at the mercy of their enemies and the elements. Bourbon ambitions in Europe could produce tragic repercussions for tribesmen in the Mississippi Valley who had never heard of the court at Versailles but whose supply lines ran back to France, while their rivals were supplied by the English. Thus the fortunes of individual tribes ebbed and flowed because of factors they could neither control nor comprehend.

From King William's War in the late seventeenth century through the War of 1812, tribal allegiances were frequently dictated by the trade situation. At a given moment a tribe might prefer its French or English Father, but if he could not put traders in their villages and his rival could, it had no alternative but to support the rival. Most Indians could not even repair a broken musket; they had to have access to traders. To return to the old way of life would be as easy for them as it would be for the average twentieth-century Manhattanite to convert to dirt farming.

Not infrequently the forerunner of the new way of life would be one of the white man's diseases which swept Indian villages, sometimes almost annihilating tribes and scattering the panic-stricken survivors. Tuberculosis, syphilis, measles, and smallpox were the principal diseases the whites inflicted on the Indian population. The Pilgrims regarded it as divine intervention that some disease, possibly smallpox left by sailors who had visited the area, had slashed eastern Massachusetts' Indian population shortly before the Pilgrims' arrival. The Cherokee medicine men attributed the smallpox epidemic which swept their nation in the 1730's to the sexual lapses of their young people, and some conservative Indians blamed the plagues on the departure from the old ways. In the next century the white man's diseases were still at work solving the Indian problem.

From the beginning there was no unanimity in the white approach to the Indian problem. The French were primarily concerned with the fur trade, and it was to their advantage to make use of the Indian's special skills as a hunter. The possibility of precious metals lured the Spanish into the area that now comprises the United States, but for the Indian the mission became the principal Spanish institution. The English sought Indian land, although the fur trade also attracted some.

The net effect of the evolving policies was most disastrous for those Indians in contact with the English. The Frenchman actually needed the Indian and cultivated him accordingly. The Spanish mission might resemble a forced-labor system and its paternalism was not designed to prepare the mission Indian for independent status in a white society, but it did preserve his life and provide a rude plenty. Although citizens of neither of these Latin Catholic nations had the pronounced racialist views of the Anglo-Saxon, discrimination did exist in Spanish America. The universities were restricted to the whites, an Indian priest was a rarity, and laws were enacted to keep horses and firearms in the hands of whites.

The average English colonist was a farmer, not a fur trader or priest, and to him the Indian was either a nuisance or a menace. If the Indian had departed peacefully, probably racial prejudice would have been only so great as to rationalize expropriating him. But he did resist and his style of warfare, braining infants against trees and torturing captives, horrified Englishmen. As a result, some assimilation did take place, but not to the degree nor with the approbation that it took place among the Spanish and French.

One fundamental problem for all colonial powers was land title. Spanish experts like Franciscus de Victoria advised that the Indian title was valid. In contrast, the Swiss jurist Vattel held that the Indian title depended upon their use of the land. Among the English colonies Vattel's view prevailed and what was generally held to have been transferred by treaty was the Indian usufruct, or right to use the land. In negotiating with each other and pre-empting for their national governments the authority to purchase land, all nations maintained the right of discovery to be paramount. In practice the results were essentially the same: if the whites needed the land, they took it.

Compared to Spanish and French, English policy was necessarily confused and contradictory, since the individual colonies contended with each other and the crown in the area of Indian affairs. One of the few unifying threads was the work among Indians sponsored by the infrequent missionary groups which did not take colonial boundaries into account. The colonial charters frequently carried a clause enjoining the grantees to convert and civilize the Indians, but, because the grantees were not investing their money for that purpose, these injunctions had little effect. The missionary impulse was not strong among Englishmen, and the tribesmen did not convert easily. One of the early missionaries gave up in disgust after three years, despairing, "Heathen they are & heathen they will remain."

In authorizing the colonization of Virginia, James I had urged the propagation of the Christian religion among the Indians. Down to the outbreak in 1622 this seems to have received more than just lip service. The Virginia Company officials directed their governor at Jamestown to use force if necessary to separate the Indian children from the unholy atmosphere of their families. Money was appropriated to educate young Indians in Virginia homes and a few were even sent to England, but little progress was made and an uprising in 1622 ended plans for two Indian schools.

The uprising forced a general reorientation of Virginia Indian policy. Virginians had assumed that in time the Indians would recognize the beneficence of civilization. The marriage of John Rolfe to Pocahontas, daughter of Powhatan, who headed the Indian confederation in eastern Virginia, had been expected to consolidate the alliance, particularly after James I, by proxy, had crowned Powhatan. But Powhatan died in 1618 and under his successor, Opechancanough, the Indians united to avenge themselves for the petty slights inflicted by the whites and to eliminate this growing menace to their territory. Although the Virginians beat off these first onslaughts, peace did not return for twelve years.

During that period the Virginia Indian policy was reoriented. The optimistic approach of coexistence disappeared in a welter of ambushes and truce violations. During the remainder of the seventeenth century the only provision for education of Indian students was for those held hostage or captive. As the Reverend Samuel Purchas rationalized Virginia's new policy, the Indian had broken natural law and was no longer entitled to consideration.

The uneasy peace was broken in 1644 by a last concerted effort to drive the Virginians into the ocean. Led again by Opechancanough, now so enfeebled by age he had to be carried on a litter, the tribesmen killed about five hundred whites in the surprise attacks that opened the war. The survivors quickly rallied and easily crushed the Indian forces. The buildup of strength in the settlements had reached the point that without outside help the Indians could not win a protracted war. For a century and a half the war whoop echoed on the Virginia frontier and captives returned to tell ghastly stories of torture and enslavement, but after Opechancanough's defeat the destined victor was obvious. For the frontiersmen the threat was very real, but for the whole colony the Indian constituted little more than a nuisance.

Before the Virginia Indians drifted into obscurity they were counseled to send some of their young men to the College of William and Mary, which had a few Indian students supported by charity and instructed in segregated classes. A spokesman declined, explaining that their young men who had been exposed to the white man's education had returned bad runners, ignorant of woodcraft, susceptible to cold and hunger, "neither fit for hunters, warriors, nor counsellors." He did offer to make men of any Virginia youths sent to the Indians for instruction. There is no record that Virginia officially availed itself of the opportunity, but generations of frontiersmen traded boots for moccasins and excelled their tutors at scalping.

The other southern colonies profited from Virginia's experience in Indian affairs. Maryland authorities were fortunate in not having to contend with a confederation as powerful as Opechancanough's, and they were more careful to leave the tribes with some feeling of compensation. The Jesuits who followed Lord Baltimore to Maryland apparently hoped to launch large-scale mission enterprises comparable to those of Spanish colonies, but discovered that Baltimore's religious zeal was not sufficient to tolerate this threat to his proprietorship.

For Carolina and Georgia, trade and imperial defense were the determining factors in their Indian relations. By 1750 Charleston was the center of the fur trade in the South and an estimated 1,250,000 deer-skins passed through that port between 1739 and 1759. Trade of this volume attracted competition and the southern colonies were frequently at odds since Virginia traders ignored South Carolina regulations.

Farther south, Georgia's early Indian relations were relatively painless owing to Oglethorpe's prestige with the Creeks. Recognizing the power of this tribe he courted their favor through Mary, a half-blood Creek woman who married successively a South Carolina trader, a Georgia militia officer, and a former Indian agent turned cleric. All of Mary's husbands, as well as Oglethorpe, profited from Mary's relation to the head of the Creek nation. These white men were not the first, nor the last, to use Indian marriages to further their economic and political objectives. Sentiment may have played a role in these connections, but it is interesting to note that white men usually contracted such liaisons only with close relatives of tribal leaders.

No such intermarriage eased the movement of the Pilgrims and Puritans into New England, but they had something far better—the assurance that God was on their side. Through the agency of the plague He had cleared the way for His chosen people and this morally justified the Pilgrims' refusal to purchase the land from the Indians. Whether at Plymouth or the settlements around Massachussetts Bay, the settlers had little difficulty identifying the Indians as agents of Satan. It required no great change in Puritan mentality to make room in their universe, already peopled with witches and saints, for these "tawny serpents" and "hideous creatures."

There were exceptions. The Pilgrims were delighted to have the advice and fellowship of Squanto. Speaking English he had learned from slave traders, Squanto served as an intermediary between the neighboring tribes and the Pilgrims, besides introducing them to native foods like planked shad and the clambake.

Roger Williams and John Eliot did not fit the pattern either. Eliot denounced his fellow Puritans for their enslavement of Indians and neglect of their missionary responsibilities. He translated the Bible into a local Indian dialect and helped establish several reservations of Christian or "praying" Indians. Roger Williams was even more heretical in New England eyes. He attacked the Puritan policy of recognizing Indian rights to land only if it were occupied by villages or under cultivation. He insisted the Indians also had a valid title to their hunting grounds.

Any debate over Indian claims to land became purely academic after the Pequot War of 1637. One of the few tribes whose strength was unimpaired by the plague, the Pequots chose to resist the movement of settlers into the Connecticut Valley. At night a small party of whites surrounded the Pequot stronghold, fired it, and over five hundred Indians were killed or burned to death, while the attackers lost but two men. The remnants of the tribe were sold into slavery. The Narragansetts, wooed by Roger Williams, had provided an auxiliary for the white squads that combed the woods for surviving Pequots. Such help was badly needed by the whites in 1637 for some of their commanders continued to think in terms of warfare as it was waged in Europe. White captains had to learn and relearn the lesson that Indian fighting required speed and stealth rather than cumbersome baggage trains and troops maneuvering in ranks in open country.

The Puritans confidently attributed their victory over the Pequots to divine intervention. One of their captains said it was "as though the finger of God had touched both match and flint," and that the Indian cries, as they succumbed to the flames and bullets, were so pathetic that "if God had not fitten the hearts of men for the service, it would have bred in us a commiseration towards them." Cotton Mather called upon his congregation to thank God, "that on this day we have sent six hundred heathen souls to hell."

Three decades elapsed before the next Indian crisis in New England, King Philip's War, 1675–76. Sparked by the Wampanoag chief Philip, it was a coalition war aimed originally at Plymouth. The usual disregard for Indian personal and property rights, attempts to enforce Indian observance of the Puritan Sabbath, and a legal code providing capital punishment for blasphemy, furnished Philip allies from the Narragansetts. Three tribes, however, furnished auxiliaries for the New Englanders. Once again the Indian allies of the whites at least shortened the war if they did not completely alter its course.

The war did tax the resources of New England to the limit. A score of settlements were wiped out and the death toll ran over a thousand. Finally victorious, the whites bloodily avenged themselves. Philip was captured, drawn and quartered; his skull remained on view on a pole in Plymouth as late as 1700. The Narragansett chief Canonchet was also captured and sentenced to be beheaded. Informed of his fate he remarked stoically that he was happy to go "before his heart was soft, or he had spoken anything unworthy of himself." Hundreds of Indians captured were not executed but sold into slavery, many of them to the West Indies. This not only rid the country of surplus Indian population but helped defray some of the expenses of the war. The Puritan conscience was not troubled by this slave traffic. The Indians were simply the agents of Satan, successful to the degree that the Puritans had strayed from grace by leniency to the Quakers or by the obsession of Puritan wives and daughters with the "cutting, curling and immodest laying out of their hair."

The Indians, as usual following one of these wars, went downhill rapidly. Brought under close surveillance, the recently hostile and friendly tribesmen alike were required to live in specified villages, arms and ammunition were denied them, and precautions were taken against their assembling. Plymouth authorities even revived the Anglo-Saxon tithing system by making one Indian in each group of ten responsible for the behavior of the others.

In semi-isolation, the New England Indians did what countless generations of tribesmen were to do later on reservations from the Atlantic to the Pacific: they degenerated. Unable to revert to their primitive practices, they picked up the white man's vices and diseases faster than they acquired his virtues. The proposition that contact with the whites corrupted rather than uplifted was demonstrated all too well in the Puritan theocracy.

The pattern of events in the middle colonies was similar to that in New England and the South. The Dutch and Swedes pioneered in that area and had virtually cleared southern New York and New Jersey of Indians by the time the English supplanted them. Governor Kieft of New Amsterdam is credited with offering the first bounty for Indian scalps, a more convenient trophy than heads. The Dutch resembled the English more than the French in their relations with their Indian neighbors. They did not dignify their relations with Indian women by marriage, and they exhibited the same lack of missionary zeal. As traders, however, they were very effective and after scattering the smaller tribes on the lower Hudson effected a mutually profitable relationship with the Iroquois which the English inherited.

The fame of the Iroquois had spread far and wide. In 1682, William Penn dispatched a letter to the "Emperor of Canada," as he addressed the ranking chief of the Iroquois, apprising him of the Quaker intention to develop Pennsylvania. Although they failed ultimately to produce a society in which the Indian could live as an equal, the Pennsylvania Quakers compiled a record of just dealings with the tribesmen clearly superior to that of the other colonists. Penn was careful to purchase Indian land claims, his first treaty on the banks of the Delaware being described by Voltaire as the only treaty not sealed by an oath, and the only treaty kept faithfully by the whites. But gradually the white pressure on Indian lands and the necessity of propitiating the dangerous Iroquois led to the expulsion of the Delawares and other small tribes from southeastern Pennsylvania. The wealthy Quaker merchants of Philadelphia were not as ruthless as the Scotch-Irish on the frontier; however, they were a far cry from George Fox and William Penn, as their behavior in the intense rivalry for the Indian trade indicated.

For the Indians this rivalry was a mixed blessing. Competition did bring higher prices for their furs, but cutthroat rivalry led to the wholesale introduction of rum and debauchery of entire tribes. Traders employed any tactics to make an immediate profit on the assumption that next year they might be crowded out. As the trade wars multiplied, and tribal rivalries were encouraged for trade purposes, they resulted in the virtual extermination of some tribes and the expulsion of others. These conditions were only intensified when the competition was between French and English, or Spanish and English traders, instead of between Georgians and South Carolinians.

These international trade rivalries provided one of the chief motivations for the struggle for control of North America. Granted that the four great wars waged between 1689 and 1763 (King William's, Queen Anne's, King George's, and the French and Indian) had their origins in European politics, they frequently did no more than give official status to what was already going on along the frontier. French and English traders contending for the furs harvested by the tribes did not need a declaration of war to recognize a state of hostility. They were continually intriguing with the tribesmen to hold the trade they had and to undercut their competition.

Although the Iroquois were sufficiently powerful to play the role of a balance of power on the New York–Canadian frontier, the average tribe simply responded to the nation able to bring the most power to bear upon it. True, the Indian found the Frenchmen less race-conscious and less covetous of Indian land, but English trade goods were generally cheaper and superior in quality. Both sides employed Indian auxiliaries. The French were dependent on them for their offensive punch because French troops were too few to be more than a stiffener for the war parties which devastated the frontier of the English colonies. Neither the French nor the English could operate in the trackless forests without Indian scouts and guides.

The aftermath of a raid on Haverhill, Massachusetts, indicates the nature of the warfare. Spurred on by indications of the treatment awaiting them in the Indian villages, three captive white women and a boy tomahawked ten of the twelve members of a war party while they slept during a break on the trail to Canada. Hannah Dustin, one of the women, then scalped their victims and returned to Haverhill with her bloody trophies and claimed the bounty offered by the colonial government.

The Indian casualty rates in these campaigns were high. In the South the Spanish mission system among the Florida Indians never recovered from the raids of the English and their Indian allies who killed and enslaved the Spanish wards. The white man's wars and need for slaves were pitting the Indians against each other and only the whites could be the winner. One agent described the tactic as setting one wolf pack against another. . . .

In 1749 one French detachment traveled down the Allegheny and the Ohio warning English traders away and trying in vain to get the tribes to expel the Englishmen from their villages. Three years later another French column surprised the Miami village of Pickawillany, captured five English traders, confiscated their goods, and killed a number of Indian allies of the English. As a salutary lesson to other Ohio tribesmen the French Indian auxiliaries boiled and ate the Miami chief. . . .

By the time colonial discontent had paved the way for a new nation the pattern of white-Indian relations in what was to be the United States had already become apparent. Scores of Indian tribes, such as King Philip's Wampanoags, had been corrupted and eliminated by the whites. The outline of events in such tragedies was clear. The traders first employed the Indians to gather furs and tribal standard of living rose as they acquired firearms and metal tools. Then as the game diminished and the frontier line pressed upon the Indian holdings the second act opened. It closed with the tribesmen having been forced or seduced into selling their land. Occasionally this act would include an Indian war with a standard script calling for an outburst of violence by the tormented natives, scalpings, burning, and the horrors of torture embellished by that early American form of literature, the captivity narrative. The third act would find the Indian resistance crushed and the inevitable treaty written ceding even more land to the whites. The principal problem remaining would be the ultimate disposition of the tribe. The Indians might settle the problem temporarily by migrating westward to compete with already established tribes for their hunting grounds and set the stage for a repetition of the last two acts. Or, if the defeat in the war had been overwhelming, the few tribesmen remaining might be absorbed by neighboring bands or located on a reservation. The usual result was that the reservation Indians frustrated their well-wishers and co-operated with their oppressors by dying off rapidly.

The role of the central government, to be played by the United States after the Revolution, had already assumed definite character as portrayed by the British Empire. Basically paternal in their approach to Indian problems, officials of the central government soon learned that when a conflict existed between the interests of the Indians and those of the frontiersmen, that the Indians had to be sacrificed. To the extent that the Revolution would produce a new nation more responsive to its citizens' pressures, the Indians would lose by the change.

CHAPTER 5

THE INFLUENCE OF THE FRONTIER ENVIRONMENT

More than 75 years ago, in July 1893, Frederick Jackson Turner, a young assistant professor at the University of Wisconsin, delivered a paper to the American Historical Association, meeting on the grounds of the Chicago World's Fair. The paper "The Significance of the Frontier in American History" is the best-known and probably the most important essay ever written in the field of American history. Turner argued that American historians, in interpreting the American past, tended to overemphasize European factors and to ignore American factors. "The true point of view in the history of this nation," he said, "is not the Atlantic coast, it is the Great West." The development of American institutions and of the American character could be explained, Turner suggested, by the "existence of an area of free land, its continuous recession, and the advance of American settlement westward. . . ."

The Turner thesis, or frontier hypothesis, was put forward as one of the possible explanations of American development. Unfortunately, until Turner's death in 1932, his views enjoyed overenthusiastic and uncritical acceptance; then, in the 1930's and 1940's his thesis was violently and unreasonably attacked by critics in history and other disciplines. In the 1950's and 1960's a "third generation" of the frontier hypothesis emerged.

In *America's Frontier Heritage,* Professor Ray Allen Billington, once a student of Turner's, seeks to summarize the findings of the "third generation" and to reappraise the entire hypothesis in the light of modern research. To accomplish these tasks, he has utilized several hundred eighteenth- and nineteenth-century travel accounts and recent studies of sociologists, anthropologists, social psychologists, and demographers.

In the next selection, Professor Billington examines the influence of both environment and heredity on man's social behavior, evaluates the role of the physical environment and the social environment in determining cultural patterns, and applies these findings to the development of American institutions and American character traits on the frontier. He suggests that the end products were determined not by the European heritage alone nor by the physical wilderness frontier alone, but primarily by the clash of traditional controls and values with a changing and innovative social environment on the frontier.

In seeking to appraise the influence of the frontier on American civilization, Professor Billington raises this fundamental question: Can a culture be basically altered by transplantation to a different physical environment? What is his answer? Does he see the development of a distinctive national character in colonial and nineteenth-century America? If so, in explaining this development, what weight does Professor Billington give to the various forces operating on the Americans—their European heritage, the wilderness frontier, and what he identifies as the social environment?

With a plethora of excellent material on this subject, students can begin with Frederick Jackson Turner, "The Significance of the Frontier in American History" (reprinted in numerous places). A provocative two-part article is Stanley Elkins and Eric McKitrick, "A Meaning for Turner's Frontier," *Political Science Quarterly,* LXIX (July 1954) and (December 1954). Billington's *America's Frontier Heritage** is a thorough and penetrating treatment of the subject.

* Available in a paperback edition.

THE FRONTIER AND THE AMERICAN CHARACTER
RAY A. BILLINGTON

Let us indulge in a thoroughly unhistorical speculation. Suppose that in the year A.D. 752 the emperor Hsiian Tsung, wearying of the brilliant scholars in his Academy of Letters and moved by the plight of his over-crowded peasantry, decided to dispatch his most experienced navigator, Bo Ko Lum, to search for a route to thinly settled Europe. Assume that Bo Ko Lum, sailing eastward with three sturdy ships, made his landfall in a gentle country that he mistook for a remote outpost of the Frankish kingdom where he was welcomed by friendly natives, called by the Chinese, Red Franks. Pretend that this newly discovered continent, later called Frankland, was occupied over the next century by hundreds of thousands of settlers from China's overpopulated mainland. They would fashion rice paddies, build their pagodas to worship at the shrine of Buddha, and slowly advance their Asiatic civilization eastward, led by venturesome fur trappers in flowing silken robes. As they moved ever onward toward the rising sun until they reached the distant Atlantic they would leave behind a new Orient, transplanted across the seas, and modeled after the Orient they had left behind.

But would this civilization be an exact replica of the old? It would not. Chinese pioneers would discover that silken robes were less resistant to wilderness wear than jackets and pantaloons of hides, that corn and wheat were more easily produced than rice, and that decrees of a distant emperor were easily ignored by a people whose unique problems demanded unique local solutions. They would, over the course of years, change in appearance, in dietary habits, and in social values as the wilderness of Frankland altered their customs and institutions. A future Chinese historian might write that they had been Franklandized by the New World environment. Yet would this transformation convert the colonists into replicas of the pioneers who actually settled the Wests? Certainly not. Trans-

SOURCE. From Chapter Three (pp. 47–61) of *America's Frontier Heritage* by Ray Allen Billington. Copyright © 1966 by Ray Allen Billington. Reprinted by permission of Holt, Rinehart and Winston, Inc. and the author.

planted cultural patterns would be too powerful to be completely sub-merged. The imaginary Frankland as an outpost of China would have borne little resemblance to the actual America as an outpost of England. But it would also show little similarity to the China from which the settlers had come.

This imagined situation brings into focus the basic question that must be answered if we are to appraise the influence of the frontier on American civilization. Can a culture be basically altered by transplantation to a different physical environment? And, if it can, how is this accomplished? To solve these problems we must weigh the relative influence of traditional cultural forces and the physical environment in shaping group cultures.

Geneticists have learned a great deal about the hereditary process. They know that traits are transmitted from parents to children through the forty-six chromosomes present in every fertilized ovum, that these chromosomes are made up of complex molecules called "genes," and that these genes are reshuffled from generation to generation, giving rise to the endless new combinations that relieve us of the unpleasant necessity of all looking alike. They also know that hereditary traits are rigidly restrained (save in the rare case of mutations) and that they are passed along by the genes from generation to generation utterly unchanged by life experiences. This means that *learned* skills or experiences cannot be inherited; we inherit only a certain physical-chemical organization observable in the form of the physical structure, intelligence, temperament, and innate drives.

Environment plays an equally important role in shaping our behavior. Actually we are influenced by two interacting environments, the "primary" or *physical* environment that comprises the world of nature about us, and the "secondary" or *social* environment provided by the human group in which we find ourselves. Of these two, the latter is more immediately important, for the social group serves as a medium through which primary environmental forces reach the individual; its influence operates within limits set by the physical environment but within these limits it plays a transcendent role. Each group has its own patterns of behavior known as a *culture,* which include the shared knowledge, beliefs, customs, and habits that have been acquired by living together over the course of generations. These "cultures" vary from group to group and account for many of the differences that distinguish peoples; they determine the nature of the skills that we acquire, the knowledge that we accumulate, the basic assumptions that we hold, and the conscious or unconscious values that govern our behavior. This means that each group has its own social environment that affects the behavior of those within the group.

The culture of any people tends to change constantly as traditional practices are eliminated and adjustments made to meet new situations. In a forming social order these changes occur frequently as the group adjusts itself to its physical environment, accustoms itself to surrounding peoples, and experiments with behavior patterns. Once established, however, these patterns tend to perpetuate themselves; although change continues, the rate of change slows as each society tends to regard its culture as proper and to resist further alteration. At this point in social evolution the group is a victim of ethnocentrism.

Thus man's social behavior is influenced by both heredity and environment. Inherited characteristics are passed from generation to generation and change so slowly as the evolutionary process operates that differences are not observable within historical periods; they are unaffected by experience, although modes of expression may be altered by cultural change. Environment is both physical and social, with the latter more determinative of social behavior within limits set by the former. Central to the social environment is the "culture" of each group. This emerges in the early stages of social organization and while changing constantly to adapt to changing conditions—in the physical environment, technology, ethnic variation, and the like—tends to solidify and to be increasingly resistant to change as ethnocentrism becomes a factor. Such changes as do occur after this point result from continuing alterations in the physical environment and from interaction with adjacent cultures that mutually influence each other.

Against this background of established theory, we can ask three questions essential to understanding the frontier process: Is the behavior pattern of the individual altered by changes in the physical environment? Is it changed by deviations in the social environment? And does an alteration in the social environment affect group behavior? Experiments conducted by anthropologists, sociologists, and social psychologists shed some light on these problems.

Social scientists are now unanimous in their belief that the physical environment is not solely determinative of human behavior. Two obvious examples will demonstrate this point. First, several different cultures have been shown to exist within one physical environment: the Hopi and Navajo Indians of the southwestern United States lived during the early nineteenth century in the same geographic province, yet the Hopi were monogamous, adept in ceramic arts, skilled weavers, and capable farmers, while the Navajo were polygamous, produced no ceramics, confined weaving to women, and supported themselves by herding livestock. Second, intruding cultures adapt differently to identical physical environments. Southern

California was occupied successively by Indians, Spaniards, Mexicans, and Anglo-Americans. The Indians developed a culture based on food gathering, the Spanish-Mexicans one resting on herding, and the Anglo-Americans one built on farming and industry. Obviously the reaction of any culture to the physical environment depends not only on the environment but on the nature of the transplanted culture.

If the geographic setting does not determine cultural patterns, are they altered by the changing social environment? Two seemingly unrelated experiments show this to be the case. In one a young ape, reared in the identical environment of a human child of his own age, learned eating and toilet habits and even the meaning of some words but could never speak, for no amount of training could offset the limitations imposed by heredity. In another a young girl who had been neglected by her parents and allowed to rear herself in a dark closet was given the best training possible when discovered, but was never able to catch up with her age group in skills, language, or mental ability. Environment blocked the mental and social growth of the girl, just as heredity blocked the mental and social growth of the ape.

Further evidence indicating the ability of the social environment to alter human behavior is provided by numerous experiments with identical twins. Having the same genetic origin, and thus the same heredity influence, any differences between such twins must depend on the different social and physical environments in which they have been reared. Studies in such cases suggest that the intelligence level as measured by IQ tests is directly proportional to the amount of education; two sisters separated at the age of eighteen months and subjected to different educational experiences showed a difference of twenty-four points on the intelligence-quotient scale at the age of thirty-five years. Similar experiments indicate that in both intelligence and personality the deviation between identical twins reared apart is as great as between nonrelated persons. These results are substantiated by studies of Negro children transplanted from the inferior schools of the segregated South to the better schools of the North; they reveal a steady improvement in intelligence and social behavior as the inherited abilities of the Negroes are altered by an improved environment. The child of a steelworker in Birmingham, England, suddenly shifted to the home of a steelworker in Birmingham, Alabama, would act and talk and think differently than if he had been raised at home. Yet the physical environment would be about the same in each instance; the principal change would be in the social environment.

Studies also suggest that social environment changes group behavior. Japanese living in Hawaii develop mannerisms different from those of their homeland, revealed especially by more individualistic and assertive attitudes. Similarly Chinese transplanted to Hawaii and to the mainland of the United States behave differently; those in Hawaii are more outward in their emotional expressions than those on the mainland, who feel restrained by the presence of unsympathetic Occidentals. The inscrutable Oriental of California's discriminatory past became a gay, laughing extrovert in Honolulu, where he felt accepted and free of social disapproval. That group traits can be modified is also shown by studies of ability in different classes in the United States; these reveal that children on high socioeconomic levels are more intelligent than those from lower classes. Research such as this, fragmentary though it may be, indicates that both individuals and groups respond to social-environmental forces.

Yet such changes when they do occur are accomplished only by overcoming a vast inertia of tradition that varies its influence with each situation. A few examples will make this clear. New Englanders originally built two-story barns on hillsides where hay wagons could drive directly into lofts on the second floor; their descendants in the flat Middle West continued to build barns in this fashion even though they had to construct an earthen runway to the second floor. Londoners in the seventeenth century adjusted to the narrow streets by building overhanging second floors; these same Londoners built identical homes in Boston where space was no problem. Roads were laid out along sectional lines in the Midwest; pioneers in mountainous country continued to follow surveyors' range lines even though highways following hill contours would have been easier to construct. Summer vacations for schoolchildren originated in farm areas where help was needed in planting and harvesting, but persist in the schools of urban America. Clearly cultural patterns, once established, can be changed only with difficulty, despite alterations in the social environment.

These conclusions can be substantiated—but by no means proved— by observations of modern groups brought face to face with conditions comparable to those that existed on the American frontier. During the 1930s the Farm Security Administration established seven communities where families from a variety of backgrounds were abruptly brought together. Their behavior in this unfamiliar situation, not unlike that of a pioneer settlement, suggests that the social environment altered behavior patterns very much as it did in the successive Wests. Social relationships tended to disintegrate, as men and women associated with others of comparable economic status or whose personalities complemented their own. The new friendships were formed with those living nearby, for a more extended time was needed to develop relations with persons of like interests living far away. Particularly marked was the tendency of families that had been most mobile in the past to leave the communities, explaining that their golden dreams had not materialized. These behavior patterns were a product of the unfamiliar social environment; notable, however, is the fact that they only slightly modified established habits.

On the basis of these modern-day studies by behavioral scientists we can advance certain hypotheses that can be applied to frontier societies:

The "primary" or physical environment did not directly determine such cultural deviations as existed on the frontier, although it laid the basis for such deviations by offering individuals a unique man-land ratio that stimulated an urge for self-advancement.

The differing *social* environment of frontier communities fostered the growth of unique folk cultures, based on but distinguishable from those of the successive Easts. This was because:

(a) The diversity of ethnic and social types attracted to pioneer settlements contributed to creating a fluid social order where ethnocentrism was lacking.

(b) Social controls and traditionalism were diminished by isolation and the dispersion of settlement, with a corresponding impetus to innovation.

(c) The absence of a solidified social order with established in-groups and out-groups allowed opportunity for greater vertical mobility.

In essence, then, the principal effect of the frontier social environment was to weaken traditional controls and values. The pioneer found himself in a fluid, ever-changing, unstabilized society, where accustomed behavior did not bring predictable results and where experimentation seemed more essential than in established cultures. Change, not tradition, was the order of life.

Just as important was the fact that the pioneers realized that in moving westward they severed their ties with tradition. The act of migration disrupted the social relationships that had assisted them in patterning their behavior in their old homes. In their new homes the sense of nonbelonging was accentuated, for most frontier communities were settled by men and women from a variety of places and social backgrounds; Yankees and Yorkers, Southerners and Northerners, natives and immigrants, all met and mingled on a common ground. Language barriers and differing social customs made cohesion difficult, for a Vermonter in Illinois might not be able to communicate with the German who lived nearby, or might feel superior to the Tennessee uplander who had taken out the next farm. Distances between neighbors, growing steadily greater as the frontier moved westward across the prairies and plains of mid-America, also heightened the feeling of removal from the group, as did the economic uncertainty of life in an untested new region. The typical frontiersman was oppressed by a sense of social weightlessness (to borrow a term from the space age), which generated a feeling of not belonging fatal to cultural cohesiveness.

The result was a mild form of mass anomie everywhere on the frontier. To some degree all pioneers, even those who succeeded most rapidly, felt a sense of social deprivation, based on their failure to establish comforting social relationships with their neighbors, the absense of defined social norms, and the failure of the new land to meet their unrealistic expectations. This was reflected in the lawlessness and disorder usual in most frontier communities, by the emotional religious practices common there, and by continuing mobility. It was revealed also by the greater degree of political participation in frontier areas as individuals sought to gain status and economic benefits by assuming leadership roles in the unstructured society. These attitudes and desires marked frontier communities as different from those with tightly structured cultures. Rarely had society been so disrupted, so fluid, and so susceptible to forces inviting change. Here was a new social environment, powerful enough to alter men and institutions.

Let no one, however, be misled into believing that the frontier could affect *major* changes in either the personalities or the behavioral patterns of frontiersmen. As in human behavior today, the bulk of the customs and beliefs of the pioneers were transmitted, and were only slightly modified by the changing culture in which they lived. This can be demonstrated by contrasting the civilizations that emerged in Spanish and English America. True, the physical environment of these two areas varied greatly. North America, with its well-watered woodlands, its fertile praries, and its vast resources in forest and mineral wealth, offered far greater opportunity for the relatively propertyless individual than less-favored South America. There rugged mountains, semiarid plateaus, and dense jungles restricted the areas where small farmers or herdsmen could utilize nature. Only on the Argentine pampas and the Brazilian plains did a temperate climate, navigable rivers, and good soil beckon exploiters, and even there government largess rather than individual initiative governed the settlement process. Yet men, not geography, explain the differences between the Anglo-American and Latin-American frontiers, for individuals of different backgrounds will respond in different ways to identical physical environments.

The ferment of the Anglo-American frontier was partly a product of the ferment of the democratic, commercial, and industrial societies in which it originated. These produced settlers who, by training and tradition, were capable of unleashing the energies of individual initiative to extract the frontier's natural resources. On the other hand, the Latin-American pioneers were governed by traditions that ill-equipped them to exploit the New World's riches, for they had been reared in a culture where the individual's freedom—politically, religiously, and economically —was rigidly restrained.

For this difference the chronology of settlement was partly responsible. Spain's New World frontier was founded, and its culture solidified, in the fifteenth and sixteenth centuries when Europe was entering its modern age. An absolute monarchy had just been imposed on the feudal nobles, middle-class capitalism was in its infancy, church and state were united under the dictates of the crown, and explosive nationalism prevailed in the wake of the expulsion of the Moors. The resulting combination of royal absolutism, a militant national church, and a martial spirit created a colonial society in which the small-propertied individual was allowed scant freedom to exploit frontier resources. He was restricted politically by all-powerful viceroys, commercially by an inflexible mercantile system, and economically by the operation of the semimanorial *mita* and *encomienda*. Moreover, a humane church policy that sought conversion rather than extermination for the Indians helped create a native labor force to monopolize jobs that might otherwise have attracted immigrants from Spain. The result was a transplanted European culture, administered by a centralized bureaucracy, and designed to enrich the monarch and his favorites rather than the individual pioneer.

England, on the other hand, entered the race for colonies in the seventeenth century, with institutions far more modern than those Spain transplanted to America. The political theories of the Stuart monarch were still those of divine right and royal absolutism, but both the promoters of England's colonies and the "adventurers" who peopled them were generally foes of this official theory and active proponents of parliamentary constitutionalism. Thus inclined, they were ready to accord the colonists a degree of self-rule, as they did when Virginia established its House of Burgesses and Massachusetts its General Court—steps that established a precedent for representative government. Political liberty was strengthened by the constitutional controversies that troubled England during the remainder of the seventeenth century. The Puritan rebellion and the Glorious Revolution were shattering blows against absolutism. That the colonists would have followed the path toward democracy, with or without a frontier environment, seems doubtful had the way not been pointed by these events.

Economic institutions emerging in England also favored the rise of a colonial spirit of individual initiative. The prevailing theories of commercial capitalism, combined with a lack of effective centralized authority at home, allowed the English colonies to be established as quasi-public enterprises founded in the hope of gain. This, in turn, permitted the colony planters to slough away the restrictive controls that shackled the economy of less developed nations—feudal land tenure, medieval guilds, and monopolistic trading concepts. Instead, private land ownership, individual handicraft trades, the wage system, indentured servitude, and private contracts became the hallmarks of the American economy, all offering opportunity to farmers, planters, merchants, and craftsmen to better themselves. The English pioneer came from a culture where he had been trained emotionally to exploit the resources of the frontier. He was equipped, as his Latin-American counterpart was not, to move whenever opportunity beckoned, and to profit by each move.

This was demonstrated as the Anglo-American frontier crept westward, for the ethnic groups that it attracted responded in different ways to the physical environment. Most who migrated directly from Europe to the West integrated rapidly into pioneer communities, thus falling at once into the social environment of the frontier. These men and women soon learned the customs and language of those about them, and within a generation or two were almost indistinguishable from their neighbors. Other Europeans, however, settled in ethnic communities where they spoke their native language and remained isolated from the practices of American pioneers. The persistence with which Old World customs and thought patterns were retained in these pockets of settlement demonstrated that the *physical* environment of the frontier did not alter newcomers. This was the function of the *social* environment alone.

The French who occupied a number of town sites in the Mississippi Valley during the seventeenth and eighteenth centuries clearly illustrate this fact. There they remained until the nineteenth century when American pioneers engulfed the lands about them, living and working as had their ancestors and revealing few of the traits of the stereotyped pioneer. By contrast with their new neighbors, the French were indolent and lazy, lacking the bustle and energy usual among small-propertied frontiersmen. They enjoyed dancing and music, and shocked the sober

Americans with their gaiety. Mobility was uncommon; they preferred to stay near their churches and families rather than seek opportunity elsewhere. Their farming habits were similarly inherited, for they tilled long fields modeled after those of manorial France, even though the landscape of the midwest was ill-suited to this division. Their farm implements were those of their ancestors rather than those developed in America.

Germans who fled the Rhenish Palatinate in the seventeenth and eighteenth centuries to establish themselves in the Pennsylvania back country, and their countrymen who filled pockets of settlements in the Middle West a hundred years later, similarly remained stubbornly resistant to the process of "Americanization" that was supposed to take place on the frontier. Their dream was of a good barn and security, not speculative profits. So they showed no tendency to move about as did the usual pioneers; the "Pennsylvania Dutch" of today offer convincing proof of their willingness to stay in one place. Because they had permanence in mind, they cleared the land thoroughly, shunning the slovenly habits of their American neighbors, and preserved its fertility by manuring and by rotating crops. Knowing that well-cared-for animals ate less, they built sturdy stone barns with overhanging eaves, even though they and their families lived for a time in hovels. While Americans were inclined to plant cash crops that would bring the greatest return, the Germans used their fields for a variety of crops to protect against the diaster that might fall through blight or a glutting of the market. This same frugal spirit compelled them to consume the produce that was less in demand, and sell the choice or most expensive products. They lived, in other words, much as their peasant ancestors had lived in Germany. The speculative, exploitive, wasteful habits of frontier America affected them not.

While Germans and French best illustrated the different responses of ethnic groups to the physical environments of the frontier, all nationalities responded in predictable ways. Contemporaries sometimes amused themselves by ranking newcomers according to their skills in pioneering. Germans and Scots were rated "the most industrious, prudent, and successful." The Irish were labeled inadequate for wilderness tasks because of indolence and love of village life, the French because they reverted to hunting, and the English because they clung so tenaciously to British customs. Tales were told of newcomers from England whose cattle died when their owners insisted that barns were as unnecessary in Pennsylvania as in Cornwall, who laboriously dug wells when sparkling water could be dipped from streams, and who insisted on migrating with all their belongings when their needs could have been supplied from the countryside. John Bull, wrote one visitor to the West, would carry with him not only every possession "but even the fast-anchored isle itself, could he but cut it from its moorings." Clearly the physical environment of the frontier did not recast newcomers into a common mold.

This was to be expected. Men instinctively resist change; traditional patterns of behavior create a comforting sense of security that is lost with innovation. Too, imitation requires far less effort than invention. Pittsburgh's founding fathers based the first municipal code of the village on the codes of other eastern cities with which they were familiar. When Louisville founded its school system a delegate was sent east to "examine the most respectable of their monitorial establishments." The first school was modeled on one in New York with modifications adapted from Philadelphia and a faculty recruited from Columbia, Yale, and London. Nostalgia also played a role in perpetuating traditional practices on frontiers, for homes that had been forsaken in the East were endowed with warmth and glamor in the imagination of homesick pioneers. Even the half-savage mountain men thought longingly of the civilized life they had forsaken. One told of riding into a grove of cottonwoods where birds sang merrily. "I laied down in the shade and enjoyed their twittering for some hours," he wrote that night. "It reminded me of home & civilisation." Added a traveler much among the pioneers of the Far West: "The thought of home is ever rolled, like a sweet morsel, under the tongues of their souls." Resistance to the corroding influence of a frontier environment was heightened by such sentiments.

No physical environment could have weakened such allegiance to traditionalism, but not even established custom could withstand the corroding impact of the frontier *social* environment. Behavioral patterns, value scales, and modes of thought that emerged in early pioneer communities and that were carried from community to community by successive waves of advancing frontiersmen proved too powerful to be resisted. Even the "ethnic pockets" that clung most doggedly to Old World habits were affected as American neighbors demonstrated the practicality of frontier-tested practices. A German traveler in the West, after noting that one of his newly arrived countrymen looked completely out of place, went on: "Visit him on his thriving farm ten years hence, and, except in the single point of language, you will find him (unless he has settled among a nest of his countrymen) at home among his neighbors, and happily conforming to their usages." Even the most hidebound Englishman learned, as one of them observed, "that he has got to a place where it answers to spend land to save labour; the reverse of his experience in England; and he soon becomes as slovenly a farmer as the American, and begins immediately to grow rich." Conformity to a unique social environment was easier than resistance. The frontier did alter individuals and institutions.

For the spatial frontier, to the visitor or new settler, was a different world. Those who crossed the borderline and recorded their impressions spoke of a cultural fault as observable as a geological fault. Beyond they found a people who behaved and thought and lived in a manner distinctly different from Easterners. Here was "a state of society wholly differing from any that we had seen before," wrote one traveler, and another felt that he was suddenly "a stranger among a people, whose modes of existence and ways of thinking are of a widely different character from those, in the midst of which he has been reared." Americans were as conscious of the division between East and West as travelers from overseas. "Language, ideas, manners, customs—all are new," observed a pioneer newly arrived in backwoods Michigan; "yes, even language; for to the instructed person from one of our great Eastern cities, the talk of the true backwoods-man is scarcely intelligible." Added another from the Ohio Valley frontier of the 1830s: "The people of the west, viewed as individuals, resemble the inhabitants of almost every clime; but taken as a whole, they are unlike every people under heaven. They have come hither from the four quarters of the globe, with manners and habits and genius and temperament, as different as the nations from which they have severally sprung. Every thing is new, just coming into existence." These observers, and others like them, were acutely aware that the social environment of the frontier was distinct from that of the East.

These differences, moreover, were altering the whole national character and converting the Americans into a people strangely unlike the Europeans from whom they sprang. "If I were to draw a comparison between the English and Americans," one English traveler decided, "I should say that there is almost as much difference between the two nations . . . as there has long been between the English and the Dutch"; another judged them to be "as unlike the English as any people can well be." Significantly, the features that most clearly marked the Americans as unique were frontier characteristics, and were found most deeply etched in the West. Travelers observed there the "slight, but perceptible peculiarities of national character which our peculiar circumstances and condition have imposed upon us"; those same traits were "least observable where the population is most mixed, and are scarcely perceptible in our larger commercial towns and cities." Lord Bryce, one of the most penetrating observers of nineteenth-century America, believed that the West was the most distinctively American part of America, precisely because the points in which it differed from the East were the points in which America as a whole differed from Europe.

Observers differed widely on the exact traits that were emerging in the American character as a result of the pioneering experience, but agreed on certain basic characteristics. One Westerner, who pondered much on the West's influence during the 1850s, believed that the frontier spawned a desire for individual self-improvement even at the expense of society, a supreme confidence that refused to recognize error, and a restlessness that led men to change their habits as often as they did their abodes. Three decades later a visitor to the Far West concluded that a capacity for self-help, a willingness to aid others in distress, a dislike of hypocrisy and pretence, and a manliness exhibited in respect to women were basic frontier traits. To Lord Bryce the Westerner was unique in his veneration of democracy, his unwavering nationalism, and his belief that the world could be reformed with his help; he was also unusual in his practicality, his materialistic philosophy, his aggressive optimism, and his go-getter attitude.

Few observers of the Western scene were capable of such penetrating observations, but many contributed their mite to the picture of the American frontiersman. To polished travelers from London or Boston he was an uncouth savage, degraded by his wilderness environment, and a traitor to the civilization in which he was reared. "As man civilizes the wilderness," wrote a visitor from Britain, "the wilderness more or less brutalizes him. In thus elevating nature he degrades himself." Indolence, profligacy, and bad manners were as truly a product of the frontier as deer hides or beaver pelts to the majority of observers. Few recognized that refinements could not flourish in a new country, and that this regression toward the primitive was only temporary.

To those who could see the true man beneath his uncouth manners, the pioneer was distinguished by a variety of traits, good and bad. He was notable for his openness, the easy manner in which he adjusted to new situations, and his attachment to freedom. Some visitors branded him as hopelessly utilitarian and dourly taciturn; nearly all marked his restless energy, his eager perseverance, and his willingness to support "every species of improvement, both public and private." Scarcely an observer but commented on his lack of attachment to place, and his tendency to roam constantly. "A restless temper seems to me one of the distinctive traits of this people," noted Alexis de Tocqueville. ". . . We have been told that the same man has often tried ten estates. He has appeared successively as merchant, lawyer, doctor, minister of the gospel. He has lived in twenty different places and nowhere found ties to detain him." Incomplete though this catalogue may be, it suggests that those who knew nineteenth-century America best recognized that a national character was developing, and that it was rooted in the frontiering background of the people.

CHAPTER 6

THE VIRGINIANS

William Byrd said "In the beginning, all America was Virginia." Yet, too often the Virginia colonial experience is slighted in courses in American history, since emphasis is focused on the New England Puritans, whose dramatic story has become part of American popular culture. Puritan contributions to the development of American institutions are usually stressed. The unfortunate aspect of the neglect of the Virginians is not that there is intrinsically great significance in the fact that Virginia was established in 1607 as the first successful English colony. More regretable is the neglect of the significance of the Virginia colonial experience and the positive contributions of Virginia to American historical development.

In this selection, Professor Daniel J. Boorstin gives meaning to the Virginia colonial experience. His emphasis in these excerpts from *The Americans: The Colonial Experience,** is on the government and the politics of colonial Virginia. The Virginia story, Boorstin suggests, is quite different from that of New England, of Pennsylvania, or of Georgia, where colonists attempted, at least partly, to escape from some aspects of the English background. The Virginians were not theorists, visionaries, or reformers; they were practical realists and men of affairs who sought to realize English ideals in the New World, and who, after a bad start, succeeded remarkably well.

Professor Boorstin does not suggest that colonial Virginia was the ideal American society, and the student reader should try to identify the weaknesses of eighteenth-century Virginia as well as its strengths. Virginia produced more of the great men of the Revolutionary generation than any other colony, and the contributions of these and other Virginians in the critical early years of the Republic were indispensable to the development of the nation. How does Boorstin explain this extraordinary achievement of Virginia during her Golden Age? How does he account for the decline of Virginian leadership in the nation after the end of the early national period?

D. Alan Williams, "Colonial Virginia: Aristocratic Self-Government," in *Main Problems in American History** (1964), edited by Howard H. Quint, Dean Albertson, and Milton Cantor, is a brief but penetrating analysis of colonial Virginia. Louis B. Wright, *First Gentlement of Virginia** (1940), and Charles S. Sydnor, *Gentleman Freeholders** (1952), are delightful as well as informative works.

* Available in a paperback edition.

TRANSPLANTERS: THE VIRGINIANS
DANIEL J. BOORSTIN

> "Thus, in the beginning, all the world was America, and more
> so than it is now. . . ."

JOHN LOCKE

> "In the beginning, All America was Virginia."

WILLIAM BYRD

Virginia is a different story. Here we see no grandiose scheme, no attempt to rule by an idea, but an earthy effort to transplant institutions.
If other colonies sought escape from English vices, Virginians wished to
fulfill English virtues. Let other colonies dazzle the world with a City
upon a Hill, inspire by a commonwealth of brotherly love, or encourage
with a vast humanitarian experiment. The model in Virginians' heads
was compounded of the actual features of a going community: the England, especially the rural England, of the 17th and 18th century. If
Virginia was to be in any way better than England, it was not because
Virginians pursued ideals which Englishmen did not have; rather that here
were novel opportunities to realize the English ideals. A middle-class
Englishman was to find space in Virginia to become a new kind of English country gentleman. An unpredictable alchemy transformed the ways
of the English manor-house into the habits of a New World republic.
Squire Westerns and Horace Walpoles underwent an Atlantic sea-change
which made them into Edmund Pendletons, Thomas Jeffersons, and
George Washingtons. What made them American was not what they
sought but what they accomplished. . . .

GOVERNMENT BY GENTRY

It would be a great mistake to assume that the cozy, aristocratic character of Virginia society had nothing to do with its civic virtues. Only a

SOURCE. Daniel J. Boorstin, *The Americans: The Colonial Experience,* New York:
Random House, 1958, pp. 97–98, 110–123, 139–141, 143. Copyright 1958 by Daniel
J. Boorstin. Reprinted by permission of Random House, Inc. and the author.

perverse hindsight has made the political institutions of colonial Virginia a leveling democracy in embryo. When George Washington feared for the preservation of self-government and the rights of Englishmen, it was the political customs of mid-18th century Virginia that he must have had in mind, for he knew no others. Those customs were the representative institutions of a Virginia-bred aristocracy, whose peculiarly aristocratic virtues nourished American representative government at its roots. And those roots reached back to Virginia's Golden Day.

Never did a governing class take its political duties more seriously: power carried with it the duty to govern. Thus, while Virginia had a restrictive suffrage throughout the colonial period, it also had a law of compulsory voting. In a few other colonies occasional statutes punished the qualified voter who did not appear at the polls, and it is uncertain how strenuously the Virginia law was enforced, but the continuous course of such legislation in Virginia from the early days till after the Revolution testifies to the persistent belief that government was a duty. If the ordinary voter was required to cast his ballot, men of greater substance were expected to carry heavier burdens. When Jefferson, under particularly unhappy circumstances in 1781, yearned for "the independance of private life," he was describing the relief for which many men of prominent Virginia families must have longed.

Just as the owner of a large plantation had thrust on him tasks of management which he could not escape—he had to lay out orchards, decide on the time to plant and to cut the tobacco, find raw materials for shoes and clothing, and look after the health of the slaves—so he had political duties which he could not shirk. The successful planter developed perforce the habit of command. He came to manage the affairs of the colony with the same self-assurance he showed in managing his private estate. If the plantation was a little colony in itself, which had to be governed with tact, authority, and prudence, the colony of Virginia was in turn ruled like a large plantation. The major dignities and decisions rested on those who held the largest stake.

The roster of the House of Burgesses is a list of leading planters. The upward political path from the seat of the vestryman or justice of the peace to the Governor's Council was guarded all along the way by the local gentry. Seeking a political career without their approval was hopeless. And the House of Burgesses, which increased in power during the colonial period until it dominated the Governor and Council, was hardly more than the political workshop of a ruling aristocracy. Here were made the major decisions about the price and quality of tobacco, taxation, education, Indian relations, and religion. It was here that men were trained and scrutinized before advancement to higher office. Freeholders elected the Burgesses, but only the Burgesses themselves had the power to advance Virginians to higher honors, and the Burgesses conscientiously sifted upper-class Virginians for the tasks of government. Although there were less than a hundred seats in the House of Burgesses in the mid-18th century, nearly all prominent Virginians of the century had served an apprenticeship in the House.

Members disagreed much less than we might suppose, and their discussions little resembled the debate of a modern legislature. Although outspoken conflict marked the years of the Stamp Act, the politics of the House did not harden into party lines. Virginians were not prepared for the idea of political parties in the early years of the new government. As the 18th century wore on, the ruling Burgesses seemed to become more harmonious and singleminded, willing to recognize leadership among men of quite different political complexions. Thus when the House, sitting as the Virginia Convention of 1774, chose its delegates to the first Continental Congress, it elected Peyton Randolph, Richard Bland, and Edmund Pendleton, who had been conservatives in the recent Stamp Act controversy, as well as their opponents, Richard Henry Lee and Patrick Henry.

Perhaps never in recent times has a ruling group taken a more proprietary attitude towards public office. During the years of the Revolution and the first decades of independence, the Burgesses selected (almost exclusively from their own membership) the Virginia governors, councilmembers, judges, military officers, and delegates to Federal conventions. Their personal knowledge of each member of the Virginia ruling class qualified them to distribute public dignities and burdens with an impressive, if not quite infallible, wisdom.

This snugness of the ruling Virginians did, of course, have its less attractive side, which was displayed in the notorious Robinson Affair. No modern journalist could have concocted anything more sensational than these sober facts. When John Robinson, Speaker of the House of Burgesses and Treasurer of the colony, died, Purdie's *Virginia Gazette* (May 16, 1766) with unintended irony declared it "a calamity to be lamented by the unfortunate and indigent who were wont to be relieved and cherished by his humanity and liberality." The embarrassing dimensions of Robinson's generosity, through long suspected, were not confirmed until the administrators of his estate began to cast up their accounts. They then discovered that Robinson, while Treasurer of the colony, had drawn on the public funds to the extent of £100,761:7:5, which he had lent out to scores of his friends. These amounts varied from

£14,921 lent to William Byrd III (who had failed to inherit his ancestors' business acumen and was unlucky at cards to boot), Lewis Burwell's £6274, Carter Braxton's £3848, and Archibald Cary's £3975, down to Richard Henry Lee's £12 and Patrick Henry's £11. Members of the Governor's Council owed Robinson nearly £16,000; those of the House of Burgesses over £37,000. Edmund Pendleton, administrator of the estate, who spent twelve of the best years of his life trying to settle it, had himself been favored with £1020. As the accounts of the estate unfolded, it appeared that there was hardly a Virginia family of prominence that had not been helped in distress by Robinson's generosity with the public funds. This vast network of indebtedness explains the reluctance of the Burgesses over so many years to separate the offices of Speaker and Treasurer or to make a thorough audit of the colony's accounts. The affable Robinson had made the public treasury a relief chest for the ruling clique.

Two peculiar facts about this affair gives us valuable clues to the morals and customs of the rulers of Virginia. First, Robinson had never used any of the funds for his personal benefit—except insofar as he was benefited by the gratitude of his friends. Second, when the facts were revealed the leading Burgesses hardly reproached Robinson for misappropriating public money; they came near praising him for his excess of virtue. When Robert Carter Nicholas (Robinson's successor as Treasurer) hinted at some impropriety, he was denounced for the suggestion; he found it politic to deny the innuendo and declared the loans "more owing to a mistaken kind of Humanity and Compassion for Persons in Distress." Governor Fauquier expressed the general sentiment when, after hearing Pendleton's report on the Robinson estate, he said, "Such was the Sensibility of his too benevolent Heart." Whatever we may think of Robinson himself, his career revealed a community where public power belonged to a privileged few.

This power did carry with it corresponding and sometimes burdensome duties. Almost from the beginning the House of Burgesses strictly required all members to be present at the opening of each session. A Burgess who failed to attend the convening of the House was, according to an Act of 1659–60 and repeated reënactments, fined three hundred pounds of tobacco for every twenty-four hours of unexcused absence. At the opening sitting, the Speaker would read letters from members explaining their absence, and their reasons would be approved or rejected. It was not unknown—as in the case of James Bray in 1691—for the House to be so offended by an explanation that the Speaker issued a warrant for the member's arrest, holding him in custody until he offered suitable apology. Special tasks, such as the election of the Speaker, made attendance at the opening session important, but the House was only slightly indulgent toward Burgesses who missed any regular session. Before the end of the 17th century the fine of two shillings and sixpence was increased to one hogshead of tobacco for each absence from a sitting. When, during the session of 1684, five members failed to answer a roll-call and were found to have gone home without consent of the House, a resolution ordered the sheriffs of their counties to collect from each negligent Burgess a fine of one thousand pounds of tobacco. They were not readmitted to the House until they had apologized.

The House of Burgesses very early (in 1666) disclaimed the right to relieve any duly elected member of his duty of attending, even when his constituents formally requested it. This doctrine survived the 18th century to plague the unhappy Jefferson in May 1782 when, just after his retirement under a cloud of censure as Governor of Virginia, the people of Albemarle County elected him delegate to the House. Weary of office and smarting from the public ingratitude, Jefferson wished to decline the office. When he sent his refusal to John Tyler, Speaker of the House, the ominous reply informed him that "the Constitution in the Opinion of the Members will not warrant the acceptance of your resignation." Tyler warned Jefferson "that good and able Men had better govern than be govern'd, since 'tis possible, indeed highly probable, that if the able and good withdraw themselves from Society, the venal and ignorant will succeed." Finally Jefferson was urged "to give attendance without incuring the Censure of being siezed."

The Virginia Burgesses were, of course, "elected." Their election, if less corrupt and more open to talent, much resembled the English "election" of members of Parliament in the same period. It was nothing like a free-for-all in which any ambitious young man could seek his political fortune; the election was a process in which freeholders made their choice from among the gentlemen. Technically the qualifications for a Burgess were no greater than those for a voter, but in practice the candidates for the House were members of the gentry.

Elections took place in an intimate atmosphere which emphasized both the munificence of the candidates and the power of the freeholders, a strange combination of protocol and conviviality. Campaign oratory seems to have counted for very little; only an unusually pompous and obtuse gentleman would orate to neighbors who had known him since childhood. Seldom was there a public debate on the "issues," but even the best known candidate could not hope for success unless he had taken the trouble to mingle with his constituents. Convention forbade a candidate's soliciting votes, or even voting for himself, and there was no party organization. A candidate was, however, expected to use indirect (usually gastronomic) means of persuasion; no one could hope for election without "treating" the voters. Large quantities of rum punch, ginger cakes, and barbecued beef or pork persuaded prudent voters that their candidate possessed the liberality and the substance to represent them properly in the Assembly. Such entertainment was expensive. Samuel Overton of Hanover County estimated his cost for two elections at £75; George Washington's expenditures when he stood for Burgess were never less than £25 and on one occasion about £50. Such a sum was several times what it would have cost a man to buy the house and land required to qualify him as a voter. A Virginia statute did, of course, prohibit anyone "directly or indirectly" giving "money, meat, drink . . . present, gift, reward, or entertainment. . . . in order to be elected, or for being elected to serve in the General Assembly," but this law seems to have been seldom enforced. A general reputation for hospitality was actually the best defense against suspicions of bribery at election time.

Voting took place in the county courthouse or, in good weather, on the courthouse green. It differed from a modern American election mainly in the publicity given to every voter's choice and in the resulting opportunity for gratitude or resentment between the candidate and his constituents. By an almost unbroken custom, candidates were expected to be present at the voting-place. At a table sat the sheriff, the candidates, and the clerks (including one for each candidate). The voters came up one at a time to announce their choices, which were recorded publicly like a box-score. Since anyone present could always see the latest count, a candidate could at the last minute send supporters to bring in additional needed votes. As each voter declared his preference, shouts of approval would come from one side and hoots from another, while the betting-odds changed and new wagers were laid. The favored candidate would rise, bow, and express thanks to the voter: "Mr. Buchanan, I shall treasure that vote in my memory. It will be regarded as a feather in my cap forever." This personal acknowledgment of the voter's confidence was so customary that in the rare case when the candidate could not be present he delegated a friend to make his obeisances for him. When George Washington's command of the Frederick militia kept him at Fort Cumberland during the 1758 election, his friend James Wood, the most influential man in the county, sat at the poll and thanked each voter individually for his compliment to the absent colonel. A less common method of voting was by a show of hands, acclamation, or some other informal expression.

The control of the gentry over elections was by no means confined to their ability to earn the favorable opinion of the voters. For the gentry chose the sheriff from among themselves, and the sheriff managed the elections. He decided whether any individual was qualified to vote; he set the date of the election; he fixed the hour for opening and closing the polls; there was no appeal from his decisions except to the House of Burgesses, which was always reluctant to override local officials.

"Gentlemen freeholders," the sheriff would finally proclaim from the courthouse door, "come into court and give your votes or the poll will be closed." Sometimes the election would be ended by two o'clock in the afternoon, but if the sheriff found that many voters had been kept away "by rain or rise of watercourses," he might prolong the election into another day. What modern candidate would not envy the Virginia gentleman his power to keep the polls open until the winning votes had been rounded up!

Virginia law permitted a gentleman freeholder to vote in every county where he possessed the property qualification. If he was qualified in three counties he could vote for three sets of Burgesses. Since a man could represent in the House of Burgesses any district where he could vote, this further widened the political opportunities of the larger planters. They could choose to run where their chances seemed best. Many great Virginians, including George Washington, Patrick Henry, John Marshall, and Benjamin Harrison, used their extensive and dispersed landholdings to advance their political fortunes.

A REPUBLIC OF NEIGHBORS

The aristocratic character of Virginia republicanism helps explain why Virginians like Jefferson and Washington had more confidence in representative government than had many of their thoughtful contemporaries from other parts of the country. John Adams, Alexander Hamilton, and Gouverneur Morris came from colonies where "The people" were a volatile city crowd: "a great beast." For Virginians a "republican" government was an intricately balanced traditional arrangement.

If a modern historian had invented an allegory to tell this story he could hardly have done better than *The Candidates; or, the Humours of a Virginia Election,* a comedy in three acts written by Robert Munford of Mecklenburg in 1770. This little play is perhaps the first to express the American talent for making sport of politics. In it a small group of voters plays an affable and passive, but by no means foolish, role. Everyone, including the candidates, is confident that these voters can judge human quality and that they will see through a designing, ambitious, or dishonest candidate.

> WOU' DBE: Well, I've felt the pulse of all the leading men, and find they beat still for Worthy, and myself. Strutabout and Smallhopes fawn and cringe in so abject a manner, for the few votes they get, that I'm in hopes they'll be soon heartily despised.
>
>> The prudent candidate who hopes to rise,
>> Ne'er deigns to hide it, in a mean disguise.
>> Will, to his place, with moderation slide,
>> And win his way, or not resist the tide.
>> The fool, aspiring to bright honour's post,
>> In noise, in shouts, and tumults oft, is lost.

The gentlemen freeholders naturally come to despise Strutabout and Smallhopes and the wealthy toper Sir John Tody, while they learn to respect Wou'dbe and Worthy.

> WORTHY: I have little inclination to the service; you know my aversion to public life, Wou'dbe, and how little I have ever courted the people for the troublesome office they have hitherto imposed upon me.
>
> WOU' DBE: I believe you enjoy as much domestic happiness as any person, and that your aversion to a public life proceeds from the pleasure you find at home. But, sir, it surely is the duty of every man who has abilities to serve his country, to take up the burden, and bear it with patience.

The well-oiled machinery of aristocracy, far from thwarting the will of the people, simply saves the people from mistakes: the sheriff is always there to close the polls at the appropriate moment. The sensible neighbors finally elect the two able candidates by acclamation. This is happy evidence, Wou'dbe rejoices, of "a spirit of independence becoming Virginians."

These customs of the Virginia countryside bred a similar independence among the Burgesses themselves. Everything that made Virginia's elections aristocratic—the tendency to inherit posts in the House of Burgesses, the self-assurance and security of the large planters—encouraged Burgesses to be reasonable and independent in their judgment. Once in the legislature they seldom glanced over their shoulders for the smile or frown of their constituency, a habit which often makes a modern representative the fragile mirror of those who elect him.

It was generally accepted in Virginia in those days that the ruling planters of good family had a prescriptive right to become ruling Burgesses, always, of course, provided they had earned the good opinion of their less substantial neighbors. "There is a greater distinction supported between the different classes of life here," observed John F. D. Smyth as late as the Revolution, "then perhaps in any of the rest of the colonies; nor does the spirit of equality, and levelling principle, which pervades the greatest part of America, prevail to such as extent in Virginia." The large planter, busy with his own affairs, was deterred from standing for Burgess less by the risk of defeat than by the certainty of victory.

This security of social position bred a wholesome vigor of judgment which made the Virginia House of Burgesses a place for deliberation and discussion rarely found among modern legislatures. Burgesses came close to Edmund Burke's ideal of the representative who owed allegiance not to the whim of his constituency but only to his private judgment. The voters in colonial Virginia had just enough power to prevent the irresponsibility of their representatives, but not enough to secure their servility. This was a delicate balance, but it had a great deal to do with the effectiveness of the legislature. In Munford's *Candidates* the virtuous Wou'dbe scrupulously avoided promising to do whatever the people wished, since the people would not have chosen him unless they had preferred his judgment to theirs. The most famous example of this Burkean independence comes from a later day: in 1788, in the Virginia Convention called to ratify the new Federal Constitution, at least eight delegates voted for the new government against the wishes of their electors.

The contrast between the atmosphere in the Virginia Burgesses and in a modern state legislature is only partly explained by the talents of the representatives. The seriousness, wisdom, honesty, and eloquence in the deliberations of the Burgesses during the crucial years of the Stamp Act—the "most bloody" debates which Jefferson, then a student at the College, heard from the door of the chamber—was not due only to the greatness of the men and the issues. These men were not satisfied to be spokesmen of their voters' whims. Their speeches were serious and sometimes subtle arguments directed to fellow-legislators. Their debate lacked that meandering and miscellaneous, if amusing, irrelevance of the modern Congressional Record and its local counterparts. In those days it was still customary for a legislator (at least in Virginia) to give more time to the deliberations of his House than to answering mail from his constituents, to making "news" in legislative committees, or to seeking jobs for faithful supporters. American folklore has only a little exaggerated: the Virginia House of Burgesses was a meeting of gods on Olympus compared to a modern state legislature.

These men were talking to each other; none of them was much impressed by the flowery phrase. With the conspicuous exception of a few like Patrick Henry, Virginia's representatives talked in sober and conversational style; there has seldom been an age of representative government when the power to orate was less important. Within the intimacy of the House of Burgesses, which any visitor to Colonial Williamsburg can sense today, persuasive argument was of first importance; demagoguery was useless. Jefferson was not an eloquent speaker, a fact which led him later to send his annual messages to Congress rather than deliver them in person; Washington and Madison were hardly better. And the leading figures in the Burgesses in the 18th century—men like Richard Bland, Peyton Randolph, and John Robinson —were all ungraceful speakers. The House of Burgesses (like its English counterpart, the House of Commons) was an exclusive club where gentlemen seriously discussed public problems.

Virginia was governed by its men of property. There was no family of substance without members in the Governor's Council, the House of Burgesses, the county court or other governing bodies; and there was no governing body of the colony that was not dominated by the men of substance. These men presumably, and usually in fact, possessed the best knowledge of the large economic and political problems of the community: the price of tobacco and the cost of producing it, the quality of essential imports, the location of indispensable markets, the character of necessary shipping, the routes of primary roads, the places of the most useful ferries.

Land—land to use, to waste, to divide among one's children—was the foundation of all the governing families and the fortunes of Virginia. The power to give or to deny land, those vast virgin tracts expected to appreciate most in the next decades, rested in the hands of the government, especially in the House of Burgesses and the Governor's Council.

The Burgesses also possessed important routine powers over already-settled land, powers which in England were held by the courts. In England if a landholder inherited entailed land which he wanted to deal with as full owner, he followed certain complicated but routine court procedures which ingenious lawyers had developed. Not so in Virginia. There any heir who wanted to get rid of such restrictions had to secure in his own name, and for that particular piece of land, a private Act of the House of Burgesses. Between 1711 and 1774 a total of one hundred and twenty-five such Acts were passed; nearly three-fourths of them for members of such leading families as the Armisteads, Beverleys, Braxtons, Burwells, Carters, Dandridges, Eppes, Pages, Tazewells, Wormeleys, Washingtons, and Yeates. All these, either in their own person or through relatives, would have been represented in the House which acted on their petition. Such private Acts of the House were a necessity for the substantial planter: without them he was not free to deal with his land, to move his labor force, or to dispose of worn-out parcels in order to acquire lands farther west.

Still more important was the power of the Burgesses and the Governor's Council over that treasure-house of the West to which they held the legal keys. There was nothing secret or underhanded about any of this. Under the prevailing system of soil-exhaustion, with fluctuating tobacco prices and the exorbitant demands of London merchants, simple prudence had made tobacco planters into land speculators. George Washington, though shrewd and ambitious, was no gambler, but he seized opportunities to enlarge his holdings. He saw that a westward-pushing population would raise the value of the fertile piedmont; it was important to be alert and acquire good land early. In June 1767 Washington advised his friend, the unfortunate Captain John Posey who had been sinking deeper and deeper into debt, to "look to Frederick, and see what fortunes were made by the Hites and the first takers up of those lands: Nay, how the greatest estates we have in this Colony were made. Was it not by taking up and purchasing at very low rates the rich back lands which were thought nothing of in those days, but are now the most valuable lands that we possess?" In the middle years of the century, after his stint with Braddock and before his Revolutionary command, Washington like many of his fellow Virginia aristocrats, was in Douglas Freeman's accurate phrase, a "land hunter."

To satisfy land-hunger in Virginia one needed not only a strong body but a shrewd political sense. The pathway to landed wealth lay, not only through uncharted tracts in the wilderness, but also through the corridors of government buildings in Williamsburg. This was the "inside track," well-worn by leading Virginians, to the fertile expanses of the unsettled south and west. There was hardly a fortune in Virginia which had not been sought out in this fashion. When William Byrd was appointed by the government to survey the dividing line between Virginia and North Carolina in 1728, he saw the wealth of the fertile bottom-land and christened it the "Land of Eden." He seized the morally dubious opportunity to buy 20,000 acres from the North Carolina commissioners to whom it had been given for their services. In 1742, he secured the again "lucky" chance to patent another 105,000 acres, which he had hoped to get free but for which he actually paid the bargain price of £525. At his death this man owned 179,440 acres of the richest land in the colony —the fruit of his "public services" as much as of his business enterprise.

In none of the "public business" which engaged Washington's interest during his early years in the House of Burgesses was he more active than in trying to secure parcels of land for himself and his fellow-veterans of 1754. Governor Dinwiddie's emergency Proclamation of February 1754 had supposedly rewarded these veterans with "200,000 acres of his majesty's lands on the Ohio," but it was Washington's activity—which included the promotion of bills in the House of Burgesses, letters to the Governor, and addresses to the Governor's Council—that eighteen years later secured the actual allotment of thousands of acres. Washington took the initiative in securing the grant, in locating the land, and in allotting the acreage among different claimants in proportion to rank. His own reward was 24,100 acres. Of this 18,500 was his personal allotment, which he himself apportioned, and 5600 came from allotments of others which his special position had enabled him to buy cheap. He also had the advantage of knowing first-hand precisely the land which would be divided; and hence he could be sure that the tracts rewarding his patriotism were not unworthy of him. Under the circumstances Washington had no reason to feel that he had unduly favored himself. "I might add without much arrogance," he wrote, "that if it had not been for my unremitted attention to every favorable circumstance, not a single acre of land would ever have been obtained." With no more immodesty Washington might have claimed credit for the thousands of acres which he and other leading Virginians were to secure through the Great Dismal Swamp Company and the Mississippi Company; in every case the help of government agencies was essential.

The weaknesses of representative government in Virginia's Golden Age were on the side of realism, practicality, and a too nice equivalence of economic and political power. These were the mistakes of men of affairs rather than of visionaries, reformers, or revolutionaries. While Virginians of great landed wealth could grow wealthier, white men at the bottom of the ladder sometimes found it impossible to reach the next-to-the-bottom rung, and the Negro had no chance to rise above servitude. It was, however, also true that their aristocracy showed as high a talent for government as that of any other community before or since. And once a man was on his way up the ladder, there was little to stop him.

How irrelevant to look to the bookish prospectuses of English or French political theorists—of Locke, Montesquieu, or Rousseau—to explain Virginia's political enthusiasms! Americans who knew the reality did not need the dream. Virginians who would fight to preserve representative government and would offer "their Lives, their Fortunes, and their sacred Honor" on the altar of the British Constitution had not produced a single important treatise on political theory. Knowing what representative government was, why should they speculate about what it ought to be? The great Virginians were in the closest touch with the world of conflicting interests. They possessed a sense of full-bodied economic and political reality, but no particular genius for the abstractions of closet-philosophy. This was to prove one of their greatest strengths.

Why should Burgesses disparage the common people—or declaim in favor of government by "the rich and the well-born"? They actually lived where the people acquiesced in government by the rich and well-born; and where the rich and well-born did not overbear the people. Those Virginians who came to show an uncritical faith in the will of the people had founded it on a solid but narrow experience: their experience of rural neighbors who trusted the political talents of their extraordinarily able aristocracy. Business, the opportunity to get rich and to get poor, had vitalized and added mobility to that aristocracy. One could move into it and, if incompetent, one would almost surely drop out of it, or at least be denied the avenue to political power.

During the 18th century there was little evidence of dissatisfaction with the way of government described here. Since the people acquiesced, the ruling Burgesses had no reason to think ill of their way of life. Although there were some minor political and economic reforms in Virginia during the latter half of the century, these were all very much within the established framework of Virginia's Golden Age. In the eyes of the more influential (and even the more Revolutionary) Virginians, the American Revolution was itself an attempt to preserve the moderate ways of that age.

As the ruling Virginians admired the ideal of the English gentleman, the genteel canon they most scrupulously followed was Moderation. Unlike some of their English gentlemen-contemporaries, they did not despise trade or labor, nor did they admire an idle aristocracy. Nor, unlike some later Jacksonian Americans or European leveling democrats, did they particularly idealize the horny-handed laborer. In Brathwait's *English Gentleman,* Virginians could read that Moderation had a threefold aspect, and must be exercised equally in matters of Mind, Body, and Fortune.

"Moderation," they learned, was "a vertue so necessary, and well deserving the acquaintance of a Gentleman, (who is to be imagined as one new come to his lands, and therefore stands in great need of so discreet an Attendant) as there is no one vertue better sorting ranke." This ancient virtue, needed for governing a community, was no less desirable in those matters of religion, over which Europeans had tortured one another for centuries. . . .

CITIZENS OF VIRGINIA

Nothing could be more misleading than to think of Virginians as "Citizens of the World." In common with American leaders since their day, they preferred to start from their own problems. Their point of departure was their location in time and space.

If George Washington seems colorless to us today it is partly because our latter-day democratic prejudices have blinded us to the colors of his Virginia. It is hard to bring ourselves to believe that the great Virginia fathers of the Republic were nourished in the soil of aristocracy, slavery, and an established church. Modern American democracy, we are told, must have had its roots in some 18th-century "democracy"; so we have looked for its seeds in the New England Town Meeting (supposed to be a microcosm of democracy) rather than in the Virginia tobacco aristocracy. But the ways of history are obscure and even self-contradictory. May not the proudly independent spirit of the Virginia planting aristocrats have been rooted in their vast plantations, in their sense of aristocratic responsibility? May not the value they placed on their individual liberties have been increased by the sharp contrast with the slavery they saw about them? May not their aristocratic habit of mind—their "habit of command" and their belief that they could make judgments on behalf of their community—have helped make them leaders of an American Revolution? Perhaps revolutions are always led by people who build, in Justice Holmes' phrase, "upon an aristocratic assumption that you know what is goods for them better than they—which no doubt you do." Perhaps a reliable toleration has its roots in the quiet catholicity of a not-too-passionate established church, rather than in the explicit liberalism of rationalists and anti-religionists.

The Virginians had indeed inoculated themselves against all strong viruses; they, least of all people, sought to grasp the truths—whether of religion, of government, or of society—suddently and as a whole. Their empirical, and even their reforming, spirit was grown in the tobacco-soil of Virginia, and not in the corrosive absolutes which poured out of Europe in their century. Traditionalism—their loyalty to the working ways of ancient England—rooted them in time; localism—their loyalty to the habits of their parish and county and to their friends and neighbors—rooted them in space. The strength of both these sentiments (and, to be precise, we should call them sentiments rather than philosophies) accounts for much of what they made of Virginia, and of what Virginia in the critical early years of the Republic gave to America. The strength of their traditionalism was before long to be expressed in the American Revolution in defense of the rights of Englishmen. The strength of their localism was expressed in the autonomy of the parish and in the federal spirit, in the Constitution and in the devotion to States' rights. The fact that their tradition was loosely stated—their model was the life of the English country gentleman—made their tie to tradition no less real. There was no part of life which an ideal so vague and so real did not touch. Their narrower, more legal traditionalism was also to have its day: in the Revolution, when they would be required to state in precise legal language how their rights as Englishmen had been violated. But the traditionalism of Virginia in the Golden Age was lived out with a quiet and pervasive intensity. Their very strength as transplanters came from their willingness to transform as they transplanted, to flavor the distant past with the local present.

Their localism has been given far too little attention and too little credit. In these days, when States' rights are out of fashion, we are too often told that a man's preoccupation with the habits of the place where he lives can only drag the national progress. We are fortunate that 18th-century Virginians thought differently. Their concern with the special requirements of their own particular place on earth not only flavored their political life and expectations; it gave all their thinking the aroma of the specific and kept all their social ideals within finite bounds. It was the seed of Federalism, without which the nation could not have lived and liberal institutions could not have flourished. . . .

The supreme irony in the story of Virginia was the last act in the colonial drama. That act occurred in the Revolution itself, in the framing of the Federal Constitution and in the rule of the Virginia Dynasty (Washington-Jefferson-Madison-Monroe) within the Federal government. The leaders of that age were the last flower of the aristocracy of mid-18th century Virginia, not the first flower of a national spirit. The Revolution which the Virginia aristocracy did so much to make and "win" was in fact the suicide of the Virginia aristocracy. The turmoil of

the War, the destruction wrought in Virginia by British troops, the disestablishment of the Church, the disruption of commerce, and the decline
of tobacco-culture all spelled the decline of the aristocracy and its institutions.

The Federal Constitution was a national road on which there was no
return. The leadership of Virginians in Federal life continued only so
long as the national government was an aristocratic camaraderie like
that of Virginia. When the United States ceased to be a greater Virginia,
Virginians ceased to govern the United States. The virtues of 18th-century
Virginia, when writ large, would seem to be vices. Localism would become sectionalism; the special interests of where a man lived would come
to seem petty and disruptive.

CHAPTER 7

THE PURITANS

With the exception of the Indian and the Negro, probably no group in colonial North America has been more misunderstood than the Puritans. Every college student knows what it means to be a so-called Puritan in the twentieth century but few know what it meant to be a Puritan in seventeenth-century New England. The fact that the Puritans were religious is unquestioned—the fact that they were prudes is a conclusion not based on historical facts or on a knowledge of the period or the people. However, the Puritans were more than merely religious. They were dedicated and committed to their faith and to the aspect of their belief that the late Professor Perry Miller refers to as their "errand." The generation of Puritans that first came to New England felt that they were called by God to do His work on His earth. And, these early Puritans hoped that it was God's work that they performed as they labored in the wilderness to establish their Zion.

Yet, the Puritans failed in their errand, and one of the questions that Professor Miller discusses is why they failed. Did the frontier defeat them? Did the lure of free land tempt them (especially, those who were born in the Bay and who never knew England)? Or, was it the failure of Oliver Cromwell to make use of their example as he established his government in Great Britain? It was discouraging to recall the suffering and deprivation they had endured only to realize that the people in England for whom the experiment had been partly intended were not interested in the results. Could it not also be possible that their failing

93

resulted from something as basic as the human condition itself? Perhaps the first generation was so zealous, so committed, so dedicated as to be unique; if this is true, then the Puritans were guilty of wishful thinking when they assumed that the second and subsequent generations could maintain this spirit.

Professor Miller, the first historian of the twentieth century to examine the Puritans in their own terms, explores the many facets of these fascinating people in *The New England Mind,** 2 Vols. (1939, 1953). Samuel Eliot Morison writes a series of engaging biographies in the *Builders of the Bay Colony** (1930). Edmund S. Morgan analyzes the history of John Winthrop in *The Puritan Dilemma** (1958), discusses daily life in *The Puritan Family** (1966), and in "The Puritans and Sex," *New England Quarterly,* XV (1942) destroys the idea of Puritan prudery.

* Available in a paperback edition.

ERRAND INTO THE WILDERNESS
PERRY MILLER

It was a happy inspiration that led the staff of the John Carter Brown Library to choose as the title of its New England exhibition of 1952 a phrase from Samuel Danforth's election sermon, delivered on May 11, 1670: *A Brief Recognition of New England's Errand into the Wilderness.* It was of course an inspiration, if not of genius at least of talent, for Danforth to invent his title in the first place. But all the election sermons of this period—that is to say, the major expressions of the second generation, which, delivered on these forensic occasions, were in the fullest sense community expression—have interesting titles; a mere listing tells the story of what was happening to the minds and emotions of the New England people: John Higginson's *The Cause of God and His People In New England* in 1663, William Stoughton's *New England's True Interest, Not to Lie* in 1668, Thomas Shepard's *Eye-Salve* in 1672, Urian Oakes's *New England Pleaded With* in 1673, and, climactically and most explicitly, Increase Mather's *A Discourse Concerning the Danger of Apostasy* in 1677. . . .

Since Puritan intellectuals were thoroughly grounded in grammar and rhetoric, we may be certain that Danforth was fully aware of the ambiguity concealed in his word "errand." It already had taken on the double meaning which it still carries with us. Originally, as the word first took form in English, it meant exclusively a short journey on which an inferior is sent to convey a message or to perform a service for his superior. In that sense we today speak of an "errand boy"; or the husband says that while in town on his lunch hour, he must run an errand for his wife. But by the end of the Middle Ages, errand developed another connotation: it came to mean the actual business on which the actor goes, the purpose itself, the conscious intention in his mind. In this signification, the runner of the errand is working for himself, is his own boss; the wife, while the husband is away at the office, runs her own errands. Now in the 1660's the problem was this: which had New England originally been—an

SOURCE. Perry Miller, *Errand Into The Wilderness,* Cambridge: Harvard University Press, 1956, pp. 2–15. Copyright 1956 by the President and Fellows of Harvard College. Reprinted by permission of Harvard University Press.

errand boy or a doer of errands? In which sense had it failed? Had it been despatched for a further purpose, or was it an end in itself? Or had it fallen short not only in one or the other, but in both of the meanings? If so, it was indeed a tragedy, in the primitive sense of a fall from a mighty designation.

If the children were in grave doubt about which had been the original errand—if, in fact, those of the founders who lived into the later period and who might have set their progeny to rights found themselves wondering and confused—there is little chance of our answering clearly. Of course, there is no problem about Plymouth Colony. That is the charm about Plymouth: its clarity. The Pilgrims, as we have learned to call them, were reluctant voyagers; they had never wanted to leave England, but had been obliged to depart because the authorities made life impossible for Separatists. . . .

Wise men thought that England was overpopulated and that the poor would have a better chance in the new land. But Massachusetts Bay was not just an organization of immigrants seeking advantage and opportunity. It had a positive sense of mission—either it was sent on an errand or it had its own intention, but in either case the deed was deliberate. It was an act of will, perhaps of willfulness. These Puritans were not driven out of England (thousands of their fellows stayed and fought the Cavaliers)— they went of their own accord.

So, concerning them, we ask the question, why? If we are not altogether clear about precisely how we should phrase the answer, this is not because they themselves were reticent. They spoke as fully as they knew how, and none more magnificently or cogently than John Winthrop in the midst of the passage itself, when he delivered a lay sermon aboard the flagship *Arbella* and called it "A Modell of Christian Charity." It distinguishes the motives of this great enterprise from those of Bradford's forlorn retreat, and especially from those of the masses who later have come in quest of advancement. . . . Were there any who had signed up under the mistaken impression that such was the purpose of their errand, Winthrop told them that, although other peoples, lesser breeds, might come for wealth or pelf, this migration was specifically dedicated to an avowed end that had nothing to do with incomes. We have entered into an explicit covenant with God, "we haue professed to enterprise these Accions vpon these and these ends"; we have drawn up indentures with the Almighty, wherefore if we succeed and do not let ourselves get diverted into making money, He will reward us. Whereas if we fail, if we "fall to embrace this present world and prosecute our carnall intentions, seekeing great things for our selves and our posterity, the Lord will surely breake out in wrathe against us be revenged of such a periured people and make us knowe the price of the breache of such a Covenant."

Well, what terms were agreed upon in this covenant? Winthrop could say precisely—"It is by a mutuall consent through a specially overruleing providence, and a more than ordinary approbation of the Churches of Christ to seeke out a place of Cohabitation and Consorteshipp under a due forme of Government both civill and ecclesiasticall." If it could be said thus concretely, why should there be any ambiguity? There was no doubt whatsoever about what Winthrop meant by a due form of ecclesiastical government: he meant the pure Biblical polity set forth in full detail by the New Testament, that method which later generations, in the days of increasing confusion, would settle down to calling Congregational, but which for Winthrop was no denominational peculiarity but the very essence of organized Christianity. What a due form of civil government meant, therefore, became crystal clear: a political regime, possessing power, which would consider its main function to be the erecting, protecting, and preserving of this form of polity. This due form would have, at the very beginning of its list of responsibilities, the duty of suppressing heresy, of subduing or somehow getting rid of dissenters—of being, in short, deliberately, vigorously, and consistently intolerant.

Regarded in this light, the Massachusetts Bay Company came on an errand in the second and later sense of the word: it was, so to speak, on its own business. What it set out to do was the sufficient reason for its setting out. About this Winthrop seems to be perfectly certain, as he declares specifically what the due forms will be attempting: the end is to improve our lives to do more service to the Lord, to increase the body of Christ, and to preserve our posterity from the corruptions of this evil world, so that they in turn shall work out their salvation under the purity and power of Biblical ordinances. Because the errand was so definable in advance, certain conclusions about the method of conducting it were equally evident: one, obviously, was that those sworn to the covenant should not be allowed to turn aside in a lust for mere physical rewards; but another was, in Winthrop's simple but splendid words, "we must be knit together in this worke as one man, wee must entertaine each other in brotherly affection." We must actually delight in each other, "always having before our eyes our Commission and community in the worke, our community as members of the same body." This was to say, were the great purpose kept steadily in mind, if all gazed only at it and strove only for it, then social solidarity (within a scheme of fixed and unalterable class distinctions) would be an automatic consequence. A society despatched upon an errand that is its own reward would want no other rewards: it could go forth to possess a land without ever becoming possessed by it; social gradations would remain eternally what God had originally appointed; there would be no internal contention among groups or interests, and though there would be hard work for everybody, prosperity would be bestowed not as a consequence of labor but as a sign of approval upon the mission itself. For once in the history of humanity (with all its sins), there would be a society so dedicated to a holy cause that success would prove innocent and triumph not raise up sinful pride or arrogant dissension.

Or, at least, this would come about if the people did not deal falsely with God, if they would live up to the articles of their bond. If we do not perform these terms, Winthrop warned, we may expect immediate mani- festations of divine wrath; we shall perish out of the land we are crossing the sea to possess. And here in the 1660's and 1670's, all the jeremiads (of which Danforth's is one of the most poignant) are castigations of the people for having defaulted on precisely these articles. They recite the long list of afflictions an angry God had rained upon them, surely enough to prove how abysmally they had deserted the covenant: crop failures, epidemics, grasshoppers, caterpillars, torrid summers, arctic winters, Indian wars, hurricanes, shipwrecks, accidents, and (most grievous of all) unsatisfactory children. The solemn work of the election day, said Stoughton in 1668, is "Foundation-work"—not, that is, to lay a new one, "but to continue, and strengthen, and beautifie, and build upon that which has been laid." It had been laid in the covenant before even a foot was set ashore, and thereon New England should rest. Hence the terms of survival, let alone of prosperity, remained what had first been pro- pounded:

If we should so frustrate and deceive the Lords Expectations, that his Covenant-interest in us, and the Workings of his Salvation be made to cease, then All were lost indeed; Ruine upon Ruine, Destruction upon Destruction would come, until one stone were not left upon another.

Since so much of the literature after 1660—in fact, just about all of it— dwells on this theme of declension and apostasy, would not the story of New England seem to be simply that of the failure of a mission? Winthrop's dread was realized: posterity had not found their salvation amid pure ordinances but had, despite the ordinances, yielded to the seductions of the good land. Hence distresses were being piled upon them, the slaughter of King Philip's War and now the attack of a profligate king upon the sacred charter. By about 1680, it did in truth seem that shortly no stone would be left upon another, that history would record of New England that the founders had been great men, but that their children and grandchildren progressively deteriorated.

This would certainly seem to be the impression conveyed by the assembled clergy and lay elders who, in 1679, met at Boston in a formal synod, under the leadership of Increase Mather, and there prepared a report on why the land suffered. The result of their deliberation, published under the title *The Necessity of Reformation,* was the first in what has proved to be a distressingly long succession of investigations into the civic health of Americans, and it is probably the most pessimistic. The land was afflicted, it said, because corruption had proceeded apace; assuredly, if the people did not quickly reform, the last blow would fall and nothing but desolation be left. Into what a moral quagmire this dedicated community had sunk, the synod did not leave to imagination; it published a long and detailed inventory of sins, crimes, misdemeanors, and nasty habits, which makes, to say the least, interesting reading.

We hear much talk nowadays about corruption, most of it couched in generalized terms. If we ask our current Jeremiahs to descend to particulars, they tell us that the republic is going on the rocks, or to the dogs, because the wives of politicians aspire to wear mink coats and their husbands take a moderate five per cent cut on certain deals to pay for the garments. The Puritans were devotees of logic, and the verb "methodize" ruled their thinking. When the synod went to work, it had before it a succession of sermons, such as that of Danforth and the other election-day or fast-day orators, as well as such works as Increase Mather's *A Brief History of the Warr With the Indians,* wherein the decimating conflict with Philip was presented as a revenge upon the people for their transgressions. When the synod felt obliged to enumerate the enormities of the land so that the people could recognize just how far short of their errand they had fallen, it did not, in the modern manner, assume that regeneration would be accomplished at the next election by turning the rascals out, but it digested this body of literature; it reduced the contents to method. The result is a staggering compendium of iniquity, organized into twelve headings. . . .

"The things here insisted on," said the synod, "have been oftentimes mentioned and inculcated by those whom the Lord hath set as Watchmen to the house of Israel." Indeed they had been, and thereafter they continued to be even more inculcated. At the end of the century, the synod's report was serving as a kind of handbook for preachers: they would take some verse of Isaiah or Jeremiah, set up the doctrine that God avenges the iniquities of a chosen people, and then run down the twelve heads, merely bringing the list up to date by inserting the new and still more depraved practices an ingenious people kept on devising. I suppose that in the whole literature of the world, including the satirists of imperial Rome, there is hardly such another uninhibited and unrelenting documentation of a people's descent into corruption.

I have elsewhere endeavored to argue that, while the social or economic historian may read this literature for its contents—and so construct from the expanding catalogue of denunciations a record of social progress—the cultural anthropologist will look slightly askance at these jeremiads; he will exercise a methodological caution about taking them at face value. If you read them all through, the total effect, curiously enough, is not at all depressing: you come to the paradoxical realization that they do not bespeak a despairing frame of mind. There is something of a ritualistic incantation about them; whatever they may signify in the realm of theology, in that of psychology they are purgations of soul; they do not discourage but actually encourage the community to persist in its heinous conduct. The exhortation to a reformation which never materializes serves as a token payment upon the obligation, and so liberates the debtors. Changes there had to be: adaptations to environment, expansion of the frontier, mansions constructed, commercial adventures undertaken. These activities were not specifically nominated in the bond Winthrop had framed. They were thrust upon the society by American experience; because they were not only works of necessity but of excitement, they proved irresistible—whether making money, haunting taverns, or committing fornication. Land speculation meant not only wealth but dispersion of the people, and what was to stop the march of settlement? The covenant doctrine preached on the *Arbella* had been formulated in England, where land was not to be had for the taking; its adherents had been utterly oblivious of what the fact of a frontier would do for an imported order, let alone for a European mentality. Hence I suggest that under the guise of this mounting wail of sinfulness, this incessant and never successful cry for repentance, the Puritans launched themselves upon the process of Americanization.

However, there are still more pertinent or more analytical things to be said of this body of expression. If you compare it with the great productions of the founders, you will be struck by the fact that the second and third generations had become oriented toward the social, and only the social, problem; herein they were deeply and profoundly different from their fathers. The finest creations of the founders—the disquisitions of Hooker, Shepard, and Cotton—were written in Europe, or else, if actually penned in the colonies, proceeded from a thoroughly European mentality, upon which the American scene made no impression whatsoever. . . .

The titles alone of productions in the next generation show how concentrated have become emotion and attention upon the interest of New

England, and none is more revealing than Samuel Danforth's conception of an errand into the wilderness. Instead of being able to compose abstract treatises like those of Hooker upon the soul's preparation, humiliation, or exultation, or such a collection of wisdom and theology as John Cotton's *The Way of Life* or Shepard's *The Sound Believer,* these later saints must, over and over again, dwell upon the specific sins of New England, and the more they denounce, the more they must narrow their focus to the provincial problem. If they write upon anything else, it must be about the halfway covenant and its manifold consequences— a development enacted wholly in this country—or else upon their wars with the Indians. Their range is sadly constricted, but every effort, no matter how brief, is addressed to the persistent question: what is the meaning of this society in the wilderness? If it does not mean what Winthrop said it must mean, what under Heaven is it? Who, they are forever asking themselves, who are we?—and sometimes they are on the verge of saying, who the Devil are we, anyway?

This brings us back to the fundamental ambiguity concealed in the word "errand," that *double entente* of which I am certain Danforth was aware when he published the words that give point to the exhibition. While it was true that in 1630, the covenant philosophy of a special and peculiar bond lifted the migration out of the ordinary realm of nature, provided it with a definite mission which might in the secondary sense be called its errand, there was always present in Puritan thinking the suspicion that God's saints are at best inferiors, despatched by their Superior upon particular assignments. Anyone who has run errands for other people, particularly for people of great importance with many things on their minds, such as army commanders, knows how real is the peril that, by the time he returns with the report of a message delivered or a bridge blown up, the Superior may be interested in something else; the situation at headquarters may be entirely changed, and the gallant errand boy, or the husband who desperately remembered to buy the ribbon, may be told that he is too late. This tragic pattern appears again and again in modern warfare: an agent is dropped by parachute and, after immense hardships, comes back to find that, in the shifting tactical or strategic situations, his contribution is no longer of value. If he gets home in time and his service proves useful, he receives a medal; otherwise, no matter what prodigies he has performed, he may not even be thanked. He has been sent, as the devastating phrase has it, upon a fool's errand, than which there can be a no more shattering blow to self-esteem.

The Great Migration of 1630 felt insured against such treatment from on high by the covenant; nevertheless, the God of the covenant always remained an unpredictable Jehovah, a *Deus Absconditus.* When God promises to abide by stated terms, His word, of course, is to be trusted; but then, what is man that he dare accuse Omnipotence of tergiversation? But if any such apprehension was in Winthrop's mind as he spoke on the *Arabella*, or in the minds of other apologists for the enterprise, they kept it far back and allowed it no utterance. They could stifle the thought, not only because Winthrop and his colleagues believed fully in the covenant, but because they could see in the pattern of history that their errand was not a mere scouting expedition: it was an essential maneuver in the drama of Christendom. The Bay Company was not a battered remnant of suffering Separatists thrown up on a rocky shore; it was an organized task force of Christians, executing a flank attack on the corruptions of Christendom. These Puritans did not flee to America; they went in order to work out that complete reformation which was not yet accomplished in England and Europe, but which would quickly be accomplished if only the saints back there had a working model to guide them. It is impossible to say that any who sailed from Southampton really expected to lay his bones in the new world; were it to come about— as all in their heart of hearts anticipated—that the forces of righteousness should prevail against Laud and Wentworth, that England after all should turn toward reformation, where else would the distracted country look for leadership except to those who in New England had perfected the ideal polity and who would know how to administer it? This was the large unspoken assumption in the errand of 1630: if the conscious intention were realized, not only would a federated Jehovah bless the new land, but He would bring back these temporary colonials to govern England.

In this respect, therefore, we may say that the migration was running an errand in the earlier and more primitive sense of the word—performing a job not so much for Jehovah as for history, which was the wisdom of Jehovah expressed through time. Winthrop was aware of this aspect of the mission—fully conscious of it. "For wee must Consider that wee shall be as a Citty upon a Hill, the eies of all people are upon us." More was at stake than just one little colony. If we deal falsely with God, not only will He descend upon us in wrath, but even more terribly, He will make us "a story and a by-word through the world, wee shall open the mouthes of enemies to speake evill of the wayes of god and all professours for Gods sake." No less than John Milton was New England to justify God's ways to man, though not, like him, in the agony and confusion of defeat but in the confidence of approaching triumph. This errand was being run for the sake of Reformed Christianty; and while the first aim was indeed to realize in America the due form of government, both civil and ecclesiastical, the aim behind that aim was to vindicate the most rigorous ideal of the Reformation, so that ultimately all Europe would imitate New England. If we succeed, Winthrop told his audience, men will say of later plantations, "the lord make it like that of New England." There was an elementary prudence to be observed: Winthrop said that the prayer would arise from subsequent plantations, yet what was England itself but one of God's plantations? In America, he promised, we shall see, or may see, more of God's wisdom, power, and truth "then formerly wee have beene acquainted with." The situation was such that, for the moment, the model had no chance to be exhibited in England; Puritans could talk about it, theorize upon it, but they could not display it, could not prove that it would actually work. But if they had it set up in America—in a bare land, devoid of already established (and corrupt) institutions, empty of bishops and courtiers, where they could start *de novo,* and the eyes of the world were upon it—and if then it performed just as the saints had predicted of it, the Calvinist internationale would know exactly how to go about completing the already begun but temporarily stalled revolution in Europe.

When we look upon the enterprise from this point of view, the psychology of the second and third generations becomes more comprehensible. We realize that the migration was not sent upon its errand in order to found the United States of America, nor even the New England conscience. Actually, it would not perform its errand even when the colonists did erect a due form of government in church and state: what was further required in order for this mission to be a success was that the eyes of the world be kept fixed upon it in rapt attention. If the rest of the world, or at least of Protestantism, looked elsewhere, or turned to another model, or simply got distracted and forgot about New England, if the new land was left with a polity nobody in the great world of Europe wanted—then every success in fulfilling the terms of the covenant would become a diabolical measure of failure. If the due form of government were not everywhere to be saluted, what would New England have upon its hands? How give it a name, this victory nobody could utilize? How provide an identity for something conceived under misapprehensions? How could a universal which turned out to be nothing but a provincial particular be called anything but a blunder or an abortion?

If an actor, playing the leading role in the greatest dramatic spectacle of the century, were to attire himself and put on his make-up, rehearse his lines, take a deep breath, and stride onto the stage, only to find the theater dark and empty, no spotlight working, and himself entirely alone, he would feel as did New England around 1650 or 1660. For in the 1640's, during the Civil Wars, the colonies, so to speak, lost their audience. First of all, there proved to be, deep in the Puritan movement, an irreconcilable split between the Presbyterian and Independent wings, wherefore no one system could be imposed upon England, and so the New England model was unserviceable. Secondly—most horrible to relate—the Independents, who in polity were carrying New England's banner and were supposed, in the schedule of history, to lead England into imitation of the colonial order, betrayed the sacred cause by yielding to the heresy of toleration. They actually welcomed Roger Williams, whom the leaders of the model had kicked out of Massachusetts so that his nonsense about liberty of conscience would not spoil the administrations of charity.

In other words, New England did not lie, did not falter; it made good everything Winthrop demanded—wonderfully good—and then found that its lesson was rejected by those choice spirits for whom the exertion had been made. By casting out Williams, Anne Hutchinson, and the Antinomians, along with an assortment of Gortonists and Anabaptists, into that cesspool then becoming known as Rhode Island, Winthrop, Dudley, and the clerical leaders showed Oliver Cromwell how he should go about governing England. Instead, he developed the utterly absurd theory that so long as a man made a good soldier in the New Model Army, it did not matter whether he was a Calvinist, an Antinomian, an Arminian, an Anabaptist or even—horror of horrors—a Socinian! Year after year, as the circus tours this country, crowds howl with laughter, no matter how many times they have seen the stunt, at the bustle that walks by itself: the clown comes out dressed in a large skirt with a bustle behind; he turns sharply to the left, and the bustle continues blindly and obstinately straight ahead, on the original course. It is funny in a circus, but not in history. There is nothing but tragedy in the realization that one was in the main path of events, and now is sidetracked and disregarded. One is always able, of course, to stand firm on his first resolution, and to condemn the clown of history for taking the wrong turning: yet this is a desolating sort of stoicism, because it always carries with it the recognition that history will never come back to the predicted path, and that with one's own demise, righteousness must die out of the world.

The most humiliating element in the experience was the way the English brethren turned upon the colonials for precisely their greatest achievement. It must have seemed, for those who came with Winthrop in 1630 and who remembered the clarity and brilliance with which he set forth the conditions of their errand, that the world was turned upside down and inside out when, in June 1645, thirteen leading Independent divines—such men as Goodwin, Owen, Nye, Burroughs, formerly friends and allies of Hooker and Davenport, men who might easily have come to New England and helped extirpate heretics—wrote the General Court that the colony's law banishing Anabaptists was an embarrassment to the Independent cause in England. Opponents were declaring, said these worthies, "that persons of our way, principall and spirit cannot beare with Dissentors from them, but Doe correct, fine, imprison and banish them wherever they have power soe to Doe." There were indeed people in England who admired the severities of Massachusetts, but we assure you, said the Independents, these "are utterly your enemyes and Doe seeke your extirpation from the face of the earth: those who now in power are your friends are quite otherwise minded, and doe professe they are much offended with your proceedings." Thus early commenced that chronic weakness in the foreign policy of Americans, an inability to recognize who in truth constitute their best friends abroad.

We have lately accustomed ourselves to the fact that there does exist a mentality which will take advantage of the liberties allowed by society in order to conspire for the ultimate suppression of those same privileges. The government of Charles I and Archbishop Laud had not, where that danger was concerned, been liberal, but it had been conspicuously inefficient; hence, it did not liquidate the Puritans (although it made halfhearted efforts), nor did it herd them into prison camps. Instead, it generously, even lavishly, gave a group of them a charter to Massachusetts Bay, and obligingly left out the standard clause requiring that the document remain in London, that the grantees keep their office within reach of Whitehall. Winthrop's revolutionaries availed themselves of this liberty to get the charter overseas, and thus to set up a regime dedicated to the worship of God in the manner they desired—which meant allowing nobody else to worship any other way, especially adherents of Laud and King Charles. All this was perfectly logical and consistent. But what happened to the thought processes of their fellows in England made no sense whatsoever. Out of the New Model Army came the fantastic notion that a party struggling for power should proclaim that, once it captured the state, it would recognize the right of dissenters to disagree and to have their own worship, to hold their own opinions. Oliver Cromwell was so far gone in this idiocy as to become a dictator, in order to impose toleration by force! Amid this shambles, the errand of New England collapsed. There was nobody left at headquarters to whom reports could be sent.

Many a man has done a brave deed, been hailed as a public hero, had honors and ticker tape heaped upon him—and then had to live, day after day, in the ordinary routine, eating breakfast and brushing his teeth, in what seems protracted anticlimax. A couple may win their way to each other across insuperable obstacles, elope in a blaze of passion and glory— and then have to learn that life is a matter of buying the groceries and getting the laundry done. This sense of the meaning having gone out of life, that all adventures are over, that no great days and no heroism lie ahead, is particularly galling when it falls upon a son whose father once was the public hero or the great lover. He has to put up with the daily routine without ever having known at first hand the thrill of danger or the ecstasy of passion. True, he has his own hardships—clearing rocky pastures, hauling in the cod during a storm, fighting Indians in a swamp— but what are these compared with the magnificence of leading an exodus of saints to found a city on a hill, for the eyes of all the world to behold? He might wage a stout fight against the Indians, and one out of ten of his fellows might perish in the struggle, but the world was no longer interested. He would be reduced to writing accounts of himself and scheming to get a publisher in London, in a desperate effort to tell a heedless world, "Look, I exist!"

His greatest difficulty would be not the stones, storms, and Indians, but the problem of his identity. In something of this sort, I should like to suggest, consists the anxiety and torment that inform productions of the late seventeenth and early eighteenth centuries—and should I say, some thereafter? It appears most clearly in *Magnalia Christi Americana,* the work of that soul most tortured by the problem, Cotton Mather: "I write the Wonders of the Christian Religion, flying from the Depravations of Europe, to the American Strand." Thus he proudly begins, and at once trips over the acknowledgment that the founders had not simply fled from depraved Europe but had intended to redeem it. And so the book is full of lamentations over the declension of the children, who appear, page after page, in contrast to their mighty progenitors, about as profligate a lot as ever squandered a great inheritance.

And yet, the *Magnalia* is not an abject book; neither are the election sermons abject, nor is the inventory of sins offered by the synod of 1679. There is bewilderment, confusion, chagrin, but there is no surrender. A task has been assigned upon which the populace are in fact intensely engaged. But they are not sure any more for just whom they are working; they know they are moving, but they do not know where they are going. They seem still to be on an errand, but if they are no longer inferiors sent by the superior forces of the Reformation, to whom they should report, then their errand must be wholly of the second sort, something with a purpose and an intention sufficient unto itself. If so, what is it? If it be not the due form of government, civil and ecclesiastical, that they brought into being, how otherwise can it be described?

The literature of self-condemnation must be read for meanings far below the surface, for meanings of which, we may be so rash as to surmise, the authors were not fully conscious, but by which they were troubled and goaded. They looked in vain to history for an explanation of themselves; more and more it appeared that the meaning was not to be found in theology, even with the help of the covenantal dialectic. Thereupon, these citizens found that they had no other place to search but within themselves—even though, at first sight, that repository appeared to be nothing but a sink of iniquity. Their errand having failed in the first sense of the term, they were left with the second, and required to fill it with meaning by themselves and out of themselves. Having failed to rivet the eyes of the world upon their city on the hill, they were left alone with America.

CHAPTER 8

THE COLONIAL
WAY OF LIFE

Our concern with the early development of American institutions and traditions, such as democracy, nationalism, and religious freedom, sometimes causes us to overlook the people who molded these institutions, and who created the American republic. Most students of American history are familiar with some of the figures who founded the English colonies, such as Captain John Smith and William Penn, and with a few others who struggled for American independence, such as Benjamin Franklin and George Washington. But what about the people who lived between the era of Smith and the era of Franklin—the pioneers who actually settled and, in so doing, shaped America?

In this selection, John R. Alden focuses on the colonial Americans. As he suggests, it was not clear to the casual observer (even on the eve of the Revolution) that the inhabitants of the English colonies were an important people. Indeed, there was so much diversity and division among the colonial Americans that any but the most astute observer might well have despaired of an attempt to find a basic unity that would have justified calling the colonists "a people." The different patterns of life in the Southern, the New England, and the Middle colonies provide the basic format for Alden's essay. He concentrates on the styles of living in the three colonial sections, examining the economic pursuits, the

class structure, the education, the arts, the religion, and the ethnic strains
of the population.

In reading this selection, concentrate on two areas of concern. First,
how did the colonial Americans differ from the Americans of today?
Were they sturdier, more virtuous, and more deeply committed to American ideals? Or were they much like us, motivated by the same basic
concerns? Second, in seeking to grasp the essence of the different patterns
of life in colonial America, try to identify those forces or factors that
tended to fuse the colonists into a common and distinct people. Professor
Alden clearly asserts that from 1607 onward the colonists were growing
together and, also, were growing apart from their European kin. Is this
argument persuasive in light of the evidence of diversity and division
presented in his essay?

Students interested in pursuing this subject will delight in John C.
Miller, *The First Frontier; Life in Colonial America** (1966). D. J.
Boorstin, *The Americans: The Colonial Experience** (1958), L. B.
Wright, *The Cultural Life of the American Colonies** (1957), and
Clarence L. Ver Steeg, *The Formative Years, 1607–1763* (1964), explore
certain aspects of this subject.

* Available in a paperback edition.

THE COLONIAL AMERICANS
JOHN R. ALDEN

When the French withdrew from North America, it was not obvious to every casual observer that the Americans were an important people. Nevertheless, it is clear enough in retrospect that their condition, except for that of the Negro slaves, was nearly as comfortable, commodious, and secure as might be in a brutal and most uncertain world. So long as the British navy continued to dominate the Atlantic—and it seemed likely to maintain its sway for decades—they did not need to fear invasion by Bourbon armies. Nor must they be fundamentally concerned about an Indian threat, even though the red-skinned warriors, with or without European allies, could create havoc and agony on the western frontiers. They were not only as safe as a people might be from alien enemies in the North Atlantic world but were endowed by the Treaty of Paris with a vast prospect of expansion, even to the shores of California. The astute Benjamin Franklin, and with him John Adams, considering the maturity, the numbers, and the wealth of the Americans, and observing their rapid and continuing increase in both population and riches, had already discerned that they would become truly powerful in the British Empire, or conceivably as citizens of an independent nation. Less penetrating eyes saw the Americans as mere colonists, thinly scattered along the edge of a vast continent; divided from one another by clashing economic interests; set apart by antagonistic social structures; linguistically and culturally diverse; provincially jealous and hostile because of quarrels over boundaries, lands, and commerce; and kept apart by distance and bad roads. It was doubted they were even a people. Were they not Yankees, Pennsylvanians, and Carolinians, rather than Americans? Unquestionably there was remarkable variety among them, and one may readily distinguish among three regions, the Southern colonies, New England, and the Middle colonies. Divergence and conflict between East and West—between Tidewater and interior—also existed. But the Americans, though heterogeneous, had much in common. Indicative of their true unity is the fact that

SOURCE. John R. Alden, *Pioneer America*, New York: Alfred Knopf, Inc., 1966, pp. 47–61. Reprinted by permission of Alfred Knopf, Inc. and the author.

they had come to be called "Americans." That name was in part applied to them for convenience. More important, it recognized that they were a people not basically different from one another, and that they were not merely Englishmen who happened to reside in North America.

To say that the Southern colonies, Maryland, Virginia, the Carolinas, and Georgia, differed economically and socially from the others is not to offer a novel or dramatic insight. The long growing season and plentiful rainfall in those regions made possible, even relatively easy, the production of tobacco in Virginia and Maryland, and of rice and indigo in the Low Country of the Carolinas and Georgia centering upon Charleston. Tobacco and rice could profitably be sold abroad; and England after 1748 paid a bounty on and supplied a market for indigo, used in the making of dyes. All three could be raised in quantity by unskilled labor, under direction. Hence the bringing in of large numbers of Negro slaves, the very cheapest of workers, at least in the short run. Hence also, in great part, the rise of plantations. After 1700, sanguinely hoping for big crops obtained at low cost and sold at high prices, many Marylanders and Virginians grew more and more of the "yellow weed," acquired more land upon which to grow it and more slaves to care for it. In the Low Country rice and indigo planters similarly dreamed of easy wealth and expanded their land and slaveholdings. The plantation owners prospered, although their debts often mounted almost as swiftly as their assets. Thus agriculture in the South acquired a special cast, and there was frequently, alas, one plantation where several homestead farmers and their families could have lived in freedom and comfort. Trade did not thrive in that region as it did elsewhere in the colonies. Charleston, colonial capital of South Carolina and busy port of the Low Country, grew into a small city. It was the only one in the entire Southern region.

The social order in the South, principally based upon its special economy, was also distinctive. It was peculiar in that its bottom was composed of a mass of Negroes, who were, with few exceptions, slaves. Nine out of every ten American Negroes lived, or at least existed, in the Southern colonies. About one third of the people in the entire South were Negro. Some of the blacks were household servants and mechanics; most of them were valued because they cared for crops and produced progeny. Above the Negroes were all the whites, among whom the English element was principal, although Scotch-Irish, Germans, and Scots were also numerous. Above all the other whites was a gentry, an untitled American aristocracy, composed almost exclusively of plantation owners. It was a relatively new aristocracy, membership in it being founded on the possession of wealth rather than patrician ancestors. The worthy person, even the unworthy one, was not barred from it because his father had engaged in commerce; a man who belonged to it might himself be occupied in trade as well as agriculture. At the end of the colonial era, gentry included George Washington, whose father was not quite of it; Edmund Pendleton, who was descended from a bond servant; and Benjamin Powell, in youth a wheelwright, a carpenter, who had earned himself the title of "Gent" by merit. Below that gentry, and often confused with it, were many not-so-rich planters and substantial homestead farmers. These, along with shopkeepers and a few professional folk, composed a middle class. This middle class has escaped the attention it deserves because it lacks the glamor of aristocracy, the brutal charm of slavery. Beneath the middle class were the bond servants, numerous only in Virginia and Maryland, whose status was, of course, temporary. Above the slaves were the "poor white trash," not yet known by that name but real enough. The "trash" should be distinguished from the many whites who were poor only in possessions. Ignorant, lazy, quarrelsome, lawless, and fecund, those degraded people were more numerous than the Southern gentry. It should be added that white men of all classes contributed to the blood stock of the Negroes, who were moving biologically toward their masters and mistresses.

Fascinating as life in the country may be, rural lanes are not the smoothest or broadest highways to learning and the arts. Roads in the Southern colonies were bad, and the region lagged in terms of educational and intellectual advance. Education largely remained a private affair, and elementary schools supported by churches and individual benevolence were available only to a minority of children. The offspring of the slaves were seldom taught more than the performance of physical tasks. The young, male and female, of plain farmers often learned only to write their names. The sons of the aristocracy were commonly instructed by tutors—their sisters learned but to read and write, to play a musical instrument, to dance, and to pursue the domestic arts. Not infrequently a young gentleman continued his studies at the College of William and Mary, founded in 1693, for several generations the only institution of higher learning in the South, or at a college to the north, or at an English private school or university. One finds some of them studying Latin at Westminster School, law at the Inns of Court in London, medicine in Edinburgh and Leyden. However, formal education at the higher levels was not easily available to the middle class, and it was not sought by the majority of young gentlemen. It could not be secured in Charleston, for there was no college there during the colonial time. Nor was Charleston remarkable as a city that nourished literary and artistic talent, although her richer residents wrote essays and verse.

Something more should be said about the males of the Southern aristocracy, for it contributed great men to America and to the world. From it came Thomas Jefferson and James Madison, who were college men, scholars, and cultivated gentlemen as well as philosophers and statesmen. However, the usual man of the gentry was less given to intellectual pursuits. He was comparable to an English squire. He belonged to the Anglican Church, which was established in all the Southern colonies, but he was not devout. He managed his lands and his slaves, hunted, danced, watched cockfights, gambled, and frequently visited his neighbors. Most important, he engaged in politics. The gentry dominated local government in parish and county, and usually both houses of the Southern colonial legislatures—not so thoroughly in North Carolina as elsewhere, for that "valley of humility between two mountains of conceit" contained fewer aristocrats and more homestead farmers than did her neighbors. The aristocrats were splendidly schooled in public affairs, read and wrote about them, acquired breadth of view in statecraft, and gained the polish of men of the world. Of such was the Virginian, George Washington. He and his like offered both sturdy and informed leadership.

In his time New England produced no heroic figure equal to Washington, but many worthy men sprang from its thin soil and stony hillsides. The Yankees, as the inhabitants of the region north of Long Island Sound and east of the Hudson River were commonly designated after the middle of the eighteenth century, varied from the Southerners in both appearance and reality. If New England was not lavishly endowed with natural resources, its people were energetic, thrifty, and ingenious, like those of the Dutch provinces and the Swiss cantons. Moreover, the Yankees commanded more good land than the Dutch, far more generous forests than the Swiss. Most of them were tillers of the soil, farmers who owned their fields, wood lots, and orchards. Many, however, were carpenters, masons, mechanics of all sorts, and traders. The same man might engage in two or more pursuits, farming and fishing, lumbering and shipbuilding, trading and tavern-keeping. Cramped by the lack of fertile soil, the Yankees made ships and went to sea. They gathered abundant crops of fish off their own coasts and on the Grand Banks of Newfoundland; and they turned to maritime commerce with singular success. It is often said that the increasingly evident affluence of Massachusetts rested upon the carcasses of codfish; underneath it also were the trunks of pines and oaks, potent rum, and the bodies of slaves carried from Africa. Merchants grew wealthy in Massachusetts, and in New England, from oceanic traffic as well as fishing.

There were few slaves in New England; few citizens equivalent to the "poor white trash"; few bond servants; and an aristocracy less conspicuous, less powerful, and less glamorous than that of the Southern colonies. Upon the stable and diversified economy of the Yankee country was based a large middle class. Its members usually had the right to vote, and their will was potent in public affairs. Aristocrats did not dominate in Massachusetts or Connecticut as they did in Virginia and South Carolina. A distinction made in the seventeenth century between the "gentleman" and the "goodman" had softened. Moreover, the Congregationalist clergy had lost prestige and influence. The men of the cloth had been, to a degree, displaced by men of money. Nevertheless, New England had its first families of wealthy merchants, landowners, officeholders, lawyers, and clergy. With strong support from the middle class, they were the leaders in that region. So firm was their grasp upon the body politic in Connecticut that they formed a "standing order" which endured for generations. Even so, Hutchinsons, Saltonstalls, Trumbulls, and Griswolds did not have the social and political stature of the Southern Lees, Carters, and Pinckneys. New England society was semi-democratic.

Before the end of the colonial time the prosperous New Englanders offered outward evidence of their wealth in their clothes, coaches, carriages, and homes. The well-to-do wore garb like that of English gentlemen and ladies, like that of Southern aristocrats. They had their wines as well as their rum, and their big houses. More impressive than their mansions were the New England churches in austere elegance; more pleasing to the generous-minded observer than those mansions were the neat, attractive homes of tens of thousands of villagers and farmers. The New England village had acquired a charm and beauty which long endured. New England also had cities—Newport, which would afterward cease to grow rapidly; and Boston, which was the second largest American city and would retain importance in commerce, in banking, in education, and in the sight of its citizens. English travelers visiting the Yankee country in the eighteenth century, and later, remarked that it bore a greater resemblance to Old England than other parts of America. Its people continued to be almost entirely of English descent until the nineteenth century was well under way.

The Yankees were also the best educated of the colonists. Elementary instruction was quite readily available to them, often at public expense. As the American Revolution approached, the New Englander was usually literate. Moreover, there were many men among the Yankees who were college graduates. Harvard was the only college in New England until

Yale was founded in 1701. Nevertheless, the two colleges sent forth hundreds of informed and thoughtful men in the eighteenth century. After 1764 the College of Rhode Island (Brown University) and after 1769 Dartmouth contributed to the supply of well-educated men in the colonies. It was further increased by private study and reading, for those who earnestly sought to learn often had access to books.

Instruction of the young, even in New England, was interrupted by the tasks of transplanting from Old England, and learning and the arts did not flourish steadily from the beginning of settlement. There was, to be sure, a transit of European civilization, at least the English variety of it. However, all of that civilization did not promptly pass over the ocean, and things physical during many decades occupied minds and energies at the expense of things intellectual and artistic in New England. So it was everywhere in America as people flooded into wild new territories. Included among those who went to New England in the second quarter of the seventeenth century were many scholars, both clerical and lay. Moreover, Harvard produced gifted and learned men even in its first years. Nevertheless, there was a cultural sag in New England; it could not and did not keep pace with the Mother Country.

Nevertheless, New England spawned scholars, writers, and even a distinguished artist in the colonial time. In the South, William Byrd II of Westover, author of charming sketches of life in Virginia and North Carolina, stands out because so few men in that region distinguished themselves in letters before the onset of the American Revolution. He would have had more literary company among the Yankees. But let us not make too much of New Englanders who studied, wrote, or dabbled in the arts. We should not praise highly men—or women—who would in no way have been remarkable on the eastern side of the Atlantic. Eschewing ancestor worship, no American will classify the New England poet Edward Taylor, who was born in Old England, with John Milton, or match Cotton Mather of Massachusetts against John Locke. Mather was only a bright star in a sequestered corner of America. If he presciently declared that disease was caused by tiny invisible animals, he also believed that witches were both real and visible. His intellect was chaotic as well as brilliant. Of the Reverend Jonathan Edwards, who has been sufficiently admired by later American generations, it may be said that he was a gifted theologian and an acute philosopher, that he put the case for freedom of the human will in the face of an omniscient God as well as the logician may do it. In the London of his day Edwards would not have been a man of small repute. Another New Englander, John Singleton Copley, of a later generation than Edwards, actually did win fame in

England. Copley went abroad to study painting, was acclaimed in London for his artistry, remained in England, and fathered a lord chancellor. His best work, however, was done before he left his native country. Portraits that he painted of various Americans are remarkable for their realism and craftsmanship. However, he is not usually ranked with his English contemporaries Sir Joshua Reynolds and Thomas Gainsborough.

Material, educational, and intellectual advances, so important in themselves, also profoundly affected the Congregational establishment in New England. Almost united with the state, except in Rhode Island, the Puritan church wielded vast power in seventeenth-century New England. The will of the orthodox Puritan clergy and laymen was dominant alike in public and personal affairs. Punishing heresy, even Anglican deviations, they most earnestly strove to preserve the true church and the Puritan way. Congregations vied with legislatures in the curbing of the unfaithful, the heedless, the willful, and the wicked. Idolatry and blasphemy were at one time capital crimes in Massachusetts, and persons who denied belief in the resurrection of the body or in the validity of infant baptism, even persons who withdrew from communion, could be banished. On the other hand, Puritan congregations formally inquired into the behavior of their members and excommunicated men and women of heretical belief and unpleasing conduct; in 1640 Captain John Underhill was driven from communion in Boston because he had committed and had tried to commit adultery—and would not offer a suitable confession. Far less heinous offenses were similarly punished. Without the confession and repentance of the parents, a child conceived before their marriage might be denied baptism. It was widely believed among the Puritans that a child born on Sunday was conceived on a Sunday and so was especially burdened with sin. The true New England Puritan feared that even he, the seemingly anointed, might at last be disappointed, and he kept both his own and his brother's conscience. It ought to be added that, to his credit, he was not a prohibitionist. Congregational clergymen drank rum, and Harvard students were daily served beer with bread and beef. The "steady habits" for which the men of Connecticut have long been famous included toping. It is claimed, in fact, that some New England towns required by law the maintenance of an ordinary, or tavern, conveniently near the village place of worship. It is notorious that the Puritans of eastern Massachusetts hanged nineteen persons found guilty of witchcraft after 1688. They were not the first to suffer for that crime in Massachusetts. One ought not exaggerate the significance of the hysteria about witches that convulsed Salem—and Boston—toward the close of the seventeenth century. Belief in witchcraft was not confined to the Puritans—nor were barbarous punishments. In England in 1765 a woman convicted of poisoning her husband was burned at the stake. The execution of innocent victims accused of witchcraft is evidence of a sort that Puritanism was in decline.

So it was, but in slow descent. The New Englanders, as their lives on earth became longer and more pleasant, worried less about their existence beyond the grave. Doubtless they became more tolerant in their beliefs as they voyaged distantly and conversed with men subscribing to creeds other than their own. Deism, which obtained many converts in Europe subsequent to the discoveries of Isaac Newton, spread to America. Even Puritan clergymen increasingly preached about the God of love, saying less about the God of justice, before whom even well-educated Puritans had bowed in utter fear. Some of the ministers slipped toward Unitarianism. Weakened by assults from worldly prosperity and secular learning, orthodox Puritanism lost communicants, especially those with social pretensions, to newly founded Anglican churches. It suffered further from schism. It was hit hard in the 1740s by a wave of pietistic and emotional revivalism, the "Great Awakening." The ravings, the rantings, and the frenzies of the "Great Awakening," which Jonathan Edwards, who ought to have known better, helped to stimulate, grievously offended the Congregationalists who clung to traditional Puritan emphasis upon religious law and logic. As the American Revolution approached, the Congregational establishment was not what it had been. In 1755 at Marblehead, Massachusetts, Mrs. John Glover confessed in open church that she had engaged in sexual intercourse with her husband before their marriage. But there is no record that Glover, later a valiant and most useful officer who served under General Washington, humbled himself in church before he defied his King.

Let it not be thought that the New Englanders internally led dark, dismal, and desperate lives. Their religious notions and moral codes were their own and hence were not utterly unsuited to them. One may not say that they were an unhappy people. Were the Spartans, with their rigid rules? Or the Samurai, because of their Bushido? If not gay or frivolous, the Yankee could nevertheless be contented, even joyful. Consider the radiant and touching lines addressed by the Puritan poet Mrs. Anne Broadstreet "To my Dear and Loving Husband."

> My love is such that Rivers cannot quench,
> Nor ought but love from thee give recompence.
> Thy love is such I can no way repay;
> The heavens reward thee manifold I pray.
> Then while we live, in love let's so persever,
> That when we live no more, we may live ever.

Between the colonial extremes were the Middle colonies, New York, New Jersey, Pennsylvania, and Delaware, moderate in climate, immoderately furnished with good soil, great rivers, and splendid harbors. They were the "bread colonies," sending grain and flour to distant places. But their lands bounteously gave forth iron as well as wheat and corn, and manufacturers of the black metal in the Middle colonies offered dangerous competition to those of Sheffield and other English cities before 1750. Water-borne craft in large numbers plowed the Hudson and the Delaware. Philadelphia and New York were centers of both river and oceanic traffic. As the era of the Revolution drew near, Philadelphia, with more than 20,000 citizens, was the largest American city, and New York threatened to pass Boston in population. Had they been located in England, the two cities would have been important there. Their well-to-do merchants, such as John Watts of Manhattan and Israel Pemberton of Philadelphia, together with country magnates, gladly supplied a gentry in the region between Connecticut and Maryland. That aristocracy was a trifle closer to the Southern aristocracy than was the patrician class of New England. Some of its members, such as the Philipses, Livingstons, and Van Rensselaers of New York, owned wide estates and dictated to numerous tenants and white servants. In Delaware the masters and mistresses of Negro slaves lived much like their counterparts in Virginia. The Middle colonies had their sharp social gradations but also a middle class almost as large proportionately as that of New England. Plain farmers who owned their good land were numerous, and artisans and traders thrived in cities, towns, and villages.

Remarkable in that early Middle America was the variety of its people, for it was the home of large non-English minorities, notably German, Scotch-Irish, and Dutch. The ancestors of the Pennsylvanians were as much German as they were English; and the Scotch-Irish settled thickly in the interior of William Penn's colony. Preachers exhorted their congregations in Dutch in several communities of New York and New Jersey until the end of the eighteenth century; and the use of German, at least of a sort, persisted in German enclaves of Pennsylvania into the twentieth century. Equally various were the churches, none of them established, except that the Anglican Church was officially recognized in three New York counties. The followers of Calvin, English, Scotch-Irish, German, and Dutch, were numerous; Lutherans, Moravians, Anglicans, Quakers, and Jews worshiped the Creator in their several ways. These were all the more diverse because the "Great Awakening" and its emotional Christianity disturbed and divided several of the sects. That Christianity of enthusiasm, of hell-fire and brimstone, indeed, spread throughout the colonies, and waves of it were to assail the American people again and again.

The "Great Awakening" does not offer testimony to educational and intellectual advance. Men and women who lost their self-control in eagerness to save their souls might speak in "strange tongues" but not in Latin. Their religious frolicking might lead them to read the Holy Scriptures but hardly the plays of Shakespeare. However, there were other awakenings in the Middle colonies. Schools maintained at public expense were less common than in New England, but many privately managed ones, often maintained by clergymen and churches, purveyed elementary instruction. That devotion to learning so characteristic of the Scots was displayed by Scottish and Scotch-Irish Presbyterians in America; the Dutch and many of the Germans also set high value upon knowledge. The task of civilizing the young was not neglected in the Middle colonies. In that region no fewer than four universities were born before the Revolution: Princeton, founded in 1746; the University of Pennsylvania, established as an academy at Philadelphia in 1751; Columbia, appearing three years later as King's College; and Rutgers, which began as Queen's College in 1766.

Those central colonies had their full colonial share of talented and learned men in the eighteenth century. In New York the Scottish-born official, Cadwallader Colden, wrote a worthy history of the Iroquois and more than dabbled in medicine and physics. He erroneously believed that he had made discoveries correcting mistakes of Newton. William Livingston of New York and New Jersey was a poet, essayist, polemicist, and politician. In Pennsylvania the Bartrams, John and William, father and son, distinguished themselves as botanists; the charming *Travels* of the younger Bartram would supply imagery for Samuel Coleridge's "Kubla Khan." By far the most distinguished man in all the colonies before the Revolution was, of course, Benjamin Franklin, Boston-born but a Philadelphian during most of his long and busy life. One may not properly describe in a brief space his many-faceted genius, his diverse achievements. Born the son of an artisan, he became a printer, philosopher, essayist, postal official, superb propagandist, inventor, politician, and diplomat. He contributed importantly to knowledge about electricity, and he wrote his classic autobiography. His education was largely informal, his donations to mankind cardinal and profuse. Not without faults—there was a strain of grating smugness in him—he was the very model of the self-made and well-made man in the American "land of opportunity."

It is apparent enough that variety and contrariety were characteristics of the American scene after the middle of the eighteenth century. Nor have all the colonial divergencies and clashes been mentioned, for they existed between East and West as well as North and South. Indeed, division between East and West, in one form or another, like that between North and South, was to endure into the twentieth century. It appeared as soon as the colonists moved inland, from the coastal plain to the Piedmont above it, into the so-called Old West. The people of the Old West, especially those from Pennsylvania southward, were poorer, less educated, less European, and more American than those of the Atlantic Tidewater. The Tidewater leaned toward the aristocratic, the Old West toward the democratic. The interior folk were often indebted to their more prosperous fellows of the coastal plain. The Tidewater did not always exert itself to help defend the Old West against the Indians; it was reluctant to give the newly settled areas representation in the colonial assemblies in proportion to numbers; and it sometimes discriminated against the people of the interior with respect to taxation. In the Southern colonies the homestead farmer of the interior, owning few or no slaves, was set against the wealthy planter to the east. Hence came political collisions, and even unsuccessful rebellions by the people of the interior. They took up arms under Nathaniel Bacon in Virginia in 1676. In Pennsylvania they marched against Philadelphia in 1764; soon afterward, as Regulators, they created uproar in the Carolinas. Bacon's Rebellion was not put down without bloodshed, and an uprising of the Regulators in North Carolina continued until they were crushed by Governor William Tryon and provincial militia in the pitched battle of the Alamance in 1771.

One may be tempted to magnify the cleavages among the colonial Americans. For they had much in common from the beginning, and they became more alike. One may think too much about their varied ancestral roots in Europe and Africa, English, Welsh, Scottish Lowland and Scottish Highland, Scotch-Irish, Irish, Dutch, Flemish, German, Swedish, Finnish, French, Swiss, Jewish, and Negro. It should be observed that virtually all of the European forebears of the colonists lived on the lands and islands north of the Pyrenees and west of the Elbe River. They were west Europeans, and both they and their descendants in America were overwhelmingly Protestant, if of many sects. Moreover, the English element in America was easily principal in the colonial bloodstock, and the English language, modified somewhat in the American environment, prevailed without serious contest over other European, and African, ones. English ways of thought, English institutions retained an easy ascendancy. Karl Schmidt became Charles Smith, and Hans Fuchs became John Fox, and the Smiths and Foxes gradually learned to think like their English-speaking neighbors. Besides, although German, Dutch, and French elements persisted, there was much intermarriage between the

English and European parts of the colonial population before the beginning of the Revolution—it would accelerate.

Tending to fuse, even with the Negroes, the colonists also became less and less like the English at home.

> Leaving the old, both worlds at once they view
> That stand upon the threshold of the new.

Not too different from one another when they emigrated to the New World, the settlers were brought closer together by common experiences and interests in America, these being other than those influencing their brethren in the Old World. From 1607 onward they encountered similar troubles in subduing Nature. They had the same enemies, the Indians, the Spanish, and the French. They had a common experience of contest with English authority. Hence they grew together, and at the same time apart from their kin on the European continent and in the British Isles. That they had become like one another and unlike their blood relatives beyond the Atlantic was recognized by the observant and assumed by the less perceptive among them well before the Americans and the English exchanged shots at Lexington. It is significant that the terms "America" and "American," to indicate Britain's colonies on the mainland of North America and one of their inhabitants, had come into everyday use by the 1760s. While it is clear that these names were increasingly employed because of convenience—there were no brief equivalent terms—they were also used because they were needed to identify a distinct area and people. Thus the question posed by J. Hector St. John de Crèvecoeur and so often quoted, "What then is this American, this new man?" To be sure, the wide and growing gap between the American and the Englishman was not yet seen by all in America or England. An American in the 1760s might still refer to the Mother Country as "home"; and an Englishman might assume that a citizen of New London, Connecticut, if not the equal of one of Old London, if only a "poor relation," was nevertheless English. But that gap between the Englishman and the American became ever greater after the collapse of the French empire in North America. After 1783, when England recognized the independence of the United States, there would be no serious question that its citizens, an incomplete compound of old breeds, had become a distinct and new one.

CHAPTER 9

COLONIAL GOVERNMENT
AND POLITICS

In this section from *The First American Revolution* (1958),* a revision of his *Seedtime of the Republic* (1953), Clinton Rossiter is concerned not with the mechanics or methods of colonial politics but, instead, with the institutions through which and around which colonial politics developed. In short, he is interested in the *political culture* of the colonies.

Much has been written about the nature of colonial politics. It has been described as a great wave of the future with political freedom as the eventual goal. It has been discussed by "Progressive" historians such as Carl L. Becker, Charles A. Beard, and Vernon L. Parrington as a radical versus conservative struggle over who "should rule at home." The "Imperial" school of historians has inferred that it was a political struggle waged in a framework of general ignorance of the problems of governing a vast empire. But in all of these interpretations only a few scholars have examined the nature of the offices and political institutions over which these struggles were waged, as does Professor Rossiter in this section.

Does the nature of political institutions alter the type of politics that take place? How? Can differences between English and Spanish colonial political and revolutionary struggles be traced to different institutions?

123

In addition to the various schools of studies mentioned above, the student might well consult studies such as Charles M. Andrews' magnificent, although slightly dated, *Colonial Background of the American Revolution** (1924) and Leonard W. Labaree, *Royal Government in America* (1930). More recent studies are Charles S. Sydnor, *Gentlemen Freeholders: Political Practices in Washington's Virginia** (1952), and Jack P. Greene, *The Quest for Power* (1963). For an excellent discussion of the importance of the *political culture* and the problems of this period as well as the literature on the subject, see Jack P. Greene, "Changing Interpretations of Early American Politics," Ray Allen Billington (ed.), *The Reinterpretation of Early American History** (1966).

* Available in a paperback edition.

SELF-GOVERNMENT BEFORE DEMOCRACY: THE PATTERN OF COLONIAL POLITICS
CLINTON ROSSITER

The bisection of early American history into the years before and after the Glorious Revolution, a favorite device of colonial historians, has special application to colonial government. The first period of political development, which lasted from the Jamestown settlement (1607) to the withdrawal, alteration, and restoration of the Massachusetts charter (1684–1691), was one of "alarum and excursion" in the mother country and self-determination in the colonies. The second, which began with the creation of the Board of Trade (1696) and ended with the outburst of resistance to the Stamp Act (1765), was one of fast-growing imperial concern in England and even faster-growing political maturity in America. The influence of the first period upon the second, of the century of neglect upon the century of oversight, was great if not indeed decisive. Habits of self-government were implanted in New England and Virginia that no new policy of empire, no matter how autocratic in conception and efficient in execution, could ever have rooted out.

Except for short terms, in isolated localities, and among small groups of pioneers, there was little political democracy in the colonial period. Generations of well-meaning historians and patriots have done the colonists no service by insisting that they and their institutions were democratic. There was a good deal of practical content injected into the ancient phrase "liberty of the subject"; there were unusual opportunities for self-government at all levels; and there was thinking and talking about democracy that outran actual performance. Yet for the most part government in the colonies was simply a less corrupt and oppressive, more popular and easygoing version of government at home, and thus was characterized by limited suffrage, aristocratic leadership, and both deference and indifference among the mass of men. The governments

SOURCE. Clinton Rossiter, *The First American Revolution; The American Colonies on the Eve of Independence,* New York: Harcourt, Brace & World, Inc., 1953, pp. 100–124. Copyright 1953, 1956 by Clinton Rossiter. Reprinted by permission of Harcourt, Brace & World, Inc., and the author.

of the continental colonies were a stage in the development of American democracy rather than democracy itself. The thoughts of good colonists were thoughts of liberty and self-government rather than of equality and mass participation. The course of political freedom was halting, full of starts and stops and discouraging retreats, yet over the generations it went slowly and painfully upward to ultimate triumph.

I

The pattern of government in each colony was determined by its "constitution," leading elements of which were the original charter, grant, or patent and its renewals, commissions, and instructions to the governor, orders-in-council and other directions from the mother country, codes of laws, and local custom and practice. The charter, grant, or patent was the basic document; there were three kinds of charter and thus three types of colony in early America:

The royal colony was, from a constitutional point of view, a political entity in which the Crown was immediately supreme and sovereign. In theory, all officials and institutions existed at the pleasure of the King; in practice, the colonists shared heavily in determining their political destinies, especially through the assembly and institutions of local government. The royal colony was easily the most satisfactory type in terms of English interests. Had the early imperialists had their way, royal government would have been installed without delay throughout the empire. Even though it was not, the trend toward centralization of power in the Crown went on apace, and by the middle of the eighteenth century eight of thirteen colonies were royal in constitution: Virginia, New York, New Hampshire, Massachusetts, New Jersey, North Carolina, South Carolina, and Georgia.

The proprietary was a colony in which political power and ownership of the land were placed in the hands of one or more private individuals. The model of such proprietaries as Maryland and the Carolinas was the county palatine of Durham, a feudal principality in which the Bishop of Durham, for reasons of state, had been granted the powers of a virtually absolute king. Because of weaknesses inherent in its constitutional structure, which took little time coming to the surface in the wilderness, the proprietary was pretty much a failure in colonial America. Some proprietorships were converted into royal colonies; others made such heavy concessions to imperial demands from above and popular urges from below as to be scarcely distinguishable from royal colonies. Although nine colonies were originally constituted as proprietorships under royal favor, only three—Pennsylvania, Delaware, and Maryland—were in existence in 1765.

Connecticut and Rhode Island, both founded without authority from the Crown, were granted royal charters of incorporation at the time of the Restoration. Despite repeated threats of judicial or legislative revocation, they clung to their corporate charters and unique status of independence throughout the eighteenth century. In these two colonies the pattern of self-government was most firmly established. Although the Crown retained considerable authority over their military, diplomatic, and commercial affairs, the extent of supervision was spotty and discontinuous. An especially sour Tory, John Mein of Boston, was not too far from the truth when he wrote of Connecticut and Rhode Island: "The people in those Colonies chuse their Governors, Judges, Assemblymen, Counsellors, and all the rest of their Officers; and the King and Parliament have as much influence there as in the wilds of Tartary." In the commonwealth period (1630–1684) Massachusetts was an extraordinary type of corporate colony—extraordinary alike in origin, form, and pretensions to independence. Although the charter of 1691 established Massachusetts as a royal colony, the corporate features were never entirely eradicated.

The governor—in the royal colonies a viceroy appointed by the King, in the proprietaries an agent selected by the proprietors, in Connecticut and Rhode Island a local gentleman chosen by the assembly—was the key official in each of the colonies. In the royal and proprietary colonies he was the focus of internal politics and external relations. As representative of the sponsoring agency in England, especially of the Crown, he exercised most of the ancient executive prerogatives: command of the forces; the summoning, proroguing, and dissolution of the assembly; an absolute veto over legislation; appointment to subordinate offices; leadership of the church wherever established; the royal prerogative of mercy; oversight, at least by instruction, in financial affairs; and often, with the council, the responsibility of serving as the colony's court of last resort. In short, he was the symbol and fact of imperial authority—a dignified chief of state, a powerful political and military official, a direct participant in legislative and judicial affairs, and the linchpin of empire.

Over against the governor, representative of England and monarchy, was set the assembly, representative of colony and people. The political and constitutional history of colonial America appears often to have been nothing so much as a huge, ill-tempered tug-of-war between governors and assemblies, and it was the latter that grew steadily more robust in the struggle for power. Some assemblies were established under royal, proprietary, or trading-company favor; others were spontaneous creations of the men on the spot. Grounded firmly in representative and electoral systems that were the direct ancestors of present American practice, converted sooner or later by circumstance into a bicameral structure (everywhere except Pennsylvania), persuaded through experience that they could wield all the traditional powers and privileges of a legislature, the assemblies were the most important instruments of popular government in colonial America. The growth of such techniques of representation as residence requirements, constituency payments, annual elections, instructions, voting by ballot, and bans on place-holding by assemblymen is evidence that the assemblies were far more advanced toward the idea of a popular legislature than was the House of Commons.

In each colony there was also a conciliar body, generally made up of twelve gentlemen of property and prestige, which exercised important functions of an executive, legislative, and judicial character. The council acted for the governor as advisory cabinet, with the assembly as upper house of a bicameral legislature, and again with the governor as highest provincial court of appeals in civil cases (and in Virginia in criminal cases as well). It was often as powerful an agent of royal authority as the governor. The normal method of appointment of councilors was by the Crown, on recommendation of the governor. The principal instance of deviation from this scheme was to be found in Massachusetts. The charter of 1691, which could not ignore the years of republican independence, provided for a council of twenty-eight to be chosen annually by the general court subject to the veto of the governor.

In its origins and early development the judicial system of colonial America paid scant attention to English precedents. In the seventeenth century the differences between the courts of one colony and the next were so pronounced that it is impossible to make any general statement about them. What existed in most colonies was a practical system of law and courts in which there was much emphasis on the colonists' own rude notions of justice and little on uniform practice or a trained bench and bar. In Massachusetts lawyers were forbidden to practice, and in all colonies the prejudice against them was surprisingly strong. In part this could be traced to English antecedents; the Fundamental Constitutions of Carolina labeled it "a base and vile thing to plead for money or reward." In part it was the natural reaction of a frontier society to a profession identified with the complexities of civilization.

In the eighteenth century, chiefly at the behest of the Crown and under the pressures of a maturing society, the trend was everywhere toward uniformity in organization and improvement in professional standards. By 1765 the judicial system in most colonies was regularized and independent, and the chief agents of the system, the lawyers, were climbing into the political saddle. The remarkable fair trial of Captain John Preston and his men for the Boston Massacre and the overwhelming resistance of the judiciary to general writs of assistance are proof of the vitality of the court system inherited by the Revolutionary generation.

II

No account of government in colonial America would be complete without some mention of the complexity of officials active in England and the colonies as agents of the Crown's belated attempt to prosecute a consistent imperial policy. The word "complexity" is used advisedly, for in the eighteenth century there were so many officials and committees engaged in overseeing the colonies that it is almost impossible to fix with exactness their powers, functions, and relations to one another. Several features of imperial administration, however, are beyond dispute. Control of the colonies was exercised in the name of the King and thus as an extraordinary assertion of the royal prerogative, which by this time had lost most of its meaning in the mother country. Parliament, which was preoccupied with weightier affairs, was quite unsure of its right to legislate in support or restraint of this last significant manifestation of the prerogative. Neither Crown nor Parliament created much in the way of special machinery for colonial affairs, and for the most part regular executive agencies expanded their activities to include the colonies. Final authority over the colonies resided in the Privy Council, but the actual task of supervision was carried on by committees of the Council, regular agencies, and one specially constituted board. The most important of these varied instruments were:

The Board of Trade, or "Lords Commissioners of Trade and Plantations," was a staff and advisory agency independent of the Privy Council. The Board was charged with drafting instructions for the governors, hearing colonial complaints, suggesting appointments, collecting information for purposes of more effective oversight and direction, and reviewing colonial laws. Although the Board was inferior in legal status and had no sanctions at its command, it wielded much influence through its correspondence with governors and through reports and recommendations to the Crown. Rarely did the Privy Council disregard its advisory verdict on the wisdom or legality of colonial legislation.

The Committee of the Privy Council, often known as "the Lords of the Committee of Council for hearing appeals and complaints from the plantations," was an agency whose functions are clear in its title. This committee provided, for those colonists able and willing to make use of its machinery, a reasonably impartial and efficient high court of appeals. Its chief purpose was not to do justice or develop an imperial common law, but to protect prerogative and mercantilism against colonial interference. . . .

Last in order, but in many ways first in importance, was the Secretary of State for the Southern Department, the chief official for colonial affairs in the developing cabinet system. The first concern of the Secretary of State was war and diplomacy with France and Spain; his conduct of office thus bore directly upon problems of security for the colonies. The makings of a unified system of colonial control were present in this office, but for several reasons—the lack of interest in colonial affairs of most incumbents, the preoccupation of the Secretary with the over-all pattern of war and diplomacy, and the rapid turnover in personnel— these potentialities were never realized.

The result of this conjunction of too much organization for detail and too little concern for unity—especially when intensified by distance, slowness of communication, inferiority of personnel, corruption, bribery, and colonial obstinacy—was a large measure of self-government for the colonies. Each of the chief weapons of imperial control—the viceregal authority of the governor, appeals to the Privy Council, and royal disallowance of colonial legislation—proved defective or inadequate in action. The governor was one thing in the instructions of the Board of Trade, quite another in Williamsburg, Boston, or New York. The system of appeals to the Privy Council was workable enough, but was confined to cases in which a sizable sum was at stake. In the entire colonial period less than two hundred cases from the American colonies were prosecuted before the Council. Whatever it was to become in later years, it was not in the eighteenth century a supreme court of empire. The extent of imperial control exercised through the technique of royal disallowance may be judged from the figures: From 1691 to the end of the colonial period roughly 8,500 laws were submitted for approval. Of these some 470, or 5.5 per cent, were disallowed. The practice of submission and examination was loose and was particularly hampered by the fact of distance. Considerable success was achieved by English authorities in blocking laws that encroached on the prerogative, affected England's commercial interests, interfered with the established church, tampered with the currency, and altered the laws of inheritance; yet for the most part the threat of royal disallowance had surprisingly little effect on the course of colonial self-government. . . .

III

If the pattern of colonial politics was marked by a growing measure of self-government and home rule, then the question arises: Who were the "selves" who did the governing? Who ruled at home? An answer can be found by considering three related problems: the nature of the suffrage in the various colonies; the extent to which the suffrage was actually exercised; the intensity of popular interest and participation in affairs of town and colony.

The history of the colonial suffrage, like the history of almost all early American institutions, was one of primitive diversity in the seventeenth century and maturing uniformity in the eighteenth. A wide variety of practice prevailed before 1690, ranging from the narrow limitation of church membership in Massachusetts to something quite close to white manhood suffrage during the first years in Virginia, Rhode Island, West Jersey, and several other localities. As the settlements developed into more stable societies, demands arose for a broader suffrage in the autocratic colonies and a narrower one in the popular. By the turn of the century, some sort of property qualification for voting had been established in every colony, and this feature of American politics continued in force until well after the winning of independence. In part the requirement of property holding was fostered by English authorities, who had begun to insist in charters and instructions that

> You shall take care that the members of the assembly be elected only by *ffreeholders,* as being more agreeable to the custome of England, to which you are as nigh as conveniently you can to conforme yourselfe.

In part it could be traced to the fact that the colonists, too, were Englishmen and therefore felt, consciously or unconsciously, the urge to conform to ancient ways. It was inevitable that men of their blood and traditions should be impelled by the rise of a propertied class to restrict the suffrage to those who were in it.

The details of these property requirements furnish yet another instance of English practice adapted to American conditions. In most colonies the basic qualification was the famous "forty-shilling freehold." Seven of them —New Hampshire, Rhode Island, New York, New Jersey, Virginia, North Carolina, and Georgia—made the possession of land an absolute requirement; the others recognized property other than real estate. Everywhere a "stake-in-society" was the door to political enfranchisement, and almost everywhere additional restrictions kept women, youths, Catholics, Jews, infidels, Negroes, Indians, mulattoes, indentured servants, and other "inferior" persons from the polls. A few, but only a very few, voices were lifted in protest against limited suffrage. Perhaps the clearest of these spoke through an advertisement in a Philadelphia newspaper in 1737:

A PECUNIARY Gratification is offered to any of the learned or unlearned, who shall *Mathematically* prove, that a Man's having a property in a Tract of Land, more or less, is thereby entitled to any Advantage, *in point of understanding,* over another Fellow, who has no other Estate, than

"THE AIR . . . *to breathe in,* THE EARTH . . . *to walk upon,* and ALL OF THE WORLD . . . *to drink of.*"

Accurate figures of the voting potential in each colony are not easy to establish. The best estimate would be that something like one out of every four white males was eligible to vote for representatives in the assembly, perhaps one out of three for elective officers in towns and in boroughs with open charters of incorporation. There were many deviations, both upward and downward, from these averages, depending, for example, upon the local price and availability of land, proximity to the frontier, and the origins and attitudes of the inhabitants. It must be emphasized that these figures are estimates only, for reliable statistics are just not to be found.

If these figures are discouraging to those who think of the colonies as a Paradise Lost of American democracy, even more discouraging are estimates of exercise of the suffrage. Again the pattern is one of extreme variation from one time and locality to the next, but in general there existed what appears at first glance to have been an attitude of astounding apathy toward campaigns and elections. Not only was but one in four white males eligible to vote; in many places but one in four of those eligible even bothered to vote. Records of the late eighteenth century show that in several supposedly hotly contested elections in Massachusetts an average of one qualified voter in five took the trouble to vote. The figures are better, but not too much better, in Virginia and the middle colonies. Apathy toward elections was a widespread feature of colonial politics, and there were no campaigns to "get out the vote."

The third point of inquiry, the intensity of popular interest and participation in affairs of town and colony, has already been largely answered. What was true of voting was doubly true of office-holding: Restrictions were many and aspirants few. In an age when breadwinning consumed all a man's time and energy, when travel was difficult and political parties nonexistent, when government was severely limited in scope and touched many men not at all, and when the pace of life went slowly, political indifference—to elections, to office-holding, and to issues—was well-nigh inevitable. Despite eloquent references to "an aroused people" in certain memorable debates in the assemblies, politics in colonial America was the province of those with particular interests to defend or with a natural flair for public action. The number of such persons was never and nowhere very large. The political apathy of the colonial press, punctured only occasionally before 1765 by a thorough airing of some local squabble, is proof of the slow pace of political life. "Publick Lethargy" was under constant attack by colonial penmen.

This does not mean that the declarations and decisions of the attentive few or the experiences and instincts of the indifferent many were any the less important to the progress of American liberty. The few in their assemblies, town meetings, and polls held the democratic future in trust and acted out on a small stage the great drama of constitutional government that was in time to call millions into the supporting cast. The many, too, had their notion of liberty and self-government: to be left alone to pursue their own destinies. When government became important or oppressive enough, they found ways other than politics to express their wishes and to influence action. Sullen resistance, riots, and "going out west" are not generally recommended as effective techniques of political freedom, but in colonial times they served a very real purpose.

These are the facts of political participation in the American colonies: Only a fraction could participate and even a lesser fraction did; the colonies were still well ahead of practice in almost all other countries; and many men never cared one way or the other about political power. Nor should it be forgotten that in a society so amazingly fluid for the age, a society where people could "move on" and where land was cheap and plentiful, the privilege of the suffrage was something that almost any white man could win. The records prove that everywhere, even in aristocratic New York and South Carolina, men of mean birth and menial occupation could aspire to political power and prominence. And that a man in eighteenth-century Virginia or New England had neither opportunity nor desire to vote or hold office did not mean that he considered himself a slave. In an age when politics was one of the least of man's worries, the poll lists were one of the lesser criteria of the progress of liberty.

IV

Seeds of contention between governor and assembly were sown with profusion in the constitutions of the eleven royal or proprietary colonies. The inherent contradiction between the interests and attitudes of the mother country and those of the distant colonies was especially apparent in this instance. On one hand stood the royal or proprietary governor—in four cases out of five an Englishman, in the fifth a loyal colonial, in any case an agent of the prerogative with a commission and instructions that made him an autocrat not beholden to colonial direction. On the other stood the provincial assembly—the articulate organ of a breed of men who were more English than the English in their obstinacy, pride, and hypersensitivity in matters of self-government. From the outset the system gaped at the middle, and the final triumph of the assembly was almost foreordained. Although the governor occupied a position of overwhelming constitutional superiority, it was undercut repeatedly by circumstances in colony and empire.

The governors got far more verbal than practical support from the authorities at home. The remoteness of colonial capitals and the lack of either an imperial policy or the will to execute it created a situation in which the governor was left pretty much on his own. It was he, not the Board of Trade, who had to live with the colonists; it was his estimate of the expedient, not the Board's demand of the impossible, that controlled decisions taken on the spot. The governor was too often left defenseless against what Governor Clinton of New York labeled the assembly's "continued Grasping at Power."

The colonists fell naturally into an opinion of their governors best summed up in Franklin's remark about "men of vicious characters and broken fortunes, sent by a Minister to get them out of the way." We know today that this was rarely the case, that the governors were neither better nor worse than the officials who carried on the public business of England. There were men as bad as Cornbury and Fletcher, but there were also men as good as Dinwiddie, the Wentworths, Spotswood, Hunter, Pownall, Burnet, Shirley, Glen, and Dobbs. No matter who the governors were, however, most colonists agreed with the New York Assembly of 1749 that they were

generally entire Strangers to the People they are sent to govern . . . their Interest is entirely distinct . . . they seldom regard the Welfare of the People, otherwise than as they can make it subservient to their own particular Interest.

In this instance the myth was more telling than the fact, and the myth was one of "men of broken fortunes, dissolute and ignorant, too vile to be employed near home," a calumny that the English press printed and the colonial press reprinted with glee. Recognition of the alien purposes of the royal governors and misrepresentation of their personal traits did much to strengthen the morale and ambitions of the colonial assemblies, not that they needed it.

Colonial legislators were persistent, clever, and vigilant, and over the years they advanced a surprisingly coherent policy in constitutional matters. The struggle for power was not always so bitter and decisive as some history books would have it, for several colonies enjoyed extended periods of political quiescence and good will. Yet the trend of power moved almost always toward the assembly, which used this power to fight its way ever higher in the name of "the people" and "our ancient and undoubted rights and privileges as Englishmen."

The lack of real toughness in the imperialists in England permitted the colonists to exploit to the limit the fatal defect of the colonial constitutions: the location of the power of the purse in colonial hands, a defect compounded by the failure of the Crown to provide a permanent civil list in any of the colonies. No one was more aware than the governor himself that, in Governor Bernard's words, "the Want of a certain and adequate civil List to each Colony" was "the Root of the American Disorders." Far too many officials, institutions, and necessities of empire were left dependent upon the willingness of the assemblies to tax friends and neighbors and thus upon the natural desire to fix conditions upon any and all grants.

Occasionally in spectacular political warfare accompanied by newspaper attacks on the governors, but more often through unpublicized day-to-day encroachments, the assemblies grasped for privileges and powers like those of the House of Commons. Several of Parliament's hard-earned privileges—control over procedure, freedom of debate, determination of disputed elections—were secured by the assemblies. Others —the "Speaker's Petition," control over sessions, regulation of elections, creation of new electoral districts—were not, and over these the struggle raged in almost every colony. The Crown defended with tenacity the governor's power to prorogue and dissolve the assembly and the final weapons of gubernatorial veto and royal disallowance. Yet the area of assembly freedom grew ever wider, especially as it came home to more and more colonists that the fight for parliamentary privilege was at bottom a fight for the liberty of the subject.

The assemblies also used the purse to pry their way into executive affairs. For example, by designating a specific person to receive the salary of an office they usurped the power of appointment; by naming their own committees and even their own treasurer to verify expenditures they encroached substantially on the governor's command of the militia and control over military stores; and by the famous expedient of tampering with the governor's salary they brought more than one recalcitrant to heel in such matters as personnel and jurisdiction of colonial courts. The governors of Georgia and Virginia were the only viceroys whose salaries were not dependent on the pleasure of the assembly or, as in the case of the North Carolina quit rents, on an unsatisfactory substitute arrangement. Especially acrimonious battles were fought in New York and Massachusetts over the assembly's calculated practice of annual grants to the governor—with the assembly emerging victorious. The provision in the Constitution of 1787 forbidding the raising or lowering of the President's compensation attests the respect in which eighteenth-century Americans held this technique.

By 1765 the assembly was dominant in almost every colony in continental America. The royal power of disallowance was still strong enough to prevent a complete overriding of the governor and other imperial officials, but shrewd observers were beginning to realize that only the full power of Parliament was now equal to the centrifugal practices of the assemblies. Most discouraging to proponents of empire was the inability of English authorities to secure positive accomplishments. The record of colonial co-operation, or rather non-co-operation, in time of war must have been hard to swallow. The assemblies recorded their most spectacular gains, especially in their campaign to control the public purse, in the French and Indian War. More than one governor must have felt that he rather than the French was the enemy to be reduced to a plea for mercy.

The struggles of the colonial assemblies provide an instructive example of the way in which men distrustful of democracy in one century can, by fighting for their own privileges and opinions, open the way to democracy in the next. Indeed, "distrustful of democracy" is the very best that can be said of cliques that controlled assemblies in New Hampshire, Pennsylvania, the Carolinas, and Virginia. The records show up many colonial parliamentarians as illtempered, petty, self-seeking, tiresome little men more often than not committed to the intolerant side of questions of religious and social freedom. Yet the assemblies also counted an unusual range of strong and able men, many of whom were genuinely progressive in their opinions. The Whigs in the colonial legislatures had a limited popularism as their goal, but in driving toward it they unloosed forces that would not be halted short of total political democracy. And their arguments proved in time to be fully convertible to democratic currency.

The colonial assemblies, like the dissenting churches, were influential schools of American political thought. The system under which delegates were chosen was one as representative of "the people" as could be erected in those days of concern for Whig ideals of liberty. The proceedings of the assemblies were open to public inspection and criticism, their journals were printed and distributed, and their exchanges with the governors, especially those of a pungent nature, got thorough coverage in the colonial press. Just about all that the people of South Carolina knew of Massachusetts was that there, too, the assembly hacked away resolutely at the governor's position and powers. There can be no argument with Charles M. Andrews's conclusion: "In the development of American political ideas and social practices, the influence of the popular assembly . . . is the most potent single factor underlying our American system of government."

CHAPTER 10

IMPERIAL POLICY: MERCANTILISM AND THE NAVIGATION ACTS

In the seventeenth and eighteenth centuries, Great Britain was one of the major imperial powers. By 1763 she had reached the zenith of her power and domination; yet, twenty years later she was forced to sign a peace treaty that stripped her of her thirteen mainland colonies in America. What brought about this sudden reversal of British fortune? The answer of American patriots of the Revolutionary era—a view long since rejected by historians but surprisingly prevalent still—was that British tyranny had prompted America's struggle for independence. What constituted this so-called tyranny? Primarily, the taxation (without representation) levied by Parliament in the 1760's and 1770's, but also the sometimes oppressive Navigation Acts and the other mercantilist regulations imposed on the colonists by the British from 1650 on.

The way in which Great Britain governed and managed her empire is clearly of major importance in explaining the coming of the American Revolution. Hence, the next two readings are devoted to considerations of British imperial policy and its implementation. In the selection below, from *Origins of the American Revolution,** Professor John C. Miller concentrates on imperial policies and practices up to 1763. Professor Miller

139

suggests that the principles of mercantilism were largely responsible for shaping the British Empire and for determining the role and the function of the British colonies. Mercantilism found its most important expression in the Navigation Acts of the seventeenth century, which formed the basis of British colonial policy. In the following pages, Professor Miller is primarily concerned with the effects of British mercantilism—in particular with the effects of the Navigation Acts—on the American colonies, and with the reactions and attitudes of the colonists to imperial policy. In conclusion, Miller seeks to determine precisely what part the Navigation Acts and the system of mercantilism played in the coming of the Revolution.

In reading this selection, the student should determine the essential nature of the British imperial system. What principles shaped this system, and how did these principles affect the English conception of the relationship between the mother country and the colonies? To what extent did this conception work toward or against the preservation of a healthy and enduring empire? The reader should also be concerned with the specific effects of mercantilist policy on the economy and the thought of the several sections of the British mainland colonies. A careful reading of the impact of mercantilism not only tells us something about the causes of the Revolutionary War but also something of the mind of the colonial American.

Carl Ubbelohde, *The American Colonies and the British Empire, 1607-1763** (1968), Oliver M. Dickerson, *The Navigation Acts and the American Revolution** (1951), Lawrence A. Harper, "Mercantilism and the American Revolution," *The Canadian Historical Review,* XXIII (March, 1942), and Curtis P. Nettles, "British Mercantilism and the Economic Development of the Thirteen Colonies," *The Journal of Economic History,* XII (Spring, 1952), offer additional treatments of this subject.

* Available in a paperback edition.

THE ECONOMIC BACKGROUND
JOHN C. MILLER

In 1763, Great Britain attained a height of power and dominion which led many Englishmen to conclude that a new Roman Empire had been brought into being through the genius of William Pitt and the valor of British arms. France and Spain, united by the Family Compact, had been decisively defeated and a large part of North America and India had been brought under British control. A period of "prosperity and glory unknown to any former age" seemed to be opening for Great Britain and her colonies. Yet those Englishmen who in 1763 regarded themselves as the heirs of Rome soon perceived a new and highly disquieting resemblance between Britain and Rome: the British Empire seemed about to go the way of the Roman Empire. It appeared probable that the same generation of Englishmen which saw the empire reach its highest point of grandeur would be the witness of its decline and fall. So swiftly did fortune turn that William Pitt, who had brought Great Britain to the zenith, died in the House of Lords fifteen years later in one of England's darkest hours.

The Englishmen who lost the American colonies were not solely responsible for the catastrophe which overtook the empire, although George III and his ministers must bear a large share of the blame. Because Americans were such good Englishmen—in the seventeenth-century mold—and held fast to the liberal traditions of English history, they made uncommonly troublesome subjects from the point of view of British imperialists. Eighteenth-century Englishmen found Americans "of a disposition haughty and insolent, impatient of rule, disdaining subjection, and by all means affecting independence"—in sharp contrast to "the remarkably pliant and submissive disposition" of the inhabitants of Bengal. As a result, the British Empire was at best, in Benjamin Franklin's words, a fragile Chinese vase which required far more delicate handling than George III and his baggage-smashing ministers gave it. Yet it is true that if the Englishmen of George III's reign blundered and muddled,

SOURCE. John C. Miller, *Origins of the American Revolution*, Boston: Little, Brown & Co., 1943, pp. 3–25. Copyright 1943 by John C. Miller. Reprinted by permission of the author.

their failure was partly owing to the fact that they had inherited a traditional conception of the relationship between mother country and colonies which proved, in the crisis, an utterly false set of rules for preserving a great empire. Many of the seeds of the American Revolution existed in the British Empire almost from its beginning. George III and his advisers ripened them and planted a new crop of grievances of their own in the colonies. They harvested the bitter fruit in 1776.

The British Empire of which George III became sovereign in 1760 was shaped largely by the principles of mercantilism. The goal of mercantilism—today it would be called economic nationalism—was the creation of a self-sufficient empire from which foreign trade and commerce were excluded; the domination of vital trade routes; and the acquisition of abundant stores of gold and silver by the mother country. Mercantilism was designed to gird a nation for war by recruiting its economic strength and crippling that of its rivals. Inevitably, mercantilism itself bred war: as the nations sought to bring vital trade routes under their control and to seize choice spots of the earth's surface and then bolt the door against foreigners, national rivalries were brought to white heat. George III's empire had not been created by the exercise of the virtues of faith, hope, and charity. Sterner stuff was required of empire-builders and the English had it in abundance. They struck down the Dutch in a series of bitterly fought naval wars; and in 1763 they succeeded in attaining a hard-won, "true, national felicity upon the ruins of the House of Bourbon."

The Laws of Trade and Navigation or Navigation Acts enacted by the English Parliament during the seventeenth century were mercantilism translated into statute law. Although these acts were only a part of English mercantilism, they were its most important expression and formed the basis of British colonial policy long after the American Revolution had demonstrated their inadequacy. By mercantilist theory, the function of the colonies was to produce raw materals for the use of the mother country, to consume its manufactures and to foster its shipping; and the purpose of the Laws of Trade and Navigation was to ensure that the English colonies fulfilled these ends. This implied, as mercantilists readily admitted, that the colonies were to remain dependent agricultural regions, closely tied to the economy of an industrialized mother country. No mercantilist saw any impropriety in consigning the Western Hemisphere to a position of perpetual economic inferiority.

In a larger sense, the purpose of the Navigation Acts was to enable England, by augmenting her national strength, to triumph over France, Spain, and Holland in the struggle for world power. In the seventeenth and eighteenth centuries, a self-sufficient mercantilist empire was thought essential to national greatness and to victory over aggrandizing rival states. The Act of 1651—the first of the Navigation Acts—was directed mainly against the Dutch who by dint of sharpness in trade, financial resources which permitted them to give more liberal credit than the English, and the quality of the merchandise they purveyed, had been able to get the better of English merchants not merely in world trade but in the English colonies themselves. To cripple Dutch competition and lay the menace of the Dutch state to England's maritime supremacy, the English Parliament declared in 1651 that no goods the growth of Asia, Africa, and America could be carried to England, Ireland, the English colonies, except in English, Irish, or colonial ships, manned by sailors "for the most part" subjects of the Commonwealth. Dutch shipping was further discriminated against by the provision that goods from Europe could enter England, Ireland, and the colonies only if they were transported in the ships of the country "in which the said goods are the growth, production, or manufacture."

But the Navigation Act of 1651, however successful in barring Dutch and other foreign ships from trade with the English colonies, fell far short of erecting a mercantilist empire. Under its provisions, the colonists were able to send their products to any foreign market and to buy manufactured goods wherever they pleased—and Americans took full advantage of this privilege. After the restoration of Charles II in 1660, the English Parliament quickly set about closing the breaches in the mercantilist walls which remained after the Act of 1651. The Navigation Act of 1660—the so-called "great Palladium" or Magna Carta of English commerce—went far towards making the English Empire truly mercantilistic. This measure prescribed that no foreign ships could engage in trade with the English colonies or import any of their products into England—a re-enactment of the Act of 1651. To guard further against the intrusion of foreign competition, all foreign merchants were excluded from the colonies. At the same time, England made clear its intention of concentrating control of the resources of her colonies in her own hands. It was ordered that certain commodities were to be "enumerated"—that is, that they could be sent only to England, Ireland and Wales, and— after the Act of Union—to Scotland. Despite the fact that it was greatly to the convenience and profit of the colonists to ship these products directly to the European market, the English government insisted that they must first pass through England, Ireland, or Wales, although from thence they might be re-exported to the European continent.

The commodities thus singled out for the mother country's monopolization were those generally regarded as essential to the wealth and power of the state which were not produced in the British Isles themselves:

sugar, tobacco, cotton, indigo, and dye woods—the oil, rubber, and steel of modern imperialism. No country could hope to attain self-sufficiency without an ample supply of these semitropical products; and by enumerating them England hoped to relieve herself of dependence upon France and Holland and, ultimately, to oblige those powers to buy from her.

Although many important products of the American colonies were not enumerated—fish, hides, and flour, for example, were never monopolized by Great Britain—and might, therefore, be carried directly to European markets, this latitude permitted colonial trade was steadily narrowed during the eighteenth century. Great Britain adopted the practice of enumerating whatever commodities strengthened her trading position in world markets, benefited British manufacturers and merchants, or added revenue to the customs. This policy led to the enumeration of rice, molasses, naval stores, and furs prior to 1764. In that year, George Grenville, the British Chanellor of the Exchequer, in his efforts to raise a colonial revenue and strengthen the mercantile system added more colonial commodities to the list than had been enumerated during the entire period since the passage of the Navigation Act of 1660.

In 1663, the structure of English mercantilism was completed with the passage by Parliament of the so-called Staple Act. This law prohibited the importation of goods direct from Europe to England's American colonies: with few exceptions, notably wine from Madeira and the Azores, European goods were required to be first carried to England, where, after payment of duties, they might be reshipped to the colonies —if Americans were still willing to pay the cost, now greatly enhanced by duties and handling charges. Thus, in their completed form, the Navigation Acts required the colonists to send many of their most important raw products to Britain and to purchase almost all their manufactured goods in the same market. As a result, British merchants and manufacturers were placed in a position to determine the prices of what Americans bought and sold. Although the sharp edge of this pincers aimed at colonial producers was blunted by the fact that British capitalism was becoming increasingly competitive and, in consequence, probably few price-fixing agreements were entered into by British merchants or manufacturers, we shall see that many colonists raised the cry that they were being cruelly exploited by the system erected by the Laws of Trade.

In this manner, British colonial policy came to be dominated by the mercantilist principle that "all plantations endamage their mother kingdom, where the trades of such plantations are not confined to the mother kingdom by good laws and severe execution of them." For the remainder of the colonial period, the British government sought to tighten the screws of commercial monopoly upon the colonists and to devise means of more strictly enforcing the Laws of Trade. Even after 1764 when the British government turned its attention to raising a revenue in the provinces, it did not lose sight of the necessity of maintaining control of colonial commerce and trade. The Acts of Trade and Navigation were upheld to the last, and even the staunchest defenders of colonial liberty in England, including William Pitt, insisted upon keeping the colonies in economic leading-strings. The monopolization of colonial trade was held to be the *raison d'être* of the empire: "If we allow France and Holland to supply them with fabric," an Englishmen said, "we may just as well give up all ideas of having colonies at all." During the revolutionary period, English propagandists learned that nothing succeeded in incensing Englishmen against the colonists as did the charge that Americans were seeking to throw off the restraints of the Navigation Acts and to establish free trade with the world.

Because British imperialism was primarily commercial, the British merchants and manufacturers regarded the empire as very nearly the best of all possible empires. Until 1764, at least, the government carefully consulted the interests of British businessmen in formulating its colonial policy. During this period, British merchants and manufacturers found the American colonists rapidly becoming their best customers. Trade with the colonies grew steadily: in 1772, the exports of Great Britain to the colonies alone almost equaled her entire exports in 1704. On the eve of the American Revolution, one third of the shipping of the British Empire was engaged in the colonial trade. "The vast cities along the coast of England and Scotland," it was said, ". . . are sprung from contemptible villages only by the American trade." "The American," observed an Englishman, "is apparelled from head to foot in our manufacturers . . . he scarcely drinks, sits, moves, labours or recreates himself, without contributing to the emolument of the mother country." In 1774, it was estimated that in the province of New York eleven out of twelve inhabitants wore clothing of British manufacture.

The spice to this feast was the fact that, thanks to the Navigation Acts, the expanding colonial market was protected from the competition of Dutch, French, Spaniards, and all other interlopers. As a result, the colonies helped cushion Great Britain against postwar depressions: when peace brought a revival of European manufacturing—with consequent loss to British businessmen who had profited hugely from the destruction of European industry—the colonies offered a market relatively free from competition. Here the merchants and manufacturers might charge what the traffic would bear, although their monopoly was tempered by American smuggling and by the reluctance of Americans to pay their debts to their British creditors. Nevertheless, British businessmen had their hands deep in Americans' pockets, and as long as the mercantilist system should endure, they looked forward to engrossing "all the money our colonists should ever possess."

This trade was financed in large part by credit advanced by British merchants to their colonial customers, whether Northern merchants or Southern planters. "Credit," observed an Englishman early in the eighteenth century, "is a profitable plant that yields more fruit to our trade than the whole specie of the kingdom." Indeed, trade between Great Britain and the colonies could scarcely have been carried on without credit, for the operating capital of American planters and merchants came mainly from this source. Northern merchants in turn were enabled to extend credit to colonial farmers and thereby push forward the area of settlement; but throughout the colonial period the base of the pyramid of debt rested upon the shoulders of British merchants and manufacturers. In consequence, the capitalists of the mother country soon acquired a huge financial stake in the American colonies. By 1760, the value of British exports to the colonies was estimated to total £2,000,000 a year; but British merchants carried over £4,000,000 of American debts on their ledgers. In the case of Southern planters, they depended largely upon the sale of future crops for repayment; as regards Northern merchants, British creditors relied upon the colonists' ability to gather enough cash from the African slave trade, the fisheries, and the West Indies to pay their debts. In both cases, the merchants could ill afford to see colonial prosperity undermined by unwise restrictions, but on the other hand they felt obliged to maintain close watch over American affairs lest the colonies evade the laws upon which the monopoly of the mother country rested or seek to make themselves unwelcome competitors of British merchants in the markets of the empire.

The imposition of the mercantilist system exacted heavy sacrifices from the American colonists during the seventeenth century. Instead of the freedom of trade with the world which they had largely enjoyed prior to 1651, they were now confined for the most part to the markets of the mother country and other parts of the empire; and the colonial consumer was delivered over to the English merchant and manufacturer. From a free-trade area, the British Empire was transformed into a highly protected market closed to foreign competition. The losses in liberty and material prosperity attendant upon this economic reorganization of the empire were borne chiefly by the colonists; from the beginning, whether mercantilism appeared beneficent or oppressive depended largely from what side of the Atlantic it was viewed.

But as the mercantilists frequently pointed out, Americans were compensated for the restrictions imposed by the mother country upon their trade and commerce. Mercantilists did not advocate the exploitation by the mother country of the colonies: their ideal was rather an empire in which every part contributed to the best of its ability toward the goal of self-sufficiency; and they insisted that the good of the whole be made the guiding principle of the mother country's colonial policy. Accordingly, in exchange for the monopoly enjoyed by the mother country in the colonies, a virtual monopoly of the English market was given the producers of certain colonial commodities. All foreign tobacco, for example, was excluded from England (although this restriction was later modified to permit the importation of some Portuguese and Spanish tobacco) and Englishmen were forbidden to plant tobacco in England—a law which was consistently violated until at the end of the seventeenth century the price of tobacco became so low that it was no longer profitable to grow it there. Moreover, tariff protection was given by the mother country to sugar, cotton, and indigo grown in the British colonies—thus placing a burden on the English consumer who, in an open market, undoubtedly could have bought cheaper. At the same time, bounties were given upon the production of naval stores, pitch, silk, and wine in the colonies—in the hope that the empire would become self-sufficient in these commodities and that Americans, if encouraged to produce raw materials, would be diverted from manufacturing for themselves.

Yet despite the benefits of mercantilism, Americans surrendered their economic liberties grudgingly. They lamented that the Dutch traders who in the seventeenth century sold goods at one-third the price charged by English merchants came among them no longer and that in their stead appeared Englishmen who, as the governor of Virginia said, would "faine bring us to the same poverty, wherein the Dutch found and relieved us." Bacon's Rebellion was caused in part by the depression that struck Virginia in the wake of the Acts of Trade. The Massachusetts General Court declared in the seventeenth century that it would not obey the Navigation Acts because the people of Massachusetts were not represented in the English Parliament and because "the lawes of England are bounded within the fower seas, and do not reach America"—a more sweeping assertion of colonial rights than was made by Americans until 1776.

As Great Britain became increasingly industrialized during the eighteenth century, the chorus of complaint in the colonies against high-priced

British goods subsided, although the Southern planters remained unreconciled to British monopoly. In general, the price of British manufactures declined and the quality improved to such a degree that it is doubtful if the colonists could have bought cheaper from their old friends the Dutch. This was not true, however, of India goods, of which large quantities were purchased by Americans, a substantial part being smuggled from Holland. But even so there was considerable foundation for the claim made by Englishmen in the eighteenth century that the Acts of Trade could not justly be regarded as a hardship by Americans inasmuch as they procured cheaper and better goods in England than could have been bought in France or Holland. Later, after the United States had achieved its independence, Lord Sheffield was to elaborate this argument into the theory— and win the British government to his view—that the young republic was so inextricably bound to English economy that it could not break its bonds regardless of how inconsiderately it was treated by Great Britain.

New England did not readily fit into the mercantilists' scheme of a rightly ordered empire. Instead of busying themselves at home producing necessities for the mother country and exchanging them for English manufactures, the Puritans took to the sea with such vigor that it was said their commerce smelled as strongly of fish as their theology did of brimstone. Except for timber and masts, New England lacked valuable staples required by the mother country. And so New Englanders derived little advantage, in contrast to the Southern colonists, from English bounties: "A Cargo of any of them [bountied commodities] will be returned to us in a few Trunks of Fripperies," they said, "and we should be Bankrupt to Great Britain every Ten Years."

The Puritans found that their salvation lay in manufacturing on their own and in pursuing that "coy mistress, trade" over a large part of the world in order to scrape together enough cash to pay for the goods they imported from Great Britain. During the colonial period, the exports of the Northern colonies to Great Britain were far less than their imports from her; but the merchants prospered despite this adverse balance of trade. By engaging in the slave trade, making rum, exploiting the fisheries, manufacturing for the Middle and Southern colonies as well as for their own use, and acting as middlemen between land-bound colonists and English businessmen, they found profitable outlet for their energy and capital. The freightage, commissions, and charges for services and credits paid by the colonial consumer helped build the American seaports and laid the foundations for many of the early American fortunes. Herein the colonial merchants came into collision with the British merchants, who, by virtue of their vast financial resources, enjoyed a considerable advantage over their American rivals. But the colonists were by no means outclassed: ships could be built cheaper in New England than elsewhere in the British Empire; New Englanders possessed a canniness in trade that staggered even the Scotch; and they were masters of the art of slipping a cargo of contraband past the inefficient and undermanned colonial customhouse.

Under these circumstances, the American merchants found little quarrel with the Laws of Trade as they were actually enforced; they grew up under the system and—except for restrictions upon their trade with the foreign West Indies—were not unduly hampered by British commercial laws. The British Empire, they learned, was, in the main, big enough to hold both themselves and the British merchants, and so long as the mother country did not begrudge them a profit or too strictly enforce its laws they were in general well content. Given the lax enforcement of the Acts of Trade—by which the door was left ajar for highly profitable smuggling—and the advantages of carrying on business within the British Empire—one of the greatest trading areas in the world—it is not probable that the Navigation Acts alone would have produced a revolutionary spirit among American businessmen. On the contrary, the conviction was strongly established among many colonists that their economic well-being depended upon remaining within the empire and enjoying the benefits of its highly protected markets.

In the Middle colonies, where a far more even balance prevailed between agriculture and commerce than in New England, the Acts of Trade inflicted little appreciable hardship. These provinces exported large quantities of cereals and lumber to the European continent and the West Indies. It is important to observe in this connection that their trade with the West Indies, like that of the New England colonies, was not restricted to the British West Indies; the most profitable branch of their commerce was with the French, Dutch, and Spanish islands. Although this trade was not prohibited by the Navigation Acts, it ran counter to every principle of mercantilism and in 1733 was virtually prohibited by an act of Parliament which, as will be seen, proved unenforceable. In studying the origins of the American Revolution, it ought to be borne in mind that the prosperity of New England and the Middle colonies depended in a large measure upon a trade which had been built up outside the walls which mercantilists sought to erect around the empire.

Neither New England nor the Middle colonies were as intimately tied to the British market as were the staple colonies of the North American continent and the West Indies. Whereas the Northern colonies failed to produce vital raw materials required by the mother country and so fell short of the mercantilists' ideal, the Southern colonies fulfilled their highest expectations. These provinces constituted a rich agricultural area which supplied the mother country with such valuable products as tobacco, naval stores, rice, indigo, cotton, and sugar—the chief staples of commerce—and received in exchange British-manufactured goods. These commodities were enumerated and the planters themselves had little opportunity to supplement their incomes by smuggling. Moreover, they were excellent customers of British merchants and manufacturers. While it is true that all the American colonies depended largely upon imports of manufactured articles from Great Britain to maintain a European living standard in the New World, the Southern staple colonies were so lacking in local industries that they were compelled to look to the mother country for virtually all their manufactured goods.

Mercantilists rejoiced in the Southern staple colonies as the jewels of the empire; but many planters found that the shoe of mercantilism pinched acutely. The tightness of the squeeze differed considerably, however, among the various kinds of planters. Although they were all more or less at the mercy of the British merchants and manufacturers who sold them goods and advanced them credit, some planters had secured preferential treatment from the mother country. In 1730, for example, the British government partially met the demands of the Carolina rice growers by permitting them to export rice—which had been enumerated by the British government in 1704—to southern Europe, although they were still forbidden to import manufactures except through Great Britain. In 1739, the sugar planters of the West Indies were likewise given the privilege of exporting sugar directly to Europe although they produced barely enough to supply the needs of the British Empire alone. This concession was won largely because of the presence in the British Parliament of a powerful bloc of absentee West India planters aided by a lobby of West India merchants. As a result, during the eighteenth century, the sugar colonies were in little danger of finding their interests sacrificed to those of the mother country or of the Northern colonies; on the contrary, the Northern colonists and the British consumer were in dire danger of being made the victims of West Indian cupidity.

No such advantages were enjoyed by the tobacco growers of Virginia and Maryland. Certainly as regards tobacco, Great Britain was not in any sense "the natural entrepôt for the American trade with the continent" which the Laws of Trade sought to make it—rather, it was a bottleneck through which the British government attempted to force colonial trade. Of the 96,000 hogsheads of tobacco sent by Maryland

and Virginia to England each year, 82,000 were re-exported to the continent, competing there with Spanish tobacco; and this re-exported tobacco paid double freight, insurance, commissions, and handling charges. Daniel Dulany of Maryland estimated that the Southern tobacco growers would have received £3 more for every hogshead they sent abroad had they been permitted to ship direct to the continent instead of through England. In addition, the British government insisted upon its pound of flesh from the planters. A heavy duty was imposed upon all tobacco imported into Great Britain; and from this source the government drew a revenue of almost £400,000 a year. The planters complained that this duty was levied upon them rather than upon the British consumer and that they were thereby more heavily taxed than even the British squires.

The reason why the planters, more than other Americans, found their lot galling under British mercantilism was partly owing to their practice of pledging future crops in exchange for credits advanced them by British businessmen. In order to protect themselves against loss, the British merchants charged the planters high prices and high interest rates. Of the £4,000,000 owing British merchants by Americans in 1760, over half had been incurred by Southern planters. It is not surprising, therefore, that from the point of view of the tobacco growers, the Acts of Trade seemed designed chiefly for the better exploitation of American producers. . . .

It became increasingly clear to Americans during the eighteenth century that the British Empire was not, as the mercantilists envisaged, a government of King, Lords, and Commons in which the welfare of the whole empire was the chief concern of imperial legislation, but a government of British merchants and manufacturers who pursued their own interests even at the expense of the colonists. . . .

By 1763, it had been made painfully evident to Americans that whenever a colonial commodity became important it was enumerated; and whenever colonial enterprise competed with powerful British interest it was struck down by an act of Parliament. To protect the monopoly of British manufacturers, Parliament forbade Americans to export colonial wool, woolens, and hats from one colony to another on pain of seizure of ship and cargo; and in 1750 the erection of plating or slitting mills was prohibited. These acts were not part of the Laws of Trade but they were a significant manifestation of mercantilism. They were the work of British manufacturers who believed that colonial manufacturing was responsible for the hard times that had befallen these industries in Old England. Mercantilists warmly espoused the cause of the distressed

English manufacturers: the colonists, they contended, must be prevented from rivaling the mother country since the very reason for their existence was to increase her wealth, not to compete with her industries. . . .

It cannot be denied that there was widespread discontent among the colonists, particularly among the Southern planters, with the workings of British mercantilism. Certainly, they regarded a larger measure of economic freedom as one of the most desirable results of the revolutionary agitation of 1765–1776. The closing of certain channels of trade essential to the well-being of the Northern colonies and the efforts of the mother country to enforce the Acts of Trade after 1764 brought Northern merchants to see British mercantilism eye to eye with the Southern tobacco growers. In the correspondence of colonial merchants and planters there is a growing volume of complaint that they were risking their capital and expending their energy for the enrichment of British merchants and manufacturers. They chafed under a system which bottled up initiative and confined trade to channels prescribed by the British government, which, as was well known, frequently acted at the behest of powerful British commercial and manufacturing interests. We shall find that as Americans progressively enlarged their demands for liberty after 1765, the Acts of Trade and the entire system of British mercantilism came to be included within their definition of tyranny. Without doubt, underlying the resounding phrases and ideals of the American Revolution, there was a solid foundation of economic grievances which played an important part in determining the course taken by both the Northern merchants and the Southern planters.

Yet it cannot be said that Americans were driven to rebellion by intolerable economic oppression. In general, after the postwar depression of 1763–1765, the revolutionary period was an era of growth and prosperity for the colonies. The British "tyranny" against which Americans rebelled did little to impede their material development; on the contrary, the population continued to double every generation by natural means and the demand for British manufactures increased apace. In many New England towns it was difficult to find a man not in easy circumstances. The colonial seaports continued to hum with business: in 1762 New York had 477 vessels; by 1772, the number had increased to 709.

CHAPTER 11

THE NEW
IMPERIAL POLICY

Of the several schools of historical thought as to why the American Revolution came, one of the more important is the "Imperial" school, whose most distinguished member is Lawrence Henry Gipson. This group of historians derives its name from its insistence that the only way to understand properly the problems of the North American colonies is to view them in the broadest perspective as members of the British Empire. When this is done, they contend, we can see that the American situation was neither onerous nor oppressive.

In this essay, Professor Gipson examines the effects on relations between the North American colonies and the mother country of the Great War for Empire (more commonly but less accurately known as the French and Indian War). In this examination, Gipson raises several questions.

The most important question is whether the American Revolution was inevitable. If so, why? Given the modified situation that victory over the French produced, could the British administrators have done anything to prevent the revolution. If so, what?

Of almost equal importance is the problem involving the time and the meaning of the revolution. Did the actual revolution occur between the years 1776–1783, during the period of combat? Or did the real revolution come about in the minds of the people earlier, perhaps from 1763 to 1776, with the war years being merely the necessarily violent demonstration to the English of the realities of the new situation?

As might be expected, the literature on this subject is enormous. Professor Gipson has conveniently summarized the results of a lifetime of study in his *The Coming of the Revolution** (1954). For a point of view different from that of the "Imperial" school, see Edmund S. Morgan, *The Birth of the Republic** (1956). For a very convenient summary of the positions and writings of the various schools, along with an up-to-date bibliography, see Esmond Wright, *Causes and Consequences of the American Revolution** (1966). An excellent short essay on the meaning of the revolution is Jack Greene, *The Reappraisal of the American Revolution in Recent Historical Literature** (1967).

* Available in a paperback edition.

THE AMERICAN REVOLUTION AS AN AFTERMATH OF THE GREAT WAR FOR THE EMPIRE, 1754–1763

LAWRENCE HENRY GIPSON

Great wars in modern times have too frequently been the breeders of revolution. The exhausting armed struggles in which France became engaged in the latter half of the eighteenth century led as directly to the French Revolution as did the First World War to the Russian Revolution; it may be said as truly that the American Revolution was an aftermath of the Anglo-French conflict in the New World carried on between 1754 and 1763. This is by no means to deny that other factors were involved in the launching of these revolutionary movements. Before proceeding with an analysis of the theme of this paper, however, it would be well to consider the wording of the title given to it. . . .

A struggle of such proportions, involving tremendous stakes, deserves a name accurately descriptive of its place in the history of the English-speaking people, and the title "the French and Indian War", as suggested, in no way fulfills this need. For the war was not, as the name would seem to imply, a conflict largely between English and French New World colonials and their Indian allies, nor was it localized in North America to the extent that the name would appear to indicate. In contrast, it was waged both before and after an open declaration of war by the British and French nations with all their resources for nine years on three oceans, and much of the land washed by the waters of them, and it ultimately brought in both Spain, allied to France, and Portugal, allied to Great Britain. While it involved, it is true, as the name would connote, wilderness fighting, yet of equal, if not greater, importance in assessing its final outcome was the pouring forth of Britain's financial resources in a vast program of shipbuilding, in the equipment and sup-

SOURCE. Lawrence Henry Gipson, "The American Revolution as an Aftermath of the Great War for the Empire, 1754–1763," *The Political Science Quarterly*, LXV, March 1950, pp. 86–104. Copyright 1950 by the editors of *The Political Science Quarterly*. Reprinted with permission of *The Political Science Quarterly* and the author.

port of the British and colonial armies and the royal navy, and in the subsidization both of allies on the European continent and of the colonies in America. . . .

The development of the war into one for the military mastery of the North American continent came with the growing conviction on the part of the British ministers that nothing short of this drastic step would realize the primary aims of the government in arriving at the determination, as the result of appeals from the colonies for assistance, to challenge the right of French troops to be planted well within the borders of the Nova Scotia peninsula and at the forks of the Ohio. One may go as far as to state that the acquisition of Canada—as an objective sought by mercantilists to contribute to the wealth of Great Britain—would have seemed fantastic to any contemporary who had the slightest knowledge of the tremendous financial drain that that great possession had been on the treasury of the French King for over a century before 1754. Moreover, the motives that ultimately led, after much searching of heart, to its retention after its conquest by Great Britain were not commercial but strategic and had primarily in view the security and welfare of the older American colonies.

In view of these facts, not to be confused with surmises, the name *"the Great War for the Empire"* seems to the writer not only not inappropriate but among all the names heretofore applied to the war in question by far the most suitable that can be used by one concerned with the history of the old British Empire, who seeks earnestly to maintain that standard of exactness in terminology, as well as in other respects, which the public has a right to demand of him. . . .

But to return to the last phases of the Great War for the Empire. The British customs officials—spurred into unusual activity in the face of Pitt's demand for the strict enforcement of the Trade and Navigation Acts in order to break up the pernicious practice of bringing aid and comfort to the enemy—were led to employ writs of assistance for the purpose of laying their hands upon goods landed in American ports and secured in exchange for American provisions sent for the most part either directly or indirectly to the French West Indies. Although in the midst of hostilities, most of the merchants in Boston showed bitter opposition to the writs and equally ardent support of James Otis' declaration made in open court in 1761 that Parliament, acting within the limits of the constitution, was powerless to extend the use of these writs to America, whatever its authority might be in Great Britain. The importance of this declaration lies not so much in its immediate effect but rather in the fact that it was indicative of the line of attack that not only Otis would subsequently follow but also the Adamses, Hawley, Hancock, and other popular leaders in the Bay colony during the developing crisis, in the laying down of constitutional restrictions upon the power of Parliament to legislate for America. Further, it is clear that, even before the Great War for the Empire had been terminated, there were those in the province who had begun to view Great Britain as the real enemy rather than France.

Just as definitely as was the issue over writs of assistance related to the war under consideration was that growing out of the twopenny acts of the Virginia Assembly. In search of funds for maintaining the frontier defensive forces under the command of Colonel George Washington, the Assembly was led to pass in 1755 and 1758 those highly questionable laws as favorable to the tobacco planters as they were indefensively unjust to the clergy. Even assuming the fact that these laws were war measures, and therefore in a sense emergency measures, it was inconceivable that the Privy Council would permit so palpable a violation of contractural relations as they involved. The royal disallowance of the laws in question opened the way for Patrick Henry, the year that hostilities were terminated by the Peace of Paris, not only to challenge in the Louisa County courthouse the right of the King in Council to refuse to approve any law that a colony might pass that in its judgment was a good law, but to affirm that such refusal was nothing less than an act of tyranny on the part of the King. It was thus resentment at the overturning of Virginia war legislation that led to this attack upon the judicial authority of review by the Crown—an authority exercised previously without serious protest for over a century. It should also be noted that the Henry thesis helped to lay the foundation for the theory of equality of colonial laws with those passed by Parliament, a theory of the constitution of the empire that most American leaders in 1774 had come to accept in arguing that if the King could no longer exercise a veto over the acts of the legislature of Great Britain, it was unjust that he should do so over those of the colonial assemblies.

But the most fateful aftermath of the Great War for the Empire, with respect to the maintenance of the historic connection between the mother country and the colonies, grew out of the problem of the control and support not only of the vast trans-Appalachian interior, the right to which was now confirmed by treaty to Great Britain, but of the new acquisitions in North America secured from France and Spain. Under the terms of the royal Proclamation of 1763, French Canada to the east of the Great Lakes was organized as the Province of Quebec; most of old Spanish Florida became the Province of East Florida; and those areas, previously held by Spain as well as by France to the west of the Apalachicola and to the east of New Orleans and its immediate environs, became the Province of West Florida. The Proclamations indicated that proper inducements would be offered British and other Protestants to establish themselves in these new provinces. With respect to the trans-Appalachian region, however, it created there a temporary but vast Indian reserve by laying down as a barrier the crest of the mountains beyond which there should be no white settlement except by specific permission of the Crown.

The Proclamation has been represented not only as a blunder, the result largely of carelessness and ignorance on the part of those responsible for it, but also as a cynical attempt by the British ministry to embody mercantilistic principles in an American land policy that in itself ran counter to the charter limits of many of the colonies and the interests in general of the colonials. Nevertheless, this view of the Proclamation fails to take into account the fact that it was the offspring of war and that the trans-Appalachian aspects of it were an almost inevitable result of promises made during the progress of hostilities. For both in the Treaty of Easton in 1758 with the Ohio Valley Indians, a treaty ratified by the Crown, and in the asserverations of such military leaders as Colonel Bouquet, these Indians were assured that they would be secure in their trans-Appalachian lands as a reward for deserting their allies, the French. As a sign of good faith, the lands lying within the bounds of Pennsylvania to the west of the mountains, purchased by the Proprietors from the Six Nations in 1754, were solemnly released. Thus committed in honor in the course of the war, what could the Cabinet Council at its termination do other than it finally did in the Proclamation of 1763? But this step not only was in opposition to the interests of such groups of land speculators as, for example, the Patrick Henry group in Virginia and the Richard Henderson group in North Carolina, both of whom boldly ignored the Proclamation in negotiating with the Cherokee Indians for land grants, but also led to open defiance of this imperial regulation by frontiersmen who, moving beyond the mountains by the thousands, proceeded to settle within the Indian reserve—some on lands previously occupied before the beginning of the late war or before the great Indian revolt in 1763, and others on new lands.

The Proclamation line of 1763 might have become an issue, indeed a most formidable one, between the government of Great Britain and the colonials, had not the former acquiesced in the inevitable and confirmed certain Indian treaties that provided for the transfer of much of the land which had been the particular object of quest on the part of speculators and of those moving westward from the settled areas to establish new homes. Such were the treaties of Hard Labor, Fort Stanwix, Lochaber, and the modification of the last-named by the Donelson agreement with the Cherokees in 1771. Nor did the regulation of the trans-Appalachian Indian trade create serious colonial irritation, especially in view of the failure of the government to implement the elaborate Board of Trade plan drawn up in 1764. The same, however, cannot be said of the program put forward by the ministry and accepted by Parliament for securing the means to maintain order and provide protection for this vast area and the new acquisitions to the north and south of it.

Theoretically, it would have been possible for the government of Great Britain to have dropped onto the lap of the old continental colonies the entire responsibility for maintaining garrisons at various strategic points in North America—in Canada, about the Great Lakes, in the Ohio and Mississippi valleys, and in East and West Florida. In spite, however, of assertions made by some prominent colonials, such as Franklin, in 1765 and 1766, that the colonies would be able and were willing to take up the burden of providing for the defense of America, this, under the circumstances, was utterly chimerical, involving, as it would have, not only a vast expenditure of funds but highly complicated inter-colonial arrangements, even in the face of the most serious inter-colonial rivalry such as that between Pennsylvania and Virginia respecting the control of the upper Ohio Valley. The very proportions of the task were an insuperable obstacle to leaving it to the colonies; and the colonies, moreover, would have been faced by another impediment almost as difficult to surmount—the utter aversion of Americans of the eighteenth century, by and large, to the dull routine of garrison duty. This was emphasized by the Massachusetts Bay Assembly in 1755 in its appeal to the government of Great Britain after Braddock's defeat to send regulars to man the frontier forts of that province; the dispatches of Colonel George Washington in 1756 and in 1757 respecting the shameful desertion of militiamen, ordered to hold the chain of posts on the western frontier of Virginia in order to check the frightful French and Indian raids, support this position, as does the testimony in 1757 of Governor Lyttleton of South Carolina, who made clear that the inhabitants of that colony were not at all adapted to this type of work. The post-war task of garrison duty was clearly one to be assumed by regulars held to their duty under firm discipline and capable of being shifted from one strategic point to another as circumstances might require. Further, to be effective, any plan for the defense of the new possessions and the trans-Appalachian region demanded unity of command, something the colonies could not provide. Manifestly this could be done only through the instrumentalities of the mother country.

The British ministry, thus confronted with the problem of guaranteeing the necessary security for the extended empire in North America, which it was estimated would involve the annual expenditure of from three to four hundred thousand pounds for the maintenance of ten thousand troops—according to various estimates made by General Amherst and others in 1764 and to be found among the Shelburne Papers—was impelled to raise the question: Should not the colonials be expected to assume some definite part of the cost of this? In view of the fact that it was felt not only that they were in a position to do so but that the stability of these outlying possessions was a matter of greater concern and importance generally to them, by reason of their proximity, than to the people of the mother country three thousand miles away, the answer was in the affirmative. The reason for this is not hard to fathom. The nine years of war had involved Britons in tremendous expenditures. In spite of very heavy taxation during these years, the people were left saddled at the termination of hostilities with a national debt of unprecedented proportions for that day and age of over *one hundred and forty million pounds*. It was necessary not only to service and to retire this debt, in so far as was possible, but also to meet the ordinary demands of the civil government and to maintain the navy at a point of strength that would offer some assurance that France and Spain would have no desire in the future to plan a war to recover their territorial losses. In addition to all this, there was now the problem of meeting the charges necessary for keeping the new possessions in North America under firm military control for their internal good order and for protection from outside interference.

It may be noted that before the war the British budget had called for average annual expenditures of six and a half million pounds; between the years 1756 and 1766 these expenditures mounted to fourteen and a half million pounds a year on the average and from the latter date to 1775 ranged close to ten million pounds. As a result, the annual per capita tax in Great Britain, from 1763 to 1775, without considering local rates, was many times the average annual per capita tax in even those American colonies that made the greatest contribution to the Great War for the Empire, such as Massachusetts Bay and Connecticut—without reference to those colonies that had done little or nothing in this conflict, and therefore had accumulated little in the way of a war debt, such as Maryland and Georgia. The student of the history of the old British Empire, in fact, should accept with great reserve statements to the contrary—some of them quite irresponsible in nature —made by Americans during the heat of the controversy, with respect to the nature of the public burdens they were obliged to carry in the years preceding the outbreak of the Revolutionary War. In this connection a study of parliamentary reimbursement of colonial war expenses from 1756 to 1763 in its relation to public debts in America between the years 1763 and 1775 is most revealing. As to American public finances, all that space will here permit is to state that there is abundant evidence to indicate that, during the five-year period preceding the outbreak of the Revolutionary War, had the inhabitants of any of the thirteen colonies, which therefore included those of Massachusetts Bay and Virginia, been taxed in one of these years at the average high per capita rate that the British people were taxed from 1760 to 1775, the proceeds of that one year's tax not only would have taken care of the ordinary expenditures of the colony in question for that year but also would have quite liquidated its war debt, so little of which remained in any of the colonies by 1770. Well may John Adams have admitted in 1780 what was equally true in 1770: "America is not used to great taxes, and the people there are not yet disciplined to such enormous taxation as in England."

Assuming, as did the Grenville ministry in 1764, the justice of expecting the Americans to share in the cost of policing the new possessions in North America, the simplest and most obvious way, it might appear, to secure this contribution to a common end so important to both Americans and Britons was to request the colonial governments to make definite grants of funds. This was the requisition or quota system that had been employed in the course of the recent war. But the most obvious objections to it were voiced that same year by Benjamin Franklin, who, incidentally, was to reverse himself the following year in conferring with Grenville as the Pennsylvania London agent. In expressing confidentially his personal, rather than any official, views to his friend Richard Jackson on June 25, 1764 he declared: "Quota's would be difficult to settle at first with Equality, and would, if they could be made equal at first, soon become unequal, and never would be satisfactory." Indeed, experience with this system in practice, as a settled method of guaranteeing even the minimum essential resources for the end in view, had shown its weakness and utter unfairness. If it could not work equitably even in war time, could it be expected to work in peace? It is, therefore, not surprising that this method of securing even a portion of the funds required for North American security should have been rejected in favor of some plan that presented better prospects of a definite American revenue.

The plan of last resort to the ministry was therefore to ask Parliament to act. That Grenville, however, was aware that serious objections might be raised against any direct taxation of the colonials by the government of Great Britain is indicated by the caution with which he approached the solution of the problem of securing from America about a third of the total cost of its defense. The so-called Sugar Act first of all was passed at his request. This provided for import duties on certain West Indian and other products. Colonial import duties imposed by Parliament, at least since 1733, were no innovation. But the anticipated yield of these duties fell far short of the desired one hundred thousand pounds. He therefore, in introducing the bill for the above Act, raised the question of a stamp duty but requested postponement of parliamentary action until the colonial governments had been consulted. The latter were thereupon requested to make any suggestions for ways of raising an American fund that might seem more proper to the people than such a tax. Further, it would appear—at least, according to various London advices published in Franklin and Hall's *Pennsylvania Gazette* —that proposals were seriously considered by the Cabinet Council during the fall of 1764 for extending to the colonies representation in Parliament through the election of members to the House of Commons by various colonial assemblies. However, it is quite clear that by the beginning of 1765 any such proposals, as seem to have been under deliberation by the ministry, had been put aside when Grenville at length had become convinced that representation in Parliament was neither actively sought nor even desired by Americans. For the South Carolina Commons House of Assembly went strongly on record against this idea in September 1764 and was followed by the Virginia House of Burgesses in December. In fact, when in the presence of the London colonial agents the minister had outlined the objections raised by Americans to the idea of such representation, no one of them, including Franklin, was prepared to deny the validity of these objections. That he was not mistaken in the opposition of Americans at large to sending members to Parliament, in spite of the advocacy of this by James Otis, is clear in the resolutions passed both by other colonial assemblies than the ones to which reference has been made and by the Stamp Act Congress in 1765. Indeed, in 1768 the House of Representatives of Massachusetts Bay went so far in its famous Circular Letter framed in opposition to the Townshend duties as to make clear that the people of that colony actually preferred taxation by Parliament without representation to such taxation with representation.

When—in view of the failure of the colonial governments to suggest any practicable, alternate plan for making some contribution to the post-war defensive program in North America—Grenville finally urged in Parliament the passage of an American stamp bill, he acted on an unwarranted assumption. This assumption was—in paraphrasing the minister's remarks to the colonial agents in 1765—that opposition to stamp taxes, for the specific purpose in mind, would disappear in America both in light of the benefits such provision would bring to colonials in general and by reason of the plain justice of the measure itself; and that, in place of opposition, an atmosphere of mutual goodwill would be generated by a growing recognition on the part of Americans that they could trust the benevolence of the mother country to act with fairness to all within the empire. Instead, with the news of the passage of the act, cries of British tyranny and impending slavery soon resounded throughout the entire eastern Atlantic American seaboard. What would have been the fate of the empire had Grenville remained in office to *attempt to enforce the act, no one can say.* But as members of the opposition to the Rockingham ministry, he and his brother, Earl Temple, raised their voices—one as a commoner, the other as a peer—in warning that the American colonies would inevitably be lost to the empire should Parliament be led to repeal the act in face of colonial resistance and the pressure of British merchants. Had Parliament determined, in spite of violence and threats of violence, to enforce the act, it might have meant open rebellion and civil war, ten years before it actually occurred. Instead, this body decided to yield and, in spite of the passing of the so-called Declaratory Act setting forth its fundamental powers to legislate on all matters relating to the empire, suffered a loss of prestige in the New World that was never to be regained.

But the Stamp Act was not the sole object of attack by colonials. To many of them not only the Sugar Act of 1764 but the whole English pre-war trade and navigation system was equally, if not actually more, obnoxious. Indeed, the unusual energy displayed by the navy and the customs officials, spurred into action by Pitt during the latter years of the war—bringing with it the condemnation in courts of vice-admiralty of many American vessels whose owners were guilty of serious trade violations, if not greater crimes—generated a degree of antagonism against the whole body of late seventeenth- and early eighteenth-century restrictions on commercial intercourse such as never had previously existed. It is not without significance that the greatest acts of terrorism and de-

struction during the great riot of August 1765 in Boston were directed
not against the Massachusetts Bay stamp distributor but against those
officials responsible for encouraging and supporting the enforcement,
during the late war, of the various trade acts passed long before its
beginning in 1754. The hatred also of the Rhode Island merchants, as
a group, against the restrictions of the navigation system as well as
against the Sugar Act of 1764, remained constant. Moreover, in December 1766 most of the New York merchants, over two hundred in
number, showed their repugnance to the way that this system was functioning by a strongly worded petition to the House of Commons in
which they enumerated an impressive list of grievances that they asked
to be redressed. Even Chatham, the great friend of America, regarded
their petition "highly improper: in point of time most absurd, in the
extent of their pretensions, most excessive; and in the reasoning, most
grossly fallacious and offensive." In fact, all the leading men in Great
Britain supported the system of trade restrictions.

Nevertheless, the determination of the government—in view especially
of the great financial burdens that the late war had placed upon the
mother country—to enforce it now much more effectively than had been
done before 1754, and to that end in 1767 to pass appropriate legislation in order to secure funds from the colonies by way of import duties
so that public officials in America might be held to greater accounta-
bility when paid their salaries by the Crown, could have only one result: the combined resistance of those, on the one hand, opposed to any
type of taxation that Parliament might apply to America and of those,
on the other, desiring to free the colonies of hampering trade restrictions.

The suggestion on the part of the Continental Congress in 1774 that
Americans would uphold the British navigation system, if exempted from
Parliamentary taxation, while a shrewd gesture to win support in England, had really, it would seem, no other significance. For it is utterly
inconceivable that the Congress itself, or the individual colonial governments, could have set up machinery capable of preventing violations
of the system at will on the part of those whose financial interests were
adversely affected by its operation. Moreover, it is obvious that, by the
time the news had reached America that Lord North's ministry had
secured the passage of the coercive acts—for the most part directed
against Massachusetts Bay and the defiant destruction of the East India
Company's tea—leading colonials, among them Franklin, had arrived at
the conclusion that Parliament possessed powers so very limited with
respect to the empire that without the consent of the local assemblies it

could pass neither constitutional nor fiscal legislation that affected Americans and the framework of their governments. It is equally obvious that this represented a most revolutionary position when contrasted with that held by Franklin and the other delegates to the Albany Congress twenty years earlier. For it was in 1754 that the famous Plan of Union was drawn up there and approved by the Congress—a plan based upon the view that Parliament, and not the Crown, had supreme authority within the empire, an authority that alone was adequate in view of framers of the Plan to bring about fundamental changes in the constitutions of the colonies in order legally to clothe the proposed union government with adequate fiscal as well as other powers.

In accounting for the radical change in attitude of many leading colonials between the years 1754 and 1774 respecting the nature of the constitution of the empire, surely among the factors that must be weighed was the truly overwhelming victory achieved in the Great War for the Empire. This victory not only freed colonials for the first time in the history of the English-speaking people in the New World from dread of the French, their Indian allies, and the Spaniards, but, what is of equal significance, opened up to them the prospect, if given freedom of action, of a vast growth of power and wealth with an amazing westward expansion. Indeed, it is abundantly clear that a continued subordination of the colonies to the government of Great Britain was no longer considered an asset in the eyes of many Americans by 1774, as it had been so judged by them to be in 1754, but rather an onerous liability. What, pray tell, had the debt-ridden mother country to offer in 1774 to the now geographically secure, politically mature, prosperous, dynamic, and self-reliant offspring along the Atlantic seaboard, except the dubious opportunity of accepting new, as well as retaining old, burdens? And these burdens would have to be borne in order to lighten somewhat the great financial load that the taxpayers of Great Britain were forced to carry by reason of obligations the nation had assumed both in the course of the late war and at its termination. If many Americans thought they had a perfect right to profit personally by trading with the enemy in time of war, how much more deeply must they have resented in time of peace the serious efforts made by the home government to enforce the elaborate restrictions on commercial intercourse? Again, if, even after the defeat of Colonel Washington at Great Meadows in 1754, colonials such as Franklin were opposed to paying any tax levied by Parliament for establishing a fund for the defense of North America, how much more must they have been inclined to oppose such taxation to that end with the passing in 1763 of the great international crisis?

At this point the question must be frankly faced: If France had won the war decisively and thereby consolidated her position and perfected her claims in Nova Scotia, as well as to the southward of the St. Lawrence, in the Great Lakes region, and in the Ohio and Mississippi valleys, is it at all likely that colonials would have made so fundamental a constitutional issue of the extension to them of the principle of the British stamp tax? Would they have resisted such a tax had Parliament imposed it in order to provide on a equitable basis the maximum resources for guaranteeing their safety, at a time when they were faced on their highly restricted borders by a militant, victorious enemy having at its command thousands of ferocious redskins? Again, accepting the fact of Britain's victory, it is not reasonable to believe that, had Great Britain at the close of the triumphant war left Canada to France and carefully limited her territorial demands in North America to those comparatively modest objectives that she had in mind at its beginning, there would have been no very powerful movement within the foreseeable future toward complete colonial autonomy—not to mention American independence? Would not Americans have continued to feel the need as in the past to rely for their safety and welfare upon British sea power and British land power, as well as upon British resources generally? In other words, was Governor Thomas Hutchinson of Massachusetts Bay far mistaken when, in analyzing the American situation late in 1773, he affirmed in writing to the Earl of Dartmouth:

Before the peace [of 1763] I thought nothing so much to be desired as the cession of Canada. I am now convinced that if it had remained to the French none of the spirit of opposition to the Mother Country would have yet appeared & I think the effects of it [that is, the cession of Canada] worse than all we had to fear from the French or Indians.

In conclusion, it may be said that it would be idle to deny that most colonials in the eighteenth century at one time or another felt strongly the desire for freedom of action in a wider variety of ways than was legally permitted before 1754. Indeed, one can readily uncover these strong impulses even in the early part of the seventeenth century. Yet Americans were, by and large, realists, as were the British, and under the functioning of the imperial system from, let us say, 1650 to 1750 great mutual advantages were enjoyed, with a fair division, taking everything into consideration, of the financial burdens necessary to support the system. However, the mounting Anglo-French rivalry in North America from 1750 onward, the outbreak of hostilities in 1754, and the subsequent nine years of fighting destroyed the old equilibrium, leaving the colonials after 1760 in a highly favored position in comparison with the taxpayers of Great Britain. Attempts on the part of the Crown and Parliament to restore by statute the old balance led directly to the American constitutional crisis, out of which came the Revolutionary War and the establishment of American independence. Such, ironically, was the aftermath of the Great War for the Empire, a war that Britons believed, as the Earl of Shelburne affirmed in 1762 in Parliament, was begun for the "security of the British colonies in N. America. . . ."

CHAPTER 12

THE GENESIS OF
AMERICAN NATIONALISM

The coming of the American Revolution too often is described in negative terms as primarily the response of the colonists to the imperial legislation of the 1760's and 1770's. This view tends either to ignore or to
de-emphasize significant internal developments in the colonies that also
must be considered if one is to understand fully the American Revolution.

Professor Max Savelle's analysis of these internal developments in
Seeds of Liberty: The Genesis of the American Mind* explores the early
origins and patterns of American culture, thought, and way of life. In the
following selection, he concentrates on the genesis and early development
of an American nationalism. He suggests that, even before 1750, Americans exhibited a common loyalty to shared American purposes and ideals.
The roots of this new American self-consciousness lay deep in the colonial
past; but, in the resistance to imperial control, the American sense of
identity was most clearly expressed and resulted in relatively unified political action. Numerous forces—economic, social, intellectual and cultural, military, and political—operated to draw the thirteen colonies together into a distinctively American entity. Professor Savelle discusses
these forces, the nature of the nascent American nationalism, and the influence of American self-consciousness on the coming of the American
Revolution.

The question of American unity in the colonial period is raised in a previous selection by Professor John R. Alden. Although Alden and Professor Savelle focus on different aspects of colonial history—Alden on the varied patterns of colonial life and Savelle on the genesis of American nationalism—do they basically agree about the colonial development of American distinctiveness and self-consciousness? What factors does Savelle emphasize as contributing significantly to the development of American nationalism, and how do these compare with the ones identified by Alden? More important, what was the nature and the extent of American nationalism? What was the ideal toward which the Americans were driven by their concept of American distinctiveness and unity? Finally, what was the influence of developing nationalism on the coming of the American Revolution?

Carl Degler, *Out of Our Past: The Forces that Shaped Modern America,** (1958), has an outstanding chapter on the awakening of American nationalism. Clinton Rossiter, *Seedtime of the Republic** [Part I: *The First American Revolution*] (1956), and Daniel J. Boorstin, *The Americans: The Colonial Experience** (1958), are also rewarding reading on this subject.

* Available in a paperback edition.

THE GENESIS OF AN "AMERICAN" NATIONALISM
MAX SAVELLE

A common loyalty to a common American purpose and ideal was beginning to emerge among the Americans even before 1750. And it was this new American self-consciousness in all things, this new loyalty to America, that was to give the Americans an intellectual and emotional sense of unity of purpose and ideal. It was the conflict with the mother country over the question of taxation, to be sure, that galvanized this American self-consciousness into dramatic literary expression and political action; but its beginnings lie farther back than that: its roots are deeply embedded in the earliest American experience.

The people of the British colonies in America did not yet, in the year 1750, constitute a homogeneous social entity. For the British Empire in this hemisphere was composed of a congeries of disparate settlements and societies from the primitive trading posts on the shores of Hudson Bay and British Guiana to the highly sophisticated societies of New York, Virginia, or Jamaica. Yet thirteen of the twenty-odd colonies were passing, more or less consciously, through a process that was at once drawing them together toward homogeneity and distinguishing them, as a single unit, from all the others. For these thirteen, located along the eastern seaboard of the continent, were being subtly fused by a number of forces that were daily becoming more powerful.

Among these forces were the influences exerted by increased commercial, social, and intellectual intercourse between colonies. As roads from one colony to another appeared, finally binding them together on one long string from Portsmouth to Savannah, the spreading consciousness of a common cultural tradition could not fail to grow. This development seems to have been an almost inevitable consequence of the expansion of populations that brought the people of one colony to rubbing elbows with the people of the next. As the means of communication were expanded and

SOURCE. Max Savelle, *Seeds of Liberty: The Genesis of the American Mind*, Seattle: University of Washington Press, 1948, pp. 564–582. Copyright 1948. Reprinted with permission of the author.

improved, travel increased; and the traveler from Boston in Charleston, for example, found that the citizens of the two places had much in common. Travel and writing led to intercolonial marriages; and as the number of colleges increased and their fame spread, more and more young men crossed intercolonial boundaries in quest of education. These intellectual and social and economic forces making for closer association were well under way by the middle of the century.

One of the most obvious of these forces was the binding effect of intercolonial trade. And the continued growth of intercolonial economic relations gave impetus to the already well-developed consciousness of the differentness of American economic interests from those of the mother country. The appearance of an American self-consciousness in the realm of economic affairs, in fact, had had its beginning very early in the history of the colonies, and had sprung originally from the realization that their economic interests diverged, at many important points, from those of the mother country. The Navigation Acts and the Acts of Trade had been efforts to force American economic life into the imperial pattern, but they had been only partially successful; and many Americans such as Franklin had begun to question, as early as about 1750, the validity of the entire system. But the formulation of a positive feeling of economic nationalism did not really appear until the conflict with the mother country over the program, initiated about 1764, to make the old imperial system really effective. The colonies, thrown on the defensive, were forced to elaborate reasons for their opposition to the mother country, and some Americans went on beyond their economic philosophy in defense of their liberties to emotional glorifications of the economic grandeur and destiny of America as a whole or of one's own province as a separate unit. Such, for example, was the sentiment of Daniel Dulany, writing in Virginia in 1765:

Let the manufacture of *America* be the symbol of dignity, the badge of virtue, and it will soon break the fetters of distress. A garment of linsey-woolsey, when made the distinction of real patriotism, is more honourable and attractive of respect and veneration, than all the pageantry, and the robes, and the plumes, and the diadem of an emperor without it. Let the emulation be not in the richness and variety of foreign productions, but in the improvement and perfection of our own. . . . I have in my younger days seen fine sights, and been captivated by their dazzling pomp and glittering splendor; but the sight of our representatives, all adorned in compleat dresses of their own leather, and flax, and wool, manufactured by the art and industry of the inhabitants of *Virginia*, would excite, not the gaze of admiration, the flutter of an agitated imagination, or the momentary amusement of a transient scene, but a calm, solid, heart-felt delight. Such a sigh would give me more pleasure than the most splendid and magnificent spectacle the most exquisite taste ever painted, the richest fancy ever imagined, realized to the view . . . as much more pleasure as a good mind would receive from the contemplation of virtue, than of elegance; of the spirit of patriotism, than the ostentation of opulence.

The solid intellectual bases for an American national feeling were being laid in the 1740's and 1750's. One of the greatest of the agencies for such a development was the post-office, of which, significantly enough, Benjamin Franklin became the head in 1753. Franklin had actively sought the office of Deputy Postmaster-General for America, partly because he thought it might be remunerative, but also, as he said in his letter to Peter Collinson, because he felt sure the post-office could be made an effective agency for the development of an active intercolonial intellectual exchange. He believed the work of the Philosophical Society would be extended by it, and that Philadelphia might well become the cultural capital of America.

There were probably not many men in America who saw the intellectual maturity of America as Franklin saw it in 1743, or believed that the colonies were culturally so mature. Yet the organization and the success and permanence of the American Philosophical Society may be taken, perhaps, as evidence that in 1743 and the years following there was enough and sufficiently widespread intercolonial interest in intellectual matters to permit of this year being used as the marker of the birth of an American cultural self-consciousness. For the exchange of ideas and associations that resulted must have given considerable impetus to the growth of a sense of a common American intellectual life.

Even if Franklin had been alone in his effort to draw the colonies together culturally, as he was not, his own sponsoring of an intercolonial cultural development was a significant manifestation of his early "Americanism"; and if in 1743 he was giving form to an American cultural life, twenty years later he was beginning to see in America the very heart and center of the culture of western civilization.

Meanwhile, a cultural self-consciousness was also appearing in other lines of literary production, one of the most notable of which was history. It is probably not without significance, and highly symptomatic of the dawning self-consciousness of the Americans, that Dr. William Douglass's *Summary, Historical and Political, of the British Settlements in North-America,* which was intended to cover the entire Anglo-American colonial area on the continent of North America, appeared between the years 1747 and 1752. The fact that it was not completed does not diminish the significance of the author's conception; for he gave the first important literary and documentary expression to an American continental self-consciousness.

One of the most important manifestations of the awakening cultural self-consciousness of the Americans was the deliberate effort of William Smith and his circle of young littérateurs and artists in Philadelphia to make for America a place in the cultural sun. All of the magazines that were launched between 1740 and 1760 show this cultural objective, in one way or another; and the *American Magazine,* published by Smith and his circle, is full of literary and historical expressions of it.

The Americans, indeed, were slowly but surely awakening to a realization of their own traditions and a sense of their own glorious future as a distinct people, in all the realms of their thinking. Already, for example, American patriots were beginning to extol the humanitarianism of America as a refuge for the poor and the oppressed, and the virtues of "The American, this new man," as the product of the melting-pot. Poor Richard expressed this popular sentiment in 1752 when he sang the praises of this country as a place

> Where the sick Stranger joys to find a Home,
> Where casual Ill, maim'd Labour, freely come;
> Those worn with Age, Infirmity or Care,
> Find Rest, Relief, and Health returning fair.
> There too the Walls of rising Schools ascend,
> For Publick Spirit still is Learning's Friend,
> Where Science, Virtue, sown with liberal Hand,
> In future Patriots shall inspire the Land.

But the love of one's country inspired by its humanitarian welcome to the poor and suffering of the world was looked upon with a jaundiced eye by those hundred-per-cent patriots who feared the possible un-American activities and influence of the foreigners on our soil. This was the sort of fear which, mixed with religious distrust, led to the passage of the Connecticut "Act Providing Relief against the evil and dangerous Designs of Foreigners and Suspected Persons"; this was the fear, also, that led William Smith to write his diatribes against the Pennsylvania Germans, and William Douglass to pour out the vials of his wrath against the Quakers in his bitter exclamation that "the pusilanimous Doctrine of not defending themselves by force against an invading Enemy is very absurd: PRO PATRIA *is not only a Law of Nations, but of Nature."*

Even Franklin, in almost the same moment when with the popular voice of Poor Richard he was extolling the national melting-pot, could privately express his fear that the Germans might prove to be too un-American in their influence to be absorbed:

This will in a few Years become a *German* Colony: Instead of their Learning our Language, we must learn their's, or live as in a foreign country. Already the *English* begin to quit particular Neighbourhoods surrounded by *Dutch* [Germans], being made uneasy by the Disagreeableness of disonant Manners; and in Time, Numbers will probably quit the Province for the same Reason. Besides, the *Dutch* under-live, and are thereby enabled to under-work and under-sell the *English;* who are thereby extremely incommoded, and consequently disgusted, so that there can be no cordial Affection or Unity between the two Nations.

The split in nationalistic pride between those who glorify the melting-pot and those who fear the un-American activities of foreigners whose ideals do not exactly coincide with their own is no new thing; it has apparently been one of the dialectical strains within American nationalistic feeling almost from the beginning. . . .

Franklin believed strongly in the educational value of history, not merely for the promotion of the social ideal and the virtues of citizenship, but also for inculcation in the student of the peculiar virtues and advantages of his own people: "If the new *Universal History* were also read, it would give a connected idea of human affairs, so far as it goes, which should be followed by the best Modern histories, particularly of our mother country; then of these colonies; which should be accompanied with observations on their rise, increase, use to Great Britain, encouragements and discouragements, the means to make them flourishing, and secure their liberties."

This was written in 1749. Yet there is unquestionably present in this recommendation a consciousness of the peculiar differentness of the colonies, of their common problems, and the preciousness of their liberties. It is this idealization of the abstract qualities of one's own people that is the essence of nationalism. If this was not nationalism itself, then it was surely the psychological germ from which an American nationalism was to grow.

But it was in the face of a common enemy that the nationalistic feelings of the Americans found the freest and most intense expression in the 1750's. For at this point "Tory" feelings and "American" feelings could merge; and the approach of the Seven Years' War was unquestionably the great catalyst that precipitated the most eloquent expressions of America's nascent nationalism. This strong anti-Gallican animosity had been vocal, in fact, since the War of the Austrian Succession (King George's War) and the thrill of general exultation that ran through all the colonies over the capture of Louisbourg in 1745 by a little band of New Englanders. . . .

This deep and intense fear and hatred of a common enemy, the sentiment that might be called a sense of the "Gallic peril," was expressed in many places and in many ways. It appears again and again in the newspapers and in the pamphlets, especially in the mid-century armed truce between 1748 and 1754. The French were the great enemy of all the colonies except the small, coast-bound provinces like Rhode Island, Connecticut, New Jersey, and Delaware; and as population had expanded even farther and farther westward, the inevitability of eventual conflict had become increasingly apparent to everybody, including the French themselves. The governors of New France repeatedly warned their mother country, especially the Marquis de la Galissonnière, of the irrepressible expansiveness of the British Americans. But the French forts built along the frontier from Crown Point in the north to Fort Toulouse in the south appeared to the British colonists only the visible evidence of an aggressive French determination at least to hem them in along the seaboard. The alarmists, however, saw a greater threat than that and warned their readers that the French would reach out to the coast itself and, it might be, one day drive the British from the Atlantic coastal plain altogether, or, worse still, reduce all the Americans to slavery. One of the easiest ways, obviously, for the French to do this, would be by alienating the "foreigners" along the frontier. The French had lately been active along the Ohio, building forts and establishing control over the Indians; since the Quakers of Pennsylvania were pacifists, it seemed to William Smith that it would be extremely easy, even what the French actually designed, to make, by way of Pennsylvania, a breach in the solid front of the English colonies.

Many Americans were in a state of deathly fear of the French and their iniquitous designs, and the sermons of the period sought to whip their audiences into a fervor of patriotic defense of American soil and liberties. Here is an example from Jonathan Mayhew:

And what horrid scene is this, which restless, roving fancy, or something of an higher nature, presents to me, and so chills my blood! Do I behold these territories of freedom, become the prey of arbitrary power? . . . Do I see the slaves of Lewis with their Indian allies, dispossessing the free-born [American] subjects of King George, of the inheritance received from their forefathers, and purchased by them at the expense of their ease, their treasure, their blood! . . . Do I see protestant, there, stealing a look at his bible, and being tak[en] in the fact, punished like a felon! . . . Do I see all liberty, property, religion, happiness, changed, or rather transubstantiated, into slavery, poverty, superstition, wretchedness!

Freedom of property, freedom to work, freedom of worship, the free pursuit of happiness; these American freedoms were threatened by Louis XV of France, monstrous symbol of dictatorial government menacing the liberty of the world, and especially American freedom! This was an ideological war; and the forces of nationalistic emotion were called upon to defend the American-English ideal of liberty against the rapacious Juggernaut of popish authoritarianism. If there ever was a war of Anglo-American aggressive expansionism, the Seven Years' War in America was that war. Yet that did not prevent the intellectual leaders from preaching, in all sincerity of conviction, and the people from believing, that it was a holy war in the name of an ideal, the ideal of "British" (American) liberty and self-government. Samuel Davies, in Virginia, could pull out all the stops on the organ of his eloquence to stir the Virginians to patriotic self-sacrifice:

and shall these Ravages go on uncheck'd? Shall *Virginia* incur the Guilt, and the everlasting Shame of tamely exchanging her Liberty, her Religion, and her All, for arbitrary *Gallic* Power, and for Popish Slavery, Tyranny, and Massacre? Alas! are there none of her Children, that enjoyed all the Blessings of her Peace, that will espouse her Cause, and befriend her now in the Time of her Danger? Are *Britons* utterly degenerated by so short a Remove from their Mother-Country? Is the Spirit of Patriotism entirely extinguished among us? And must I give thee up for lost, O my Country! and all that is included in that important Word? . . .

Many of the Americans, if not all, were being drawn swiftly and deeply into the continental mood of nationalistic self-defense. The Albany Congress, with its plan for intercolonial union, was more a practical effort at defense than a sounding-board of psychological nationalism; yet its members were moved by the same patriotic sentiments that were moving the souls of so many other Americans; and William Livingston reported that "The speakers [at the conference] . . . were not many; but of those who spoke, some delivered themselves with singular energy and eloquence. All were inflamed with a patriot spirit, and the debates were nervous and pathetic [fervent]. This assembly . . . might very properly be compared to one of the ancient Greek conventions, for supporting their expiring liberty against the power of the Persian empire, or that Lewis of Greece, Philip of Macedon."

Samuel Davies probably expressed the common mood of most Americans when he said, in 1756: "Now what can be more important, what more interesting, than our country! Our country is a word of the highest and most endearing import: it includes our friends and relatives, our liberty, our property, our religion: in short, it includes our earthly all. And when the fate of our country and all that it includes, is dreadfully doubtfull . . . every mind that has the least thought, must be agitated with many eager, dubious expectations. This is the present situation of our country. . . ." . . .

The final climax of American nationalistic conviction eventually came in the realm of political thought, which epitomized the whole struggle of the Americans and their culture-complex for self-expression. And this trend toward a political nationalism looked two ways; for while it was expressing itself positively along the lines of the struggle for political self-direction, it was also expressing itself negatively in the increasing resistance to control by the mother country.

Thus in the same years in which the colonists were beginning to sense the reality of their common cause and purpose toward their French and Indian enemies, they were also awakening to a consciousness of the common nature of their problems toward the mother country. Hitherto, of course, and even now, the American's highest loyalty was to England and to his King. But these years marked the moment of his awakening, in the course of his struggle over the prerogative, over the regulation of commerce, and over taxation, to the fact of his differentness from Englishmen: the fact that, somehow, the American and the Englishman, though ruled by the same King, were not the same men, that England and America were not the same society; and that for the American, though he might still be supremely loyal to his King, the society in which he breathed and had his being was American, not English; and his loyalty to his King was really a symbol of his loyalty to his colony, and through it, eventually, to "America." Jonathan Mayhew's sermon on unlimited submission was a clear warning to the English crown to govern the colonies according to the social compact between them, delivered without for a moment contemplating a reduction of American loyalty. With the same candor within the bounds of "British" loyalty Franklin was criticizing the mother country for her shortsightedness in insisting upon the Navigation Acts. A wise mother he said, would not do it; and he was speaking for all the colonies, not just one or several.

That some such feeling of differentness was taking shape in Franklin's mind between 1750 and 1755, despite his enthusiastic expansionist imperialism, is clear from his writing during this period touching upon the relations of the colonies to the mother country, economic as well as political. For he not only criticized the unwisdom of Parliamentary restraints upon colonial trade, but, more positively, suggested a greater imperial union, with the colonies enjoying a much more important place in imperial deliberations, representation in an imperial parliament, and greater recognition of the uniqueness of the way of life of the colonies as a distinct unit in the Empire. In his eighteenth-century quest for a natural order in human affairs corollary to the order in the physical universe, he was discovering, or thought he was, the natural processes by which societies are formed. The American society had been formed by the natural process; it was different from the society from which it sprang; and it must be respected as being so. There began to be implicit in Franklin's criticisms of England a principle, the nationalistic counterpart of his sociological and economic thinking, of the naturalistic origins and peculiarities of nations. This principle, gradually becoming clearer in his own mind as it found expression in his political thoughts on the nature of the British Empire between 1765 and 1775, did not, as yet, conflict with the principle of loyalty to the King. Franklin was an ardent and patriotic Briton; but he was also a patriotic American, fired with a sense of the future greatness of his native land.

The growing feeling of criticism of England and the nebular beginning of an intercolonial solidarity were not confined to the struggle of the assemblies against the prerogative, nor even to politics. The manifold activities of the colonial agents in England also reflect the increasing complexity of the problem of forestalling interference in colonial affairs; and the agents were now finding it increasingly to their advantage to present a common front. A very significant case of this sort of co-operative action took place between 1750 and 1753, when the northern colonial agents in London found themselves lined up in a solid front against the sugar-planters of the British West Indies and their agents for the preservation of the trade of the northern colonies with the French West Indies. The proposed restrictions upon that trade, said the northern agents, would paralyze the northern colonies economically; moreover, the restrictions would constitute a violation of the American's rights as Englishmen. Significantly, their protest was based upon the economic differentness of the colonies from England.

This united effort of the agents was successful. The passage of the Sugar Act in 1764 brought the agents together again, and from then on they were regularly instructed to co-operate on questions of common interest; after the Stamp Act of 1765 they met together regularly to formulate joint policies. The significant development here was, of course, the emergence of a united, co-operative front toward the mother country among the colonies through their agents in England. The common front represented in the colonial mind the idea of common interests and a common cause.

During the Seven Years' War in America the feeling of difference between "Americans" and "Englishmen" was heightened by their relationships in military operations. The British soldiers and officers looked down upon their cruder American cousins and infuriated them by their own discrimination and patronizing attitude. This is well illustrated at the time of Braddock's defeat, when, though everybody deplored the disaster itself, there was more than a little grim satisfaction in American commentaries which pointed to it as a lesson to teach the supercilious British that the Americans knew more about warfare in America and claimed that British honor was saved, after all, by the Americans, without whom the disaster would have been far greater than it was.

This mood of American importance in imperial affairs was no passing fancy, either. For there were numerous Americans who felt that it was to the colonials that victory was due, and that the mother country actually owed them a debt of gratitude for making possible so great an expansion of the Empire. . . .

The ideas and sentiments in this curious "Who won the war?" argument are clearly the impulses of a young and bumptious nationalism, the more clearly so because they were the feelings of not just one American, but probably most of them. The Americans were thinking of themselves now as different from their English cousins and as entitled to the respect due to a people that has arrived at political and cultural maturity. As Franklin put it in a letter to Lord Kames in 1767:

Every man in England seems to consider himself a piece of a sovereign over America; seems to jostle himself into the throne with the King, and talks of *our subjects in the colonies.* . . . But America, an immense Territory, favored by nature with all the advantages of climate, soils, great navigable rivers, lakes, &c., must become a great country, populous and mighty; and will, in a less time than is generally conceived, be able to shake off any shackles that may be imposed upon her, and perhaps place them on the imposers. . . . And yet there remains among that people so much respect, veneration, and affection for Britain, that, if cultivated prudently, with a kind usage and tenderness for their privileges, they might be easily governed still for ages, without force or any considerable expense. But I do not see here a sufficient quantity of the wisdom, that is necessary to produce such a conduct, and I lament the want of it.

Franklin was warning England of the psychological facts. But a subtle and significant change had now taken place in his mind. He no longer spoke of Americans as identical with Britons, or of the colonies as part of England. They were separate; they had only respect and reverence for the great traditions and ideals of the British way of life and all that that could mean; but they were now a separate people, among the other British peoples.

The loyalties of the Americans were becoming more and more sharply divided. The American mentality was growing conscious of this divergence, thinking of itself as a distinct, "American" entity within the Empire, and of England and its people as alien to itself. This was a psychological phenomenon, a factor of profound importance for the future of the Empire and for America. From Franklin's position of 1767 it was but a short step to Jefferson's position of 1774, which spoke of Englishmen as foreigners to America, and to the eloquent Patrick Henry's "I am an American." Or to that of John Randolph, who warned the mother country, on the eve of the Revolution:

The Histories of dependent States put it beyond a Doubt that America, when she is able to protect herself, will acknowledge no Superiority in another. That she will be capable, some Time or other, to establish an Independence, must appear evident to every One, who is acquainted with her present Situation and growing Strength. But although it must be apparent to everyone that *America* will, in short Period, attain to a State of Maturity, yet, if *Great Britain* could be prevailed on to govern her Colonies to their Satisfaction, from the force of Habit, and the good Impressions which a pleasing Intercourse must occasion, I am persuaded that she would procrastinate our Separation from her, and carry on an exclusive Trade with us, so long as she is able to maintain her Weight in the political scale of *Europe;* but, on the contrary, if she persevere in her Rigour, and the Colonies will not relax on their Part, the Parent will probably soon be without a Child, and the Offspring become unable to support itself.

What the Americans were driving for was a recognition, by the mother country, of the now self-confident American national personality. The child had grown up and become a man. Psychologically, the American Revolution was a war to force the mother country to admit this basic fact. The Americans were perfectly willing, even anxious, given the mother country's admission of their national maturity, to remain members of the imperial family. But that was just the tragic point at which British nationalism found itself in conflict with British-American nationalism, and since neither one could accept the ideal and the point of view of the other, the British-American mind became the American mind, simply.

Thus the ardent national feeling that burst into flame in the Revolution was but the culmination of a long development, the explosion that marked the climax of a long smoldering fire of increasing intensity. It had had its birth within the folds of "British" patriotism; but, beginning as a loyalty to one's province, it had grown into a consciousness of problems and ideals common to all the provinces, first in matters of defense, then in cultural relationships, and finally in the problems of relationship with the mother country. Had Britain been wise enough to understand this aspect of the American mind and to accommodate British colonial policy to it, as it did a century later in the case of Canada, there is every reason to suppose that the colonies might have become the first associated nation in a new British Commonwealth of Nations. But, as Franklin sadly lamented, there wasn't enough of that sort of wisdom in Britain.

The American consciousness of national selfhood that was beginning to show its rudimentary forms by about 1750 was thus not merely allowed to grow naturally, but was actually forced into a flaming patriotic growth by the policies of the mother country. As it existed in its primitive form in 1750 it was a still nebular consciousness of, and loyalty to, the more heroic aspects of American life: the military exploits at Louisburg; the common fear of the common enemies, French and Indian, to the westward; a sense of the glorious manifest destiny of America beyond the mountains and as the future seat of the arts and sciences on this continent. As yet in 1750 and 1760 it was a glorification of Britain in America; by the end of the Seven Years' War loyalty to America was sharply distinguished, by some at least, from loyalty to Britain. As the sixties wore on into the seventies American patriots began to see that there were actually two nationalities involved, with their respective nationalisms.

It was this sense of the ineffable beauty and splendor of America and its promise to the world that inspired Philip Freneau to mark the culmination of American nationalistic felling in his *Poem on the Rising Glory of America* in 1771. Freneau was no rebel; he had no more thought of throwing off British allegiance in 1771 than most other Americans. But he envisioned his America as a nation within a British family of nations. His poem assumed the sort of British Empire that Benjamin Franklin was at that moment beginning to define as a federation of quasi-independent or autonomous states; his patriotism was the prototype of the intra-imperial patriotism of a Canada or an Australia of a later day:

> To mighty nations shall the people grow
> Which cultivate the banks of many a flood,
> In chrystal currents poured from the hills
> Apalachia nam'd, to lave the sands
> Of Carolina, Georgia, and the plains
> Stretch'd out from thence far to the burning Line,
> St. Johns or Clarendon or Albemarle. . . .

> And here fair freedom shall forever reign.
> I see a train, a glorious train appear,
> Of Patriots plac'd in equal fame with those
> Who nobly fell for Athens or for Rome.

It should be emphasized that this American nationalism of 1770 was not a nationalism of independence. It was a nationalism that expected to find self-expression within the framework of the Empire. For conflicts of economic interest and ideologies alone were not necessarily and inevitably productive of civil war; neither, indeed, was conflict in religion, or in culture, or even politics. All these things might be adjusted peaceably; but when pride was pitted against pride, emotion against emotion; ideal of American "liberty" against ideal of an imperial unity to be imposed by force, if necessary, then, and then only, civil war was, in the nature of men and things, inevitable. This germinal American nationalism was nationalism in its best sense—national self-realization, pride in national tradition and achievement, and a sense of the greatness of the national destiny—a sort of national self-respect or pride that made it impossible to submit to the benighted stubbornness of George III and his ministers. Given the men, their convictions, and their mood, given, that is, the self-consciousness and the self-confidence of the American national mind, the outcome could hardly have been otherwise. For these thirteen of the British colonies in America had become a nation. And Patrick Henry, like so many other Americans fired by the discovery of his own America and driven to desperation by the utter inability of Britain to comprehend the nationhood of America, burst out with his famous cry: "The distinction between Virginians, Pennsylvanians, New Yorkers, and New Englanders, are no more. I am not a Virginian, but an American."

CHAPTER 13

THE WAR OF

INDEPENDENCE: THE

INTERNAL "REVOLUTION"

As Professor Alden points out, there is more to winning independence than winning a war. If, in addition, the country is embarking on a social revolution, then the problem becomes even more complex. Not only must order be restored but also the basic nature of society must be modified. The old rulers must be displaced and the new ones must be phased in without destroying the good order of society any more than necessary. This transfer of power and authority must often be made at a time when interior disunity and confusion are at their maximum and exterior pressure, or its imminent threat, is also intense. This was the situation that faced the colonists during the period covered by this selection.

It is hardly surprising that the colonists, under these conditions, borrowed from their old charters, did not submit their new governing documents to the voters, and exhibited the conservatism mentioned by Alden. The fact that any innovations appeared under these conditions is more surprising. But, as Alden points out, important reforms and innovations took place at the state level during the war.

This dichotomy of important change and temporary patchwork has led historians of this period to pose this question: Exactly how revolutionary was the Revolution? This question, in turn, raises another one: Were these revolutionary changes consciously revolutionary, or were the colonists merely removing the vestiges of British rule without contemplating the consequences?

The best description of the processes by which the new governments were formed is Elisha Douglass, *Rebels and Democrats: The Struggle for Equal Political Rights and Majority Rule During the American Revolution** (1955). Although older, Allan Nevins, *The American States During and After Revolution, 1775–1789,* is still valuable. The classic statement on the revolutionary nature of the change is found in J. Franklin Jameson, *The American Revolution Considered As A Social Movement** (1926). This study has been closely examined by Fredrick B. Tolles in "The American Revolution Considered as a Social Movement: A Re-Evaluation," *American Historical Review,* LX (1954), and found to be basically sound but overstated. Louis B. Hartz, *The Liberal Tradition in America** (1954), and Daniel J. Boorstin, *The Genius of American Politics** (1953), do not agree with Jameson or Tolles. See also Jackson Turner Main, *The Upper House in Revolutionary America* (1968), which complements Jameson's study of social forces from a political perspective.

* Available in a paperback edition.

REFORMATION IN THE STATES
JOHN R. ALDEN

While the Continentals and militia fought against Britain, other patriots, assuming ultimate victory, remolded their political and social institutions. They created written constitutions both for the several states and for the United States; made careful provision for the protection of personal liberties; struck at religious privilege; assailed barbarous punishments for crime; moved haltingly in the direction of political democracy; redistributed land; and even ventured to attack the institution of Negro slavery. They initiated an "Internal Revolution" which continued beyond the war and exercised an enduring influence.

The War of Independence was hardly begun when the patriots began to try to form legal and permanent governments in the colony-states. Overturning regimes sanctioned by Britain, they were often forced for a time to govern through revolutionary and extralegal—if not illegal—conventions and committees. But they desired political institutions more stable, more ordered, and better calculated to preserve and enhance their own liberties, if not those of the Tories. Very generally, in part because of their long acquaintance with colonial charters, they looked upon the written constitution as indispensable. In the fall of 1775 John Adams developed a model constitution; early in 1776 Tom Paine proposed another. Even before Paine's model appeared, the New Hampshire patriots adopted for temporary use a written constitution which endured until 1784. The South Carolina patriots adopted a temporary constitution in March, 1776, one intended to be permanent in 1778. Two such documents designed for long use were actually promulgated before the Declaration of Independence, in Virginia and New Jersey, and six others before the close of 1777. Rhode Island and Connecticut continued in effect their colonial charters with minor revisions. Massachusetts similarly, but temporarily, operated its charter until 1780, when a carefully drawn basic document was put into effect.

SOURCE. John Richard Alden, *The American Revolution, 1775–1783,* New York: Harper & Row, Publishers, 1954, pp. 150–163. Copyright 1954 by Harper & Brothers. Reprinted by permission of Harper & Row, Publishers, and the author.

It is a striking fact that the early state constitutions were neither prepared by conventions especially elected for the purpose nor submitted to the voters for approval. In a few instances they were drawn up and declared in operation by legislative bodies chosen in elections in which constitution-making was not an issue. More commonly, they were conceived and declared in effect by legislators to whom the voters had entrusted the tasks of fashioning statutory and fundamental law. Thus even those who enjoyed the privilege of the ballot had little or no opportunity to voice their desires. This fact was a matter of concern to many patriots, including Jefferson, who insisted that any constitution intended to be more than temporary should be sanctioned by the voters.

That the basic law guaranteeing the rights of the individual and establishing the framework of state government might be adopted without ratification aroused the citizens of Massachusetts. When, in September, 1776, the towns of that state were asked whether they would permit the General Court to draft a constitution, Concord as well as other towns vigorously replied in the negative. Concord insisted that a prime purpose of such a document was "to secure the subject in the possession and enjoyment of their rights and privileges, against any encroachments of the governing part." If a General Court could mold a basic document, then another such assemblage could later alter it at will. Of what avail then a fundamental law? Accordingly Concord urged that a convention be specially elected to draw up a constitution and that the citizens of the state be given an opportunity to inspect and comment upon the result before it should be put into practice. A mass meeting at Pittsfield proposed that a constitution should become valid only when approved by a majority of the voters. The General Court decided to draft such a document, which it submitted to referendum, but its handiwork was overwhelmingly defeated at the polls. In consequence the legislature called a state constitutional convention, which met in 1779–80 and which at least pretended to submit its product to the voters. More than a year earlier the first such convention had met in New Hampshire, but its work had been disapproved by the towns of that state. In 1783 another New Hampshire convention produced a document which received their consent. Massachusetts and her neighbor thus inaugurated the familiar and exceedingly important devices of the constitutional convention and the constitutional referendum. Further, since their method of constitution-making implied the supremacy of constitutions over legislative acts, the road was opened for the development of judicial review.

The Revolutionary state constitutions were often hurriedly drafted in the midst of other business, even by legislatures in flight before advancing

British troops. In some cases there was little quarreling regarding their provisions, in others heated controversy. Nevertheless, on the whole, the work was amazingly well done, since the majority of the constitutions intended for permanent use remained in force for a generation or more.

On the surface, the new basic state laws were much alike. As a general rule, they contained a Bill of Rights; all provided for an elected legislature, usually consisting of two houses; all arranged for a governor (or president) elected either by the voters or by the legislature; all granted the suffrage only to property owners or taxpayers; and most of them gave at least lip service to the principle of separation of powers. But if the governments set up by these documents differed little in form, there were important variations in substance. In some instances these constitutions were devised by patriots who wanted little or no change beyond separation from Britain —by Conservatives; in others, they were composed by patriots who desired independence and alterations in the direction of political democracy and social equality—by Radicals; in still others, neither the influence of the Conservatives nor that of the Radicals was decisive.

In the main, the forms of government under the new state constitutions were patterned after those in vogue in the colonies before 1775, with elected governors and senates replacing governors and councils chosen by the crown or the proprietors. The substance was largely derived from the colonial experience of 150 years and from the doctrines of natural rights and compact so splendidly asserted in the Declaration of Independence, and again in the Massachusetts constitution of 1780. In the latter document it is declared that "The body politic is formed by a voluntary association of individuals; it is a social compact, by which the whole people covenants with each citizen, and each with the whole people that all shall be governed by certain laws for the common good"; and also, that "The people alone have an incontestible unalienable, and indefensible right to institute government, and to reform, alter, or totally change the same when their protection, safety, prosperity, and happiness require it." These ideas were derived from study of the writings of a galaxy of British and European political theorists, especially those of John Locke. From Locke, and perhaps more particularly from Montesquieu, came another concept of great importance, separation of powers among the branches of government in order to prevent any one of them from becoming dominant and tyrannical.

Although the makers of the first state constitutions quite uniformly subscribed to Lockeian principles, they did not agree with respect to their meaning and their application. The drafters quarreled little about statements inserted in the Bills of Rights guaranteeing trial by jury, the right of petition, freedom from self-incrimination, and other rights familiar to English law. They fought, and often bitterly, over provisions regarding religion, the suffrage, qualifications for office-holding, the powers of the governor as against those of the legislature, and other crucial issues. In fact, the Conservatives and the Radicals were seriously at odds regarding the political and social goals of the Revolution.

In essence, the Conservatives, though devoted to the ideal of independence, feared excessive change. In the seats of authority formerly occupied by royal appointees, they now wished to place the propertied, the educated, and the socially qualified. They despised and dreaded majority rule because they conceived the humbler and less learned patriots to be incapable and even depraved. They opposed "mob rule" as leading to anarchy or dictatorship. Not a few of them defended established churches, feudal arrangements of primogeniture and entail, and privilege generally for the select and the superior. Had they been able to impose their will, the great planters, the wealthy merchants, and a portion of the clergy—the upper middle class—would have formed an American aristocracy and an American oligarchy. The Conservatives read their Locke as the British landed aristocracy and the British merchants read him after the Glorious Revolution of 1688. In the compact mechanics, small farmers, and slaves were not full and equal partners.

The Radicals refused to concede that the only great purpose of the patriots was separation from Britain. They would not admit that their rights—the rights of mankind—would be secured by the mere disappearance of royal and proprietary officials. To them Lockeian philosophy was a system of thought which sanctified neither rule by Britain nor domination by privileged Americans. They argued that all citizens were equal participants in compact. They were likely to look upon government as at best a necessary evil and to seek to limit its powers. They insisted that the suffrage should be generously granted, even that it should not be denied to any adult white male. They demanded just apportionment of legislative seats, so that the vote of the farmer and the frontiersman in the interior would have equal weight with that of the seaboard merchant and planter—tidewater areas were then frequently over-represented. The Radicals would place power in the legislature rather than in the executive or the judiciary, since the legislature would be most responsive to popular will. Conceding that the wishes of a minority should be given thoughtful consideration, they were prone to insist upon majority rule.

Nor was Radical thought confined to things political. Enlightened "leftists" of the War of Independence demanded complete religious freedom; they inveighed against hereditary aristocracy and legal and customary arrangements which favored the eldest son at the expense of his brothers and sisters. They asked at least a modicum of free public education for the sons and daughters of all free men. They urged reform of civil and criminal law to prevent injustice and cruel punishments, and they assailed brutal treatment of prisoners. Some even attacked the institution of Negro slavery as inhumane and unwarranted either by Locke or by God. In short, many Radical leaders, and at least a portion of their followers, entertained views which may be described as liberal or progressive and as logical.

To be sure, all the Radicals were not occupied with altruistic designs for present and future improvement—they were not all Jeffersons. Some were shiftless, irresponsible, and unprincipled folk who found in the Revolution opportunity to evade payment of taxes and debts, to pull down to their own level envied neighbors, and to exalt themselves without resort to toil. Nor were all the Conservatives mere crass devotees of personal and class interests. A number, among them Henry Laurens of South Carolina, were troubled because they were fighting for the rights of man while continuing to hold Negroes in bondage. Many of them desired religious freedom. Indeed, many Conservatives were moderate men hardly to be distinguished from the milder Radicals. In fact, no hard and fast line can be drawn between Conservatives and Radicals. Within both groups there were infinite variations, and some individuals shifted from one camp to the other.

In the struggle between the Conservatives and Radicals the latter group possessed important advantages. The Tories, who in the main would have been natural allies of the Conservatives, were commonly excluded from public life and even from the ballot. Moreover, many men who had not been permitted to vote before the war had been allowed to help choose Revolutionary conventions and legislatures. These clung to the ballot as more permanent regimes appeared. The Second Continental Congress itself advised "a full and free representation of the people" in constitution-making; and the influence of the new voters is to be discerned in the basic state documents. Inevitably, the majority of these suddenly enfranchised men joined the Radicals. In addition, the Conservatives, crying out against Britain, had come forth in defense of the rights of man and against taxation without representation, and had thus supplied their fellow patriots with ammunition which could be used against themselves. They could hardly deny the logic of the demands by the Radicals that the franchise be given to many of those voteless in colonial days; nor could they easily counter Radical arguments for redistricting of seats in the legislatures. The interior regions, "the Old West," had long been so patently underrepresented in the colony-states, especially in Pennsylvania, Virginia, and South Carolina, that the justice of those arguments was obvious. Yet in giving way to the Radicals on these points the Conservatives suffered serious diminution of their influence, not only because the new voters were inclined toward the Radicals, but also because "the Old West" was their stronghold. In sum, the Conservatives found it impossible to control the patriots as a whole and to insist that the only great goal of the war was severance from Britain.

Among the patriots were divisions along socio-economic lines. The small and tenant farmers, the frontier folk, and unpropertied people of the seacoast towns and cities tended to oppose the planters and merchants in the camp of the Conservatives. Class lines were not always clearly drawn, however. Jarring concepts were debated rather than settled by force; conflicting interests were compromised rather than decided by blows; and the Radicals found their most effective leaders among planters and certain merchants, lawyers, and other men of wealth, such as Jefferson, Richard Henry Lee, George Mason, George Wythe, Franklin, George Bryan, Thomas McKean, and Elbridge Gerry.

The influence of the Radicals may readily be discerned in the provisions of the new state constitutions concerning the ballot and qualifications for office-holding. Under these any taxpayer in Pennsylvania, Delaware, North Carolina, Georgia, and Vermont could vote. Any Virginian owning twenty-five acres of improved soil or five hundred acres of undeveloped land possessed the ballot. In the other states the suffrage was less generously offered to men who possessed either land or personal property in some quantity, or paid fairly substantial amounts in taxes. Very commonly, higher qualifications in the way of property or payment of taxes were required for members of the lower house of the legislature, still higher ones for membership in the upper house, and occasionally even higher ones for persons serving as governors. Office-holding was thus frequently reserved for men of means; no state conceded manhood suffrage; and plural voting on the basis of ownership of land was still possible in several states. But if political democracy had not been achieved, it is nevertheless true that the voting population was larger than it was in colonial days. Land was cheap, and the privilege of the ballot was often easily within the reach even of the poor. Since the Tories were usually disfranchised and since many sought safety in exile, there came a more or less permanent swing to the left in American politics.

The influence of the Radicals is also to be observed in the provisions of the early constitutions concerning the powers of the respective branches of government. While expressions of respect for the principle of separation

of powers were freely offered, authority was usually centered in the legislature, and especially in the lower house. The Radicals feared strong
executives and distrusted independent judiciaries. As a result the governor
was given an effective veto only in Massachusetts, and he was in some
states a mere figurehead. In several states judges were chosen by the
legislature, and for very short terms. The Radicals believed, and not
without reason, that the legislatures would be more responsive to the
public will, particularly since they were also able in a number of states
to require frequent elections. The political systems set up in states where
Radicals were dominant—for example, Pennsylvania, Virginia, and North
Carolina—were accordingly ill balanced and not too efficient. They were,
however, far more democratic than those established in states under Conservative domination—for example, Maryland.

Much redistricting in the direction of political justice and democracy
is also to be found in these constitutions. In Pennsylvania the southeastern
counties, almost absurdly overrepresented before 1775, lost their special
and privileged position. In Virginia the Piedmont and Shenandoah regions
received for the first time representation in accordance with their numerous population. Sectional favoritism was also eliminated in North Carolina. Concessions were made to interior folk in South Carolina and Massachusetts, although the Lowlands about Charleston continued for some
years to hold a favored position. Frontier democracy was given larger
opportunity to express itself, an opportunity which was not wasted.

The makers of fundamental law in the Revolutionary period also took
long strides toward religious freedom. Before the war there was
a relatively large measure of toleration everywhere in the Thirteen Colonies, but complete religious freedom nowhere except in Rhode Island.
In no fewer than nine colonies there were established tax-supported
churches, enjoying privileges varying greatly from place to place. In New
England, except for Rhode Island, the Congregational Church had the
support of the state, while the Anglican Church was official in a few
counties of New York and in all the colonies from Maryland to Georgia.
It was usually difficult and sometimes impossible for a member of a dissenting sect to escape taxation for the support of the established church
in his colony; and he who was attached to no religious organization could
not evade it. Universally, save in Rhode Island (which in the eighteenth
century restricted the political activities of Catholics and Jews), there
were discriminations of one sort or another, relatively mild in Pennsylvania
and Delaware, onerous in Congregational New England and Episcopalian
Maryland and Virginia. Connecticut law still required church attendance;
Roman Catholics could not hold office in Maryland.

The movement for disestablishment was facilitated by the fact that in no state were the Anglicans in a numerical majority. Except in Virginia, it was easy to reduce the Church of England to the level of other churches, for Presbyterians, Lutherans, Baptists, Roman Catholics, its own laymen, and deists (numerous among the leaders of the patriots) joined in the attack upon it. In Virginia, where the Anglicans formed perhaps half of the churchgoing population and included the bulk of the planters, there was a bitter struggle. However, Anglican clergymen in the upper South were distinguished for neither piety nor learning, and they were frequently Tories. Finally, the Church was definitely disestablished in the Old Dominion. The Congregational state churches in New England were less vulnerable; they lost some of their privileges, but were not deprived of all vestige of official sanction until the nineteenth century was well under way.

Disestablishment was, of course, not the equivalent of complete religious freedom, which was not attained in most of the states for some years. Thus New Jersey and the Carolinas continued to require that officeholders be Protestants; Massachusetts insisted that they declare themselves to be Christians; and Delaware demanded from them, and also from members of the legislature, that they declare their belief in the Holy Trinity. These and similar restrictions were soon to disappear. The trend was toward total religious liberty, with Jefferson and James Madison pointing the way in Virginia. In the Old Dominion the principle of toleration was incorporated in the Declaration of Rights of 1776. In the following year statutes requiring church attendance and the use of public money to support the Episcopal Church were repealed. The Episcopal Church fought bitterly against disestablishment and received powerful assistance from other Protestant sects, which desired that public funds be devoted to the maintenance of all the major Christian churches. Although the Episcopalian Church was deprived of all official status two years later, Patrick Henry, young John Marshall, and apparently Washington joined the ranks of those who wished to compel all citizens to help finance the Christian sects. Henry was able to mobilize a large majority in the assembly in favor of the scheme, but Jefferson, James Madison, and George Mason fought it persistently and imaginatively. At length the proposal was dropped, and the Statute of Religious Liberty, drawn up by Jefferson and sponsored by his friends, became law in 1786. In a long, rhetorical, and yet moving preamble the act condemned utterly all efforts to employ the power of government in behalf of any species of religion and affirmed that "truth is great and will prevail if left to herself. . . ." It was accordingly enacted "that no man shall be compelled to frequent or support any religious worship, place or ministry whatsoever, nor shall be enforced, restrained, molested, or burthened in his body or goods, nor shall otherwise suffer on account of his religious opinions or beliefs; but that all men shall be free to profess, and by argument to maintain, their opinion in matters of religion, and that the same shall in no wise diminish, enlarge, or affect their civil capacities." Jefferson was justly proud of his contribution to religious freedom.

The Revolutionary generation, seeking to assert the natural rights of mankind, could not but be conscience-stricken when it considered the lot in America of some of the children of Nature's God, the Negroes, who composed one-fifth of the total population and half of that of South Carolina. Almost all of the Negroes were slaves. Generally they were held in mild subjection. Nevertheless, slavery then, as later, had its horrors, the worst of which was the traffic in human bodies between Africa and America. That brutal commerce had aroused indignation before the war, and the importation of slaves had been halted in Rhode Island, Connecticut, and Pennsylvania, but the British government and its representatives in the colonies had prevented the passage of similar laws in the royal colonies. When Britain and British officials could no longer interfere, American legislatures, with that of Delaware leading the way in 1776, undertook to put an end to the traffic. During and immediately after the war the introduction from foreign lands of enslaved blacks was forbidden in all the states, save for South Carolina and Georgia. Even in the far South there was much sentiment in favor of such action, and importation was temporarily forbidden in South Carolina in 1787 and again in 1788.

The patriots did not content themselves merely with endeavors to destroy the oceanic slave trade. In the spring of 1775 there was formed at Philadelphia the first antislavery society in America, and many patriots, Conservative and Radical, including Washington, Jefferson, Madison, Patrick Henry, and Horatio Gates, were soon afterward urging the outlawing of Negro bondage. Economic interest, ignorance, feelings of racial superiority, and fear of the consequences of emancipation usually postponed or prevented action. Nevertheless, a few Negroes received their freedom in return for honorable military service in the war; and many thousands obtained it by manumission, made relatively easy by law in Virginia in 1782 and also by other states in the South. Moreover, Pennsylvania provided for gradual emancipation by a law of 1780; and statements of the Massachusetts Bill of Rights of the same year, including one which declared that "All men are born free and equal," were construed three years later by the highest court of that state to mean that slavery was outlawed. Certain other Northern states soon followed the examples of Pennsylvania and Massachusetts. Others did not act until after the close

of the century. In the South, however, where there were both proportionately and absolutely many more slaves, sentiment began to swing after
the war toward protecting that institution.

If the patriots indirectly gave support to the concept of aristocracy by
their failure to abolish slavery, they struck hard at that concept nonetheless. Provisions that there should be neither a privileged class nor hereditary offices were inserted in several of the first state constitutions. Two
denied the legislature the power to create titles of nobility! Georgia even
refused the privileges of voting and office-holding to persons claiming
titles. Manorial rights and quitrents vanished. What was more important,
the patriots demolished those twin props of landed aristocracy, primogeniture and entail. At the beginning of the war entailment, though forbidden
in South Carolina, was more or less legal elsewhere. Primogeniture
flourished in New York and the Southern colonies; in Pennsylvania, Delaware, New Jersey, and New England the eldest son received a double
share in inheritance. With Jefferson and Virginia once again leading the
way, these arrangements so well calculated to preserve family estates collapsed before the assaults of the reformers. By 1786 entails had been
abolished or rendered innocuous in every state; by 1792 primogeniture
had disappeared; indeed, by that time equality in intestate succession was
universally established. The results of these wholesale changes are difficult
to measure, but in some areas they may have contributed to a more
equitable distribution of land. Whatever the actual results, the social structure had been altered in the direction of equality.

The importance of redistribution of land, as Jefferson fully appreciated,
can scarcely be overestimated. Ownership of soil brought relative economic independence, and with it advance in social and political status.
More owners meant more democracy, social and political. Happily, redistribution proceeded during and immediately after the War of Independence, not only through the eradication of laws forcing and permitting
concentration of ownership, but also through the abolition of British authority over the trans-Allegheny West and the confiscation of Tory property. The bars to westward settlement set up by the Proclamation of
October 7, 1763, and later British restrictive measures vanished. Moreover, the great speculators in lands beyond the mountains, highly favored
under the royal regime, found it somewhat more difficult to secure large
grants from the state and federal governments at the expense of the
small farmer. Thus the path of the humble to landownership in the eastern
part of the Mississippi Valley was made somewhat broader and smoother.
To be sure, this result was hardly discernible until the war had ended
and large-scale expansion beyond the mountains began.

The effects of confiscation of lands owned by Tories, however, appeared almost immediately. On November 27, 1777, the Continental Congress recommended that the states seize and sell the estates of Loyalists, the proceeds to be used to finance the war. The idea of paying for the war in part at the expense of the Tories was a popular one among the patriots. Indeed, some states had already begun the process of confiscation. Now it was greatly hastened, and every state without exception declared Tory lands forfeited or at least subject to forfeiture. The result was a spate of sales of those lands which continued even after the close of the conflict. Whatever may be said about the treatment thus meted out to the supporters of Britain and the widespread corruption attendant upon such sales, many large estates were broken up and dispersed in smaller holdings among the patriots. In New York the lands of Tory James De Lancey became the property of 275 different persons; those of Tory Roger Morris went to nearly 250; and large tracts owned by Tories in the central and northern parts of the state were sold to poor farmers in quantities from one hundred to five hundred acres. Since many of the Loyalists sooner or later went into exile (although some returned), it may be said that conservatism was permanently weakened both by their departure and by the fact that the less affluent were often enabled to acquire their properties and to move upward economically and socially.

If this analysis of change in the states accompanying and resulting from the war is already lengthy, it should nevertheless be recalled that the era of the Revolution brought increased pressure for more lenient treatment of debtors, for improvement in prison conditions, and for the revision and modernization of civil and criminal law. Certainly, education, in some part at least because of Revolutionary ferment, entered upon a new course. The concept of education at public expense received added impulse. In 1776 John Adams declared that "Laws for the liberal education of youth, especially of the lower class of people, are so extremely wise and useful, that, to a humane and generous mind, no expense for this purpose would be thought extravagant." Jefferson, who was equally convinced with Adams of the values of education and of the desirability of spreading widely its benefits, proposed three years later that Virginia establish public schools for elementary instruction and remold the College of William and Mary into something approaching a university. Five Revolutionary state constitutions urged that provision be made for schools, in some instances specifically for free schools. It was apparent to many patriot leaders that the new American society in process of formation required diffusion of education, if for no other reason to the end that the less affluent citizens who were wielding influence in public affairs should be sufficiently enlightened to carry their burdens. Although the war temporarily interfered with the operations of schools and colleges, and although the proposals of Jefferson, and others like him, were temporarily set aside, the concept of a freer and more democratic educational system gained converts. Indicative of the future was the action of the legislature of Georgia in 1783 giving one thousand acres of land to every county for the support of schools.

CHAPTER 14

THE NEW NATION UNDER THE ARTICLES OF CONFEDERATION

It can hardly be argued that the decade of the 1780's was not a critical period in the history of the United States. Yet there is considerable doubt that it was *the critical period of American history,* as claimed by John Fiske in his widely influential book of that title. The traditional, or Fiske interpretation of the 1780's held that an exceptionally weak and inept Articles of Confederation government was responsible for bringing the nation to the brink of disaster, from which it was rescued only by the magnificent efforts of the "founding fathers." Revisionists counter that the period was much more complex than the traditional view would indicate. They suggest that the major disruptive forces of the decade— post-war demobilization, economic dislocation, and fundamental political conflict—would have operated regardless of the government in power.

The strength and effectiveness of the government under the Articles is difficult to determine with any degree of exactitude. In this selection, Professor Merrill Jensen, a leading critic of the Fiske viewpoint, suggests that the government was not nearly so defective as earlier historians believed. Jensen argues persuasively that it was not the imminent collapse of the Confederation which led to the calling of the Constitutional

Convention of 1787 and the creation of a new Constitution. These developments represented instead the victory of one political group in the fundamental political conflict which Jensen sees as the essence of the period of the 1780's.

In reading this selection the student should consider carefully three basic matters. First, does Professor Jensen's terminology for the two opposing political groups help to clarify or to obscure the basic nature of the political conflict of the period? What characteristics does Jensen ascribe to the opposing groups? Which group represented the cause of democratic government? Second, what was the precise nature—particularly the central issue—of the disagreement between the two groups? Third, was the conflict finally settled in the 1780's, or anytime thereafter? If not, what has been the nature of the continuing disagreement? Has this disagreement always been, as Professor Jensen argues it was in the 1780's, over the issue of democracy as a way of government for the United States?

The student wishing more information on this topic should begin his reading in Jensen, *The Articles of Confederation** (1940), and *The New Nation** (1950), from which this selection is taken. Also he, at least, should sample John Fiske, *The Critical Period of American History* (1916, second edition), to get a taste of the other side of the debate. A modern analysis that disagrees with Jensen is found in Oscar and Mary Handlin, "Radicals and Conservatives in Massachusetts after Independence," *New England Quarterly,* XVII (1944). The standard biographies of men such as George Washington, John Adams, Thomas Jefferson, James Madison, and Alexander Hamilton can be read profitably for a knowledge of the period. See also the bibliography and selection for Chapter 16 of this volume.

* Available in a paperback edition.

THE SIGNIFICANCE OF THE CONFEDERATION PERIOD

MERRILL JENSEN

This book is an account of the first years of the new nation that was born of the American Revolution. Like every other segment of time, the history of the United States from 1781 to 1789 was an integral part of the past in which it was rooted and of the future into which it was growing. It was a time when men believed they could shape the future of the new nation, and since it was also a time in which they disagreed as to what that future should be, they discussed great issues with a forthrightness and realism seldom equalled in political debates. The history of the Confederation is therefore one of great inherent importance for the study of human society if for no other reason than that during it men debated publicly and even violently the question of whether or not people could govern themselves.

Aside from its inherent importance, the history of the Confederation has been of enormous significance to one generation of Americans after another in the years since then. Repeatedly Americans have turned to that history in the course of innumerable social and political struggles. They have done so because it was during those years that the Articles of Confederation were replaced by the Constitution of 1787. In order to explain their Constitution, Americans have appealed to the history of the period out of which it came. In the course of such appeals, sometimes honestly for light and guidance and sometimes only for support of partisan arguments, Americans have usually found what they sought. As a result the "history" has been obscured in a haze of ideas, quotations, and assumptions torn bodily from the context of fact that alone gives them meaning. Again and again political opponents have asserted that the founding fathers stood for this or that, while their writings have stood idly and helplessly in volumes on shelves or have lain buried in yellowed manuscripts and newspapers.

SOURCE. Merrill Jensen, *The New Nation: A History of the United States During the Confederation, 1781–1789,* New York: Alfred A. Knopf, Inc., 1950, pp. vii–xiv and 422–428. Copyright 1950 by Alfred A. Knopf, Inc. Reprinted by permission of A. A. Knopf, Inc. and the author.

Since the founding fathers themselves disagreed as to the nature of the history of the period and as to the best kind of government for the new nation, it is possible to find arguments to support almost any interpretation one chooses. It is not surprising therefore that conflicting interpretations have filled thousands of pages and that all this effort has never produced any final answers and probably never will, for men have ever interpreted the two constitutions of the United States in terms of their hopes, interests, and beliefs rather than in terms of knowable facts.

The conflict of interpretation has been continuous ever since the first debates over the Articles of Confederation in the summer of 1776. Men then differed as to the kind of government which should be created for the new nation. They continued to debate the issue during the 1780's. The members of the Convention of 1787 differed as to the need for and the amount of constitutional change. When the Constitution was submitted to the public in October 1787 the controversy rose to new heights. Men talked in public meetings and wrote private letters and public essays in an effort to explain, justify, or denounce what the Convention had done. They disagreed as to what had happened since the war. Some said there had been chaos; others said there had been peace and prosperity. Some said there would be chaos without the new Constitution; others that there would be chaos if it were adopted.

Once it was adopted Thomas Jefferson and Alexander Hamilton, with two opposed ideals of what the United States should be, laid down two classic and contradictory opinions of the nature of the Constitution. These two basic interpretations may be simply stated. Jefferson held that the central government was sharply limited by the letter of the Constitution; that in effect the states retained their sovereign powers except where they are specifically delegated. Hamilton argued in effect that the central government was a national government which could not be restrained by a strict interpretation of the Constitution or by ideas of state sovereignty. These rival interpretations did not originate with Hamilton and Jefferson, for they had been the very core of constitutional debate ever since the Declaration of Independence, and even before it, for that matter.

Jefferson and his followers used the states rights idea to oppose the plans of the Federalists when they passed the Alien and Sedition Acts in 1798. But when Jefferson became president and purchased Louisiana, he justified his actions by constitutional theories that even Hamilton hardly dared use. Meanwhile Jefferson's opponents seized upon his earlier theories in a vain attempt to block the expansion of the United States. They did so again during the War of 1812 when the Federalists of New England became out-and-out exponents of "states rights" and threatened secession because they were opposed to the war.

In the decades before the Civil War, Daniel Webster and John C. Calhoun carried on the dispute, each having changed sides since his youthful years in politics. Webster, who had been a states rights spokesman during the War of 1812, became the high priest of nationalism, while Calhoun, a leading nationalist in 1812, became the high priest of the states rights idea which he elaborated to defend the slave-owning aristocracy of the South.

The Civil War itself was the bloody climax of a social conflict in which the ultimate nature of the Constitution was argued again and again in seeking support for and arguments against antagonistic programs. But even the Civil War did not finally settle the constitutional issue. The stresses and strains that came with the rise of industrial and finance capitalism produced demands for social and regulatory legislation. The passage of such legislation by the states involved the interpretation of the nature of the Constitution, for business interests regulated by state governments denied their authority and appealed to the national courts. Those courts soon denied the power of regulation to state legislatures. Then, when regulatory laws were passed by the national government, the regulated interests evolved a "states rights" theory that limited the power of the central government, and the national courts once more agreed.

Throughout American history the courts have drawn boundary lines between state and national authority. The pose of judicial impartiality and finality assumed by the courts cannot hide the fact that they have shifted those boundary lines with the shifting winds of politics, and always with sufficient precedents, if not with adequate grace. As a result they had created by 1900 a legal and constitutional no man's land in which all sorts of activity could be carried on without effective regulation by either state or national governments.

The crash of American economy in 1929 once more posed in imperative terms the problem of the nature of the Constitution. How should it, how could it deal with the potentiality of chaos inherent in unemployment, starvation, and bankruptcy, and ultimately, the loss of faith in the utility of the economic and political foundation of the society itself.

As the national government began to act where, plainly, state and local governments had failed to or were unable to act, the question of constitutionality was raised. For a time the courts once more listened to and heeded states rights constitutional theories which were expounded by opponents of the New Deal. New Deal lawyers, in turn, adopted as weapons John Marshall's nationalistic interpretations of the Constitution for ends which Marshall himself would have fought to the death. President Roosevelt, in his fight on the Supreme Court, declared that the Constitution was not a lawyer's document; yet some of the ablest lawyers who ever lived in America wrote it. New Deal publicists wrote tracts in the guise of history to prove that there had been a "national sovereignty" in the United States from the beginning of the Revolution. Therefore, they argued, the courts could not stop the New Deal from doing what needed doing by following a strict interpretation of the Constitution. Both the New Dealers and the Republicans insisted that they were the sole heirs of the legacy of Thomas Jefferson, while Alexander Hamilton went into an eclipse from which he has not yet emerged.

The most recent appeal to the history of the Confederation Period has come from those who support some form of world government. Adequate arguments for such a government can be found in twentieth-century experience, but, like most men, its backers turn to history for analogies and lessons.

When the League of Nations was set up at the end of the First World War men turned to American history after the American Revolution as a parallel experience. At that time books were written to show the "chaos" of the Confederation Period and the happy solution that came with the Constitution of 1787. Among them was a book by a great authority on international law with the title *James Madison's Notes of Debates in the Federal Convention of 1787 and their Relation to a More Perfect Society of Nations*. The book was widely distributed by the Carnegie Endowment for International Peace. This and other books like it had little relation to the realities of world politics in the 1920's and 1930's, but despite this supporters of the United Nations and of various plans of world government have again turned to the history of the American states after the American Revolution. . . .

Even if it can be granted that most appeals to the history of the Confederation have been sincere, let it also be said that they have seldom been infused with any knowledge of the period or its problems. The result has been the drawing of lessons the past does not have to teach. This is a luxury too expensive in an age when men have discovered how to unhinge the very force that holds matter itself together but have advanced very little beyond cave men in their notions of how to live peacefully with one another.

Yet it is little wonder that such false lessons have been drawn in the twentieth century because most of them have come from John Fiske's

The Critical Period of American History, a book of vast influence but of no value as either history or example. Fiske, a philosopher and popular lecturer, wrote the book "without fear and without research," to use the words of Charles A. Beard. As long ago as 1905, Andrew C. Mc-Laughlin, an impeccably conservative historian of the Constitution who wrote a far better book on the same period, said that Fiske's book was "altogether without scientific standing, because it is little more than a remarkably skillful adaption of a very few secondary authorities showing almost no evidence of first hand acquaintance with the sources."

The story told by Fiske and repeated by publicists and scholars who have not worked in the field—and some who have, for that matter—is based on the assumption that this was *the* "critical period" of American history during which unselfish patriots rescued the new nation from impending anarchy, if not from chaos itself. The picture is one of stagnation, ineptitude, bankruptcy, corruption, and disintegration. Such a picture is at worst false and at best grossly distorted. It is therefore important to attempt a history which makes an effort to examine the sources, which is concerned with the nature of political and economic problems rather than with proving that one side or another in the innumerable political battles of the period was "right" or "wrong." Nothing is to be gained by following a "chaos and patriots to the rescue" interpretation. We have too long ignored the fact that thoroughly patriotic Americans during the 1780's did not believe there was chaos and emphatically denied that their supposed rescuers were patriotic. The point is that there were patriots on both sides of the issue, but that they differed as to desirable goals for the new nation. At the same time, of course, there were men as narrow and selfish on both sides as their political enemies said they were.

If one approaches the history of the Confederation in this way, if one tries to see it as men who lived in it saw it and to write of it in their terms, one may achieve some semblance of reality. It is not the task of the historian to defend or attack the various groups of men whose conflicts were the essence of the period, but to set forth what they believed and what they tried to achieve. This can be illustrated no better than in the definition of terms. Throughout this book the words "federalist" and "nationalist" are used to describe two opposed bodies of opinion as to the best kind of central government for the United States. In so doing I have followed the members of the Convention of 1787. Those men believed that the Articles of Confederation provided for a "federal" government and the majority of them wanted to replace it with a "national" government. The fact that the men who wanted a national government called themselves Federalists after their work was submitted to the public is relevant to the history of politics after 1787, not to the discussion of the nature of the central government prior to and during the Convention of 1787.

Whatever the confusion since then, there was none at the time. Gouverneur Morris stated the issue concisely in the Convention when he "explained the distinction between a federal and a national, supreme government; the former being a mere compact resting on the good faith of the parties; the latter having a complete and compulsive operation." This explanation was in answer to those members of the Convention who wanted to know what Edmund Randolph meant in his opening speech when he spoke of the "defects of the federal system, the necessity of transforming it into a national efficient government. . . ."

The issue was not, as has been argued from time to time, whether there was a "nation" before the adoption of the Constitution of 1787. That was not the question at all during the 1780's. There was a new nation, as the men of the time agreed: they disagreed as to whether the new nation should have a federal or a national government. They did so from the outset of the Revolution and men have continued to do so ever since. The Constitution of 1787 was, as Madison said, both national and federal. And while this fact has led to innumerable conflicts of interpretation, it has also been a source of strength; for as one political group after another has gotten control of the central government it has been able to shape the constitution to its needs and desires. Thus with the single exception of the Civil War, peaceful change has always been possible, and as long as Americans are willing to accept the decisions of ballot boxes, legislatures, and courts, the Constitution will continue to change with changing needs and pressures. . . .

The foregoing pages indicate that the Confederation Period was one of great significance, but not of the kind that tradition has led us to believe. The "critical period" idea was the result of an uncritical acceptance of the arguments of the victorious party in a long political battle, of a failure to face the fact that partisan propaganda is not history but only historical evidence. What emerges instead is a much more complex and important story in which several themes are interwoven. It was a period of what we would call post-war demobilization, of sudden economic change, dislocation, and expansion, and of fundamental conflict over the nature of the Constitution of the United States. Each of these themes is so interwoven with the others that any separation is arbitrary but, taken separately or together, they are better keys to an understanding of the period than the traditional one.

At the end of the war Americans faced innumerable problems arising from it. What should be done with war veterans? Should the Loyalists return to their homes? What should be our relations with foreign friends and foes? Should commerce be free or should there be discrimination, and if so, against whom and for whose benefit? How would peace affect the economy? How should the war debt be paid? What kind of taxes should be levied to pay it, and who should pay them? When the war-boom collapsed, why did it? What should the state or central governments, or both, do about it? Should government encourage one form of economic enterprise over another or should it keep hands off? What about discontented groups: should government ignore them, cater to them, or forcibly suppress those who might revolt?

Such questions or others like them have probably been asked after every great war in history. They were asked, debated, and given various solutions during the 1780's. The significance of those debates and solutions has often been misunderstood. This is no better illustrated than in the case of the national debt during the 1780's which is usually discussed only in terms of depreciation and nonpayment of interest. Actually much more was involved than this. The debt was fantastically low compared with the national debt of today—about twelve dollars per capita as compared with seventeen hundred—and the nation had vast untouched natural resources with which to pay it. Multitudes of accounts had to be reduced to simple forms so that they could be paid, and this the Confederation government managed to do. But even more important that the economics of the national debt was its politics: should it be paid by the states or the central government? A fundamental assumption of every political leader was that the political agency which paid the debt would hold the balance of power in the new nation. Hence, the supporters of a strong central government insisted that the national debt must be paid by Congress while their opponents insisted that it should be divided among the states and paid by them. The latter group was on the way to victory by the end of the 1780's, for they were supported by clamoring creditors. The result was that one state after another assumed portions of the national debt owing to its citizens. Thus the traditional story is so out of context as to be virtually meaningless. This is true of other traditions as well. Most of the ports of the world were open, not closed, to American citizens. Reciprocity and equal treatment of all United States citizens was the rule in the tonnage and tariff acts of the states, not trade barriers.

To say that many of the pessimistic traditions are false is not to say that all Americans were peaceful and satisfied. The holders of national and state debts wanted bigger payments than they got. The merchants wanted more government aid than was given them. The farmers, hit by high taxes and rigid collection of both taxes and private debts, demanded relief in the form of lower taxes and government loans from state legislatures. Such demands kept state politics in an uproar during the 1780's. However, the often violent expression of such discontents in politics should not blind us to the fact that the period was one of extraordinary economic growth. Merchants owned more ships at the end of the 1780's than they had at the beginning of the Revolution, and they carried a greater share of American produce. By 1790 the export of agricultural produce was double what it had been before the war. American cities grew rapidly, with the result that housing was scarce and building booms produced a labor shortage. Tens of thousands of farmers spread outwards to the frontiers. There can be no question but that freedom from the British Empire resulted in a surge of activity in all phases of American life. Of course not all the problems of the new nation were solved by 1789—all have not yet been solved—but there is no evidence of stagnation and decay in the 1780's. Instead the story is one of a newly free people who seized upon every means to improve and enrich themselves in a nation which they believed had a golden destiny.

Politically the dominating fact of the Confederation Period was the struggle between two groups of leaders to shape the character of the state and central governments. The revolutionary constitutions of the states placed final power in the legislatures and made the executive and judicial branches subservient to them. The members of the colonial aristocracy who became Patriots, and new men who gained economic power during the Revolution deplored this fact, but they were unable to alter the state constitutions during the 1780's. Meanwhile they tried persistently to strengthen the central government. These men were the nationalists of the 1780's.

On the other hand the men who were the true federalists believed that the greatest gain of the Revolution was the independence of the several states and the creation of a central government subservient to them. The leaders of this group from the Declaration of Independence to the Convention of 1787 were Samuel Adams, Patrick Henry, Richard Henry Lee, George Clinton, James Warren, Samuel Bryan, George Bryan, Elbridge Gerry, George Mason and a host of less well known but no less important men in each of the states. Most of these men believed, as a result of their experience with Great Britain before 1776 and of their reading of history, that the states could be best governed without the intervention of a powerful central government. Some of them had programs of political and social reform; others had none at all. Some had a vision of democracy; others had no desire except to control their states for whatever satisfaction such control might offer. Some were in fact as narrow and provincial as their opponents said they were. However, the best of them agreed that the central government needed more power, but they wanted that power given so as not to alter the basic character of the Articles of Confederation. Here is where they were in fundamental disagreement with the nationalists who wanted to remove the central government from the control of the state legislatures.

The nationalist leaders from the Declaration of Independence to the Philadelphia convention were men like Robert Morris, John Jay, Gouverneur Morris, James Wilson, Alexander Hamilton, Henry Knox, James Duane, George Washington, James Madison, and many lesser men. Most of these men were by temperament or economic interest believers in executive and judicial rather than legislative control of state and central governments, in the rigorous collection of taxes, and, as creditors, in strict payment of public and private debts. They declared that national honor and prestige could be maintained only by a powerful central government. Naturally, not all men who used such language used it sincerely, for some were as selfish and greedy as their opponents said they were. The nationalists frankly disliked the political heritage of the Revolution. They deplored the fact there was no check upon the actions of majorities in state legislatures; that there was no central government to which minorities could appeal from the decisions of such majorities, as they had done before the Revolution.

There were men who veered from side to side, but their number is relatively small and their veering is of little significance as compared with the fact that from the outset of the Revolution there were two consistently opposed bodies of opinion as to the nature of the central government. There was, of course, a wide variation of belief among adherents of both points of view. There were extremists who wanted no central government at all and others who wanted to wipe out the states entirely. There were some who wanted a monarchy and others who would have welcomed dictatorship. But such extremists are not representative of the two great bodies of men whose conflict was the essence of the years both before and after 1789.

While the federalist leaders gradually moved to a position where they were willing to add specific powers to the Articles of Confederation, the nationalist leaders campaigned steadily for the kind of government they wanted. During the war they argued that it could not be won without creating a powerful central government. After the war they insisted that such a government was necessary to do justice to public creditors, solve the problems of post-war trade, bring about recovery from depression, and win the respect of the world for the new nation. Meanwhile their experience with majorities in state legislatures merely intensified their desire. They became desperate as state after state in 1785 and 1786 adopted some form of paper money that could be loaned on farm mortgages and be used to pay taxes, and in some cases private debts as well. When they were able to hold off such demands and farmers revolted, as in Massachusetts, they were thoroughly frightened.

They looked upon such events as evidence of the horrors of unchecked democracy and they said so in poetry, private letters, newspaper essays, and public speeches. The problem, they said, was to find some refuge from democracy. They worked hard to control state legislatures and they were often successful, but such control was uncertain at best, for annual elections meant a constant threat of overturn and the threat was realized repeatedly.

We may not call it democracy, but they did. Edmund Randolph put their case bluntly in his opening speech in the Convention of 1787. He said, "our chief danger arises from the democratic parts of our constitutions . . . None of the [state] constitutions have provided a sufficient check against the democracy. The feeble senate of Virginia is a phantom. Maryland has a more powerful senate, but the late distractions in that state, have discovered that it is not powerful enough. The check established in the constitutions of New York and Massachusetts is yet a stronger barrier against democracy, but they all seem insufficient." Outside the Convention General Knox was saying that a "mad democracy sweeps away every moral trait from the human character" and that the Convention would "clip the wings of a mad democracy." James Madison in the *Federalist Papers* argued that the new Constitution should be adopted because a "republican" form of government was better than a "democracy."

The debate was white-hot and was carried on with utter frankness. It was white-hot because for a moment in history self-government by majorities within particular political boundaries was possible. Those majorities could do what they wanted, and some of them knew what they wanted. Democracy was no vague ideal, but a concrete program: it meant definite things in politics, economics, and religion. Whatever side of the controversy we take, whether we think the majorities in state legislatures governed badly or well—the fact to face is that men of the 1780's believed that the issue was democracy as a way of government for the United States of those days.

They faced the issue squarely. They thought hard and realistically about the problems of government. They understood that society is complex and that the truth about it is multifold rather than simple. James Madison summed it up as well as it has ever been done. There are, he said, many passions and interests in society and these will ever clash for control of government and will ever interpret their own desires as the good of the whole. Men like Madison and John Adams believed, as Madison said, that the "great desideratum which has not yet been found for Republican governments seems to be some disinterested and dispassionate umpire in disputes between different passions and interests in the state." In the tenth number of *The Federalist,* after citing various origins of political parties, Madison said that "the most durable source of factions [parties] has been the various and unequal distribution of property. Those who hold and those who are without property have ever formed distinct interests in society. Those who are creditors and those whose are debtors, fall under a like discrimination. A landed interest, a manufacturing interest, a mercantile interest, a monied interest, with many lesser interests, grow up of necessity in civilized nations, and divide them into different classes, actuated by different sentiments and views. The regulation of these various and interfering interests forms the principal task of modern legislation, and involves the spirit of party and faction in the necessary and ordinary operations of the government."

The constitutional debate of the 1780's was thus carried on by men with a realistic appreciation of the social forces lying behind constitutional forms and theories, by men who were aware of the relationship between economic and political power. This realistic approach was lost sight of in the nineteenth century by romantic democrats who believed that once every man had the right to vote the problems of society could be solved. It was lost sight of too by those who came to believe in an oversimplified economic interpretation of history. In a sense they were as romantic as the democrats, for they assumed a rationality in the historic process that is not always supported by the evidence.

If the history of the Confederation has anything to offer us it is the realistic approach to politics so widely held by the political leaders of the time, however much they might differ as to forms of government and desirable goals for the new nation. Throughout the Confederation men with rival goals pushed two programs simultaneously. The federalists tried to strengthen the Articles of Confederation; the nationalists tried to create a new constitution by means of a convention, and thus avoid the method of change prescribed by the Articles of Confederation. The movement to strengthen the Articles failed on the verge of success; the movement to call a convention succeeded on the verge of failure. The failure of one movement and the success of the other, however we may interpret them, is one of the dramatic stories in the history of politics.

CHAPTER 15

THE FRAMING OF
THE CONSTITUTION

One of the ancient truisms of American History is that the United States Constitution is a "bundle of compromises." In the literature on the subject it is easy to find authorities who wish it were otherwise, but it is easier to find ones who see in those compromises the strengths of the document and of the nation. Although Professor Holcombe probably belongs to the second group, this study describes the end products of the compromises and does not point with pride or view with alarm.

The first two principles of the Constitution which Holcombe discusses are fairly obvious. For instance, nowhere in the Constitution is there a section headed "Federalism," or one entitled "Checks and Balances," but they can readily be inferred from the text itself. The third principle, "Pluralism," is much more subtly ingrained in this organic law. You can search the Constitution from preamble to the final period and find not the slightest mention (either directly or by inference) of the concept of pluralism or of the political party, which is its practical manifestation. In fact, it is so well concealed that other documentation, especially *Federalist Ten,* is essential for a clearer view. In *Federalist Ten,* a most remarkable essay on the development and workings of a republican government, James Madison (frequently called the "Father of the Constitution") laid out, in 1788, the workings of our party system with such clarity and sophistication that one cannot understand the workings of our system of government unless one understands Madison's argument.

Carefully read, this selection can be of great value in understanding the operation of our Constitution. It will be helpful to keep several questions in mind as you read. How are these abstract principles currently functioning and are they operating as the founders intended? How do political parties affect Holcombe's other constitutional principles? How and why can pluralism be a "constitutional principle" if it is neither mentioned nor inferred in the document?

The literature on the Constitutional Convention and its offspring is monumental. For an understanding of both, one would do well to begin with Holcombe's *Our More Perfect Union* (1950). Most, if not all, of the contemporary accounts of the convention are to be found in Max Farrand, *The Records of the Federal Convention of 1787**, 4 Vol. (1911), although the casual student is more likely to finish and enjoy Farrand's *The Framing of the Constitution of the United States** (1913). Charles A. Beard's epochal study, *An Economic Interpretation of the Constitution of the United States** (1913, 1935, 1962), has been subjected to detailed and telling criticism in Robert E. Brown, *Charles Beard and the Constitution** (1953), and Forrest McDonald, *We the People: The Economic Origins of the Constitution** (1958). However, Professor Beard is not without his defenders; see, particularly, Jackson Turner Main, *The Anti-Federalists: Critics of the Constitution, 1781–1788** (1962).

* Available in a paperback edition.

THE CONSTITUTIONAL PRINCIPLES OF 1787
ARTHUR N. HOLCOMBE

The Virginia Plan was designed to provide a general government for the whole body of people in the United States which would do for the more perfect Union what well-ordered state governments were expected to do for their respective states. To this end all necessary powers were to be granted to a new central government dependent for support directly on the people of the Union and not at all, or as little as possible, on the state governments. The Congress under the Articles of Confederation was to be replaced by a new national legislature, representative of the people and responsible to them, which would be supreme in its proper sphere. There was to be also a supreme executive, as independent as possible of the legislative branch of the central government, and a supreme court. This was what the Virginia leaders meant by a national government and was their justification for calling themselves Nationalists.

FEDERALISM

The details of the plan were somewhat indefinite. The members of the Virginia delegation were not agreed upon the qualifications of the voters who would elect representatives to the proposed national legislature nor upon a formula for the apportionment of representatives among the states. They proposed to divide the Congress into two branches, the upper branch to represent the more substantial property owners and to be elected by the lower out of candidates nominated by the state legislatures, but they did not agree upon the amount of the property qualification for membership in the upper branch. They were not agreed upon the structure of the executive, some favoring a single chief executive, others preferring a plural executive. They did not agree upon the functions of the Supreme Court, though all seemed to favor giving the judges, like the executive, some part in the making as well as in the interpretation of the laws.

SOURCE. From *Securing the Blessings of Liberty: The Constitutional System* by Arthur N. Holcombe, New York: Scott, Foresman and Company, 1964, pp. 63–86. Copyright 1964 by Scott, Foresman and Company. Reprinted by permission of Scott, Foresman and Company and the author.

The debates later in the Convention disclosed that the differences of opinion within the Virginia delegation on some of these points were serious. But there seemed to be at the beginning no important differences among the Virginians concerning three basic features of their plan, to which great opposition promptly developed within the Convention. This opposition resulted in the eventual abandonment of these features by the Virginians or in their defeat by the Convention. The first of these was a proposal for the coercion of the states by military force, if necessary, to secure their compliance with the decisions of the national government. The second was a proposal to endow the supreme legislature with a general grant of lawmaking power, the extent of the national authority in particular cases to be defined by the national government. The third was a proposal for legislative guardianship of the supremacy of the national government rather than the assertion of a judicial supremacy such as might have been expected from statesmen devoted to the principle of a reign of law.

These proposals, if adopted, would have established a highly centralized form of government, which in the light of later events can now be seen to have been unacceptable to the American people. It is difficult to understand the original support of these proposals by the Virginia delegation, unless the Virginians expected the government of the more perfect Union to be dominated by the representatives of a state as great and powerful as was Virginia at that time. Virginia then included the present states of West Virginia and Kentucky, comprising a share of the total population of the United States equal to that of the present states of New York and California together. It is not surprising that the great Virginia planters, producers of the country's principal money crop, should have thought of themselves as the leading interest in national politics. Naturally the Virginians were Nationalists. . . .

In the Committee of the Whole the Nationalists controlled only two delegations, those from Virginia and Pennsylvania. Four other delegations, however, that from Massachusetts and those from the three states to the south of Virginia, supported the leadership of the Nationalists without subscribing to all their political theories. They were ready to abandon the Articles of Confederation and to oppose all efforts to maintain equality of representation for all states in the Congress, or in any branch of it, if the bicameral system should be adopted. They made no attempt to draft a plan of their own and probably could not at this stage have agreed upon such a plan if they had tried. Delegates from three of these states, however, were to play important parts in the parliamentary maneuvers which later culminated in the rejection of the Virginians' plan for a nationalistic upper branch of the proposed supreme legislature.

At the opposite end of the scale for measuring the distribution of power between the states and the Union were those delegates who advocated unlimited sovereignty for the states. Among them Luther Martin of Maryland was the most vocal and the most dogmatic. This doughty foe of centralized government claimed that each of the former colonies had acquired sovereign power with its independence from Great Britain and had surrendered no part of this power under the Articles of Confederation. According to this view the Congress was a mere conference of ambassadors rather than the principal organ of a genuine government, and the Confederation was no true state but rather a voluntary association of sovereign states organized primarily to implement a military alliance. An impressive number of the delegates showed unrestrained impatience both with Luther Martin's long-winded exposition of his political theories and with his particular brand of opposition to the formation of a more perfect Union.

Another faction among the opponents of the Virginia Plan consisted of those delegates who based their opposition on strictly practical considerations. They argued, first, that the Convention was not authorized under the call issued by the Congress to do more than revise and strengthen the Articles of Confederation; and secondly, that the people of the United States would not accept a form of government so highly centralized as that proposed by the Virginia Nationalists. The case against the Virginia Plan was set forth on these grounds by William Paterson of New Jersey, when he presented the New Jersey Plan to the Committee of the Whole. Paterson, an able lawyer and later a justice of the Supreme Court by appointment of President Washington, did not discuss at length the details of this plan upon their merits, preferring to play the role of an opportunist in Convention politics. The members of this faction showed little interest in the doctrine of state sovereignty and in general seemed to be governed more by expediency than by principle. To distinguish them from the strict states' rights faction, these delegates might be called Confederationists. Among them Judge Sherman of Connecticut was the most active participant in the debates on the floor of the Convention and in the work of the committees.

These Confederationists were the original Federalists in national politics. At the end of the Convention, however, all the supporters of the finished Constitution were calling themselves Federalists, and the word had lost its original meaning. This change of meaning is a principal clue to what really happened in the federal Convention of 1787. The Philadelphia Convention was in fact a national convention as well as a federal convention. The acceptance of the appellation Federalist by all factions except the states' rights dogmatists marked the formation of what we would now call a national political party. This party led the fight for ratification of the

Constitution. Their defeated opponents became known in history as Anti-federalists.

A third faction among the supporters of the New Jersey Plan consisted of delegates from small states who objected to all Nationalist schemes that threatened to submerge their states in one centralized leviathan. They were not necessarily opposed to plans for forming a more perfect Union by substituting a new central government for the old Congress under the Articles of Confederation; but the new Union, in order to meet their criticisms of the Virginia Plan, would have to be a union of states as well as a union of the American people. Prominent among the members of this faction was John Dickinson of Delaware, formerly of Pennsylvania. As the celebrated author of the *Letters of a Pennsylvania Farmer,* an early and outstanding statement of the colonial case against King George III's government, Dickinson had been a national leader before the Revolution, and, as chairman of the Annapolis Convention which had first issued the call for the Constitutional Convention of 1787, he had become an outstanding advocate of a more perfect Union. He was an admirer of the British Constitution and liked many features of the Virginia Plan, but he could not give it his support until it was modified so as to allay the fears of the delegates from the small states.

Despite the diversity of reasons for supporting the New Jersey Plan in the Committee of the Whole, the plan contained some important features which proved of general interest in the subsequent development of the Federalist constitutional system. Instead of building the new system around a new national house of representatives, as the Nationalists proposed, the authors of the New Jersey Plan proposed to keep the Congress as it was, adding to its powers those deemed necessary to correct the weaknesses of the government under the Articles of Confederation and establishing a separate federal executive and federal judiciary. The proposed federal executive was to be a plural executive, elected for fixed terms by the Congress and restricted to the enforcement of the laws, without any participation in their making, by means of a veto power or otherwise. The federal judiciary was to consist of a single supreme court appointed by the executive to serve during good behavior and vested with final authority to interpret the laws and presumably also the new Articles of Union. This federal executive would obviously have been a comparatively weak organ of the new government, but the new supreme court would have had a stronger position than that proposed in the Virginia Plan.

By proposing no direct representation of the people in the new constitutional system, the New Jersey planners misjudged the temper of the

Philadelphia Convention. The combination of state-rights dogmatists, state Confederationists, and delegates from small states could control only four state delegations—New York, New Jersey, Delaware, and Maryland. The other seven states rejected the New Jersey Plan, and the Committee of the Whole reported to the Convention that further proceedings should be based upon the proposals of the Virginians, objectionable though their plan was in several important respects. But the New Jersey planners had presented a scheme for maintaining a reign of law to which the Convention would return. When a way should be found for combining this scheme with another for establishing the sovereignty of the people in some suitable form, the first task of the Convention would be achieved.

This achievement was accomplished under the leadership of the delegation from Connecticut. Judge Ellsworth and Dr. Johnson cast the vote of Connecticut for proceeding under the Virginia Plan, because they shared the Virginians' desire for a national House of Representatives to protect the national interest as understood by a majority of the people. But they could not share the Virginians' desire for an upper branch of the supreme legislature dedicated to the protection of the special interests of property owners, especially the owners of large amounts of property. They believed that the state governments were the best servants of the people within their proper sphere of action. They were not interested in forming a highly centralized national government in order to protect the people of the states against the abuse of power of their own state governments. They were more concerned with preserving sufficient authority in the states to protect their peoples against the abuse of power by a strong national government. To effectuate this purpose it was essential to utilize the upper branch of the proposed national legislature as the special agent of the states in the government of the more perfect Union.

History has no particular name for these Connecticut delegates, who were the principal contributors to the solution of the problem of distributing power between the new and stronger central government and the existing state governments. In default of a name sanctioned by ancient usage we may most conveniently call them Unionists. Their special contribution rested upon their belief that sovereign power could be divided in a properly designed constitutional system between the central government and the local governments in the states. In the nineteenth century the so-called positive school of jurists convinced themselves that sovereignty is indivisible and hence must be located either in the central government or in the state governments. But in the eighteenth century, when belief in the ultimate supremacy of a law higher than any man-made law was widespread and deeply rooted, there was no difficulty in accepting the doctrine that sovereignty in the realm of man-made law is not absolute but limited and hence divisible. The more perfect Union, therefore, should be both a union of states and a union of people. Instead of a national government or a federal government in the original sense of the term, there should be a general government of a national-federal union.

The Connecticut delegation, as experienced parliamentarians and skillful political tacticians, accepted the Virginia Plan as a point of departure in designing a stronger and more suitable central government for the more perfect Union, because they also believed that they could more easily get agreement upon the kind of union they wanted by amending the Virginia Plan than by substituting for it an alternative plan based upon a radically different principle. Their first tactical move was to substitute for the expression, *national government,* the more equivocal but also more politic expression, *government of the United States.* But their main emphasis lay upon the importance of making what came to be known as the Senate of the United States a body in which the states should be represented in their corporate capacity as separate bodies politic. The Connecticut delegates, since they represented a state which at that time was not strictly speaking a small state but one of the middle rank, were not greatly concerned whether the states were represented in the Senate equally or in proportion to some rough measure of their relative importance. In either case, being an average state, Connecticut would get the same representation. But the Connecticut delegates preferred equal representation of the states in the Senate, because equality would be more consistent with their view that the states should be represented as separate bodies politic and not as divisions of the whole body of the American people. They believed in popular government for the more perfect Union, based upon the concurrence of majorities both of the whole nation and of the peoples of the several states.

The concept of the new constitutional system held by the Connecticut delegation may be further defined by comparison with the positions of the other factions which were critical of the Virginia Plan. The Unionists rejected as excessively unrealistic the dogmatic devotion to the doctrine of state sovereignty best represented by Luther Martin. They rejected as untimely opportunism the extreme caution exhibited by the Confederationists. They rejected as unseemly un-Americanism the extreme devotion of the small-state faction to the interests of the small states. They could not go along with the authors of the New Jersey Plan when the latter were supporting a plan which made no provision for a national House of Representatives. . . .

The triumph of what American history has called federalism was not of course a victory for federalism as the term was understood at the beginning of the Convention. But it was a victory for the spirit of moderation in politics, for even-tempered leadership, and for that opportunistic sense of what is possible that has usually characterized the most successful American politicians. So close were the votes in the Convention which led to the adoption of the Connecticut Compromise that a superficial critic might ascribe the outcome to accident or chance rather than to sound political judgment and astute tactical leadership. But it is clear that the final result was more acceptable to the American people than the alternative would have been, and that the delegates were moved by a subtle perception of popular sentiment more potent than formal arguments on the Convention floor. Washington's intervention on the last day of the Convention, for the purpose of giving a somewhat more popular cast to the arrangements for establishing the bicameral legislative system in the new Constitution, shows his awareness of the essential character of the American way in politics. But the American way put an end to the use of the word *federalist* to describe a specific category in a logical classification of forms of government. For Americans, federalism means simply that special mixture of original federalism and nationalism which is embodied in the actual constitutional system It is not a rational but an empirical concept.

CHECKS AND BALANCES

If the first purpose of sound constitutional planning is to create a government capable of controlling the governed, the second, the authors of the Virginia Plan believed, is to oblige the government to control itself. This way of thinking inclined a large majority of the delegates toward the favorite political idea of the eighteenth century in the English-speaking world. It is the experience of the ages, the French political philosopher Montesquieu had written in his celebrated work, *L'Esprit des Lois,* that every man is capable of abusing power and, if he attains it, is likely to do so. He presses forward until he finds his limit. If power is not to be abused, Montesquieu concluded, then in the nature of things it is necessary that power be made a check to power. The authors of the Virginia Plan were convinced that American experience was in harmony with that of the ages. They agreed with Montesquieu that the political maxim which he derived from universal experience was indeed consistent with the nature of things.

The Virginia planners allowed no exception to this maxim for governments based on the principle of popular sovereignty. A majority of the people in a popular government, like lesser portions of mankind, they believed, were capable of abusing their power and were likely to do so unless restrained by suitable constitutional limitations. Most of the framers, though born loyal subjects of a king, had come to believe in popular government. Few believed, however, that the representatives of a sovereign people would be wholly free from the natural faults which they associated with all possessors of governmental power. As Madison put it, "a dependence on the people is, no doubt, the primary control of the government, but experience has taught mankind the necessity of auxiliary precautions."

The Virginia planners proceeded upon the assumption that the most important "auxiliary precaution" would be an efficient system of checks and balances. They proposed, therefore, that the danger of the abuse of power by a supreme house of representatives should be met by three different kinds of checks which they hoped would keep the national government in a durable state of balanced equilibrium. The first of these would be produced by a division of the supreme legislature into two branches, one of which would be designed to represent that particular minority of the nation which they deemed most likely to be the victim of the abuse of power by the representatives of a majority of the people. The second would be produced by the creation of a strong and independent executive branch of the government. The third, by the creation of a strong and independent judiciary.

The Virginia planners' belief, that the minority of the nation most in need of special protection against the abuse of power by the representatives of a majority of the people would be the larger property owners, was expressed by several of the Nationalist delegates with astonishing candor. Foremost among the advocates of special representation for property owners in the proposed bicameral Congress was Alexander Hamilton. Expounding his personal political philosophy in an elaborate speech on the floor of the Convention, he declared, according to Madison's *Debates*, that "in every community where industry is encouraged there will be a division of it into the few and the many. Hence separate interests will arise. . . . Give all power to the many, they will oppress the few. Give all power to the few, they will oppress the many." . . .

The representatives of the rich in the Convention of 1787 were apparently in a position to frame a government which would assure them of protection against the poor, if they had deemed it right and proper to do so. Two thirds of the delegates were wealthy planters or merchants, or professional men connected with the families of wealthy planters or merchants and largely dependent upon these groups for clients and professional success. They composed a majority of the delegations from nine of the states represented in the Convention. If these delegates had wished to act as Gouverneur Morris asserted that the rich were universally disposed to act, they could easily have dominated the proceedings in their own interest. In fact, the arguments of Hamilton and Morris seemed to fall on deaf ears, and their ideas for the structure of the Senate were rejected by the Convention. Doubtless circumstances conspired against them. Be that as it may, there is no evidence from the record of debates that the Convention was interested in theoretical speculations concerning the nature of the class struggle.

In the state ratifying conventions there were some discussions of the class struggle among the American people. A view strongly represented in these discussions was that the essential character of the American class system was determined by the existence of three rather than merely two classes. These were the upper class, the lower class, and an intermediate or middle class. The former consisted of the relatively few who were rich; the second class, of the more numerous groups who were poor. But the bulk of the population, the independent farmers in the open country and the more or less skilled handicraftsmen and tradesmen in the towns, formed a middle class which in most parts of the country, the argument ran, was more numerous than the poor and much more influential in local politics. . . .

In the federal Convention there were no small farmers or artisans, although there were more than a few delegates who had begun life in humble circumstances. Approximately one third of the delegates, mostly lawyers, were not directly connected with wealthy landowners or mercantile families and were well qualified to speak for the middle class or for the average man both in the open country and in the towns. Outstanding among them was Franklin, who had left a middle-class home in Boston to seek his fortune in what was then the frontier town of Philadelphia. Franklin's sensational success qualified him for a place in the aristocracy, if he had wished it, but he retained throughout his long life a natural sympathy with the average man which enabled him to speak for that typical American with greater authority than any other member of the Convention. In the debate on the qualifications of voters for representatives in the popular branch of the Congress, he stressed the importance of keeping the requirements low so that the United States would continue to attract the better sort of immigrants from Europe, who liked the country because of its liberal treatment of the common people and who contributed greatly to its prosperity. No delegate ventured to contradict him, and his interposition in the debate brought it to an end. Unspoken awareness of the importance of the middle class in the politics of the states and of the necessity of procuring its consent to the projected new constitutional system was a silent but impelling factor in all the Convention deliberations relating to the principle of checks and balances. . . .

The problems of the Nationalists were further complicated by strong opposition to any system of checks and balances. Franklin, who had enjoyed ample opportunity to study the vaunted British parliamentary system of checks and balances at close range and had formed a low opinion of its alleged merits, was an avowed leader of this opposition. He would doubtless have preferred something like the system of ministerial leadership and cabinet government which eventually developed in Great Britain, but no one in 1787 could imagine such a system, though it was actually beginning to develop at that very time under the inspired guidance of the younger Pitt. Judge Sherman, another active leader of the opposition to the checks and balances system, would apparently have preferred something more like the present Swiss system of a plural executive. But he and other leading Confederationists contented themselves at this stage of the proceedings in the Convention with advocating an important rival principle of government, that of the separation of powers.

The principle of the separation of powers was embodied with exemplary logic in the New Jersey Plan. Each of the three kinds of power —legislative, executive, and judicial—was to be vested in a separate branch of the proposed general government. No one of these branches was expressly endowed with any portion of the power of the other branches. There was no question of a balance between them. The New Jersey Plan would have led directly to a system of legislative supremacy. The chief protection against an abuse of power by the Congress would have been a strict interpretation of the lawmaking authority to be expressly delegated to it by the revised Articles of Confederation. Presumably the framers of the New Jersey Plan relied on patriotic jurymen, encouraged and guided by suitable declarations of rights, to refuse to convict persons prosecuted under federal legislation which in their opinion might be unconstitutional. . . .

The immediate question was, will the Convention give the judicial branch of the new central government a sufficiently independent and strong position to enable it to make effective use of its novel power? To provide an acceptable answer to this question was the task of the Committee on Postponed Matters and Unfinished Business, the last of the Grand Committees appointed to work out suitable compromises between the contending factions in the Convention. Judge Brearley was the chairman of this committee, Judge Sherman was an active member, and John Dickinson was also present. The original Nationalists, as well as the original Confederationists, were also strongly represented. The result was a compromise which was warmly supported by these two leading factions. It was equally acceptable to the leading Unionists. Its adoption cemented the union of all those delegates who now agreed to call themselves Federalists.

The independence of both the executive and the judiciary was made as secure as was possible under the conditions of the age. Instead of being named by Congress, the President was to be elected by a novel and complicated process intended to reduce the influence of the Congress to a minimum. Since direct popular elections in a single nation-wide constituency were deemed impracticable under the then existing conditions, the committee devised a scheme for choosing state electoral colleges with a membership equal to the total number of a state's representation in the Congress in a manner to be determined by each state for itself and authorizing them in turn to vote for two candidates for President. The electors were forbidden to vote for two candidates from the same state, thus insuring a wide distribution of the electoral votes. . . .

The committee was more happily inspired in providing for the independence of the judiciary. Instead of the election of the Supreme Court by the Senate, the judges were to be appointed by the President, subject to the approval of the Senate. Thus a firmer foundation was supplied for the development of the judicial veto. On the other hand, the Supreme Court was deprived of its previous jurisdiction over impeachments. This potentially political exercise of the judicial power was transferred to the Congress, where it might serve to counterbalance the potentially political exercise of the power of judicial review of legislative and executive acts. These changes were obvious departures from the principle of the separation of powers. They were, however, potentially important contributions to an effective system of checks and balances.

The Convention, impatient as usual with theoretical discussions, gave little attention, when the report of this last of the Grand Committees was under discussion, to the comparative merits of the two great principles, that of the separation of powers and that of checks and balances. The former was embodied most emphatically in the text of the Constitution. The executive power was vested in the President of the United

States. The judicial power was vested in the Supreme Court and in such inferior courts as the Congress might establish. All legislative powers granted to the new central government were vested in the Congress. But portions of the executive and judicial powers were also in fact granted to the Congress. The Senate, for instance, was authorized to advise the President in the matter of appointments to office and to veto (by withholding its consent) those it should deem inadvisable, and both branches of the Congress were made judges of the elections and qualifications of members.

On the other hand, the exercise of legislative powers by the Congress might be checked by the separate executive and judicial vetoes. Whether an effective balance would result would depend on the way these potentially important powers should be used. Doubtless the Convention thought of them primarily as weapons for the defense of the executive and judicial branches against trespasses on their independence by aggressive Congresses. But they might be used as offensive weapons by ambitious and vigorous chief executives and judges bent on enforcing their own views of sound public policy. Washington and his leading associates in the Convention did not try to pierce the mysteries of a distant future. They seemed content that the new Constitution should have good prospects of lasting long enough to give the reconstructed constitutional system a fair trial. This, they believed, would be a reasonable expectation, if the Constitution were ratified by at least nine of the thirteen states. . . .

In view of all these uncertainties the framers of the Constitution could not be sure how the system of checks would operate in practice or whether an effective balance between the principal constitutional officers would be established. On the whole, nevertheless, the protagonists of the principle of checks and balances seemed to have put their mark on the finished document more heavily than those of the principle of the separation of powers. The original Nationalist leaders together with their new allies, operating under the name of Federalists, succeeded in procuring support for the new Constitution by accredited spokesmen for all the states represented in the Convention at its close, and, subject to the implicit promise of an eventual bill of rights, they managed to obtain its prompt ratification by conventions in eleven of the thirteen states. They won for themselves the opportunity to make a fair trial of its merits. It was a magnificent performance in the art of practical politics which has justly earned for them a high place in the history of the science of government.

PLURALISM

The third of the "auxiliary precautions," which Madison, writing in *The Federalist* in support of the new Constitution, considered necessary for preventing the abuse of power by popular majorities in a government of a sovereign people, involved a reliance upon a principle which we would now call *pluralism*. Madison's primary "precaution" against what he considered a dangerous preponderance of power in the proposed national House of Representatives was of course the system of checks and balances. A secondary "precaution," namely federalism, had been forced on the Nationalists by the exigencies of the struggle in the Philadelphia Convention to form a more perfect Union. The final "precaution," to which Madison gave no particular name, was more agreeable to his way of thinking.

Pluralism, regarded as a constitutional principle, is based on the observation that there are natural limits to the power of numerical majorities of the people in a popular government. These natural limits spring from the natural differences among the people in a population large enough to constitute a durable sovereign state. The larger the state, the greater the variety and importance of these differences will normally be, and the greater also, therefore, will be their limiting effect on the formation of popular majorities capable of exploiting their power for the advancement of their own special interests. In general their effect, Madison believed, would be to put substantial obstacles in the way of organizing popular majorities into factions or parties capable of dominating representative bodies. Thus he reached the comfortable conclusion that in a state the size of the more perfect Union this "precaution" would be more effective than in any single state or combination of states within the Union. . . .

The whole proceedings in connection with these compromises showed how right Madison was in thinking that the variety of special and local interests in a country as large as the United States would offer formidable obstacles to the formation of durable combinations of factions capable of dominating the legislative process in the national House of Representatives.

Nevertheless the timely and impressive success of the Committee on Postponed Matters and Unfinished Business made General Washington the leader of the first national political party in the more perfect Union. The original Nationalists contributed two states to the support of his leadership. The original Confederationists and their small-state allies contributed four more. The Unionists of various kinds contributed the other five states which composed the Convention at this stage of its proceedings. It was a masterly performance in the rare art of making a revolution without resort to physical force and violence. . . .

The successful fight for ratification of the Constitution confirmed the ascendancy of the Federalists, but it did not lead immediately to a two-party system in national politics. Many of the necessary conditions for a two-party system were present at the time, but one important condition was lacking. The opposition to Federalist leadership and policies was not a national opposition but rather an unorganized group of state oppositions. Those oppositions represented the first appearance of the great American West in national politics, but it appeared in the form of local factions which may be described as uncoordinated "state wests." Their time would come with the arrival on the national political scene of leadership capable of organizing them into a single national party.

In the Philadelphia Convention there was little consideration of national party systems. The principle of pluralism encouraged the belief that durable national parties would be exceedingly difficult to organize and the hope that the organization of more than one at a time would be impracticable. A few imaginative members of the Convention, notably Gouverneur Morris and Oliver Ellsworth, speculated on the prospects for national parties. They observed that the "outs" would strive to combine against the "ins" in order to take their places in the government, but they did not venture to predict the kind of party system that might emerge from such factious strife. No delegate, as has been noted, foresaw the effect on factiousness and partisanship of the novel scheme finally adopted for nominating the electing Presidents. No one indeed seems to have anticipated the commanding role which presidential nominations and elections would eventually play in the organization of parties. With the advantage of hindsight it is clear that the peculiar system which was provided for choosing the chief executive made a two-party system of national politics inevitable. But at the time, the Federalist chieftains were preoccupied with the task of making a success out of an improvised one-party system. An unplanned party system of this kind formed an indispensable component of the new constitutional system.

The truth is that the framers of the Constitution of 1787 did not contemplate a system of party government for the more perfect Union. They looked forward to government by superior persons, a natural aristocracy, rather than to a constitutional system which they would have called democratic. They gave little thought to the eventual development of an unwritten constitution, which would supplement and in part transform the written Constitution which they had produced with so much effort and—it must be recognized—skill. But they did produce a national political party as well as a national-federal Constitution. It was a major, though unplanned, contribution to the development of the American constitutional system.

CHAPTER 16

THE FOUNDING FATHERS

In the foregoing selection, we examined the framing of the Federal Constitution in light of the basic constitutional principles that emerged in that document. In Chapter 14, we considered national affairs under the Articles of Confederation and were introduced to the "revisionist" view of the founding fathers as self-interested conservatives who feared democracy and repudiated the political heritage of the Revolution. The nineteenth-century traditional image of the framers of the Constitution as an assemblage of all-wise, farsighted demigods who, in a single stroke, produced the world's greatest political document is still prevalent. A third generation of historians of the Revolutionary era accepts neither the traditionalist nor the revisionist point of view.

The next selection focuses directly on the founding fathers. Stanley Elkins and Eric McKitrick, members of the third generation of historians, are unsatisfied with the two older, symbolic images of the founding fathers—the traditional "father" image and the revisionist "conservative" image. In their article, "The Founding Fathers: Young Men of the Revolution," they point out that recent research and writing on the framers is still in progress, and that, as yet, no new, clear, and systematic point of view has emerged. Elkins and McKitrick suggest that the new work will not be complete nor satisfactory until a new, symbolic image of the Founding Fathers is created to replace the old tired ones. In this selection, these authors search for such an image.

The first question which the student should consider in reading this selection is why, in the opinion of the authors, a fresh *symbolic* image of the Founding Fathers is necessary to an understanding of the Revolutionary era of United States history. Do you agree with this basic contention of the authors? Second, in what aspects of the history of this period do the authors find the basis for a new image of the Federalist framers and supporters of the Constitution? Third, what constituted the real struggle between the Federalists and the Anti-Federalists? In seeking to identify the basic source of conflict over the Constitution, what do Elkins and McKitrick suggest about the revisionist argument that the fight was fundamentally one between the conservatives and the democrats, between the man of property and the propertyless, and between the nationalists and the champions of localism? Finally, do you believe that this selection tends to humanize the Founding Fathers, thus making them more understandable to us today?

Cecilia Kenyon, "Men of Little Faith: The Anti-Federalists on the Nature of Representative Government," *William and Mary Quarterly,* XII (January, 1955), and Merrill Jensen, *The New Nation** (1950), present ideas that Elkins and McKitrick find useful. Both can be read with profit by the interested student. Carl Degler has an excellent, broadly interpretive essay on the Revolutionary and Constitutional eras in *Out of Our Past: The Forces that Shaped Modern America** (1958).

* Available in a paperback edition.

THE FOUNDING FATHERS: YOUNG MEN OF THE REVOLUTION
STANLEY ELKINS AND ERIC McKITRICK

The intelligent American of today may know a great deal about his history, but the chances are that he feels none too secure about the Founding Fathers and the framing and ratification of the Federal Constitution. He is no longer certain what the "enlightened" version of that story is, or even whether there is one. This is because, in the century and three quarters since the Constitution was written, our best thinking on that subject has gone through two dramatically different phases and is at this moment about to enter a third.

Americans in the nineteenth century, whenever they reviewed the events of the founding, made reference to an Olympian gathering of wise and virtuous men who stood splendidly above all faction, ignored petty self-interest, and concerned themselves only with the freedom and well-being of their fellow-countrymen. This attitude toward the Fathers has actually never died out; it still tends to prevail in American history curricula right up through most of the secondary schools. But bright young people arriving at college have been regularly discovering, for nearly the last fifty years, that in the innermost circle this was regarded as an old-fashioned, immensely oversimplified, and rather dewy-eyed view of the Founding Fathers and their work. Ever since J. Allen Smith and Charles Beard wrote in the early years of the twentieth century, the "educated" picture of the Fathers has been that of a group not of disinterested patriots but of hard-fisted conservatives who were looking out for their own interests and those of their class. According to this worldlier view, the document which they wrote—and in which they embodied these interests—was hardly intended as a thrust toward popular and democratic government. On the contrary, its centralizing tendencies all reflected the Fathers' distrust of the local and popular rule which had been too little restrained under the Articles of Confederation. The authors

SOURCE. Stanley Elkins and Eric McKitrick, "The Founding Fathers: Young Men of the Revolution," *The Political Science Quarterly,* LXVII (June 1961), pp. 181–216. Reprinted by permission of the authors.

of the Constitution represented the privileged part of society. Naturally, then, their desire for a strong central government was, among other things, an effort to achieve solid national guarantees for the rights of property—rights not adequately protected under the Articles—and to obtain for the propertied class (their own) a favored position under the new government.

This "revisionist" point of view—that of the Founding Fathers as self-interested conservatives—has had immeasurable influence in the upper reaches of American historical thought. Much of what at first seemed audacious to the point of lèse majesté came ultimately to be taken as commonplace. The Tory-like, almost backward-turning quality which this approach has imparted to the picture of constitution-making even renders it plausible to think of the Philadelphia Convention of 1787 as a counter-revolutionary conspiracy, which is just the way a number of writers have actually described it. That is, since the Articles of Confederation were the product of the Revolution, to overthrow the Articles was—at least symbolically—to repudiate the Revolution. The Declaration of Independence and the Constitution represented two very different, and in some ways opposing, sets of aspirations; and (so the reasoning goes) the Philadelphia Convention was thus a significant turning-away from, rather than an adherence to, the spirit of the Declaration.

In very recent years, however, a whole new cycle of writing and thinking and research has been underway; the revisionists of the previous generation are themselves being revised. The economic ideas of the late Professor Beard, which dominated this field for so long, have been partially if not wholly discredited. And yet many of the old impressions, intermingled with still older ones, persist. Much of the new work, moreover, though excellent and systematic, is still in progress. Consequently the entire subject of the Constitution and its creation has become a little murky; new notions having the clarity and assuredness of the old have not as yet fully emerged; and meanwhile one is not altogether certain what to think.

Before the significance of all this new work can be justly assessed, and before consistent themes in it may be identified with any assurance, an effort should be made to retrace somewhat the psychology of previous conceptions. At the same time, it should be recognized that any amount of fresh writing on this subject will continue to lack something until it can present us with a clear new symbolic image of the Fathers themselves. The importance of this point lies in the function that symbols have for organizing the historical imagination, and the old ones are a little tired. The "father" image is well and good, and so also in certain respects is the "conservative" one. But we may suppose that these men saw themselves at the time as playing other rôles too, rôles that did not partake so much of retrospection, age, and restraint as those which would come to be assigned to them in after years. The Republic is now very old, as republics go, yet it *was* young once, and so were its founders. With youth goes energy, and the "energy" principle may be more suggestive now, in reviewing the experience of the founding, than the principle of paternal conservatism. . . .

IV

The work of Merrill Jensen, done in the 1930's and 1940's, has suffered somewhat in reputation due to the sweep and vehemence of the anti-Beardian reaction. Yet that work contains perceptions which ought not to be written off in the general shuffle. They derive not so much from the over-all Beardian traditions and influences amid which Jensen wrote, as from that particular sector of the subject which he marked off and preëmpted for his own. Simply by committing himself —alone among Beardians and non-Beardians—to presenting the Confederation era as a legitimate phase of American history, entitled to be taken seriously like any other and having a positive side as well as a negative one, he has forced upon us a peculiar point of view which, by the same token, yields its own special budget of insights. For example, Jensen has been profoundly impressed by the sheer force, determination, and drive of such nationalist leaders as Hamilton, Madison, Jay, Knox, and the Morrises. This energy, he feels, created the central problem of the Confederation and was the major cause of its collapse. He deplores this, seeing in the Confederation "democratic" virtues which it probably never had, finding in the Federalists an "aristocratic" character which in actual fact was as much or more to be found in the Anti-Federalists, smelling plots everywhere, and in general shaping his nomenclature to fit his own values and preferences. But if Professor Jensen seems to have called everything by the wrong name, it is well to remember that nomenclature is not everything. The important thing—what does ring true— is that this driving "nationalist" energy was, in all probability, central to the movement that gave the United States a new government.

The other side of the picture, which does not seem to have engaged Jensen's mind half so much, was the peculiar sloth and inertia of the Anti-Federalists. Cecilia Kenyon, in a brilliant essay on these men,[1] has

---

[1] "Men of Little Faith: The Anti-Federalists on the Nature of Representative Government," *William and Mary Quarterly,* XII, 3rd ser. (January 1955), pp. 3–43.

shown them as an amazingly reactionary lot. They were transfixed by the specter of power. It was not the power of the aristocracy that they feared, but power of any kind, democratic or otherwise, that they could not control for themselves. Their chief concern was to keep governments as limited and as closely tied to local interests as possible. Their minds could not embrace the concept of a national interest which they themselves might share and which could transcend their own parochial concerns. Republican government that went beyond the compass of state boundaries was something they could not imagine. Thus the chief difference between Federalists and Anti-Federalists had little to do with "democracy" (George Clinton and Patrick Henry were no more willing than Gouverneur Morris to trust the innate virtue of the people), but rather in the Federalists' conviction that there was such a thing as national interest and that a government could be established to care for it which was fully in keeping with republican principles. To the Federalists this was not only possible but absolutely necessary, if the nation was to avoid a future of political impotence, internal discord, and in the end foreign intervention. So far so good. But still, exactly how did such convictions get themselves generated?

Merrill Jensen has argued that the Federalists, by and large, were reluctant revolutionaries who had feared the consequences of a break with England and had joined the Revolution only when it was clear that independence was inevitable. The argument is plausible; few of the men most prominent later on as Federalists had been quite so hot for revolution in the very beginning as Patrick Henry and Samuel Adams. But this may not be altogether fair; Adams and Henry were already veteran political campaigners at the outbreak of hostilities, while the most vigorous of the future Federalists were still mere youngsters. The argument, indeed, could be turned entirely around: the source of Federalist, or nationalist, energy was not any "distaste" for the Revolution on these men's part, but rather their profound and growing involvement in it.

Much depends here on the way one pictures the Revolution. In the beginning it simply consisted of a number of state revolts loosely directed by the Continental Congress; and for many men, absorbed in their effort to preserve the independence of their own states, it never progressed much beyond that stage even in the face of invasion. But the Revolution had another aspect, one which developed with time and left a deep imprint on those connected with it, and this was its character as a continental war effort. If there is any one feature that most unites the future leading supporters of the Constitution, it was their close engagement with this continental aspect of the Revolution. A remarkably large number of these someday Federalists were in the Continental Army, served as diplomats or key administrative officers of the Confederation government, or, as members of Congress, played leading rôles on those committees primarily responsible for the conduct of the war.

Merrill Jensen has compiled two lists, with nine names in each, of the men whom he considers to have been the leading spirits of the Federalists and Anti-Federalists respectively. It would be well to have a good look at this sample. The Federalists—Jensen calls them "nationalists"—were Robert Morris, John Jay, James Wilson, Alexander Hamilton, Henry Knox, James Duane, George Washington, James Madison, and Gouverneur Morris. Washington, Knox, and Hamilton were deeply involved in Continental military affairs; Robert Morris was Superintendent of Finance; Jay was president of the Continental Congress and minister plenipotentiary to Spain (he would later be appointed Secretary for Foreign Affairs); Wilson, Duane, and Gouverneur Morris were members of Congress, all three being active members of the war committees. The Anti-Federalist group presents a very different picture. It consisted of Samuel Adams, Patrick Henry, Richard Henry Lee, George Clinton, James Warren, Samuel Bryan, George Bryan, George Mason, and Elbridge Gerry. Only three of these—Gerry, Lee, and Adams—served in Congress, and the latter two fought consistently against any effort to give Congress executive powers. Their constant preoccupation was state sovereignty rather than national efficiency. Henry and Clinton were active war governors, concerned primarily with state rather than national problems, while Warren, Mason, and the two Bryans were essentially state politicians.

The age difference between these two groups is especially striking. The Federalists were on the average ten to twelve years younger than the Anti-Federalists. At the outbreak of the Revolution George Washington, at 44, was the oldest of the lot; six were under 35 and four were in their twenties. Of the Anti-Federalists, only three were under 40 in 1776, and one of these, Samuel Bryan, the son of George Bryan, was a boy of 16.

This age differential takes on a special significance when it is related to the career profiles of the men concerned. Nearly half of the Federalist group—Gouverneur Morris, Madison, Hamilton, and Knox—quite literally saw their careers launched in the Revolution. The remaining five—Washington, Jay, Duane, Wilson, and Robert Morris—though established in public affairs beforehand, became nationally known after 1776 and the wide public recognition which they subsequently achieved came first and foremost through their identification with the continental war effort. All of them had been united in an experience, and had formed commitments, which dissolved provincial boundaries; they had come to full public maturity in a setting which enabled ambition, public service, leadership, and self-fulfillment to be conceived, for each in his way, with a grandeur of scope unknown to any previous generation. The careers of the Anti-Federalists, on the other hand, were not only state-centered but—aside from those of Clinton, Gerry, and the young Bryan—rested heavily on events that preceded rather than followed 1776. . . .

The logic of these careers, then, was in large measure tied to a chronology which did not apply in the same way to all the men in public life during the two decades of the 1770's and 1780's. A significant proportion of relative newcomers, with prospects initially modest, happened to have their careers opened up at a particular time and in such a way that their very public personalities came to be staked upon the national quality of the experience which had formed them. In a number of outstanding cases energy, initiative, talent, and ambition had combined with a conception of affairs which had grown immense in scope and promise by the close of the Revolution. There is every reason to think that a contraction of this scope, in the years that immediately followed, operated as a powerful challenge.

V

The stages through which the constitutional movement proceeded in the 1780's add up to a fascinating story in political management, marked by no little élan and dash. That movement, viewed in the light of the Federalist leaders' commitment to the Revolution, raises some nice points as to who were the "conservatives" and who were the "radicals." The spirit of unity generated by the struggle for independence had, in the eyes of those most closely involved in coördinating the effort, lapsed; provincial factions were reverting to the old provincial ways. The impulse to arrest disorder and to revive the flame of revolutionary unity may be pictured in "conservative" terms, but this becomes quite awkward when we look for terms with which to picture the other impulse, so different in nature: the urge to rest, to drift, to turn back the clock.

Various writers have said that the activities of the Federalists during this period had in them a clear element of the conspiratorial. Insofar as this refers to a strong line of political strategy, it correctly locates a key element in the movement. Yet without a growing base of popular dissatisfaction with the status quo, the Federalists could have skulked and plotted forever without accomplishing anything. We now know, thanks to recent scholarship, that numerous elements of the public were only too ripe for change. But the work of organizing such a sentiment was quite another matter; it took an immense effort of will just to get it off the ground. Though it would be wrong to think of the Constitution as something that had to be carried in the face of deep and basic popular opposition, it certainly required a series of brilliant maneuvers to escape the deadening clutch of particularism and inertia. An Anti-Federalist "no" could register on exactly the same plane as a Federalist "yes" while requiring a fraction of the energy. It was for this reason that the Federalists, even though they cannot be said to have circumvented the popular will, did have to use techniques which in their sustained drive, tactical mobility, and risk-taking smacked more than a little of the revolutionary. . . .

Whether or not the years between 1783 and 1786 should be viewed as a "critical period" depends very much on whose angle they are viewed from. Although it was a time of economic depression, the depressed conditions were not felt in all areas of economic life with the same force, nor were they nearly as damaging in some localities as in others; the interdependence of economic enterprise was not then what it would become later on, and a depression in Massachusetts did not necessarily imply one in Virginia, or even in New York. Moreover, there were definite signs of improvement by 1786. Nor can it necessarily be said that government on the state level lacked vitality. Most of the states were addressing their problems with energy and decision. There were problems everywhere, of course, many of them very grave, and in some cases (those of New Jersey and Connecticut in particular) solutions seemed almost beyond the individual state's resources. Yet it would be wrong, as Merrill Jensen points out, to assume that no solutions were possible within the framework which then existed. It is especially important to remember that when most people thought of "the government" they were not thinking of Congress at all, but of their own state legislature. For them, therefore, it was by no means self-evident that the period through which they were living was one of drift and governmental impotence.

But through the eyes of men who had come to view the states collectively as a "country" and to think in continental terms, things looked altogether different. From their viewpoint the Confederation was fast approaching the point of ruin. Fewer and fewer states were meeting their requisition payments, and Congress could not even pay its bills. The states refused to accept any impost which they themselves could not control, and even if all the rest accepted, the continued refusal of New York (which was not likely to change) would render any impost all but valueless. Local fears and jealousies blocked all efforts to establish uniform regulation of commerce, even though some such regulation seemed indispensable. A number of the states, New York in particular, openly ignored the peace treaty with England and passed discriminatory legislation against former Loyalists; consequently England, using as a pretext Congress' inability to enforce the treaty, refused to surrender the northwest posts. Morale in Congress was very low as members complained that lack of a quorum prevented them most of the time from transacting any business; even when a quorum was present, a few negative votes could block important legislation indefinitely. Any significant change, or any substantial increase in the power of Congress, required unanimous approval by the states, and as things then stood this had become very remote. Finally, major states such as New York and Virginia were simply paying less and less attention to Congress. The danger was not so much that of a split with the Confederation—Congress lacked the strength that would make any such "split" seem very urgent—but rather a policy of neglect that would just allow Congress to wither away from inactivity.

These were the conditions that set the stage for a fresh effort—the Annapolis Convention of 1786—to strengthen the continental government. The year before, Madison had arranged a conference between Maryland and Virginia for the regulation of commerce on the Potomac, and its success had led John Tyler and Madison to propose a measure in the Virginia Assembly that would give Congress power to regulate commerce throughout the Confederation. Though nothing came of it, a plan was devised in its place whereby the several states would be invited to take part in a convention to be held at Annapolis in September, 1786, for the purpose of discussing commercial problems. The snapping-point came when delegates from only five states appeared. The rest either distrusted one another's intentions (the northeastern states doubted the southerners' interest in commerce) or else suspected a trick to strengthen the Confederation government at their expense. It was apparent that no serious action could be taken at that time. But the dozen delegates who did come (Hamilton and Madison being in their forefront) were by definition those most concerned over the state of the national government, and they soon concluded that their only hope of saving it lay in some audacious plenary gesture. It was at this meeting, amid the mortification of still another failure, that they planned the Philadelphia Convention.

The revolutionary character of this move—though some writers have correctly perceived it—has been obscured both by the stateliness of historical retrospection and by certain legal peculiarities which allowed the proceeding to appear a good deal less subversive than it actually was. The "report" of the Annapolis meeting was actually a call, drafted by

Hamilton and carefully edited by Madison, for delegates of all the states to meet in convention at Philadelphia the following May for the purpose of revising the Articles of Confederation. Congress itself transmitted the call, and in so doing was in effect being brought to by-pass its own constituted limits. On the one hand, any effort to change the government within the rules laid down by the Articles would have required a unanimous approval which could never be obtained. But on the other hand, the very helplessness which the several states had imposed upon the central government meant in practice that the states were sovereign and could do anything they pleased with it. It was precisely this that the nationalists now prepared to exploit: this legal paradox had hitherto prevented the growth of strong loyalty to the existing Confederation and could presently allow that same Confederation, through the action of the states, to be undermined in the deceptive odor of legitimacy. Thus the Beardian school of constitutional thought, for all its errors of economic analysis and its transposing of ideological semantics, has called attention to one element—the element of subversion—that is actually entitled to some consideration.

But if the movement had its plotters, balance requires us to add that the "plot" now had a considerable measure of potential support, and that the authority against which the plot was aimed had become little more than a husk. Up to this time every nationalist move, including the Annapolis Convention, had been easily blocked. But things were now happening in such a way as to tip the balance and to offer the nationalists for the first time a better-than-even chance of success. There had been a marked improvement in business, but shippers in Boston, New York, and Philadelphia were still in serious trouble. Retaliatory measures against Great Britain through state legislation had proved ineffective and useless; there was danger, at the same time, that local manufacturing interests might be successful in pushing through high state tariffs. In the second place, New York's refusal to reconsider a national impost, except on terms that would have removed its effectiveness, cut the ground from under the moderates who had argued that, given only a little time, everything could be worked out. This did not leave much alternative to a major revision of the national government. Then there were Rhode Island's difficulties with inflationary paper money. Although that state's financial schemes actually made a certain amount of sense, they provided the nationalists with wonderful propaganda and helped to create an image of parochial irresponsibility. . . .

We have already seen that nineteenth century habits of thought created a ponderous array of stereotypes around the historic Philadelphia conclave of 1787. Twentieth century thought and scholarship, on the other hand, had the task of breaking free from them, and to have done so is a noteworthy achievement. And yet one must return to the point that stereotypes themselves require some form of explanation. The legend of a transcendent effort of statesmanship, issuing forth in a miraculously perfect instrument of government, emerges again and again despite all efforts either to conjure it out of existence or to give it some sort of rational linkage with mortal affairs. Why should the legend be so extraordinarily durable, and was there anything so special about the circumstances that set it on its way so unerringly and so soon?

The circumstances *were,* in fact, special; given a set of delegates of well over average ability, the Philadelphia meeting provides a really classic study in the sociology of intellect. Divine accident, though in some measure present in men's doings always, is not required as a part of this particular equation. The key conditions were all present in a pattern that virtually guaranteed for the meeting an optimum of effectiveness. A sufficient number of states were represented so that the delegates could, without strain, realistically picture themselves as thinking, acting, and making decisions in the name of the entire nation. They themselves, moreover, represented interests throughout the country that were diverse enough, and they had enough personal prestige at home, that they could act in the assurance of having their decisions treated at least with respectful attention. There had also been at work a remarkably effective process of self-selection, as to both men and states. Rhode Island ignored the convention, and as a result its position was not even considered there. There were leading state particularists such as Patrick Henry and Richard Henry Lee who were elected as delegates but refused to serve. The Anti-Federalist position, indeed, was hardly represented at all, and the few men who did represent it had surprisingly little to say. Yates and Lansing simply left before the convention was over. Thus a group already predisposed in a national direction could proceed unhampered by the friction of basic opposition in its midst.

This made it possible for the delegates to "try on" various alternatives without having to remain accountable for everything they said. At the same time, being relieved from all outside pressures meant that the only way a man could expect to make a real difference in the convention's deliberations was to reach, through main persuasion, other men of considerable ability and experience. Participants and audience were therefore one, and this in itself imposed standards of debate which were quite exacting. In such a setting the best minds in the convention were accorded an authority which they would not have had in political debates aimed at an indiscriminate public.

Thus the elements of secrecy, the general inclination for a national government, and the process whereby the delegates came to terms with their colleagues—appreciating their requirements and adjusting to their interests—all combined to produce a growing esprit de corps. As initial agreements were worked out, it became exceedingly difficult for the Philadelphia delegates not to grow more and more committed to the product of their joint efforts. Indeed, this was in all likelihood the key mechanism, more important than any other in explaining not only the peculiar genius of the main compromises but also the general fitness of the document as a whole. That is, a group of two or more intelligent men who are subject to no cross-pressures and whose principal commitment is to the success of an idea, are perfectly capable—as in our scientific communities of today—of performing what appear to be prodigies of intellect. Moving, as it were, in the same direction with a specific purpose, they can function at maximum efficiency. It was this that the historians of the nineteenth century did in their way see, and celebrated with sweeping rhetorical flourishes, when they took for granted that if an occasion of this sort could not call forth the highest level of statesmanship available, then it was impossible to imagine another that could.

Once the Philadelphia Convention had been allowed to meet and the delegates had managed, after more than three months of work, to hammer out a document that the great majority of them could sign, the political position of the Federalists changed dramatically. Despite the major battles still impending, for practical purposes they now had the initiative. The principal weapon of the Anti-Federalists—inertia—had greatly declined in effectiveness, for with the new program in motion it was no longer enough simply to argue that a new federal government was unnecessary. They would have to take positive steps in blocking it; they would have to arouse the people and convince them that the Constitution represented a positive danger.

Moreover, the Federalists had set the terms of ratification in such a way as to give the maximum advantage to energy and purpose; the key choices, this time, had been so arranged that they would fall right. Only nine states had to ratify before the Constitution would go into effect. Not only would this rule out the possibility of one or two states holding up the entire effort, but it meant that the Confederation would be automatically destroyed as an alternative before the difficult battles in New York and Virginia had to be faced. (By then, Patrick Henry in Virginia would have nothing but a vague alliance with North Carolina to offer as a counter-choice.) Besides, there was good reason to believe that at least four or five states, and possibly as many as seven, could be counted as safe, which meant that serious fighting in the first phase would be limited to two or three states. And finally, conditions were so set that the "snowball" principle would at each successive point favor the Federalists.

As for the actual process of acceptance, ratification would be done through state conventions elected for the purpose. Not only would this circumvent the vested interests of the legislatures and the ruling coteries that frequented the state capitals, but it gave the Federalists two separate chances to make their case—once to the people and once to the conventions. If the elected delegates were not initially disposed to do the desired thing, there was still a chance, after the convention met, of persuading them. Due partly to the hampering factor of transportation and distance, delegates had to have considerable leeway of choice and what amounted to quasi-plenipotentiary powers. Thus there could be no such thing as a fully "instructed" delegation, and members might meanwhile remain susceptible to argument and conversion. The convention device, moreover, enabled the Federalists to run as delegates men who would not normally take part in state politics.

The revolutionary verve and ardor of the Federalists, their resources of will and energy, their willingness to scheme tirelessly, campaign everywhere, and sweat and agonize over every vote meant in effect that despite all the hairbreadth squeezes and rigors of the struggle, the Anti-Federalists would lose every crucial test. There was, to be sure, an Anti-Federalist effort. But with no program, no really viable commitments, and little purposeful organization, the Anti-Federalists somehow always managed to move too late and with too little. They would sit and watch their great stronghold, New York, being snatched away from them despite a two-to-one Anti-Federalists majority in a convention presided over by their own chief, George Clinton. To them, the New York Federalists must have seemed possessed of the devil. The Federalists' convention men included Alexander Hamilton, James Duane, John Jay, and Robert Livingston—who knew, as did everyone else, that the new government was doomed unless Virginia and New York joined it. They insisted on debating the Constitution section by section instead of as a whole, which meant that they could out-argue the Anti-Federalists on every substantive issue and meanwhile delay the vote until New Hampshire and Virginia had had a chance to ratify. (Madison and Hamilton had a horse relay system in readiness to rush the Virginia news northward as quickly as possible.) By the time the New York convention was ready to act, ten others had ratified, and at the final moment Hamilton and his allies spread the chilling rumor that New York City was about to secede from the state. The Anti-Federalists, who had had enough, directed a chosen number of their delegates to cross over, and solemnly capitulated.

In the end, of course, everyone "crossed over." The speed with which this occurred once the continental revolutionists had made their point, and the ease with which the Constitution so soon became an object of universal veneration, still stands as one of the minor marvels of American history. But the document did contain certain implications, of a quasi-philosophical nature, that make the reasons for this ready consensus not so very difficult to find. It established a national government whose basic outlines were sufficiently congenial to the underlying commitments of the whole culture—republicanism and capitalism—that the likelihood of its being the subject of a true ideological clash was never very real. That the Constitution should mount guard over the rights of property— "realty," "personalty," or any other kind—was questioned by nobody. There had certainly been a struggle, a long and exhausting one, but we should not be deceived as to its nature. It was not fought on economic grounds; it was not a matter of ideology; it was not, in the fullest and most fundamental sense, even a struggle between nationalism and localism. The key struggle was between inertia and energy; with inertia overcome, everything changed.

There were, of course, lingering objections and misgivings; many of the problems involved had been genuinely puzzling and difficult; and there remained doubters who had to be converted. But then the perfect bridge whereby all could become Federalists within a year was the addition of a Bill of Rights. After the French Revolution, anti-constitutionalism in France would be a burning issue for generations; in America, an anti-constitutional party was undreamed of after 1789. With the Bill of Rights, the remaining opponents of the new system could say that, ever watchful of tyranny, they had now got what they wanted. Moreover, the Young Men of the Revolution might at last imagine, after a dozen years of anxiety, that *their* Revolution had been a success.

CHAPTER 17

WASHINGTON:
THE FIRST PRESIDENT

He is "Freedom's myth" and "more than man," Virginia poet James Barron Hope wrote of Washington in 1858. Although not as well known as "Light-Horse Harry" Lee's eulogistic "first in war, first in peace and first in the hearts of his countrymen," Hope's words are more suggestive of Washington's apotheosis, the process by which, through the years, a mere mortal has become America's immortal Father-Hero. The Washington myth is so entrenched in the minds of Americans that Washington the man is virtually unknown, and his real greatness is generally unappreciated.

In this selection, J. A. Carroll seeks a more human Washington. Although Washington was well known to his contemporaries, and although his Administrations have been thoroughly researched by historians, the figure of Washington is still obscure. In particular, a persistent vagueness exists about his role as President. Professor Carroll suggests that an assessment of that role is not an easy task. Washington's character, he believes, is "better sensed than analyzed." Washington was a doer rather than a thinker, and he does not "emerge spontaneously in a pattern" but "appears gradually in a procession of events." Hence, Professor Carroll is concerned with the achievements of Washington's Administrations, concentrating on American avoidance of involvement in European wars. In the story of these achievements, a viable picture of Washington as a man as well as a President emerges.

In reading this essay, attempt to determine the kind of man Washington was and the kind of President he made. What were his major characteristics? To what extent was he his own President? Equally important, how can we explain the rise and the strength of the Washington myth? Here, the student should consider carefully Professor Carroll's suggestions about the relationship of reality to the creation and persistence of the legend.

Indispensible in a consideration of this topic is Bernard Mayo's delightful and penetrating essay on Washington in *Myths and Men: Patrick Henry, George Washington, Thomas Jefferson** (1959). Excellent interpretative essays on Washington and his administrations are found in Marcus Cunliffe, *The Nation Takes Shape: 1789–1837** (1959), and Esmond Wright, *The Fabric of Freedom: 1763–1800** (1961). Among the many useful biographies are Bernhard Knollenberg, *Washington and the Revolution* (1940), and D. S. Freeman, *George Washington,* 5 Vols. (1948-1952).

* Available in a paperback edition.

GEORGE WASHINGTON
JOHN A. CARROLL

Close to ten o'clock on the morning of April 16, 1789, a tall man in his fifty-seventh year, dressed for travel in blue broadcloth and black boots and holding a tricorn hat in his hand, stood for a very brief moment on the piazza at Mount Vernon. From here on a clear day he could see some distance down the several miles of river that bordered his plantation, and the broad and quiet Potomac always rested his spirit. But there was no time left to contemplate the view. Makers of history, unlike those who study it, seldom are allowed the pleasures of retrospection.

General George Washington, soldier of the Revolution and Virginia's foremost farmer, was ready to make a journey that would put him into a new career. Two days earlier he had received notice of his elevation, by the vote of every elector, to the office of President of the United States— and now his carriage was waiting. "I bade adieu to Mount Vernon, to private life, and to domestic felicity," he wrote that night in his diary, "and, with a mind oppressed with more anxious and painful sensations than I have words to express, set out for New York . . . with the best disposition to render service to my country in obedience to its call. . . ." A few miles up the road at Wise's Tavern, the citizens of Alexandria honored their neighbor with a farewell dinner. "Go," Mayor Ramsay exhorted the President-elect, "and make a grateful people happy."

As it soon proved, the people of the United States were grateful indeed in 1789 that General Washington had consented to serve as chief magistrate of their new republic. His eight-day journey to New York, the first capital city, was in the manner of a triumphal procession of a Roman conqueror. At Baltimore, at Wilmington, at Philadelphia, at every town and coach stop along the route he was fêted with the pealing of bells, gun salutes, toasts and huzzas, gratulatory speeches and odes, parades and public banquets, and pyrotechnics through the night. The people of Trenton, eager to excel in their demonstration, provided a caparisoned

SOURCE. J. A. Carroll, "George Washington," in Morton Borden, ed., *America's Ten Greatest Presidents,* Chicago: Rand McNally, 1961, pp. 5–30. Copyright 1961 by Rand McNally & Co. Reprinted by permission of Rand McNally & Co. and the editor.

white horse which Washington rode as ladies sung to him and children threw flowers in his path. Finally, after crossing Newark Bay in a festooned barge with a train of flag-flying small craft in his wake, the President-elect was met at the Battery by thousands of New Yorkers. The crowd was so dense, and so determined to applaud and admire, that it took Washington almost an hour to make his way from the wharf to the "Executive Mansion" nearby at No. 3 Cherry Street. If this was adulation in the extreme, if it was almost idolatry, it was something deeper also. Here, unmistakably, was a manifestation of the ebullient hopes of a people recently free and a nation freshly born.

Of the several presidents of the United States who have served their countrymen memorably in critical periods, none experienced so full a measure of public esteem in the hour of inauguration as George Washington. No chief executive has entered office better known to his contemporaries. From New England to Georgia in 1789 Washington was celebrated as the American Atlas, the American Fabius, the Cincinnatus of the Western Hemisphere; for almost a decade now he had heard references to himself as "Father of his Country." In 1783, upon retirement to his farm after eight years as Commander in Chief of the Continental Army, he was by all odds the most famous man in America. Even as proprietor of Mount Vernon he had been conspicuous, a kind of national host whose beautiful home on the Potomac became, as he said, a "well-resorted tavern" for unexpected and unannounced travelers of every type. His appearance at the Philadelphia Convention in 1787 brought him again into public view, and the architects and advertisers of the Constitution were quick to dramatize the fact that General Washington had presided at the rebuilding of the old Articles of Confederation into the "New Roof of Federalism." So familiar was his name by 1788 that no other could be mentioned seriously for the highest office in the new system of government. . . . The first presidential election was a formality in the strictest sense, and unanimity was inevitable. The soldier-farmer from Virginia was the one American that his fellow-citizens, be they Federalists or "anti-Feds," knew best of all.

It is curious, then, that perhaps no president has proven more mysterious to posterity than the first. Historians have found it reasonably easy to chronicle the events of Washington's two administrations because the records and literary remains of the years 1789-97 are abundant. They have been able to dissect and to understand the opposite philosophies, social and economic, of the dominant personalities of the period, Alexander Hamilton and Thomas Jefferson. In detailed monographs they have shown how the clashing concepts of these two men ignited a political fire which, despite Washington's avowed determination to "walk on a straight line" and to act as "President of all the people," quickly divided the nation into sectional parties—Federalists following Hamilton north-ward and eastward, Republican-Democrats following Jefferson southward and westward. Scholars have identified party strife in the United States with the revolutionary upheavals that convulsed Europe in the 1790's, and possibly some have gone too far in ascribing "Anglomania" to Feder-alist leaders and "Gallomania" to Republicans. Washington's administra-tions, in any case, have been much discussed by modern historians. Their specialized studies fill a long shelf, and their conclusions are distilled accurately in many textbooks. Yet, to Americans in the twentieth century, President Washington presents something of an enigma. Confi-dent as we may be that we understand the period, we do not always understand the man. . . .

Like a good poem, George Washington's character is perhaps better sensed than analyzed. It is better, in any case, to contemplate Washington in full size than to examine him by synthetic lens. Washington was not an architect in ideas; he was essentially a man of deeds. His thoughts do not array themselves in a convenient constellation that may be understood in outline; rather they form a massive milky way that must be considered from end to end. Washington does not emerge spontaneously in a pattern; he appears gradually in a procession of events. He is best portrayed not in composite overview, but by scrutiny of his thoughts and interpretation of his actions at climactic moments of his career. . . .

Reduced to enumeration, the achievements of Washington's administra-tions count to not less than ten. During his presidency the United States government gained its executive and legislative precedents, appended a bill of rights to the Constitution, established its credit at home and abroad, fostered manufacturing and encouraged commerce, survived a serious in-surrection in the mountains of Pennsylvania, secured the transmontane frontier against Indian depredations, effected the removal of British troops from the Old Northwest, checked Spanish encroachments in the Old Southwest and obtained transit rights on the Mississippi, forged a policy for the disposition of public lands, and avoided involvement in the vortex of European wars. Analysis will reveal that Washington's hand was large in many of these accomplishments, and that in several his role was decisive. Proud of their record, Federalists were quick to acknowl-edge this: Washington's leadership was never nebulous to them. "Such a Chief Magistrate," said Fisher Ames, "appears like the pole star in a clear sky. . . . His Presidency will form an epoch and be distinguished as the Age of Washington." Ames was an orator who arranged his words nicely, but he was also as intuitive and straight-speaking a Federalist as there was in the party. However reluctantly, Republicans came to the same conclusion. In 1796 Jefferson expressed it simply: "One man outweighs them all in influence over the people."

Yet, by the eyes of posterity, Washington's role has not been seen in so sharp a light. It has long been a fashion to regard President Washington's administrations not so much his as Alexander Hamilton's. Critical research in the twentieth century has established beyond question that the genius and energy of Hamilton were responsible for much that the Federal government did—and, indeed, for much of what happened in the United States—between 1789 and 1797. As Senator William Maclay, dour Republican of Pennsylvania, remarked testily, "Mr. Hamilton is all powerful and fails in nothing he attempts." No student of the period would deny Hamilton's significance, but it may be that emphasis on the brilliance of the "Young Lothario" of the Federalists has worked to the disadvantage of a deeper consideration of the President's own part in the affairs of the new republic. In its business, great and small, the President was always there. He was neither listless nor dull, as sometimes he has been portrayed, and neither too old nor too deaf to participate fully. "He was an Aegis," Hamilton admitted, "very essential to me."

Surely it is not incorrect to think of the Federalist era as the heyday of Hamiltonian ideals. But it is quite wrong to suppose that Washington loved the pomp and ceremony with which his aides surrounded him, that his attitudes were more English than American, or that he concurred readily with Hamilton's extreme and often-quoted remark on the necessity of rule by the "rich and well-born." And it altogether wrong to imagine that the President responded automatically to Hamilton's every suggestion, that he permitted a Svengali-like control to be exercised over him, or that he turned to Hamilton in helpless frustration when the pressures of office became too great.

Washington did none of these things. Instead, as chief executive, he developed to a remarkable degree the science of deliberate and responsible consultation. While Hamilton served as secretary of the treasury and Jefferson as secretary of state, Washington solicited advice from them almost equally. In 1789 and 1790 he consulted the "heads of departments" individually on specific matters, and made his decision largely on one officer's specific advice. By the end of 1791, however, he was calling them together for discussion of larger problems. The Cabinet met several times in 1792, and many times during Washington's second term. Washington's closest friend in the Cabinet was neither Hamilton nor Jefferson but rather his old military comrade, General Henry Knox, the secretary of war. It may be argued reasonably that Knox, who served until 1795, was a convenient mirror for Hamilton's views; but in these same years the President's thinking over a wide range of major problems more nearly approximated that of Edmund Randolph than of any other member of the Cabinet. This gifted Virginian was in no way a Hamiltonian Federalist—and, according to Jefferson, not very much of a Republican, Jefferson thought Randolph "indecisive" and a "chameleon." Washington thought him impartial and sound. . . .

Of the ten enumerated achievements of Washington's administrations, the last in the list is perhaps the first in significance. Nothing that the Federalists did between 1789 and 1797 was of larger moment then, or deserves the larger gratitude of posterity, than their efforts to keep the United States out of the wars of the French Revolution. Whether their sympathies incline to the Federalists or to the Republicans, historians have been in general agreement that American participation in the wars which erupted in Europe in 1793 would have proven disastrous. The American Union, then just four years old, scarcely could have survived such an experience. No man in the United States saw this more clearly in 1793 than George Washington. And in no instance during his tenure as chief executive did Washington demonstrate his role in the government so abundantly, or his greatness in statecraft so dramatically, as in the decisions he made—and in the manner he made them—early in that year. The preservation of American neutrality was Washington's mightiest personal achievement as President of the United States. In February, March, and April of 1793 he forged the neutral rule in its fundamental form, and through the next four years his every policy was built on it. Of the several examples that might be used to indicate the active hand of Washington in the great affairs of government, this one has been chosen as much for its illustrative value as for its importance.

On March 4, 1793, in the Senate chamber at Philadelphia, Washington took the presidential oath for the second time. The first Federal administration, he could be sure, had accomplished much. Procedures had been established and many precedents set, the Constitution had been enlarged with the Bill of Rights, the stature of the central government had been assured, the machinery of national finance put into motion, and plans had been laid for a permanent capital city to be erected on the north bank of the Potomac. With these specifics and with the rapid rise of manufacturing and commerce that augered so well for the prosperity of the nation, Washington was immensely pleased. "A spirit of improvement displays itself in every quarter," he declared, "and principally in objects of the greatest public utility . . . things which seem eminently calculated to promote the advantage and accommodation of the people at large." The young republic had come far since 1789; further progress, the President felt, was certain if citizens would fix their minds and fasten their energies on such internal and immediate goals as inland navigation, road and bridge building, and settlement of the frontier. Then suddenly, in the opening weeks of his second term, the United States approached the precipice of war. The appeal of the French Revolution now threatened to draw the new American nation into a global conflict that would obliterate its fairest prospects.

Satisfied as he was with the results of his first administration, Washington entered his second term in a mood of apprehension. The national progress in which he took such pride had been gained, he knew, only at a very dear price. The bills on funding, assumption, residence, the excise, and the national bank—each one a device of Hamilton's to engross the prestige of the Federal government and multiply its powers under the Constitution—had loosened a torrent of opposition, criticism of Hamilton and Vice President Adams as "monocrats," and denunciation of all Federalists as "speculators" and "corruptionists." In Congress and in every city the Federalist followers of Hamilton and the Republican disciples of Jefferson were arguing vociferously, hurling epithets in their newspapers, and straining for advantage in what Fisher Ames now aptly styled "the pitched battle of parties." And, as political strife came to high tide in the vice-presidental contest of 1792 between the Federalist Adams and the candidate of the Republicans, Governor George Clinton of New York, Washington realized that the ebb of controversy soon would wash against his own door. No longer could he regard himself as "President of all the people," and he hardly could expect the same immunity in his second term that had shielded his office and his person from public censure in the first. "Convulsed as we are," Edmund Randolph warned him early in 1793, "I cannot but believe that there is scarcely a man in the Government whom party will not sooner or later destine for an attack."

Washington was past sixty, his health uncertain and his hearing impaired, and he longed for the shade of retirement at Mount Vernon more fervently now than ever. Still, because both Hamilton and Jefferson had urged him to do so—and because both Secretaries promised to remain in the Cabinet—he consented to a second term. "The motives which induced my acceptance," he wrote to a friend, "are the same which have ever ruled my decision, when the public desire (or, as my countrymen are pleased to denominate it, the *public good*) are placed in the scale against my personal enjoyment or private interest." But now, he might have added, Hamilton and Jefferson seemed farther than ever from agreement on just what constituted the "public good," and at this moment his countrymen were exhibiting a "public desire" that alarmed and dismayed him. The anxiety of Americans for news of the French Revolution was so intense as to be frightening. Did the people of the United States feel such communion with the cause of France that they might actually wish to plunge into the European conflagration? . . .

Washington scarcely would have denied that the good will of the French was precious to him. His personal gratitude to the soldiers of France for their unstinting aid in the war of American independence could never be dimmed. Without quibble he approved Jefferson's official reply to formal notification of the establishment of the French Republic: "The Government and the citizens of the United States . . . consider the union of principles and pursuits between our two countries as a link which binds still closer their interests and affections." But beyond this the President would not go. He did not agree with Jefferson that America's experiment in representative government was tied irrevocably to the French Revolution. As Washington walked alone in High Street, taking his exercise in the early mornings of March, he saw the tricolor on display in Philadelphia windows and knew that his nation was drifting into a storm of difficulties, a tempest of diplomatic problems blowing together with domestic ones, that would put to an ultimate test his wisdom and skill as national helmsman. If Washington was the "indispensable" leader, as his admirers had insisted in 1789 and again recently, this was the crisis that would show it. If his first term had been disfigured somewhat by conflicting attitudes in his Cabinet and the subsequent rise of parties, factionalism would now thicken and spread under new stimuli from abroad. The questions of policy would be large, complex, fraught with peril. Anticipating them, the President let the whole business filter through his mind time and again. Finally he was resolved on two points: Whatever developed in Europe, the United States must remain strictly neutral; whatever developed in the Cabinet or in the public temper, the President must remain impartial and dispassionate. The pilot must steer a safe and constant course. . . .

On April 4 [1793] the post to Mount Vernon brought a note from Jefferson, who expressed his feeling that recent stories of Anglo-French hostilities were exaggerated—and that it was more probable that England faced a civil war. Eight days later the President opened a letter from Hamilton which could leave "no room for doubt" that a global conflagration was raging. Marie Antoinette had been executed, Hamilton wrote, and on February 1 the French Republic had formally declared war against the British Empire, the Spanish Empire, and The Netherlands.

Hamilton's letter was sent on April 5; Jefferson wrote on the seventh that a general war was now "extremely probable" and the United States should "take every justifiable measure for preserving our neutrality" while providing France with "those necessaries for war which must be brought across the Atlantic." On the same day that he received Hamilton's communication, and before Jefferson's had arrived, the President penned his instructions. "It behooves the Government of this country," he wrote the Secretary of State, "to use every means in its power to prevent the citizens . . . from embroiling us with either [belligerent]"; would Jefferson, therefore, please give "mature consideration" to a plan which would insure "a strict neutrality"? In the same post he placed notes to Hamilton and Secretary of War Knox which made unmistakably clear the President's wish for "immediate precautionary measures." The next morning, April 13, his coach left for Philadelphia by the shortest possible route, and Washington was in High Street by late afternoon on the seventeenth.

When Jefferson appeared at the President's office early the next day, he had in hand four dispatches from Thomas Pinckney at London—each many weeks old and of trivial content. These the Secretary of State presented, but he had prepared no memorandum and could offer no plan to guarantee the nation a neutral role in the European war. If Washington's temper rose, he kept it in leash. Later the same day he saw Hamilton, and the Secretary of the Treasury spread before him the detailed draft of a program for "perfect" neutrality. Hamilton had a set of questions on paper, and the logic behind them in his mind; he even had ready a suggested "proclamation," the text of which Chief Justice John Jay had written hastily at his request. It was obvious that the Secretary of the Treasury had been feverishly occupied for some time in business that properly belonged to the Secretary of State; it was equally obvious that the two Cabinet officers had conferred not at all on the vital business in point. The President did not know the extent of Hamilton's dabbling in diplomatics; he was unaware of Hamilton's confidential assurances to the British envoy at Philadelphia, George Hammond, that the United States would maintain—as the Englishman reported to his superiors—"as strict a neutrality" as possible because "any event which might endanger the external tranquility . . . would be fatal to the systems he [Hamilton] has formed. . . ." Whatever the indiscretions of the Secretary of the Treasury, they would not blur the blueprint he advanced at this moment. The President had decided on neutrality. What he needed was a prescription for it. Hamilton had that in hand, and Jefferson did not.

No time was to be lost. Washington copied out Hamilton's interrogatories, labeled them "sundry questions . . . arising from the present posture of affairs in Europe," and sent identical lists to Jefferson, Knox, and Randolph with a request that the Cabinet meet at his house the next morning, April 19, at nine. The President's covering note did not indicate that Hamilton had originated the questions; but this is not to imply, as some historians have, that Washington was attempting to deceive his advisers. He could hardly have been able to conceal their authorship; nor would he have tried. . . .

The questions totaled to thirteen, but essentially the "doubts" were three. Should the President issue a proclamation to the American public, and should it include an explicit "declaration of neutrality"? Should Genêt, who would arrive soon as minister of the new French government, be formally accredited; and, if so, should his reception be "absolute" or "qualified"? Could and should the United States either disavow or suspend the Treaties of Alliance and Commerce made with France in 1778? The second and third points, Washington realized, would be highly antagonistic to Jefferson. They challenged the legitimacy of the Republic of France and suggested that the French Revolution ultimately would fail—as Hamilton plainly expected it would. Should the *de facto* government in France be recognized forthwith? Should the United States in 1793 be free to annul treaties concluded in 1778 with a monarchy that was now overturned, or were those treaties always to be valid because they existed between the *peoples* of nations rather than between the *governments* of nations? By their nature these considerations were central to the whole problem of erecting a permanent neutrality for the United States. Washington saw this and was grateful to Hamilton for raising pertinent points which soon would have to be discussed at length and in depth by the Cabinet. No precedent stood as a sure guide on the question of recognition, and likewise none on the validity of treaties. The President might anticipate long legalistic arguments and much heated opinion in his Cabinet before a decision could be wrought on either point.

There need be no delay, however, in adopting "immediate precautionary measures" against possible participation by Americans in the European war. To Washington this was the immediate issue, the paramount one. Questions of *de facto* recognition and the status of treaties could be, as they were, "postponed for further consideration" to "another day"; but the first question could not. What should the President do to prevent unneutral acts by Americans which might propel the United States into war? If American enthusiasm for the cause of the French Revolution was as intense as it appeared to be, a belligerent act might occur at any hour in any of a dozen seaports. The slightest unneutral gesture might be seized upon by the English, and America again might be fighting for her own freedom. It would be too late then to argue on the finer distinctions of international law, and Washington did not wish to debate them in detail until he had taken "immediate precautionary measures" to insure that no accident or irresponsible act would bring war to the shores of the American republic. This was the crisis of Friday, April 19, 1793—and George Washington did not mistake it.

Should the President, then, issue a public proclamation, and should it include a "declaration of neutrality"? Hamilton, Knox, and Randolph considered an immediate proclamation to be imperative. Jefferson acquiesced, but insisted that a "declaration of neutrality" would amount to "a declaration that there should be no war," and, he said, only Congress had the right to determine that question. "If on the one hand the Legislature have the right to declare war," Hamilton answered, "it is on the other the duty of the Executive to preserve peace till the declaration is made." But Jefferson had another argument, a compelling one, against any "premature declaration" that the United States would remain neutral. "It would be better," he reasoned, "to hold back the declaration of neutrality as a thing worth something" to each side. This was the same logic on which the Secretary of State had premised his opinion regarding Miranda's possible attack on Spanish Louisiana—that the United States must be "free to act" in pressing for diplomatic concessions—and now Jefferson wished to wring from the British "the broadest privileges" that American neutrality would buy. Redcoats of His Majesty's Canadian regiments still occupied seven forts on American soil in the Northwest; this might be a way to get them out. Washington liked the idea, and on his preference the decision of April 19 was made: the President would issue a proclamation immediately, but it would not contain an explicit "declaration of neutrality." It would serve as a positive warning to American citizens against "all acts and proceedings inconsistent with the duties of a friendly nation toward those at war," but it would avoid words and phrases that might negate the bargaining power of the United States in the market place of diplomacy.

The decision of April 19, 1793, established an important precedent in American history, but neither Hamilton nor Jefferson took particular satisfaction in the day's work. . . . Hamilton's friend, Senator Rufus King of New York, expressed the attitude of most Federalists in his reaction: "I could have wished to have seen in some part of it the word 'neutrality' which everyone would have understood and felt the force of. . . . We must not become entangled with this mad war." James Madison's response characterized that of ardent Republicans: "It wounds the popular feelings by a seeming indifference to the cause of liberty." And President Washington, a few hours after he had issued the proclamation, explained his decision in these words: "To administer justice and receive it from every power will, I hope, be always found the most prominent feature in the administration of this country; and I flatter myself that nothing short of imperious necessity can occasion a breach with any of them." It was, he said, "the sincere wish of the United States to . . . live in peace and amity with all the inhabitants of the earth."

The work of George Washington as a statesman has been obscured to posterity not only by Alexander Hamilton's ascendancy in the 1790's, but equally as much by the very legend that attaches to his name. That legend is essentially military, and has been so from its seeding. . . .

This fact does much to explain why his achievements as president are not as obvious to posterity as they should be. Washington was a statesman fully as long as he was a soldier, and his achievements in council were fully as significant as those in the field. But he was first a soldier, and primacy is vital in legend-making. So is drama, and so also is an undisputed leading role. The campaigns of the Revolution can be rendered infinitely more interesting than the problems of statecraft in the formative period. And, as a soldier, Washington occupied the center of the stage. . . .

Washington's popularity as a biographical subject is easily explained. He was America's first hero in war. John Adams, who was capable of descending to a certain level of bitterness during the years that he served inconspicuously as vice president in Washington's administrations, put it this way: "The history of our Revolution will be one continued lie from one end to the other. The essence of the whole will be that Dr. Franklin's electrical rod smote the earth and out sprang General Washington, that Franklin electrified him with his rod, and thence forward these two conducted all the policy, negotiations, legislatures, and war." Neither Benjamin Franklin's admirers nor Washington's have ever advanced this theory, but certainly the Commander in Chief of the Continental Army emerged from the war of independence with a major share of credit for its success. Then, as many Americans delighted in depicting it, the General followed the noble example of the Roman soldier Cincinnatus by retiring modestly to his farm and plow in the bright hour of victory—and this, above victory itself, emblazoned him with greatness in the eyes of the people. . . .

Like the flora of his Virginia, the legend of George Washington was early to blossom. Within a half dozen years of his death in 1799, American readers already had the choice of two biographies. One was a thin, simple book of eighty pages which presented the fiction of the cherry tree and the prayer in the snow at Valley Forge, and in the last paragraph ushered its subject through the Pearly Gates and into the Kingdom of the Angels. Few biographers of any hero have dared to go this far, but Mason Locke Weems was a self-styled clergyman and he was unfettered by footnotes. His *Life of General Washington* earned "Parson" Weems an emperor's ransom in royalties and a reputation as one of the most pleasant and plausible charlatans in American literature. Such success with Washington prompted Weems to consider the careers of other champions of the Revolution, and he did not lay down his prolific pen for many years. . . .

While the legend of Washington has been heavy with the laurels of the soldier, it nonetheless has communicated a valid impression. For all the ardor of their researches, modern historians have not turned up evidence that Washington in life was appreciably less than the great American patriot imaginatively painted in words by Weems. Catch-penny debunkers appear occasionally, to be sure, but they are compensated for their efforts as much in ridicule as in royalties. This is as it should be. Washington's life and times have been rigorously researched, his silhouette has been exposed to different light by different scholars, and we may be certain today that he is quite deserving of the halo that has been his. Weems, so fictitious in detail, was authentic in spirit: George Washington was a great and good man, great in the largest sense and good in the deepest. . . .

However deep the roots of any legend, it will die in poor ground. The legend of George Washington did not wither because its soil was uniquely rich. In an oration at St. Paul's Church in New York, Gouverneur Morris spoke a sentence that goes far to explain its endurance. "Born to high destinies," said Morris, Washington was "fashioned for them by the hand of nature." Had this not been so perfectly true, it is doubtful that this legend would have flowered as it did. More than any personage of his time and more perhaps than any American who followed him to the national stage, Washington presented an ideal subject for adulation. In him, physically and psychologically, were the elements of heroism. In seeing Washington, in meeting him, Americans and Europeans alike received the same spontaneous impression. Many described it, but none better than Jefferson who saw him daily for several years. As the first Secretary of State appraised the first President, "His person was fine, his stature exactly what one would wish," and more:

His mind was great and powerful, without being of the very first order; his penetration strong, though not so accurate as that of a Newton, Bacon, or Locke; and as far as he saw, no judgment was ever sounder. It was slow in operation, being little aided by invention or imagination, but sure in conclusion. . . . Perhaps the strongest feature in his character was prudence, never acting until every circumstance, every consideration, was maturely weighed; refraining when he saw a doubt, but, when once decided, going through with his purposes whatever obstacles opposed. His integrity was most pure, his justice the most inflexible I have ever known, no motives or interest or consanguinity of friendship or hatred being able to bias his decision. . . . On the whole, his character was in its mass perfect, in nothing bad, in few points indifferent; and it may truly be said that never did nature and fortune combine more perfectly to make a man great, and to place him in the same constellation with whatever worthies have merited from man an everlasting remembrance. . . .

CHAPTER 18

THE NEW NATION
IN THE WORLD

While the new administration of George Washington was striving to establish the new government outlined in the Constitution, it was seeking to establish the infant United States as a nation of the world. This was not an easy task, since the very survival of the new federation was uncertain. American foreign affairs reached a particularly critical stage in 1793 when England and France once again went to war, and most of the diplomacy of the young nation was concerned with this European conflict.

But domestic conditions and policies also influenced American foreign relations. Wayne S. Cole discusses these internal factors in this selection. In describing the American nation in its formative years, Cole seeks to pinpoint the distinctive internal characteristics that had important influences on foreign policy. He deals with the population—its density, its composition, and its distribution—with the economy, with the ideological patterns of Americans, and with the internal aspects of the administration and conduct of foreign affairs.

In this study the student will not find a blueprint for systematically measuring the impact of domestic influences on American foreign affairs. However, with an increased understanding of the basic patterns in American activity and thought before 1815 and with a general knowledge of the important events in the foreign affairs of the period, he can consider the major questions raised by this essay. What specifically were the domestic factors that influenced the nation's foreign relations, and just how did these factors influence the direction of American foreign policy? What does the knowledge that the entire population of the United States in 1775 was less than the population of Chicago today, and that the Department of State had a staff of five in 1790, tell us about the capacity of the nation to be effective in the power diplomacy of the late eighteenth century? Does this knowledge bring home an awareness of how different the America of these years was from the America of today?

For a brief, but excellent characterization of Washington's America see Esmond Wright, *Fabric of Freedom, 1763–1800** (1961); indispensable for the interested student is Henry Adams' brilliant classic *The United States in 1800** (1955 reissue). Thomas A. Bailey is particularly concerned with domestic influences on foreign relations in his *A Diplomatic History of the American People* (first edition, 1940).

* Available in a paperback edition.

THE NEW NATION: DOMESTIC INFLUENCES ON AMERICAN FOREIGN RELATIONS TO 1815

WAYNE S. COLE

The United States before 1815 differed radically from twentieth-century America. And those distinctive internal characteristics helped account for the foreign policies of the young nation.

THE PEOPLE

Some of the differences may be seen in population totals, composition, and distribution. With only about 2.5 million people when the Revolution began in 1775, the population was considerably less than the present city of Chicago. Even at the close of the War of 1812, with less than 8.5 million, the United States had a smaller population than New York City today.

The ethnic and racial composition of the population differed too. By 1815 there were approximately 1.5 million Negroes in the United States —most of them in the South and most of them slaves. There were almost no Orientals in America and native Indians generally were outside organized white society. Very few Americans in those years were of Latin or Slavic descent. The overwhelming mass of the people were immigrants or descendants of immigrants from the Anglo-Saxon and Germanic countries of northern and western Europe—from England, Scotland, Ireland, and Germany. And those Anglo-Saxons dominated politically, economically, and culturally.

Reflecting the ethnic composition, most Americans with religious affiliations then were Protestants. The Irish and some of the Germans were Roman Catholic, and there were a few Americans of Jewish faith. They were only a tiny minority, however, and the great influx of Catholic and Jewish immigrants did not begin until much later.

SOURCE. Reprinted with permission from Wayne S. Cole, *An Interpretive History of American Foreign Relations* (Homewood, Ill.: The Dorsey Press), 1968, pp. 22–39. Copyright 1968 by The Dorsey Press. Reprinted by permission of The Dorsey Press and the author.

Geographically most Americans lived east of the Appalachian Mountains—generally very close to the Atlantic coast. In the eighteenth century, Scotch-Irish and German settlers moved down the valleys of the Appalachians, and some began to locate west of the mountains during the Revolution. Vermont, Kentucky, and Tennessee became states while Washington was President. Ohio became a state in 1803 and Louisiana in 1812—making a total of eighteen by the close of the period. But most of the present area of the United States was not settled by whites when the War of 1812 ended. Except in Louisiana and in some Spanish-held lands in the far Southwest, there was very little white population west of the Mississippi River in 1815, and substantial areas east of that river were still unsettled. Indiana, Illinois, Wisconsin, Michigan, Alabama, and Mississippi, for example, were not yet states.

Before 1815 most Americans lived on farms, on the frontier, or in small towns—in striking contrast to the highly urbanized society of the United States in the twentieth century. The first census in 1790 classified 95 percent of Americans as rural—living on farms or in small towns. Even the so-called urban people lived in cities tiny by present standards. The largest city during the American Revolution was Philadelphia with about 30,000 people. Despite its growth and influence, New York City had fewer than 150,000 inhabitants as late as 1815.

THE ECONOMY

Like the population, the American economy before 1815 also differed greatly from that of today. For purposes of analysis most individuals in those years may be divided into two broad categories: the shipping-commercial group; and the farmer-agrarian group. They overlapped, and their interests were not mutually exclusive, but the division was real. The economy was much less complex than today. Each of the two broad economic groups requires some analysis in terms of impact on American foreign affairs.

The smaller of the two—the shipping-commercial group—included merchants and traders who owned their own ships, fishermen (particularly from New England where fishing was a major industry), shipbuilders, and the bankers and creditors who helped finance the trading and shipping enterprises. Before 1815 that group included very little commercial manufacturing. There was some manufacturing, of course, and both the American Revolution and the War of 1812 promoted the growth of industry. But manufacturing was weak in productivity, wealth, and power relative to the total economy. Geographically the shipping-commercial group was most numerous in New England and in eastern portions of the Middle Atlantic states. On a much smaller scale that group was in the Southern coastal cities such as Charleston and New Orleans. Politically the members of that group tended to work through the Federalist Party. Among its many prominent and able political spokesmen were John Adams of Massachusetts, and Alexander Hamilton and John Jay of New York.

The characteristics of American foreign trade before 1815 were strikingly different from the patterns today. First, foreign trade played a larger role relatively in the economy before 1815 than in any other major period of American history. Second, since the United States had little commercial industry of its own, most imports consisted of manufactured and semimanufactured products. Third, since most Americans were farmers, exports consisted largely of agricultural commodities such as wheat, flour, tobacco, and cotton. Fourth, most foreign trade was conducted with Europe, and particularly with Great Britain. Britain, of course, had dominated American trade during the colonial period, but that continued long after independence. American traders became increasingly active in non-English parts of the world. They traded more with continental Europe. The China trade began in the 1780's and was lucrative to some merchants. Despite legal obstructions, trade with the West Indies continued active and profitable. United States trade with Latin America began while Spain still had its empire, and it expanded after Latin America won independence. Despite expansion of non-English trade, however, Europe and particularly Great Britain continued to receive most American exports and send most of its imports. That was not due primarily to government controls but, instead, resulted from the fact that England manufactured products that Americans wanted, while England needed many of the commodities that American farmers produced. Fifth, the United States before 1815 generally had an "unfavorable" balance of trade—that is, it imported more products than it exported. Sixth, most foreign trade was carried in ships owned and operated by Americans. The United States had one of the leading merchant fleets in the world. Those ships not only transported products in American trade but also engaged in the carrying trade between other countries. The profits from the carrying trade helped fill the gap left by the unfavorable balance of trade. Until the beginning of the War of 1812 American foreign trade, and the profits from that trade, generally increased—in spite of (and partly because of) the European wars and the interference by European belligerents with American ships.

Throughout those years the United States had a debtor status in international finance—that is, foreigners loaned and invested much more money in the United States than Americans loaned and invested abroad.

Private lenders and investors from Great Britain provided most of that foreign capital. That influx of capital helped fill part of the gap left by the unfavorable balance of trade and also helped finance America's rapid economic growth.

The interests and activities of members of the shipping-commercial group directly affected their attitudes toward foreign policies. Understandably, the members of that group supported policies that would promote and protect American foreign trade. In that connection they wanted commercial treaties, an efficient consular service, and a large and effective navy. Many of them wanted protection and subsidies for the fishing industry. They considered peace with Great Britain essential at almost any price. Since most trade was with Britain, war with that country would have disastrous direct effects on American foreign trade. Furthermore, Britain's powerful navy could, in the event of war, destroy America's trade with other countries as well. Generally the group opposed westward territorial expansion by the United States. Most of them would not profit directly from western expansion. New lands in the West might reduce the labor supply in the East and increase its cost. Westerners might buy fewer European products and produce less for export (at least at first) than if they remained in the East. And politically, westward expansion might lead to the creation of more agrarian states that would weaken the relative political power of the shipping-commerical interests. A few merchants and traders supported the westward movement. Some of them were also land speculators. Others became active in the New Orleans trade that benefited from westward movement. Those were exceptions, however, and most merchants and their political representatives opposed westward territorial expansion.

The second (and by far the larger) of the two broad economic categories before 1815 was the farmer-agrarian group. It included small farmers, planters, fur traders, and land speculators. A very large precentage of Americans engaged in land speculation, from small farmers to city financiers. Most major figures in the era—including Patrick Henry, Benjamin Franklin, and George Washington, among others—were in various land speculation schemes. In other words, the farmer-agrarian group included most people in the United States before 1815. Geographically they were in every section of the country—including New England and the Middle Atlantic states. But they were most numerous and powerful in the South and West ("West" meaning the Piedmont, valleys of the Appalachians, and the Ohio-Mississippi Valley in those years). Politically they generally supported the Anti-Federalist, Democratic-Republican, or Jeffersonian Republican Party. Their greatest political spokesman was Thomas Jefferson of Virginia.

The interests and activities of the farmer-agrarian group directly affected foreign policy attitudes. Farmers (then and now) needed foreign trade. They bought manufactured products from abroad, and many of their farm commodities eventually reached other parts of the world. Foreign interference with ships flying the American flag aroused their patriotism. In general, however, farmers attached much less importance to the expansion and protection of foreign trade than did the shipping-commercial group. They were not so directly involved in buying and selling abroad, and they did not particularly care whether foreign or American merchants handled (and profited from) the products entering and leaving American ports. The China trade and the fishing industry had little appeal to most of them. Members of that group tended to be anti-British and pro-French. In contrast to the shipping-commerical faction, the farmer-agrarian group generally urged American westward territorial expansion. Some hoped for additional cheap lands. They wanted the United States to control the mouths of rivers (such as the Mississippi) through which their products went to markets. Territorial expansion might facilitate control or defeat of hostile Indians. Some hoped to benefit from land speculation in the West. And still others wanted to expand their fur-trading operations. In general they favored low tariffs on the manufactured products they had to buy. And most of them wanted the Indians ruthlessly controlled, driven out, or (if need be) killed off.

Much of the history of American foreign affairs to 1815 became meaningful in terms of the influence of those two economic groups.

POLITICAL PATTERNS

For purposes of convenience the political history of the United States to 1815 may be divided into four distinct periods. The first was the American Revolution, from 1775 to 1783. The Second Continental Congress and its appointees and committees provided such central government as there was during the Revolution before 1781. But that Continental Congress (though it got the job done) amounted to little more than a meeting of representatives of sovereign states.

The Articles of Confederation, from 1781 to 1789, provided the second period of American political history. That first constitution authorized relatively weak, decentralized authority with sovereignty residing in the states. There was no President. Committees and department secretaries performed the executive functions. There was no central supreme court. The Articles provided for a one-house legislature representing the states, with equal voting powers for all states and extremely limited power for the legislature. It did have authority to control foreign affairs, however, and to raise an army and navy, make treaties, wage war, and send and receive diplomats. The government under the Articles of Confederation was much criticized then and later, but it was more effective than many of its critics conceded and more democratic than they wanted.

During the Revolution various factions struggled inconclusively for dominance and for control of domestic and foreign policies. In the 1780's, however, the shipping-commercial group (in alliance with large southern planters) gradually gained the upper hand. One result was the drafting and adoption of the present Constitution of the United States by 1789.

The next period in American political history (the first under the new Constitution) was the Federalist Era, from 1789 to 1801. Two Americans served as President in the period—Washington from 1789 to 1797, and John Adams for one term from 1797 to 1801. They and others hoped permanent political parties would not evolve, but they did anyway. And the dominant party then was the Federalist Party with Alexander Hamilton as its greatest leader. It was strongest in the Northeast and drew its most important support from the merchant-trader-creditor groups in the cities, with additional support coming from the wealthiest of the southern planters. It tended to be conservative, pro-business, pro-English, "elitist," and somewhat undemocratic on the issues of the day. Dominant from 1789 to 1801, the Federalist Party provided vigorous minority opposition after 1801 until it disappeared with its defeat in the elections of 1816.

The next period in American political history (the second under the Constitution) was the Jeffersonian Era, from 1801 to 1817. Two men served as President—Thomas Jefferson from 1801–1809, and James Madison from 1809 to 1817. The party they led was the Democratic-Republican or Jeffersonian Republican Party. It drew its greatest support from farmers and small planters of the South and West. Under Jefferson's leadership it represented (in comparison with the Federalist Party) a relatively democratic, pro-farmer, pro-French, and territorial expansionist point of view. Its sympathies did not extend very much to the small urban working class. For sixty years (from 1801 to 1861) the farmer-agrarian group, working first through Jefferson's Republican Party and later through Jackson's Democratic Party, controlled politically most of the time. And in those decades both the domestic and foreign policies of the United States reflected, to a considerable degree, the needs, interests, and aspirations of the farmer-agrarian group.

IDEOLOGICAL PATTERNS

The challenging and exhausting tasks of conquering a new land, of surviving and making a living in the New World, were not conducive to systematic philosophizing. Widespread illiteracy, limited news media, and poor transportation and communication facilities inhibited the distribution of ideas and information. Preoccupation with personal, local, and state problems were commonplace for the upper classes and the masses alike. Perhaps a third of those living in America during the Revolution played no role in it and thought (and cared) little about the issues involved.

The extent of public apathy should not be exaggerated, however. Most people were innocent of the reflective thought and great learning of a Jefferson. Precise details and subtle theories may have escaped them. But even the illiterate were not without conceptions of the true, the good, the beautiful, and the possible—however unsophisticated those conceptions may have been. Furthermore, those views, whether eloquently expressed or crudely "felt," affected the attitudes men and women took toward America's relations with the rest of the world.

To some degree the ideas of Americans (then and now) were rooted in their own experiences and interests—experiences and interests that helped them to see truth in certain ideas and not in others. One of the ideas present from the beginnings of American colonial history and deeply rooted in experience has come to be called "isolationism." Most immigrants came partly to escape evils in Europe—religious persecution, economic hardships, wars, or personal problems. And most of them hoped for something better in America. Thus from the beginning there was implicit the assumption (or at least the hope) that the New World was better than the Old. Many literally saw America as a Promised Land reserved by God for His chosen people. The long and arduous trip to America magnified the geographic (and moral) separateness of America.

During the American Revolution the belief that America should keep out of Europe's wars was common. John Adams in 1775 said that America ought "to maintain an entire neutrality in all future European wars." Thomas Paine wrote that America should "steer clear of European contentions." Responsible and informed leaders sometimes expressed very extreme views along those lines. In 1785 Jefferson suggested that

America should "practice neither commerce nor navigation, but . . . stand with respect to Europe precisely on the footing of China. We should thus avoid war, and all our citizens would be husbandmen." At the same time John Adams wrote that "If all intercourse between Europe and America could be cut off forever, if every ship we have were burnt, and the keel of another never to be laid, we might still be the happiest people upon earth, and, in fifty years, the most powerful." Both Jefferson and Adams, however, knew that the commercially active United States could not actually follow the policies they described. But President Washington was advancing an old and widely held view when, in his "Farewell Address" in 1796, he urged: "The great rule of conduct for us, in regard to foreign Nations is in extending our commercial relation to have with them as little *political* connection as possible. So far as we have already formed engagements let them be fulfilled, with perfect good faith. Here let us stop." He did, however, approve "temporary alliances for extraordinary emergencies." If informed Americans had such thoughts, it is understandable that the views appealed to the semiliterate frontiersman working from dawn to dusk to clear fields in the forest and to coax the virgin soil to produce a crop so that he and his family might survive.

So-called "isolationist" views may have seemed a bit less valid to the merchant whose ships touched distant ports or to the family in a coastal city whose husband or father traveled the world over as a merchant seaman. The oceans not only separated the New World from the Old; they also served as avenues linking the New and the Old. Personal memories, family ties, trade, learning, tradition, and personal experience bound many to Europe. And even those who would have preferred "isolation," found that the violence, ideologies, and passions of the Wars of the French Revolution and the Napoleonic Wars made it impossible for America to turn its back on France completely.

Some in those years had interests, ideas, and emotions that made them sympathetic with England and hostile to its enemies. Those Anglophiles were most numerous in the Federalist Party and its forerunners and included such able Americans as Alexander Hamilton and John Jay. Many considerations accounted for those pro-British inclinations. Some had been Loyalists or Tories during the Revolution and had never wanted to separate from the British Empire in the first place. Some conservatives had not been enthusiastic about the War for Independence but had gone along with it to prevent it from going to extremes contrary to their interests and ideas. Most Anglophiles were of English descent and had ethnic, cultural, family, and emotional ties with England. Many merchants were moved partly by economic considerations. And finally, an important explanation for the pro-British sympathies of many Federalists lay in their political and philosophical attitudes. Many of those conservatives had not been enthusiastic about the advanced ideas in the Declaration of Independence—including the idea that "all men are created equal," the natural rights of man, and the compact theory of government. In that same context, many of them believed the Articles of Confederation was too democratic and did not sufficiently restrain the "excesses" and "passions" of the masses. That is not to say that those Federalists wanted to return to divine right monarchy; most of them did not want that. At the same time, however, many of them feared democracy and wanted some form of constitutional government that could be controlled by an "aristocracy of talent"—or at least by men of property. Intellectually many of them were more in tune with Britain's Edmund Burke than with Voltaire, Rousseau—or even Jefferson. Given those attitudes, understandably many were less than enthusiastic about the French Revolution.

At the same time, many other Americans sympathized with France as opposed to Britain. Those Francophiles and Anglophobes generally were Anti-Federalists and later Jeffersonian Republicans. They were most numerous and vocal in the agrarian South and West. Their attitudes were influenced by the Enlightenment or "Age of Reason" as it extended from Europe to America. The Enlightenment in Western civilization frowned on reliance on traditional authority. It minimized the supernatural and inclined toward Deism in theology. It de-emphasized original sin and stressed the essential goodness and dignity of man. It included an earnest concern for human welfare and a belief in the inevitability of progress. The Enlightenment included a faith in the capacity of man through reason, science, and education to understand and control his environment for the betterment of himself and society. Emphasis was on practical progress for mankind on earth rather than on life after death. In politics it embraced the natural rights theory, the compact theory of government, and belief in the right of revolution.

In that context the views of Anglophobes resulted partly from the American Revolution itself. Wartime hatred of the British continued long after independence was assured. Though the French acted out of self-interest, some Americans realized that French assistance had made independence possible. Since America gained its independence through revolution and the Declaration of Independence endorsed the right of revolution, it was easy for Americans to view foreign revolutions with sympathy and even enthusiasm. Struggles to overthrow monarchy seemed intrinsically moral and right—whether the tyrant was George III or Louis XVI. Americans and Frenchmen were seen as partners in the universal struggle for freedom and the rights of man against monarchy and oppression. Idealistic enthusiasm for the French was cooled rapidly by the antics of Edmond Genêt, the execution of the King, the bloodletting in the Reign of Terror, and by the rise of a new tyranny in the person of Napoleon Bonaparte. In general, however, the intellectual and political followers of the author of the Declaration of Independence, Thomas Jefferson, found more common ideological ground with the French after 1789 than with the British.

Furthermore, some Republicans either lacked the ethnic ties to England or had ethnic origins that predisposed them to hate the English. For example, Germans living in Pennsylvania (the so-called "Pennsylvania Dutch") may have had no overpowering reason to hate the British, but neither did they have any strong reasons for liking them. At the same time, the Scotch-Irish frontiersmen had substantial reasons for hating England. They or their ancestors had suffered extreme discrimination and hardship at the hands of the British before they fled from North Ireland to America.

The importance of economic ties with England was felt less keenly by farmers in the South and West than by merchants in the Northeast. To be sure, many farm products were sold to Britain, and farmers needed English manufactures. But many in the West were subsistence farmers or sold largely on local markets. And even those whose products eventually found their way to England were less directly aware of the importance of foreign markets—at least until these markets were cut off by British, French, or American actions.

Politics also entered into consideration for many. It was easy to be anti-British and pro-French when political opponents, the Federalists, were such Anglophiles. The Federalists, for their part, found it expedient to charge Republicans with being more enamored of France than of America. That was not the last time in American history that foreign affairs and domestic politics became entangled.

Concern with Anglophobes and Anglophiles, with Francophobes and Francophiles, should not be overemphasized, however. Most Americans were preoccupied largely with their own personal welfare, and with that of their state and nation—not with Britain, France, or any other foreign country. With only rare exceptions, even the most fervent Anglophiles did not want to rejoin the British Empire or submerge America's future with that of England. And all but the most ecstatic supporters of the French Revolution did not wish to endanger American security and interests by waging war on behalf of the French. For various reasons, many Americans sympathized with the English or the French, insofar as American policies touched on the European conflagration. At most, however, their concern for the European belligerents was subordinate to their interest in themselves and the United States.

That was true even though a real spirit of American nationalism developed only very slowly in those years. Up to 1815 most Americans were much more attached emotionally to their particular locality, state, or section than they were to the United States as a nation. Gradually, however, the emotions and symbols of nationalism began to emerge. Some of the roots of that nationalism could be traced to the fact that Americans or their ancestors had originally fled evils in Europe to make their way in the New World where they hoped to find greater opportunities or freedom. The pride many felt in the local area or state (its natural beauty, its rich soil and resources, the vigor of its people) was broadened into a pride in America. Common problems, struggles, and accomplishments in winning independence and conquering the frontier gave many a feeling of oneness and unity that evolved into nationalism.

Some writers and intellectuals added their influence. The geography books published in 1784 and after by New England's Jedediah Morse put America at the center and emphasized the superiority of American soil, climate, and resources. In his spelling books, first published in 1783, and in his dictionary, Noah Webster encouraged use of distinctly American words, spelling, and usage. Historians, too, aroused nationalism. They described the American Revolution as a struggle by noble and valiant Americans against the evil tyranny and oppression that was George III's Britain. Some (like Parson Weems) wrote so-called biographies of American leaders that had as much fiction as truth. Weems's story of young George Washington and his cherry tree contributed nothing to knowledge of the nation's first President, but helped magnify America's heroes into Godlike figures. In sermons and essays many clergymen encouraged the belief that Americans were a chosen people and that the hand of God was guiding the nation inevitably toward a sacred destiny.

Political bases for American nationalism were provided by the Constitution adopted in 1789, by Alexander Hamilton's economic policies, by the new capital city separate from any state, and by the Supreme Court's decisions under Chief Justice John Marshall. Many politicians in their quest for votes helped stimulate chauvinism. Despite the many military reverses on land and sea, the War of 1812 aroused the spirit of nationalism—and even provided what later became the national anthem. Foreign visitors noted the boastfulness of Americans, their boundless faith in the nation's future, and their belief in the superiority of all things American. That growing American nationalism reenforced the ideological and emotional bases for both isolationism and expansionism. The belief in America's moral superiority encouraged the conviction that little but harm could come from involvement with the corruption and tyranny of monarchical Europe. At the same time, however, chauvinism and its intrinsic self-righteousness inspired the belief that the United States had an almost divine destiny to lead the world toward democracy, freedom, and the good life. Most Americans in those years would have restricted the nation's leadership to the power of example outside of North America. That is, by developing democracy, freedom, and economic prosperity the United States might serve as a beacon for less fortunate peoples to follow out of their misery and darkness. Few Americans before 1815 would have had the United States commit its military, diplomatic, or economic resources to accomplish that utopia in foreign lands. Confidence in American superiority and faith in the power of example were not inconsistent with so-called "isolationist" attitudes as they evolved. In any event, among the myriad domestic influences affecting foreign affairs were ideas and the emotions surrounding them.

MILITARY FORCES

The United States won its independence in war with Great Britain and maintained it in undeclared naval wars with France and the Barbary States, and in the War of 1812 against Britain. Nevertheless, the armed forces of the young nation before 1815 were tiny and weak relative to those of the major European countries. A professional military caste, traditional in Europe, did not exist in America. Financial and industrial resources for raising and equipping military forces were severely limited. Localism and state pride opposed efforts to build national military forces. State militia generally were badly trained, inadequately equipped, and poorly led. Faith in democratic "citizen soldiers" sometimes was misplaced. "The spirit of 1776" moving men to heroic sacrifices in battle often was conspicuous by its absence. The flamboyant confidence and nationalism of Henry Clay's congressional War Hawks in 1812 generally was not reflected in enlistments or victories after war began. Generalship in the Revolution rarely was better than adequate; in the War of 1812 it was often miserably incompetent. In peacetime (for example, under the Articles of Confederation) national military forces sometimes almost ceased to exist. Anti-Federalists and Jeffersonian Republicans in the agrarian West and South greatly feared the dangers to democracy posed by a permanent military establishment. They doubted the necessity for a navy adequate for more than coastal defense. President Jefferson's fleet of more than 150 one-gun, 45-foot "gunboats" symbolized that agrarian attitude—and was inadequate even for the task it was supposed to serve. American military weakness helped to account for diplomatic difficulties and failures.

At the same time, however, a multitude of circumstances prevented that weakness from having the disastrous consequences one might have anticipated. Supply and command difficulties for European military forces operating across the Atlantic were considerable. Military targets in America were so scattered and decentralized, transportation and communication facilities were so poor, and the populace in the countryside was so hostile, that it was hard for foreign forces to strike decisive blows. European overconfidence was a liability at times. Furthermore, Britain had to content with European belligerents while fighting America. The United States could not have prevailed in the Revolution without French economic, military, and naval support. Napoleon (not the United States) absorbed most of Britain's military resources from 1812 to 1814. Lack of popular enthusiam and political support for war with America inhibited Britain during both the Revolution and the War of 1812. Furthermore, if "citizen soldiers" were inadequate at times, they were not always so. If there were incompetent generals, there were also Washingtons and Jacksons. Despite the views of agrarian Republicans, coastal Federalists pushed successfully for naval appropriations in 1794 and after, and created a separate Navy Department in 1798. Jefferson's administration founded the United States Military Academy at West Point. Even state militia occasionally performed superbly—as under Andrew Jackson at New Orleans in January, 1815, after the peace treaty with Britain had been signed. American diplomacy was handicapped by military weakness, but special circumstances in Europe and America prevented that weakness from being so decisive and unfortunate as it might have been.

ADMINISTRATION AND CONDUCT OF FOREIGN AFFAIRS

The colonial period before 1775 provided Americans with very little practical experience in the administration and conduct of foreign affairs. Merchants and shipowners negotiated in their commercial dealings with officials and businessmen in foreign lands. Benjamin Franklin, Arthur Lee, Silas Deane, and others obtained useful experience when they served as colonial agents or "lobbyists" in London. But the British government reserved to itself authority for formal diplomatic matters of its empire.

During the Revolution the Second Continental Congress was responsible for conduct of foreign affairs until 1781. The Congress in 1775 created a Committee of Secret Correspondence under the initial chairmanship of Franklin to conduct correspondence with friendly Europeans. In 1777 the Committee's name was changed to Committee for Foreign Affairs. The change reflected official American independence. Perhaps it was also a tacit admission that there was very little "secret" about the Committee and its agents. The combined effectiveness of the British Navy, spies, and cooperative Loyalists in America rendered the term inappropriate. The personal secretaries of America's representatives in France often were British spies. Most famous and successful of those agents was Dr. Edward Bancroft of Massachusetts. As secretary first to Silas Deane, then to Franklin, and later to the joint commission in France, he had access to the most secret information. He lived in the same house with Franklin and Deane, and even worked for Franklin during the peace negotiations in 1782–1783. On occasion he pretended to spy on England for America, but it was Britain he truly served. Arthur Lee, a member of the commission, suspected and distrusted Dr. Bancroft—but did not know that his own personal secretary was also a British spy. The enemy commonly obtained copies of secret American documents before they reached the intended American hands. Some spies were apprehended, but after the Revolution Dr. Bancroft lived out his remaining years as a respected citizen in the United States. His double role was not discovered until many years after his death.

American diplomats during the Revolution were, of necessity, inexperienced "shirt-sleeved diplomats" and were essentially political appointees. Some were inept, some failed, and Silas Deane even deserted to the enemy. Others, like John Jay, John Adams, the naturalized Dutchman Charles Dumas, and particularly Benjamin Franklin, proved to be impressively able. As always, though, success came most easily (even for the talented) when the circumstances were right.

The powers of the central government under the Articles of Confederation were severely limited, but it did have exclusive authority for the conduct of foreign affairs—including power to send and receive ambassadors, make peace or war, and make treaties (subject to approval by a vote of at least nine in the legislature). Under the Articles, the Congress in 1781 created a Department of Foreign Affairs to administer foreign relations. The first man chosen to head the Department as Secretary of

Foreign Affairs was Robert R. Livingston, Jr. He was succeeded by the able and strong-willed John Jay in 1784. Since under the Articles the secretaries were appointed by and responsible to Congress, the British pattern of ministerial responsibility might have evolved had not the Articles been abandoned.

Under the new Constitution adopted in 1789 the federal government had exclusive authority for control of foreign affairs. The President was given primary responsibility for foreign affairs, but his powers under the Constitution were distinctly limited. In the first place, he was authorized to receive ambassadors and (subject to approval by the Senate) to appoint them. Following the precedent set by the first Secretary of State, Thomas Jefferson, the United States consistently followed the *"de facto* theory of recognition" until early in the twentieth century. That is, the United States based its decision to recognize on the foreign government's effective control of the state and its capacity to bind that state in its dealings in international affairs. The decision to extend recognition was not based on the morality or legality of the government or the means by which it came to power. Second, the Constitution gave the President authority to make treaties with the advice and consent of the Senate providing two thirds of the senators present concurred. Washington sought the advice of the Senate on certain treaties but found the procedure difficult. Since then Presidents generally have not sought the "advice and consent" and have simply submitted treaties to the Senate for approval or rejection after they were signed. Third, under the Constitution the President was commander in chief of the armed forces. Conceivably he could use that power to reinforce diplomatic negotiations. He could (as Polk did in 1846) use the power to make war inevitable. Presidents even conducted undeclared wars—as Adams did against France and as Jefferson did against the Barbary States. Fourth, the President had the power to issue state of the union and other messages. The Monroe Doctrine, for example, originated in a message to Congress. And finally, the President executed laws and treaties—and diplomacy is essentially an executive function.

Presidential authority in foreign affairs was not only very limited, but the Constitution also gave important powers to Congress. Those legislative powers were largely negative, but they were important nonetheless. For example, under the Constitution the Senate could refuse to approve diplomatic appointments. Second, treaties were not binding until approved by a two-thirds vote of the Senate. Third, Congress (both houses, by a simple majority) had exclusive power to declare war. Fourth, Congress had the power to levy taxes and make appropriations—

increasingly important for American foreign policies. Congress might pass other legislation affecting foreign affairs—neutrality legislation, for example—and could adopt advisory resolutions. The powers of Congress under the Constitution that related to foreign affairs were by no means insignificant.

The Constitution is a living document, and practices under it have changed as circumstances and leaders changed. The long-term tendency has been for presidential power in foreign affairs to increase relative to that of Congress. That tendency is most striking in the twentieth century, however, and was much less conspicuous before 1815. Presidential powers began to expand as soon as the Constitution went into effect under Washington. But a combination of circumstances (including the temperaments and philosophies of the men who were president) inhibited (but did not prevent) the growth of presidential authority in foreign affairs.

In contrast to the President and Congress, the United States Supreme Court played only a minor role in American foreign affairs. Conceivably the Court could declare treaties or foreign policy legislation unconstitutional as it did domestic legislation. In practice, however, the Supreme Court seemed to assume that control of foreign affairs was outside its jurisdiction. In any event, the Supreme Court did not exercise any significant restraining influence over the President or Congress in foreign affairs. When forced to rule, the Court sustained federal authority in foreign affairs in general and presidential power in particular.

Under the President the main responsibility for the actual conduct of foreign affairs rested with the Department of State under the Secretary of State. In the twentieth century the Department of State has become a huge, complicated organization employing thousands. Before 1815, however, and throughout the nineteenth century, it was extremely small. In 1790 it had a staff of only five, and as late as 1820 it employed only fourteen persons in Washington in addition to the Secretary of State. The Secretary of State, the top position in the President's Cabinet, was always a political appointee, but generally he was selected from among the more prominent, able, and respected leaders of the majority party. John Jay served briefly until Thomas Jefferson took over as Secretary of State in Washington's first Cabinet. The importance of the Secretary of State in foreign affairs relative to that of the President varied depending upon the abilities and personalities of the two men involved. Until the late 1820's the position was often a stepping-stone to the Presidency. Jefferson, Madison, Monroe, and John Quincy Adams all served in that important Cabinet post before they gained the Presidency. Most of those early secretaries had had diplomatic experience—a pattern that did not generally prevail during the rest of the nineteenth century.

Two general categories of foreign service officers served the United States (and other countries) overseas—diplomats and consuls. Diplomats were the official representatives from one government to another and normally resided in the capital city of the foreign state. Traditionally there were four grades of diplomats: ambassadors (residing in an embassy), envoys extraordinary and ministers plenipotentiary, ministers resident (residing in legations), and chargés d'affaires (subordinate or temporary officers). Americans commonly distrusted diplomats, and some early congressmen did not even wish to maintain permanent diplomatic posts abroad. Even President Washington did not wish to send many diplomats and, for a time, preferred only chargés. Since the ambassador traditionally was the personal representative of a monarch, the United States sent only ministers and chargés during the first century of its constitutional history—providing American representatives with less status than those of other countries. Not until the 1890's did the United States begin to use the rank of ambassador.

In the eighteenth and nineteenth centuries the United States did not have a professional career foreign service. Generally American diplomats were political appointees; often they were little qualified by experience or ability for their responsibilities. Commonly they did not know the language of the country to which they were assigned. Salaries were too low to support diplomats at major posts, so the best appointments went to men who were wealthy enough to be able to accept them—often planters or businessmen. Some able and distinguished men represented the United States in diplomatic posts before 1815—Jay, Franklin, Jefferson, Madison, John Quincy Adams, and others—but many other American diplomats were most inadequate. At the same time, foreign diplomats did not consider appointments to the United States particularly appealing. Before 1815 the dusty, drab, unsophisticated town of Washington, D.C., did not compare favorably with the major European capitals. Nor did the power or status of the new nation impress foreign statesmen. Consequently, foreign governments often sent third-rate diplomats to represent them in America.

In addition to diplomats, consuls were economic and social agents of a government sent to serve the interests of their compatriots living, traveling, or doing business abroad. Consuls were assigned to major population and business centers—not simply to capital cities. Traditionally there were four grades: consul general, consul, vice consul and consular agent. Before 1815 the United States relied largely on consular agents.

In those years the nation had a very inferior consular service. The predominantly agricultural society did not attach very high priority to business or travel abroad. Often American agents were simply businessmen who performed consular duties on the side. Others were political appointees. Until 1855 they were paid only on a fee basis. In general, despite important exceptions, neither the diplomats nor the consuls of the United States before 1815 were equal to their counterparts from other lands.

CHAPTER 19

THE DEVELOPMENT OF THE TWO-PARTY SYSTEM

During the first half of the twentieth century most students of American history assumed that the political parties that arose under Hamilton and Jefferson had their origins in the struggle over the ratification of the Constitution; some even assumed that parties derived from the loyalist-revolutionary disputes of the early 1770's. Thus, Hamilton and his followers were the reluctant revolutionaries who supported the Constitution. Jefferson and his supporters led in the revolutionary struggle but opposed the Constitution.

The basis for this belief was more than just a repetition of the name "Federalist," and more than a general knowledge of the political philosophies of the men involved. It was firmly rooted in a major work, *The Economic Origins of Jeffersonian Democracy** (1915), by one of America's greatest historians, Charles A. Beard. In the 1950's, this view came under strong attack with the posthumous publication in book form of a series of articles, *The Origins of the American Party System** (1956), by a very promising historian, Joseph Charles. The battle was shortly joined by a number of other scholars, including political scientists and sociologists as well as historians.

It is now well established that the political issues that gave rise to the new factions or parties were of an immediate nature rather than of historical origin. However, the importance of the nature of American political institutions in this development is not well established. In an earlier selection in this volume, Arthur Holcombe suggests that party development is inherent in the Constitution. What bearing does the present selection have on that contention? Could our constitutional system function without parties? What historical and personality factors were responsible for the emergence of parties?

In addition to the works cited above, the student should also examine Manning Dauer, *The Adams Federalists** (1953), and such general studies of the development of American political parties as Herbert Agar, *The Price of Union** (1950), Roy Nichols, *The Invention of the American Political Parties* (1967), Seymour M. Lipset, *The First New Nation** (1963), and William N. Chambers, *Political Parties in a New Nation** (1963).

* Available in a paperback edition.

THE GENESIS OF MODERN PARTIES
WILLIAM N. CHAMBERS

In 1790 Alexander Hamilton, as Secretary of the Treasury in the new government of the United States, proposed to Congress the first in a long series of measures aimed at the economic development of the new nation. Before he was finished he had brought into being a powerful political engine to advance his program, to support his determined effort to shape the destiny of the infant republic. In effect, he had founded the Federalist party. He began this task fourteen years after the declaration of American independence, seven years after the treaty of peace which followed the Revolutionary War.

In 1797 Thomas Jefferson boarded a coach at Monticello, the gracious home he had built on a Virginia hilltop. After three years of retirement devoted mainly to agricultural experiments and to country life, he was on his way to the nation's capital to assume fresh duties as Vice-President. Yet the trip of a week or so was more than just a return to the chores of office. It was a crucial stage in a political odyssey which was to bring him at last to full acceptance of active leadership in the opposition Republican party, a political force which was unique for its time.

The two events symbolize the genesis and ultimate establishment of national political parties on the American scene. These political engines were not only the first parties to adventure on the precarious ground of politics in an emerging nation but also the first true parties of modern times, appearing well before such formations developed in England or other European countries. They were shaped slowly and painstakingly, as part of a general progress in which the American states moved from colonial dependence and revolutionary uncertainties to become a stable democratic, modern republic. Like the nation itself, parties were the work not only of Hamilton and Jefferson, and of other great leaders like George Washington, the industrious James Madison, and the conscientious John Adams, but of nameless lesser workers as well. The final result was not

SOURCE. Abridged from *Political Parties in a New Nation: The American Experience, 1776–1809*, by William N. Chambers, New York, 1963, pp. 1–2, 36–44, 53–67, and 106–107. Copyright 1963 by Oxford University Press, Inc. Reprinted by permission of Oxford University Press and the author.

only parties but a system of competing parties in interaction. Yet no man could have said in advance just what the outcome would be.

Indeed, the whole national and party progress was beset by the difficulties and hesitations of exploration. It was fortunate that most of the new nation's leaders were men not only of high public faith and national vision, but of a profoundly pragmatic ability to learn and invent as they went along. . . .

II

In his advocacy, political management, and nation building, Hamilton brought together the elements that came to constitute the Federalist party. He did not consciously set out to do so, but such was the ultimate result.

It took some time to set the government going, first briefly in New York and then after 1790 in Philadelphia as temporary capitals. The first session of Congress was devoted mainly to establishing the executive departments and the judicial branch, and to other housewarming chores. It was not until 1790 and 1791 that Hamilton presented his proposals, and a new political era opened. . . .

In this effort, he was favored by an unusual political context. Not only did he move in the protective shadow of Washington's prestige. He was also able to "produce the event" so brilliantly at the outset—only in the tariff did he fall much short of his goals—largely because he could "march at the head of affairs" along comparatively open ways. In a new governmental system still being formed and in an unstructured national politics, he found ready opportunity for his purposes.

At the outset, the legislative branch Hamilton addressed was a leaderless herd. Composed almost entirely of "Federalists," in the sense of men who had supported the Constitution of 1787, Congress set no direction of its own for the new government. During the first session of April–September 1789, in a nearly free flow of legislative individualism, members had agreed or disagreed as issues came and went. There was sharp cleavage over proposals by Vice-President Adams to establish a "high-toned" government by giving grandiose titles to the president and other such devices, but alignments on the issue disappeared with the defeat of Adams's proposals. The choleric "Billy" Maclay of Pennsylvania, an Ishmael in the Senate who smelled conspiracy in any alliance however temporary, noted periodic instances of "caballing and meeting of members in knots." Yet even he could find little consistency beyond certain joint exertions by the "mercantile interest," or the support that Pennsylvania, New Jersey, Maryland, and Delaware members gave proposals for imports to encourage manufactures, or the tendency of "the New England men" to join together in opposing molasses duties. The ramblings of individual views and shifting relationships were only occasionally joined into blocs representing particular interests or sections. Otherwise, there were not even clear factional divisions. A summary comment by Maclay on early Congressional behavior was not far from the mark: "The mariner's compass has thirty-two points; the political one, perhaps as many hundreds."

The sessions of 1790 and 1791, however, revealed the stamp of Hamilton's firm leadership. The law creating the Treasury Department had sketched unusual ties between the head of that department and Congress in the reports and interchange of information it required. Beginning with the debt-assumption issue, Hamilton elaborated these formal ties into the bonds of informal executive-legislative leadership, utilizing, in Maclay's phrase, "every kind of management." His "reports" were calls to action, and he and his assistants provided arguments and statistics for Congressional debates. He followed legislative affairs with the utmost care, keeping a sharp eye on timing, favorable committee appointments, and chances for maneuver. He met privately with members, and discreetly arranged informal conferences to draw his followers together. Everything "is prearranged by Hamilton and his group," Maclay cried in the anguish of opposition.

Although Maclay exaggerated, he was right in perceiving that the debt and bank issues, with the prestige of Washington's "name," had produced a "court faction." Its genesis in Hamilton's executive or "ministerial" leadership marked the beginnings of coherence and order in politics in the new nation's capital.

III

The emergence of management at the capital brought strong responses across the country. In the process, what began as a capital faction soon became a national faction and then, finally, the new Federalist party.

From the national center, ties of common interest and action were extended into the states, counties, and towns. Again Hamilton played a prominent role, weaving a web of correspondents out of his wartime associates, his business connections and friends, and the many individuals whom, as Secretary, he was able to oblige. His personal contacts and personal influence were used to draw together a new political formation, which eventually became less personal. The Federalists also drew on the first American veteran's association, the Society of the Cincinnati, a strongly knit organization of Revolutionary War officers and their descendants. Such notable figures as Fisher Ames and Theodore Sedgwick in Massachusetts, John Jay and Rufus King in New York, John Marshall in Virginia, or Robert Goodloe Harper in South Carolina joined the cause, along with many others. Thus Hamilton's original faction reached out into the countryside and developed into a national political structure which could support its capital leadership by undertaking the labors of propaganda, electioneering, and other political tasks. Its key local leaders were men of position and high respectability in their communities: former military officers everywhere, or mercantile magnates in New York; the Congregational divines in Massachusetts and Connecticut, or Episcopalian ministers in the Middle Atlantic region and in the coastal plains of the South; captains of finance in Philadelphia, or great planters in Maryland or South Carolina. From the Federalists' center at the capital to their periphery in the counties and towns, relationships among established notables provided the strong strands of the emerging Federalist structure. Such notables drew in other participants, and together they soon formed the ranks of the active workers or "cadre" of the emerging party.

Yet the party-in-the-making also rested on a broad combination of interests and opinions. Like any open major party in a pluralistic society, it came to include in its following a substantial range and significant density of groups and individuals. Domestic merchants, men in the shipping trade and shipbuilders, holders of public debt securities, bankers, investors and financiers generally, owners of struggling manufactories, great Tidewater planters, dependent business and professional men—all could look happily to Hamilton's promotion of enterprise under the protection of government action. Furthermore, most of these groups had already enjoyed sufficient economic development to enable them to support their interests with significant political power. Yet the Federalist appeal was not limited to capitalist or proprietary interests. Many wage earners, particularly in shipbuilding along the coastal rivers, where a man might farm part of the time and work in the shipyards another part, could see employment and higher wages in Hamilton's proposals. Modest farmers who looked to the export market could also anticipate prosperity and higher prices as a result of Federalist policy, although ultimately the great weakness in the Federalist fabric proved to be an insensitivity to the concerns of agriculture as a whole. The assumption scheme had a strong appeal in states that had incurred heavy Revolutionary debts and failed to pay them off. This special issue operated in Hamilton's favor in debt-ridden South Carolina as well as in mercantile New England. Indeed, Massachusetts and South Carolina became the early Northern and Southern foundations of Federalist strength.

Their emerging structure and broad base gave the Federalists a position of effective influence in the electoral arena. Working through their network of notables and lesser leaders, and through Hamilton's web of correspondents, beneficiaries, and officeholders, the Federalists were able to put forward candidates and mobilize voters for them. Though they tended to look upon elections largely as opportunities for the public to ratify their policies, Federalist managers knew that co-ordinated action in election contests was essential to maintaining power.

The Federalists also drew support from an imposing propaganda array. In 1789 Hamilton and Senator Rufus King of New York raised funds to enable John Fenno to establish the *Gazette of the United States,* which became the semi-official national Federalist organ, published first in New York and then in Philadelphia. In 1790 the *Columbian Centinel* in Boston, under the editorship of Benjamin Russell, began a long career as polemical spokesman for New England partisans. In 1793 gifts from Federalist merchants in New York launched the *American Minerva,* under the great grammarian and lexicographer Noah Webster, as the city's first daily. These and other major presses gave the lead to lesser sheets, and the Federalists could soon count a majority of the nation's editors on their side. Early newspapers were overwhelmingly political in character; and taken together they constituted a major force for factional or party cohesion, communicating partisan information and views from the centers of power to the outlying communities. Thus the Federalists undertook another key function of parties: influencing or polarizing national opinion, on particular issues as they arose or around their program as a whole. In the process, they brought additional measures of order into national politics.

The Federalists' achievement of full party status came with the development of emotional attachment to the party as such. The concerns of interest, economic as in Hamilton's proposals or otherwise, provided critical strands for party formation; but something more was also necessary. This was the emergence of unifying faiths and loyalties, of exclusive and distinctive "in-group" attitudes, of emotional commitments, of at least the beginnings of an ideology. Here again the charisma of Washington, his aura as a providential agent of national independence and national identity, supplied "an *Aegis very essential"* to Federalist party development. At the outset of his Administration the President gave an ear to the divergent views of a cabinet which included Jefferson as well as Hamilton and played a chairman-of-the board role, deliberating and deciding among alternative policy suggestions. As time passed, however, Washington himself and his Administration as a whole became more and more partisan; and by 1793 he was seeking advice almost entirely from a limited number of Federalist-minded leaders. Meanwhile, his portentous name was increasingly used as a distinctively Federalist symbol. Thus the Father of His Country became also the father figure of Federalist propaganda, a focus for partisan faiths, sentiments, and loyalties.

Reactions to new issues furthered the development of ideological ties. The French Revolution, at first widely hailed in America, ran its course toward regicide, radical republicanism, and (in February 1793) war with Great Britain. Determined to avoid involvement, Washington proclaimed a policy of official neutrality, a course Jefferson at the State Department accepted reluctantly in the face of treaties of commerce and alliance with France which had been signed in America's own hour of revolutionary trial. Yet to most Federalists the issue had become one of sanity against madness, stability against chaos, and their sentiments lay with the established order they thought England represented. The whole controversy prompted a war of words in which, as it intensified over the years, Federalist "Anglomen" came to stigmatize opponents with the cry of "Jacobin!" while opposition "Gallomen" responded with "Monocrat!" Though group or economic interests were not absent from the French-British issue in America, the controversy once again brought an emotionalized, philosophical, or symbolic cleavage of deeper faiths, convictions, and loyalties. In the ideological controversy the Federalists could perceive their party as a knightly band of saviors, the true champions of society, stability, and the nation. Irrational as attachment to Washington as father figure may have been, exaggerated as the logomachy over the French-British question was, these symbolic reactions and emotional ties completed the great transition from a Federalist faction to a Federalist party, as part of a general transition from old-style faction politics to modern party politics. They did so by reinforcing the seams of structure with crucial threads of emotional *élan,* of Federalist party spirit.

Throughout the long shaping of the Federalist formation, Hamilton played a curious though commanding role. In effect he had initiated the whole effort with his vision and advocacy, and throughout its early years he stood forth as the party's unquestioned spokesman and leader. Yet at no time, apparently, despite his energy and brilliance, did he see himself in full consciousness as a man who was building a party. Like his colleagues, he had no pattern of party in mind to go by, and had to devise what amounted to party practices as party structure took form. His purposes, as he saw them, were to point the new nation in the "right" direction, place its new government on firm foundations, mobilize support for his management in that government, and thwart such political foes as might appear. Furthermore, even while these goals brought him to act as a bold party leader, he could condemn the very idea of party. To be sure, what he usually had in mind by the term was a "factious opposition"; it was as much the idea of a co-ordinated opposition as the idea of party that he feared, and he and other Federalists tended to use the terms "party" and "party spirit" more and more as stigmas to damage their opponents. Nonetheless, the labors of Hamilton and his allies did make a party also—the first modern party of Western history, and a remarkably effective one at that.

Indeed, its early achievements in structure, following, and ideology make the Federalist formation a powerful political phalanx, and marked it for initial success. Yet certain characteristics that grew out of its origins also marked it for ultimate failure in the American context. It began as, and remained, a "party of notables," in Max Weber's phrase, despite its wide early following. It was such because it was led by and found its center among men of established property, position, and power; and the attitudes of such men gave the Federalist outlook a particular cast. Hamilton himself had remarked, "The mass of the people are turbulent and changing—they seldom judge or determine right." Such attitudes of elitist condescension, which became typical of the Federalists, ultimately offended the mass of voters. These attitudes also led the Federalists themselves to resist the development of broad, public organization as a means to mobilize mass support. Such organization as the Federalists did achieve was largely oligarchic and more than half clandestine.

Thus, to their chronic weakness of appeal to the bulk of the nation's small farmers, the Federalists added an elitist structure, corresponding attitudes of condescension, and disdain of popular organization. As time strengthened the new democratic impulse in American society, such characteristics were to prove fatal flaws. For some years, however, their party remained dominant.

Viewed in historical analysis and against the retrospect of American faction politics in the 1770's and 1780's, the emergence of the Federalists reveals a transition from the older "connexions" of fluid factions, family cliques, or juntos to the newer, modern connection of party. . . .

IV

As the Federalist party originated with action by Hamilton at the Treasury, so the first clear impetus of opposition came in reactions led by James Madison in Congress. The opposition, however, began not only as a self-styled "Republican" group at the capital, but as a popular Republican movement in the states and communities. . . .

It was the junction of Madison's Republican faction at the capital with this indigenous opposition that ultimately made the Republican party. Yet the formation of that party was a slow process of discovery and invention for the men who came to lead it, and it was some years before its shape was fully apparent.

No bold innovative protagonist, Madison nonetheless was a dogged antagonist to "Belcour."* He was a Virginia planter's son and scholarly graduate of the College of New Jersey, which was later renamed Princeton. Barely five feet, four inches tall, soft-spoken and a bit fussy, he lacked commanding flair, and his leadership depended on the fact that he was shrewd, ready to meet the challenge Hamilton presented, and immensely industrious. He took the floor in the House of Representatives more frequently than any other member; and he was also busy behind the scenes, trying to persuade other members, carrying on a substantial political correspondence, and devising strategy. As early as the second session of Congress in 1790, the philosopher of the Constitution had established himself as the chief spokesman against what Hamilton wanted to make of the national character.

V

It was a circumspect, slow-forming sort of opposition. Like Jefferson, for example, Madison was willing to compromise on the debt assumption question if he could, even without the bait of establishing the capital on Virginia's border which had been offered by Hamilton to get assumption through. Furthermore, despite Madison's activity in Congress, opposition remained for some time fluid, undisciplined, and scattered. Only by late 1791 and early 1792 were lines discernible between Hamilton's "court faction" on the one hand and a reasonably consistent anti-Administration bloc on the other. Even so, as late as 1794 a fifth or more of the members in the House showed no consistent attachment to any faction or bloc. . . .

Generally, the Republicans took a negative stand on Hamilton's program for positive action to promote economic development. To the Republicans, the gains from Hamilton's policies for capitalist enterprisers were more than counterbalanced by their cost to agriculturists. On the whole, the opposition in addition saw no pressing need for rapid industrial advances. In their view planters, plain farmers, and many other elements

* A polemical reference, made in 1790, to Alexander Hamilton. (Eds.)

in the population could be happy and prosperous if they were provided the elementary protections of government, not overburdened by taxes, and then left alone. Republican economic policy thus became a policy of "equal rights for all, special privileges for none," as Jefferson put it—of opposition to Hamilton's measures as a panoply of "special privileges," and insistence on a political economy that amounted to "hands off." They were aware that, to succeed, a government must be effective and must provide satisfaction to important interests in the society; but they were convinced that a policy of *laissez faire* could best serve both agricultural interests and the principle of equality, and could also "succeed." Ultimately the forces of industrialization, economic development, and capitalism were to triumph in the sweep of modernization; and the process was to bring new outpourings of goods and services which soon raised American living standards above those of contemporaneous European nations. In the 1790's, however, the ordinary American was already relatively comfortable in comparison with his European counterpart; and thus Americans were not swept so strongly into the current of rising economic expectations which was to characterize later emerging peoples, as they looked to their own contemporaries, the modern industrial nations. In this situation, the new American nation as a whole did not find itself so pressed for the payoff of forced economic development as other new nations have been. In this situation also, the Republican economic outlook could win broad popular support from groups who could see Hamilton's measures as a threat to agrarian ways and to equality.

As the years passed, meanwhile, the Congressional opposition broadened its scope and found increased co-ordination. In 1790 Maclay in the Senate, who could see only "caballing" in Hamilton's "management," was somewhat naïvely startled to discover the peculiar role a Virginian-turned-Pennsylvanian was playing behind the scenes. This was the discreet go-between John Beckley, former mayor of Richmond and now Clerk of the House, who was intimate both with Speaker Frederick Augustus Muhlenberg of Pennsylvania and with Madison, as well as with other members. Thus Billy Maclay found that he could, "through this channel, communicate what I please to Madison." After 1791, Madison was also flanked by other leaders such as, in the Senate, his former opponent Monroe of Virginia and Burr of New York, and, in the House, the bold polemicist William Branch Giles of Virginia and the gentle, simple-republican Nathaniel Macon of North Carolina. Again and again, Giles in particular was effective as a critic of Federalist policies, from the national bank to lesser measures such as the "favoritism" of bounties to aid cod fisheries. Early in 1793 he offered a set of nine resolutions censuring virtually all of Hamilton's official conduct, and aimed at forcing him out of office. For the moment, Federalist fire was directed less against Madison and his faction than against "Giles and his junto."

The bitter Federalist orator of the House, Fisher Ames (of Massachusetts and Harvard) cried out against the new force of opposition. Writing at the beginning of 1793 to a fellow ultra-Federalist, Timothy Dwight (of Connecticut, and President of Yale), he protested: "Virginia moves in a solid column, and the discipline of party is as severe as the Prussian. Deserters are not spared. Madison is become a desperate party leader." Intolerant of any opposition, particularly opposition tinged with democratic "evil," he was exaggerating. But an anti-Administration Congressional faction existed by 1792 and 1793, and Virginia men composed its core.

Changes in relationships between major figures in the national government also exacerbated political cleavage. Quite early Madison had concluded that Adams was hopelessly embroiled in an "anti-republican" (meaning Federalist) course and had written him off. More important, as Washington himself was drawn ever more deeply into the Federalist cause, his trust in Hamilton was strengthened and his ties with Madison and Jefferson were weakened. Late in 1791 Madison's role in establishing Philip Freneau—"that rascal Freneau," Washington called him—as an anti-Hamilton editor had caused a severe chill in relations between the President and the Congressman. Finally, when by 1793 Madison's opposition role became fixed, confidential exchanges with Washington came to an end. At the same time Jefferson, slow to oppose as he was, found it increasingly difficult to get along with Hamilton; and the years brought cankers of difference which even Washington's continued tactful efforts could not heal. In 1791 both men gave the President opinions on the national bank proposal, Hamilton defending his brain child, Jefferson raising doubts on strict-constructionist constitutional grounds. Other questions sharpened the animosity: patronage contentions; differences on financial policy, with Jefferson listing for Washington in 1792 a bill of twenty-one objections to Hamilton's views; and a personal condemnation of Jefferson by Hamilton in 1792. When Jefferson left the cabinet at the end of 1793, rupture at the executive as well as the legislative centers of government was complete.

Meanwhile, events brought increasing collaboration between Jefferson and Madison. In 1791 Jefferson was inadvertently drawn into a press-and-pamphlet controversy in which John Adams was accused of being the author of an anonymous attack on Thomas Paine's pamphlet defending the French Revolution, *The Rights of Man*. Having written a letter praising the pamphlet, Jefferson could condemn (as did Paine) "the doctrine of king, lords & commons," and see Adams as its sponsor. Yet he also regretted that he had been brought into the controversy with his old friend of Revolutionary days, and proclaimed "my love of silence & quiet, & my abhorrence of dispute." By mid-1793, however, Jefferson was aghast at the pro-British, anti-French, executive-prerogative doctrines Hamilton, as "Pacificus," was expounding in a series of articles defending Washington's neutrality proclamation. He urged Madison: "For God's sake, my dear Sir, take up your pen, select the most striking heresies and cut him to pieces in the face of the public." As "Helvidius," Madison did so, urging the role of Congress in the treaty and war powers against Hamilton's penchant for executive authority. In a dramatic Congressional debate on a report Jefferson had submitted at a propitious moment concerning commercial relations with Great Britain and France, Madison directly echoed Jefferson's views. On the other side William Loughton Smith of South Carolina, working from a document Hamilton had put into his hands, took the floor as the Federalist voice. The emergence of Madison as Jefferson's spokesman, balancing Smith as Hamilton's agent, represented a significant crystallization of factional ties between executive and legislative leaders. Although the actual debate had to wait until 1794, just after Jefferson's retirement, the Madisonian Congressional faction was becoming a general capital faction—and turning to foreign as well as domestic issues. . . .

This characteristic,* plus what Jefferson had come to stand for as chief author of the Declaration of Independence, as a moderate liberal-reform governor in Virginia, and as the informal philosopher of democratic-republican convictions, inevitably made him a reference point and symbol for the opposition to Hamilton's doctrines. Even in his retirement to his Monticello home in Virginia he was, willy-nilly, the focus of the republican cause and its potential gentle hero. As factional lines drew tighter, he necessarily began to assume a qualified role of leadership, although the main direction of affairs remained with men like Madison or Beckley.

Another landmark in the emergence of resistance at the capital was the establishment of an opposition press. It began with "that rascal Freneau" in October 1791. A poet, a Princeton man also who was friendly there with such future Republicans as Madison and Burr, Philip Freneau was also an effective journalist. Largely at Madison's instigation, but with Jefferson's approval and aid, he was brought to Philadelphia to establish the *National Gazette.* He also served as printer for official

* Jefferson's charm and strong personal appeal.

State Department papers, just as John Fenno of the earlier *Gazette of the United States* acted as printer for Treasury papers. The *National Gazette* joined the bank fray with a series of essays by Madison. On the issues of world politics and ideology it was strongly pro-French, full of praises for Paine and brickbats for Burke, as champion and critic respectively of the French Revolution. Generally more "radical" and inclined to ideological blacks and whites than either Jefferson or Madison, Freneau was a vigorous catalyst for opposition reactions. He was also an early example of the use of patronage for political purposes, serving not only as printer for Jefferson's State Department but also as a clerk-translator with almost a sinecure in the department itself.

Politically, the *National Gazette* was an instrument of Republican cohesion. It communicated the words and deeds of factional leaders at the center of government to emerging local leaders and followers across the country, thus promoting a national tone. It did this in part directly, in part by playing oracle to local editors, who clipped generously from it. Never so blessed with presses as the Federalists, the inchoate Republican impulse could count on only a few large papers like the *American Advertizer* in Philadelphia and the *Independent Chronicle* in Boston, but numerous country weeklies followed Freneau's lead. The *National Gazette* remained a factional rather than a party organ, however; and it was short-lived, yielding in 1793 to the Philadelphia *Aurora* under Benjamin Franklin Bache. When Jefferson withdrew from the cabinet cockpit, Freneau withdrew from national prominence to lesser journalism in New Jersey and to composing nature lyrics.

VI

In the states, counties, and towns, meanwhile, forces of interest and opinion that could be combined into a complex political entity were beginning to gather.

In Virginia, for example, wily old Patrick Henry, during the movement for a new Constitution, had "smelled a rat." Near the end of 1790, convinced that his fears had been confirmed, he carried a series of strong resolutions through the Virginia legislature at Richmond. They condemned Federalist policies for spawning a "moneyed interest" inimical to agriculture and proper commerce, and as an excessive exercise of national power at the expense of the states. Privately, Hamilton grumbled, "This is the first symptom of a spirit which must either be killed, or it will kill the Constitution." The Federalists might act and assemble for their purposes, but it was presumably not fitting for an opposition to do so.

Again, at Pittsburgh, in western Pennsylvania: "The cause of France is the cause of man, and neutrality is desertion." These stirring words appeared in a public letter sent to President Washington by H. H. Brackenridge in May 1793, after the manifesto of neutrality between warring England and France.

Such expressions revealed a humus of national sentiment that promoted the growth of a popular Republican opposition, a ferment not only of immediate issues but also of larger moral and political questions.

Before long, the opposition had achieved some organization which revealed a strong ideological bent. In 1793 eleven popular political associations calling themselves Democratic Societies or Republican Societies were formed, and by 1794 another two dozen were established. Ten flourished in Pennsylvania, seventeen grew up in the hospitable soil of the South, and in every state but one the Societies flowered. Their political hue was vibrantly anti-Federalist. Though other interests were also intertwined in the movement—merchants looking to the French trade, or some speculators in western lands who saw Hamilton's exise tax as an obstacle to settlement, or dissident sugar or tobacco planters— the appeal of the Democratic or Republican clubs was particularly directed to the mass of "farmers" in the countryside and to "mechanics" in the towns. The latter term included such diverse callings as self-employed craftsmen, ship-carpenters, and mariners. Indeed, one ultra-populist outburst was a printed "Feast of Merriment," in which hearty mariners were heroized in pornographic anecdote while figures of Federalist respectability were subjected to salacious jibes. Yet the Societies had respectable leaders of their own, particularly urban and urbane doctors, editor-"printers," and teachers—intellectuals who gave the Society movement much of its ideological coloration. Several, like James Hutchinson and Benjamin Rush (founder of the Philadelphia Dispensary) in medicine, or Freneau and Benjamin Franklin Bache in letters or journalism, were eminent in their fields. Few lawyers, however, and only a negligible number of ministers joined the movement. Its broad liberal character was less appealing than Federalism to traditionalist-oriented men. . . .

From the Societies or insurrection to philosophical flowerings, the humus of popular antagonism was producing a lusty growth, despite bitter counterattacks evoking the magic of Washington's name. A new movement was at hand.

The whole development brought to the fore the difficult question of an opposition faction or party. Under Hamilton's leadership, the Federalists were building a "government" party, a party of stability, dedicated to the idea that the first imperative for government in a new nation was that it must govern and sustain itself. By contrast, the rising Republican movement was maintaining, in effect, that the new polity should also provide room for counteraction, for effective representation of interests and opinions that were slighted or discountenanced in the government party. In addition, the emerging Republicans were "going to the people," in a virtually unprecedented attempt not only to represent popular interests and concerns but also to mobilize popular opposition to those who held power. If they had their way, if their appeal to planters, farmers, and "merchanics" was broadened sufficiently to succeed, it would end by displacing the Federalists in power and substituting a new set of governors. It would do so, however, not by intrigue or violence but by peaceful means, by the weight of votes in elections, by popular choice or decision. In its notion of opposition and the possibility of a peaceful transfer of power, effected by peaceful democratic action, the emerging Republican movement represented a radically new outlook in political history.

Despite its commitment to peaceful means, opposition brought strains in national unity. It was perhaps fortunate as well as inevitable that the Federalists, with their emphasis on stability and consolidation, came first on the scene and held power first; that the Republicans appeared later and were slower to gain the strength that made them contenders for public power; and that both formations still reached only limited numbers of voters, instead of achieving immediately the full mobilization of popular masses in party competition. If the new polity had begun its political life with two full-blown parties, both stirring broad mass action in their behalf, the frictions of party combat might have proved unmanageable. It was also certainly fortunate that the opposition which looked to Madison or Jefferson was moderate rather than extreme, able to work within a developing national tradition rather than bound to deep social cleavages or to intransigent positions. In fact, the views of Republicans and Federalists were not "wide as the poles asunder." If they had been, or if the methods of the Whiskey Rebellion had been commonly employed, the nation might have been disrupted or opposition might have been snuffed out long before a two-party system could develop. Even as it was, it was years before the nation as a whole came to full acceptance of the idea of a governing party on the one hand and an opposition on the other.

At the outset, meanwhile, the opposition did not yet constitute a party. The Republicans were at most a capital faction that was beginning to find sympathy and support in the countryside in a congeries of dissenting elements, bodies of opinion, associations, and groups. Even more than with Hamilton and the Federalists, the ultimate Republican formation was the end result of a long and halting process of searching and of experimentation in workable ways to meet immediate problems. Although

Madison and others spoke of a "Republican party" from time to time in the early years of opposition, the term at first meant little to them beyond sympathy and some co-ordination among like-minded men; and Jefferson remained unconvinced of the wisdom or necessity of party. What the Republican leaders wanted to do at the beginning was to oppose what they took to be wrong measures and win sufficient support to block them. It was some time before they advanced to the point where they arrived at some conception of a popularly-based party in a full sense and began to fill the new roles it called for. When they did so, they brought about a new kind of political formation or institution—but it was not to spring forth in a day. . . .

It is in terms of relationships between structure and following that the Republicans may be thought of as a new kind of political institution. The Federalists achieved party structure earlier and found a substantial popular power base; and yet they never quite transcended their ministerial, English-oriented, elitist origins. They represented interests, shaped opinion, and offered choices to the electorate; but they were not given to encouraging intraparty popular participation. They always depended on a comparatively close nucleus of leaders in government, and their attitude toward the public and electorate was always an uncertain mixture of condescension and fear. The Republicans on the other hand, although slower to form, finally established a close rapport between leaders and followers.

The difference is manifest in various facets of the Republican formation. Like the Federalists, the Republicans built out from a nucleus at the center of government, many of their early leaders also were notables, and Jefferson frequently showed at least a trace of condescension in his attitude toward the people, despite his republican philosophy. Yet the coruscations of republican sentiment in currents of opinion, in the Democratic and Republican Societies, and in the furor over foreign policy, before there was a Republican party, gave the party a broad potential power base in advance. Furthermore, from the outset the Republican leaders, cadres, and actives included a large number of "politicians," of men who made their careers and achieved prominence in politics, as contrasted with notables; and the Republicans were very nearly a "party of politicians," in Max Weber's term. In this situation, the party's leaders came to look to public opinion and to the electorate as vital powers to which the party should be responsive or responsible. Thus the Republican outlook developed in terms of leaders not only acting on their following but also interacting with it. The Republican founders were the first modern party-builders to conceive of a party in a distinctively democratic role, and thus the first to create a genuinely "popular" party.

CHAPTER 20

THOMAS JEFFERSON: HIS HERITAGE TO AMERICA

All American political figures on all sides of all questions customarily have appealed to the authority of Thomas Jefferson. His words were used by Southerners in support of secession, but they were also used by Abraham Lincoln in support of human freedom. Today, he is much quoted by states' righters, but the ringing phrases of the Declaration of Independence are used repeatedly by those in the Civil Rights Movement. His words and sentiments have been adopted by anti-Communist right-wingers and by left-leaning liberals; by Democrats and Republicans; and by traditionalists and progressives. Different generations of Americans have viewed Thomas Jefferson in a variety of ways, as the historian, Merrill D. Peterson, shows in his study, *The Jefferson Image in the American Mind** (1960).

Dumas Malone attempts to bring clarity to this confused picture by using a "common sense" approach to determine the meaning that Thomas Jefferson has for us today. Professor Malone examines Jefferson's acts, policies, and words in the area of world affairs, his presidential administrations, his views of the functions of government and, finally, the words and deeds that Jefferson himself believed had the "quality of timelessness": the items included on his tombstone. Malone specifically argues that we cannot find the relevance of Jefferson by taking him out of his times and by directly applying his policies to today's problems. We must consider him in his own setting of time, place, and circumstance.

This selection raises and answers important questions about the nature and uses of history. What does Malone say about the widespread use of Jefferson's name in direct support of politicians and causes? In view of the prevalent misuse of history in the direct application of Jefferson's words and policies to modern circumstances, what more valid approach and criteria does Malone use to determine Jefferson's relevance for the modern world? Do you agree that this is the "common sense" approach to the relevance of Jefferson? What are the constant factors in history that Malone considers of major significance in the process by which historical personalities speak to subsequent generations across the years and centuries? Finally, what relevance does Thomas Jefferson have for us in the last half of the twentieth century?

Students wishing to explore this topic further should read (in addition to the Peterson volume cited above) two brilliant essays: Carl Becker, "What is Still Living in the Political Philosophy of Thomas Jefferson?," *American Historical Review,* XLVIII (July, 1943), and Dumas Malone, "Mr. Jefferson to Mr. Roosevelt; An Imaginary Letter," *Virginia Quarterly Review,* XIX (Spring, 1943). D. J. Boorstin, *The Lost World of Thomas Jefferson** (1948), is an outstanding study of Jefferson's thought.

* Available in a paperback edition.

THE RELEVANCE OF MR. JEFFERSON
DUMAS MALONE

In almost the last year of his long life, replying to a query about the Declaration of Independence, Thomas Jefferson wrote a letter which is worth recalling. Certain people, especially people who did not care for his politics, had suggested that in fact that famous document was not original. When he was eighty-two years old he made a statement about its objects—that is, his own objects in writing it—which I quote in part:

Not to find out new principles, or new arguments, never before thought of, not merely to say things which had never been said before; but to place before mankind the common sense of the subject. . . .

The present utterance can hardly be compared to the immortal Declaration, and I do not presume to address it to all mankind, but, without pretense of originality, I hope to set forth the common sense of the matter in dealing with Mr. Jefferson himself. While many true and wonderful things have been said about this inexhaustible man since his death, a considerable number of things have been said that should really be described as nonsense. Perhaps it would be fairer to say of many of these that they are partial truths which have been paraded as whole truths, deriving from the law and gospel. At all events, confusion is confounded when an historic personage is quoted on opposite sides in a contemporary controversy, as Mr. Jefferson repeatedly has been. Instances will quickly come to mind in connection with the presidential campaign of 1960, when it was solemnly announced that he would have voted for both candidates; or in connection with the New Deal, which he is said both to have opposed and favored.

It is not my purpose to declare which side he was on, since I really have no way of knowing. Also, I recognize the likelihood that I should arrive at the pleasant conclusion that he always agreed with me. The proneness of the human mind to rationalize can hardly be exaggerated. In view, however, of the well-authenticated fact that contradictory state-

SOURCE: Dumas Malone, "The Relevance of Mr. Jefferson," *The Virginia Quarterly Review* (Summer, 1961), XXXVII, pp. 332–349. Originally delivered as The Founder's Day Address at the University of Virginia in the spring of 1961. Reprinted by permission of *The Virginia Quarterly Review* and the author.

ments have been made about him ever since his death I am disposed to ask certain questions. What meaning does he really have for *us* in our present situation? Are his words and actions relevant to *our* circumstances, or irrelevant? If he is relevant in certain respects and irrelevant in others, what is the ground of distinction? How is anyone to know? On this confused situation I should like to turn what the late William S. Gilbert called "The hose of common sense." Surely the common sense of the matter is to try to distinguish between those words and actions which related solely or primarily to his own time, and those which have the quality of timelessness. That is, we need to separate what is or may be properly regarded as dateless from what is necessarily dated.

In this connection, I do not need to focus attention on him as a human being. Human nature seems to have changed little in the course of recorded history, and human personality defies barriers of space and time. In spirit we can live intimately with persons from the past whenever their words and deeds are sufficiently recorded for us to know them. We soon forget that their clothes were unlike ours and that they wore their hair quite differently. We have to allow for changes in manners and morals, and even when they employ our own language we may detect a certain quaintness in their speech. But the common denominator of human nature and individual experience is so large that great personalities can speak to us across the generations, even across the centuries, in language that is understandable since it is the language of life itself.

By precept and example the father of the University of Virginia can still teach anyone who will take the trouble to listen to him and observe him. Many things can we learn from him about the fine art of living. Not the least of these is that once an apostle of equality lived a notably elevated life, an extraordinarily rich, perennially interesting, endlessly generous, and ceaselessly useful life, in a society which he himself had made more democratic. He exemplified excellence, not the dull level of mediocrity; individuality, not unthinking conformity. He dared to build his house upon a mountain and to be himself, surveying the universe in personal independence. As a human being he has real meaning for our time: in his own person he reminds us what man can do with freedom.

Though human nature and human personality seem to be the most constant factors in history except the earth and the waters round it, along with the seasons and the tides, they manifest themselves in widely varying circumstances, of course, and no human being of either the past or the present can be fully understood apart from his particular environment. We should be foolish to assume that Mr. Jefferson would make precisely the same domestic arrangements at Monticello if he were living there now as he made a hundred and fifty years ago; or that, if one of his grandchildren became ill today, he would be as dubious as he was then about the value of medical services; presumably he would not now suggest that doctors may do more harm than good. We can appreciate the realism which enabled him to appraise them so well in his day, but we should be unwise to seek his *specific* advice in the conduct of our personal affairs, medical or otherwise.

Anything that may be said about considering a human being, in his personal life, on the background of his own environment has to be heavily underlined when we speak of him as a public man. We *have* to view statesmen, past and present, in their own settings of time, place, and circumstance. To do otherwise would be to render them a grave injustice. For forty years, with only a few interruptions, Mr. Jefferson was a public official—burgess, delegate, governor, minister to a foreign country, secretary of state, vice president, and president. During all these years he was dealing with current public affairs and day-to-day problems. More than most statesmen, he tried to take the long view and to guide his steps by enduring principles, and if he had not done so better than most men his fame would have been less enduring. Nonetheless, he could not escape the necessity, and no statesman ever can, of adjusting policies to the existing situation. Public affairs are not conducted in a vacuum. It is of the utmost importance, therefore, to seek a fair understanding of the public situation he had to face.

Since he devoted a very large part of his time and labors to foreign relations, and world affairs are of such vital concern to us today, we can profitably take a quick look at the general world situation in his era. Even in his slow-moving age that situation changed, to be sure, but certain of its features were relatively constant during most of his public life. Some of these features were so similar to what we ourselves have faced that his age seems positively familiar. Most of his career was set on a background of general war. The conflict which broke out in Europe when he was secretary of state and lasted, with only slight interruption, considerably beyond his presidency, if not world war in our sense, came nearer being that than any that our planet was to know until the twentieth century. In his day this planet was a less dangerous place than it has been in our era of world war, total war, cold war, and threat of nuclear destruction. Furthermore, because of the slowness of movement and communication, peril was less imminent. There was not the same sense of desperate urgency, and statesmen could be less hurried. That is one thing the statesmen of this day can deeply envy them. Nonetheless, the dangers faced in the two eras were strikingly similar, even if in our time they have been greatly intensified.

His age was one of revolution which touched virtually all parts of the globe that our country was concerned with. Indeed, it was commonly regarded as *the* age of revolution until our generation pre-empted the title. In our day the revolutionary spirit has spread to continents which were still slumbering in his time. It has taken on social and economic forms which were little dreamed of by our forefathers when they proclaimed revolution in the name of political independence, and which were not approached even in revolutionary France. But his time was also one of great political and considerable social convulsion. Thus one can say that, in its international aspects, no other period in American history can so fitly be compared to ours as the age of Washington and Jefferson. I have been particularly struck with what may be called the psychological parallels. Human nature being much the same, personal and social reactions to war and revolution show a great deal of similarity. This is frequently reflected in language: many of the things that were said in manifestos and resolutions, in newspapers and in private letters, sound like utterances of our time if you change the names and places.

There were numerous differences, however, and we can readily recognize the paramount importance of one of them. The position from which Mr. Jefferson and others charged with the national interest and security viewed a warring and revolutionary world was virtually the reverse of the one our leaders now occupy. The potential giant of the West was then only a stripling, a weakling among the Powers, while today our Republic is in all respects gigantic. They had to lead from weakness, where we can lead from strength. The policy which will always be associated with the names of Washington and Jefferson was to keep out of the raging power struggle in so far as possible, regardless of personal predilections one way or the other, regardless of ideology. Thus was born the classic American doctrine of neutrality or non-involvement, which, despite occasional aberrations, endured for generations. It arose from the necessities of national security, and its wisdom at that time cannot be doubted. Everybody knows that the policy has been completely reversed in our century, also because of the necessities of national security.

What does this signify about the bearing of the acts, the policies, the words of Mr. Jefferson on the world problems of our day? Can we really learn anything from him? In my opinion, we can learn much. As an example I will cite the year 1793, when the European war broadened so as to threaten us, when the French Revolution passed into its greatest excesses, when this young Republic entered upon its historic policy of neutrality. To consider the activities of Mr. Jefferson, the Secretary of State, in one of the most momentous years in modern history, observing his incessant labors, his extraordinary patience amid frustrations, his unflagging patriotism, and his basic wisdom, is to share a tremendous experience. Regarding the controversy into which he, a friend of France, was drawn in 1793 with the insolent envoy of the French revolutionary government, one of the greatest of his successors in the office of Secretary of State, John Quincy Adams, said that his papers on that controversy "present the most perfect model of diplomatic discussion and expostulation of modern times." This was American diplomacy at one of its highest points, revealing rare skill and a realistic appraisal of the existing situation which should command the admiration of anyone dealing with international problems in any age.

Yet the policy at which President Washington and Secretary Jefferson arrived has had to be repudiated in our century, when at length we reluctantly assumed the rôle of world leadership which destiny imposed upon us. Conceivably it might have been reversed sooner, to the advantage of mankind, but for the sad human proclivity to learn the wrong lessons from history and miss the right ones. As an exemplar of the skillful and realistic conduct of foreign affairs, which he generally was, Mr. Jefferson is very relevant. So far as specific policies go, however, time has rendered him quite irrelevant. To be sure, some people in our century have sought specific answers to the problems of contemporary foreign policy in the Neutrality Proclamation of 1793, Washington's Farewell Address of 1796, and Jefferson's First Inaugural of 1801. In a world that has been turned upside down, that sort of reliance on sharply dated pronouncements, wonderful as they were when written, hardly seems the common sense of the matter. Indeed, one is inclined to ask, as Elmer Davis used to: "How silly can you be?"

II

Now let us turn from the world situation to the home scene. When we fly on the wings of the spirit back into Mr. Jefferson's America, of course we can recognize many landmarks—the configuration of the coasts, the rivers flowing to the sea, the mountains on the western horizon. We can quickly perceive that he and his contemporaries were persons of like passions and vanities with ourselves. In his day political organization —party organization, for example—was rudimentary from our point of view, but the minds of politicians worked very much as they do right now and they used the same sort of wiles—slogans, name-calling, and various devices designed to show that they were more honest and more patriotic than their rivals. All of this is very familiar and should make us feel at home. But it is difficult for us to realize how few people there were or how scattered, and how slowly they got around. When Jefferson became President the population of New York did not greatly exceed that of present-day Charlottesville. If he could see the national metropolis today he would no doubt regard it as an incredible monstrosity. It took him ten days to come home to Albemarle from Philadelphia; and the post rider from Richmond was so erratic that he sometimes didn't get to Charlottesville with the mail for three weeks, although Mr. Jefferson insisted that the roads were generally passable to a carriage and always, he believed, to a man on horseback. Getting out of one's locality and keeping in touch with the outside world was an exceedingly difficult thing, and it is no wonder that so much government devolved upon the county court in Virginia, or that the town meeting was so important in New England. To a degree which is hard for us to conceive, emphasis *had* to be laid on the locality and the self-reliance of individuals. By our standards that society was amazingly simple, delightfully simple, though by the same standards life was extraordinarily inconvenient and must often have been extremely dull.

The fact is that the series of non-political revolutions which have so profoundly affected the physical conditions of existence and have transformed our economy and society occurred *after* Mr. Jefferson's public career was over. The industrial revolution had begun in Europe by his time, but it did not really get started in this country until the very end of his presidency, and even then our industries were only infants. The successive revolutions in transportation and communication all came later. Fulton's steamboat, the *Clermont,* plied the Hudson in his second term, but it has been aptly said that Jefferson, like Nebuchadnezzar, never saw anything faster than a horse.

It would be rather absurd for me to attempt to describe the various revolutions in science and technology which have followed one upon another with ever-increasing speed. I have had difficulty in adjusting my mind to the ones that have occurred in my own lifetime, finding some of them utterly bewildering. Indeed, I escape from them nearly every day into the age of Mr. Jefferson. The air seems clearer there, and the unhurried pace leaves more time for thought. In the uncrowded country there were no huge factories—scarcely any at all, in fact; there were no immense aggregations of capital and formidable organizations of labor. There were sailing vessels in the harbors and merchants in the ports and inland centers, but nearly all the workers in this farflung country were tillers of the soil. This was no Golden Age of health, comfort, and convenience, but perhaps it may be regarded as a sort of heyday of individualism. Human beings may have been dwarfed by the vastness of the land, though relatively few had traveled over much of it; they were *not* dwarfed by any of the works of man.

Almost exactly one hundred and sixty years ago the rawboned country gentleman who had been chosen head of this predominantly agricultural republic delivered his first inaugural address in the Senate chamber, the only part of the capitol that was yet finished in the straggling wilderness village that went by the name of Washington. It is said that few in the audience could hear him, he spoke so low; but his speech could be read afterwards in the newspapers, and it proved to be one of the few to which historians recur. Does it have any present bearing on *our* problems?

It was admirably suited to its particular circumstances. One of the important conflicts in the previous campaign had been over the right to oppose, to criticize the existing government—a thing the group in power had sought to prevent by means of the notorious Sedition Act. Historians often say that, whatever else Jefferson's election signified, it vindicated the legitimacy of political opposition. But terrible things had been predicted if this man should be elected; Bibles might be confiscated. Accordingly, he felt impelled to speak words of reassurance, and some of these are still fresh after more than a century and a half. He announced one principle which he called sacred and which may be regarded as timeless, I think, in any self-governing society: "that though the will of the majority is in all cases to prevail, that will, to be rightful, must be reasonable; that the minority possess their equal rights, which equal laws must protect, and to violate which would be oppression." It is a great pity that Abraham Lincoln did not quote those words in *his* first inaugural. They would have been eminently appropriate then, as they would have been on January 20, 1961.

There are other nuggets of abiding wisdom in Mr. Jefferson's address, and there is some deeply moving language. I am most concerned here, however, with what he said in the year 1801 about the way he meant to conduct the government. Since he never wrote anything like a systematic treatise on government but scattered his ideas throughout his profuse writings, the things he said here have been regarded by many as a handy summary of his working political philosophy. Judging from this address, he believed that the federal government should devote itself largely to the conduct of foreign affairs, which were always important in his era. With special reference to domestic matters he summed up federal functions in a passage which has been quoted for more than a century and a half:

Still one thing more, fellow citizens—a wise and frugal government, which shall restrain men from injuring one another, which shall leave them otherwise free to regulate their own pursuits of industry and improvement, and shall not take from the mouth of labor the bread it has earned. This is the sum of good government. . . .

That is, the federal government, outside the conduct of foreign relations, was to be little more than a policeman and an umpire. It was to grant special privileges to none and secure equal and exact justice for all—an obligation requiring diligence as well as forebearance—but if we take these words at their face value its functions were to be essentially negative. From the vantage point of today, the "sum of good government" as thus described is very small.

Even at that time some intelligent people thought it dangerously small. Midway in his first term his ancient antagonist, Alexander Hamilton, lamented that the Constitution was a "frail and worthless fabric," despite all his own efforts to prop it up. He believed that under Jefferson's interpretation the government could withstand no serious strain; and he had little hope that it would further the economic development of the country in the directions he himself had pointed. Hamilton wanted to stimulate that part of the economic society now described as "business," which by modern standards was then little more than rudimentary. He was particularly interested in banks, the facilitation of trade, the creation of fluid capital; and if anyone deserves to be described as the father of American capitalism surely it is Hamilton. He wanted to use the government, and when in office he did use it, for the development of business. He thought Jefferson uninformed in these matters—indifferent, even hostile to this development. In my opinion, he did not fully understand his great rival; it seems to me that the bitter feeling of the Eastern merchants and emerging financiers of that time toward Jefferson went beyond the point of reason. He certainly knew little about banks and deplored speculation in securities; to him property pre-eminently was real property, that is, land; but he unquestionably knew a great deal about foreign commerce, and he was an economic nationalist in his own way. Nonetheless, I think I can understand why to the Hamiltonians he often seemed an old-fashioned farmer who was blind to the wave of the future. It can be argued that John Marshall did not sufficiently recognize the flexibility of his distant kinsman in the face of actual circumstances. Yet it is not hard to see why the Chief Justice sought to counter the centrifugal tendencies he perceived in the Jeffersonian philosophy by asserting through a long generation the scope of national authority.

How well adjusted the policies of President Jefferson really were to the conditions of his own time is a matter of historical judgment. In his own person he was certainly not negative or lethargic; this incessantly active and extraordinarily dynamic man cannot be rightly regarded as the historical prototype of Calvin Coolidge. Actually, his administration was more economical than Coolidge's, but if anybody should be disposed to think that his main service was that of counting pennies in the Executive Mansion, or that his rôle was primarily that of a caretaker, that person should take a look at the map. There was a large element of luck in the Louisiana Purchase, as well as some theoretical inconsistency on Jefferson's part—or at least this has been alleged; but no one can properly deny to him the credit for doubling the area of his country. The domestic consequences of his actions were to prove momentous. He left to his successor a different country from the one he had begun to govern at the age of fifty-eight; and as soon as new states began to emerge from this huge domain the Union began to be a different sort of Union. The balance of power within it was bound to shift, and in the long run it shifted decisively against his own Virginia. There was no little irony in the course of later events, but this majestic achievement, this creation of what he happily termed an "empire for liberty," makes it impossible to think of him as the caretaker of an old order, or as one whose main function was to put brakes on the wheels of progress.

One of his undoubted purposes, as expressed in his own words, was to "lead things into the channel of harmony between the governors and governed," and in this he was conspicuously successful. He gave his countrymen what most of them wanted, and I think he gave his country what it then needed most—which was mainly a chance to grow without either aid or interference. The immediate task and the dominant desire was to possess the land. He handed out no subsidies to farmers or anybody else, but to his land-hungry generation he pointed the door of unparalleled opportunity, seeking to maintain approximate equality of opportunity but otherwise largely leaving human nature to take its course. He hoped that the vast preponderance of his countrymen would be self-supporting farmers, whom he regarded as the best citizens and the freest and happiest men on earth. His countrymen liked the idea; indeed, they embroidered it into the legend which long survived the circumstances which gave it birth. It became a myth which invested agricultural problems of later generations with nostalgia.

What present reality is there in his pronouncement of one hundred and sixty years ago about limiting the functions of government? Does this mean today that the federal government ought to be small even though everything else has become gigantic—that the best way to solve our national political and economic problems is to set down a pigmy among the giants? And all this in a time of world crisis to which we can see no end? It would hardly be fair to Mr. Jefferson to claim that he would favor that degree of impotence. This is not to say that he would like all of our huge organizations, or any of them. The processes of consolidation in all departments of life have been greatly accelerated in our time by the series of wars and crises we have gone through. Mr. Jefferson would certainly not rejoice that we have had to adjust all our institutions to the needs of these, and he might not like the way we have done it. Very likely he would approve of Lord Acton's well-known dictum: "Power tends to corrupt; absolute power corrupts absolutely." His entire career reflects his distrust of power as well as his undying concern for freedom, and it is just as true now as it ever was that the price of liberty is eternal vigilance. But when speaking of the threat of tyranny, he kept on talking about kings, who are not much of a menace now. Tyranny changes its face from age to age, and every era has to decide for itself where the greatest and most imminent danger to the freedom of the individual really lies. The contradiction which we face arises from the dreadful circumstance that the very survival of liberty at home and abroad depends on the employment of power such as Mr. Jefferson never dreamed of and which inevitably carries within itself a threat to personal freedom. We can't expect him to resolve this contradiction. He would be bewildered by this strange new world, this wonderful and terrible new world. In his day he was an alert sentinel and generally, though not always, a sagacious guide. But he is well beyond the age of retirement and we can't expect him to chart our course for us.

He himself summed things up sufficiently in one of the most important of his sayings: "The earth belongs always to the living generation." Whatever opinions he may have held at one time or another about specific problems, he held tenaciously to the conviction that the present need not and should not be guided by the dead hand of the past. We can learn greatly from past experience, but we must not ask too much of history. It often provides suggestive analogies, but rarely if ever can we find in it an answer to a specific question, a precise solution for a contemporary problem. It offers us no detailed road map to guide the traffic of today. The common sense of the matter is that the particular policies or methods Mr. Jefferson announced one hundred and sixty years ago are now essentially irrelevant, if not wholly so. The same can be said, of course, of the historic policies of George Washington and Abraham Lincoln. And the saying goes for Queen Elizabeth I, Julius Caesar, Alexander the Great, and Pericles, though the careers of all of them are well worth studying.

III

The undiscriminating use of the past has had unfortunate consequences on Mr. Jefferson's reputation. This incessant builder, who was ceaselessly striving to advance knowledge and improve society, has often been cast in the rôle of perpetual obstructionist. One of the signers of the Declaration of Independence was known as "the great objector"; that was not Mr. Jefferson, though no one more than he insisted on the right of any man to object to anything on the merits of the case. There is an even greater danger than that of judging him unfairly: in stressing what is actually irrelevant, people tend to overlook or disregard acts and words of his which do have the ring of timelessness and are applicable to our age or any other. He left us no road map, but, more than any public man in our history, he pointed us to the star by which our course should be guided. It would be a pity if, while following some ancient and long-abandoned trail, we should fail to see what is shining overhead.

He has left us in no doubt whatever about the way to separate the temporary from the enduring elements in his heritage to posterity. He explicitly stated that he wanted no public offices listed on his tombstone—not even the Presidency of the United States. He knew that his official actions were necessarily dated, that policies could not be expected to last forever. He wanted to be remembered for words and deeds which had the quality of timelessness about them, and there can be no possible doubt that he made a wise selection.

The Declaration of Independence, which he listed first, has a date, to be sure—our most famous date since it marks the birthday of our Republic; and this was identified with him all the more irrevocably when he died fifty years later on July 4, as though by Divine Providence. Part of the document itself is unmistakably dated: historians do not accept all those charges against King George III as eternal truth. But the part of the Declaration we know best and prize most was undoubtedly regarded by its author as timeless and universal. How can you date truths which you regard as eternal and self-evident? By virtue of their birth into the world as human beings, all men are equal—not in status certainly, and surely not in ability, but in rights. The implications of the assertion that everybody is a human being and should be treated as one were not fully perceived by all who approved the historic pronouncement of our national faith, but these words have gone ringing down the generations. They were still vibrant words when we answered the mad ravings of Adolf Hitler and countered the arrogant cruelty of the German Nazis. (At the time many historians must have reflected, as I surely did, that history offers no more striking antithesis than that between Adolf Hitler and Thomas Jefferson.) No ways and means are specified in the great Declaration; these must be determined by every living generation for itself in the light of its own circumstances. But those phrases, which we have heard a hundred times, have in them the perennial freshness of the spring; today as in 1776 they breathe undying faith in human beings. Many people, many high-minded people, find it hard to extend that faith to groups they have long regarded as "lesser breeds without the law"; and it is difficult indeed to uphold the freedom and dignity of all men when so many are unworthy and so many abuse their freedom. But we need not look to our historic Declaration for soothing words, for words that condone complacency or excuse any form of arrogance. We can find there no specific solution for any of our immediate problems, but we can find an eternal summons to proceed upon unfinished tasks.

To this timeless document we can also turn for a sense of values—for an everlasting criterion by which to judge all human institutions. So far as my knowledge and judgment go, history provides none better. Man was not made for government, but government was made for man; and the final criterion of its actions or its inaction is the degree to which it supports the freedom, upholds the dignity, and promotes the happiness of individual human beings. This is our answer to Communism and to any form of totalitarianism, whether of the right or left. Man was not made for organization—business, labor, professional, or any other; these were made for man, and the only proper test of them is what they do for him. We should think of this when we consider these giants of government, of business, of labor which our society has nurtured, and which so often seem to dwarf human beings. Surely the purpose of government should never be to augment power for its own sake, of business to produce profits solely for themselves, of labor to increase wages merely for the sake of wages. What is the product worth in terms of human happiness? When change is not productive of human happiness, surely it is not progress. This is no mere matter of material things, though no one can question their importance. "Man shall not live by bread alone," was said by a greater teacher than Mr. Jefferson. The challenge of our times and of all times is to humanize institutions—*all* institutions.

The Virginia act establishing religious freedom was adopted by the General Assembly on a particular date, but the date is unimportant. Actually, Jefferson drew his bill some years before it was passed, and it is just as fresh in the twentieth century as it was on the day he drew it. Here, even more clearly than in the Declaration, perhaps, can one perceive the essence of his philosophy. Above all things, he was a champion of the freedom of the human spirit, and by this he meant even more than the right to worship God in any way one likes—supremely important as that is. He meant the entire freedom of the mind, the sacred right of any man to his own opinions, whether these be popular or not, whether they be moderate or radical or conservative. There was no mistake in choosing the key quotation for the Jefferson Memorial and in putting it as a motto on a postage stamp. He was eternally hostile to all tyrannies but most of all to tyranny over the human mind. I sometimes wonder if some of the people who take his name on their lips really like this, the most typical of all Jefferson quotations. I doubt if the Communists even begin to comprehend it, but surely it is in his insistence on the freedom of men to think that he becomes most dangerous to the monolithic state and the philosophy of complete conformity.

The University of Virginia, with which he ended his select list of memorable achievements, was chartered on a particular date, and we are not yet warranted in describing it as immortal. But in the Western world universities have been exceedingly long-lived; they flow on like so many streams, and this one may be expected to flow as long as our civilization shall endure. Besides being virtually timeless, any university, to be worthy of its name, must in spirit be universal. In his own lovely county, amid its eternal hills, this lifelong student institutionalized his undying faith in intelligence and knowledge. Nothing that he ever did was more characteristic of this inveterate builder—of this ardent farmer who prized the harvest of the mind beyond all others. If I understand him aright, he would not expect his academic heirs to pay much heed to specific things he once said about courses and regulations, but he would want them to apply to their life and learning the final tests of value. Not only does learning languish in the air of conformity and complacency; not only does it fail if it does not liberate the spirit; learning becomes a sterile thing when it loses its humanity.

Nothing is immutable but "the inherent and inalienable rights of man," he said. "The earth belongs always to the living generation." Times change, needs change, policies and methods change with them. But human beings remain, always. And the star of liberty still shines over Monticello. That star and the people it shines on are what he would most want us to see.

CHAPTER 21

THE SEARCH FOR
AMERICAN IDENTITY

Many American history texts suggest that the United States went to war in 1812 to sever the apron strings that still bound the new nation to the "Mother Country"; the War of 1812, then, was a second war for American independence, in part brought about by American nationalistic feeling. But most texts are unable to devote much attention to the theme that a developing sense of nationhood was a significant force in American history in the early nineteenth century. Thus, students are left with unanswered questions whose answers are fundamental to a better understanding of American history. To what extent was the young nation really a nation at key points in its early history—in 1789, or in 1812, or even in the 1820's? To what extent did countervailing forces, particularly those of sectionalism and state sovereignty, prevent the full development of American nationalism?

The next selection, from *The Nation Takes Shape: 1789–1837,** helps students come to grips with these questions and their implications. Marcus Cunliffe, in this fresh and provocative essay, concentrates on the search for American identify. Cunliffe discusses the symbols of the national spirit—"Liberty," the flag, the American eagle, the memory of Washington, and many others—employed by American patriots; comments on the outward manifestations of the American national consciousness; and outlines the forces opposing the development of nationalism.

Today, there are new nations in which nationalism is a self-conscious creation, in which rejection of former mother countries leads to distorted images and the imposition of a narrow, compulsory loyalty, and in which forces in opposition to nationalism create tensions and even warfare. In reading this selection students should reassess contemporary American nationalism. To what extent do large groups of Americans still identify with localities, states, or regions, thereby creating strong forces operating against the establishment of a nationalism rooted in the "affections of the people?"

For further reading on this subject, students should consult Hans Kohn, *American Nationalism: An Interpretive Essay** (1957), Merle Curti, *The Roots of American Loyalty** (1946), and P. C. Nagel *One Nation Indivisible: The Union in American Thought, 1776–1861* (1964). Invaluable for students wishing to examine the concept of nationalism from a broad perspective is Seymour M. Lipset, *The First New Nation: The United States in Historical and Comparative Perspective** (1963).

* Available in a paperback edition.

NATIONALISM AND SECTIONALISM
MARCUS CUNLIFFE

In the view of Henry Adams, whose study of the administrations of Jefferson and Madison led him to publish a nine-volume survey of that sixteen-year epoch, "the scientific interest of American history centred in national character, and in the workings of a society destined to become vast, in which individuals were important chiefly as types." Since he wrote, seventy years ago, we have become less impressed by "scientific" theories of history. However, his massive analysis is still unsurpassed as a guide to the early years of the nineteenth century. The reasons seem to be that, coupled with a polished, ironical style and a capacity for sustained research, Adams had a tireless curiosity about larger themes, and that two of the themes on which he dwelt with special persistence—nationality and democracy—were indeed as fundamental as he thought. The making of the American nation is accordingly the subject of the present chapter, and the next, chapter vii, is concerned with American democracy.

The evolution of American national feeling is nicely illustrated in a small, unofficial ceremony that took place at Göttingen in Germany. The date was July 4, 1820, and the participants were two American students, of whom one was the Boston historian-to-be George Bancroft. John Adams wrote to his wife in 1776 that July 2, when independence was actually agreed upon by Congress, was the *"Day of Deliverance"* that ought to be celebrated by succeeding generations as "the great anniversary festival." However, within a few years July 4 was singled out as *the* great day on which to commemorate America's national origins. By 1789 it was already a sacred point in the American calendar, to be marked with firecrackers, militia parades, dinners, recitals of the Declaration of Independence, and formal speechmaking.

In their German exile Bancroft and his companion were therefore very much in tradition. No American was more fervently and consciously patriotic than Bancroft, who was to narrate the story of his country's birth

SOURCE. Marcus Cunliffe, *The Nation Takes Shape: 1780–1837,* Chicago: The University of Chicago Press, 1959, pp. 122–137. Copyright 1959 by the University of Chicago. Reprinted by permission of the University of Chicago Press and the author.

in ten proudly lyrical volumes. He more than any other American scholar during the first half of the nineteenth century strove to impress upon his readers the meaning and mission of the United States as a phenomenon without parallel in history.

Several of the symbols of the national spirit he later labored to inculcate are displayed in Bancroft's Göttingen "banquet." They are enumerated for us in the toasts to which the young men raised their glasses. The list included "the sweet nymph Liberty," the heroes of the Revolution, the flag, the American eagle, the Constitution, "the memory of Washington," and "the literary prospects of America." Each is worthy of comment.

"Liberty" is one of those words that have become faceless through overuse, like a coin handled and handled until its insignia are worn away. But to Bancroft and his fellow Americans it was still in 1820 one of the strongly emotive words in the American tongue, which together with "freedom," "union," and others quickened the pulse when they were spoken. Crowded with association, incantatory, they conveyed more in the first thirty years of American independence than, say, "democracy." They struck deep, so deep that when Daniel Webster employed them in a famous speech of 1830, his "LIBERTY AND UNION—NOW AND FOREVER—ONE AND INSEPARABLE" was treated not just as compelling oratory but as great literature, as holy writ.

The practical accomplishment of liberty was the work of the "heroes of the Revolution." Washington, naturally, was foremost. Yet there was no lack of other figures and of moving incidents to awaken the pride of Americans and to fill out the pages of their children's textbooks. A Revolutionary veteran, a little more wrinkled and a little more vague and grandiloquent in his recollections as each year went by, was an indispensable exhibit in Independence Day processions. On one such occasion at Indianapolis in 1822 it turned out that the old soldier in question, though he had undoubtedly fought in the Revolution, had done so as a Hessian on the British side. The embarrassing discovery was overlooked in the mellowness of the moment and in consideration of the fact that he had after all remained behind at the end of the war to become a good American. This story may be apocryphal, since the incident has also been ascribed to other dates and places. However, it has an element of poetic truth. The authentic veteran could tell stirring anecdotes of the discomfiture of the British redcoats at Lexington and Concord, of the audacious descent on Quebec by Montgomery and Benedict Arnold, the exploits of Ethan Allen at Ticonderoga and of George Rogers Clark at Vincennes, the misery at Valley Forge, the bloody onslaught of Mad Anthony Wayne at Stony Point, the British surrenders at Saratoga and Yorktown.

Cherished slogans entered the national heritage from the war—Israel Putnam's "Don't fire until you see the whites of their eyes," John Paul Jones's "I have not yet begun to fight." Articles of national faith were consecrated by the war. One was that Americans, having defeated the strongest nation in the world, were therefore by tournament rules the champions in valor and military ability. As the British minister to the United States, Robert Liston, wrote home in 1799, Americans had such an "overweening idea of American Prowess and American Talents that they do not scruple to talk of the United States as an overmatch for any nation in Europe." Another article of faith concerned the superiority of the American volunteer fighting man to the professional. If the Massachusetts minutemen and militia could give so good an account of themselves against trained European troops at Concord and Bunker Hill, or the farmers of Vermont against Burgoyne's men at Bennington, or the southerners under Morgan against Tarleton at Cowpens, then America possessed an invincible civilian army which she could summon from the plow at a few days' notice and disband with equal simplicity.

The flag that Bancroft toasted was the Stars and Stripes. Fifty years later, in irreverent chophouse slang, the expression signified a plate of ham and beans. In 1820 such levity would probably have been unthinkable. The flag's origin was complicated; though chosen by Congress as the national flag in 1777, it was devised in the first place as a naval ensign during the Revolutionary War and not adopted by the American army until 1834. Francis Scott Key's "Star Spangled Banner" was written in 1814, under the stimulus of a British bombardment near Baltimore, but it did not become accepted as an (unofficial) national anthem until the Civil War. The composition of the flag and the idea of adding a star for each new state while restricting the quantity of stripes to thirteen (in honor of the founding states) was not finally decided upon until 1818. However, the flag was one of the emblems of nationhood that the young United States venerated.

To a lesser extent, the American eagle was also a familiar emblem. It was the American bald eagle, a different species from the heraldic birds embodied in so many European crests. The difference was not very striking at a casual glance, and Benjamin Franklin—himself among the monuments of early American patriotism—suggested half-humorously that the turkey would have been a better choice, being "a much more respectable bird, and withal a true original native of America." However, the eagle was the preferred creature. Clutching arrows in one talon and olive branches in the other, the eagle appeared on the official seal of the United States, together with the official motto "E Pluribus Unum"; on some of the coins produced by the United States mint; and in all sorts of unofficial places as a decorative device.

Slogans, flag, eagle—though all had their importance in contributing to the image of American nationhood, none bulked as large as the Constitution. In a Fourth of July oration at New Haven in 1788 Simeon Baldwin invited his audience to

turn your attention to that venerable body [the Philadelphia Convention of 1787]—examine the characters of those illustrious sages . . . see them *unfolding* the volumes of antiquity, and carefully examining the various systems of government, which different nations have experienced, and judiciously extracting the excellence of each . . . hear the mutual concessions of private interests to the general good, while they keep steadily in view the great object . . . and then glory, Americans, in the singular unanimity of that illustrious assembly of patriots in the most finished form of government that ever blessed a nation.

In his address Baldwin, like most other eulogists of the Constitution, emphasized its recency in order to maintain that it drew upon all previous forms of government and was therefore, as the most sophisticated model, better than all others. He also, in typical fashion, managed to speak of the Constitution as though it were an ancient affair. Less than twelve months after the Constitution had been drawn up, he talked of its makers as if they were all Methuselahs, whereas Hamilton, Madison, Edmund Randolph, and several other prominent delegates were well under forty years of age. Poetically, Baldwin's description was correct. In the American time scale, logarithmic in range at the formative stages, the Declaration of 1776 and the Constitution of 1787 tended to be represented as closer to, say, the Magna Carta of 1215 than to the actual events of the decade after 1787. The documents, being of eternal significance, were in a sense out of time altogether.

Something of this holy aura also enveloped George Washington, whose memory Bancroft invoked. His leading part in the War for Independence, his presence in the chair at the Philadelphia Convention, his imposing demeanor, and his integrity while President combined to elevate him after his death—and even during his own lifetime, though not so unanimously—to a status not far short of deification. His birthday, February 22, came second to July 4 as a national holiday. "Boston with every other considerable town in this state," wrote one of its citizens in 1796, "has marked . . . the last birthday with uncommon demonstrations of glee. It appears that our beloved President still reigns in every breast where genius, virtue, and patriotism are implanted." (Thanksgiving, which Washington ordained in 1789, was maintained as a special day by John Adams and James Madison also, but on widely varying dates; not until the Civil War did President Lincoln firmly institute the custom of an annual national Thanksgiving.) His Farewell Address of 1796, which is still read aloud in Congress every year on February 22, at once became a part of the sacred literature of American nationalism. It embodied the commandments enjoined on those who would keep the faith. Without embarrassment or thought of blasphemy, one or two writers even hinted that Washington had certain of the attributes of Jesus Christ: thus, the mother of each was named Mary, and Washington had led a singularly blameless life.

As for Bancroft's salute to "the literary prospects of America," part of what he had in mind is forcibly expressed in the words of Noah Webster. Webster, a Connecticut scholar, declared in his *Dissertations on the English Language* (1789): "A *national language* is a band of *national union*. Every engine should be employed to render the people of this country national; to call their attachments home to their own country; and to inspire them with the pride of national character. . . . Let us then seize the present moment, and establish a national language, as well as a national government." Webster felt that "Great Britain, whose children we are, and whose language we speak, should no longer be *our* standard." He did not contend that the United States should invent some entirely new tongue for herself, but rather that she should, while introducing local expressions, go back to the pure English which the mother country had corrupted. "I do not innovate but *reject innovation*," he told a correspondent in 1809. "When I write *fether, lether,* and *mold,* I do nothing more than reduce the words to their original orthography, no other being used in our earliest English books." It is a characteristic assertion in the story of American nationalism; the new land claims to be the rightful heir to an immemorial heritage; not revolution but conservation is its aim. Being mainly a lexicographer, Webster was less concerned than some authors with the wider problem of what Americans were to write about. Ardently patriotic men of letters such as Philip Freneau insisted that the national character and destiny would not be complete until there was an independent American literature. They did not necessarily mean literature devoted to the United States, but rather authorship *by* Americans, whether the field be poetry, history, philosophy, or scientific investigation.

There was similar intense concern in some circles for the development of painting, sculpture, and architecture. As with literature, the discussion involved a double argument: first, that America should have a culture respectable enough to set beside that of other nations and, second, that her culture should be unmistakably *American*—in idiom, theme, and so on. It seemed fitting that in the new "Federal City" (Washington, D.C.) an attempt was made in the Capitol building at sculptural innovation. Some of the columns in the Supreme Court wing, though based on the Corinthian principle, illustrated the leaf and blossom of the American tobacco plant, while other columns in the Senate wing rotunda were fluted like American cornstalks, with corncob capitals.

Bancroft's toast list of national symbols could be added to. There was, for instance, the cartoon symbol of "Brother Jonathan," who seems to have originated as a contemptuous British nickname for Americans as early as 1776. The character of that name in Royall Tyler's *The Contrast* (1787)—which deserves to be regarded as the first play written by an American and staged successfully in the United States—is still a rather crudely comical person, in fact, a servant. But he is at heart honest and shrewd, like his master "Colonel Manly," and the "contrast" of the title is between them and an absurdly Anglophile master and manservant. Accepting the British taunt, the patriotic American shaped it to his own satisfaction, so that Brother Jonathan—lean, gawky, laconic, unpretentious—emerged as the caricaturist's counterpart to the fat, ruddy, blustering, conceited figure of the British "John Bull." He was a useful conception for others than writers and artists. Oddly for a nationalistic people, the Americans had no precise, convenient name for their country. "The United States" was cumbersome and sounded temporary; "America" was not a country but a continent. The obvious choice was "Columbia," which Freneau recommended and to which Joseph Hopkinson addressed his patriotic song "Hail Columbia" in 1798. But though "Columbia" sufficed eventually for the name of the federal district, of a river, of a college (in place of the old designation of "King's College"), and of another sovereign state (Colombia) on the American continent, it never lost its faintly literary taint for inhabitants of what remained, awkwardly yet permanently, the United States.

So designations like "Brother Jonathan" formed convenient synonyms as well as symbols. "Uncle Sam" was an acceptable addition. Its sense was not quite the same. Brother Jonathan represented either the whole United States or the typical individual American. Uncle Sam represented only the government of the United States. Though there are other suggested derivations, it seems to have been an extension of the initials U.S. The earliest known reference comes in a Troy, New York, newspaper in 1813: "This cant name for our government has got almost as common as 'John Bull.' The letters U.S. on the government waggons, &c are supposed to have given rise to it."

"Uncle Sam" was born in the War of 1812. The conflict made various contributions to the folklore of American nationalism. It provided some vivid fresh slogans. Young Oliver Hazard Perry, the American naval commander who defeated the British on Lake Erie in 1813, announced his victory in the famous message, "We have met the enemy and they are ours." His flagship *Lawrence* was named after an American captain who in another engagement of the war uttered as his dying words, "Don't give up the ship." These words were inscribed on Commodore Perry's flag.

Perry's and Lawrence's mottoes, like John Paul Jones's, redounded to the credit of the American navy, not the army. The regular army had its academy at West Point, whose name awoke echoes of the Revolutionary War, and there was no naval academy until the 1840's (when Bancroft, then Navy Secretary, conjured it into being). But the United States Military Academy, founded in 1802, was subject to some sharp criticism as an outpost of "aristocracy" and was not able to make an effective reply to its critics until the Mexican War. Up to 1837, neither it nor the regular army had as high a place as the navy in patriotic legend.

A special place was, however, accorded to the spectacular victory of Andrew Jackson over the British at New Orleans in 1815. Even more conclusively than Bunker Hill or Cowpens, the contest at New Orleans was held to prove that the American militiamen, the civilian warrior, was invincible. Moreover, the "Kentucky riflemen" of New Orleans were *western* heroes, a new national type whose spontaneous, rough-and-ready virtues were thought to be epitomized in their leader Jackson. He in his own right became a prime American hero—second only to Washington in éclat—who according to Bancroft "by intuitive conception . . . shared and possessed all the creative ideas of his country and his time."

The battle itself was a source of enormous pride to Americans. It set the seal on a war which, said Albert Gallatin, "has renewed . . . the national feelings and character which the Revolution had given. . . .The people have now more general objects of attachment. . . .They are more Americans; they feel and act more as a nation." The September, 1815, issue of *Niles' Register,* the first to be "printed on beautiful new type of *American* manufacture," also felt that "the people begin to assume, more and more, a NATIONAL CHARACTER; and to look at home for the only means, under divine goodness, of preserving their religion and liberty."

Some outward evidences of the American national consciousness have been indicated. To a dedicated patriot like Bancroft the United States held deeper significance. Richard Hofstadter remarks that "it has been our fate as a nation, not to have ideologies but to be one." For Bancroft, as for many of his countrymen, the American ideology had to do not only with words such as "liberty, union and democracy," but also with "providence, asylum, posterity, nature." They discerned unmistakable signs—of which one was the complete triumph at New Orleans, with shattering losses for the British and at negligible cost to Jackson's men—that the United States was under the special care of God. She had a special mission to perform, that of setting an object lesson to the rest of the world in tolerance, order, equality, and prosperity. She must therefore provide an "asylum for the oppressed"; the phrase recurs often in American speeches of the period, though not necessarily as an invitation to unlimited numbers of immigrants. The story was still being told; so its climax was invariably left to the imagination, to be disclosed fifty, a hundred, two hundred years hence, to a grateful posterity. This appeal to the future applied alike to the development of culture, commerce, population, in unlimited vistas of conjectural extrapolation.

By way of national sentiment, then, it could be said that Americans had a simultaneous attachment to yesterday and to tomorrow, the one invested with all the glamor of antiquity though its events belonged to recent history, the other with all the mysterious promise of futurity though Americans expected, so to speak, to live to see the future. However, if challenged to produce some present sign of American greatness, they could always (and did frequently) expatriate on nature in the United States. Nature meant many things—the sheer bigness of the country, the novelty of its fauna and flora, the abundance of life, the sense of room to spare, the conviction that the outdoors would be the domain of American art and letters, the definition of American character in terms of what was large, generous, informal, self-taught, non-European.

The vision was in some aspects raw and xenophobic: witness the naval officer Stephen Decatur's toast of 1816, "Our country! In her intercourse with foreign nations may she be always right; but our country, right or wrong." Thomas Low Nichols wrote of his schooling in New Hampshire in the 1820's:

The education we got was solid enough in some respects, and superficial in others. In arithmetic, geometry, surveying, mechanics, and such solid and practical matters, we were earnest students; but our geography was chiefly American, and the United States was larger than all the universe beside. In the same way our history was American history, brief but glorious. . . . We were taught every day and in every way that ours was the freest, the happiest, and soon to be the greatest and most powerful country in the world. This is the religious faith of every American. He learns it in his infancy, and he can never forget it. For all other countries he entertains sentiments varying from pity to hatred; they are the downtrodden despotisms of the old world.

One wonders whether Nichols was exposed in the classroom to a bizarre *Historical Reader* of the War of 1812 written by Gilbert J. Hunt (1817). Hunt, whose book was designed for use in schools and went into several editions, couched it in biblical style, even breaking the chapters up into numbered verses. Thus, the President figures as "James, whose sir-name was MADISON," and Congress as "the GREAT SANHEDRIM"; Satan abets the wicked British; and, according to this latter-day American version of the holy scriptures, Jackson at New Orleans (chapter liv, verse 13)

> . . . spake, and said unto his captains of fifties, and his captains of hundreds, Fear not; we defend our lives and our liberty, and in that thing the Lord will not forsake us:
> 14. Therefore, let every man be upon his watch. . . .
> 15. And ye cunning back-woodsmen, who have known only to hunt the squirrel, the wolf, and the deer, now pour forth your strength upon the mighty lion, that we may not be overcome.
> 16. And as the black dust cast upon a burning coal instantly mounteth into a flame, so was the spirit of the husbandmen of the backwoods of Columbia.

No doubt it was essential to reject Europe in order to form a national character; yet the rejection was accomplished by setting up a distorted image of Europe. Out of rawness, too, American patriotism was sometimes given a narrow, compulsory definition. What did not conform was denounced as un-American and therefore as verging on treason. Washington, himself, while President, came near to asserting that the political opponents of Federalism were traitorous. A generation later, efforts at the promotion of trade unions were castigated as subversive, "foreign" activities.

American nationalism was a self-conscious creation. Other nations had grown slowly; the United States had swiftly and deliberately to invent her own symbols of nationhood. The necessity was clearly understood. Note, for instance, the charge to a jury by Judge Addison of Pennsylvania, during Washington's first administration: "The laws and Constitution of our government ought to be regarded with reverence. Man must have an idol. And our political idol ought to be our Constitution and laws. They, like the ark of the covenant among the Jews, ought to be sacred from all profane touch." Robert Liston said of the nationwide memorial ceremonies held on February 22, 1800, only two months after Washington's death:

> The leading men in the United States appear to be of the opinion that these ceremonies . . . elevate the spirit of the people, and contribute to the formation of a *national* character, which they consider as much wanting in this

country. And assuredly, if self-opinion is . . . an essential ingredient in that *character* which promotes the prosperity and dignity of a nation, the Americans will be gainers by the periodical recital of the feats of their Revolutionary war, and the repetition of the praises of Washington.

American nationalism was more than merely self-conscious: it was a counterstatement, a plea, a continuing debate with hostile forces. Some factors in the situation strengthened the Union; others threatened to throw it apart by centrifugal action, or at least to prevent it from becoming a fully independent nation.

To deal with the last of these groups of factors first, America's cultural nationalism suffered painful setbacks. The confidently awaited American authors and artists did not arrive on the scene as promptly as had been foretold, and when they did arrive they complained of a cool reception from their countrymen. In order to gain a hearing in the United States, they had to win a previous reputation in Europe. As poets and novelists, most of them struggled in vain to compete with Walter Scott, Byron, and a multitude of other gifted and famous Europeans. Washington Irving seemed to achieve international renown only at a price—that of becoming half-European. Fenimore Cooper, while he sturdily defended America in Europe, lived there for a prolonged interval and on returning home behaved—so his enemies thought—like one corrupted by European notions of aristocracy. These men wrote in an "English" idiom; there was hardly a sign, except in comic writing of a subliterary sort, of an "American" language. Webster's *Dictionary* and *Spelling-Book* were widely used, but his American contemporaries hesitated to adopt either the local American terms he recommended or the traditional spellings he had rediscovered. Culturally, they were alarmed by his radical *and* his conservative boldness. Some believed that America was bound to reflect her recent cultural inheritance and to reveal her cultural immaturity.

Whatever their attitudes, they were vulnerable to British jibes in the quarterly reviews and elsewhere. Seen unsympathetically, American cultural pretensions were absurd; to appreciate the full overtones of the American predicament called for more detachment than either side could usually muster. One of the ironies, for example, was that the corncob capital, symbol of native genius, was carved by an Italian craftsman imported by Jefferson to work on the embellishments to the new Capitol. For that matter, most of the early patriotic statuary, from Houdon's figure of George Washington to the productions of Causici or Canova, was commissioned from foreigners. Another irony was that despite outbursts of belligerent nationalism, the United States was surprisingly reluctant to commemorate her heroes or heroic episodes. In part her caution arose from a feeling that it was dangerous to the cause of republicanism to pay too much tribute to individuals, in part from low aesthetic standards among congressmen, and in part from the erratic ways of American government. Though the Continental Congress voted an equestrian statue to George Washington some years before he became President, it was not finished until fifty years after he was dead; and the Washington Monument, projected in 1800, took even longer to complete. Jefferson did not get his memorial in Washington, D.C.—admittedly a lavish one when it came—until he had been in the grave a full century. John Browere, an American who took life masks in plaster of Jefferson and others in order to compile a national portrait gallery, exhausted his savings in the task and could not persuade President Madison to provide money for casting the likeness in bronze. Browere's collection was not rescued from oblivion until the very end of the nineteenth century, when it was found tucked away in a New York farmhouse.

But such slights were trivial in comparison with the immediate dangers to the Union. During the administrations of Washington, Adams, Jefferson, and Madison there were successive moves to dismember some portion or other of the Union, and the menace returned, after a crisis weathered by Monroe, to darken the presidency of Andrew Jackson. . . .

How can all this be reconciled with enthusiastic nationalism? Certainly there was a major contradiction within American society, this "piebald polity," in Thomas Moore's phrase, "of slaving blacks and democratic whites." The situation is accurately expressed by Tocqueville's image of nationalism and sectionalism as two separate currents "flowing in contrary directions in the same channel." Both were strong currents. Both were, in a way, artificial currents. If it was comforting to reflect that sectionalism might prove merely a temporary phase, it was disturbing to realize that the same might be said of American nationalism. Most Americans contrived to believe in both *ism's,* simultaneously or in rapid succession, as the situation dictated.

The Union had gained enormously in strength and coherence during the half-century. Washington referred to it as an "experiment." When Jackson claimed that the experiment had succeeded, he was correct by every index of material well-being. The affection for the Union shown by the new states and the nationwide enthusiasm aroused by Lafayette's visit in 1825 were heartening signs of solidarity. We should not exaggerate the extent of sectional feeling—or of its somewhat incompatible companion, desire for state sovereignty—before 1837. The states that lifted their voices in support of South Carolina did so only in a ragged, wavering, and quickly silenced chorus. Even Calhoun's own South Carolina was far from unanimous in its defiance of the federal government. The many Americans who, on one occasion or another, raised the specter of secession were fully aware of the awfulness of the threat. They could be compared to men in the Middle Ages who achieved a similar effect by invoking the devil.

More compelling than all the symbols of Americanism, however, were the physical evidences of the nation's prosperity. It was an unequal prosperity; the West and South were less well provided than the North with schools, colleges, hospitals, jails, and other signs of high civilization. But they too were growing, active regions. The United States, clearly, was a going concern, whose inhabitants' noisy verbal warfare with one another testified to an essential vigor. Nor should we overlook the relative unconcern of many Americans. They were a busy people, engrossed in local and day-to-day problems. Often they remained indifferent to what was being fought over by their legislators. They could be aroused to fury, but their emotions died away rapidly.

It was also true, as Jackson admitted, that the foundations of union "must be laid in the affections of the people." American nationalism had still to be expressed as an imperative; yet he knew that in the last analysis unity could not be enforced. Washington failed to appreciate this fully, so concerned was he to deny that any significant diversities ought to exist in the United States. By Jackson's day Americans were accustomed to the inescapable reality. The country *was* divided; behind the formal niceties of constitutional theory were shifting coalitions of interests. The task of American politics was to reach acceptable compromises. The prayer of American patriots was that the American "national character"—in the ambiguous terminology they employed—would also be a nationalist character. In any case, the search for American identity—national, sectional, individual—would no doubt be protracted. Mercifully, perhaps, the average American remained unaware that he was living in a quandary. There was much to be said for simply ignoring problems in the hope that they would eventually go away. Of no other country could it be so plausibly maintained that matter-of-factness was on occasion more valuable than intellectual discourse.

CHAPTER 22

THE DEVELOPING
AMERICAN ECONOMY

The international situation at the end of the War of 1812 and at the end of the Napoleonic Wars caused the American people to look inward for their economic growth and development. The result was a period of almost unbelievable economic growth coupled with a remarkable increase in population, and the participation of an increasing number of Americans in a great migration westward. In the following selection, Professor Jones describes this growth in its many forms.

This phenomenal and multifaceted growth leads to some important questions. What was the role of the federal government in this growth? Was this period the golden age of *laissez faire* economics in the United States? Impressive as this period of development was, could it have been more impressive if the government had exercised more positive control on the economy? What was the role of the railroad boom in the growth of the entire economy? In view of the prominence of cotton in the American economy, was the South justified in thinking that it could parlay this all-important staple into an independent Confederacy? Which region was actually becoming stronger and more stable—the North with its diversifying industrial economy, or the South with its single crop dependent on the world market?

The literature covering this economic history is rich and varied. For general economic histories of this period see, especially, Douglass C. North,

Economic Growth in the United States, 1790–1860* (1961), and Stuart Bruchey, *The Roots of American Economic Growth** (1965). For a description of the growth of transportation and its importance during this period, see George R. Taylor, *The Transportation Revolution, 1815–1860** (1951). A Pulitizer Prize-winning study is Bray Hammond, *Banks and Politics in America from the Revolution to the Civil War** (1957). Thomas Govan's *Nicholas Biddle* (1959), is an important biography of one of the shakers and movers of the economy during this period.

* Available in a paperback edition.

THE PRE-CIVIL WAR MARKET
PETER D'A. JONES

The War of 1812

That Anglo-American war, sometimes called the 'Second War of Independence,' had profound effects on the United States economy, and marked the end of America's international role as a neutral leader. The British Navy blockaded the Atlantic ports south of New London, and very effectively reduced United States imports, causing severe depression and hardship in the West. Smuggling from Canada was probably extensive, but the only genuine hope was for Americans to be free of dependence on foreign imports, to develop their own manufacturing industries. War did help to overcome many of the old agrarian and seafaring prejudices against investment in native industry. There was some surplus capital too, lying idle for want of investment opportunities—Yankee merchant capital, denied its normal outlet in foreign trade by the naval blockade. Industrial development was a long-term affair, however, and in the meantime New Englanders stood to lose a great deal. They tried to prevent the outbreak of war with Britain. It is true that much fuss had been made by the seaboard states about 'maritime rights' and a series of cold-war incidents between British and American sailors. It is also true that the Royal Navy thought nothing of violating the three-mile limit, and 'arresting' American sailors on the high seas, practically in full view of the United States coast. But northeastern merchants had strong British connections and were highly suspicious of the French, whether in Canada or in Europe. . . . Was not the Anglo-American disagreement a product of Napoleon's machinations? What is more, trade was New England's lifeblood: war with Britain could prove even more crippling than the disastrous Embargo of 1807. . . .

A great psychic victory for the frontier nationalists, the War of 1812 also saw a temporary growth of native industry. Two years of blockade and warfare, with imports closed off again, threw Americans onto their

SOURCE. Peter d'A. Jones, *The Consumer Society; A History of American Capitalism,* London: Penguin Books Ltd., 1964, pp. 45–57, 64–68. Copyright 1964 by Penguin Books Ltd. Reprinted by permission of Penguin Books Ltd., and the author.

own resources. Capital, released from shipping and foreign trade, was set to work drawing native raw materials into the market economy to be processed for home demand—iron and nonferrous metals, cottons and woolens. But America's wealth was not yet to be in manufacturing. The war impetus was something of a false start, because domestic industrialists were well-nigh ruined altogether after the Treaty of Ghent: an enormous inflood occurred of imported European goods, made with cheaper labor and a more advanced British technology. United States imports multiplied overnight as British manufacturers, starved of markets during the long war and the Continental System, exploited their comparative advantage with heavy exports of finished goods (especially textiles from Lancashire) to American ports. Thriving import houses in New York, Philadelphia, and Baltimore handled about $113 million worth of products in 1815—twice the prewar figure of 1811, and many times the wartime low of 1814 ($13 million). The exports of 1815 ($53 million) were somewhat lower in value than those of 1811, but were greatly in excess of the wartime low of 1814 ($7 million). This great and rapid expansion of American trade, although it set back the emergence of native industry, was nevertheless the chief source of American wealth in the first half of the nineteenth century.

Cotton Exports and the Atlantic Economy

The main component of United States exports from the War of 1812 to the Civil War was cotton. The southern crop represented over a third of total exports in value down to the crash of 1819, rose to two-thirds in the late 1830's, and remained well over half the total until the outbreak of hostilities in 1861. In contrast, America's traditional exports—tobacco, rice, naval goods, lumber, and fish—declined as a percentage of total exports. The sale of American manufactures abroad remained very small and even declined in the 1830's before beginning a gradual rise. Wheat and flour were exported by the middle Atlantic states and made up an unsteady one-tenth of total exports down to 1820, declining afterward. It was rising cotton prices in foreign markets that underlay the economic expansion of the immediate postwar years and of the 1830's, and even in the boom of the 1850's in which many other factors are to be seen—the westward push of the frontier, the Industrial Revolution in the Northeast, gold discoveries in California, waves of immigration—the rising figures of cotton production and cotton exports are still a good guide to the general health of the economy.

Almost half of America's total exports before the Civil War went to help sustain the economy of Britain during its first and greatest period of revolutionary change. France, being slower to industrialize, took on average up to one-sixth of United States exports; the West Indies, no longer a major American customer, bought a steadily declining percentage. Since the export trade was dominated by southern cotton, the chief American consumer was the North of England textile industry. In fact, Eli Whitney's cotton gin, patented in 1794, became available to increase the productivity of southern plantations at a time when the demand for cotton in Britain was increasing voraciously. Of all the economic changes that made up the classical Industrial Revolution in Britain in the late eighteenth and early nineteenth centuries, none were swifter or more powerful than those in the cotton textile trades of Lancashire. The key industry of the British economic revolution and the key export staple in United States economic growth were very heavily interdependent. Justifiably, economists have called the international system that emerged the 'Atlantic Economy.'

There was more to the Atlantic Economy than the cotton trade, as we shall see later. But that trade itself is comprehensible only in an international setting. After the boom of the 1830's, conditions were changing, and with the coming of a more permanent native American industrialism, internal improvements such as canals and railroads, and an extension of the home market, the United States economy would in time become less dependent. After the Civil War the source of American wealth was a vast and growing domestic demand for industrial products. However, even in that stage of its economic history, in the last quarter of the nineteenth century and long after its 'take-off' into self-sustaining growth, the American economy remained a functional part of the wider Atlantic Economy, with the export of foodstuffs (grain and meat) and the 'new immigration' from eastern and southern Europe playing rather similar roles (on a larger scale) to those played previously by cotton and the northwest European immigration.

America's Merchant Navy

In the 1820's transatlantic trade was cut into very heavily by the post-1819 depression. America's chief wealth-producing changes took place internally rather than externally. The river steamboat was perfected, for instance, and in 1825 the magnificent Erie Canal was completed—boosting the growth of the two great ports, New Orleans and New York. External recovery was very slow up to about 1830. Then came a seven-year foreign trade boom, the result of a fundamental general increase in population and productivity, as well as of such specific factors as tariff reductions, international trading agreements, a growing American domestic surplus of foodstuffs, and innovations in ocean transportation.

This new expansive surge of the 1830's was brought to an end by the panic of 1837, which was international in scope, a faltering of the Atlantic Economy. But just before news of the crash broke upon the market, United States imports were worth $129 million and United States exports $190 million. Only three years later, America was already on the road to recovery, though trade fluctuated continually down to 1846. In that year American foodstuffs were urgently demanded by the British government to save the unhappy Irish peasant population from total famine and death through disastrous failure of the potato crop. The Prime Minister, Sir Robert Peel, climaxed his great series of free-trade budgets by abolishing at last the import duty on imported foreign grain, the infamous 'Corn Law' (originally imposed in 1815 by a Parliament of landlords). Britain was now free to import American grain to help ease the Irish situation. Events in other parts of the world gave American commerce a further fillip—gold discoveries in Australia, Colorado, and California coinciding with falling United States tariffs.

So the 1840's witnessed an abnormal production of American shipping to meet trade demands. Regular oceangoing steamship services brought New York nearer to Liverpool and northern Europe. But the most dramatic development was the brief flowering of the beautiful three-masted Yankee 'clipper ship'—narrow-beamed, six times as long as it was broad, with concave sides, a prodigious height and spread of canvas and a sharp, streamlined prow—the most graceful and the fastest sailing ship afloat. Donald McKay's *Flying Cloud* plowed through the ocean from Boston to San Francisco in 89 days and 8 hours—a speed not equaled even by steamships for many years to come. This speeding up of economic transfers between the east and west coasts of the continent was by far the most significant service the Yankee clipper made to United States economic growth.

But it was trade with the Orient that first stimulated the building of clipper ships before 1848. Americans had long taken the lead in opening up the Far East to Western trade and culture, and as early as 1784 the United States *Empress of China* had sailed from New York to Canton. In 1836 Siam gave special trading rights to Yankee merchants; in the forties and fifties Anglo-Chinese wars threw part of the China trade out of British and into American hands, especially since China's ports were more open to all comers after 1844. In addition, in 1849 Britain relaxed her Navigation Laws, and fast New England clippers were allowed to compete in carrying tea to the London market, where the first delivery of the season's tea crop brought a fabulous price. Five years later (1854) Commodore Perry broke through the self-spun cocoon of Japanese cultural isolation and dragged that nation out into world trade.

The mid-nineteenth-century shipbuilding boom gave the United States a merchant-marine gross tonnage not much below that of Britain herself, the high point of 1861 (5½ million tons) not being equaled again until 1901. A cost advantage in cheap timber underlay the extraordinary growth of the American shipbuilding industry, but as forests near the Atlantic seaboard were steadily depleted of pine and oak, timber prices rose and formerly marginal timber was drawn into use. Yankee builders turned to the less suitable chestnut and birch, and British consumers turned toward Scandinavian and Russian suppliers as the advantageous price differential between the United States and Europe fell drastically. The clipper ship in any case was always expensive to build, and with limited hold space was profitable only for cargo of low bulk and high value or perishability. Circumstances had favored the ship: gold discoveries in California (1849) and in Australia (1851), war (in the Crimea as well as in China), and the European revolutions in 1848. But its days were numbered. Circumstances would soon destroy it—the decline of old trade routes (Brazilian coffee capturing the United States market at the expense of Oriental tea, for instance); the perfection of the steamship in the bulky transatlantic trade markets and the cheap mass-migration passenger field; the Civil War and the preceding Panic of 1857 which was a foretaste of general decline in a shipbuilding industry that lost the initiative and was unprepared for the changeover to steel ship production. Americans lost out to better British clipper designers even before the Civil War, and Britain, since it possessed the world's most highly developed iron industry, used its cost advantage to take the lead in the increasing use of metal ships. United States capital sought new outlets in manufacturing industry and in railroad construction. America turned away from her merchant marine and foreign commerce to the subjugation and internal development of her native wealth.

GROWTH OF THE HOME MARKET

Although United States foreign trade increased noticeably down to 1860 and the export sector played a strategic role in general economic growth, the home market expanded enormously and far more dramatically. The 'extent' of the market depends on density of population (absolute size and degree of urbanization) and on the efficiency of economic transfer (movement of the factors of production: resources, men, and capital). Both these forces were at work in the United States during the first sixty years of the nineteenth century. Population grew by natural increase and by immigration, with greater urbanization; a network of trails, turnpike highways, canals, and railroads linked the sections and facilitated factor mobility. Moreover, by 1853 United States territorial expansion on the North American continent was almost complete. The purchase of Alaska from Russia after the Civil War (1867) brought the continental United States up to well over three million square miles in area —three or four times the size of the young Republic of 1790. Population was nine times greater: 36 million when the war ended (1865) as opposed to under 4 million in 1790. As the federal Constitution guaranteed there were to be no internal tariffs or artificial barriers to trade among the states, the United States became a huge free-trade domestic market.

The Web of Sectionalism: Interregional Economic Flows

The size and geographical variety of this market, and its three great sections (Northeast, South, and West) with their differences in 'comparative advantage,' led to area specialization based on the clearly patterned though changing interregional flow of economic activity. The South devoted itself to plantation staples for the export trade and for the growing textile manufacturing industry of New England, buying much of its food supply from western farmers by way of that great river artery the Mississippi, and obtaining its manufactured goods from the Northeast by sea. The West came to specialize in grain and cattle production to feed the South and the Northeast. The Northeast (New England and the middle Atlantic states) performed a function similar to that of Britain a hundred years earlier for the thirteen colonies: it supplied finished goods, tools and equipment, commercial and building know-how, foreign imports and capital.

It was after the 1812–1814 War that a regional pattern of mutual interdependency became clear. The river steamboat, by accelerating and making rather more certain the tricky passage of the Mississippi River both downstream and upstream, had much to do with this. The flow of domestic trading established before the 1830's depended heavily on the great river flowing north-south from the interior of the continent to the Gulf, which bound the West to the South with the umbilical cord of economic need. Western products floated down the wide, muddy stream through Arkansas, Tennessee, Mississippi, and Louisiana, and very often never reached the port of New Orleans, being landed informally and sold on the way. Cotton, sugar, rice, tobacco—the southern staples—were shipped from New Orleans by coastal vessels to the northern states. In turn the latter provided for southern farmers banking, insurance, transportation, and brokerage services, and manufactured articles. As for the West before 1830, the most valuable eastern manufactured goods could afford to be sent there by the expensive wagon routes, but bulkier products of necessity went first by sea to New Orleans and then by river upstream.

Drastic changes took place after 1830 or so when this web of economic relationships was struck sideways by the 'transportation revolution.' Internal improvements like the Cumberland Turnpike, the Erie and Ohio canals, and the great railroad systems such as the New York Central, the Erie, the Baltimore and Ohio, and the Pennsylvania linked the industrial, commercial Northeast with the agrarian and frontier West. Major economic flows changed direction; the alliance between West and South was badly weakened at a crucial period in the history of American sectionalism.

After about 1835 western lumber, cattle, and grain reached Buffalo and was transshipped to eastern consumers and exporters. Since 1825 the Erie Canal had served mainly to bring the output of western New York State to the tables of eastern families. Now the completion of the Ohio canal (1832) brought products from much farther west, and the railway networks of the early fifties completed this transition.

Western trade with the South continued to rise absolutely. Indeed, the antebellum decade was a bouyant era in the economic history of the Mississippi Valley. New Orleans remained America's principal export center as late as 1860, with the port of New York running second, followed by three southern ports—Mobile, Charleston, and Savannah—involved in the heavy coastal traffic, shipping raw staples from Dixie to the eastern states. But New Orleans was increasingly dependent on these regional staples of its immediate hinterland. In 1843 Buffalo had the very first grain elevator, and three years later was transshipping more wheat and flour from western states to eastern markets by way of the Erie and canals farther west than New Orleans could receive from upstream. The river was simply inadequate for ever-growing western needs. In the fifties Ohio's farmers sent the vast bulk of their grain eastward by way of canals, using the southern route only for whiskey and meat products. Buffalo's receipts tell a forceful story, with a moral for the South: in 1836 she received from the West 139,000 barrels of flour and 500,000 bushels of grain; in 1860, well over 1,000,000 barrels of flour and over 31,000,000 bushels of grain. Consequently the volume of trade at St Louis (destined for New Orleans) declined steadily after the boom of the 1850's. The transportation revolution had assured the future of New York and sealed the fate of New Orleans.

The Mechanism of Trade and the Growth of Cities

American domestic trade, like manufacturing industry in later years, was not only subject to sudden and revolutionary change but also revealed a wide variety of conditions. Sharply contrasting marketing systems existed simultaneously, from frontier barter in, say, the southern Appalachians, to the complexities of international transfers in Philadelphia or New York. Well-nigh self-sufficient backwoodsmen could transport low bulk and high value products (furs, whiskey, potash) to market by horse; in areas of more settled agriculture the sale of bulk farm surpluses was dependent on river and lake navigations before the canal and railroad era. At the local level in all parts of the country the essential mechanism of trade was the ubiquitous 'country store' with its useful extension of 'book credit' to individual farmers. From the 1830's onward, manufacturers and wholesalers in the cities began a great American tradition by sending out traveling salesmen. And of course the 'Yankee peddler' was encountered everywhere, in the North, the East, the South, and the West, bearing his load of clocks, 'notions', and Connecticut hardware.

Large-scale grain, cattle, and cotton marketing on a national and international basis called for more sophisticated and elaborate sales organization, with a hierarchy of middlemen and specialists—all of which usually implied some ultimate degree of control from New York. That city developed the greatest amount of marketing specialization: brokers, jobbers, commission houses, wholesalers, public auctioneers, and even embryo department stores. A. T. Stewart helped to introduce departmental organization into the retail dry-goods business, using the so-called 'one price system' that eliminated the haggling of the marketplace—all prices being plainly marked on goods. (Macy's, opened in the city in 1858, followed the same policy, and such famous firms as Arnold Constable and Lord & Taylor were already established, with buyers combing Europe and their stores offering a wide variety of dry goods to the fortunate city dweller.) New Yorkers controlled the export of southern raw cotton and the distribution of New England cotton textiles alike, as Boston directed in no more seemly fashion the wool trade and boots and shoes.

Meanwhile the Ohio Valley economy gave birth to Cincinnati, Pittsburgh, and Louisville, and the commerce of Lake Erie nurtured Detroit, Toledo, and Cleveland. All these growing communities were strategically located on nodal points in the western river and lake navigation systems. Farther west, St Louis sprang into being where the Missouri, still untamed after flowing hundreds of miles east and south from the Rockies across the Great Plains, pours into the Mississippi. St Louis commanded the very heart of a 4,000-mile-long river system and was the natural place of transshipment where cargo from the major steamboats serving New Orleans and Memphis was transferred to smaller vessels for distribution up far-distant streams. But the coming of the railroad gave Chicago greater advantage. Much better located for control of westward railway traffic, and enjoying a wonderful stretch of navigable lakes and canals eastward, Chicago after mid-century rapidly outrivaled both St Louis and New Orleans. To about 1850, however, western trade was dominated in fact by Cincinnati, the great meat-packing center on the Ohio, linked in 1845 to Lake Erie (Toledo) by many miles of state-owned canal.

The Transportation Revolution

The great cities that fought for control of America's growing wealth in the early century owed their existence, many of them, to the transportation revolution. For in United States history transportation innovation was not only a 'linking factor' that articulated the whole process of economic development, but very often the essential precondition of the opening up and subjugation of the continental interior. Turnpike highways reached their greatest growth period between about 1790 and the 1812–1814 War. Meanwhile, from about 1807, the river steamboat came on the national scene; its hey-day was the 1850's. Canal building was most significant between 1817 and 1850, and railroad construction from the 1830's onward.

Revolutionary changes such as these were not accepted with complete approval by Americans. When internal improvements were encouraged and aided by federal and state authorities at public expense, they became the object of heated sectional and group politics; rarely were they considered as necessary 'social overhead capital,' except when private and public interest combined. Generally western farmers in dire need of communication with eastern markets supported the enterprises, as did northeastern coastal communities with growing industrial populations demanding cheaper foodstuffs. Land speculation was mixed up with transport history through the federal and state land-grant policy and the soaring land values in turnpike, canal, and railway development areas. But leaving aside politics and finance, the creative force of the transportation revolution is undeniable, not merely supporting but locating and creating human settlements and drawing human and natural resources into the growing market economy. Railway construction in particular often preceded settlement; after about 1850 the companies themselves organized migration from the East and from Europe to the areas flanking their lines. And the political benefits of economic integration were equally obvious, especially with the advent of the transcontinentals and increased use of the telegraph once the Civil War was over. Never was Adam Smith's dictum on the extent of the market illustrated so spectacularly. . . .

Coming of the Railroad

If the United States was rather slow to take the British example in the matter of canal construction, she certainly made it up in the adoption of railroads. T. P. Kettell, the southern publicist, said of these years:

The excitement in relation to canals and steamboats was yet at its zenith, when the air began to be filled with rumour of the new application of steam to land carriages and to railroads. . . . In 1825 descriptions came across the water of the great success of the Darlington railroad, which was opened to supply London with coal, and which had passenger cars moved by steam at the rate of seven miles per hour.

Before the Stockton-Darlington line was built in Britain, there had been several native American experiments, but this foreign achievement and the later Rainhill Trials of 1829 were an enormous stimulus to Americans. 'The most animated controversy sprang up,' wrote Kettell, '. . . [and] with the national energy of character, the idea had no sooner become disseminated than it was acted upon.'

A British engine, the *Stourbridge Lion,* was the first locomotive to operate on a commercial track in the United States, but like most British engines imported in this early period it was, strange as it may seem, too heavy for American needs. So the Baltimore and Ohio used on its thirteen miles of track in 1830 a much lighter United States engine, Peter Cooper's *Tom Thumb,* while still experimenting with horse traction and sails. The second commercial railroad in the United States was built in 'the agrarian South'—the Charleston and Hamburg, connecting the major port of South Carolina with the Savannah River in the hope of diverting some of the rich cotton trade from the Georgia port of Savannah at that river's mouth. The Charleston and Hamburg had a regular passenger service from 1831, and claimed in 1833 to be the longest existing railroad in the world (136 miles).

In the Northeast the seaboard states followed a pattern of rivalry similar to that of canals. The Massachusetts legislature chartered three railroad companies to build outward from Boston in 1831, and ten years later had a through connection to the Hudson—making good its failure to do the same by canal. Pennsylvania rapidly gained ground with four lines in the 1830's going out in all directions from Philadelphia to nearby towns like Columbia, Trenton, Reading, and, farther out, to Baltimore. In fact, by 1840 all the larger eastern states except Maine had significant mileage. Though the Appalachian barrier remained to be conquered, total United States railroad mileage in 1840 equaled that of canals. Ten years later it was almost three times greater (9,000 miles), and the problems were of a different order. The question now was: How soon to the Pacific coast? A through connection to the Great Lakes was made by the New York Central in 1850. In 1853 Chicago and in 1855 St Louis were joined to New York city, and a year thereafter a railroad bridged the Mississippi. The same decade saw New Orleans linked to Chicago and Memphis, Tennessee with a through connection to the Atlantic coast of Virginia.

No transcontinental railroad could be built until Congress was able to agree. The idea had been in the air since the twenties, but politicians split on sectional lines, and the cities of Chicago, St Louis, and Memphis were keen rivals in the congressional struggle, each claiming prior right to a transcontinental connection. A line was built across Nicaragua in 1855, but nothing more. Southern secession and Civil War resolved the issue a few years later. By that time several lines stretched to the very cutting edge of the western frontier, and total United States mileage of road actually being operated was well over 30,000 miles.

Public Aid to America's Railroads

This immense network was built within the space of three decades, 1830–1860. How was such an immense program financed? Obviously, private enterprise capital alone could not handle such a feat of economic development. It is true that in the thirties private funds were used and foreign loans at high rates were much supported in London by British capitalists and investors. But however locally important this foreign investment was, it proved ultimately inadequate, especially after the debt-repudiation fiascoes of 1837; its function was to help initiate economic developments that would eventually have occurred in any case, if somewhat more slowly. Government stepped into the breach—first state and local authorities and, later on, more massively, federal authority.

Almost all the initial state charters gave wide privileges to the railroad companies, and few, if any, placed restrictions on fares or securities. Professor Milton Heath, a most distinguished student of the South, has shown that the bulk of railroad investment in that section came from government agencies and not from private enterprise. Yet some states went so far as to grant monopoly rights to railroad companies—as did Georgia, South Carolina, Kentucky, Louisiana, New Jersey, and Massachusetts—sweeping aside normal American fears of monopolistic privilege in the scramble for riches. Between New York and Philadelphia the Camden and Amboy Railroad was given the exclusive rights to provide rail transportation. Such relaxations, spurred on by city and state rivalries, were accomplished by tax exemptions, free grants of rights-of-way and permission to establish railroad banks.

This was not all. Huge amounts of outright financial aid were given by state and local governments to private railroad companies. Counties, towns, cities, and states bought railroad securities directly with public money. State debts attributable to railroads totaled $43 million in 1838, and local aid probably exceeded this figure. In the East and West, as well as in the South, tax money was lavished on railroad loans and investments. In the antebellum South this amounted to $144 million by 1861, over 95 per cent of which came from local and state governments; the state of Virginia had supplied $21 million, Missouri over $25 million. State authorities did not stint in doling out public land either; Texas alone gave away five million acres to stimulate railroad construction.

Meanwhile, the federal government was not exactly idle in this field. Army engineers surveyed and even directed the building of some lines, free of charge. Tariffs on imported British rails and other necessities were canceled (1830–1843) by a thoughtful Congress. But it was from 1850 onward that federal aid became massive, and took the form of Gallatin's proposal of 1808: land grants. A temporary alliance of southern and western states pushed through Congress a demand for land to support a north-south railroad from northern Illinois to Mobile, Alabama. The Act of 1850 gave the states of Illinois, Alabama, and Mississippi alternate sections of land in a strip six miles wide on each side of the proposed line. The states were then to give the land to the railroad companies, who either sold it or sold bonds secured by a mortgage on it. In this way constitutional difficulties over the role of the federal government were neatly sidestepped. The land—almost four million acres— eventually made up parts of the Illinois Central and the Mobile and Ohio railroads. In return the companies promised to convey federal troops and property without charge, and Congress was to fix the rates for mail. Having established a precedent, Congress acted upon it in the years that followed, and by 1857 had handed out to 45 railroad companies (through the intermediary of 10 states) about 18 million acres of the public domain. And this was nothing compared with the enormous land grants to the transcontinental lines after the Civil War. One could perhaps twist an old phrase around and call the American system of railroad financing one of 'public enterprise for private profit,' without being too far from the truth.

The Railroad and the United States Market

The railroads did everything to extend the American market that the turnpikes and canals did, only more so. The *Preliminary Report* of the Eighth Census (1860) declared that

. . . our railroals transport in the aggregate at least 850 tons of merchandise per annum to the mile of road in operation. Such a rate would give 26,000,000 tons as the total annual tonnage. . . . At $150 per ton, the aggregate value of the whole would be $3,900 million. Vast as this commerce is, more than three-quarters of it has been created since 1850.

A mere decade of growth! Railroads in the United States had much more to give, and their impetus was not exhausted so soon as in Britain, for the westward movement brought various repeat performances of the original impact, with the lateral extension and sequential growth of the economy. The roads that became part of the northwestern empire of James J. Hill did for Minnesota, North Dakota, and Montana in the eighties and nineties what the Chicago, Burlington and Quincy consolidation (1855) did earlier for the Midwest, and what the pioneer lines did for the Atlantic seaboard in the thirties.

More than any other single factor, the rate of public and private investment in the railroads drew unused natural resources into the market economy on a large scale, and within the physical framework of a favorable land-man ratio, created high living standards for the American worker. As a geographically widespread form of social capital, the railroads created jobs all over the nation and even found the labor to fill them. By deliberate 'colonizing' and by building in anticipation of traffic, the companies drew into the productive process human as well as physical resources. In any case the very building and maintenance of the network was in itself a major industry with insatiable demands for iron rails, timber, coal (eventually), engines and rolling stock, bridge and tunneling materials, and a wide range of human skills, to say nothing of huge aggregations of mobile capital. A large part of all foreign investment in nineteenth century America was tied up in railroads. New financial techniques and institutions had to be evolved, and in the process agriculture became commercialized, growing urbanization became a structural factor in American social history, the domestic market and foreign trade were metamorphosed. Externally, United States exports were cheapened and latent foreign demand for foodstuffs allowed its full expression; internally, division of labor on a continental scale became a reality—the regional specialization that has already been discussed.

In sum, the railroad created unprecedented demands for all the factors of production, and the economic, political, and psychological disturbance it caused brought successive waves of social change for years to come.

CHAPTER 23

THE NEW WEST

Frederick Jackson Turner, in his famous essay of 1893, suggested that Americans should look to the West for their heritage. In the preceding selection, Peter Jones suggested that the settlement of the West was one of the important factors in the rapid growth of the American economy. In the study that follows, George Dangerfield describes the area and its people.

The American West, which then included Ohio, Indiana, Illinois, and points South, has been blamed and praised for a number of influences on the American way of life. It has been credited with being the cradle of the unique qualities of American life. It has been praised as the birthplace of our democratic institutions and has been damned as the source of our propensity for violence. In this essay little praise or blame of this nature is assigned. Professor Dangerfield seeks rather to analyze the Western mind and to explore the influence of the West upon American life in the years immediately after 1812. How does Dangerfield define the West? What characterized Western thought (or instinct)? How does Dangerfield explain the great migration to the West? What major impact did the West have on American political development in this period?

In the 75 years following Turner's essay, the old and the new West have been studied by many historians. The West has been the subject of some of the finest history written in the United States. The non-specialist in this area needs a guide through this mountain of material. Ray Allen Billington provides such a guide to the latter part of the period in *The Far Western Fronties, 1830–1860** (1956). The eastern and older aspects of the area and period are discussed in Francis S. Philbrick, *The Rise of the West, 1754–1830** (1965). The Billington volume contains a complete and annotated bibliography, and the Philbrick work includes (as an appendix) a critical commentary on the Turner thesis.

    * Available in a paperback edition.

THE WEST
GEORGE DANGERFIELD

The Peace of Ghent was a victory for the West. No Eastern demand was satisfied by it; but once the British had withdrawn their claim to the sources of the Mississippi and the control of the Northwest, the triumph of expansionism was complete. All serious territorial disputes were now confined to the northeast frontier, about which the West cared little, and the Oregon country, about which it cared much, but knew less. At the same time, the Peace of Ghent marked the beginning of a release from Europe. The time was gone when the thunders of a Trafalgar or an Austerlitz, a Jena or a Wagram, stealing across the Atlantic, could rattle the windows of American merchants and legislators; when the fortunes of an Administration seemed to rise and fall with the fluctuations of a campaign in the Spanish Peninsula; and when some obscure and secret change in the policies of Whitehall was sooner or later translated into extravagant uneasiness along the Wabash. The connection was still intricate and sensitive, as the events of the next few years were to show, and it was never for one instant severed; but it was evidently loosened, by the pull of the Pacific Ocean and by the influence of that star which marked the center of population as it ascended from the coastal plain and climbed toward the summit of the Alleghenies.

What the deliberations of Ghent had proved—and they had done so with all the elaborate arguments that commonly attend the proving of the truth of an axiom—was that the United States of America must not be considered a European appendage. American axioms, to be sure, were not always very clear to European minds; but if further arguments were needed, one was immediately supplied by the increase in the velocity of the westward movement.

SOURCE. George Dangerfield, *The Era of Good Feelings,* New York: Harcourt, Brace & World, 1952, pp. 105–112, and 115–121. Copyright 1952 by Harcourt, Brace & World, Inc. Reprinted by permission of Harcourt, Brace & World, Inc. and the author.

I

This movement had been checked to some extent by the War of 1812. Rumors of Indian uprisings halted the pioneer upon his frontiers and even pressed him back; but by 1814 the more potent influence of taxation and commercial depression had reasserted itself. Farmers, mechanics, artisans, and tradesmen, fleeing the ogres of monopoly and debt, turned their faces westward; and the frontier resumed its irregular advance. With the coming of peace, the advance became a migration. It was one of the greatest migrations in history and in its early stages was one of the most imaginative, for its impulse was centrifugal, and a centrifugal impulse favors the imaginative mind. Competition, of course, was the essence of the frontier, and there was probably no place in the Mississippi and Ohio valleys where industry, thrift, and luck were stronger than callousness, cunning, and scoundrelism. The frontier offered many awful examples of what a highly acquisitive mentality can do when it is permitted to change its environment by any means that come to hand. But the means were still crude in the 1820's; and though the implementing of ideals by practices that negated them was an exercise the frontier always performed with a certain adroitness, it cannot be denied that in the 1820's the high ideals were as noticeable as the low practices. The frontier uttered with conviction the language of the great American dream. This dream was essentially the adaptation of political ideals to territorial opportunities; and it was not called into question so long as environment took the shape, or seemed to take the shape, of vast spaces of unoccupied land. It was a dream that foresaw the simultaneous achievement of two dissimilar objectives: a maximum of political liberty and a maximum of material well-being; and those who were possessed by it were always a little impatient of the innumerable adjustments necessary to bring these two great objectives into some kind of focus. Nowadays we have learned through painful experience that the two objectives are on different planes; but in 1817, and for many years after, this fact was more inconvenient than apparent.

The tutelary geniuses of the westward movement were Necessity and Hope, which have always provided the motive force for human beings. It would be wrong to underestimate the importance of the latter. Hope is an instinctive apprehension of the fact that everything is in the process of becoming, that all things change, that nothing can be undone; and it is natural enough that this fact, admitted into the drama of human affairs, should take on some extravagant forms. The westering migrant, for example, was drawn across the Alleghenies by a strand of rumors. Some of these rumors were obviously put out by the land-speculating fraternity;

some were old and magical. In very early days, the American West was said to be full of "savannas"—Hesperian meadows of rich grass, bosom-high, and perfumed by exotic flowers and trees. The early Spanish explorer, with his lean and fantastic vision, had looked for them; but no man had ever found them. They retreated as mankind advanced; and when the news came from Lewis and Clark, and from Zebulon Pike, that beyond the Missouri lay a treeless desert, it was generally conceded that the savanna had passed beyond the reach of the pioneer farmer. In the 1820's the mythical "desert" was like the dragon of the Hesperides, all dry rustling scales and fiery breath, guarding the approaches to the promised land. None the less, the savanna, like a memory or a spell, still haunted the westward movement as it spilled into the Mississippi Valley. Men still cherished the belief that at the end of the journey lay the incomparably good life; and they continued to cherish this belief even after they had arrived at their destination.

Oddly enough, the pioneer farmer avoided the real savanna whenever he encountered it. The prairie was found in Illinois, in Indiana, even among the forests of Ohio; but the westward movement into the Ohio and the Mississippi valleys was still in the grip of seventeenth- and eighteenth-century agriculture. For two centuries, or thereabouts, the forebears of the nineteenth-century pioneer had themselves been pioneering in the forest. Girdling, grubbing, log-rolling, burning, and the building of log houses were inherited techniques. William Cobbett has testified to the extraordinary proficiency of Americans with the ax: he said that they could do ten times more work with that tool than any Englishman he ever saw, and they were very active and hardy—"they will catch you a pig in an open field by *racing* him down; and they are afraid of nothing." But he added that they knew little of such delicate skills as hedging or the use of the bill-hook; it was in forest farming that the Americans excelled. They put great faith in their ability to select a soil by the character of its forest cover; hardwood, for example—a heavy growth of it—was certain evidence of a "strong" soil. But at the prairies and treeless savannas they looked askance. They suspected a soil where no timber had ever grown; they feared the open solitude, the exposure to winds and storms. The game they coveted lived in the forests; from the forests they obtained the walls of their houses, their fuel, their fences, the wooden pins they used for nails, the wooden hinges and door latch, the wooden chimney, the hollow log that curbed their wells. The immense difficulty involved in digging a deep well with picks and shovels made the prairie hateful; and the expense of breaking up the prairie sod, which required three or four yoke of oxen and a heavy plow, was prohibitive, and the return was slow. Prairie soil had to lie fallow for a whole season until the grass roots had thoroughly rotted; whereas in the forest the pioneer, armed only with an ax and a hoe, could girdle the trees, grub out the undergrowth, plant his corn, and have a good crop the first year.

A well-found emigrant would go into the wilderness with an ax, a gun, a few household goods, a cow, a yoke of oxen or a horse, a few sheep, and some pigs. Or he might have acquired the characteristic small wagon, with its blanket "tilt," which Birkbeck noted on his westward journey in 1817, and which was the sure sign of a man with some farming experience and a little capital. Such travelers were the sober realists of the movement. Others, less prosperous, trudged westward with a single pack-horse, carrying all their household effects, while the barefoot wives followed behind with the babies. Or the family cow may have been the beast of burden. More often than not, the migrant was a man with no farming experience—a mechanic, or artisan, or merchant's clerk. A handcart on four plank wheels carried his smaller children and the family clothes, skillet, bed-quilt, and bag of corn meal; or a wheelbarrow would serve this purpose; or in cases of extreme destitution a man would carry all his property on his back. Was he driven by necessity, or drawn by hope?

Early in the spring, in the season of courage and of dreams, the rude pilgrims from the seaboard turned their faces west, and, as soon as they struck the great highways, melted into an almost continuous stream of wagons, carts, and foot parties. The journey that lay ahead was immense and terrible. William Cobbett, who never ventured out of the East, recoiled from it with the instinctive horror of a Surrey yeoman. "The rugged roads, the dirty hovels, the fire in the woods to sleep by, the pathless ways through the wilderness, the dangerous crossings of the rivers." And as for the destination! "To boil their pot in the gipsy-fashion, to have a mere board to eat on, to drink whiskey or pure water, to sit and sleep under a shed far inferior to . . . English cowpens, to have a mill at twenty miles' distance, an apothecary's shop at a hundred, and a doctor nowhere." Few English families, he thought, could put up with such conditions or could even cope with them. Did not an American farmer mend his plow, his tackle of all sorts, his household goods, his shoes? Did he not, if need be, *make* them? Could an Englishman do this? Could he live without bread and, worse, without beer, for months at a time? The whole business horrified him; it was a "transalleganian romance," he said bitterly; and he hoped his country-men would have nothing to do with it. Let them settle in the Atlantic states, near the great cities on the coast. Many settlers, no doubt, would have agreed with Cobbett. "It was on the 6 of May we came here," an anonymous woman wrote to President Monroe, from Barnsville, Ohio; "we had no other food for our horses nor cows but what they could procure in the woods. It took nearly all the time of one of our grown sons to hunt the cattle (the little ones are of no use for this purpose). Your patience sir will not hold out while I would describe swarms of large flies which inhabit these uncultivated lands and which stinging the cattle nearly drive them to madness. Unsound corn, sick wheat and mills seven miles off and then only going in times of great moisture. Indeed last summer the whole settlement were supported by one hand mill for several months. You will conclude we did not eat much bread— and neither we did." But the Americans had a saying that the cowards never started, and the weak died by the way. Few of them, once they had set out, turned back again. Thomas Jefferson told Adam Hodgson that he never knew a person to leave the coast for the Western country and then return to the seaboard. . . .

II

The words "West and "frontier" are almost interchangeable for the 1820's. The West was the lurch of Christendom along the shortest route between western Europe and eastern Asia, and it was led by the fur-trade—conducted by men of extreme daring and organized by men of extreme cupidity—the produce of which was still the most likely medium of exchange between China and the United States. The frontier was anywhere across the Alleghenies where subsistence farming predominated: thus in the 1820's the frontier was moving out of Ohio, but could still be found in western Pennsylvania. Or again the frontier could be the barrier—as in western Georgia, eastern Alabama, and the northern two thirds of Mississippi—that Indian lands opposed to the advance of cotton. It was extremely fluid; but it also settled into stagnant pools along the mountain ridges in eastern Tennessee and Kentucky, and away from the rivers and the coast it lingered in the lower South like a state of mind—abandoned, primitive, and obstinate.

In 1817, the frontier was advancing along the lines of least resistance, following the rivers, and thrusting out slender fingers towards the West. If the pioneer had a processional, it was choired by rivers. The great movement hastened up the Wabash and the Kaskaskia; up the Mississippi towards the mouth of the Des Moines; up the Missouri, the Arkansas, the Washita, the Red; and down the Pearl, the Pascagoula, the Alabama, and the Chattahoochee. Behind it, like unsubmerged islands, lay the rough mountain regions of the Adirondacks and the Alleghenies of northwest Pennsylvania; it swerved aside from the swamps of northwest Ohio, western Indiana, and southern Georgia; it recoiled a little from the malarial flood plains along the lower course of the Mississippi. It was a ragged affair, but formidable, inspired, and inspiring. Only where the Missouri crossed the boundary of the present state did it suddenly stop; for here began the arid region, or so the readers of Zebulon Pike believed, where a treeless and waterless prairie swept away into some fearful Sahara that heaved its sands to the feet of the Shining Mountains.

The trapper, the elemental spirit of expansionism, already knew that the stories of the great American "desert" were false. But he did not write books. Although, in 1840, the westward movement had at last completely emerged from the forest into daylight, and had reached and reconciled itself to the prairie region, it waited even then upon the line of the ninety-seventh meridian until the railroad pushed on forward in the decade 1850–60. In the 1830's pioneers had begun to settle in savannas of Ohio and Indiana, and the large prairies of Illinois, Michigan, Wisconsin, and Missouri; but in the 1820's it is safe to say that pioneer farming was, with but few exceptions, forest farming. In the shade of the forest men grew sallow and sickened, but ideals flourished; and it was not until it left the forest that the frontier lost its innocence. . . .

III

In any case, the majority of settlers, upon reaching a destination, began by hewing out a clearing in the midst of the forest. It may be taken for granted that from the beginnings of settlement until after 1850 the great proportion of farms were cleared out of forest land. After this, if a settler were fortunate enough to have accessible neighbors, which was by no means always the case, he summoned them to a "raising," with whisky and a frolic, and the log cabin was built by a communal effort. He then proceeded to "girdle" or deaden an additional tract, by cutting a ring through the bark around the lower portion of the tree-trunks to prevent the sap from rising. The branches then withered and, after they had been burned, the first crop of corn and vegetables was planted. The new clearing, with its gaunt and menacing trees, wore a dismal look, as if it had been blasted by cannon or withered by fire and disease. Generally, five acres were cleared in this way, half an acre being given to the vegetable garden, half an acre to wheat, and the rest to the corn patch. Corn was the chief support of the settlers, and was almost always the first crop on newly cleared land. Such livestock as there was ran loose in the woods, each owner recognizing his animals by their earmarks; and although careful farmers made up winter feed out of Indian corn and pumpkins, in most cases the animals shifted for themselves. That image of hunger, the "wind-splitter," the fabulous hog of the Western forest, was the product of this treatment.

The pioneer farmer raised his own wool, cotton, and flax for his summer and winter clothing, which his women spun and wove and made into garments; his cap was fashioned out of raccoon fur; he was shod from the skins of deer or cattle. His household furniture, his farming utensils, his harness, were all homemade; and his wooden cart, without tires or boxes, and run without tar, would be heard creaking a mile or more away. The valiant women helped with the planting, the hoeing, and the raking at harvest time; and if there was milking to be done, they did that too—for except in Yankee families no settler, man or boy, could be persuaded to milk a cow.

Such was the Western Arcadia, and had it not been for the fever that flitted through the woods, the ague distilled by the swamps and river mists and the desecrated leaf-mold, the malaria and milk sickness, the loneliness, the corroding poverty, and the inevitable squalor, such an Arcadia might have justified even the optimistic rumors that traveled back from it towards the Eastern seaboard. But the forest left its mark. Where the primitive frontier reigned, as in Indiana, the traveler noticed that the cleared land was rich and valuable, but the people pale and deathly looking. An Englishwoman, traveling up the lower Mississippi in 1827, shrank in horror from the bluish-white complexions of the people who crept from their squalid settlements at every landing.

And yet, unless the sickness seized them with too fierce a grip, the pioneers often impressed the passerby in quite another way. The most shiftless of them—it was odd, but it was true—seemed to be the most buoyant. "Everyone in the West walks erect and easy," said one traveler; "impudent and lazy," said another. Both remarks reflect the independence of the frontier, its belief that no man was its master. As for its imagination, the expression of that was naturally crude and *farouche*. The backwoodsman who dragged his wife and children on and on into the forest, and away from the face of civilization, was a highly imaginative type—"half wild and wholly free"—a curious variant of the classical cenobite. The "generals, colonels, majors" who infested land-office towns like Kaskaskia were not obsessed with some idea of social distinction; while they probably used these self-bestowed titles as a screen for some very sharp practices, they were just as probably expressing their belief in the uncommonness of the common man. For it was the common man who, like a giant, subdued the wilderness, and the frontier never forgot it. . . .

V

Thus a fear of centralization must be considered as one of the instincts of the frontier: but it was an instinct only—a fear that is felt by individualists, not a fear that is formulated by doctrinaires. Just as the good people of Maria Creek smelled aristocracy in the Baptist Board of Foreign Missions, so the West in general saw in the Administration of James Monroe the sign of a social elite, of a dynasty of Virginians, with the inevitable entourage of professional office-holders and heirs-apparent. When depression settled upon the West after the panic of 1819 this instinct found its voice in "a general impression that there was something radically wrong in the administration of the Government." But the early West never went farther than that. It had its own brand of militant nationalism, a potent influence in the 1820's, which was oddly compounded of Jeffersonian phrases, expansionist sentiments, and a sure conviction that there was nothing wrong with centralization when it favored the debtor and the farmer, and everything wrong with it when it did not. When centralizing energy appeared in the form of a contraction of credit, as in 1819, the West was enraged; when it showed itself as a protective tariff, or a national scheme of internal improvements, the Westerner was hard put to make up his mind. There was, he believed, centralization and centralization; and he could say no more.

VI

"Old America," said the English speculator, Morris Birkbeck, in 1817, "seems to be breaking up and moving westward." His statement, on the face of it, is a trifle glib—he had acquired over 26,000 acres in Illinois and was anxious to dispose of them to likely purchasers in England—he had, indeed, written a book for that purpose. But the break-up of Old America—an idea Mr. Birkbeck advanced as a useful and legitimate piece of salesmanship—was, in a limited but extremely important sense, actually taking place. The westward migration represented, if anything, the diaspora of the American Enlightenment; for the westward migrant, trudging along his terrible roads towards his improbable wilderness, carried with him the great principles of Liberty and Equality, the twin torches that had flared and smoked through the eighteenth century and now lighted him fitfully along his way.

The pioneer and the migrant saw themselves not as wage-earners but as property owners; and surely the conflicting philosophies of the Enlightenment agreed at least upon one thing—that the property owner must be free to follow his own self-interest. As an agrarian property owner, the pioneer naturally carried farther and farther into the West some fragments of the enlightened nationalism of Thomas Jefferson, which was essentially an agrarian nationalism, and which believed that an evangelizing nation was fully as important as a self-contained one.

"We feel that we are acting under obligations not confined to the limits of our own society," Jefferson wrote. "It is impossible not to be sensible that we are acting for all mankind." An old gentleman, writing to his Congressman son in 1819, expressed this ideal with equal force. "You must not loose sight," he wrote, "that you are ligislating for a great Nation whose Decisions may be a president for ages to come." All Americans believed that they were setting precedents for ages to come, and none held this belief more firmly than did the Western pioneer. Necessity drove him, it is true: the trails he blazed through the forest were trails that led away from exhausted soils, discriminating laws, limited suffrage, unlimited slavery; but the vitalizing notion that he was the standard-bearer of a new freedom accompanied him all the way. He was convinced that somewhere in the wilderness lay the solution for the ills of the Old World. And so, while the party of Thomas Jefferson slowly disintegrated along the Eastern seaboard, or aligned itself more and more with the interests of the Southern slave-holder, the ideals of Thomas Jefferson were being carried into the wilderness.

The old nationalism of the Enlightenment, however, had already reached its apogee in 1807 with the announcement of the Embargo doctrine—the very gospel of enlightened self-interest. It was never to appear again in so concentrated a form. It was the victim of a lamentable, but oddly enough almost universal, unwillingness of self-interest to be enlightened. Thereafter, dispersed along the roads and streams leading to the Ohio and Mississippi valleys, it lost in power what it gained in mobility; for dispersal is never strength.

The pioneer, after all, was a civilizing influence only to the extent that he modified his environment as quickly as he could. For this essential purpose the Jeffersonian notion that all men are created equal was extremely useful; indeed, the pioneer could hardly have got along without it. It was a very complex notion—it may have originated in John Locke's curious misunderstanding of the nature of perception—but the society the pioneer evolved construed it into an equalitarian democracy that Jefferson himself must have thought alarming. All the new states in the West and Southwest showed a fondness for manhood suffrage which exercised a disturbing but salutary influence on the rest of the country. None the less, there is much peril in the equalitarian doctrine; for its devotees are often lulled into forgetting that political equality does not mean economic equality; and the early West was frequently woken from its social trance by sharp reminders of this simple fact. One might almost go as far as to say that this fact—which is the bug-bear of all political democracies—bewildered and provoked the pioneer at every turn.

The pioneer's solution was not a Jeffersonian one. He did not condemn central government—which in those days was taken to be the purveyor of economic inequality—but he sought to dominate it wherever he could. He represented a centrifugal energy, and central government represented a gravitational one. It was there to see that pioneer society did not fly off into space. The laws relating to the public lands are very instructive in this respect. In 1817, when a settler wished to purchase public lands, the minimum purchase allowed him by law was a quarter section (160 acres), and the minimum price per acre was $2.00, one fourth to be paid down, and the rest payable in four annual installments. This was a scheme to raise revenue, rather than a plan to assist the settler, for the credit system encouraged speculation, and the debt on the public lands rose from $3,042,613.89 in 1815 to $16,794,795.14 in 1818. The great land boom collapsed in 1819, and the settler was in a fair way of being ruined when a Senate Committee on Public Lands, all of whose members but one were from the West, brought in a thoughtful report recommending the abolition of the credit system. This was accomplished by the famous Act of April 2, 1820, which also reduced the minimum purchasable tract to 80 acres, and set the minimum cash payment at $1.25. A farm of 80 acres could now be purchased for $100. This was the first effort to legislate for the settler rather than for the Treasury; and on September 30, 1822, the debt on public lands had sunk to $10,544,454.16.

By the apportionment of 1822, the Western representation was increased to forty-seven members in the House of Representatives, which, with a delegation of eighteen in the Senate, made a formidable group: and legislation favoring the settler continued all through the 1820's, culminating in the pre-emption laws of 1830. These laws officially changed the status of the squatter from one of public pest to one of public benefactor. The squatter, supreme individualist who ranged far ahead of the government surveyors, and occupied the best of the unsurveyed lands without going through the formality of paying for them, had always been protected by frontier opinion and to some extent by Congressional sentiment. The pre-emption laws made him free of the whole public domain in the sense that he was given the right to purchase his lands, no matter how valuable they might be, at the minimum price and before anyone else could bid for them in the public auction.

Thus there was a close relationship between pioneer society and the bounty of the general government, which lasted long after the debt on public lands was extinguished in 1832. Yet the relationship was never a comfortable one. The West, considered as a centrifugal force, longed for complete control of the public land system, while the general government, as a gravitational pull, yielded this control with the utmost reluctance. Eastern capitalists, Western speculators, and Southern planters were all opposed to a liberalization of the land laws; and although the movement of American history was towards the Pacific, it was not until 1862 that a Homestead Act finally committed this movement into the hands of the common man. And by then it was too late. No society of free pioneering farmers could survive the attack of the railroad interests or disentangle itself from the nets of price-fixing monopolists.

VII

Meanwhile, in the 1820's, the West maintained an ambivalent attitude towards the general government, and expressed a nationalism that was all its own. The addition of six new states between 1816 and 1821, all but one of them in the West or Southwest, was a visible triumph for the expanding frontier, and indicates, even more than do population figures or ratios of increase, the great velocity of the westward movement. Both those who believed in a strict adherence to State Rights, and those who favored a stronger central government, professed themselves satisfied with this new development. The former welcomed to the fold six new sovereigns who would resist the pretensions of consolidation, while the latter believed that economic nationalism would, as a consolidating force, be increased rather than diminished by the addition of new states with neither the strength nor the traditions to resist it. The issues involved were not academic. Agrarian philosophy contended that if the general government grew too strong, it would inevitably align itself with the financial and investing interests; and had its professors lived until the 1870's, they would have been amply justified in all their predictions. Even centralizing opinion feared the West. The conservative financier, for example, thought that the new states were a constitutional sanction of the procreative instinct, an instinct which he was inclined to discourage on economic grounds, for he believed that "the creation of capital is retarded, rather than accelerated, by the diffusion of a thin population over a great surface of soil. The West itself oscillated in a most confusing way between the two points of view. Its several states were the creatures of the national government, deriving their very existence from an Act of Congress. It was not likely that they would have such a delicate sense of States Rights as did the more doctrinaire of their elder sisters; that they would always resist the rough advances of consolidation; or that when they did resist them they would invariably do so from the highest motives. On the other hand, they were all agrarian and debtor states; and in moments of crises or depression it was their instinct to suspect that there was some connection between the central government and the creditor interest. This confusion of sympathies was increased by the great drama of the Missouri Compromise, which began to divide the West on the free soil question.

When the Western mind was actually confronted, in the 1820's, with a program of national consolidation, its response was an odd mixture of enthusiasm and fear. Between 1816 and 1832, Henry Clay was engaged in developing his American System; and by 1824 its main features were evident for all to see. It was composed of protective tariffs; a national system of internal improvements financed by the sale of public lands; and the centralizing influence of the United States Bank. Henry Clay was a Westerner, and a man notably possessed by the great American dream: might not this system be called an answer to the needs and aspirations of the West? So Mr. Clay argued. He contended that a protective tariff, by fostering the country's industries, would provide a domestic market for the country's produce; that the internal market thus provided for could not be organized without a complex of roads and canals efficient enough to reduce the cost of transportation; and that domestic exchanges could never be regulated without a stable currency. Did not his system provide for all these things? He advanced this system with all the warmth and magic of his oratory, which have not, alas, survived the touch of cold print, and the answer to this question, as it congeals upon the cold page, would seem to be that Mr. Clay's system was an adroit commingling of the less precise formulations of the Enlightenment with some of the more exacting demands of the business community. No man touched the chords of Liberty and Prosperity with a defter, indeed with a more sincere, finger than did Mr. Clay; but somehow or other they did not harmonize with the rest of his music. He was a great man and a generous man, and he never ceased to fascinate his countrymen; but his American System was consolidation at its brassiest. Certainly, as the 1820's advanced, the country became more and more aware of the need for internal improvements; and the Western farmer, whose progress depended upon the production and marketing of an agricultural surplus, was more aware of it than anyone else. None the less, Western farming in the 1820's was still largely subsistence farming. The agricultural market was roughly organizing itself through the increased demand from Southern slave-holders for Western produce, and a program of economic nationalism with a strong financial emphasis could not be expected to find complete favor after the panic of 1819, when the agrarian West was continuously striving, by some piece of frenzied legislation, some stay law or replevin law, to gain a brief respite from the waters of debt. Might it not be said that, if Mr. Clay dreamed the great American dream, he did so with one eye open, and that the open eye was in rapt contemplation of the interests of Eastern monopoly? In any case, the Western instinct against centralization seems to have been aroused, and though Mr. Clay never ceased to command the affection of the West, as was only right and proper, it is safe to assume that after 1824 he began gradually to lose its confidence.

VIII

The West—the flow of human beings from the Alleghenies at one end to the prairies and the Gulf at the other—was a great and wonderful influence upon American life in the 1820's. It was perhaps the last time in all history when mankind discovered that one of its deepest needs— the need to own—could be satisfied by the simple process of walking towards it. Harsh as the journey was, and cruel as the wilderness could be, this movement could not help but be a hopeful one. In the 1820's, the West sank into debt; but still its inhabitants professed, in the midst of their discontents, to see some evidence of promise in the individual human being, and to look for a human being, rather than a set of principles, who should constellate this evidence for them. The Westerner was a Rousseauesque figure. While on the one hand he offered the world an inspiring picture of courage, simplicity, and ingenuity, on the other hand he became the very symbol and representative of the congregated discontents of a nation. He spoke for the Eastern mechanic; for the debtor in his cell; for the rural democrat of New England and New York; for any man who considered himself abused, cheated, or misunderstood. His nationalism, therefore, though exuberant, was a visionary nationalism, speaking with many tongues and little clarity.

The dreams of Mr. Clay were too capitalistic to satisfy this kind of nationalism; the Jeffersonian philosophy, though highly quotable, was held to be too impractical to cope with the imperatives of the practical life;

the Virginia Dynasty, lingering on in Washington in the person of Mr. Monroe, was considered too narrowly professional to provide a leadership. To whom could the hopeful and the discontented turn? In the early twenties, Andrew Jackson began to emerge as just such a man. It was true that little was known about him; and that his political beliefs and economic habits, had they been carefully examined at the time, would not have satisfied either the debtor, or the antislavery man, or any of the more exacting of his followers. But the materials for a careful examination were not readily accessible; and what was known against him was always glossed over. The outline was clear, the details were mysterious; and the mystery carried its enchantment. Only one thing was certain about General Jackson—in moments of crisis he invariably behaved as the imaginative man, of the extreme martial type. This type was a Western ideal; and because it was a Western ideal it summoned, like a magnet, all sorts of aspirations that were not Western at all.

When the Monroe Administration, in 1818, turned the General loose upon the Seminoles and Spaniards of Florida, it could not possibly have foreseen all the consequences of this action. The General was a powerful weapon in 1818, and did all that was required of him. It was only later that the weapon turned upon Monroe's heir and dealt him a mortal wound.

CHAPTER 24

THE RENEWAL OF
AMERICAN NATIONALISM

Although nationalism was one of the causes of the War of 1812, the war itself renewed the sense of national self-consciousness that first found clear expression in the Revolutionary era and that had been so consciously promoted by the patriots of the early national period. The end of the War of 1812 marked a turning point in the history of the United States. Now the young nation could turn its back on the Old World and the kind of history that it represented and could devote its energies to the development of the New World. As the historian, George Dangerfield, points out in the following selection from *The Awakening of American Nationalism,** the Peace Treaty of Ghent significantly altered American relations with the one nation—Great Britain—that might have prevented this change of direction. This treaty, and the negotiations preceding it, caused the decay of British mercantilist concepts and paved the way for American expansion.

The decade following the War of 1812 is confusing and contradictory to the student of history. It was an "Era of Good Feelings," but it produced the first full-fledged sectional controversy—the Missouri controversy of 1819–1820. It was a period dominated by Jefferson's Republican party (the party that had championed limited government), but now the party's leaders advocated a uniform national currency, a national bank, a protective tariff, and a national system of roads and canals. It was a period in which South Carolina's John C. Calhoun, later a great defender of states' rights, was a nationalist, and Massachusetts' Daniel Webster, the great Unionist, voted for purely sectional interests.

Professor Dangerfield, author of *The Era of Good Feelings** (from which the preceding reading is taken), seeks to put this period in its proper perspective. To what extent was the era one of good feelings? Was the program of the new Republican party really neo-Federalist or Hamiltonian in spirit? What was the nature of postwar nationalism, and what were its limits?

Indispensable to further work in this area are the two Dangerfield volumes. Also *The Twilight of Federalism* (1962) by Shaw Livermore, Jr. should be consulted.

* Available in a paperback edition.

MADISON, CONGRESS, AND AMERICAN NATIONALISM

GEORGE DANGERFIELD

Peace with Great Britain was proclaimed in Washington on February 18, 1815; and with the passing of the War of 1812, the shadow of political Europe withdrew from the scene which it had darkened and confused for many years, and a new light seemed to fall upon the map of the United States. As Henry Adams put it, with pardonable hyperbole: "The continent lay before [the American people] like an uncovered ore-bed." The continent, it is true, or all that part of it which lay west of the Mississippi and east of the Perdido, was still claimed by the King of Spain, and much of this was then believed to be a waterless desert. But "ore-bed" admirably describes the objective of a forward-looking state of mind. The American people, in 1815, endeavored to turn their backs upon Europe, insofar as Europe represented the kind of world history they most detested. For if the Napoleonic Wars constituted (as surely they did) a world war, then the War of 1812, their penultimate phase, could not be entirely freed from this character. It was now over for the Americans, and they naturally preferred to see it as nothing more than a quarrel between themselves and Great Britain. Whether this quarrel was or was not (as to its American origins) an expansionist adventure is still debated; but if there was an element of expansionism in it, then the Peace of Ghent was an ample fulfillment of this healthy impulse. Superficially, to be sure, the peace treaty which the Senate ratified on February 14 left everything much as it had been before the war began: time alone was to be the arbiter of Anglo-American relations, and the expression "not one inch ceded or lost" would be a more than adequate summary of the treaty's achievements. To the modern student of the negotiations which preceded the treaty, however, a very different idea presents itself; the treaty has become an eloquent register of historical process, because

SOURCE. George Dangerfield, *The Awakening of American Nationalism, 1815–1828*, New York: Harper & Row Publishers, Inc., 1965, pp. 1–16. Copyright 1965 by George Dangerfield. Reprinted by permission of Harper & Row Publishers, Inc. and the author.

one can observe, in the negotiations themselves, the decay of British mercantilist concepts. If the treaty meant anything at all, beyond a mere end of hostilities, or (as some Anglophobes thought) at best an armistice, it meant that in the future Britain would cease to regard the United States as a colony which paid its own expenses, and that she would look upon American expansion with a favorable eye, so long as it provided an enlargement of British industrial opportunity. In this sense, a whole new world had come into being, and for the Americans the first task was to describe the terms upon which, in America, it was to be organized.

The bonfires, the cannon, the church bells which celebrated the Peace of Ghent constituted less a shout of triumph than a sigh of relief. The American character had not so far been of a militarist nature: no militarists could have endured the mismanagement, the lukewarmness, the disaffection which marred almost every feature of the late war. As a nonmilitarist nation in 1812–15, the Americans put forth just enough energy to get the work done, and when all was over they showed no disposition to make themselves more formidable in a military sense. Efficiency and, soon enough, economy became their goals.

Moreover, the United States was, for a brief while, genuinely at peace with itself. As for the Old World, on the other hand, one has only to contemplate the Final Act of the Congress of Vienna to see that, although it had all the finality of a completed jigsaw puzzle, it was actually an instrument full of chinks and crannies, through every one of which there glared and squinted the Argus eyes of revolution. The effort to avert this dire inspection by filling these gaps with repressive laws varied widely from state to state in Europe, but it served to show that there was no longer a common tradition between the rulers and the ruled. In a community like the United States, now ready and anxious to make new experiments in self-government, it was precisely the emergence of a common tradition that counted most. The very Congress which, in 1815, took up the task of postwar readjustment was composed, as to more than one-third of its membership in both houses, of Federalists; and some of these were not a little tainted with wartime disloyalty. They sat down with their Republican opposites to discuss and to organize the peace; and since their opposition was neither very mischievous nor very resolute, they presumably acquiesced in what was done.

The Federalists, of course, remained a suspect group throughout the period of one-party rule which now began; and although their diminishing numbers and influence, and their accommodating behavior on the federal level, scarcely justified their reputation for persistent conspiracy, their efforts to inflame Republican faction in the several states did something to keep it alive. But they were not very skilled at party warfare; and even in those States where they had a real chance of survival, they were manifestly on the defensive and betrayed every anxious symptom of decline. It might be said that in the brief "Era of Good Feelings," which really ended with the Panic of 1819, the United States was free from those political and social fears which, in one form or another, haunted the Old World. The fact that the only suspect groups in America were those connected with wealthy men merely serves to emphasize the difference.

In short, as Albert Gallatin put it in 1816, "the War," and one ventures to presume that he also meant the peace, "has renewed and reinstated the national feelings which the Revolution had given and which were daily lessened. The people have now more general objects of attachment with which their pride and political opinions are connected. They are more American; they feel and act more like a nation; and I hope that the permanency of the Union is thereby better secured." In the Old World the concept of nationalism was either imperialistic or subversive of the counterrevolution, or could be accepted only in the terms—even truer for 1815 than for 1845—of Disraeli's "Two Nations."

Albert Gallatin was a most acute observer of the American scene, and he may have confined his ideas on American nationality to his own recollection: he did not arrive on these shores until 1780. Or he may have taken it for granted that national feelings and character were not actually "given" until 1776 or 1775. Like many historical axioms, this is open to technical reproach; but what Gallatin does suggest, and very forcibly, is that the postwar American had a renewed sense of a common national experience, real or imagined, with which he could face the future.

The Peace of Ghent undoubtedly bestowed upon the American nation a status among the family of nations which it had not hitherto enjoyed, but it was a status with a difference. "The mere existence of such a nation," it has been well said, "was a threat to the continuance of class government and special privilege in other countries." To the conservative and reactionary rulers of Europe the United States was little more than a grimy republican thumbprint upon the far margin of that page of history which, at Vienna, they were so ingeniously writing backward. The Tsar of Russia was possibly a friend; the British Tories were soon obliged to regulate their political behavior in terms of an American market they could not afford to antagonize; the others had simply come to accept the fact that if the thumbprint was grimy, it was also ineffaceable. That was the point in 1815.

The problem of readjustment to peace did not, at first, present the Americans with many difficulties: the Jeffersonian establishment, which had been so shaken by the Embargo of 1807 and had almost dissolved by the end of 1814, was now, all of a sudden, both strong enough and flexible enough to restate its old positions and to adopt a new one. The era of the "new Republicans" had begun. One need look no further for this than the Seventh Annual Message of President Madison, submitted to the Fourteenth Congress on December 5, 1815.

Some fourteen months before, in circumstances of great indignity, Madison had left his capital and fled like a partridge into the Virginia hills, pursued by a British army whose leaders jested that they proposed to catch him and take him back to London "for a curiosity." His prestige, already dim, had thereupon become totally invisible to all but the most friendly eyes. He was now addressing the Congress, in the language of a victor, and in terms which must have occasioned some surprise to the more doctrinaire members of his party.

Throughout his long career, from the early days when he had been a delegate to the Second Continental Congress, Madison had displayed a certain predilection—one might use a stronger term—for nationalist expedients. Had he not told Thomas Jefferson in 1787 that the Constitution "will neither effectually answer its *national object,* nor prevent the local mischiefs which everywhere excite disgust against the State Governments"? It is true that he had never gone so far along the road to centralization as Robert Yates suggested in his *Secret Proceedings and Debates,* or as he himself seems to have proposed in his Number 44 of *The Federalist;* and in his subsequent battles with Hamilton and with Adams he had often discarded his nationalist weapons for the outrageous slings and arrows of particularist dispute. Between the coauthor of *The Federalist* and the writer of the Virginia Resolutions there certainly exists a wide gulf, yet during his later years of executive power he was able to straddle it without too much discomfort. His was a subtle and athletic mind, which only became baffling in his later years. In 1815, much as he may have suffered in reputation from his handling of the War of 1812, he was a victorious statesman; and his Seventh-Annual Message is remarkable, not merely for being statesmanlike, but for its candid acceptance of the likelihood that it would sooner or later be called something else.

The Message, in its three more significant passages, is not exactly a ringing document: under the circumstances, it could hardly have been that. But it is an admirable mixture of constitutional prudence and enlightened common sense.

It is [he wrote] essential to every modification of the finances that the benefits of an uniform national currency should be restored to the community. . . . If the operation of the State banks can not produce this result, the probable operation of a national bank will merit consideration; and if neither of these expedients be deemed effectual it may become necessary to ascertain the terms upon which the notes of the Government (no longer required as an instrument of credit) shall be issued upon motives of general policy as a common medium of circulation.

[And again:] In adjusting the duties on imports to the object of revenue the influence of the tariff on manufactures will necessarily present itself for consideration. However wise the theory may be which leaves to the sagacity of individuals the application of their industry and resources, there are in this as in other cases exceptions to the general rule. . . . Under circumstances giving a powerful impulse to manufacturing industry it has made among us a progress and exhibited an efficiency which justify the belief that with a protection not more than is due to the enterprising citizens whose interests are now at stake it will become at an early day not only safe against occasional competitions from abroad, but a source of domestic wealth and even of external commerce.

[And finally:] Among the means of advancing the public interest the occasion is a proper one for recalling the attention of Congress to the great importance of establishing throughout our country the roads and canals which can best be executed under national authority . . . requiring national jurisdiction and national means . . . and it is a happy reflection that any defect of constitutional authority which may be encountered can be supplied in a mode which the Constitution itself has providently pointed out.

It has often been said that this tripartite scheme was more Hamiltonian than anything else, or, at best, that it endeavored to employ Hamiltonian means for Jeffersonian ends. But, in truth, the national bank was the only Hamiltonian feature in it—a feature, to be sure, of a startling prominence; and even here it should be remembered that the rechartering of the First Bank of the United States in 1811 had not met with Madison's disapproval or that of Gallatin, and that it failed for other reasons. Aside from the national bank, which (together with its alternative solution of a national currency in terms of treasury notes) required no little boldness in its advocate, there was nothing especially Hamiltonian in the rest of Madison's program. Did not the great *Report on Manufactures* show that Hamilton really preferred bounties to tariffs; but did not Jefferson, in his Second Inaugural, propose a scheme of internal improvements to be financed by tariff receipts? Would Gallatin's superb *Report* on internal improvements have been relegated to a dusty shelf if the government and the nation had not been bemused and divided by the war fever of 1807 and its aftermath? And in his suggestion that no national system of internal improvements would be valid without a constitutional amendment Madison—like his great predecessor—sounded a note of caution: his nationalism retained a distinctly Jeffersonian bias.

A vast and varied experience, needless to say, had interposed itself between Jefferson's Second Inaugural and Madison's Seventh Annual Message. The Message was a document which had been created by the Napoleonic Wars: it was what an unmilitary nation required if it was to profit from all that it had so recently and so painfully learned. For example, the Treasury had become bankrupt in 1814 because the national currency had fallen into such disorder that revenues could not be moved from one place to another. This immobility had been repeated in another realm, by a difficulty in moving and subsisting the nation's troops: bad currency, with only a local circulation, had found its counterpart in bad roads, with only a local usefulness. As for manufactures, they had been nourished by embargo and war into an infancy so vigorous that to expose them to free trade might well have seemed a cruelly Spartan measure. Thus a national bank and a system of internal improvements might be seen as an effort to remedy those weaknesses which the War of 1812 had revealed, and a plan for protective tariffs as an effort to preserve what the war had fostered.

The Fourteenth Congress, having been elected in the final autumn of the war, and in the shadow of disaster, was fortunately well qualified to act upon this program: the people had submitted their affairs to their ablest men, of whatever persuasion. The best of the war party were back in the House: Henry Clay, William Lowndes, John Forsyth, Peter B. Porter, Richard M. Johnson, Samuel Ingham, John Caldwell Calhoun. Only Felix Grundy and Langdon Cheves were missing; neither had cared to stand for re-election. The stalwarts of the peace party were also present: Timothy Pickering, Daniel Webster, Thomas P. Grosvenor, John Randolph. In the Senate the old obstructionists, Michael Leib, Samuel Smith, David Stone, Joseph Anderson had all vanished; the President would hardly recognize it for the same body which, since 1808, had practiced so successfully upon his peace of mind.

Once it had swallowed the hard morsel of a continuance of the direct tax, Congress turned its attention to the question of a central bank. The President's carefully qualified proposals in the Annual Message had been implemented by a more direct plea from his Secretary of the Treasury, A. J. Dallas. In a letter to John Caldwell Calhoun, of South Carolina, chairman of the House Committee on National Currency, Dallas outlined a plan for a national bank and, like the President, refrained from discussing the constitutionality of such a measure.

Certainly, if the government were to regain some control of the national currency—which not everyone thought a necessity—it would have been quixotic indeed if it had set constitutional traps for itself in its own messages. Nor was Dallas the man to have thought them necessary. Born in Jamaica of Scots parentage, a graduate of Edinburgh University, married to the daughter of a British general, he had reached British-occupied New York, by way of the West Indies, in June, 1783. He had then found his way to Philadelphia, and in Pennsylvania, after some preliminary difficulties, he had founded a legal career of mingled brilliance and unpopularity. He was an odd kind of Jeffersonian. A tall and courtly personage, with powdered hair and exquisitely oldfashioned clothes, he never overindulged his courtliness: he never concealed his belief that he was in every respect superior to the usual run of politicians. As a member of the Republican party, he was for ordinary purposes a liability. It was only in a season of despair, when Secretary Campbell had resigned from the Treasury after confessing his own incompetence, that the Thirteenth Congress—then meeting at the Patent Office, the solitary public building which the British had spared—could bring itself to accept the Pennsylvanian as Campbell's successor. In a mordant report upon the difficulties of the Treasury's situation, which was one of virtual bankruptcy, Dallas could only suggest the creation of a national bank; but as Daniel Webster put it all too truly, he founded his bank upon the discredit of the government and then hoped to enrich the government out of the insolvency of the bank. Dallas' best support, in this preposterous dilemma, was the fact that behind him there loomed the figures of John Jacob Astor, Stephen Girard, and David Parish. In April, 1813, Parish and Girard had taken $7,055,800 of Government 6 per cent stock at 88, and Astor had taken $2,056,000 at the same figure. Jacob Barker had also contracted for a huge sum, $5 million, but could find no one to join him: in the March 16, 1814, issue of the *National Intelligencer* he had called for a national bank. One need not impugn the patriotism of these capitalists, who were, after all, willing to venture large sums to maintain the nation's credit; but it would be flouting the long annals of financial behavior to suppose that they would not endeavor to protect themselves against the consequences of patriotism, should these prove to be unfortunate. They proposed, in short, to appreciate the price of government bonds by making them exchangeable for stock in a national bank; their plans had been maturing since early 1814; and it is reasonably certain that the influence of Astor and Girard upon the President, and upon certain members of Congress, had been in some measure responsible for Dallas' appointment.

The energetic Calhoun had of course been privy to their plans, and although he had not seen eye to eye with Dallas in matters of detail, in principle they were agreed. When the war came to an end, Dallas was still Secretary of the Treasury and Calhoun was one of the most prominent nationalists in the House of Representatives. Thus, in support of Madison's modest proposal, there existed an alliance between the Treasury, on the one hand, and the Committee on National Currency, on the other. In a very real sense, this was the surviving monument to the efforts of Astor, Girard, and Parish; for while these three were still influential among capitalists, the initiative now lay with Madison, Dallas, and Calhoun, and with a phenomenon which defies exact analysis—the political climate itself.

It was a warm, beneficent climate, eminently suited to the shedding of inconvenient creeds. Now that the war had been, somehow or other, won, now that the Republican party was, somehow or other, still in the saddle and likely to stay there—it was useless to insist upon constitutional quibbles. The Republicans were now administering a state of affairs in which, Albert Gallatin wrote in December, 1815, "we are guilty of a continued breach of faith towards our creditors, our soldiers, our seamen, our civil officers. Public credit, heretofore supported simply by common honesty, declines at home and abroad; private capital placed on a still more uncertain basis; the value of property and the nature of every person's engagements equally uncertain; a baseless currency varying every fifty miles and fluctuating everywhere."

The obvious remedy for this, if the banks could not be persuaded to resume specie payments, was a national institution with regulatory powers, and James Madison, who had fought the chartering of the First Bank of the United States on constitutional principles in 1791, was now ready, on expedient ones, to consent to the chartering of a second.

Very few men possessed Albert Gallatin's sensitive financial conscience, but Madison's broadmindedness was quite in keeping with the new mood of the times. On January 8, 1816, Calhoun introduced a bill to incorporate the subscribers of a Bank of the United States; Henry Clay, descending from the Speaker's chair, reminded the House that in 1811 he had sternly opposed the rechartering of the First Bank on the grounds that Congress had no right to incorporate such an institution. "The force of circumstance and the lights of experience," he now said, had convinced him that Congress actually did have this "constructive power." A penitential garb of some kind the Speaker had to wear on such a painful occasion; one cannot say that loose construction was ill-chosen or unbecoming.

The Federalist opposition, at any rate, was purely formal; and that of the unreconstructed Jeffersonians was led by John Randolph of Roanoke, who happened to be more suspicious of the state banks than he was of the projected national one, and who contented himself with insinuations.

The bill passed the House, 80 to 71, on March 14 and, after certain Senate amendments had been concurred in, received the President's signature on April 10, 1816.

When the First Bank was incorporated in 1791, it was the North which had supported it and the South which had opposed it. Now their positions were reversed. Combining the votes of both houses, the New England and middle states gave 44 votes for the Bank and 53 against it; the southern and western states gave 58 for it and 30 against. In other words, "Jeffersonian policy had got itself into a position where a national bank was as essential to it as it had been to the Federalists twenty-five years before." To judge from the temper of the debates in House and Senate, and from the regional distribution of the votes, nobody was really eager to call this position into strict account.

As for the Bank which now emerged, it had a capital of $35,000,000, of which the government owned $7,500,000, and the government was to receive a bonus of $1,500,000 payable in three installments during the first years of operation. The head office was to be in Philadelphia; its directors were authorized to establish branches where they saw fit; and its charter was to run for twenty years. It was to be the principal depositary of the United States Treasury, was to report to the Treasury, and was to be subject to Treasury inspection. There were to be twenty-five directors, of whom five were to be appointed by the President, with the approval of the Senate. Finally, in order to fix a day for the resumption of specie payments, a resolution was adopted requiring payment of all government revenues in legal tender after February 20, 1817. Here one may leave the Bank, for the moment a symbol of financial chastity and nationalist order; its relapses will be examined later on.

Having agreed to this substantial and statesmanlike reform, the Fourteenth Congress was not likely to make heavy weather out of protective tariffs. A demand for protection had been more or less coeval with constitutional government itself, and never did it appear more justified than after the Peace of Ghent. The metaphor of a peaceful nation which now turned its face toward the West is historically sound, but only if one concedes that this nation was constantly looking over its shoulder. In fact, the United States was now exposed to the mercies of a world market, as Americans began to contemplate the strange phenomenon of a Europe at peace, "a Europe that had the whole world in which to buy supplies, a Europe that was able to do much of its own ocean carrying, and an England that had new and well-developed manufactures."

To the planters, the farmers, and the land speculators of America this change in world relations had, for the time being, a hopeful aspect. Europe, already blighted by the marching and countermarching of its locust armies, was now subjected to the calamity of poor harvests, and the demand thus created for American staples was further enhanced by a European propensity to gamble in tobacco and cotton. The American manufacturer, on the other hand, the latest child of the Industrial Revolution, was now in danger, through British dumping, of being smothered by his own parent. Madison's call for protective tariffs was statesmanlike, since it recognized the difficulties of adjusting from a state of war to a state of peace, but he did not expect the adjustment to be a lengthy one; he assumed that some equilibrium would soon be established between the forces of American and of British industry. Dallas' report, less mechanistic, was more forthright. He proposed, for example, a duty of 33⅓ per cent on cotton products and 28 per cent on woolens; the Committee of Ways and Means, which had not blenched at adopting a duty of 56 per cent on sugar, reduced both cotton and woolen duties to 20 per cent; and it was only after some striking scenes in the committee that the 20 per cent was raised to 25 per cent.

The debates in the House were acrimonious, as is the nature of tariff debates, but they were not divisive. There was an underlying agreement which could be expressed in three ways. In the first place, a tariff *did* answer the needs of a wide variety of interests.

War industries, suffering from the dumping of British manufactures, were crying for protection, from which almost every section of the country expected to benefit. In New England few cotton manufacturers managed to survive the fall in prices unless they adopted improved spinning machinery and the power loom. The few experimental mills in the Carolinas were staggering. Pittsburgh, already a flourishing smelter for iron deposits of the northern Appalachians, was eager to push its iron pigs and bars into the coastal region, in place of British and Swedish iron. In Kentucky there was a new industry of weaving local hemp into cotton bagging, which was menaced by the Scottish bagging industry. . . . The shepherds of Vermont and Ohio needed protection against English wool; the granaries of central New York, shut out of England by the corn laws, were attracted by the home market argument. Even Jefferson, outgrowing his old prejudice against factories, wrote, "We must now place the manufacturer by the side of the agriculturalist."

In the second place, the tariff as enacted on April 27, 1816, was a very temperate piece of legislation. The duty of 25 per cent on cottons and woolens was to continue until June 30, 1819, after which, it was assumed, a duty of 20 per cent would be sufficient to repel the competition of British manufacturers. A duty of 30 per cent was imposed upon rolled bar, leather, hats, writing paper, and cabinetware, and a specific duty of 3 cents a pound on sugar. But the only protective feature in the whole act was the principle of minimum valuation on coarse cottons: all cotton goods whose value was less than 25 cents a square yard should be considered as having cost that sum. (Its object was to exclude all low-grade prints and East Indian fabrics; and, since the price of these imported cottons tended to fall with the price of raw cotton and the use of the power loom, this importation gradually ceased.)

In the third place, the voting in the House was not exactly partisan: 63 Republicans voted for the tariff and 31 against; 25 Federalists were for it, 23 against; and the state divisions themselves were more perplexing than factious. It might seem ironical that maritime New England voted against a principle from which, in due time, it would be the first to benefit, and that congressmen from states that would later prefer secession to protection were disposed to support the protection of 1816. But here the real meaning of Madison's nationalistic program begins to reveal itself. The South considered that it alone had given the War of 1812 a substantial and decisive support; it identified itself in spirit with the successful outcome of the war; and it observed the nation's readjustment to peace with a benevolent eye. If the Tariff of 1816 had, as its chief beneficiary, the northern manufacturer, did he not deserve to be protected against the dumping practices of the late enemy? It could only have been on patriotic considerations such as these that representatives from southern districts which had no interest whatsoever in manufacturers gave, as many of them did, their votes for potection. Moreover, the southern leaders still believed that they controlled the triumphant Republican party, and with it the machinery of the central government: their nationalism rose and fell with this sense of control, so that one could say, without risking a paradox, that in the last two years of James Madison's Presidency the congressional South was most nationalistic when it was most sectional.

A Utopian element in the mild Tariff of 1816 can be detected, not only in the peculiar character of southern nationalism at this point, but more specifically in a speech which John Caldwell Calhoun delivered on April 4. He believed that the South would soon participate in New England's industrial development, and he argued that in the event of another war with England—which he did not consider unlikely—the interests of the army and navy imperatively required a balanced domestic economy. Should there be no war, however, into what channels could the vast accumulations of capital, themselves derived from a state of war, be peacefully directed? Obviously into manufactures. At this point any doctrinaire Jefferson might have protested that a system of manufactures would return America precisely to that kind of history from which, since the beginning of her national existence, his party had sought to divorce her. But Calhoun maintained that despotism and pauperism in England were due, not to England's industrial system, but to bad laws and excessive taxes. He foresaw a national state, in which commerce, navigation, agriculture, and manufacturing would be mutually, indeed serenely, dependent. The most trenchant criticism of Calhoun's quasi-corporate state was uttered by a man who was preternaturally quick to detect, though not to correct, an error. "On whom bears the duty on coarse woolens and linens, and blankets, upon salt and all the necessaries of life?" said John Randolph. "On poor men and on slaveholders." From this question and its answer there was never to be an escape, but Randolph was a kind of male Cassandra, more feared than honored; and in spite of his predictions or maledictions, the Tariff of 1816 was the symbol of consensus not conflict.

Into this happy state of affairs there intruded itself one incongruous but most significant event. Since the First Congress itself, surely nobody had been more able or more energetic than the Fourteenth. It seems to have decided that its labors should be rewarded in some fitting way. It therefore proposed and passed a Compensation Bill, which changed the emolument of Congressmen from $6 per diem to $1,500 per annum. There were sound reasons for this change; but the open nerve in the bill was soon touched by Calhoun, a statesman to whom intelligence and tact were not granted in equal measure, and who said that its real purpose was "to attract and secure ability and integrity to the public service . . . and any people, as they use or neglect them, flourish or decay."

The people, strange to say, did not agree. What they perceived in the Compensation Bill was an effort on the part of Congress to turn itself into an elite. The result was that in the fall elections, two-thirds of the representatives were replaced. "That this remarkable body of men should have incurred almost instantly the severest popular rebuke ever visited on a House of Representatives, could not have been mere accident." Nor was it. The people evidently wished their House of Representatives to represent them as they were, not as they ought to be; a strain of democratic or egalitarian nationalism was beginning to show itself, and legislators who distinguished themselves even with such modest laurels as a stipend of $1,500 simply did not conform to this.

CHAPTER 25

THE MARSHALL COURT
AND AMERICAN
NATIONALISM

Robert McCloskey demonstrates, in *The American Supreme Court** (1960), that Chief Justice Hughes' statement that the Constitution "is what the Supreme Court says it is" is certainly true when it is applied to the Marshall Court. Under the leadership of John Marshall (one of the most remarkable of a remarkable generation of Virginians), the Supreme Court created for itself a position in the power structure of American government that it occasionally has mislaid but never has permanently lost.

John Marshall had no blueprints and few tools when he constructed this position for the Court. The Court's broad duties are vaguely stated in the Constitution, but its more specific duties are left to the discretion of Congress—the Court's potential rival. Moreover, the Court has no institutional means of enforcing its decisions, particularly in a conflict with one of the states (for example, *Fletcher* v. *Peck*) or with the national government *(Marbury* v. *Madison)*. The Court must use sound reasoning, solid logic, majestic language and, on occasion, must "row to its objective with muffled oars." McCloskey shows that John Marshall and his associates were masters of these techniques. But this selection also indicates that Marshall—with all his understanding of the nuances of political power—was too fine a jurist to forget that "it is a Constitution we are expounding."

However, in spite of Marshall's judicial genius, significant questions arise when we study the record of his Court. Was the Court actually fulfilling the function that the founding fathers intended for it in the framework of the national government? Did its decisions, with their emphasis on increasing the national power, conflict with the framers' view of the nature of state-federal relations? Did the nation and the economy change sufficiently by 1815 to make the new interpretations imperative?

There are a number of good, general constitutional histories available. Among them are Alfred H. Kelly and Winfred A. Harbison, *The American Constitution: Its Origins and Development* (third edition, 1963). For a detailed study of Marshall, both as man and as a judge, see Albert J. Beveridge's classic, *The Life of John Marshall*, 4 vols. (1916–1919). Edward S. Corwin, one of this century's greatest constitutional historians, wrote a briefer, but excellent study, *John Marshall and the Constitution* (1919).

* Available in a paperback edition.

THE MARSHALL COURT AND THE SHAPING OF THE NATION

ROBERT McCLOSKEY

So far the story of the Supreme Court has been largely prelude. The judges have been deviled by uncertainties about their own status in the young American polity and about the power and malevolence of the forces that might imperil that status. Since the constitutional agreement of 1789 was inexplicit about the nature and scope of judicial authority, the Court has inherited the responsibility for drawing up its own commission, one line at a time, and the task has been delicate. Only gradually has it become apparent that the Court is being accepted as a symbol of constitutionalism and can therefore count on a solid measure of public support. Only with experience has it become clear to Marshall and his judicial brethren that the Republicans are not after all savage revolutionaries, that their bark is worse than their bite, and that the rule of law can therefore survive even though the Federalist party may not. In such a prelude, amid such uncertainties, the Court has been able to lay the argumentative bases for future accomplishments; it has fashioned some of the tools which may later be used to help govern America. But it has not yet been in a position to exert much real influence on the course of affairs. It has built its own fences with some cunning, but has not so far done much to build the nation.

However, with the War of 1812 and its immediate aftermath a new stage in the Court's history was inaugurated. We have seen that the slow accretion of precedents and confidence culminated in 1810, when the judges at last felt secure enough to hold a state law unconstitutional. Logically, the Court was then ready to begin to make its weight felt in the political order, to defend and foster in a concrete way the principle of national union. Now this logical development was stimulated and strengthened by the war's impact on American attitudes and political alignments.

SOURCE. Robert McCloskey, *The American Supreme Court,* Chicago: University of Chicago Press, 1960, pp. 54–71, 77–80. Copyright 1960 by the University of Chicago. Reprinted by permission of the University of Chicago Press and the author.

Many of the old Federalists, especially in New England, had fiercely opposed "Mr. Madison's war," had talked darkly of seceding from the Union, and had espoused a states' rights position strangely reminiscent of the extreme Republicanism of the Virginia and Kentucky resolutions. The politically dominant Republicans, on the other hand, were forced, in defending their war, to embrace the idea of nationalism, and to abjure in part their own localist tradition. Since they were in the ascendancy, this meant that the creed of nationalism enjoyed an unprecedented, if temporary, popularity and—the other side of the coin—that localism was for the moment bereft of really powerful defenders. To be sure localist sentiment soon revived and its exponents were as vocal as ever. But the nationalist spirit, once awakened, could not be dismissed at will. These events had intruded a cross-current in the Republican ideology; leaders like Madison and Monroe though by no means unqualified nationalists were not consistent localists either; the tradition they spoke for was now ambivalent on the great question of the nature of the Union.

This ambivalence persisted for some years and gave John Marshall his opportunity to use the judicial instruments he had been preparing. But his way, though now passable, was still far from easy. The Court after all was in the process of attaining a position more exalted than any attained by a judicial tribunal in modern world history; great tasks were impending. For one thing it was necessary both to confirm and to extend the Court's claim to authority, to transmute "judicial review" into "judicial sovereignty." Granted that it was proper for the Court to adjudge questions of constitutionality, did this imply that the Court's judgment was final? Did it imply that the judges could call the other branches to account even when the question of constitutionality was doubtful? Did it imply that the Court would exercise a general supervision over some governmental affairs that fell outside the traditional judicial orbit?

To Marshall it implied all this, for he was firmly convinced that the more America was guided by judges the happier and more just its system would be. But others, in politics and out, were not ready to bear the Chief Justice's mild yoke, and there was always a threat that overweening judicial power would encounter resistance or counterattack more formidable than its recently established independence could withstand. Though moving onward and upward, then, the Court must still tread carefully.

Secondly and simultaneously, the Court of Marshall's remaining years was engaged in using its still nascent authority to establish the substantive constitutional principles on which the American polity should rest. It was interpreting the document of 1789 so as to provide maximum protection to property rights and maximum support for the idea of nationalism.

Usually these two objectives were conjoined, so that a pro-nationalist constitutional doctrine best served the cause of property rights and vice versa. The national government was not at this time much inclined to interfere in commercial affairs, whereas the states, one or the other, presented a constant threat to the stability of currency, the sanctity of debts, or the freedom of business enterprise. Thus Marshall, happily for his peace of mind, was able to assure himself that he made property rights more secure when he deprived the states of power by enhancing the power of the nation. If these two primary values of his had conflicted, his soul-search would have been agonizing. But they seldom did conflict, and his historic achievements in the cause of union were therefore not clouded by confusion of motives.

He had troubles enough without adding internal uncertainty to them. The antinationalist front of the Republicans (soon to be called Democrats) had indeed been impaired, but specific and bitter centers of opposition still developed when specific provocations aroused them, and almost every major decision was met by a storm of intemperate denunciation from some politically potent quarter. Even worse, as the 1820's neared their end, it became increasingly apparent that the tide of states' rights sentiment was rising if not in volume at any rate in intensity. From time to time he was compellingly reminded of a fact that all Supreme Court justices must learn to live with: that the Court's decrees are backed only by its own prestige and ultimately by the willingness of the President to help enforce them. Over and over he was reminded that Congress could destroy in a day the judicial independence that had been building for decades.

In this context Marshall faced his great task of augmenting the judicial power and shaping the Constitution into a charter for nationalism. These two interwoven themes run through nearly all his decisions; each case raises the question of the Court's authority together with that of nation-state relationship, and the Court must always decide one question in the light of the other, taking care that its nationalist zeal does not compromise its own status or that claims for judicial power are never so extreme as to vitiate the crusade for nationalism. And little by little, in spite of the delicacy of this balancing feat, in spite of the deep antagonism of affected litigants, in spite of the rising wave of states' rights sentiment, the job is done. The Court's empire of decision is extended and stabilized as firmly as it ever can be in a governmental arrangement that rests on inference and acquiescence rather than on final definition. The great operative phrases of the Constitution—the supremacy clause, the contract clause, the necessary and proper clause, the commerce clause—are im-

pregnated with the nationalist meanings so dear to Marshall's heart. And
most important of all, these judicially contrived mutations in the character
of American constitutionalism are generally accepted by the nation they
are designed to guide.

How were these remarkable results achieved? How was the Court able,
in the face of these adversities, to have its way? Partly the answer goes
back to factors mentioned in previous chapters—the American attachment to the idea of fundamental law and the gradual identification of the
Supreme Court with that idea. Partly the answer is to be found in the
judges themselves and most of all of course in Marshall—the judicial
sense of strategy and timing, the rhetorical virtuosity which should never
be undervalued, the capacity to engender respect even among those who
disagreed. Partly, as has been said, the difficulties were eased by the
temporary ambivalence of Republican opinion on the nature of the Union.

But the Court's progress was also aided by a basic disability of the
localist movement—its very lack of unity. The states were so individualistic
that they defeated themselves, for it was (and is) a peculiarity of the
states' rights doctrine that its partisans were devoted to it only when
their own oxen were being gored, when nationalism presented a specific
threat to a concrete interest. If states' rights could be associated with a
common and long-term economic issue like slavery or the tariff, then
the affected states would stand long and firm against their mutual ad-
versary. But if Virginia had a problem today that Maryland did not
share, Virginia's outraged protest in the name of states' rights would
attract little support from Maryland any more than Maryland's similar
protest tomorrow would bring Virginia rushing to her standard. Both
states were being true to the fractional principle that lay at the heart of
states' rights doctrine. But, because of their adherence to that principle,
the Supreme Court, with its eye steadily on a single target, was spared
the calamity of confronting a united opposition. The Court left such
potentially unifying issues as the tariff and slavery pretty much alone,
and it was not even necessary, then, to divide to conquer, for the opposition had thoughtfully divided itself.

THE COURT OVER THE STATES

One of the Court's great problems was presented either by direct or by
implied challenge in nearly every significant case of the era: the problem
of its right to review decisions of state courts involving the validity of
acts undertaken by the state governments. Such a right was granted to
the Court under Section 25 of the Judiciary Act of 1789; state court
decisions that denied a claim made in the name of the federal Constitu-

tion, laws, or treaties could be reviewed by the Supreme Court by a "writ of error." And of course if the state court was thought to have erred, its judgment could be reversed and any state law it rested on invalidated.

That was the Supreme Court's nominal statutory authority, but it was one thing for Congress to pass such an empowering act and another thing to persuade the states to yield to it. From the first, localists had contended that Section 25 involved an unconstitutional encroachment on state sovereignty, and although the Court had several times exercised this supposedly unwarranted power with comparative impunity, the rumbles of protest had never quite been stilled. The case of *Martin* v. *Hunter's Lessee* in 1816 compelled the Court, which had so far tried to ignore arguments against Section 25, finally to meet them head on.

The case involved the title to some 300,000 acres of Virginia land which had once belonged to Lord Fairfax but which had been confiscated by the state in Revolutionary times partly on the ground that Fairfax and his heirs were enemy aliens. Virginia had proceeded to grant a section of the land, which it now claimed as its own, to David Hunter, who later sought in the courts of Virginia to eject the Fairfax heirs. But in the meantime of course the Revolution had ended, the Treaty of Peace with Great Britain had been signed, the national Constitution had come into being, and the new national government had been endowed with the power to make treaties. It was argued that both the Treaty of Peace and Jay's Treaty of 1795 confirmed the titles of British subjects to land in America and that the Fairfax title was therefore still valid.

In spite of this, the Virginia Court of Appeals held against the Fairfax heirs, and the Supreme Court of the United States, having granted review of this holding on a writ of error, ordered it reversed. The Virginia court, which was headed by Spencer Roane, an ardent states' righter and bitter foe of Marshall, pondered this order for a while and then decided to ignore it, arguing that Section 25 was itself unconstitutional. The Virginia judges conceded of course that they were bound to observe the federal Constitution, but they insisted that the meaning of the Constitution was for them to decide and that the Supreme Court had no power to impose its own interpretation upon them. It was this contention, so fatal to the prospects for both judicial supervision and centralism, that faced the Court in *Martin* v. *Hunter's Lessee*. If the Constitution was to mean whatever the various states wanted it to mean, the cause of national union was lost at the outset.

Justice Story spoke for the Court, Marshall having disqualified himself because he had been financially involved with the Fairfax interests. Story had been appointed by Madison in 1811 as a New England Republican; but now, after five years on the Court, he was as nationalistic in his views as Marshall himself. Indeed the supreme bench consisted of two Federalists and five nominal Republicans, and yet Marshall was seldom to have much difficulty enlisting his fellows in the nationalist crusade. His success in doing so has often been attributed to the witchcraft of his strong and charming personality; Jefferson had once predicted that "it will be difficult to find a character with firmness enough to preserve his independence on the same bench with Marshall." There can be no doubt that Marshall was an immensely attractive and convincing colleague, but it seems reasonable to suppose that the judges who came to share his nationalist views were beguiled not only by him but by a growing awareness that the Court's status and their own depended on the strength of the Union. It is hardly surprising that the Supreme Court, an intrinsically national institution, should be drawn to the doctrine of nationalism.

Story's powerful opinion in this case followed a pattern which can be traced through most of the great nationalistic decisions of the era. In the first place, he felt called upon to argue, or rather to assert, that the Constitution was the creation of "the people of the United States" as the Preamble says, and not of the several states. This contention, which may seem merely abstract, was essential to his purpose. Since at least 1776, most Americans had conceded that the people were the ultimate source of sovereignty and that the people could therefore, as Story says, "invest the general government with all powers which they might deem proper and necessary." If the Constitution was the work of the people, the powers it granted the national government *could* be as extensive as sovereignty itself. But if, on the other hand, the states had created the Constitution, it was arguable that the powers of the national government must stop at the point where they encroached on state sovereignty, and this very argument had been insisted upon by the embattled Virginians. The assertion that the Constitution represented the higher sovereignty of the people enabled Story to controvert the argument that state sovereignty is inviolable; if the people, in enacting the Constitution, wanted to modify state sovereignty, they had an incontestable right to do so.

The second great step in the opinion was to contend that the people *did* want to modify state sovereignty and had given evidence of that desire in the language of the Constitution. Article III extends the judicial power to all *cases* arising under the Constitution, laws, or treaties. There is no suggestion that the judicial power must stop short if a case originates in a state court rather than a federal. Since the language is general and is not restricted by the context or by necessary implication, it must be assumed that any case presenting a federal question is within reach of the judicial power, whatever may be the tribunal in which it arises.

This opinion contains, in more or less explicit statement, practically all the major items in the bag of tricks the Marshall Court was to use in future years against the minions of disunion. It invokes the doctrine of popular sovereignty to accomplish traditionally Federalist ends, a gambit that was particularly frustrating to the Court's Republican opponents, who were accustomed to think of themselves as the champions of that doctrine. The doctrine is then used by Story to deprecate the idea that state sovereignty was left intact at the time the Union was formed. Next he sets forth the proposition that national powers should be construed generously, a notion disastrous to states' rights when its implications are developed. From these principles "in respect to which no difference of opinion ought to be indulged," as Story says, he is able to infer a supervisory power for the Supreme Court so broad that it embraces all state tribunals. And finally this panoply of authority is used to defend property rights against spoliation by a capricious public. Each of these themes will be echoed over and over in the decisions of the future; each of them serves a vital purpose in the judges' struggle to make America the nation they believed it ought to be.

The specific problem of the *Martin* case—whether the Court's power under Section 25 could be maintained—was not of course entirely settled by Story's argumentative dexterities. In the years that followed, whenever a state felt aggrieved by a Court decision, the familiar cry against Section 25 was again heard. In 1821, in *Cohens* v. *Virginia,* Marshall not only reiterated Story's basic points but interpreted the Eleventh Amendment, that supposed warranty of states' rights, so as to permit individuals to appeal to the Supreme Court even though a state was the other party in the litigation. The Amendment, said Marshall, prevents individual suits against states only if the action is "commenced" by the individual; if the state has initiated the action (for instance, by arresting a person), the person can still bring the state into the Supreme Court to defend itself against an appeal.

At this point, the Virginian defenders of states' rights felt that judicial sophistry has surpassed itself, since not even a constitutional amendment had arrested its course. They urged that the Court's authority be curbed by statute or by more carefully drawn amendment, and hereafter throughout the 1820's hardly a session of Congress went by without a proposal to modify, in one way or another, the doctrine of judicial control. These threats were serious enough to alarm the Court and its friends, but in truth none of them ever came very close to succeeding. As John Taylor of Caroline complained, the apathy of the "sister states," when one of their number was assailed, for a long time made a united front of states' rights sentiment impossible to assemble. Meanwhile, decision after decision accustomed the nation to accept the Court's view of its own function; each year that passed, each holding that was submitted to, made it a little harder to question that view. When South Carolina radically assailed the whole principle of nationalism in the Nullification Ordinance of 1832, its formidable adversaries included not only Andrew Jackson but a federal judiciary which had become a focus of public respect and a symbol of Union.

THE ENHANCEMENT OF NATIONAL POWER

One handicap of the Supreme Court during these early years and indeed throughout its history was its divorce from the sources of political power. Seven men in Washington, armed with nothing save their robes and their intellects, seem pitiful rivals to state legislatures, congresses, and presidents who command the machinery of government and are backed by the mighty force of the electoral process. But the Court's apparent weakness was also, as we have seen, a kind of opportunity. Because it was an independent, small, cohesive body, it could maintain a long-term view that gave it a decided advantage over opponents divided between a variety of special, temporary concerns and often confused in the basic premises of their opposition.

This advantage is further illustrated by the great Marshallian decisions involving the question of national legislative authority. Story's argument in the *Martin* case that national powers should be liberally construed enabled him to contend that Congress had a right to pass Section 25 and thus to make the Court the dominant tribunal of the nation. But his interest and Marshall's in the doctrine of liberal construction went far beyond its use to bolster judicial status. They wanted to enhance national power in all respects, partly because this would simultaneously restrict the power of the states, but partly too because they anticipated awesome tasks for the nation and wanted to insure that it was constitutionally equipped to deal with them. And the Court's success in accomplishing this aim must be attributed in no small degree to self-contradiction among the forces that opposed it.

McCulloch v. *Maryland* in 1821 is by almost any reckoning the greatest decision John Marshall ever handed down—the one most important to the future of America, most influential in the Court's own doctrinal history, and most revealing of Marshall's unique talent for stately argument. It involved a state tax on note issues of the Bank of the United States, which had been incorporated by act of Congress in 1816. The government argued that such a tax on a federal instrumentality was invalid and need not be paid. The state replied that the incorporation of the Bank exceeded Congress' constitutional powers and that in any event the states could tax as they willed within their own borders. These contentions raised vast and difficult questions both for the present and the future. The Bank was viewed with special loathing by the states' rights advocates; any decision upholding its claim to exist and denying the state's claim to tax could be counted on to infuriate them. And not the least of their heated objections would be the familiar one that the Court had no power in spite of Section 25 to entertain the cause. On the other hand, it was clear to Marshall, as it has been to posterity, that a national government restricted in its powers by Maryland's narrow interpretation would be incapable of the great tasks that might lie before it.

Speaking for a unanimous Court, Marshall therefore upheld the constitutionality of the Bank's incorporation, and in doing so set down the classic statement of the doctrine of national authority. The argument he advanced was not new; its main outlines had been endlessly debated since the first Congress and Hamilton's famous paper urging the Bank's establishment; and much of it had been given judicial expression by Story in 1816. But Marshall deserves the credit for stamping it with the die of his memorable rhetoric and converting it from a political theory into the master doctrine of American constitutional law.

Because the argument is logical it lends itself to summary, falling into three major phases. The first is concerned with the problem of the nature of the Constitution itself. Two crucial premises are laid down: First, the Constitution emanates from the hand of the sovereign people and speaks in broad language so that it can "be adapted to the various crises of human affairs." We must never forget that "it is a *constitution* we are expounding." These premises infuse the second phase, which concerns the nature of the national government the Constitution created. The people made that government supreme over all rivals within the sphere of its powers (Art. VI), and those powers must be construed generously if they are to be sufficient for the "various crises" of the ages to come.

The third phase is simply the application of these weighty principles. The power to incorporate the Bank is upheld under the clause endowing Congress with the power to make all laws "necessary and proper" for carrying into execution the other powers (Art. I, sec. 8); the words "necessary and proper" are interpreted generously, in accord with the principles advanced, to mean "appropriate" and "plainly adapted." The Maryland tax is invalidated, because since "the power to tax involves the power to destory," to uphold the tax would grant the state the power to defeat the national government's supremacy; an inferior (in these matters) would be empowered to destroy a superior. But no summary can convey the air of high seriousness that pervades the opinion, the magisterial dignity with which it marches to its conclusions, the sense of righteous certitude with which it announces them. It was such qualities as these that made it persuasive to contemporaries and to the generations to come; and to appreciate these qualities the reader must go to the opinion itself.

The reaction was what might have been expected. In the North and the East the decision was praised; in the South and West, where the Bank was especially unpopular, the Court was roundly condemned. But even in Virginia, the fastness of such philosophers of Republicanism as Jefferson, Roane, and Taylor, the assailants curiously compromised their own position by putting the immediate issue of the Bank ahead of the broader issue of principle. Most of them denounced the Court for *not* holding the incorporation statute unconstitutional, thus of course tacitly conceding that the Court had the power to do so. Yet surely if the Court had the exalted power of overthrowing an act of Congress, it was not unreasonable to suppose that it also had the right to disapprove state laws. And if it did have these high prerogatives the Court must have some discretion in exercising them, that is, it could not be condemned merely because Spencer Roane, wielding the same power, would have decided the case differently.

In short most of the critics conceded too much for the good of their own criticisms. Their proper course would have been to deny that the Court had any business judging the validity of either national or state laws. But as usual they were more concerned about the immediate, concrete issue than they were about such a general doctrine as judicial sovereignty or even states' rights; and once again the Court profited from the fact that it alone seemed to understand the value of consistency and generality.

Much the same lesson can be drawn from the "Steamboat Monopoly Case," *Gibbons* v. *Ogden* in 1824, in which the Court was confronted for the first time by the problem of interpreting the commerce clause. A quarter-century before, the New York legislature had granted Robert R. Livingston and Robert Fulton the exclusive right to steamboat navigation in the waters of New York, and in the course of time the monopoly had extracted a similar privilege from Louisiana. The value of this controlling position in the two great port states of the nation was of course enormous, and rival states were deeply resentful of the arrangement. The *Gibbons* case involved an action for encroachment on the monopoly, and the defendant contented that the state had no right to grant it in the first place, because navigation is "commerce among the several states," which is the business of Congress.

This contention raised a series of questions that were destined for long and checkered careers in the development of constitutional law. First, what *is* interstate commerce? Does the term cover only buying and selling, or does it apply to such activities as navigation? Second, once we have determined what interstate commerce is, what is the extent of the power to regulate it? Third, what is the effect on the states of this grant of power to Congress? Must they stay out of the field altogether, or do they have a concurrent right to control it? It is not too much to say that the future of America as a nation depended on the answers that were given to these questions.

And Marshall, with his usual foresight, was well aware that he stood at another major constitutional crossroad. The opinion, like so many of his great ones, is a deft blend of boldness and restraint. In answer to the first two questions, he advanced the kind of broad, nationalistic definitions that the Hamiltonian tradition approved. Commerce, he said, is not merely buying and selling; it includes "every species of commercial intercourse," and this is true whether we are talking of either interstate or foreign commerce. Nor does interstate commerce stop at state boundaries; a journey that begins in Boston and ends in Philadelphia is subject to congressional power from start to finish. Of course, so inclusive a definition amply covers navigation. As for the extent of Congress' power to regulate a subject, once it is found to be in interstate commerce, that power is "complete in itself, may be exercised to its utmost extent, and acknowledges no limitations other than are prescribed in the Constitution." It is no less than the power "to prescribe the rule by which commerce is to be governed."

Perhaps only in the perspective of the future can it be understood how much these words meant; a twentieth-century observer looking back on them is impressed because he knows that the definitions have proved elastic enough to justify all the extensive commercial enterprises in which the national government has since engaged. But to contemporaries the most urgent question was yet to come: are the states precluded from acting in the commercial area thus defined? And at this point Marshall grew curiously evasive. He stated sympathetically the argument that the commerce power is exclusive, remarked that it had "great force" and said: ". . . the court is not satisfied that it has been refuted." He came as close to formally approving the doctrine as he could without quite doing so. But, he went on, it is not now necessary to decide this issue, because the New York monopoly law conflicts with a federal coasting license statute. Whether or not the commerce clause alone would in-validate the state law, surely it must be admitted that the federal coasting license law does, for the Constitution makes congressional enactments "the supreme law of the land." The lucrative but controversial monopoly was thus at last brought to an end.

Once again, as so often in the past, Marshall had managed to achieve imperishable results while side-stepping the area of greatest controversy. In other commerce clause cases he refined the notion of interstate (and foreign) commerce somewhat further by holding that goods were still subject to national control so long as they remained in their original shipping packages (the "original package doctrine"); and confused the question of state regulatory power still more by allowing a state to main-tain a dam that blocked a navigable stream. No watchful guardian of states' rights could contend that Marshall had erected constitutional bar-riers to all state commercial regulation. Surely he had implied that some such regulation might be prohibited by the commerce clause alone, and surely his dicta about the extent of the commerce power had opened up the possibility of prodigious congressional regulation in this field. But it was present actualities, not implications and possibilities, that most con-cerned his contemporaries, and they found it hard to condemn a judicial stroke that slew the hated monopoly, whatever the flourishes that ac-companied it. Jefferson and a few like him were horrified by *Gibbons,* but in general the decision was welcomed; the fact that it did after all overthrow a state law and hammer a few more nails in the coffin of state sovereignty was easy to minimize in the face of its immediately popular conclusion. . . .

THE ACHIEVEMENT OF JOHN MARSHALL

Few intellectual feats are more difficult than the assessment of history while we are living it, and perhaps the problem is all the greater for those who are themselves playing the leading roles. In his last years, Marshall was beset with misgivings about America's future, full of gloomy convictions that he had failed in his campaign to establish judicial sovereignty and to cement the bonds of national union. The states' rights movement was waxing ever stronger and more vocal under the ministrations of John C. Calhoun; the Court had recently been defied in two spectacular cases by Georgia, and President Jackson's unwillingness to back the judges had underlined the Court's ultimate dependency on ex-ternal support. The old Federalist dream of rule by "the wise, the rich, and the good" seemed more chimerical than ever, as the spirit of Jack-sonian democracy swept the nation.

But, ominous though these developments appeared, Marshall was wrong to think that they spelled the failure of his programs. Not even he, the architect-in-chief, realized how securely the cornerstones of American constitutionalism had been laid. His error probably was that he hoped for absolute certitude in a system that had been dedicated by its framers to the principle of relativism. We cannot say that the doctrine of judicial sovereignty was established beyond the shadow of doubt by *Cohens* v. *Virginia* in 1821, or that the broad construction of national powers was settled once and for all by *McCulloch* v. *Maryland* and *Gibbons* v. *Ogden,* or that the *Dartmouth* case stilled all uncertainties about the contract clause. We cannot say that at one moment the constitutional basis for union was an aspiration and at the next a firm reality, for constitutional history does not move in this way. The vagueness of the Constitution on these issues gave the Court its chance to be creative, but by the same token it was decreed that the creations would never be final and perfect. The Court's title to power, being inferred rather than explicitly stated, must always be somewhat tentative; interpretations of the Constitution, being fashioned by the historical context rather than by the fiat of 1789, must submit to the verdict of later history, as well as the past. With all this subtlety and shrewdness, Marshall's mind was attracted by absolutes, and the contingency of the constitutional universe never ceased to trouble him.

But if we can tolerate, as Marshall could not, a world of half-certainty (and if we enjoy, as he did not, the perspective of the future), we can see that his forebodings were excessive, and his accomplishments greater than he knew. The doctrine of judicial sovereignty was still subject to occasional challenge in moments of stress; men like Jackson and Calhoun were unwilling to admit that the Supreme Court was the *only* authority on the Constitution's meaning. But surely the judicial monopoly, though imperfect, was very impressive. The nation in general thought of the Court as the principal authority and conceded its right to supervise the states in most matters. When the Court impinged on the great primary interest of a state or region, a line might be drawn; but in the considerable distance before that line was reached judicial sovereignty held its ,sway. The Supreme Court was now far more serene and formidable than the precariously balanced institution Marshall had taken over in 1801. America's devotion to the idea of fundamental law and the Court's ability to capitalize on opponents' errors had made sure of that.

This establishment of judicial hegemony was itself a highly important victory in the struggle to promote the principle of national union, for it meant (with the qualifications already mentioned) that the Constitution spoke with one voice throughout America. But the other substantive principles Marshall had laid down also served that purpose and were also more solidly fixed than Marshall, in his somber old age, imagined. The national-power doctrines of *McCulloch* and *Gibbons* were to have their great day in a more remote future when the national government felt inclined to use the constitutional sinews Marshall's court had provided; until then their significance was more moral than practical. But the corollary doctrine—that the states may not encroach on these federally reserved realms—was well accepted and immediately relevant. These limitations on state power based on the doctrine of national supremacy, plus such specific limitations as those derived from the contract clause, helped open the way to the development of commercial enterprise on a national scale in the next half-century.

Marshall was right in thinking that he had failed to resolve for America the great problem of nation-state relationships. No court could finally settle an issue of such dimensions, an issue that had already brought the nation near the brink of civil war. But he might justifiably have felt that he and his Court had made a priceless contribution to its settlement, had fashioned out of judicial materials an ideology of seasoned strength to which those who cared for the Union could repair, had established a pattern of control that would help to shore up the Union even though nothing but bloodshed could ultimately save it. He could have comforted himself with the thought that no court in world history had every done so much to affect the destiny of a great nation.

CHAPTER 26

JOHN QUINCY ADAMS AND AMERICAN EXPANSIONISM

In the introductory chapter of *When the Eagle Screamed,** William Goetzmann of the University of Texas covers the expansionist foreign policy of John Quincy Adams in order to set the stage for his interpretation of United States expansionism in the 1830's, 1840's, and 1850's. Adams' historical reputation has not been based primarily on his performance as President. Before 1824 he was the country's brightest diplomat and, following his term in the White House, he began a career in the House of Representatives where he acquired the title "Old Man Eloquent." However, it is his diplomatic career that concerns us here.

As Secretary of State under James Monroe, Adams certainly must be ranked as one of America's outstanding diplomats. His handling of the English during the period when he formulated the Monroe Doctrine places him among the outstanding Secretaries of State. Yet, as Goetzmann demonstrates, the Adams-Onis Treaty is probably Adams' greatest achievement. During these negotiations, he performed a series of diplomatic bluffs that must have pleased Henry Clay—one of this country's finest political poker players. Adams simultaneously and judiciously threatened the Spanish with (1) the forcible acquisition of both East and West Florida, (2) the recognition of the independence of the rebellious republics of South America, and (3) the pressing of our Louisiana

Purchase claims to Texas. Moreover, Adams constantly encouraged Monroe not to lose faith or to show signs of backing down. As a result of Adams' bargaining, the United States received a peaceful and cheap title to the Floridas and strengthened its claims to the Oregon country. Shortly after the Spanish accepted this treaty, the United States became the first power to recognize the independence of the former Spanish colonies in the New World. Thus, all that the nation gave up for this grant of territory and claims was a very dubious claim to the Texas country and, within twenty-five years, this area, as well as the Oregon country, had become United States territory. In the long run, the nation gave up nothing and gained much. Although Adams did not negotiate the later territorial acquisitions, there is little doubt that his expansionist policies stood his successors in good stead—serving not only as examples but also, in the case of the Oregon country, giving his successors strong diplomatic grounds on which to stand.

In reading this account, the student should seek to determine the relationship between Adams' diplomacy and the developing American nationalism discussed in previous selections. To what extent did Adams' chief policies, expressed in the Adams-Onis Treaty and the Monroe Doctrine, reflect the mood and temper of the nation? Were these two policies connected? If so, how? Finally, what can be learned from this essay about the nature of nineteenth-century diplomacy?

Adams has an outstanding biographer in Samuel Flagg Bemis, whose *John Quincy Adams and the Foundations of American Foreign Policy* (1949), is a study of Adams both as a man and a diplomat. The basic study of the Monroe Doctrine is Dexter Perkins, *The Monroe Doctrine** (1927). For additional insights on the Adams-Onis Treaty see R. W. Van Alstyne, *The Rising American Empire** (1960), and Henry Nash Smith, *Virgin Land** (1950).

* Available in a paperback edition.

CLEAR-EYED MEN OF DESTINY
WILLIAM H. GOETZMANN

The foundations of American expansionism were laid by two very different men, who nevertheless had much in common—Thomas Jefferson and John Quincy Adams. Jefferson, the Virginian, stood for the agrarian way of life. As a farmer and local politician he believed that "those who till the earth are the chosen people of God." And as a young surveyor, he had traveled in the backcountry enough to learn something of the needs, indeed the demands, of the sturdy Scotch-Irish pioneers who were pushing westward regardless of the dangers and the niceties of national jurisdiction. But the image of Jefferson the simple agrarian can be misleading. He was also a cosmopolite—a romantic child of the eighteenth-century Enlightenment, who had been to France, who had absorbed much of the science and learning of the day, and whose imagination was therefore global. Even in his Revolutionary days his instinct, and that of many of his associates, was to address himself to "a candid world." His friends were veterans of the world's political battlefields—Joseph Priestly, the Marquis de Lafayette, and Tom Paine. Later, following Franklin, he became president of one of the most important world organizations of the time, the American Philosophical Society—modeled successfully on its more famous English counterpart, the Royal Society of London. His house, built atop a mountain in the Virginia wilds, was a Palladian villa with a simulated Roman ruin in the garden. It was the height of fashion and sophistication, but it stood on the edge of a wilderness facing West. Jefferson, therefore, combined the values of the republican and agrarian democrat with the instinct, taste, and knowledge of a man of the world.

John Quincy Adams of Braintree, Massachusetts, has always seemed the more provincial of the two. Adams was almost a caricature of the staunch, introspective New England puritan. He arose before dawn to

SOURCE. William H. Goetzmann, *When the Eagle Screamed: The Romantic Horizon in American Diplomacy, 1800–1860*, New York: John Wiley & Sons, Inc, 1966, pp. 1–3, 9–20. Copyright 1966 by John Wiley & Sons, Inc. Reprinted by permission of John Wiley & Sons and the author.

read his Bible and study his Latin classics, and was dyspeptic throughout the day if, on a rare occasion, he failed to beat the sun. However, he was also a man of the world. From the beginning, thanks to the advantage of being a child of the Revolution and having a presidential, one might say "founding," father, John Quincy Adams was keenly aware of the intricacies and perils of world diplomacy. He was among the first, for example, to note the dangers of prolonging the Revolutionary alliance with France, and at an early age expressed his sentiments in speeches and letters to the editors of various Boston papers, a gesture more effective then than now. In 1794, at the age of 31, he was appointed by Washington as an envoy to the Hague and thus began his long career in the foreign service. He went to Holland, then London, then Prussia, and then to Russia where he secured the friendship and allegiance of the Czar to the American cause. He was one of the negotiators of the Treaty of Ghent ending the War of 1812, and just before becoming Secretary of State under President Monroe, he was Minister to the Court of St. James, the premier position in the American diplomatic service. Therefore, although Adams loved New England—loved it enough to place the plight of codfishermen and poor impressed seamen, and the fortunes of sea otter hunters and whalers uppermost in his mind, he was also a man of the world. He was no stranger to continental and intercontinental strategy. He, too, was a devotee of European science and learning and, like Jefferson, he worked to advance these enterprises in America. He was not an agrarian, however. He represented the maritime interests of New England; but he was enough of a strategist to realize that America's maritime interests could best be served by a policy of continentalism that looked westward to the Pacific. And so, along with Jefferson, he became one of the architects of American westward expansion.

The vision of these two men of the world—the one looking toward development of an inland and democratic empire, the other looking toward eventual command of the sea—became the cornerstone of American expansionism. They set the pattern, and a daring pattern it was, for the fledgling American empire that flung itself brashly and boldly across the romantic world horizon, and from which to this day there has been no retreat. . . .

Although the acquisition of Louisiana was a master stroke for American continental diplomacy, it nevertheless raised serious problems which remained to be solved in the future. It forecast the dispersion of people and energies over a vast territory which, through lack of communications, would be but loosely held. "We rush like a comet into infinite space" wailed the Federalist Fisher Ames with this very danger in mind.

In addition to the dispersion and disunity that might result, possession of Louisiana inevitably brought the United States once again into direct confrontation with Spain and, more importantly, with England, the most powerful nation on earth. These twin confrontations drew the perilous lines of continental diplomacy virtually until mid-century.

II

The burden of these later anxieties was assumed by the gentleman from Braintree, John Quincy Adams. In the course of his career he was to extend American continental commitments even farther, and although he was successful, he did nothing to lessen the tensions between the United States and its two powerful rivals. When Adams assumed his post as Secretary of State he faced several severe problems which related to the question of expansion. To begin with, according to the agreement signed at Ghent, all territories seized by the British or the Americans were to revert back to their *status quo ante bellum*. In the Northwest this presented a particularly acute problem for during the war Canada had moved south. British agents and traders controlled virtually the entire near Northwest, and it was only through the valiant efforts of Manuel Lisa, the St. Louis fur trader, who mobilized the Sioux against them on the Upper Missouri, that the British were not able to move south as far as St. Louis. In the far Northwest, Astoria had fallen to a ragtag and bobtail brigade of Northwest Company men who came out of the woods and down the Columbia to demand its surrender. Fearing British military conquest, the Astoria partners had sold Astoria to the Northwest Company. But since this was a private commercial venture they had no right to bargain away American political claims to the Columbia region and they did not do so. Sometime later when the British Man-of-War H.M.S. *Raccoon* put in at Astoria, its commander found to his dismay that the fort was already in British hands and he could not have the "glory" of capturing it. So he contented himself with raising the Union Jack and sailing away. However, by the Treaty of Ghent, Astoria should properly have been returned to the United States, and the near Northwest cleared of British officials. Adams helped to accomplish these two things.

Albert Gallatin and Richard Rush, the two men sent in 1818 to negotiate with England concerning these and numerous other postwar difficulties, such as impressment of sailors and the Newfoundland fishing rights, under Adams' orders also held fast to the northern boundary line of the 49th parallel from the Lake of the Woods to the crest of the Rockies, thus denying British traders the easy access to the Missouri and the Mississippi which they once enjoyed. A short while before this, out in St. Louis, William Clark, the Governor of Louisiana, began the practice of licensing would-be fur traders, which was an on-the-spot means of excluding Canadian competition. Earlier, in 1795, the federal government had established a group of government-owned trading posts in the region to assert federal control over the Indian trade—a measure that proved somewhat ineffective. In addition, however, after Major Stephen Long surveyed a series of frontier defense posts, John C. Calhoun, the Secretary of War, began planning what came to be called the Yellowstone Expedition. It was to be an expedition in force up the Missouri River which would establish a strategic military outpost at the mouth of the Yellowstone River on the upper Missouri. Although this expedition ultimately proved to be a dismal failure, rumors of an American show of strength in the North Country undoubtedly helped to expedite the agreements of 1818.

On the political front the enthusiasm of the American, if not the British, negotiators was also spurred by the series of articles published by the young western politician, Thomas Hart Benton, in the St. Louis *Enquirer*. Benton, speaking for the St. Louis fur trade interests, for John Floyd of Virginia, and for a number of western-minded men, demanded that the United States government do something about the upper-Missouri situation, and also take steps to acquire Oregon. Following Jefferson, as he did most of his life, Benton felt that the United States could probably not extend its sovereignty to Oregon—indeed he pictured the "fabled god Terminus" astride the Rocky Mountains preventing future mass migrations in that direction—but he saw Oregon and the Columbia as a strategic trading outpost on the road to India: hence of supreme importance to American interests. A settlement of republican-minded emigrants from the United States at the mouth of the Columbia would give the new nation a window on the Pacific, keep the British out, and make the Columbia, and what came to be the Oregon Trail (discovered by Robert Stuart in 1813) a vital path of inland commerce between the Mississippi Valley and the Pacific with its sea otter and China trade. Benton's grandiose rhetoric in defense of this aggressive plan more than matched the audacity of the plan itself, which had once been the dream of John Jacob Astor and of Thomas Jefferson.

Given these pressures, the results of the negotiations of 1818 were at least satisfactory. No boundary west of the Rocky Mountains was agreed upon. In August, 1818, Astoria was returned to American sovereignty and an official American claim was established north of the Columbia River, although it took a warship, the U.S.S. *Ontario,* to do it. And finally the negotiators agreed to a joint occupation treaty to extend for ten years which left both the British and Americans free to trade in the Oregon country, but which did not prejudice the claims of either nation to political sovereignty over the region. Spanish interests in the Northwest were for the time being ignored.

Adams was not, however, unmindful of Spain. The object of his immediate attention was Florida, both East Florida, "the pistol pointed at the heart of the United States," and West Florida, the region extending from the Mississippi to the present-day Florida line. The latter, Spain claimed, was not properly part of the Louisiana Purchase, and the former, though she held it loosely under tolerance from the Indians, she regarded as having great strategic if not sentimental value. Both of these areas were troublesome to the United States because from them, spurred on by British and Spanish soldiers of fortune and agents of the Panton-Leslie Company, bands of brigands, red men and white, terrorized settlements on the American southwestern frontier. It fell to Adams to extinguish these conflagrations by acquiring the Floridas by any peaceful means possible. In performing this task he had powerful aid from his future lifelong political antagonist, General Andrew Jackson.

Under Monroe's orders Jackson employed the doctrine of "hot pursuit" and invaded Florida, capturing Pensacola and St. Mark's. There, with 3,000 men he chastised the Indians, humiliated the Spanish officials, and precipitated a serious international crisis by executing two British filibusters, Armbrister and Arbuthnot—one by hanging and the other by the firing squad. Weak-minded, vindictive or politically opportunistic members of Monroe's cabinet wished to disavow or publicly condemn Jackson's actions. But Adams persuaded Monroe against this action, despite the possibility of war with England and Spain. This course proved to be an expedient one. Lord Castlereagh and the British negotiators in London acknowledged the justice of Jackson's actions and proceeded in good spirits to negotiate the other issues of the treaty of 1818. Spain, on the other hand, although she protested vehemently, saw clearly that the Floridas were beyond her practical control. This increased her willingness to trade them for some more secure piece of property, in point of fact Texas, and if possible the entire Trans-Mississippi West, as far north as the upper Missouri.

Adams' negotiation of the transcontinental boundary treaty of 1819 thus began as a swap: Texas (whatever that was) for the Floridas. As a student of history, Adams could not help being aware of Spain's insecurity over Texas and New Mexico. In 1806, Zebulon Pike was captured on the upper Rio Grande and held prisoner, his papers and maps were confiscated, and he was summarily sent back to the United States by the quickest possible route. Shortly afterward, in 1807, Captains Freeman and Sparks were turned back on the Red River. That same year the fur trader Anthony Glass was repeatedly threatened by Spanish authorities as he intruded on what they regarded as their territory. An 1812 trading expedition by Robert McKnight to Santa Fe landed him in a Chihauhau prison for nine years. The Gutierrez-Magee filibustering expedition into Texas in 1813 was put down and its leaders executed. In 1818 the fur trader Auguste Chouteau and his parter Jules De Mun were captured on the upper Arkansas. Their furs were confiscated; they were forced to kneel and kiss the document sentencing them; and then they were sent home with a bare minimum of equipment. These were convincing demonstrations of Spanish insecurities regarding Texas, but what made them seem outrageous to the United States was the fact that, if the limits of the Louisiana Purchase included the watershed of the Mississippi, then the territory to the headwaters of the Arkansas and Red Rivers belonged to the United States. Indeed, certain enthusiasts with a poor knowledge of geography claimed even the Rio Grande on this basis.

Needless to say, faced by a threatened American penetration of its territories, Spain, by 1819, was ready to negotiate a boundary that would give her a buffer against American invasion. Though Adams never knew it, she was willing to retreat all the way to the Rio Grande.

The negotiations with the Spanish minister Onis, a harried but tenacious diplomat, who awoke one morning to find a dead chicken tied to his doorbell rope, began with Adams offering a Texas boundary and indemnity for the Floridas. The Spanish sought a larger buffer to the West, however, and attempted to extend the Texas border from the high point of land between two creeks near Natchitoches, Louisiana, north to the Missouri River. In this way they could acquire most of Louisiana in exchange for the Floridas, which they could not hold in any case. This strategy, however, caused Adams to revise his own thinking. Previously he had been concerned with southern and southwestern problems; now the vision of a continental empire arose, and he shifted ground. If in exchange for Texas he could acquire the Floridas and also an extension of Louisiana in a wide swath to the Pacific, he would have opened the way to an American empire on the Pacific and gained the key to the continent.

Thus began a series of new negotiations, with the implied threat of an American invasion of the Floridas and Texas hanging in the background. On July 16 Adams, using Melish's inaccurate map of 1818, offered a line up the Colorado River of Texas to the Red River, and then across from the Red River to the crest of the Rocky Mountains, thence along the 41st parallel to the Pacific. Onis countered with a line northward from Natchitoches to the Missouri, then along the Missouri to its headwaters at the Three Forks, the line west from there not specified. And so the negotiations went throughout the fall and winter of 1818-1819, with Onis trying ultimately to get a Missouri-Columbia line to the Pacific with rights of trade on these rivers, and Adams stumping for the Colorado River of Texas or the Sabine River and the 41st parallel. Even an ultimatum offer of October 31, 1818, made at the behest of President Monroe, who had grown impatient, failed to impress Onis. Then Monroe began to give ground and seemed almost inclined to accept Onis' proposal of February 1, 1819, which was a line up the Arkansas River to the mythical San Clemente River, to the 43rd parallel and along it to the sea. But Adams held firm, and eventually on February 22, 1819, he had his transcontinental boundary treaty. The major provisions of the treaty included the Spanish cession of the Floridas, East and West, to the United States, the assumption by the United States of American claims against Spain up to $5 million, and a western boundary line which began at the mouth of the Sabine River, continued north along the western bank of that river to the 32nd parallel of latitude, thence by a line due north to the Red River, thence westward up the south bank of the Red River to the 100th meridian of longitude, thence across the Red River due north on the 100th meridian to the south bank of the Arkansas River, thence up that river to its source in latitude 42° north, and westward from that point along the 42nd parallel to the Pacific, as laid down in Melish's map of 1818.

Adams had thus bartered away Texas, but he had gained the Floridas and, equally important, he had gained his coveted transcontinental corridor to the Pacific. In accomplishing this he had served the New England sea traders well. But, in addition, despite much western opposition, he had served the West equally well since the acquisition of the Spanish claims to the Northwest opened the way for the development of the Rocky Mountain fur trade. However, Westerners fretted that he had given up Texas and the potential riches of the Southwest. Present-day knowledge of Spanish documents indicates that he had indeed done so.

But Adams could not have known this at the time, and thus he did the best he could. As his biographer remarks,

Even without Texas the Transcontinental Treaty with Spain was the greatest diplomatic victory won by any single individual in the history of the United States.

III

One further course of diplomatic events that took place while Adams was Secretary of State continued—indeed exaggerated—the emergence of America on the horizon of world diplomacy. This involved the development or formulation of an American policy for the entire western hemisphere that culminated in the Monroe Doctrine.

During the time Adams was negotiating with Spain, the countries of Latin America, encouraged by tradesmen from England and the United States, revolted against Spain, and in a long series of civil wars succeeded in establishing a de facto independence. Since the delicate negotiations with Spain were in progress, Adams was reluctant to recognize the new revolutionary nations although, like Jefferson, he sympathized with their desire for independence. As a New Englander, however, Adams also deplored the outfitting by the new countries of privateers which preyed on world shipping, including that of neutrals. He stood for the principle of freedom of the seas, and the violation of that principle by any power, however just its cause, threatened the principle itself. At least during the Spanish treaty negotiations the canny Braintree moralist used this as an agrument to counter the enthusiastic trumpetings of Henry Clay, who was demanding immediate recognition of the new republics, partly out of sincerity and partly because of a desire to embarrass the Monroe administration.

Eventually the new Latin republics ceased their privateering. American business representatives were established in the major ports. And, in 1821, Spain ratified the transcontinental treaty. Between 1822 and 1826 the United States recognized the independence of the seven new Latin American countries, although not all of them were republics patterned after the Jeffersonian democratic model. The United States was the first major nation to recognize formally the independence of the Latin states, and she did so at the risk of offending the major powers of Europe.

After the defeat of Napoleon, the chief continental powers led by the Czar of Russia formed the Holy Alliance with the avowed purpose of keeping peace in Europe through pacts of mutual assistance. Although we now know that there was little chance of a continental nation coming to the aid of Spain in her attempt to regain her lost New World colonies, this did not necessarily appear to be the case when the United States extended its recognition. Rather than a feat of diplomatic daring, however, the recognition of the Latin states appears to have been a response to demands by American trading and maritime interests for official government support in their competition with Britain for the trade of South and Central America.

While these events were occurring, Adams faced still another challenge to his dream of a continental empire. In 1816 the Russians had landed at Bodega Bay north of San Francisco and established a colony, Fort Ross. Subsequently Russia claimed all of the Pacific coast from Alaska to the latitude of Fort Ross, which of course encompassed the newly won Spanish claims above the 42nd parallel. Adams sternly rebuked the Russian expansionists in a note which was later to become the model for the Monroe Doctrine. He wrote to the Russian minister in Washington that the United States contested the right of Russia to her coastal claims, and furthermore he declared, "We should assume distinctly the principle that the American continents are no longer subjects for any new European colonial establishments." Russia retreated from her untenable and unprofitable position in the face of opposition not only from the United States but also from Britain, and in 1824 concluded a treaty with the United States limiting her territorial aspirations to 54° 40', the present Alaskan boundary. In 1825 a similar treaty with Britain was consummated. Adams had forestalled still another threat by a major power, although the United States had no way of defending her position by anything like the force of arms.

The Monroe Doctrine grew out of this anti-European position. Interested in maintaining good trade relations with South America, the British Minister, George Canning, proposed in 1823 that the United States join with England in making a declaration against any further attempts by the continental powers to colonize the New World. At Adams' insistence Monroe refused to join the British plan. Instead he issued an independent American statement, since known as the Monroe Doctrine, although Adams claimed to be its primary author. The Monroe Doctrine declared:

(1) That the United States did not wish to take part in the politics or wars of Europe.

(2) That the United States would regard as manifestations of an unfriendly disposition to itself the effort of any European power to interfere with the political system of the American continents, or to acquire any new territory on these continents.

The Monroe Doctrine, at first hailed by the new countries of Latin America, now much maligned by the same countries and transgressed by Soviet intrusions into the Caribbean, was something more and something less than tradition has made it seem. Enforcement of the doctrine depended, of course, in the main, on the British fleet, and in this sense many have considered it a hollow gesture although it was a true commitment. Later generations have seen it as a weapon or facade behind which the United States was able to interfere unduly in the internal affairs of its neighbors, and it has also on occasion served this purpose. Still others regard it as one more inflexible American principle that by its unyielding quality has limited American maneuverability in Latin American affairs, and this is certainly correct. But understood in the context of its own day, the Monroe Doctrine would appear to have several other legitimate purposes. First, it was a refusal to allow Latin America to become exclusively a British protectorate. Second, it reinforced American trading interests in the hemisphere. Third, it announced America's emergence as a power among nations that had to be reckoned with. Fourth, it was a gesture of genuine goodwill and concern for the new Latin republics. Fifth, it was a continual renunciation of European political alliances and a strategic refusal to play the balance-of-power game on Britain's terms. And finally, it was a rallying cry, a nationalistic symbol for Americans at home, that drew the nation together in terms of its ultimate ideals of republican democracy for all. Only the fact of slavery beclouded the lofty pretensions of such a democratic mission.

By the time Adams became president, the United States had acquired a continental empire of its own that looked both inward and outward, south toward the Caribbean, and west toward China and the Pacific. It had, moreover, taken an important place in the world family of nations and, following Jefferson's prophecy, it had spawned sister republics based on the American model as far as Cape Horn. The French had been ousted from North America, and the British, Spanish, and Russians severely circumscribed. This was not the work of a nation that sought or needed a comfortable security. It was the missionary impulse of individuals who had fought their way to freedom and independence, and therefore appreciated their virtues, an impulse making itself felt for the first time around the world.

CHAPTER 27

THE DISINTEGRATION AND REESTABLISHMENT OF THE AMERICAN PARTY SYSTEM

Wilfred Binkley's *American Political Parties: Their Natural History* is one of those rare books to which the student constantly returns, not only for its detail but also for its many insights. The following excerpt is not an exception. In the scope of a single chapter, Binkley discusses the election of James Monroe, the demise of the once powerful Federalist party, the congressional caucus and its decline, the election of 1824 (in which four men campaigned), and, finally, the election of Andrew Jackson in 1828 and the rebirth of two party politics.

In covering this mass of material, Binkley raises a number of intriguing questions concerning the nature of the political process in the United States—questions that apply both to the period under discussion and to the political process in general. Why did the Federalist party vanish by the 1820's? Of course the party was damaged by its opposition to the War of 1812, but the Democratic party did not dissolve following the Civil War (certainly a more cataclysmic event than the War of 1812). How were the Jacksonians able to "canalize mass movements" during this period, considering the primitive nature of their communication facilities? If the Jacksonians had not used the tactics that Binkley views with

405

disfavor in 1825 to 1828, could they have won in 1828? Or, more important, could they have developed their organization without using public antipathy toward John Quincy Adams and without amplifying the "moral outrage" of his "corrupt bargain" with Henry Clay? This leads to the question of how a political organization is created down to "even the rural school district."

There is a growing library devoted to such questions. An excellent study of the period is Robert Remini, *The Election of Andrew Jackson** (1963). For a first-rate discussion of the problems inherent in the building of a national political party, see Richard P. McCormick, *The Second American Party System: Party Formation in the Jacksonian Era** (1966). Arthur M. Schlesinger, Jr., *The Age of Jackson** (1946), is very readable.

* Available in a paperback edition.

ONE-PARTY GOVERNMENT

WILFRED E. BINKLEY

We are about to behold an administration of the Jeffersonian Republicans, who after conducting the War of 1812 with incredible ineptitude, emerged from the conflict covered with glory at the very moment when their Federalist opponents experienced irreparable ruin. Left unchallenged masters of the political field after 1816, the Republicans were to discover presently the disintegrating effect on a multi-group party of the disappearance of a common enemy, a vigorous political opposition. The "War Hawks" of 1811-12 evolved in the post-war period into supernationalists, literally contemptuous of the prescriptions of the Constitution and irrepressible in their determination to convert the Federal government into a paternalistic institution providing a powerful standing army, a great navy, a new Bank of the United States, government-built roads and canals, and protective tariffs. Here, however, was a program that stirred in the hearts of the older Jeffersonians memories of the Virginia and Kentucky Resolutions—the bible of the original Republicans, which had proclaimed the anti-national dogma of state rights. In little more than a decade this ideological clash was to produce two distinct factions of the Jeffersonian party, the National Republicans and the Democratic Republicans, from which were to evolve in due time the Whig and Democratic parties of the thirties.

Eventually, then, the Federalists were to behold their ideal of a partyless or one-party government achieved not, as they had so fondly hoped, by eradicating the opposition, but instead by the gradual dispersal of their own forces and their leaving the field to the triumphant Republicans. The pre-war policy of non-intercourse and embargoes had baffled the party of mercantile capitalism, but war against their chief customers induced a madness that led to their ruin.

Possessing the bulk of the nation's financial resources, these New England Federalists deliberately refused to finance the war and presently

SOURCE. From Wilfred E. Binkley, *American Political Parties: Their Natural History,* New York: Alfred A. Knopf, Inc., 1943, pp. 94–115. Copyright 1943, 1958 by A. A. Knopf, Inc. Reprinted by permission of the publisher.

placed the government in a desperate financial predicament. Nor would the New England states contribute their militia for the conquest of Canada and the consequent creation of new agrarian states, with increased congressional delegations and votes in the electoral college certain to reduce their own section to a still more hopeless minority. So disaffected, indeed, did New Englanders become that the British navy refrained from blockading their coast until almost the end of the war, and news of allied—that is to say, British—victories across the sea were celebrated by the fatuous Federalists. Commodore Stephen Decatur even complained that blue-light signals, set on dark nights to warn British war vessels, had prevented his running the blockade and putting out to sea from New London in 1813. Never were these luckless partisans to hear the last of the opprobrious epithet, the "Blue Light" Federalists. In the fall of 1814 their discontent culminated in the convention of delegates at Hartford, assembled to air their grievances and to seek means of redress. Fortunately the extremists among them, the Essex Junto, stark disunionists, were in the minority and the resolutions adopted, consisting of the proposal of some amendments to the Constitution, sound moderate enough today. Collectively they constitute the swan song of the Federalist Party. . . .

During Monroe's first term all but the irreconcilable Federalists moved over into the Republican column and were presently modifying that party's agrarianism by the pressures of once Federalist interests. Indeed, the Republican Party, in time, "became almost as much a party of business groups as the old Federalist party had been," thus confirming John Taylor's dictum that the business interests were devoid of principle and would combine with any party. It was an outstanding Federalist leader, Josiah Quincy, who gave utterance to the poignant lament that the Republicans had "out-Federalized Federalism." Even that staunch Federalist, John Marshall, had been tempted to vote for Madison, but he repressed the impulse and cast no vote for President from 1800 to 1824, when he voted for John Quincy Adams.

In the absence of an opposition the Republicans gradually lost their party discipline and their organization on a national scale. There is no better evidence of the disappearance of the old party alignments than the fact that Republican newspapers in 1816 reprinted in support of the second Bank of the United States Hamilton's argument for the first bank. This was simply using, in support of a Republican measure in 1816, the identical Federalist reasoning of 1791 that had aroused the opposition then and even contributed to the origin of the Republican Party. Thus cavalierly was Jefferson's historic opinion against the chartering of the first bank, including his classic statement of the dogma of strict construction, given the *coup de grâce* by his own disciples. And to make the topsy-turviness of politics complete, Webster and other Federalists opposed the chartering of the new bank.

When the time came to nominate presidential candidates in the spring of 1820, there were invited to the congressional caucus not only Republicans but all Congressmen who saw fit to attend. Even the old New England Federalists were satisfied with Monroe, and the incorporation of Federalists within the Republican fold seemed to be practically complete. The Massachusetts presidential electors in 1820 consisted of seven old-line Republicans and eight former Federalists, among whom were ex-President John Adams and Daniel Webster; and all, of course, voted for the re-election of Monroe.

It had now become as fashionable for Republicans as it once was for Federalists to disparage political parties as such. Paradoxical as it may seem, it was that later prince of partisans Andrew Jackson who was to give authentic expression to this prevailing sentiment in a letter of advice to President-elect Monroe in 1816. Concerning the choice of cabinet members he advised: "In every selection party and party feeling should be avoided. Now is the time to exterminate the monster called party spirit. By selecting characters most conspicuous for their probity, virtue, capacity and firmness, without any regard to party, you will go far to, if not entirely, eradicate those feelings which, on former occasions, threw so many obstacles in the way of government; and perhaps have the pleasure of uniting a people heretofore politically divided. The chief magistrate of a great and powerful nation should never engage in party feelings. His conduct should be liberal and disinterested, always bearing in mind that he acts for the whole and not a part of the community. By this course you will exalt the national character and acquire for yourself a name as imperishable as monumental marble. Consult no party in your choice."

Monroe reciprocated the sentiment in a letter to Jackson, writing: "We have hitherto been divided into two great parties. That some of the leaders of the Federalist party entertained principles unfriendly to our system of government, I have been thoroughly convinced; and that they meant to work a change in it, by taking advantage of favorable circumstances, I am equally satisfied."

Intimately related to the disappearance of political parties was the concurrent decline in the significance of the presidential office. Since the President is the focus of American party conflicts, under the circumstances then obtaining the office sank to comparative insignificance. It was no snap judgment of R. V. Harlow's that "Madison could scarcely have played a less significant part during those eight uncomfortable years if he had remained in Virginia." Had the office then possessed its present pre-eminent importance, Monroe could not have been re-elected without opposition in the midst of the nation-rocking controversy over the admission of Missouri to the Union and just as the economic depression starting in 1819 was spreading disaster throughout the length and breadth of the land. Since then no President has been re-elected following a term of his in which a depression began. During this quarter of a century not only had Congress overshadowed the President, but it had, in every case, determined the choice, either directly through election by the House of Representatives or through nomination by the congressional caucus, which in the absence of any significant opposition was tantamount to an election.

The revival of a two-party alignment was involved in the fact that the Virginia dynasty had now run its course. The tobacco plantation of the Old Dominion had produced its last outstanding statesman-President. Powerful interests in other sections were ready to bid for the stakes of power inherent in the presidential office. Their particular candidates were about to engage in a severe competition for the presidency. Universal manhood suffrage had swept the frontier, forcing the older settlements to consider its adoption in the hope of discouraging somewhat the tide of western migration. The aspirant to the presidency was now compelled to adapt his appeal to a rapidly expanding electorate in which the common man was becoming a distinct force. No longer would the congressional caucus that had so long maintained the Virginia dynasty by mechanically promoting the Secretary of State to the presidency be complacently accepted. Nor could the legislatures of half the states hope to continue much longer to choose presidential electors instead of permitting the people to elect them.

With the restoration of a free competition for the presidency in the middle twenties, aspirants were being compelled to search for issues or combinations of them with a nationwide popular appeal. The most ingenious of these was the so-called "American System" of Henry Clay, which he began to formulate soon after the Peace of Ghent in 1815. The end of the war marked the beginning of a new era, in which Americans stopped calling each other "Anglomen" and "Gallomaniacs." The colonial psychology had given way to a conviction of genuine American independence. Public opinion found its focus on the domestic issues of currency, banking, tariff, transportation, public lands, and western migration. The dogma of state rights proved unsuitable for dealing with these problems, and national needs now induced the resurgence of nationalism, already noted.

The war and its aftermath had demonstrated so convincingly the vulnerability of American prosperity that Henry Clay believed his fellow countrymen were ready for a planned national economy based on a protective tariff. Nor should it be assumed that this plan was merely the revival of an old Federalist dream. The center of gravity in that party combination had been the merchant shipowners of the Atlantic ports from Boston to Charleston. These men certainly wanted no artificial restrictions placed on either incoming or outgoing cargoes. As shipowners they did not relish the early protection of hemp, cordage, flax for sail duck, and iron, all used in shipbuilding. Nor did they welcome the establishment of industries here that could not fail to reduce their import trade. When Henry Clay presented his American System he found himself in controversy with the champion of the New England shipping interests, the Federalist Daniel Webster, who could see nothing "American" about it. . . .

A native of Virginia, young Henry Clay had migrated to frontier Kentucky, grown up with the community, and, like Lincoln later, whose exemplar he was to be, deliberately cultivated an inherent talent for politics. Law was then the high-road to political preferment, and Clay so fascinated his juries that it was said no person ever hanged where he spoke for the defense. Perused in cold print today, his speeches seem tame, but so magnetic was the personality of this master of men that for five decades he led Kentucky emotions and reason captive. "In his understanding of human nature, in his ability to appeal to the common reason, and in his absolute fearlessness in stating his convictions, he was unexcelled by any of his contemporaries." Having served his legislative apprenticeship in the Kentucky lower house, he came in 1811 to the national House of Representatives, there to be elected at once to the speakership, where his mastery was to be impressed no less on the incorrigible John Randolph than on the complaisant President Madison, whom we have seen obliged to come out for war with England as virtually the price of a second term.

Clay's well-matured exposition of the American System, set forth in the House of Representatives as the presidential competition of 1824 developed, resembled that of the "Open Door at Home" revived by Charles A. Beard more than a century later. "Now our people," declared Clay, "present the spectacle of a vast assemblage of jealous rivals, all eagerly rushing to the seaboard, jostling each other on their way, to hurry off to glutted foreign markets the perishable produce of their labor. The tendency of that policy, in conformity with which this bill is prepared, is to transform these competitors into friends and mutual customers, and, by reciprocal exchange of their respective productions, to place the confederacy upon the most solid of all foundations, the basis of common interest." The presidential aspirant counted on attaching to himself practically every section and interest in the nation. Through adequate protection there might be created the home market for farm products on the one hand and for manufactured products on the other. Reduced prices of the output of factories, once they were firmly established, was held forth. Revenues from tariff duties would finance the network of canals and highways required for this internal traffic.

The Middle and Ohio Valley states, realizing that the European market was now gone beyond recall, had developed an almost childlike faith in the protection of wool, hemp, flax, wheat, and corn. The frustration of Ohio Valley farmers at seeing their marketable surpluses rot for lack of transportation united them on internal improvements as on no other issue. Already there were, according to McMaster's estimate, 2,000,000 factory workers becoming impressed by the argument for protection as a maintainer of wages and a means of keeping the mills running. If only Clay could manage to convince the farmers, shepherds, road and canal contractors, factory-owners, mill hands, and handicraftsmen of a common interest in his American System, the grand prize of the presidency might be his reward.

Unfortunately for Clay, the post-war nationalist enthusiasm had already spent its force when he presented his formula, and the South never found it acceptable. The cotton-planters wanted no restrictions on the free flow of foreign trade in and out. Moreover, nature had provided their states with magnificent systems of river transportation. Not only would protection favor particular industries, but the planter was convinced that he would, as John Randolph put it, "only get much worse things at a much higher price," and the funds extracted from him at the detested custom house would be used to construct Northern canals and highways. In short, it was, to the planters, a system of vicious class legislation. Nor was the West swept off its feet by the Clay formula. After all, its appeal was to the intellect and not to the feelings. "Its acceptance carried no intoxication" and "could not be adapted to the western style of exhortation." Confronted by the dynamic personality of Old Hickory, then emerging as a presidential possibility, the emotion-starved pioneer lost interest in Clay's elaborate argument.

The West had taken, in the early twenties, a keen interest in discussing the relative strength of the followings of Clay and Jackson. The section was ready for a leader who could sense, phrase, and symbolize the needs of the depression-vexed West as well as those of the Eastern urban masses now beginning to stir uneasily under their social subordination. Clay's essay at this was his American System. What had others to offer in this first free-for-all competition for the American presidency? In 1822 *Niles' Register* found sixteen or seventeen candidates, but a year later only half a dozen remained in the field. Easily first among these was William H. Crawford, Secretary of the Treasury, whose candidacy enjoyed the blessing of no less a notable than the aged Jefferson himself. Macon, Madison, Randolph, Van Buren, and Marcy also backed him and he was given the formal nomination of the congressional caucus which made him the official party nominee, the candidate of the regular Republican politicians. Regionally regarded, he was the candidate of the cotton-planters, who were insisting upon the removal of the Indians from the fertile black belts. Ideologically he was the legatee of the Jeffersonian tradition, standing on the extreme ground of the Kentucky Resolutions with their "rightful remedy" of "nullification." The wide appeal of these Resolutions was evident from the fact that the legislature of Ohio was just then using them in its protest against the Supreme Court decision that it could not tax the branches of the Bank of the United States located in Ohio.

Crawford revealed the regional candidate's typical reaching out for a nation-wide union of interests in his support of moderate tariffs and the maintenance of the Bank of the United States. Presently it was Crawford against the field, which "ganged up" on him and proceeded to "smear" him as the candidate of the "undemocratic" congressional caucus, while other candidates were nominated instead by state legislatures presumed to be more immediate agents of the popular will. In any case Crawford was eliminated by a paralytic stroke in the midst of his campaign.

That Andrew Jackson should even be considered for the chair so long occupied by a line of distinguished Virginia statesmen seemed at first thought utterly preposterous to most men, not even excepting General Jackson himself. "Do they think I am such a damned fool as to think myself fit for the presidency?" he asked in 1821 when for the first time he saw his name mentioned in that connection in a newspaper. "No, sir," he continued, "I know what I am good for. I can command a body of men in a rough way, but I am not fit to be president." Yet the smoke of the Battle of New Orleans had scarcely more than cleared away when his availability had been perceived by one of the keenest practical politicians of that day. In 1815 Aaron Burr, eager to find a candidate around whom might be rallied the forces to overthrow the Virginia "oligarchy," had suggested Jackson in a letter to his own son-in-law, Joseph Alston.

It was the depression of the twenties that had provided the seed-bed of what has since come to be known as the Jacksonian movement. Keen political observers perceived deep-seated stirrings of both the rural and the urban masses accentuated by the prevailing hard times. A profound conviction that the ruling class had betrayed the people's interests was taking possession of the common man. A new species of politicians expert in canalizing mass movements began to emerge and sweep the horizon in search of a national leader. That a man of Jackson's background should be called upon for this purpose would have seemed preposterous to any but these new politicians. This Nashville ex-judge, sound-money man, and creditor distinctly distrusted the turbulent masses and had habitually sided with the haves and against the have-nots. Nevertheless the "Nashville Junto" of designing politicians decided to ignore the party machinery, on which, in any case, the Crawford men had an iron grip, and boldly proclaim their fellow citizen as the hope of the underdogs, the champion of the masses then groping for leadership.

Ever since his victory at New Orleans there had not been a more widely known celebrity in the United States than General Jackson. To the depression-frustrated ordinary citizen, whether urban worker, yeoman, or frontiersman, he was a veritable miracle-worker, invincible in battle against Indians, British, or "hard times." Even the illiteracy of voters worked to his advantage, because, as one of his supporters wrote in a letter, "they are illy acquainted with the character and qualifications of the other candidates" and need no education to know of "the glorious exploits which have crowned the career of Jackson."

Nor was Andrew Jackson in 1824 by any means a mere novice in politics. The general, passing down the tense lines in the pitch darkness of one o'clock in the morning before the Battle of New Orleans and picking out by voice and calling by name the soldiers who spoke to him, whether he realized it or not was already practicing the great art. Called upon to give his opinion of the tariff measure pending in the campaign year of 1824, he wrote with an eye keenly alert to all the interests concerned: "So far as the Tariff before us embraces the design of fostering, protecting, and preserving within ourselves the means of national defense, I support it . . . Providence has filled our mountains and our plains with . . . lead, iron, and copper, and given us a climate and soil for growing hemp and wool. These being the grand materials of our national defense, they ought to have extended to them . . . protection, that our manufacturers and laborers . . . may produce within our own borders a supply . . . essential to war. . . ." What candidate in any decade could, with such verbal economy, make a neater bid for the support of seven different interests and, at the same time, base his argument on the universal and fundamentally sound argument of national defense?

Measured by experience, learning, intelligence, and sheer devotion to the public interest, John Quincy Adams was best fitted of all the competitors for the presidency in 1824. Moreover, according to established precedent he was the heir apparent to the high office. As Secretary of State he occupied the position from which every President for almost a quarter of a century had been promoted. "I am a man of reserved, cold, austere and forbidding manners," confessed this unbending Puritan; "my political adversaries say, a gloomy misanthrope; and my personal enemies an unsocial savage." Despite these handicaps here is the candidate who in the end captured the grand prize. Nor was this capable stateman utterly innocent of the game of practical politics. He gave dinners, owned a newspaper, found loans for its editor and public printing for its support.

Since Adams's views corresponded closely with Clay's American System, their candidacies tended to split the vote of the interests soon to form the National Republican Party. When the results of the balloting in the fall of 1824 were available, it was seen that Adams had captured all the counties in New England and those in New York and Ohio wherever the New England stock predominated. Some scattered counties in New York and Missouri gave Clay majorities, but his strength, though far from uniform, lay largely in the Ohio Valley. . . .

Jackson's astonishing showing was due to the support of his fanatically devoted fellow Scotch-Irish scattered throughout Pennsylvania, the upland South, and the entire West south of the Mississippi and St. Lawrence divide, the Germans of Pennsylvania and Ohio, and everywhere the underdog marshaled by Jacksonian politicians who knew how to utilize the popular ferment of the twenties. Jackson's vote in the electoral college was 99 to 84 for Adams, while Crawford received 41.

In case of the failure of any candidate to obtain a majority in the electoral college, one of the highest three would be elected by the House of Representatives, with each state casting one vote as the Constitution prescribed. Clay was, of course, disappointed at his exclusion, for he must have considered his chances good in an election by the House, of which he was the Speaker and in which, of course, he possessed an enormous influence. As it now turned out, he and his following in Congress consciously held a balance of power between Jackson and Adams and were thus in a position to determine the next President. For weeks Clay seemed undecided whether to express his loyalty to the West by supporting Jackson or, for his own future advantage, to endeavor to eliminate his Western rival by supporting Adams. Whatever his motives, his influence ultimately made Adams President, and since the views of the men were so similar on the American System, the action might be regarded as logical and indeed the fulfillment of what amounted to practically a referendum on the paramount issue of the campaign of 1824.

To the Jackson men there was nothing at all logical about the election of Adams. None of them doubted that the House had been morally bound to elect the one who ranked first in the electoral college. Then, too, it was argued that the popular vote carried a like mandate. Even though the legislatures and not the voters had chosen the presidential electors in half the states and despite the fact that in only four states had the electorate voted on all four candidates, nevertheless, for the first time in our history, estimates of the total popular vote for each candidate were published. These seemed to indicate that Jackson had received a plurality of forty-two percent of the votes. The reaction of the masses to the publication of these data betokened the new force in American politics. Jackson's followers, among whom the Scotch-Irish were most partisan, maintained that the House had flouted their cherished doctrine of popular sovereignty. It was as their peculiar spokesman that Jackson eventually was to recommend the popular election of the President in every one of his eight annual messages to Congress. We have here in fact a germinal dogma of emerging Jacksonian Democracy and it was to be dinned into the ears of the public daily during the four years of Adams's presidency.

Thurlow Weed has given us the opinion of a contemporary expert in party politics that the new President was no practical politician. "Mr. Adams," said he, "during his administration failed to cherish, strengthen, or even recognize the party to which he owed his election; nor as far as I am informed, with the great power he possessed did he make a single influential friend." Adams had indicated a willingness to have Andrew Jackson considered the vice-presidential candidate with him "on correct principle—his fitness for the place, the fitness of the place for him and the peculiar advantages of the geographical situation." Utterly oblivious of the incipient renaissance of political parties, he offered cabinet appointments to all his rivals for the presidency, only to be repulsed by all except Clay, whom he made Secretary of State. This appointment proved to be a fatal error since it served only to confirm the conviction of the Jacksonians that Clay had made a "corrupt bargain" whereby he would make Adams President in return for his own appointment to the office of Secretary of State. The significance attached to this appointment was due to the fact that the office had become the established stepping-stone to the presidency, so the cry at once arose: "Clay is in the succession."

The Jacksonians stubbornly insisted that Adams was thereby dictating the choice of his successor to the "sovereign" people—or, at any rate, assuming to do so.

Ill fortune dogged every move of President Adams during his four miserable years in the White House. His first annual message seems commonplace today, but it rent the country asunder. The President's grandson, Brooks Adams, saw in it a revival of Washington's dream of tying the West to the East with a system of canals, thereby checking the growing sectionalism of the North and South by diversifying the industries of Virginia and Maryland. Adams's message proposed canals, highways, harbor improvements, a stronger navy, military schools, a strengthened militia, a national university, and an observatory, all at Federal expense. This terrifying program, in the opinion of W.B. Giles, published in the Richmond *Enquirer,* created "a crisis involving the liberty and happiness of all future ages." Nor did the President's message catch the popular favor even of the North, where it was only reminiscent of a post-war nationalism that had already subsided, and prophetic of an enthusiasm for the Union yet to develop and find classic expression in Webster's sonorous periods.

A "minority" President who would remove no enemy from office, not even his Postmaster General, busy employing patronage against him, who prevented his supporters from copying the public record of the court-martial decision on the six militiamen Jackson had executed, for fear it "would be construed as a measure of hostility against General Jackson," but who persisted with inflexible Puritan sternness in the performance of his duty, simply played into the hands of the anti-Adams men. These had no scruples against arousing the pioneer's prejudice against the administration's unprecedented expenditures of $14,000,000 in four years of peace. The absurd rumor that part of this money had been spent on a billiard table installed in the White House for the amusement of the President's son set Western tongues wagging. The Scotch Presbyterians scarcely knew whether to be more incensed over the waste of taxpayers' money or the sin of the game, but thrifty Pennsylvania Dutch puzzled over no such alternative. It was in fact a four-year "smear" campaign in which the Jacksonians converted "a personal prejudice into a political force that was positive, aggressive and effective." So contemptible, in fact, was the propaganda employed that one distinguished recent historian wondered whether it would not have been more honorable for Jackson to have lost than won in 1828.

John Quincy Adams was the first of our Presidents to be confronted by a Congress deliberately organized against the administration. Clay's alleged "corrupt bargain" was aired *ad nauseam,* and filibustering against the President's measures was unblushingly carried on. The crowning device intended to overwhelm Adams was the Tariff Act of 1828. It was an over-clever politician's intrigue for snaring votes, which, as crabbed John Randolph averred, "referred to manufactures of no sort or kind except the manufacture of a President of the United States." The stake was the protectionist vote of Pennsylvania and the West. Jacksonian politicians, with diabolical ingenuity, framed a high-protection bill so loaded with provisos damaging to New England's interests as to invite the Adams men to vote it down. If they did so, the Pennsylvania protectionists would be turned against Adams, while if the measure passed, the Democrats were the champions of protection anyhow. If the tossed coin came up tails, Adams lost; if it turned up heads, Jackson won. To the discomfiture of the Jacksonian politicians, the New England Congressmen accepted the measure, and when passed, Adams signed it.

The transformation of these anti-Adams men into Jacksonian Democrats constitutes a landmark in the history of American party politics. The traditional revolutionary machinery of the committees of correspondence was utilized in order to overthrow the ruling class. The Jacksonian politicians organized the now enfranchised masses through conventions, caucuses, and committees down into the county, the township, and even the rural school districts. National politicians were learning to weave the local sectional and class interests into intricate national patterns. "Their cross sections instead of displaying a few simple colors, were a jig-saw puzzle of radicalism and conservatism, national and state rights, personal loyalties and local issues. Party strategy was directed toward accumulating as many bundles as possible; and statesmanship was the art of finding some person or principle common to all the bundles that would make them forget their differences and in union find strength."

On a national scale the politician *par excellence* of his generation was Martin Van Buren, who perfected his art in the severe competition of the factions in New York politics. "Few men in American life," wrote Turner, "so united the ability to make political combinations and the power of critical analysis of underlying principles. Suave and conciliatory, Van Buren was perhaps the highest type of New York politician. He rose to national greatness and achieved a reputation as a statesman by his ability to think in national terms, to formulate Democratic party principles that remained substantially unchanged down to recent years and at times to make decisions hazardous to his career and to abide by them."

CHAPTER 28

THE TRIUMPH OF DEMOCRACY

A traditional American legend assumes that democracy, like religious freedom, sprang up full-grown when European colonists set foot on the soil of the New World. But we have learned from previous readings that colonial and revolutionary America were far from being democratic. Property and other qualifications limited the suffrage and office-holding. A fairly well-defined privileged class, composed of those with a "stake in society," dominated American government, society, and the economy. Yet from its beginning, America was significantly different from Europe. Economic opportunity was more widespread, more people owned property and thus could vote, the American ruling class lacked the traditional and legal roots of European aristocracy, and a degree of class mobility existed even during the colonial period. Some of these seeds of democracy developed fully during the first half of the nineteenth century.

In this selection from *Out of Our Past: The Forces that Shaped Modern American**, the historian, Carl Degler, concentrates on the extension of American democracy. His emphasis is on the democratization of politics and government—the expansion of suffrage and office-holding, new attitudes toward majority rule, acceptance of the principle of rotation in office, and the strengthening of the office of President. Professor Degler also comments on the increased commitment to the ideal of the

419

equality of man and to a more equalitarian and a more open society. He not only describes the growth of democracy but also explores the factors that made this growth possible.

In this, the latter half of the twentieth century, we might well try to evaluate America as a democratic society in light of Degler's treatment of Jacksonian America. To what extent is the nation more or less democratic than it was over a hundred years ago? What are the forces operating to expand or curtail democracy? Are we still shielded from the reality of American society by the myth of democracy?

For a brief critical summary of recent scholarship on this topic, see Marcus Cunliffe, *The Nation Takes Shape: 1789–1837** (1959). Another good, general treatment is Gilman Ostrander, *The Rights of Man in America, 1606–1861** (1960). Also, read Alice Felt Tyler, *Freedom's Ferment: Phases of American Social History to 1860** (1940).

* Available in a paperback edition.

THE GREAT EXPERIMENT
CARL N. DEGLER

Even before the first settlers had arrived, America was an object of curiosity to Europeans; but in the thirties, forties, and fifties of the nineteenth century the United States was as interesting to Europeans as Soviet Russia was to the world a hundred years later. Scores of foreign travelers made the Grand Tour of America in those years, dutifully recording their impressions for the edification of their less fortunate, but no less curious, fellow Europeans. This was the era of Tocqueville, Mrs. Trollope, Charles Dickens, Harriet Martineau, Charles Lyell, Fredrika Bremer, and Captain Hall. And whatever else America may have been in the writings of visitors, all seemed agreed that the United States was the great experiment in democracy. To English Chartists, struggling to democratize English government, the United States appeared as "the bright luminary of the western hemisphere whose radiance will extend across the Atlantic's broad expanse and light the whole world to freedom and happiness."

It was in the course of these years that the Democratic Dogma, as Brooks Adams was to call it later, was pushed to its outer limits. The common people came into their own as political arbiters and participants; majority rule was invested with a kind of sanctity. By the time the era was over, new, popular colors had been added to the bare outline of American politics inherited from the Revolutionary Fathers. The modern party system was in being, the Presidency bore the indelible marks of Andrew Jackson and James K. Polk, and the principle of a people's administration of government had been permanently implanted in American political thought.

"LET THE PEOPLE RULE"

Even during the eighteenth century, as we have noticed, more people could vote, proportionately, in the United States than in England and

SOURCE. Carl N. Degler, *Out of Our Past: The Forces that shaped Modern America,* New York: Harper & Row Publishers, Inc., 1959, pp. 136–146. Copyright 1959 by Carl N. Degler. Reprinted by permission of Harper & Row Publishers, Inc. and the author.

other European countries. But in the years after 1815, Americans deliberately expanded the suffrage in order to rest their governments upon the consent of all the governed.

By the decades of the 1830's and 1840's this movement reached flood tide, as the states altered their constitutions in conformity with the principle that manhood, not property, was the most just basis for political rights. This was a new view, one which constituted a sharp departure from colonial and early republican theory and practice. "The pretense has been that none but the rich have a stake in society," James Fenimore Cooper wrote. But this is wrong, he insisted. "Every man who has wants, feelings, affections and character, has a stake in society." Hence he is entitled to vote. It was precisely this abandonment of the traditional assumptions regarding the suffrage which renders this period significant; goodly numbers of people had always voted in America, where property was widely distributed. Now, however, even property was removed as a limitation. Once it was conceded that the basis for the suffrage was mere citizenship, then it was possible for any group or class to advance a claim to participation in government. The floodgates of democracy were open. In due time, on this basis, women, Negroes, and eighteen-year-old youths would be accepted as voters.

The shift away from the stake-in-society conception of politics was dramatic because it was accomplished so rapidly. In 1800, only three of the fifteen states of the Union granted the vote to all white men, regardless of property; by 1860, in a Union of thirty states, all but seven states extended the ballot to all white men, rich and poor alike. Property holding as a test of fitness to hold office was also discarded. Most of the new states in the early years of the century entered the Union without such requirements, while the original states gradually dropped theirs: Maryland began in 1810, Pennsylvania followed in 1838, then New Jersey in 1844, and so on.

The suffrage was only one of the several governmental innovations which embodied the upsurge in democratic ideals. Governors, for example, were now popularly elected instead of being chosen by the legislature. Maryland in 1837, North Carolina in 1835, New Jersy in 1844, and Virginia in 1850 all made changes in this direction. A large number of other offices were also made elective; indeed, it might be said that during this period the "long ballot" came into being, for a host of minor and middling offices were newly opened to election on the state and local level.

Most striking as a measure of the belief in the validity and value of a wide suffrage was the subjection of the judiciary to popular election.

Between 1846 and 1853, thirteen states made various of their judges subject to the direct pleasure of the people—an extension of the democratic ideal which probably none of the Founding Fathers would have sanctioned.

The democratic faith was also extended to the making of the state constitutions. At the time of the Revolution only two states had found it necessary to submit their constitutions to the people for ratification; by the Age of Jackson, however, such a procedure was the usual practice; only an occasional state failed to seek the people's judgment on a constitution. The principle that just government derives from the consent of the governed was taken literally in this democratic age.

Faith in the infallibility of the people's judgment was the sun around which American political thought now revolved. Andrew Jackson, for example, upon retiring from the Presidency in 1837, told the people in his Farewell Address that they should "Never for a moment believe that the great body of the citizens of any State can deliberately intend to do wrong." It is true, he confessed, that they may be misled, "but in a community so enlightened and patriotic as the people of the United States, argument will soon make them sensible of their errors" and they will therefore rectify them. Martin Van Buren, Jackson's successor, was widely known for his dictum that "the sober second thought of the people is never wrong." And George Bancroft, Democratic theoretician, historian, and politician, contended that "true political science does indeed venerate the masses. . . . Individuals are of limited sagacity; the common mind is infinite in its experience. . . . Individuals are time-serving; the masses are fearless." To Bancroft the new democratic upsurge meant that "the day of the multitude is now dawned." "Democracy is the cause of Humanity," proclaimed the first number of the radical Democratic organ *The United States Magazine and Democratic Review.* "It has faith in human nature. It believes in its essential equality and fundamental goodness. It respects, with a solemn reverence to which the proudest artificial institutions and distinctions of society have no claim, the human soul. It is the cause of philanthropy." The virtues of the common man as a class were often said to be superior. At the New York Constitutional Convention of 1821, for example, it was asserted that "more integrity and more patriotism are generally found in the labouring class of the community than in the higher orders."

Such a deeply held belief in the people's wisdom was something new in conservative America; neither Thomas Jefferson nor even Tom Paine would have gone to such extremes, for both these advocates of the people saw the flaws as well as the beauty in humankind. To be sure, there still were many who would not accept the new-found democratic oracle; the Whig party in general for a while stood against such doctrine. But by the election of 1840 even the Whigs, at least publicly, were throwing their money and their oratory in the same direction as the Jacksonians—that is, in outright flattery of the people. After 1840 no political party would again dare to doubt the wisdom of the people as the Federalists and even some of the Whigs had done in earlier years. Charles Francis Adams, for example, while editing his grandfather's works in 1851, bemoaned the fact that candid political criticism was no longer possible in America. ". . . The fact is certain," he wrote, "that no leading political man" since John Adams' day "has been known to express a serious doubt of the immaculate nature of the government established by the majority." America was now committed to the dubious dogma that wisdom in politics was in direct proportion to the participation of the people.

The people did not need politicians to bolster their self-esteem; they demanded not only the ballot but access to appointive office as well. Even before Jackson's administration there was popular demand for a rotation of officers among the people. Jackson, however, gave the movement intellectual footing when, in his first annual message to Congress, he justified the removal of many old civil servants. "I cannot but believe," the new President wrote, "that more is lost by the long continuance of men in office than is generally gained from their experience." And it was true that many officeholders were superannuated in both mind and body. (Not insignificant in Jackson's motivation was the patent fact that a good number of the officeholders thought "the wild man from the West" a real danger in the White House after the incumbency of cultivated John Quincy Adams.) Moreover, many of them had come to think of their offices as a species of personal property—as Englishmen were wont to do in the eighteenth century. "In a country where offices are created solely for the benefit of the people," Jackson argued in lofty democratic tones, "no one man has any more intrinsic right to official station than another. Offices were not established to give support to particular men at the public expense."

Though the rotation of public office among the people opened the gates for an increasingly vicious spoils system, it also faithfully mirrored the American democratic philosophy that any citizen could adequately perform the work of government. Nor was this rather naïve conception of governmental work without truth. While today the tasks of government bureaus are infinitely complex and technical, in the early years of the Republic the bulk of the employees were little more than clerks, postmasters, and the like. The vast proportion of the jobs of the government could be effectively and efficiently carried on by the average citizen.

Jackson's deliberate removal of the old and the partisan from the offices of his administration brought forth a flood of aspirants for the vacancies. Thus was initiated the burden of the patronage system, the weight of which, in the course of subsequent years, has almost borne down the Presidency. Whig Daniel Webster said in 1835: "No one can deny that office of every kind is now sought with extraordinary avidity. . . ." Convinced that theirs was a people's government, the people were not hesitant in demanding their places. The policy initiated under the Democrats was continued by the Whigs in 1841, the faithful rushing "pell-mell to Washington, every man with a raccoon's tail in his hat" to identify himself as a supporter of William Henry Harrison. Such men, John Quincy Adams wrote with distate in 1842, were "wolves of the antechamber, prowling for offices." President after President struggled hopelessly and unendingly with the "wolves" until the murder of a Chief Executive in 1881 by a disappointed office-seeker startled the American people from their unconcern. It was only then that civil service reform got an opportunity to lighten the crushing burden of the patronage.

Though the rotation system unquestionably wasted much of the Presidents' time and threatened to reduce officeholding to the work of party hacks, something of value, nevertheless, came out of it. Principally this was democratization of administration on both the federal and state levels. There would never grow up in America any remote civil service which was divorced from the people or which conceived of itself as a superior caste or class, outside or above the main body of the citizenry, as, for example, occurred in Germany to the detriment of the democratic Weimar Republic. Americans made sure, in this period, that their government, like the society at large, reflected their firm belief in the equality of men. Undoubtedly, a democratic administrative structure has been a prop and a succor to the whole democratic way of life in America.

At first glance it appears incongruous that in this very period when popular control of government was at its height, the office of the President, occupied as it is by a single person, should also attain new strength and prestige. This consequence is largely the result of two men's influence upon the people and upon the office. It is true that George Washington, as the first President, did more than any other incumbent to create the mold from which the Chief Magistracy of the Republic would thereafter be cast. But if the austere and essentially aristocratic Washington bequeathed dignity, independence, and high prestige to the Presidency, it remained for Andrew Jackson and James K. Polk to make it also an expression of the democratic spirit of the American people.

It was Jackson, for instance, who first declared that "the President is the direct representative of the people" and no less capable of speaking for the people than the Congress. In practice, Jackson did not hesitate to appeal to the people to sustain policies which the Congress opposed, as, for example, when he vetoed the Bank recharter bill in 1832. Polk, who with reason was often called "Young Hickory," made no secret of following Jackson's conception of the President as the Tribune of the People. "The President," Polk wrote, "represents in the executive department the whole people of the United States, as each member of the legislative department represents portions of them." As early as 1824, ardently democratic Senator Thomas Hart Benton advocated changes which would bring the President closer to the people than the cautious Founding Fathers had intended. Stigmatizing indirect election through the Electoral College as a "favorite institution of aristocratic republics," Benton urged that the people be able to vote directly for the Chief Magistrate. Jackson himself, in his first annual message, also urged the amending of the Constitution in order to permit the people to elect the President directly. Though nothing came of either Benton's or Jackson's proposals regarding election, the nomination of the President was democratized in the early 1830's. The Anti-Masonic party held the first Presidential nominating convention in the United States in 1831; within a few years the two major parties abandoned the old caucus system in favor of the more popular convention.

It was Jackson who conclusively established the right of a President to control his Cabinet, even though the Congress may have legislated otherwise. At the time of his war against the Bank of the United States in 1832–33, Jackson, despite Congress' deliberate effort to make the Secretary of the Treasury responsible to the legislature, successfully compelled two Secretaries of the Treasury to resign because they would not implement his policies. Congress protested vehemently and the Senate, in an extraordinary procedure, formally censured the President. But Jackson was vindicated and the President's power enhanced when a more friendly Senate later, in a dramatic ceremony, expunged the censure from its records. Since that time all Presidents, with the exception of the befuddled Grant, have been encouraged by the example of Jackson to fight vigorously against any congressional efforts to control the Cabinet.

It was left to James Polk to explore the immense reservoir of power inherent in the President as Commander in Chief of the armed forces. The Mexican War, as Leonard White has pointed out, was really fought from the White House: Polk named the generals, set forth the grand strategy which won the war, cajoled and bullied the Congress into granting the necessary credits and support, and finally drew up the peace terms. All this was achieved with a minimum of consultation with or dependence upon the Congress. When faced with a much greater military challenge, Abraham Lincoln would find encouraging precedent in Polk's use of the Presidential power.

Under imaginative handling by Jackson and Polk, even an essentially negative power like the veto was made to strengthen the authority and prestige of the Presidency. For the first forty years of the Republic it was more or less assumed, from the precedent set by Washington, that the veto was merely a check on unconstitutional legislation and not a weapon which the President could use to enforce his own views. All the Presidents prior to 1829 used their negatives so sparingly that Jackson's vetoes numbered more than all those of his predecessors combined. More important, Jackson made no effort to conceal the fact that the motives behind his vetoes were at best a compound of constitutional scruple and expediency. It is true that he said he doubted the constitutionality of the Bank when he vetoed the recharter bill. But a perusal of his veto message made it clear to everyone that his opposition stemmed from his distrust of the Bank as such and not from any questions of constitutional niceties concerning an institution which, after all, had functioned for almost forty years.

The new Democratic view of the veto power was not discarded by John Tyler, the first Whig President. And even though Tyler was threatened with impeachment for daring to veto legislation which the Congress considered constitutional, the Jacksonian conception of the veto prevailed then and later. In vetoing a river and harbors bill Polk did not find it necessary to offer any justification for his act other than his mere disapproval. The power and prestige which the Jacksonian veto added to the arsenal of the President is best appreciated when it is realized that no veto was overridden by Congress until 1866.

Such an accretion of Presidential power was possible only after the President had been transformed into the Tribune of the People. Prior to that time, the unlimited exercise of the veto smacked of the royal prerogative and of the flouting of the will of the people's representatives. But once the President was accepted as a representative of the people, then the augmentation of his power, even during a period of expanding popular participation in politics, was quite possible and in conformity with democratic ideals.

Indeed, it might be said that the expansion of Presidential power during these years, as well as the increasingly popular character of the office, bear testimony to the realistic political judgment of the American people. Rather than being jealous of the power of the executive, the people seemed to recognize the vital role which strong executive leadership must occupy in any democratic polity which seeks to avoid the deadly paralysis of factionalism. As a result, twentieth-century Americans enjoy an executive unparalleled in its independence and power, yet one responsive to the people's will.

"ALL MEN ARE CREATED EQUAL"

The democratization of politics and government was only one of the signs spelling out the Rise of the Common Man; the new democratic spirit was apparent throughout society. Dixon Ryan Fox went so far as to entitle his history of these years *The Decline of Aristocracy*. But that is a phrase which almost sacrifices accuracy to neatness. For as we have seen, it is doubtful that an aristocracy, as the term has meaning in European history, ever existed in America, much less declined. Any ruling class which may have existed in this country has always been tempered by the fact that it could lay no claim to a long tradition of wealth and power such as European aristocracies enjoyed and which is the true soil of an aristocracy.

But even if Fox's phrase somewhat overstates the situation, it does serve to accentuate the fact that in the years between 1820 and 1860, Americans made it quite clear that theirs was to be an equalitarian and open society. Earlier expressions of this sentiment had been sporadic and moderate; in the Age of Jackson it was blatantly and continuously proclaimed. "The equality of Man is, to this moment," wrote British traveler Alexander Mackay in 1842, the "cornerstone" of American society. Earlier Alexis de Tocqueville concluded that democratic societies like America were "ardent, insatiable, incessant and invincible" in their passion for equality. "They will endure poverty, servitude, barbarism, but they will not endure aristocracy."

A symptomatic expression of this strong distaste for privilege was evident in the attacks upon West Point during the mid-1830's. Tennessee, for example, in a resolution of the legislature, stigmatized the Military Academy as "this aristocratical institution." And the Ohio legislature declared that West Point was "wholly inconsistent with the spirit and genius of our liberal institutions." And so sure were Americans of their "liberal institutions," wrote Mrs. Trollope, that she "once got so heartily scolded for saying that I did not think all American citizens were equally eligible" for the Presidency "that I shall never again venture to doubt it."

The source from which the reservoir of American faith in equality was constantly being replenished was opportunity. "The United States are certainly the land of promise for the labouring class," wrote Michel Chevalier in 1834. "After landing in New York, I thought every day was Sunday, for the whole population that throngs Broadway seemed to be arrayed in their Sunday's best." Even prickly Mrs. Trollope bore witness to the opportunities of the new country. "Any man's son may become the equal of any other Man's son," she admitted, "and the consciousness of this is certainly a spur to exertion." Harriet Martineau thought she saw unlimited horizons for the lowly in America: "an artisan may attain to be governor of the state, member of Congress, even President," she said. "It is extremely seldom," Englishman Alexander Mackay observed, "that the willing hand in America is in want of employment."

The opportunities open to Americans were reflected in how well the average citizen lived. "I saw no table spread, in the lowest order of houses," Harriet Martineau recalled, "that had not meat and bread on it. Every factory child carried its umbrella; and pig-drivers wear spectacles." Michel Chevalier related the story of a newly arrived Irishman who showed his employer a letter he wrote to his family in the old country. " 'But Patrick,' said his master, 'why do you say that you have meat three times a week, when you have it three times a day?' 'Why is it?' replied Pat; 'it is because they wouldn't believe me, if I told them so.' " Other observers remarked on the notable absence of beggars. There were poor in America, to be sure, for while some men prospered others slipped and fell. And already the tenements of the burgeoning cities were open for inspection and the slum was no longer a European monopoly. But even with such qualifications, and especially when compared with European social conditions, this country opened new economic vistas for Everyman. As Emerson said, "America is another word for opportunity."

One immediate consequence of the breadth of opportunity was the looseness of class lines. We have noticed already a tendency in this direction all through American history; during the first half of the nineteenth century, however, this blurring of classes was a fact and a boast. "We have no different estates," Erastus Root told the New York Constitutional Convention of 1821, "having different interests, necessary to be guarded from encroachment by the watchful eye of jealousy. We are all of the same estate—commoners. . . ." New citizen Achille Murat said that "the lines which divide" Americans "are so delicate that they melt into each other; and that . . . there are neither castes nor ranks." European social patterns do not fit in the United States, German immigrant Francis Lieber wrote home. "In America there is no peasant. . . . He is a farmer, and may be rich or poor; that is all the difference."

In a country in which most men possessed "a competence," as Alexander Mackay put it, property was in no danger. Where acquisition of property is relatively easy, as it was in America, the demand for equality of holdings is rarely heard. It is significant that at no time, insofar as the great majority of Americans was concerned, did "equality" signify an equal division of wealth; too many men owned wealth, or soon expected to, to become involved in schemes or theories which might someday be fashioned into weapons with which to wrest from them their tangible goods. "There will be no attack on property in the United States," Harriet Martineau correctly prophesied. Because property was distributed throughout the various levels of society, no philosophy or organization fundamentally opposed to private property, be it Brook Farm or "agrarianism," was able to win the support of the American people.

CHAPTER 29

JACKSONIAN DEMOCRACY

Few men in American history have been more controversial during their lifetimes and afterward than Andrew Jackson. He was both despised and idolized by Americans living in the 1820's and 1830's, and historians differ sharply in their interpretations of him. Some historians have viewed Jackson as the democratic champion of the common man; others have considered him as a conservative and wealthy demagogue. Some historians attribute his political success to his appeal to Western frontiersmen and Southern farmers; others attribute it to the support he received from Eastern and urban workers. Some writers argue that Jackson was an anticapitalist; others argue that his aim was to open doors for the emerging capitalists and entrepreneurs.

If Jackson is controversial, so is the meaning of Jacksonian Democracy. This term is illusive and difficult to define because historians have used it to mean many different things. For our purposes it will be used to designate the aims, the approach, the style, and the program of Jackson and his administration. Gilman Ostrander devotes a chapter of *The Rights of Man In America, 1606–1861** to Jacksonian Democracy. He seeks to answer questions that must be answered if we are to achieve a better understanding of the Jacksonian era and of the man who dominated and symbolized that vigorous period of American History.

As you read this selection, keep these questions in mind. What kind of man was Andrew Jackson, and what was he really trying to do? Was his primary concern personal political power or the welfare of the nation?

Or both? Were Jackson's actions based on firm commitment to principles, or were they determined by expediency and opportunism? Was Jacksonian Democracy a broad reform movement with Jackson as its symbolic and actual leader, or was it something else? Finally, how do you explain the general agreement of historians that Jackson was an outstanding President? Do you agree?

The literature on Jackson is voluminous. The interested student should begin with one of Charles Grier Sellers' essays on Jacksonian historiography, *Jacksonian Democracy** (Service Center for Teachers of History, 1958), and "Andrew Jackson versus the Historians," *Mississippi Valley Historical Review,* XLIV (March 1958). James L. Bugg has compiled an excellent collection of readings on the subject entitled *Jacksonian Democracy: Myth or Reality?** (1962). Arthur M. Schlesinger, Jr., *The Age of Jackson** (1945) is a work of major significance. Marvin Meyers, author of *The Jacksonian Persuasion** (1960), approaches his subject from the vantage point of intellectual and social history.

* Available in a paperback edition.

JACKSONIAN DEMOCRACY
GILMAN OSTRANDER

The election [of 1828] brought to the Presidency a man who, at the age of sixty-two, was broken in health. It was doubted that he would live out his term of office. If he did, it was generally assumed in political circles, he would remain merely titular President, to be manipulated by the professionals who had conducted his campaign. Jackson's campaign, from the first, had been managed by others with little more than his passive consent. He had been willing clay, as James Parton wrote, in the hands of a few friendly potters. Until his defeat in 1824, by what he was convinced had been a corrupt bargain, Jackson had seemed almost indifferent to his own candidacy. After Adams' election by Congress, Jackson's heightened interest appeared to be little more than a personal desire for vengeance against Adams and Clay. Once in the Presidency, however, Jackson gathered into his hands the authority of the office, augmented by his own popularity. The first President to be elected by the people, he became in his own eyes the special guardian of the people by the divine right of majority assent. In the view of conservatives he became the dreaded demagogue, that fearful threat to republican institutions which the founding fathers, through the contrivance of the electoral college, had so carefully defended against.

James Parton concluded his biography of Andrew Jackson with an equivocal reflection.

Respecting the character of Andrew Jackson and his influence, there will still be differences of opinion. One fact, however, has been established: during the last thirty years of his life, he was the idol of the American people. His faults, whatever they were, were such as a majority of the American citizens of the last generation could easily forgive. His virtues, whatever they were, were such as a majority of American citizens of the last generation could warmly admire. It is this fact which renders him historically interesting. Columbus had sailed; Raleigh and the Puritans had planted; Franklin had lived; Washington

SOURCE. Gilman Ostrander, *The Rights of Man in America, 1606–1861*, Columbia, Missouri: The University of Missouri Press, 1960, pp. 183–198. Copyright 1960 by the Curators of the University of Missouri. Reprinted by permission of the University of Missouri Press and the author.

fought; Jefferson written; fifty years of democratic government had passed; free schools, a free press, a voluntary church had done what they could to instruct the people; the population of the country had been quadrupled and its resources increased ten fold; and the result of all was, that the people of the United States had arrived at the capacity of honoring Andrew Jackson before all other living men.

That, as Parton said, is the fact that renders Jackson historically interesting. He personified the American idea to the American people as no other President until General Eisenhower. "Other men are lenses through which we read our own minds," Ralph Waldo Emerson write in *Representative Men*. Among all of America's Presidents these two generals emerge as Emerson's "representative men."

Jackson was the visible sign of the prople's triumph. His inauguration is remembered, not for what he said, which was very little and to no clear point, but for the motley crowd of farmers and mechanics who obtruded themselves upon a ceremony which formerly had been reserved for gentle folk. Traveling by horse and by foot over roads made all but impassable by spring rains, these common people converged on Washington by the thousands, some of them coming as far as five hundred miles for the occasion. Muddy and unmannerly, they crowded their way, uninvited, into the post-inauguration reception, threatening to reduce the White House to shambles, until they were diverted by tubs of punch hastily carried out to the White House lawn. They announced their sovereignty to the world.

There were hostile observers who found this inauguration of democracy disgraceful and fittingly so. As Alexis de Tocqueville noted, many Americans of wealth, position, and education privately despised democracy. Publicly, however, these men were compelled to accept the prevailing democratic shibboleths. Privately they might be guided by sensible and decorous religious conventions; publicly they were obliged to conduct themselves in such a way as to give no offense to the prevailing mores of the evangelical religions. They might profess to despise a society which made money the naked measure of social position, but the southern gentleman who disdained the counting house sometimes found his place in society pre-empted by his overseer. And however much certain rich men might despise the democratic process, the age of Jackson taught them the hard lesson that if they desired the political power to which they felt their position entitled them, they would have to go to the people to get it. As a class the aristocracy had become separated from the national character, which was democratic.

I

What followed Jackson's White House reception was anticlimax. The nation, awaiting the outcome of the Jacksonian revolution, waited in vain for any startling political changes. It turned out that Thomas Jefferson had disturbed himself unnecessarily over the possibility of a Jacksonian *coup d'etat* against the republic. The new President and his chief lieutenants thought of themselves, not as political innovators, but as good, safe Jeffersonians, whose duty it was to safeguard the people against dangerous centralizing tendencies in the national government.

The Jacksonians pledged themselves to reduce government personnel and introduce other economies to the end that the national debt be paid off, the government freed from the grasp of the money power, and the burden of taxation be lifted from the people. The Constitution should be strictly construed to the end that the states be protected in their rights from the encroachments of Federal power. The Federal government should always act in the general interest; never in the interest of a special group.

Where Jackson departed from the Jeffersonian tradition, the difference was often largely a matter of style. Where Jefferson believed that a good government was one which operated so quietly as to go almost unnoticed, Jackson acted on the principle that a good democratic government ought to trumpet forth in the name of the people now and then. Where Jefferson, fearing the city mobs, placed his reliance upon those "who labor in the earth," Jackson presented himself as the spokesman for the workingman as well as the farmer. In practice, however, the two followed very similar policies toward those who labored in the shops and mills. The Jeffersonians had eagerly made common cause, both with the urban radicalism of the Democratic-Republican societies, and with the urban political machinery of the Tammany Society. Jackson, on the other hand, while drawing political strength from these same elements, showed no marked interest in the problems which were peculiarly those of the city worker. It was his successor, Van Buren, who set out to secure the workingman's vote by adopting measures, notably the ten-hour working day, which were demanded by urban workers particularly, rather than by laboring classes as a whole. Most Americans were still farmers in Jackson's day, and most of the laborers in whose name Jackson spoke were those who labored in the earth.

The most startling novelty to occur during Jackson's first year in office, his defense of the spoils system, was, at the time, largely academic. Concerning the inevitable redistribution of political offices which accompanied the change in administrations, Jackson presented an aggressive defense on democratic grounds. Rotation in office, he said, freed the nation's government from control by an entrenched bureaucracy. To argue that public offices should remain in the hands of those trained by experience to perform them was to call democracy itself into question. "The duties of all public offices are, or at least admit of being made, so plain and simple that men of intelligence may readily qualify themselves for their performance." Jackson's defense of the spoils system shocked those who were prepared to be shocked by anything that this plebian President said, and certainly it was a world apart from Jefferson's idea of a natural aristocracy. In practice, however, Jackson showed considerable restraint in his redistribution of the patronage. The turnover in personnel was roughly comparable to that which had taken place under Jefferson. After Jackson, President Van Buren, who, of course, inherited an administration he himself had helped to staff, made only eighty removals. It was not until the forties that the spoils system really came into its own.

No part of the Jackson administration has been so widely and uncompromisingly denounced by historians as Jackson's defense of the spoils system; yet, as Carl Russell Fish pointed out, the system was essential to the very existence of democracy. Some citizens there no doubt were who would exert themselves politically with no thought of patronage, but they would be exceptional. The people as a whole could be expected to play an active and effective role in the maintenance of their governments only through political parties which could keep discipline based upon expectations of future rewards. In the Old South, Fish noted, democracy, in terms of a broad suffrage, existed everywhere by the eve of the Civil War, but it existed without elaborate party organization and without the spoils system, and the aristocracy did not find it difficult to control the state governments.

There remained a further basic difference between Jeffersonian republicanism and Jacksonian democracy: Jackson rejected the Jeffersonian idea that government was a necessary evil and by its very nature an abridgement of liberty. "There are no necessary evils in government," he declared. "Its evils exist only in its abuses. If it would confine itself to equal protection, and, as Heaven does its rains, shower its favors alike on the high and the low, the rich and the poor, it would be an unqualified blessing." Jefferson, with his generation, feared the tyranny of the majority. Jackson supposed that the nation was secure against tyranny so long as it was under majority rule. As the first President literally to represent the popular will, Jackson conceived of himself as the embodiment of the majority, and in its name the special guardian of the Constitution.

It was in his emphasis upon the sovereign will of the majority that Jackson departed farthest from Jeffersonian republicanism. While Jefferson, with John Locke, had viewed sovereignty as residing in the will of the majority, those two political philosophers of the enlightenment had proceeded from the original assumption that men were endowed by their Creator with inalienable rights, and that the purpose of governments was to secure them in these rights. What was to be done if the majority asserted its sovereignty for the purpose of depriving individuals of their inalienable rights? Locke did not meet this problem, but there can be no doubt as to how he would have resolved it. For Locke and for Jefferson the whole purpose of society was to secure the liberty of the individual. For Jackson this was not the case. The individual already was sufficiently secure in his rights, protected by common law, by the first nine amendments to the Constitution, by the balance of powers within the Federal government, and by the balance of powers between the Federal and the state governments. These arrangements, devised by America's "sages and patriots," were accepted by Jackson as "sacred." At the same time, all of these arrangements together did not entitle the individual to flaunt the will of the majority. For Jackson, and for Jacksonian democracy, those citizens who opposed the will of the majority were the enemies of democracy, and, the sacred principles of the Constitution aside, they should be treated accordingly.

Jacksonian democracy demanded social as well as political conformity to the will of the majority. The man who differed from his neighbors publicly in matters of dress, speech, morals, or religion risked a tarring and feathering, and rightly so. The history of Joseph Palmer is a case in point, though no doubt an extreme one. Palmer, an eccentric Massachusetts farmer, was "Persecuted for Wearing the Beard," as his gravestone testifies. Palmer wore a full beard during the Age of Jackson, at a time when it was customary to go about cleanshaven. This defiance of accepted convention was more than the democratic community of Fitchburg, Massachusetts, could tolerate. Palmer's physician told him to shave; that he was spreading disease. Ministers labored to bring him out of his waywardness, and the minister of his own church attempted to prohibit him from receiving communion. When argument did not suffice, Palmer was set upon by men of the town, who attempted to shave him forcibly.

When some of his assailants were injured in the struggle, Palmer was jailed on charges of unprovoked assault. Refusing to pay his fine, he remained in jail, where the jailer and the prisoners attempted unsuccessfully in their turn to force him to shave. He remained in jail for a year, until unfavorable publicity resulted in his release. A temperance man, abolitionist and advocate of a wide number of reforms, he moved on to help Bronson Alcott found a utopian community, Fruitlands. To Alcott and the Transcendentalists, Palmer's brand of crusty individualism was a vital part of American democracy. That was not the view of the democratic majority, however. To the majority, the ideals of democracy called for identification with the community and conformity to the accepted social and moral code.

Amid the fierce sectarian struggles of the period, Jacksonian democracy demanded at least an outward show of conformity to Christian belief. Jefferson, a religious liberal, understood religious liberty as including the right to be a professing atheist. Jacksonian democracy did not join him in this view. The nation accepted the doctrine of separation of church and state necessarily, in the face of the fact that no sect was sufficiently dominant to establish itself against the competition of rival sects. But the view that an atheist could be a good American was not widely held. Jackson personally accepted the principle of religious liberty as part of the sacred order of things. That was not to say that he was ever quite easy with it. On Sunday mornings, Parton relates, Jackson would say to his guests, "Gentlemen, do what you please in my house; *I* am going to church." Among Jackson's advisers there were religious liberals and outright materialists, but the religious views of these men were suffered, rather than gladly tolerated, by Jackson and by Jacksonian democracy.

II

Jackson's first administration was a democratic pageant; his second was a democratic crusade. Until the veto of the bank bill late in his first term, Jackson led a party without a political program of its own, and it was no doubt the deep desire of his political lieutenants that he avoid ever arriving at a program. Jackson had been elected by high-tariff and low-tariff men, by broad nationalists and states-rights men, by inflationists and hard-money men, and by friends and foes of internal improvements. Under such circumstances the interests of the party seemed best served by doing as little as possible about anything.

Jackson, himself, seemed to think that he possessed a political program and, furthermore, that he had presented it to the public in his first annual message to Congress. The message contained no specific recommendations concerning domestic legislation, however, and it led to the passage of no bill. The Peggy Eaton episode was by far the most important event of Jackson's first three presidential years, when the chivalrous President used the full weight of his office to defend the wife of his friend the Secretary of War, John Eaton, against the snobbery and aspersions of Washington society. The event was important because it contributed to the political break between Jackson and Vice-President Calhoun, the husband of Washington's leading socialite. As the most important event to follow the democratic revolution of 1828, however, the Eaton episode was significantly lacking in ideological import.

Second in importance to the Eaton episode during those years was the Maysville Road bill veto, which placed Jackson in opposition to Federally financed intrastate internal improvements, on grounds of both economy and constitutionality. Jackson broke no new political ground with the veto, however. He merely reaffirmed a principle established by several of his predecessors. Nor did the veto commit Jackson to any very clear policy in the field of internal improvements, for subsequently he signed other very similar measures, on the grounds that they were national rather than local in scope, and the Federal internal improvements program did not diminish during his administration. Not even his chief Whig opponent Henry Clay could find in Jackson's vigorously worded veto a campaign issue for 1832. Jackson's treatment of the tariff question was similarly vague, cautious, and middle-of-the-road. He signed both the tariff of 1832 and the compromise tariff of 1833, but neither of them was passed as an administration measure. They were associated rather with his presidential rival Clay. They hardly could serve to separate the Jacksonians from their political opponents.

Had Jackson not been presented by Congress with a bill rechartering the United States Bank in 1832, he would have entered the campaign for re-election as little involved in any real political issues as he had been four years earlier. As it happened, Nicholas Biddle, director of the bank, called for a new charter four years before the expiration of the existing one. Biddle and Congressional leaders, knowing Jackson's hostility to the bank, reasoned that political considerations would force Jackson to sign the bill, if it were presented to him before the election. Jackson returned the bill to Congress with what has remained the most famous veto in American history, and he launched an attack which continued throughout his second term, serving, more than any other circumstance, to crystallize the national political forces at last into two separate organized political parties of Whig and Democrat.

In vetoing the bill Jackson followed his own private convictions. Typically, the veto for him was as much a private matter between himself and Biddle as it was a matter of political principle. "The bank is trying to kill me," Jackson told Van Buren, "but I will kill it." As Richard Hofstadter writes, the challenge aroused the dueling instinct in Jackson. The glove was thrown down, and Jackson picked it up—and instinctively in the name of the people and against the forces of wealth and privilege. The bank war made Jackson the hero of radical democrats, many of whom had shown little previous enthusiasm for the old hero of Horseshoe Bend. In American financial history the bank bill veto was a disastrous error which committed the nation for a century to the least serviceable banking system of any major industrial nation in the world. In the history of American democracy it was a heroic attack by the people's President against the bastion of wealth and privilege. With the bank bill veto, Jacksonian democracy at last went into action on a national scale.

Jackson's veto was vigorously forthright in style, and electric with ideology.

It is to be regretted that the rich and powerful too often bend the acts of government to their selfish purposes. Distinctions in society will always exist under every just government. Equality of talents, of education, or of wealth can not be produced by human institutions. In the full enjoyment of the gifts of Heaven and the fruits of superior industry, economy, and virtue, every man is equally entitled to protection by law; but when the laws undertake to add to these natural and just advantages artificial distinctions, to grant titles, gratuities, and exclusive privileges, to make the rich richer and the potent more powerful, the humble members of society—the farmers, mechanics, and laborers—who have neither the time nor the means of securing like favors to themselves, have a right to complain of the injustice of their Government.

This line of argument, although it represented the dominant economic radicalism of democratic America, was neither novel nor peculiar to American democratic thought, except in its aversion to titles and its pointed concern for the farmers, mechanics, and laborers. With those exceptions, the statement might well have been presented more than two centuries earlier amid loud cheers to that Elizabethan House of Commons which in 1601 successfully forced the Queen to rescind certain chartered monopolies.

Considering the strength of the anti-monopoly spirit in English tradition, the wonder is that the spirit emerged so late in American history and remained relatively so impotent. Part of the reason no doubt lies in the fact that almost all of the American colonies came into existence as state or private monopolies, and that colonial and frontier conditions necessitated a large measure of government supervision. Then, once independence was won, the American people tended to the view that they controlled their own governments and therefore had little to fear from the monopoly-creating power. The United States began life with a long-established tradition of government economic regulation to the minutest detail, including government-chartered local monopolies over a wide variety of economic activities.

The Bible of economic liberalism, Adam Smith's *Wealth of Nations* was published in the same year that Jefferson wrote the *Declaration of Independence*. The *Wealth of Nations* was the economic declaration of independence for the British businessman, who went on to win England to free trade over the opposition of the landed interests during the second quarter of the nineteenth century. Jacksonian America, meanwhile, experienced a somewhat similar struggle with the sides roughly reversed. The landed interests of the Cotton Kingdom won a partial victory for free trade over the opposition of the tariff-minded business community. Economic liberalism, in the sense of free trade, was never accepted by the American businessman, and, if it was accepted privately by Jackson, he did not advocate it as President.

Jackson did place himself at the forefront of the anti-monopoly fight with his bank bill veto, but he did so in a highly qualified manner. The veto lashed out at the principle of monopoly itself, but specifically it was an attack upon a national, as opposed to a state, monopoly. Indeed one of Jackson's arguments against the bank was that it infringed upon the rights of the less powerful banks which had been chartered by the states. The monopolistic state banking interests fully appreciated this argument, as their strong support of Jackson indicated in 1832.

The truth is that even in the heyday of Jacksonian democracy the anti-monopoly spirit, although it dominated one wing of the Democratic party, did not triumph in the nation. As the industrial revolution progressed, the scope of government regulation widened, and the chartering of government monopolies of banks as well as of bridges, canals, turnpikes, and then railroads, continued. These monopolies brought criticism, but they were nevertheless accepted as the most expeditious means of exploiting the resources of the nation. The nearest approach to the triumph of liberal capitalism in the age of Jackson was the passage of uniform laws of incorporation in various states, giving any group an equal chance to enter a field of economic activity—banking for instance —providing it fulfilled the general requirements of the law. In the pre-Civil War period, however, most corporations continued to operate under special charters.

In the meantime, the Jacksonian Supreme Court handed down a series of decisions, most notably the Charles River Bridge case, attacking the vested interest of old chartered companies, where their assertion of monopoly rights interfered with the rights of the community, in a country "free, active, and enterprising, continually advancing in numbers and wealth." To spokesmen for vested interest, the Charles River Bridge case was a Jacobinical attack upon the rights of private property. Actually it was a sensible decision which, as Charles Warren has written, encouraged "all business men who contemplated investments of capital in new corporate enterprise and who were relieved against claims of monopoly concealed in ambiguous clauses of old charters."

The notion that economic liberalism emerged hand in hand with political liberalism in America outside the planting states is absurdly false, as recent studies of Massachusetts, Pennsylvania, Georgia, and Missouri make abundantly clear. In each of these states down to the Civil War the governments engaged themselves vigorously and un-self-consciously in regulating, financing, and even administering, a bewildering variety of economic activities. "Massachusetts observers," wrote Oscar and Mary Handlin, "conceived of the beneficent hand of the state as reaching out to touch every part of the economy." The Locofoco movement in attacking monopolies was not proposing *laissez faire*. The Locofocos accepted government control, and they did not oppose government support for private enterprise. They simply wished, as Jackson said, to live under a government which would "shower its favors alike on the high and the low, the rich and poor." Jefferson the Physiocrat was an advocate of *laissez faire,* and he was joined in this doctrine by other southern planters, who wished to be let alone on their lordly plantations. The doctrine did not fail altogether to win its converts in the North as well, especially in academic circles, but it was no significant part of Jacksonian democracy. Its strength remained with the broadcloth party of southern Whig planters.

In one respect, however, Jackson was curiously Jeffersonian in his economic views. A successful career as lawyer, land speculator, and merchant had failed to win him away from the ascetic policy of hard money. To the enterprising America of Jacksonian democracy banking institutions were absolute necessities. The railroad age was unthinkable without the existence of extensive credit; yet Jackson, with the left wing Locofoco Democrats, was opposed to all banks. Metallic currency was the only honest currency. Bank notes were means by which the wealth produced by labor was syphoned off to the financial manipulators—the monocrats. Jackson favored the entire elimination of banking institutions, and he was joined in this wish by certain of his leading advisers and supporters, including Thomas Hart Benton, Roger B. Taney, and Van Buren. Their views, as Bray Hammond has written, "belonged with an idealism in which America was still a land of refuge and freedom rather than a place to make money," the land of Jefferson's golden dream, where commerce and industry would remain the handmaidens of agriculture, in a nation of self-sufficient farmers.

Upon this subject Jacksonian democracy was divided, however, and so were Jackson's lieutenants. Among his closest advisers Jackson counted men who had been closely connected with state banks and who represented the more enterprising wing of the party. These easy money Democrats, especially the state banking interests, disliked the United States Bank, not on hard money grounds, but on grounds that the bank imposed a restraint upon their own lending activities. They wished to destroy the bank to free themselves from all central control. Facing the election of 1832, Jackson worded his veto in such a way as to commit himself to neither wing of his party. The veto made no criticism of the state banks or of banks as such, and it suggested no alternative to the United States Bank. It straddled the issue so successfully that Jackson entered the campaign with the enthusiastic support of both the hard money men and the state banking interests.

Jackson's policy toward the bank during his second administration reflected the ambivalent character of his political following. Upon his reelection Jackson struck at the bank by removing Federal funds and distributing them among "pet" state banks. The banks were requested not to use the funds for speculative purposes, but nothing was done to enforce the request. The banks naturally followed their inclinations, and a rapid extension of credit ensued. At the same time, the national debt was paid off, and Congress enacted the Jacksonian policy of distributing the surplus revenue among the states, thus further accelerating the inflationary tendency. Then, during his last year on office, Jackson reverted to his hard-money principles with the Specie Circular, requiring specie payments for public lands, and helping to trigger the panic of 1837. The panic broke upon the country several months after Jackson went into retirement in the Hermitage.

Inheriting the panic as well as the concerted animosity of the dominant economic interests of the nation, Jackson's successor, Van Buren, moved unsuccessfully to settle the crisis according to hard-money principles. An independent treasury would be established to hold government funds where they could not be used for speculative purposes. Against the hard-money program of Van Buren the business interests struggled without final success until the Civil War, when southern secession gave them the opportunity to pass new laws authorizing the establishment of banks under a uniform national charter.

Within the Jacksonian ranks the bank war revealed the fundamental conflict between the Jeffersonian ideal of the simple, virtuous, agrarian society and the democratic reality of an acquisitive society which could call upon its government to assist in the exploitation of a continent. Senator Benton indignantly declared that he "did not join in putting down the Bank of the United States to put up a wilderness of local banks." It did not matter. His old-fashioned intentions were powerless to alter the fact. In attempting to make democratic practice conform to Jeffersonian theory he was attempting the impossible. Democratic America believed with Abraham Lincoln that "it is best for all to leave each man free to acquire property as fast as he can," and the motto for democratic government was, "boost; don't knock."

CHAPTER 30

JACKSON, CALHOUN, AND CLAY: THE CRISIS OF UNION

In reviewing the career of Andrew Jackson, historians are of divided opinions concerning the effectiveness of Jacksonian policy on the major issues that confronted the nation. The consensus of recent historians is that Jackson's veto of the bank was detrimental to the nation's economic development, and that his stand on nullification was a major contribution to the maintenance—at least temporarily—of the Union. There is much less agreement on the long-range results of Jacksonian policy upon the welfare of the nation.

Agar's opening sentences are, perhaps, overly harsh on Jackson's failure to solve the growing issues of sectionalism and Southern separatism. No political leader, either before or after this period, solved these problems. Only in the tragedy of war was a final "decision" rendered—hardly a desirable course. Historians have also failed to emphasize (and here Agar is less at fault than most) the caliber of the opposition faced by Jackson and the Jacksonians. In the 1950's, when the United States Senate chose the five greatest senators of all time, Clay, Calhoun, and Webster were included in that select group. On every major issue of his career, Jackson could count on at least two of this triumvirate either to oppose actively his policy, or (for example, in the case of Clay and nullification) to attempt to modify his policy for their personal political gain. When the opposition's level of competence is considered, the political skill of Jackson and the Jacksonians becomes more obvious.

Yet, one can legitimately question the correctness of Jackson's policies and positions. As Bray Hammond shows in *Banks and Politics in America from the Revolution to the Civil War** (1957), Jacksonian monetary policy was a major mistake. Agar suggests that the constitutional grounds on which Jackson chose to meet the nullifiers also may have been unwisely chosen. Here the critic is on much shakier ground. As Agar suggests, Jackson's stand on the Constitution against nullification placed him in a vulnerable position. But in view of the widespread veneration of the Constitution, an appeal to it offered a much more solid platform from which to rally support than an argument based on "what was wise." And the President and his advisers must choose the strongest arguments possible to take to the people.

Out of this reading a few pertinent and basic questions arise. What opinions were available to Andrew Jackson on nullification and the public lands? What were the political consequences of these options? Were these consequences an acceptable price?

In addition to the studies mentioned in preceding introductions, the interested reader should peruse Marquis James, *The Life of Andrew Jackson**, 2 vols. (1938). The careers of two of Jackson's principal Congressional leaders are covered admirably in William N. Chambers, *Old Bullion Benton: Senator from the New West* (1956), and Charles G. Sellers, *James K. Polk: Jacksonian* (1957). Excellent biographies of two Jackson antagonists are Margaret L. Coit, *John C. Calhoun: American Portrait** (1950), and Clement Eaton, *Henry Clay and the Art of American Politics** (1957). William W. Freeling has brought the latest scholarship to bear on nullification in *Prelude to Civil War: The Nullification Controversy in South Carolina** (1966).

* Available in a paperback edition.

THE JACKSON MEN IN ACTION
HERBERT AGAR

Jackson's second important effort, the fight on nullification, suffered from the same weakness as the fight on the Bank: Jackson knew what to attack, but he had no remedy to offer. He could destroy the Bank, but he could not build a just money system; he could oppose nullification, but he could not diminish the sectional injustices and jealousies which were poisoning the national life. He did not know how to build a government which would give enough power to the sections to protect them from oppression, and yet leave enough power in Washington to conduct the public business.

Unhappily, the struggle over nullification was discussed in terms of what was constitutional, not in terms of what was wise. The constitutional argument could satisfy nobody, for it was well known that Jackson, like Webster and like most Americans, was himself a nullifier whenever it suited him—as in the case of the unhappy Cherokees. Relying on the treaties which concluded Jackson's Indian campaigns in 1813 and 1814, the Cherokees had settled peacefully on the lands left to them. Because of their rapid advance in civilization and the arts of peace, and because the cotton gin was giving a new value to their lands, they were soon hated by their white neighbors. Hostile and savage Indians were a nuisance—but only a temporary nuisance, because they could be defeated and ousted. Peaceful and friendly and settled and civilized Indians were more than a nuisance, they were a catastrophe, for if they persisted in behaving themselves it might be difficult to take the land which had been guaranteed them by the United States Government—especially since one of the federal treaties which gave this guarantee had been signed by Andrew Jackson.

Just before Jackson became President, the state of Georgia tore up the federal treaties and annexed the land of the Cherokees and the Creeks. Mississippi and Alabama followed suit, expropriating the Choctaws and Chickasaws. The Cherokees engaged William Wirt of Baltimore, former Attorney General, to take their case before the federal court on the ground

SOURCE. Herbert Agar, *The Price of Union*, Boston: Houghton Mifflin Co., 1950, pp. 262–274. Copyright 1950 by Herbert Agar. Reprinted by permission of the Houghton Mifflin Company and the author.

that it is unconstitutional for a state to annul a federal contract, whereupon Jackson made a trip into the Indian country to tell the chiefs that their case was hopeless, that even if they won in the courts they would be robbed by their white neighbors. It was a question of robbery with or without murder, and a wise chief would choose the latter.

The Chickasaws and Choctaws gave in; they abandoned seventeen million acres of land in Mississippi and Alabama and moved west across the river. The Cherokees put their faith in the Supreme Court of the United States and stayed where they were. The state of Georgia extended its jurisdiction over their territory. The Supreme Court upheld the rights of the Indians and ordered Georgia to desist. Georgia paid no heed, and neither did the President.

Another case, arising when Georgia for the second time extended its power over the doomed Cherokees, came before the Supreme Court in 1832. The Court held that Georgia was without authority over the Indians. It is on this occasion that Jackson is reported to have said, "John Marshall has made his decision, now let him enforce it." There is some doubt as to this neat statement of the nullifier's creed; but there is no doubt that Jackson wrote: "The decision of the Supreme Court has fell still born, and they find it cannot coerce Georgia to yield."

It would seem to follow that if the federal government made a law, a decision, or a treaty, which was disliked by the citizens of a state, those citizens might refuse to obey and the President would do nothing. Yet when Calhoun urged the South Carolinians to refuse to obey a federal tariff, Jackson talked of treason and of hanging. The sanction of a law, in other words, depended upon whether the President liked the law. Jackson might have had trouble putting the idea into philosophic terms, yet it was good American doctrine. Jefferson, Madison, Webster, Jackson, Calhoun himself, all found that the demands and decisions of the federal government were sacred when they agreed with them, tyrannous when they didn't. Or to use the language of the American Revolution, they found these demands and decisions backed by natural law when they agreed with them, and opposed by eternal principles when they didn't.

The Tariff of Abominations, as we have seen, led Vice-President Calhoun to write the South Carolina *Exposition;* but he kept the authorship secret and urged his followers to wait for an attempt at peaceful repeal. He thought Jackson, the incoming President, would prove a friend and ally, and it was two years before he knew he was wrong. Meanwhile, in 1829, the *Exposition* was defended in the Senate during a debate on Western land.

The North and the South were bidding for Western votes—the first to maintain, the second to abolish, the tariff. The West wanted cheaper land, or free land if possible. The North could not offer free land, for fear too many of its own factory hands should turn pioneer; so it proposed as an alternative to distribute the proceeds from land sales among the states, with a bonus to those states wherein the lands lay. The ingenious Henry Clay thought this would satisfy the West and at the same time get rid of the surplus revenue, so that the high tariff could not be attacked on the ground that it brought in too much money. The South, on the other hand, felt free to support the West in throwing open the public domain if the West would vote for a reduction in the tariff. "On the outcome of this sectional balance," wrote Professors Morison and Commager, "depended the alignment of parties in the future: even of the Civil War itself. Was it to be North and West against South, or South and West against North?"

In December, 1829, this momentous question came before the Senate. Foot[1] of Connecticut suggested restricting the sale of public lands to those already on the market. Benton of Missouri opposed the resolution as a typical piece of Eastern hostility toward the West, and called upon the South for help. Hayne of South Carolina responded, precipitating the most famous debate in Congressional history. Hayne quickly got away from the problem of public land onto the problem of the Constitution. He defended the Calhoun doctrine that a state may defy a federal law if it is convinced that the law is unconstitutional. If the federal government was the judge of its own power, argued Hayne, the states were impotent; and if the states were impotent a numerical majority of voters living in the industrial Northeast might impose unbearable conditions upon the entire southern region.

Here was the old problem which had called forth the resistance of Kentucky and Virginia to John Adams, and the resistance of New England to Jefferson: men might submit to a majority of their neighbors, but they would not submit to a majority living a thousand miles away. "Of what value is our representation here," said Hayne, attacking the tariff, when "the imposition is laid, not by the representatives of those who pay the tax, but by the representatives of those who are to receive the bounty?" South Carolina, he argued, was trying to save herself from federal laws which had wrecked her economy and which would soon reduce the South to ruin. By devising means to frustrate an unjust majority, South Carolina was safeguarding the Union.

[1] Senator Samuel Augustus Foot, like his father before him, spelled the name without a final *e*. His descendants have adopted the longer form.

On January 26, 1830, Daniel Webster replied. The power which Senator Hayne would bestow upon the states, said Webster, belonged to the federal Supreme Court. The Court alone should decide whether Congress had the power to make a law, otherwise the federal government became a rope of sand. In one state the tariff would be null and void; in another state it would be legal; there could be no consistency, and in the end no Union. Nullification was treason, and neither a state nor a man could commit treason with impunity. Webster, whose amazing presence made his speeches far more important than the arguments they contained,[2] concluded with the peroration about "Liberty and Union, now and forever, one and inseparable." Generations of school children were to recite those sonorous lines. They helped to attach men's patriotism, in the North and West, to the national rather than the local community. They may well have helped to turn the sentimental Andrew Jackson from the support of state rights, which he had once seemed to favor, to the support of the Union.

On April 13, 1830, a few months after the Hayne-Webster debate, the leaders of the Democratic Party attended a Jefferson Day dinner. It was expected that Jackson, when he spoke, would make clear which side of the debate he favored. The question was vital for the assembled politicians; Jackson's choice would settle whether Calhoun was to be the next President, and whether for the immediate future the Constitution was to be administered according to the logic of Webster or of Hayne. When the time came for the President to give a toast, Jackson rose and pledged "Our Federal Union, it must be preserved!" The nullifiers were undone. Calhoun's plan to unite the South in resistance to centralization was delayed for twenty years, until the slave question had overshadowed the problem of government. The Democratic Party was committed, temporarily, to a nationalism as complete as that of Clay and Webster and John Quincy Adams.

Although Jackson's toast meant that Calhoun would not yet rule the Democratic Party, he still ruled the state of South Carolina. Nullification

---

[2] Carlyle described Webster's "crag-like face; the dull black eyes under the precipice of brows, like dull anthracite furnaces, needing only to be *blown;* the mastiff mouth accurately closed." Robert Lytton saw Webster when he visited America as a youth in 1850–52. Years later he wrote *(Personal and Literary Letters of the Earl of Lytton,* vol. I, p. 32): "Webster I think on the whole the greatest speaker, or rather the greatest orator, I ever heard. . . . He had a singularly musical and mellow voice. . . . He had a wonderful, an awful, face, with eyes set in caverns, and one might certainly say of him what Sydney Smith said of Lord Thurlow, that the Almighty never made any man as wise as he looked." It was Fox, not Sydney Smith, who made the remark about Lord Thurlow.

was defeated as a national solution to the problem of minorities; but it was not defeated in its birthplace. During the summer of 1831 Calhoun issued an *Address to the People of South Carolina,* a restatement of the argument in the *Exposition.* When in July, 1832, Clay won the votes of the West for a new high tariff, Calhoun abandoned passive resistance. In the autumn elections the nullifiers swept the state. The legislature called a convention which passed an "Ordinance of Nullification" declaring that neither the "Tariff of Abominations" nor the new tariff of 1832 was binding upon the people of South Carolina. The legislature also decreed that if goods were seized by federal officers for nonpayment of duties, the owners of the goods might recover twice their value from the officials who seized them. The governor was authorized to call out the militia, and early in 1833 he summoned ten thousand citizens to be ready to repel invasion.

Jackson was the last man in America to be impressed by a threat of force. He prepared the Navy and the Army, talked bravely about hanging Calhoun,[3] and in December, 1832, issued his Proclamation to the people of South Carolina (the work of Edward Livingston).

Admit this doctrine [said the Proclamation] and every law for raising revenue may be annulled. . . . I consider, then, the power to annul a law of the United States, assumed by one state, incompatible with the existence of the Union, contradicted expressly by the letter of the Constitution, unauthorized by its spirit, inconsistent with every principle on which it was founded, and destructive of the great objective for which it was formed. . . . To say that any state may at pleasure secede from the Union is to say that the United States is not a nation. . . . Disunion by armed force is treason. Are you really ready to incur its guilt? If you are, on the heads of the instigators of the act be the dreadful consequences.

Those are strong words. They did not lead to strong deeds because the country was averse to treating Calhoun and his followers as traitors. South Carolina stood firm; but the rest of the country was of divided mind. In Virginia the powerful group represented by John Tyler was in sympathy with the nullifiers. Opinion in New York was divided. Georgia, Mississippi, and Alabama would not have supported Jackson against South Carolina had he not recently helped them nullify the federal treaties which favored the Indians. Except for the fiery President, there were few

[3] Marquis James and Hugh Russell Fraser have shown that Jackson was not the cheerful swashbuckler he has often been pictured, when he threatened to hang Calhoun. On the contrary, he was much worried as to what might happen to the country if he was driven to strong measures.

who would have executed the leaders of South Carolina with a clear conscience. The country wanted a compromise.

Clay, the skilled and happy compromiser, used his influence to secure a
bill which would reduce the tariff over a period of nine years until it stood
at twenty per cent. At the same time, as a sop to the nationalists, a
"Force Act" was passed, giving the President authority to call out the
army and navy to enforce the laws of Congress. South Carolina, having
won the reduction of the tariff, repealed her Nullification Ordinance but
declared the Force Act null and void. Temporarily the crisis was at an
end.

The crisis was at an end, and there was no comment from John Randolph. For the first time in thirty-four years an important political event
was not annotated by that singular mind. Randolph of Roanoke was
dying. The most faithful of the "Old Republicans," he had broken his
career and denied his friendships out of loyalty to the principles of 1798.
All his life he had labored to weaken the power of the central government,[4] and all his life he had watched that power grow: sometimes at the
hands of his fellow Virginians, sometimes at the hands of a hated Northerner, but most of all at the hands of "this wretched old man," as he
described Jackson during the nullification fight. In his last days he saw
the start of a new challenge to central power, led by a man as implacable
as himself and far more competent. Perhaps he took hope from knowing
that the fight would go on; but probably not, since he had long foretold
that the fight was lost, that centralization must conquer, and that "my
country," as he called Virginia, must fall. Nevertheless, he offered to join
the army of South Carolina if Calhoun went to war. Instead of such
melodrama, he lived just long enough to see his detested Henry Clay
make another compromise. He was too tired to fight. We do not know
what baleful flashes of vision and of invective the nation was spared;
but we do know that Randolph was not the man to praise a compromise.[5]

At the height of the conflict Calhoun had resigned the vice-presidency,
and in January, 1833, he replaced Hayne in the Senate. The day he took
his oath he was looked upon as a brave man who might soon pay with his
life for his opinions; but two months later he emerged from the shadow of
the gallows with a new prestige. He also emerged as the ally of a new
political party. With several of his disciples, Calhoun made overtures to
the Whigs. He was warmly welcomed by Henry Clay, for the only conviction demanded of a Whig was that he should dislike Andrew Jackson.

---

[4] Except when he supported the Louisiana Purchase.
[5] He was buried at Roanoke with his face to the West. According to legend,
this was so he could "keep an eye on Clay."

Nevertheless Calhoun's association with the new party was to be brief and embarrassed. As we have seen, it was virtually at an end by 1837.

III

Calhoun was born in the South Carolina uplands where Jackson had been born fifteen years before. They both had the same dour Scotch-Irish blood. Unlike the Jacksons, the Calhoun family had been settled for two generations and begun to prosper. The ambitious boy, therefore, did not push West but stayed at home and married his cousin, Floride, whose mother was Floride Bonneau of the tidewater aristocracy. Calhoun was educated at Yale College and became a lawyer. After his marriage he had enough money to devote himself to public life. He began his Congressional career as a "War-hawk," a nationalist, a promoter of internal improvements to avoid "that greatest of all calamities . . . disunion." During the eighteen-twenties he watched with distress the growth of economic and cultural antagonism between North and South. He sought constitutional means for protecting his minority region. With all his ardent being he still hoped to hold the nation together—but not at the sacrifice of South Carolina. If nationalism meant the exploitation of the farm by the factory, he must abandon nationalism and give allegiance to his state. It was the greatness of Daniel Webster that he could feel (and make others feel) the beauty and the hope for man that lay in the federal Union; it was the strength of Calhoun that when the choice had to be made his heart had to be given to the hills and villages of his youth. For him, South Carolina was the only unit small enough to be known the way a man should know his country, small enough to be loved. And it may not be irrelevant that the Union, for Massachusetts, meant wealth, but for South Carolina, poverty. Or so it seemed to Calhoun, unless he could exempt his people from the laws passed to benefit other regions, with other interests, climates, institutions.[6]

[6] Calhoun exaggerated when he spoke as if the South was suffering "oppression." After the North had accepted Clay's compromise tariff bill of 1833, the South had no serious economic grievance. And in any case, she was to control the federal government most of the time until the Civil War. But Calhoun was alarmed by the growing population of the North, and wished to ensure a minority veto for his state or region while there was still time. In speaking of a future danger as if it were already present, he had good American precedent. Colonial discontent, beginning with the Stamp Act and culminating in the Revolution, was based more upon fear of what Great Britain intended than upon anything that had been done. Professor Samuel Eliot Morison writes (*The American Revolution, 1764–1788, Sources and Documents,* p. xiv): "It is a fair question whether potential rather than actual oppression did not produce the ferment in America."

He saw America as a nation of dangerous and growing diversity, stretching from the sub-tropical Gulf to the sub-arctic continental plains and containing many races, religions, and economies. The clash of these interests must either split the Union, or subject some regions to a colonial economic status, or else the clash must be restrained. It could not be restrained by force, since if the use of force were permitted those who controlled it would run the country for their own advantage and suppress dissent. How, then, could man's lust for power and wealth be kept from ruining America? Only, he decided, by an agreement that each important interest and each important region must consent to every act of government which impinged upon its affairs. This might be done by giving to each state the right to nullify federal laws which displeased it, or it might be done by constitutional amendment. In either case, the result would be what Calhoun called the rule of the concurrent majority: rule by the agreement of all interested parties.

The fact that such a rule, embodied formally in the Constitution, would thwart all government action did not bother Calhoun. As a traditional American he felt that a government incapable of acting at all would be better than a government free to act as it chose—especially if a mere numerical majority was to do the choosing.[7] In this, he was a devout "Old Republican," a faithful son of 1798. But he allowed his logic to triumph over his political wisdom when he asked that the federal government formally commit itself to impotence. The rule of the concurrent majority is a fair description of how the government of a federal empire must operate; it is a fair description, as we shall see, of how in normal times the modern American Government does operate—but only informally, only by custom, and gentlemen's agreements, and the subtle refinements of the party system. All these can be overridden in time of emergency; but in an emergency Calhoun's rigid plan would have condemned the nation to death. Calhoun was a doctrinaire, not a politician in the Anglo-American tradition of practical compromise.

Calhoun was the stern, pessimistic leader of a doomed cause. He was the sleepless enemy of Leviathan; but Leviathan could not be destroyed. If Webster looked too wise for this world, Calhoun looked too tragic. It was not a pose, for he foresaw accurately the ruin of his hopes. Henry Clay pictured him as "tall, careworn, with fevered brow, haggard cheek

[7] In the *Address to the People of South Carolina*, July 26, 1831, he wrote that the "dissimilarity and, as I must add, contrariety of interests in our country . . . are so great that they cannot be subjected to the unchecked will of a majority of the whole without defeating the great end of government, without which it is a curse—justice."

and eye, intensely gazing, looking as if he were dissecting the last and newest abstraction which had sprung from some metaphysician's brain, and muttering to himself, in half-uttered words, 'This is indeed a crisis!' "

Ciay did not believe in crises or in abstractions. He did not believe in the logic by which Calhoun learned that day by day the nation moved closer to disunion. Clay was the assured politician, adept in the conciliations whereby "inevitable" crises were postponed, "inevitable" issues evaded. This time he seemed to be wrong; this time the issue could not be dodged. America was either a nation or a cluster of sovereign states, and some day she must decide which. Yet even so, even where Calhoun's logic was right, Clay was to triumph in the end by temporizing and compromising and denying the plain facts until it was too late for Calhoun to get his way without force, and too late for the force to be effective. Calhoun would have had the South a free nation by 1850; but Clay and the other compromisers postponed the issue until the North was strong enough to win a civil war. Clay did not plan it that way. He merely planned to avoid head-on collisions as long as possible, in the hope that something might turn up. By so doing he became a savior of the Union.

IV

The problem of the public domain had been exacerbated rather than settled by the Hayne-Webster debate. The Land Act of 1820, as we saw, had allowed settlers to buy tracts as small as eighty acres, and for a dollar and a quarter an acre. This was a victory for the Western school (which wanted to dispose of the lands quickly, for the benefit of settlers and speculators alike) over the school of John Quincy Adams (which wanted to hold the lands for a fair price and to use the money for internal improvements and education). Yet even a dollar and a quarter an acre seemed excessive to the West, as the day approached when the national debt would be extinguished. According to the school of Benton, when the federal government no longer needed the money it should either give the land away or give the proceeds to the states. So in 1832 six states asked Congress to sell them the public domain within their own borders and to divide the money among all the states in the Union. The request led to a show of political chicanery which was a warning to the new democracy.

The Jackson men in the Senate referred the matter to the Committee on Manufactures, of which Clay was chairman, rather than to the Committee on Public Lands. "I felt," said Clay, quite correctly, "that the design was to place in my hands a many-edged instrument which I could could not touch without being wounded." It was in this report that Clay, unable to persuade his Eastern allies to lower the price of the lands, suggested distributing the proceeds among all the states with a bonus to the states in which the lands lay. The suggestion was ingenious; but the Jackson politicians had only played half their hand. When the Clay report was in, the Senate voted to refer the whole matter, for reconsideration, to the Committee on Public Lands, where it should have gone in the first place. That committee brought in a report written by Thomas Hart Benton, attacking Clay for putting revenue ahead of the interests of the settlers. The Benton report said the price of the lands should be reduced to a dollar an acre, and in five years to fifty cents an acre.

Clay defended his plan in a good speech, and again nothing was done except to reduce the size of the minimum tract from eighty to forty acres. The Jackson men, however, had procured a Clay-Whig report and a Benton-Democratic report to circulate through the Western country, so that the settlers could see which party was willing to offer them the best terms. "The old school of politicians," wrote Claude G. Bowers in discussing this episode, "still gauged public opinion by the roll-calls of the Congress. The new school, which came in with Jackson, were least of all concerned with the views of the politicians at the capital. They were interesting themselves with the plain voters, and were devising means for reaching these in the campaign to follow." Unhappily, the "new school" did not interest itself in the plain voters with an eye to what would do them good, but with an eye to what would trick them into voting for the members of the school.

Nothing useful resulted from the elaborate game which had been played upon Clay. The moment when the proceeds from the public lands were no longer needed to pay the national debt was the moment to face the problem of a permanent land policy. Instead of seeking to deal with the problem, the "new school" treated itself to some low japery and left the matter where it was. Neither the Adams plan nor the Benton plan was adopted. The lands were not used to endow a democratic educational system for the entire nation. Neither were they made secure, at the lowest price, for genuine settlers. They were left at the mercy of the speculator. And the land problem was left, like other major problems, to become entangled with the slavery fight and thus help promote the catastrophe of war.

As late as the decade of 1840–50 the question of free land was discussed apart from the question of slavery. "Hayne of South Carolina, Thomasson of Kentucky, Smith and Ficklin of Illinois, Murphy of New York, McConnell of Alabama, and Andrew Johnson of Tennessee all advocated the principle in one form or another. The important point . . . is that the demand came from every quarter; . . . but in the next decade the question became strictly sectional."

In 1851, Andrew Johnson introduced a homestead bill[8] which was supported by thirty-three Southern members of the House and opposed by thirty. In 1859 the same bill received only three Southern votes—one each from Kentucky, Tennessee, and Missouri. The merits or demerits of free land no longer mattered. The Southerners were against it; the new Republican Party was solidly for it; slavery had made even the use of land into a sectional struggle. The reason usually given is that the South awoke to the knowledge that the Homestead Act would favor the small farmer rather than the planter, and thus encourage free labor rather than slave labor. It is hard to see why this should have become clear in the eighteen-fifties if it was not clear in the eighteen-forties. Professor Webb offers a more plausible reason. Profitable large-scale slavery, on the whole, was confined to the cotton plantation, and by 1850 the cotton kingdom in its westward march had almost reached the 98th meridian—that fateful divide in American climate, geography, and life. West of 98° lay the Great Plains, where there was no timber and the rainfall dropped to less than twenty inches a year, and in places to less than ten. West of 98° the animals, the plants, the Indians, the life of the white man, changed radically; in fact, the white man jumped this vast region at first, carrying the frontier straight to the Pacific Ocean, not seeking to settle the Plains until he had devised new institutions and new machinery: the cattle ranch, the stock farm, barbed wire, the tin windmill, and the Colt six-shooter. There was no place for the cotton kingdom, with its pampered institution of slavery, in the rough world west of 98°; and the cotton plantation was already prevented from spreading north, both by law and by climate.

The southern opposition to the Homestead Act [wrote Professor Webb] grew out of the fact that it was to apply in a region from which plantations, and therefore, slaves, were barred by the laws of nature. By 1850 the cotton kingdom had expanded about as far as it could go to the West. . . . It was bounded on the north by cold; it was bounded on the west by aridity. . . . Had the southern portion of the Great Plains been suitable to cotton, the South would have had possession of it before an issue arose, and would have continued in favor of free land as it was in the beginning. The point that has been overlooked is that the land was useless to the South, even though it was free.

In 1832, however, the frontier was well east of the 98th meridian. In 1832, the land question might have been solved forever, without sectional bitterness, if the politicians had been less crafty.

[8] Granting free land to genuine settlers.

When the South turned decisively against free land, in the eighteen-fifties, the North espoused it. The long opposition of Eastern industry was silenced by the argument that free land was the price of Western votes for a high tariff. "Vote yourself a farm" and "Vote yourself a tariff" became the campaign cries during the election which put Lincoln into the White House. The South had bought almost thirty years of low tariff by offering very cheap land; the North was now to buy generations of high tariff by offering land for nothing. So the final alignment was North and West against South: an alignment which created desperation in the South and thus made disunion more likely.[9] The difficulties of maintaining a federal empire had been needlessly aggravated by the failure to deal with the Western lands in time. . . .

VI

At the end of his second term, in 1837, Jackson retired to "The Hermitage," his farm near Nashville, Tennessee. He did not seek to maintain in retirement the influence over his old associates which Jefferson had kept up until the end. Perhaps he felt that his work was done, that his task had been to alter institutions, rather than to make policy. He and his friends had remodeled the Executive and the political parties; they had changed the nature of the American Government; but they had not succeeded in using the new forms to deal effectively with the old problems. They failed to solve the money question, though at least they prevented it from being solved badly. They failed to solve the question that lay back of nullification—how to run a country the size of an empire, on democratic principles, without sacrificing regional minorities to the greed of the people who can muster the most votes. They failed to solve the tangled problem of the public lands. And for the most part they failed even to admit the problem of slavery.

One intangible asset they bequeathed to the future: the symbolic figure of Jackson. In the American mind the word "Jackson" means the buoyant and hopeful youth of democracy. It means a fighting friend for the people, a friend who could not be terrorized. It means a proper contempt for the power of mere finance. From the time of Jackson, no American has doubted that a man working for the people's good can be as relentlessly stubborn as any tyrant.

Andrew Jackson died in 1845. It is a legend in Tennessee that one of his slaves was asked if he thought the General had gone to heaven. The reply came without hesitation: "Of course he went to heaven—*if he took a mind to.*"

[9] As we shall see, this alignment was greatly strengthened by the Southern failure to compete with the North in railway-building.

CHAPTER 31

EVANGELICAL RELIGION
AND AMERICAN REFORM

The America of the 1830's, 1840's, and 1850's was exuberant, restless, and optimistic. It was a society in ferment. Americans had come to believe fervently that they could perfect themselves and their institutions. Because some Europeans shared this belief (to a degree, at least), the United States was thought of as the political laboratory of the world. Certain European thinkers came to America to participate in the experiments in human perfectibility; some came to observe; and some were content to let America serve as the beacon to progress and happiness, while they remained at home.

It is difficult to conceive of a significant aspect of life that Americans of this period did not try to perfect by the process of reshaping or reforming. Major reform movements were concerned with politics, education, the treatment of criminals and the insane, women's rights, temperance, slavery, international peace, and with the very structure of American religion and society. The two most important impulses to reform were dynamic democracy and evangelical religion. In this selection from her pioneering book, *Freedom's Ferment,** Alice Felt Tyler is concerned not with specific reforms, but with the impetus to reform. What, she asks, gave this particular generation that extraordinary "faith in man and in the perfectibility of his institutions?" One factor important to the development of this attitude, Tyler suggests, was the potency of the democratic ideal, which had grown through the years and which, in the Jacksonian period, was increasingly put into active political practice. In the following excerpt, Tyler concentrates on the other major impulse to reform—evangelical religion. The American religious experience reinforced the democratic faith. Together they touched off the great reform crusades that seemed to link the perfection of mankind with America's national destiny.

In reading this selection, students should focus on these questions. How does Tyler account for the exuberant optimism and the extraordinary faith in man and in the perfectibility of his institutions that were characteristic of the young American republic? Were these characteristics a reflection of a broadly-based, deeply-rooted nationalism, discussed in the previous selections? What were the major features of evangelical religion on the frontier, and how do these features explain the success of particular churches in the new settlements? A fundamental question deserves particular attention: How did evangelical religion serve as a major impulse to reform? Finally, what is the connection, if any, between the two forces prompting reform activity—emotional perfectionist religion and the American democratic faith?

Alice Felt Tyler, *Freedom's Ferment**, is the best, general treatment of the reform movement. Also consult A. M. Schlesinger, *The American as Reformer** (1950), *W. R. Cross, The Burned-Over District** (1950), and John L. Thomas, "Romantic Reform in America, 1815–1865," *American Quarterly,* XVII (Winter, 1965). A classic study is Ralph H. Gabriel, *The Course of American Democratic Thought* (1940). Evangelical religion is touched on in William Warren Sweet, *Revivalism in America** (1944), in Bernard A. Weisberger, *They Gathered at the River** (1958), and in William S. McLaughlin, *Modern Revivalism* (1959). A fine biography illustrating the confluence of revivalism and reform (in this case antislavery) is Benjamin P. Thomas, *Theodore Weld* (1950).

* Available in a paperback edition.

THE FAITH OF THE YOUNG REPUBLIC: EVANGELICAL RELIGION

ALICE FELT TYLER

The time has come when the experiment is to be made whether the world is to be emancipated and rendered happy, or whether the whole creation shall groan and travail together in pain. . . . If it had been the design of Heaven to establish a powerful nation in the full enjoyment of civil and religious liberty, where all the energies of man might find full scope and excitement, on purpose to show the world by one great successful experiment of what man is capable. . . . where should such an experiment have been made but in this country! . . . The light of such a hemisphere shall go up to Heaven, it will throw its beams beyond the waves; it will shine into the darkness there, and be comprehended—it will awaken desire, and hope, and effort, and produce revolutions and overturnings until the world is free. . . . Floods have been poured upon the rising flame, but they can no more extinguish it than they can extinguish the flames of Aetna. Still it burns, and still the mountain murmurs; and soon it will explode with voices and thunderings, and great earthquakes. . . . Then will the trumpet of jubilee sound, and earth's debased millions will leap from the dust, and shake off their chains, and cry, "Hosanna to the Son of David!"

With this vision of the future as a new and glorious epoch Lyman Beecher a hundred years ago voiced the exuberant optimism of the young American republic in which he lived. In that time, if ever in American history, the spirit of man seemed free and the individual could assert his independence of choice in matters of faith and theory. The militant democracy of the period was a declaration of faith in man and in the perfectibility of his institutions. The idea of progress so inherent in the American way of life and so much a part of the philosophy of the age was at the same time a challenge to traditional beliefs and institutions and an impetus to experimentation with new theories and humanitarian reforms.

SOURCE. Alice Felt Tyler, *Freedom's Ferment: Phases of American Social History to 1860,* Minneapolis: University of Minnesota Press, 1944, pp. 1–4, 23, 33–45. Copyright 1944 by the University of Minnesota. Reprinted by permission of the University of Minnesota Press and the author.

The period was one of restless ferment. An expanding West was beckoning the hungry and dissatisfied to an endless search for the pot of gold. Growing industrialization and urbanization in the East, new means of communication and transportation, new marvels of invention and science, and advance in the mechanization of industry, all were dislocating influences of mounting importance. And increasing immigration was bringing into the country thousands of Europeans who were dissatisfied with the difficult conditions of life in their native lands. Nor did religion place any restraint on the unrest; recurring revivals, emphasis on individual conversion and personal salvation, and the multiplicity of sects, all made religion responsive to the restlessness of the time rather than a calming influence upon it. The pious editors of the writings of a Shaker seeress asserted in their preface to her revelations:

Let any candid people, endowed with a common share of discernment seriously examine the signs of the times, and view the many wonderful events and extraordinary changes that are constantly taking place in the moral religious and political world, as well as in the natural elements, through the operations of Providence, and they cannot but consider the present age as commencing the most extraordinary and momentous era that ever took place on earth.

Each in his own way the citizens of the young republic recognized the ferment of the era and made answer to its challenge. Itinerant revivalists and the most orthodox of clergymen alike responded with missionary zeal. For an influential few transcendentalism proved to be a satisfying reconciliation between the rationalism of their training and the romanticism of the age, while among the less intellectual, adventism, spiritualism, Mormonism, and perfectionism each won adherents who founded churches and preached their creeds with fervor. To these sects were added the cults and communities transplanted from abroad. The combination of religious toleration, overflowing optimism, and cheap lands caused Europeans of unorthodox faith or unusual social ideas to seek asylum in America. Each such sect, each isolated religious community, each social utopia, was an evidence of the tolerant, eclectic spirit of the young republic, and each made its contribution to the culture of the land that gave it sanctuary.

The desire to perfect human institutions was the basic cause for each sect and community, and this same desire lay at the roots of all the many social reform movements of the period. The American reformer was the product of evangelical religion, which presented to every person the necessity for positive action to save his own soul, and dynamic frontier democracy, which was rooted deep in a belief in the worth of the individual. Born of this combination, the reformer considered reform at once his duty and his right, and he did not limit his activities to one phase of social betterment. Education, temperance, universal peace, prison reform, the rights of women, the evils of slavery, the dangers of Catholicism, all were legitimate fields for his efforts.

The American reformer knew that he did not work alone. He recognized that each cause he espoused was a part of a world of progress and aspiration, but peculiarly his was the freedom to experiment, for in his homeland there was room and hospitality for adventure. Happy in his privilege, he acknowledged his duty and accepted for his age the sign of his crusade. It is with him, his quest for perfection, and his faith in his right to be free that this story deals.

The sources for the story are many and varied. Such was the volume of contemporary material on the American scene that one hardy author introduced his own book with these verses:

> O books! books! books! it makes me sick
> To think how ye are multiplied,
> Like Egypt's frogs, ye poke up thick
> Your ugly heads on every side.
> If a new thought but shakes its ear
> Or wags its tail, tho' starved it look,
> The world the precious news must hear
> The presses groan, and lo! a book.

In its first half century the United States was visited by scores of curious European travelers who came to investigate the strange new world that was being created in the Western Hemisphere. In their accounts of the experience they praised, or condemned, the institutions and national characteristics spread out before them, seized avidly upon all differences from the European norm, and worried each peculiarity beyond recognition and beyond any just limit of its importance. Americans themselves, with the keen sensitiveness of the young and the boasting enthusiasm natural to vigorous creators of new ideas and institutions, examined the work of their hands and, believing it good, reassured themselves and answered their calumniators in a flood of aggressive replies. Every American interested in a reform movement, a new cult, or a utopian scheme burst into print, adding another to the rapidly growing list of polemic books and pamphlets. From this variety of sources it is possible to recapture something of the inward spirit that gave rise to the more familiar and more tangible events of America's youth. . . .

The religious heritage of the young republic was as important in the development of nineteenth-century ideas as were the liberties won in the struggle with civil authorities. "When the common man has freed himself from political absolutism, he will become dissatisfied with theological absolutism." The cold and repressive doctrines of Calvinism could not win the hearts of those who escaped from its control when its dictatorial governmental power came to an end. Moreover, the rationalism of John Locke and the French philosophes had the same dislocating effect on religious thinking as on political ideas. Calvin's doctrine of total depravity might have sufficed an older generation as an explanation of the presence of evil in human society, but man's reason found other causes, and his common sense rejected the idea that he and his neighbor were utterly depraved. The idea of progress and of the importance of the individual undermined the old doctrines of election and predestination. The consequent dissatisfaction with Genevan dogma, coupled with the aridity and dullness of New England cultural life, caused the people to turn with eagerness to evangelical Protestantism. Rebellion against Calvinism forced into the open field of battle a question that was fundamental both in theology and in political and cultural life: Is the will of man completely free or is it wholly subject to the "stable" will of God? . . .

So much were the Western revivals and the religious awakening in the older sections of the country parts of the same movement that it is difficult to be sure whether the lines of influence extended from the East westward or whether the movement beginning in the West about 1800 was the spark that set off the Eastern quickening of interest. Perhaps it is better to think of the two as spontaneous movements occurring at nearly the same time, with the same fundamental causes, each having great effect upon the other, and both combining to exert a tremendous influence upon the social history of the nation throughout the following century.

The settlers who made their way across the mountains during and immediately after the Revolution cut themselves off from the churches of the Eastern states, and for a time the isolation of the families lost in the little forest clearings was one of the greatest hardships of Western life. But settlement rapidly increased, and the frontiersmen, eager to take advantage of every opportunity for community life, welcomed the missionary and flocked to revival meetings. The Presbyterians were in a good position to assume responsibility for missionary work, for they were already entrenched in the Allegheny region in the Scotch-Irish settlements that stretched from Pennsylvania to Georgia. The Congregational church, too, might well have been expected to flourish wherever emigrants from New England settled extensively. Both the Congregational and the Presbyterian churches insisted upon an educated clergy and endeavored to bring culture to the Western communities as rapidly as possible, and both considered missionary activity in the West a patriotic as well as a religious duty. Their appeal to the frontiersman, however, was decidedly less than that of the Baptist and Methodist churches.

The Baptist church, which had spread rapidly after the Great Awakening, went over the mountains with the pioneers, and its simplicity of doctrine and organization fitted into the frontier atmosphere. The Baptist preachers were indigenous—from the ranks of the frontier farmers themselves—and were, at least at first, self-supporting, tilling their own soil five or six days a week. The Baptist insistence on immersion was a tangible issue that appealed to the frontier, and it figured large in frontier theological discussions, serving to distinguish the Baptists from sects very similar to them in other respects.

The Methodist church was the most vigorous in Western enterprise, and Methodist churches were soon the most numerous. Their organization was autocratic and centralized, and their first American bishop, Francis Asbury, was an aggressive, restless, incredibly active and vigorous person, well fitted to direct a flock of circuit-riding evangelists. Methodist doctrine, however, was exceedingly democratic, emphasizing the gospel of free will and free grace, the belief that men are equal before the Lord, and the tenet that each must obtain his own salvation through conversion. The ideal of Methodism was the "creedless religion of the heart."

In the West the Methodist church made wide use of the circuit rider —a practice that was copied by other churches. The circuits were long and the life arduous. Preferably unmarried, practically without a home, the circuit rider and his horse traversed the back country. Not awaiting the arrival of Methodist settlers, he organized Methodist "classes" wherever he found settlers interested in any religious service. Each rider supervised twenty to thirty such local units, preaching almost every day of the week. The riders themselves came up from the ranks. Vigorous young lay preachers were encouraged to "exercise their gifts" and were given exhorting licenses by the presiding elders. Some of them became circuit riders and rendered long years of hard service. Western elders, too, and even bishops were for all practical purposes circuit riders, for they found it necessary to travel extensively to keep in touch with their far-flung districts.

The few Catholics in the West were served by itinerant priests except in the French settlements. John Carroll of Maryland was made the first American Catholic bishop in 1789, but his communicants numbered only

about thirty thousand at that time. The Catholic church looked to immigration from Catholic countries for recruits and was not of much
significance in the West until the purchase of Louisiana added French
Catholics and the following years saw the beginning of Irish and German
immigration. The early Western travelers noted that there were almost
no Episcopalians on the frontier. It was not until after 1815 that Bishop
Chase established both churches and schools in the Ohio-Illinois
country.

CAMP-MEETING REVIVALISM

When the godlessness of the backwoodsmen began to be a matter of
concern to the missionaries and the circuit riders, drastic measures were
used to bring conviction of sin, repentance, and conversion. Upon men
accustomed to the terrors of the wilderness—loneliness, wild animals,
Indian raids—mild homilies had no effect, but vivid pictures of hell-fire
and damnation contrasted with the happiness and peace of salvation, if
used with sufficient dramatic force, would bring the strong man to his
knees. As Ralph Leslie Rusk says, the Protestant sects succeeded in the
West in inverse ratio to their intellectual attainments and in direct ratio
to their emotional appeal.

Frontier religion was an intensely individual experience. Its major
tenets were these: Before conversion man's soul is shackled by sin;
acceptance of religion means freedom from bondage; salvation must
come through conversion consciously experienced at a definite time and
place. This revivalistic type of Christianity was not created by the
frontier, but there is found its natural habitat and ran riot in every
extreme of emotion and in primitive abandon. A militant evangelical
Protestantism preached by itinerant ministers often as illiterate as those
who listened to them was the force that exhilirated, united, and at the
same time tamed the frontier. Such a West was ripe for the excitement
of the camp meeting and the efforts of the revivalist. So much alone,
the frontiersman was peculiarly susceptible to crowd psychology; leading
a violent life, he reacted violently to the vigorous preaching of the frontier evangelists. The revival was to him both a social event and an intense religious experience.

The revival movement began soon after the Revolution in the back
country of North Carolina, Virginia, and Maryland. In 1787 a revival
at the Jones' Hole church in Virginia was accompanied by the violence
and physical manifestations later characteristic of the Western camp
meetings. In the midst of the screaming, groaning, and dancing a part

of the church wall collapsed. Impervious to the falling bricks and mortar, the frenzied people continued their excitement until exhausted, and later one man proudly proclaimed that just before he experienced conversion the Lord himself hit him with a brick. Thirty-five hundred converts were claimed for this and other revivals of the period. In Maryland the Methodists gained so many adherents that other sects were alarmed lest "at this rate the Methodists will get all the people."

Coincident with the revival movement just starting in the New England churches, this Methodist and Baptist expansion in the South greatly increased the desire of all churches to carry religion and salvation to the "Godless West." On the frontier missionaries from the Northeast met the representatives of the Allegheny Presbyterian synods and the circuit-riding Methodist preachers. They were, for the most part, eager young men; afraid of the worldliness of the seaboard states and convinced of the wickedness and desperate need of the West, they wished to dedicate their lives to the preaching of salvation.

Such a frontier preacher was James McGready, who came over the mountains from the Carolinas into southwest Kentucky in 1796. Logan County had long been known as "Rogue's Harbor,"and its collection of horse thieves, murderers, highway robbers, counterfeiters, fugitive bond-servants, and runaway debtors were not easily won. Meetings were well attended, but no conversions were made. Then in the summer of 1799 McGready held a sacramental meeting at the Red River from which he hoped to secure better results. Two young preachers, brothers by the name of McGee, one a Methodist and one a Presbyterian, happened by and came to assist in the preaching. And there, much to the astonishment of congregation and preachers alike, began a revival that was to develop into one of the greatest religious excitements of all time. A letter from John McGee to a presiding elder of the Methodist church describes the scene—soon to be typical of Western revivals:

William felt such a power come over him that he quit his seat and sat down on the floor of the pulpit. I suppose not knowing what he did. A power which caused me to tremble was upon me. There was a solemn weeping all over the house. At length I rose up and exhorted them to let the Lord God Omnipotent reign in their hearts, and submit to Him, and their souls would live. Many broke silence. The woman [*sic*] in the east end of the house shouted tremendously. I left the pulpit and went through the audience shouting and exhorting with all possible ectasy and energy, and the floor was soon covered with the slain.

This time the excitement did not collapse after the meeting ended but spread like wildfire through Kentucky and Tennessee. The next summer so many people flocked to the Gasper River sacramental meeting that it was necessary to hold the services outdoors. This first camp meeting, for the services were held from Friday to Tuesday, was the scene of violent preaching and much shouting and weeping. Preaching, praying, and singing went on all through the day and night except for the hours from midnight to dawn. Little attention was paid to food and still less to rest. When Saturday morning broke, the "slain"—those struggling with conviction of sin—were lying in anguish all about the camp, and by the end of the session the conversions were many.

Ten such camp meetings were held in southwest Kentucky during that season and still more the next summer. One of them was attended by Barton Stone, the pastor of the Cane Ridge church in Bourbon County, who then went home and vividly described the camp-meeting revival he had witnessed. Catching his excitement, the members of the Cane Ridge church made arrangements for a camp meeting of their own. It was a union meeting of Presbyterians and Methodists and lasted from Friday to Wednesday. More than twenty thousand people attended, and the excitement was intense. The diary of the Reverend Mr. Lyle, who was present, described the crowd as rushing hysterically from preacher to preacher and swarming about those who were "fallen" in the agonies of their conviction of sin.

Two young men, Peter Cartwright and James Finley, later the most famous of all the backwoods preachers, were present at the Cane Ridge meeting. Finley was converted on this occasion and wrote of it in his *Autobiography* in vivid terms:

> The noise was like the roar of Niagara. The vast sea of human beings seemed to be agitated as if by a storm. I counted seven ministers all preaching at once, some on stumps, others in wagons, and one . . . was standing on a tree trunk which had, in falling, lodged against another. Some of the people were singing, others praying, some crying for mercy in the most piteous accents, while others were shouting most vociferously. . . . At one time I saw at least five hundred swept down in a moment, as if a battery of a thousand guns had been opened upon them, and then immediately followed shrieks and shouts that rent the very heavens.

After the Cane Ridge meeting the contagion spread rapidly. Through the summers of 1802 and 1803 the frontiersmen flocked to meetings held in dozens of forest clearings. By 1805 the fever had greatly diminished, and as the years went by it became intermittent, although there were annual camp meetings in many districts throughout the century.

There is only occasional mention in contemporary accounts of camp meetings in the East—one even of a meeting on Long Island—but it is obvious that the evangelical, romantic type of religiosity was carried back from the frontier to the Eastern states. Yet methods and manifestations differed greatly in the East. Where churches were more numerous and population less scattered, revivals were usually held indoors in the form of protracted meetings conducted either by the resident ministers or by an imported evangelist. Western camp-meeting methods and measures were used to some extent—bolder preaching, praying for individuals by name, insistence upon public evidence of conversion, and a pledge that the penitent would "serve the Lord." There were interdenominational meetings, mass conversions, and mass admissions to the church. But there was less "shouting" in the East and fewer physical manifestations of religious excitement.

These physical extremes of religious enthusiasm were peculiarly a camp-meeting phenomenon. A special terminology was quickly evolved. All such manifestations of excitement were called "exercises." The falling exercise has been mentioned, the shouting exercise is obvious, the jerking exercise came a little later but was perhaps the most prevalent. All observers gave detailed descriptions of the "jerks." Peter Cartwright's *Autobiography* includes a full account of this form of religious hysteria, concluding with the story of the unrepentant sinner who swore he would "drink the damned jerks to death." His arms jerked so violently that he dropped his whiskey bottle and could not pick it up again. His curses filled the air until his head jerked with such force that he broke his neck. Cartwright piously comments, "I always looked upon the jerks as a judgment sent from God."

The barking exercise seems to have been common, too. As the name indicates, the afflicted often dropped on all fours and barked like dogs. In packs they would dash at a tree as they had seen dogs do when treeing an opossum. This was called "treeing the devil." The running, rolling, and laughing exercises need no description; the last became so prevalent that the "Holy Laugh" seems to have been almost a part of the services. Often the preachers encouraged dancing to relieve the tension, and the solemn prancing about reminded observers of the services of the Shaker communities. Some accounts mention local variations that indicate the vivid imaginations of certain of those under conviction. At one camp meeting several men dropped on their knees in the aisles and played marbles in literal obedience to the admonition, "Except ye be converted, and become as little children, ye shall not enter into the kingdom of heaven." An Irish preacher named McNemar crawled on the ground saying, "I am the serpent that tempted Eve." A canny Scot, unaffected by the hysteria, thereupon stepped on his head with the quotation, "The seed of woman shall bruise the serpent's head." Along with this wide variety of physical phenomena came genuine trances and visions.

The attitude of the preachers usually determined the quantity and the variety of the extravagances. The better educated preachers, especially the Presbyterians, opposed the most intense excitement. Where the preachers themselves were calm and controlled there were few excesses; a period of quiet prayer was a sure cure for an incipient epidemic of jerks. The Methodist and Baptist itinerant preachers used the physical exercises to procure conversions. Hysterical preachers had a hypnotic effect upon the people, and their ranting was often the signal for mass hysteria. Those with a sense of humor, even though the humor may have been crude and coarse, held their audiences in control and relieved the intensity of emotion with gibes and apt stories. Forceful and competent evangelists like Finis Ewing and Peter Cartwright used much practical psychology in managing their huge audiences. They were utterly fearless, sturdy, honest, and self-controlled.

Taking stock after the initial wave of revival had swept across the Middle West, the churches found that, even with some allowance for backsliding, they had gained many new members, the Methodists and Baptists having reaped the largest harvest. With the same tendency to emotionalism that had characterized the revivals, the frontiersman turned to a survey of religious doctrine. His militant individualism made him the ardent champion of whatever dogma he found interesting. The results were schism within the churches and a galaxy of new sects. The Methodists with their autocratic church government and relatively uncomplicated creed had the least difficulty, whereas the Baptists with their independent local church organization and the absence of real control in their associations split into numerous groups. There were Hard- and Soft-Shell Baptists, United Baptists, Particular and General Baptists, Primitive and Free-Will Baptists, while the Disciples of Christ, the Christian church, and the Campbellites (followers of Thomas and Alexander Campbell) were offshoots of the Western Baptist church. Usually the differences were upon minor points—immersion versus sprinkling, infant versus adult baptism—but the quarrels were hot. Even such minor issues as the use of the psalms in the church services led to disputes and schism. Many of the new sects were short-lived; some were permanent.

The Presbyterians, too, had serious doctrinal difficulties in the West. One schism that occurred in the Cumberland region was occasioned by a dispute over the ordination of preachers who had not met the usual Presbyterian standard of training and over the whole matter of revivalistic methods. Those who advocated adopting Methodist doctrines and methods seceded and formed the Cumberland Presbyterian church which grew rapidly in the West because of its circuit-riding and camp-meeting methods. Another Presbyterian schism came because of the promulgation of New Light doctrines in the West. A group of ministers who, in direct contravention of all Calvinist doctrine, placed their emphasis upon God's love for the whole world and the possibility of salvation for all sinners, were forced out of the church and formed a sect called simply the Christians, which later was merged with the Campbellite Disciples.

The close union between American political and religious faith is shown in the infinite tolerance accorded this apparently endless multiplication of sects. James Fenimore Cooper wrote that it was a mistake to think that America's liberality on religious subjects was due to the lack of an established church. "On the contrary," he said, "the fact that there is no establishment is owing . . . to the sentiment of the people." Even more explicitly, Emerson Davis, in a book published in 1851, said: "Men are free, and claim the right to think for themselves in religious as well as in political matters."

During the excitement over the affairs of war-torn Europe there was a temporary subsidence of religious enthusiasm, but with the return of peace in 1815 came a renewal of interest in camp meetings, and the resulting revivals had an effect upon the Eastern states, too. Western New York was visited by so many waves of religious emotion that it acquired the name of a "burnt" district where it was difficult to create any excitement. But it was in western New York that Charles Grandison Finney in the mid-1820's began the evangelical work that was to continue throughout his life. His published memoirs are one long chronicle of revival meetings conducted in most of the Eastern cities and throughout the upper Middle West—a chronicle of the successes of the eloquent preacher whose hypnotic eye and terroristic imagery swept hundreds of converts into the fold in an upsurge of religious excitement that came to be known as the Great Revival.

Although he was not a camp-meeting evangelist, Finney used many of the tactics of the Western itinerant preacher. He preached not only salvation but reform, and many who came under his influence turned to the abolition and temperance societies and made of them crusades as vigorous as Finney's own. Indeed, the Great Revival was the fountain of energy from which came much of the impetus for the various reform movements. The whole-souled young reformers of this period disregarded the doctrinal disputes of earlier days and threw their energies into social reform.

This religious fervor may itself have been in part responsible for the development in the same period of free-thought and atheistic agencies to voice the opinions of its opponents. Frances Wright and Robert Dale Owen led the way with their *Free Enquirer,* the German rationalistic groups in their Turnvereins followed, and in the 1840's there was even some attempt at national organization with scantily attended conventions in 1845 and 1847. This movement made little appeal except in the cities, where it was militant and where it allied itself with the socialism that was being adopted by some of the workingmen. It scarcely threatened the grip of the clergy, but they swept at once into an attack upon "infidelity," closing their ranks against the common enemy with public meetings and sermons and with attempts to stifle the atheist press.

OBSERVERS AND CRITICS

The frank and open adoption of emotionalism in religion and the sensational methods of revivalists did not go unnoticed by American and European contemporary commentators. Margaret Bayard Smith in describing a revival in Washington in 1822 stated that the preachers were

introducing all the habits and hymns of the Methodists into our Presbyterian churches . . . that they were going through the highways and hedges, to invite guests . . . into every house exhorting the people, particularly into all the taverns, grog-shops, and other resorts of dissipation and vice. Whether all these excessive efforts will produce a permanent reformation I know not; but there is something very repugnant to my feelings in the public way in which they discuss the conversions and convictions of people and in which young ladies and children display their feelings and talk of their convictions and experiences. Dr. May calls the peculiar fever, the *night* fever, and he says almost all cases were produced by night meetings, crowded rooms, excited feelings, and exposure to night air.

A somewhat less naïve explanation of revivalistic phenomena was made by Bishop Hopkins of Vermont, who stated that revivalists secured conversions solely because of the terror induced by their exhortations. Disapproval of such tactics seems to have been prevalent among the Episcopalian clergy, one of whom Captain Marryat quoted as saying that revivals were

those startling and astounding shocks which are constantly invented, artfully and habitually applied, under all the power of sympathy, and of a studied and enthusiastic elocution, by a large class of preachers among us. To startle and to shock is their great secret power.

But the American clergy in general probably felt that the revival had come to stay and could be made a valuable part of the religious program of the Protestant churches.

European travelers almost invariably were taken to camp meetings, especially in the West, and reacted to the experience in accord with their own temperaments. Captain Marryat drew back in disgust from the preacher who began his prayer with the words "Almighty and diabolical God," and deprecated all the excesses and extravagances of evangelical religion. Frances Trollope made many caustic comments about both revivals and preachers. Always suspecting the worst, she felt sure that such sessions must turn at times into sex orgies, although the only ocular evidence she had was the sight of a preacher whispering consolation into the ear of a sobbing and distraught young feminine convert.

James Stuart was much impressed by the perfect decorum of the audience, the "faultless" sermons, and the magnificent singing. The revival he attended, however, was on Long Island; he was not exposed to the crudities of a genuine frontier camp meeting. It is more surprising to find the usually censorious Thomas Hamilton commending the camp meeting as an agency of civilization.

In a free community [he wrote] the follies of the fanatic are harmless. The points on which he differs from those around him are rarely of a nature to produce injurious effects on his conduct as a citizen. But the man without religion acknowledges no restraint but human laws; and the dungeon and the gibbet are necessary to secure the rights and interests of his fellow-citizens from violation. There can be no doubt, therefore, that in a newly settled country the strong effect produced by these camp-meetings and revivals is on the whole beneficial. The restraints of public opinion and penal legislation are little felt in the wilderness; and, in such circumstances, the higher principle of action, communicated by religion, is a new and additional security to society.

Two of the most detailed descriptions of camp-meeting revivals are those of Francis Lieber and Fredrika Bremer, written nearly twenty years apart and published in 1835 and 1853. Lieber was repelled by the emotionalism of the camp meeting he attended and was shocked by the "scenes of unrestrained excitement," but the Swedish traveler, Fredrika Bremer, was much impressed by the immense crowd of both white and colored people at the Georgia camp meeting she witnessed in the early 1850's. The grandeur of the night meeting in the forest, the eight fine altars, the campfires of resinous wood, the superb singing of the thousands of Negroes, the wails of the penitent, the thunder and lightning of an approaching storm—all, she said, combined to make the night one never to be forgotten.

The effects of the absence of state control and the consequent multiplicity of sects seemed to interest all foreign observers. Many of them mention the lack of religious intolerance in the United States and the easy "live and let live" philosophy apparent in the attitude of most men. Alexander Mackay, who traveled extensively in America in the 1840's, was so impressed that he wrote:

It is true that the insulting term "toleration" is but seldom heard in America in connexion with the religious system of the country. To say that one tolerates another's creed, implies some right to disallow it, a right that happens to be suspended or in abeyance for the time being. The only mode in which the American manifests any intolerance in reference to religion is that they will not tolerate that the independence of the individual should in any degree, be called in question in connexion with it.

On the more fundamental question of the connection between the American democratic faith and the emotional perfectionistic religion that had swept over the United States the observers seemed in agreement. Again and again missionaries and patriots identified democratic with religious faiths and asserted that neither could stand alone, that combined they furnished an invincible bulwark for American freedom. Timothy Flint, writer and missionary preacher of the first decade of the century, emphasized always that missionary enterprise in the West was for the good of the whole country; the West must not fall into Godless anarchy, for the representative institutions of the East would then also perish. As the Western missionary told De Tocqueville, "It is, therefore, our interest that the New States should be religious, in order that they may permit us to remain free."

In an essay published in 1851, Mark Hopkins, president of Williams College, expressed the same feeling that democracy must be linked with Christianity:

Man himself is the highest product of this lower world, those institutions would seem to be the best which show, not the most imposing results of aggregated labor, but humanity itself, in its most general cultivation and highest forms. This idea finds its origin and support in the value which

Christianity places upon the individual, and, fully carried out, must overthrow all systems of darkness and mere authority. Individual liberty and responsibility involve the right of private judgment; this involves the right to all the light necessary to form a correct judgment; and this again must involve the education of the people, and the overthrow of everything, civil and religious, which will not stand the ordeal of the most scrutinizing examination and of the freest discussion.

Regardless of their differences as to details, European and American observers alike were insistent upon the prominence of the part played by religion in the Western World. They saw that the same intensity of faith vivified both the democracy and the religious experience of many Americans, and they realized the potentialities of that combination. The mind and heart quickened by the "lively joy" of a vital religious experience were easily turned toward social reforms, and the spirit of inquiry and soul-searching that animated the revival had a dynamic social significance. The American faith in democratic institutions found its alter ego in the romantic evangelical spirit of American religious life. Together they gave to the Americans of the first half century of the republic their conviction that their institutions could be perfected and their national destiny be fulfilled.

CHAPTER 32

MANIFEST DESTINY

In this chapter from *Ideas, Ideals, and American Diplomacy** (1966), Arthur Ekirch easily demonstrates that, in the 1840's, the nation reaped the unharvested fruits of J. Q. Adams' diplomacy. During the earlier days of our nation we were expansionist but, after 1815, we avoided the risk of war. By the middle of the 1840's we were not only expansionist but were prepared to fight for additional territory, if necessary. This reading from Ekirch's work and the blunt fact of the Mexican War document this change in attitude.

Moreover, as this reading shows, we, as a nation, tend to identify our acquisitive interest with moral imperatives. In other words, any acquisition or occupation of territory and any military intervention by the United States is defended as absolutely necessary for the good of the entire world. The irony of this global moral posturing is that, generally, it has been accepted as valid only by ourselves.

This sense that the United States is doing God's work in the world did not originate in the Mexican War period. It is probably one of the least desirable heritages of our Puritan forefathers. (However, we should point out that it has also undergirded efforts to improve American society.) Neither did it vanish at the end of the era under discussion. We need only read a recent debate on American foreign policy to realize that the participants still evoke varying concepts of the national "mission." Only in the 1840's and 1850's, however, did the idea of

mission became so central to the events of the period that both contemporaries and historians have given it a specific title—"Manifest
Destiny."

It was this spirit that led to the annexation of Texas, the Mexican war,
and the war's result—the subsequent acquisition of New Mexico, Ari-
zona, California, and parts of Utah, Nevada, and Colorado. Although
there was a peaceful settlement of the Oregon question, it was preceded
by a long, bellicose period. Probably, this spirit might also have led
to the acquisition of such Caribbean islands as Cuba and Santo Domingo and, perhaps, even more of Mexico if even stronger social forces
—sectionalism and slavery—had not entered the political arena. A
quarreling North and South could not unite on further expansion. Here,
again, the irony of history enters the picture since, in part, the acquisitions of the 1840's caused the nation's growing awareness of the particular
needs of the "Peculiar Institution." The future of slavery in the territories became the fateful disruptive issue.

In reading this essay, students should consider these important questions.
First, how does Professor Ekirch define manifest destiny? Was it merely
a popular phase of justification for American expansionism, or were the
words the outward expression of a deeply-rooted pattern of thought that
had wider ramifications? If so, what were these ramifications? What were
the basic characteristics of manifest destiny? Was it broadly idealistic
or narrowly nationalistic? Was it passive or aggressive? Finally, what
influence did it have on the subsequent course of American foreign
policy?

Several volumes stand out in the literature of this period. Of course,
essential to this topic is Albert Weinberg, *Manifest Destiny: A Study of
National Expansionism in American History** (1935), with its detailed
examination of the degree to which the concept permeated American
thinking of the period. Frederick Merk, *Manifest Destiny and Mission in
American History** (1965), is a collection of essays and articles dealing
with this period and this concept. R. W. Van Alstyne in *The Rising
American Empire** (1960), discusses expansionism as one of the central
themes of American diplomatic history. William Goetzmann, *When the
Eagle Screamed: The Romantic Horizon in American Diplomacy, 1800–
1860** (1966), covers the entire period in delightful prose.

* Available in a paperback edition.

MANIFEST DESTINY
ARTHUR EKIRCH

The concept of manifest destiny is particularly associated in American history with the aggressive diplomacy of the 1840's. In this decade the continental limits of the United States were carried westward to the shores of the Pacific and as far south as the Rio Grande. The national domain was rounded out by the accession of vast and valuable territories, and the United States could be said to have achieved its "natural boundaries." Thus, in a short span of time, the United States had already moved to fulfill the prediction of Tocqueville, when he wrote:

At a period which may be said to be near,—for we are speaking of the life of a nation,—the Anglo-Americans alone will cover the immense space contained between the polar regions and the tropics, extending from the coasts of the Atlantic to those of the Pacific Ocean.

The first widely noted use of the phrase "manifest destiny" seems to have occurred in 1845 in an editorial by John L. O'Sullivan in the *Democratic Review.* Under the title "Annexation," O'Sullivan declared that God had marked out Oregon, Texas, and the remaining continental territories for possession by the United States. Even though other reasons were not wanting, he contended that the recent United States annexation of Texas was justified by the intrusion of foreign nations into this American matter "for the avowed object of thwarting our policy and hampering our power, limiting our greatness and checking the fulfillment of our manifest destiny to overspread the continent allotted by Providence for the free development of our yearly multiplying millions." Some years earlier another O'Sullivan essay in the *Democratic Review,* depicting America as "The Great Nation of Futurity," not only foreshadowed his use of the phrase manifest destiny, but also exemplified the transition from the peaceful idea of American mission to the aggressive concept of territorial expansion.

SOURCE. From *Ideas, Ideals, and American Diplomacy: A History of Their Growth and Interaction* by Arthur Ekirch, Jr., pp. 40–45, 50–60. Copyright 1966 by Meredith Publishing Company. Reprinted by permission of Appleton-Century-Crofts and the author.

The far-reaching, the boundless future will be the era of American great-ness. In its magnificent domain of space and time, the nation of many nations is destined to manifest to mankind the excellence of divine principles. . . . Its floor shall be the hemisphere—its roof the firmament of the star-studded heavens, and its congregation a Union of many Republics, comprising hundreds of happy millions, calling, owning no man master, but governed by God's natural and moral law of equality, the law of brotherhood—of "peace and good will amongst men."

O'Sullivan's 1845 editorial reflected the view that Great Britain, by its continued occupation of Oregon and recognition of the Lone Star Re-public of Texas, had interfered with American territorial progress. The Democratic party in 1844 had seemed to gauge correctly the strength of this American expansionist sentiment when it picked James K. Polk as its candidate and adopted a platform which included the resolution:

That our title to the whole of the Territory of Oregon is clear and unquestion-able; that no portion of the same ought to be ceded to England or any other power, and that the re-occupation of Oregon and the re-annexation of Texas at the earliest and practicable period are great American measures, which this convention recommends to the cordial support of the Democracy of the Union.

"These were the days," diplomatic historian Thomas A. Bailey has writ-ten, "when Manifest Destiny was a dynamic force—when it was widely believed that America's multiplying millions were manifestly destined to spread their republican institutions, though not necessarily by force, over at least the whole continent. These were the days when men talked of 'the universal Yankee nation' and 'an ocean-bound republic'; when the eagle was made to scream and the buffalo to bellow."

Popular support for the notion of manifest destiny received tangible encouragement from a number of factors which, for the first time in American life, seemed to come together in the 1840's. Developing rail-road lines and the experimental work in electricity which culminated in the Morse telegraph and promised better communication with the Far West overcame early American fears that the Pacific Coast could not be integrated with the rest of the nation. "The magnetic telegraph," the exuberant O'Sullivan wrote in 1845, "will enable the editors of the 'San Francisco Union,' the 'Astoria Evening Post,' or the 'Nootka Morning News' to set up in type the first half of the President's Inaugural before the echoes of the latter half shall have died away. . . ." At the same time the belief that much of the plains and the mountain area within the Louisiana Purchase—the so-called "Great American Desert"—was unsuited for agricultural settlement gave rise to an uneasy feeling that additional territories might be needed to satisfy the demands of land-hungry American pioneers and planters. Meanwhile the economic problems of the frontiersmen had been heightened by the hard times following the Panic of 1837. Texas and Oregon accordingly might offer a fresh start on the way to wealth. Finally, the prospect of bringing distant regions under the American flag had a jingoistic appeal for many citizens. A young and growing population, convinced of the reality of material progress, proved an eager audience for the expansionist propaganda of the penny press—the mass media of the new democracy. Andrew Jackson himself, the hero of this democracy, was an ardent expansionist who, in his own person and career, glamorized the spirit of manifest destiny.

Although the term manifest destiny proved a popular and useful phrase of justification and rationalization for the expansionist course of American foreign policy in the 1840's, the ideas and philosophy behind the words had wider ramifications. In the first place, manifest destiny conveyed a strong impression that American expansionism was inevitable and providential. Americans were a chosen people intended by Heaven to spread across the continent. Secondly, manifest destiny transformed such broad concepts as the idea of progress into the specific terms of a law of natural territorial growth. Third, it gave a new dynamic and positive value to the older doctrines of isolationism and the American mission. Neither isolation nor missionary ideas were discarded. Instead, under the guiding hand of manifest destiny, they were imbued with greater nationalist vigor and precision. Thus the further accessions of territory in North America in the 1840's were viewed as strengthening the position of the United States and making its independence of Europe more certain. At the same time, the vague ideal of the American mission to spread democracy by example was translated into the actuality of the reach of free institutions across the continent.

In changing in this way the general into the specific, American foreign policy was, of course, also losing something of its idealistic and universal significance and appeal. While the concept of an American mission embraced a concern for the well-being of all nations and peoples, the doctrine of manifest destiny stressed the welfare of the United States. Moreover, despite the argument that expansion was the inevitable and inexorable fate decreed by Providence for the American people, there was actually a good deal of human will and effort which had to be called upon before the goals of manifest destiny could be reached. For example, much political agitation and propaganda, war, and threat of war, had to take place before the territorial aspirations of the advocates of manifest destiny were achieved.

Manifest destiny was an expression of exaggerated nationalism in American foreign policy. This expansionism of the 1840's was nationalist, not in the sense that it enjoyed the united support of all Americans, but in the way in which the nation selfishly pursued its own interests at the expense of other nations. While isolationism and the concept of an American mission were, of course, also nationalistic, neither concept was as aggressive as that of manifest destiny. Isolationism stressed the defense and security of the American Republic in a world of hostile European monarchies. And the idea of mission, though expansionist, emphasized on the whole the peaceful export of American ideology and the realization of the natural rights of man through the spread of American political institutions. In contrast, the concept of manifest destiny implied expansion in a more belligerent manner. It turned the defensive and idealistic notions of isolationism and mission toward the course of a unilateral, nationalist, political and territorial expansion. And, in so doing it also transposed broader, more universal values of genuine international importance—the natural rights philosophy, for example—into a narrower doctrine of the special rights of Americans over and against other peoples.

In pursuit of its goals the United States had the immense advantage of being able to work out its destiny without the serious opposition of other world powers. At the very birth of American expansionist designs in the first years of the Republic, Europe was absorbed in the French Revolutionary and Napoleonic struggles. Thus American foreign policy was able to profit immediately from the strife of Europe. As J. Fred Rippy points out, not only is it "doubtful indeed whether the United States would even have been born," but "A harmonious Europe would never have permitted the United States to extend its boundaries and its political dominance from the Appalachians to the Pacific Ocean and from the tropical Caribbean to the snows of Alaska."

Finally, it should be noted that the doctrine of manifest destiny not only implied inevitability, but it also indicated that the process of expansion was unlimited in time or place. Once the Pacific Coast had been reached, Americans looked outward across the waters to the islands and shores beyond. And then, as the desire for new territories and overseas dependencies eventually waned, manifest destiny was increasingly identified with the search for foreign markets and the desire to exercise a dominating military and ideological influence in world affairs.

Thus the general philosophy and outlook of manifest destiny became one of the major controlling assumptions underlying American foreign policy in both the nineteenth and twentieth centuries.

In the course of the contemporary justification of manifest destiny as distinct from the more material factors which also influenced expansionism, the American people invoked, as Albert K. Weinberg's massive scholarly study of nationalist expansion has shown, a wealth of argument and illustration, touching virtually every aspect of American foreign policy. From the natural rights philosophy of the American Revolution to the assertions of world leadership in the twentieth century, American spokesmen described at length what they understood to be the destined direction of United States expansion. Except briefly in the crisis of the Civil War, American confidence in the manifest destiny of the nation hardly wavered. For, in the words of Franklin Roosevelt, the American people quite literally always believed that they had a rendezvous with destiny. . . .

Increasingly in the 1840's arguments used to justify the progress of manifest destiny in relation to the Indians proved useful as well to support American policies with respect to Mexico and Oregon. At the expense of the Indian tribes the national domain of the United States was gradually being increased without the addition of new foreign territories, but merely through the acts and treaties by which the Indians' land claims were extinguished. Louisiana and Florida had also been acquired by treaty, but in the mid-forties the workings of American diplomacy no longer seemed so inexorable or automatic. Mexico refused to recognize the annexation of Texas, and Great Britain continued to be reluctant to yield all of Oregon. At this juncture, as the Polk Administration called upon the country to prepare for war to defend what was regarded as its true title to both Oregon and Texas, American expansionists invoked the higher sanction of an appeal to democracy. Possession of Texas and Oregon, it was said, would extend the area of freedom and further the progress of civilization.

This incantation to democracy to justify American acquisition of Texas and Oregon was a relatively new form of the expansionist argument. Jefferson, it is true, had referred to the idea of "an empire for liberty" to include Canada, Florida, and even Cuba, but democracy as a positive ideal was seldom used to support the case for American territorial expansion until the 1830's and '40's. Although Jefferson expressed the view that possession of an extensive territory would strengthen American democracy by minimizing the divisive force of selfish local interests, he also shared the widespread feeling that the growth of free institutions could be achieved best by peaceful example rather than through force. Thus there seemed to be a distinction in the American mind between the general mission to advance democracy and free institutions and the specific desire to annex new lands.

The extension of democracy had not been an important factor in the early American expansionist interest in Louisiana or Florida. And, in the case of the inhabitants of New Orleans, the United States had acted tardily in enabling them to benefit from the American practice of local self-government. But the opinion of many of the Revolutionary and Founding Fathers that a republican form of government and free institutions could not well be extended over large areas was gradually weakened as the United States gained new territories and indulged in expansionist dreams in the War of 1812. "The expansion of our Union over a vast territory can not operate unfavorably to the States individually," President Monroe declared in 1822. "With governments separate, vigorous, and efficient for all local purposes, their distance from each other can have no injurious effect upon their respective interests." By the 1830's all remaining American apprehensions of this incompatibility of democracy and territorial growth virtually disappeared in the midst of the strong desires of the country to gain Canada, Cuba, Texas, Oregon, and California.

Important additional support for the linkage of democracy and expansion was provided by American concern over European ambitions in North America. As Professor Rippy has remarked, "manifest destiny never pointed to the acquisition of a region so unmistakably as when undemocratic, conservative Europe revealed an inclination to interfere or to absorb." Although the Texas Republic already enjoyed political freedom, British commercial interests there encouraged American expansionists to call for annexation in order to preserve democracy. Some Texans, it is true, resented such a patronizing attitude on the part of their fellow Americans to the north, and abolitionists and antiexpansionists also complained vigorously that the United States wished to extend the area of freedom by enlarging the area of slavery. Once the Texas question became a part of war with Mexico, however, expansionists were able to contend that the boundaries of political freedom were being extended over regions hitherto suffering from Mexican misrule.

In the course of the Mexican War, United States interest in carrying the benefits of democracy south of the Rio Grande became intertwined with the contention that the war was necessary as a part of an American mission of regeneration for the Mexican people. Under the spell of the idea that the Anglo-Saxon countries were destined to conquer the world, American nativists considered the Mexicans an inferior people. While some expansionists, desiring only territory, warned that the United States would be corrupted by intimate contact with a non-Anglo-Saxon race, others were eager to accept responsibility for the regeneration of so-called lesser nationalities. When the results of the war left American armies of occupation in command of large areas of Mexican territory, the editors of prominent Democratic publications were quick to accept the mission of regeneration for the United States. "The latter expectation," Weinberg comments, "perhaps showed more optimism than the previous history of military occupations warranted." But the enthusiasm of the *New York Herald,* at least, was undaunted:

> The universal Yankee nation can regenerate and disenthrall the people of Mexico in a few years; and we believe it is a part of our destiny to civilize that beautiful country and enable its inhabitants to appreciate some of the many advantages and blessings they enjoy.

As the appetite for expansion grew with the war, some Americans came around to the view that even all of Mexico might safely be absorbed by the United States. The *Democratic Review,* which had previously opposed such complete annexation, now declared in February, 1848:

> Whatever danger there may be in blending people of different religions into one nation, where religion is established by law,—or in annexing by conquest, under arbitrary governments, which trample upon the rights of all their subjects, and conquer only to enslave,—a free nation, which shows equal toleration and protection to all religions, and conquers only to bestow freedom, has no such danger to fear.

In their acceptance of an American destiny to regenerate the Mexican people and extend the benefits of freedom to their Government, the expansionists of the 1840's were anticipating the argument, fifty years later, of the white man's burden. Meanwhile, in the midst of nativist hostility to European immigrants, the doctrine of an Anglo-Saxon civilizing mission to all lesser races became in a sense the positive aspect of American pride and prejudice. As the national feelings toward the Indians and Mexicans demonstrated, an egocentric and ethnocentric intolerance was becoming an important part of the philosophy of manifest destiny. In the 1840's and 50's the rationale of manifest destiny in all of its varied ramifications gave vital backing to the aggressive goals of American foreign policy. And, at the same time, the angry protests of those who opposed this expansionism were effectively countered by the claim that American arms and diplomacy carried in their wake the blessings of democracy and civilization.

In Oregon the pressure of the pioneers taking the westward trail in the 1840's made untenable joint occupation of the territory with Great Britain. The farmers of the Northwest associated an expanding frontier with American individualism and economic opportunity. Oregon, it was said, "must be occupied for poor men who needed homes and for the extension of free institutions," and this economic individualism "perhaps did more than anything to cement the association between democracy and expansion." To the pioneers democracy meant economic opportunity as well as a form of government. British fur trading interests in the Northwest as well as British monarchy were, therefore, a threat to American democratic expansionism. While England wanted to keep Oregon "for the benefit of the wild beasts as well as of the savage nations," John Quincy Adams, in upholding the American claims to 54° 40′, asserted that the national purpose was "To make the wilderness blossom as the rose, to establish laws, to increase, multiply, and subdue the earth. . . ."

In his denunciation of British imperialism in Oregon, Senator William Allen of Ohio declared that exclusive American occupation would give the United States "the first place in the modern system of the world, . . . leading it on to that social regeneration, which promises the delivery of mankind from the miseries of antiquated monarchy." "Expansionism, later to be depicted by anti-imperialists as a means to economic exploitation and slavery, was seen in this period as a means to economic liberty. Economic freedom had become as important as political freedom to the philosophy of democracy. . . . Freedom for the American nation; freedom for the American State; freedom for the American individual; such then were the principal elements in the fundamentally egoistic program of extending the area of freedom."

The extravagant hopes of the American pioneer in the West were illustrated in the career of a young soldier and journalist, William Gilpin. Gilpin was a personal friend of Andrew Jackson, who appointed him to West Point. Later he came into contact with such ardent Western expansionists as Thomas Hart Benton and John Charles Frémont. Returning to Washington in 1844 from an expedition to the Oregon country with Frémont, Gilpin found employment as an expert adviser to Benton, Buchanan, Polk, and other expansionist-minded Democratic statesmen.

Then, after Army service in the Mexican War and a later stint of fighting against the Pawnees and Commanches, Gilpin turned to writing and speaking about the West. In one of the first examples of his literary work Gilpin summed up in grandiloquent fashion the millenium that he foresaw if the workings of manifest destiny were fulfilled:

> The *untransacted* destiny of the American people is to subdue the continent—to rush over this vast field to the Pacific Ocean—to animate the many hundred of millions of its people, and to cheer them upward . . . —to agitate these herculean masses—to establish a new order in human affairs . . . —to regenerate superannuated nations— . . . to stir up the sleep of a hundred centuries—to teach old nations a new civilization—to confirm the destiny of the human race—to carry the career of mankind to its culminating point—to cause a stagnant people to be reborn—to perfect science—to emblazon history with the conquest of peace—to shed a new and resplendent glory upon mankind—to unite the world in one social family—to dissolve the spell of tyranny and exalt charity—to absolve the curse that weighs down humanity, and to shed blessings round the world!

In language as extravagant as Gilpin's, James D. B. De Bow, the New Orleans magazine editor, in the journal that bore his name, exclaimed in 1850:

> *We have a destiny to perform,* a 'manifest destiny' over all Mexico, over South America, over the West Indies and Canada. The Sandwich Islands are as necessary to our eastern, as the isles of the gulf to our western commerce. The gates of the Chinese empire must be thrown down by the men from the Sacramento and the Oregon, and the haughty Japanese tramplers upon the cross be enlightened in the doctrines of republicanism and the ballot box. The eagle of the republic shall poise itself over the field of Waterloo, after tracing its flight among the gorges of the Himalaya or the Ural mountains, and a successor of Washington ascend the chair of universal empire! These are the giddy dreams of the day. The martial spirit must have its employ. The people stand ready to hail tomorrow, with shouts and enthusiasm, a collision with the proudest and the mightiest empire on earth.

The territorial growth which Americans proudly rationalized in the extraordinarily elastic meanings that they assigned to the concept of manifest destiny had been accomplished with an abnormal amount of speed in the 1840's. But the winning of Texas, Oregon, and California for the American flag did not curtail the activities of American expansionists. The success of the Mexican War, instead of satiating, merely whetted their appetite for more territory. Even though the regions already acquired seemed to be in excess of any immediate national needs, Southern slaveholders, for example, were far from satisfied. Thus the early 1850's saw the climax of American efforts to annex Cuba and other lands deemed suitable for the extension of slavery.

That the sole expansionist achievement of the 1850's was the purchase of a strip of southwest territory by Gadsden's Treaty was, it has been suggested, more a matter of lack of luck than of boldness. President Pierce, as a representative of the "Young America" expansionist wing of the Democratic party, frankly favored an aggressive foreign policy. In his Inaugural Address he announced that the policies of his adminis- tration would "not be controlled by any timid forebodings of evil from expansion. . . . The apprehension of dangers from extended territory, multiplied States, accumulated wealth, and augmented population has proved to be unfounded," he declared. Pierce accordingly gave his support to the Perry expedition to Japan, initiated by his Whig predecessor, and only the renewed sectional dispute over slavery following the Kansas- Nebraska bill forestalled more ambitious expansionist projects in Cuba and the Caribbean. By antagonizing antislavery opinion the Kansas- Nebraska bill insured the opposition of the North to the longstanding American hopes of acquiring the island of Cuba, and the Pierce adminis- tration had to admit the defeat of its expansionist dreams.

Although prospects for territorial growth in specific areas were therefore dim by the mid-fifties, the overall confidence of the advocates of mani- fest destiny was hardly diminished. "Expansion," said President Buc- hanan, "is in the future the policy of our country, and only cowards fear and oppose it." Whatever their temporary disappointments, American expansionists could take refuge in their unassailable confidence that growth was the law of nature for all healthy nations. The historic exten- sion of American territory and the ever-increasing American population were assurances that this natural growth was indeed the destined future of the Republic. To themselves, Americans felt, the famous observation of Humboldt was applied with particular force: "It is with nations as with nature which knows no pause in progress and development, and attaches her curse on all inaction."

Even those who drew back from the more extreme notions of manifest destiny were content to accept the accessions that might be expected to come from the natural growth of the American national domain. Thus Edward Everett, the scholarly Secretary of State in the anti-expansionist Fillmore Administration, in countering an Anglo-French proposal to tie American hands in regard to Cuba, adroitly suggested that in contrast to the foreign policies of the Old World, that of the United States was subject to "the law of American growth and progress." Like Everett a man of peace, Parke Godwin, in his book of political essays published in 1854, wrote:

Precisely, however, because this tendency to the assimilation of foreign ingredients, or the putting forth of new members, is an inevitable incident of our growth . . . there is no need that it should be especially fostered or stimulated. It will thrive of itself; it will supply the fuel of its own fires; and all that it requires is only a wise direction. . . . The fruit will fall into our hands when it is ripe, without an officious shaking of the tree. Cuba will be ours, and Canada and Mexico, too—if we want them—in due season, and without the wicked imperative of a war.

Less forbearing and patient than Everett or Godwin, the Democratic expansionists of the late 1850's were continually hopeful that this law of natural growth and expansion would once again receive official political encouragement. Southern annexationists and their supporters, in particular, refused to concede that the Kansas-Nebraska question had doomed all chance for the acquisition of Cuba and other potential slave territory. Sympathetic with these expectations and convinced that Mexico, and perhaps Cuba, lay within the path of American destiny, Caleb Cushing asked:

Is not the occupation of any portion of the earth by those competent to hold and till it, a providential law of national life? Can you say to the tide that it ought not to flow, or the rain to fall? I reply, *it must!* And so it is with well-constituted, and therefore, progressive and expansive nations. They cannot help advancing; it is the condition of their existence.

A Senate report, advocating the purchase of Cuba in 1859, declared: "The law of our national existence is growth. We cannot, if we would disobey it. While we should do nothing to stimulate it unnaturally, we should be careful not to impose upon ourselves a regimen so strict as to prevent its healthful development." And on the eve of the Civil War, retired Congressman J. F. H. Claiborne, in defending the American filibusters who sought to liberate Cuba, asserted:

We proceed upon the theory that the condition of a republic is repose. What an error! That is the normal condition of absolutism. The law of a republic is progress. Its nature is aggressive.

We are in the restless period of youth; the law of the age is progress; let our flag be given to the winds, and our principles go with it wherever it is unfurled. Conquest is essential to our internal repose. War sometimes becomes the best security for peace.

Not only was natural growth the manifest destiny of the American nation, but the attempt to violate this law could be the harbinger of disaster. The nations that failed to advance with the progress of civilization could not expect to enjoy the repose of stability. Instead, the alternative to progress was swift descent in a retrograde motion. In making out his case for the accession of Cuba, a writer in the *Democratic Review* for 1859 observed:

'We are governed by the laws under which the universe was created;' and therefore, in obedience to those laws, we must of necessity move forward in the paths of destiny shaped for us by the great Ruler of the Universe. Activity and progress is the law of heaven and of earth; and in the 'violation of this law there is danger.'

This same thought in connection with expansionist ambitions was expressed earlier by the magazine writers who pointed out:

Civilization is a progressive work—there is no standing still—its principle is continual advancement. The nation that ceases to go forward must certainly go back.

National glory—national greatness—the spread of political liberty on this continent, must be the thought and action by day, and the throbbing dream by night, of the whole American people, or they will sink into oblivion.

Thus the advocates of manifest destiny found support for their ambitious views in the philosophical concept of the idea of progress. The law of progress for nations, as for individuals, indicated growth and activity as the only alternative to decline and death.

As the Civil War cast its shadow over the land to disrupt the course of American manifest destiny, American expansionists were forced to postpone their conviction that Cuba, Canada, Mexico, and other regions in the New World would eventually come under the American flag. But confidence in the force of American political gravitation and in the inevitability of the American destiny was not lost. While the Civil War armies were joined in their fearful struggle, Darwinian concepts of evolution and competition emerged to provide new arguments for growth, and to create a bridge from the manifest destiny of the early nineteenth century to the imperialism of later years. At the same time the achievement of a stronger national union as a result of the Civil War reinforced American security and helped to establish thereby the foundations for the development of the United States as a major world power.

CHAPTER 33

THE PECULIAR
INSTITUTION: THE IMPACT
ON SLAVE PERSONALITY

One of the most exciting, productive, and rapidly growing fields of American history is the study of the American Negro. This relatively new area of interest has focused strongly on slavery in the United States. Recent studies have greatly expanded the historiography of American slavery; historians have begun to approach it from various points of view, to utilize the conclusions of modern social sciences, to rely on new materials, including psychological and social data, and to employ cross-cultural approaches.

One of the most provocative of the recent studies is Stanley Elkins' *Slavery: A Problem in American Institutional and Intellectual Life** (1959). Professor Elkins suggests that the time has come to employ fresh approaches and to ask new questions in exploring the problem of slavery. He believes that historians—including the authors of the two classic studies of American Negro slavery (U. B. Philips, *American Negro Slavery**, 1918, and Kenneth Stampp, *The Peculiar Institution**, 1956)—have engaged, for too long a time, in the same debate on slavery as the abolitionists and proslavery proponents of the ante-bellum years. The rhythm of "right" and "wrong" has dominated the discourse to the point of diminishing

491

returns. Hence, Elkins attempts to utilize a different line of argument. Borrowing a technique from Frank Tannenbaum, *Slave and Citizen** (1948), he systematically compares the institutions of slavery in Latin America and the United States. In addition, he attempts to study the effect of bondage on slave personality by examining the responses of victims in another kind of stressful, dehumanizing situation—confinement in Nazi concentration camps. This is a daring method of dealing with the past, but it produces some stimulating, hard-to-gauge results.

Several key questions must be considered in reading this selection. First, what basic difference does Professor Elkins see between the institutions of slavery in Latin America and in North America? Second, what does he suggest about the basic influence of North American slavery on personality formation for large numbers of slaves? Third, what evidence does Elkins present to justify his conclusions?

In considering these basic questions, students should be particularly careful to identify the features of North American slavery most responsible for producing personality adjustment, to perceive clearly the precise nature of the Elkins' analogy between slavery and German concentration camps, and to understand how the plantation system might have operated to produce "Sambos." What implications does Elkins' essay have for modern America? Are there similarities between the author's description of the "old inmates" and the traditional and still prevalent stereotype of the Negro in the United States? Finally, does "Sambo" still exist as a personality type; or have modern deviations from the system of white control and the rise of a new black assertiveness reversed the process of personality adjustment?

The literature on slavery is enormous and greatly varied. An excellent beginning point would be the outstanding collection of readings by Allen Weinstein and Frank O. Gatell, *American Negro Slavery: A Modern Reader** (1968). In addition to the works cited in this introduction, students may want to consult Winthrop D. Jordan's monumental *White Over Black: The Development of American Attitudes Toward the Negro, 1550–1812* (1968). Students should read the U. B. Phillips and Kenneth Stampp works referred to above, and they will enjoy two popular books by J. C. Furnas: *Goodbye to Uncle Tom** (1956) and *The Road to Harper's Ferry* (1959). A fictional account that deals sensitively with the development of slave personality is William Styron, *The Confessions of Nat Turner** (1967).

* Available in a paperback edition.

SLAVERY AND PERSONALITY
STANLEY ELKINS

PERSONALITY TYPES AND STEREOTYPES

An examination of American slavery, checked at certain critical points against a very different slave system, that of Latin America, reveals that a major key to many of the contrasts between them was an institutional key: The presence or absence of other powerful institutions in society made an immense difference in the character of slavery itself. In Latin America, the very tension and balance among three kinds of organizational concerns—church, crown, and plantation agriculture—prevented slavery from being carried by the planting class to its ultimate logic. For the slave, in terms of the space thus allowed for the development of men and women as moral beings, the result was an "open system": a system of contacts with free society through which ultimate absorption into that society could and did occur with great frequency. The rights of personality implicit in the ancient traditions of slavery and in the church's most venerable assumptions on the nature of the human soul were thus in a vital sense conserved, whereas to a staggering extent the very opposite was true in North American slavery. The latter system had developed virtually unchecked by institutions having anything like the power of their Latin counterparts; the legal structure which supported it, shaped only by the demands of a staple-raising capitalism, had defined with such nicety the slave's character as chattel that his character as a moral individual was left in the vaguest of legal obscurity. In this sense American slavery operated as a "closed" system—one in which, for the generality of slaves in their nature as men and women, *sub specie aeternitatis,* contacts with free society could occur only on the most narrowly circumscribed of terms. The next question is whether living within such a "closed system" might not have produced noticeable effects upon the slave's very personality. . . .

SOURCE. Stanley Elkins, *Slavery: A Problem in American Institutional and Intellectual Life,* Chicago: University of Chicago Press, 1959, pp. 81–82, 86–89, 102–115, 128–133. Copyright 1959 by the University of Chicago. Reprinted by permission of the University of Chicago Press and the author.

It will be assumed that there were elements in the very structure of the plantation system—its "closed" character—that could sustain infantilism as a normal feature of behavior. These elements, having less to do with "cruelty" per se than simply with the sanctions of authority, were effective and pervasive enough to require that such infantilism be characterized as something much more basic than mere "accommodation." It will be assumed that the sanctions of the system were in themselves sufficient to produce a recognizable personality type.

It should be understood that to identify a social type in this sense is still to generalize on a fairly crude level—and to insist for a limited purpose on the legitimacy of such generalizing is by no means to deny that, on more refined levels, a great profusion of individual types might have been observed in slave society. Nor need it be claimed that the "Sambo" type,[1] even in the relatively crude sense employed here, was a universal type. It was, however, a plantation type, and a plantation existence embraced well over half the slave population. Two kinds of material will be used in the effort to picture the mechanisms whereby this adjustment to absolute power—an adjustment whose end product included infantile features of behavior—may have been effected. One is drawn from the theoretical knowledge presently available in social psychology, and the other, in the form of an analogy, is derived from some of the data that have come out of the German concentration camps. It is recognized in most theory that social behavior is regulated in some general way by adjustment to symbols of authority—however diversely "authority" may be defined either in theory or in culture itself—and that such adjustment is closely related to the very formation of personality. A corollary would be, of course, that the more diverse those symbols of authority may be, the greater is the permissible variety of adjustment to them—and the wider the margin of individuality, consequently, in the development of the self. The question here has to do with the wideness or narrowness of that margin on the ante-bellum plantation.

The other body of material, involving an experience undergone by several million men and women in the concentration camps of our own time, contains certain items of relevance to the problem here being considered. The experience was analogous to that of slavery and was one in which

---

[1] Elkins delineates the characteristics of the "Sambo" type elsewhere in his book: "Sambo . . . was docile but irresponsible, loyal but lazy, humble but chronically given to lying and stealing; his behavior was full of infantile silliness and his talk inflated with childish exaggeration. His relationship with his master was one of utter dependence and childlike attachment: it was indeed this childlike quality that was the very key to his being." p. 82. (Eds.)

wide-scale instances of infantilization were observed. The material is sufficiently detailed, and sufficiently documented by men who not only took part in the experience itself but who were versed in the use of psychological theory for analyzing it, that the advantages of drawing upon such data for purposes of analogy seem to outweigh the possible risks.

The introduction of this second body of material must to a certain extent govern the theoretical strategy itself. It has been recognized both implicitly and explicitly that the psychic impact and effects of the concentration-camp experience were not anticipated in existing theory and that consequently such theory would require some major supplementation. It might be added, parenthetically, that almost any published discussion of this modern Inferno, no matter how learned, demonstrates how "theory," operating at such a level of shared human experience, tends to shed much of its technical trappings and to take on an almost literary quality. The experience showed, in any event, that infantile personality features could be induced in a relatively short time among large numbers of adult human beings coming from very diverse backgrounds. The particular strain which was thus placed upon prior theory consisted in the need to make room not only for the cultural and environmental sanctions that sustain personality (which in a sense Freudian theory already had) but also for a virtually unanticipated problem: actual change in the personality of masses of adults. It forced a reappraisal and new appreciation of how completely and effectively prior cultural sanctions for behavior and personality could be detached to make way for new and different sanctions, and of how adjustments could be made by individuals to a species of authority vastly different from any previously known. The revelation for theory was the process of detachment.

These cues, accordingly, will guide the argument on Negro slavery. Several million people were detached with a peculiar effectiveness from a great variety of cultural backgrounds in Africa—a detachment operating with infinitely more effectiveness upon those brought to North America than upon those who came to Latin America. It was achieved partly by the shock experience inherent in the very mode of procurement but more specifically by the type of authority-system to which they were introduced and to which they had to adjust for physical and psychic survival. The new adjustment, to absolute power in a closed system, involved infantilization, and the detachment was so complete that little trace of prior (and thus alternative) cultural sanctions for behavior and personality remained for the descendants of the first generation. For them, adjustment to clear and omnipresent authority could be more or less automatic—as much so, or as little, as it is for anyone whose adjustment to a social system begins at birth and to whom that system represents normality. We do not know how generally a full adjustment was made by the first generation of fresh slaves from Africa. But we do know—from a modern experience—that such an adjustment is possible, not only within the same generation but within two or three years. This proved possible for people in a full state of complex civilization, for men and women who were not black and not savages. . . .

SHOCK AND DETACHMENT

The thoroughness with which African Negroes coming to America were detached from prior cultural sanctions should thus be partly explainable by the very shock sequence inherent in the technique of procurement. But it took something more than this to produce "Sambo," and it is possible to overrate—or at least to overgeneralize—this shock sequence in the effort to explain what followed. A comparable experience was also undergone by slaves coming into Latin America, where very little that resembled our "Sambo" tradition would ever develop. We should also remember that, in either case, it was only the first generation that actually experienced these shocks. It could even be argued that the shock sequence is not an absolute necessity for explaining "Sambo" at all.

So whereas the Middle Passage and all that went with it must have been psychologically numbing, and should probably be regarded as a long thrust, at least, toward the end product, it has little meaning considered apart from what came later. It may be assumed that the process of detachment was completed—and, as it were, guaranteed—by the kind of "closed" authority-system into which the slave was introduced and to which he would have to adjust. At any rate, a test of this detachment and its thoroughness is virtually ready-made. Everyone who has looked into the problem of African cultural features surviving among New World Negroes agrees that the contrast between North America and Latin America is immense. In Brazil, survivals from African religion are not only to be encountered everywhere, but such carry-overs are so distinct that they may even be identified with particular tribal groups. "The Negro religions and cults," Arthur Ramos adds, "were not the only form of cultural expression which survived in Brazil. The number of folklore survivals is extremely large, the prolongation of social institutions, habits, practices and events from Africa." Fernando Ortiz, writing of Cuba in 1905, saw the African witchcraft cults flourishing on the island as a formidable social problem. One of our own anthropologists, on the other hand, despite much dedicated field work, has been put to great effort to prove that in North American Negro society any African cultural vestiges have survived at all.

ADJUSTMENT TO ABSOLUTE POWER
IN THE CONCENTRATION CAMP

A certain amount of the mellowness in Ulrich Phillips' picture of ante-bellum plantation life has of necessity been discredited by recent efforts not only to refocus attention upon the brutalities of the slave system but also to dispose once and for all of Phillips' assumptions about the slave as a racially inferior being. And yet it is important—particularly in view of the analogy about to be presented—to keep in mind that for all the system's cruelties there were still clear standards of patriarchal benevo-lence inherent in its human side, and that such standards were recognized as those of the best Southern families. This aspect, despite the most drastic changes of emphasis, should continue to guarantee for Phillips' view more than just a modicum of legitimacy; the patriarchal quality, whatever meas-ure of benevolence or lack of it one wants to impute to the regime, still holds a major key to its nature as a social system.

Introducing, therefore, certain elements of the German concentration-camp experience involves the risky business of trying to balance two necessities—emphasizing both the vast dissimilarities of the two regimes and the essentially limited purpose for which they are being brought to-gether, and at the same time justifying the use of the analogy in the first place. The point is perhaps best made by insisting on an order of classifi-cation. The American plantation was not even in the metaphorical sense a "concentration camp"; nor was it even "like" a concentration camp, to the extent that any standards comparable to those governing the camps might be imputed to any sector of American society, at any time; but it should at least be permissible to turn the thing around—to speak of the concentration camp as a special and highly perverted instance of human slavery. Doing so, moreover, should actually be of some assistance in the strategy, now universally sanctioned, of demonstrating how little the prod-ucts and consequences of slavery ever had to do with race. The only mass experience that Western people have had within recorded history compar-able in any way with Negro slavery was undergone in the nether world of Nazism. The concentration camp was not only a perverted slave system; it was also—what is less obvious but even more to the point—a perverted patriarchy.

The system of the concentration camps was expressly devised in the 1930's by high officials of the German government to function as an instrument of terror. The first groups detained in the camps consisted of prominent enemies of the Nazi regime; later, when these had mostly been eliminated, it was still felt necessary that the system be institutionalized and made into a standing weapon of intimidation—which required a continuing flow of incoming prisoners. The categories of eligible persons were greatly widened to include all real, fancied, or "potential" opposition to the state. They were often selected on capricious and random grounds, and together they formed a cross-section of society which was virtually complete: criminals, workers, businessmen, professional people, middle-class Jews, even members of the aristocracy. The teeming camps thus held all kinds—not only the scum of the underworld but also countless men and women of culture and refinement. During the war a specialized objective was added, that of exterminating the Jewish populations of subject countries, which required special mass-production methods of which the gas chambers and crematories of Auschwitz-Birkenau were outstanding examples. Yet the basic technique was everywhere and at all times the same: the deliberate infliction of various forms of torture upon the incoming prisoners in such a way as to break their resistance and make way for their degradation as individuals. These brutalities were not merely "permitted" or "encouraged"; they were prescribed. Duty in the camps was a mandatory phase in the training of SS guards, and it was here that particular efforts were made to overcome their scruples and to develop in them a capacity for relishing spectacles of pain and anguish.

The concentration camps and everything that took place in them were veiled in the utmost isolation and secrecy. Of course complete secrecy was impossible, and a continuing stream of rumors circulated among the population. At the same time so repellent was the nature of these stories that in their enormity they transcended the experience of nearly everyone who heard them; in self-protection it was somehow necessary to persuade oneself that they could not really be true. The results, therefore, contained elements of the diabolical. The undenied existence of the camps cast a shadow of nameless dread over the entire population; on the other hand the *individual* who actually became a prisoner in one of them was in most cases devastated with fright and utterly demoralized to discover that what was happening to *him* was not less, but rather far more terrible than anything he had imagined. The shock sequence of "procurement," therefore, together with the initial phases of the prisoner's introduction to camp life, is not without significance in assessing some of the psychic effects upon those who survived as long-term inmates.

The arrest was typically made at night, preferably late; this was standing Gestapo policy, designed to heighten the element of shock, terror, and unreality surrounding the arrest. After a day or so in the police jail came the next major shock, that of being transported to the camp itself. "This transportation into the camp, and the 'initiation' into it," writes Bruno Betelheim (an ex-inmate of Dachau and Buchenwald), "is often the first torture which the prisoner has ever experienced and is, as a rule, physically and psychologically the worst torture to which he will ever be exposed." It involved a planned series of brutalities inflicted by guards making repeated rounds through the train over a twelve- to thirty-six-hour period during which the prisoner was prevented from resting. If transported in cattle cars instead of passenger cars, the prisoners were sealed in, under conditions not dissimilar to those of the Middle Passage. Upon their arrival—if the camp was one in which mass exterminations were carried out—there might be sham ceremonies designed to reassure temporarily the exhausted prisoners, which meant that the fresh terrors in the offing would then strike them with redoubled impact. An SS officer might deliver an address, or a band might be playing popular tunes, and it would be in such a setting that the initial "selection" was made. The newcomers would file past an SS doctor who indicated, with a motion of the forefinger, whether they were to go to the left or to the right. To one side went those considered capable of heavy labor; to the other would go wide categories of "undesirables"; those in the latter group were being condemned to the gas chambers. Those who remained would undergo the formalities of "registration," full of indignities, which culminated in the marking of each prisoner with a number.

There were certain physical and psychological strains of camp life, especially debilitating in the early stages, which should be classed with the introductory shock sequence. There was a state of chronic hunger whose pressures were unusually effective in detaching prior scruples of all kinds; even the sexual instincts no longer functioned in the face of the drive for food. The man who at his pleasure could bestow or withhold food thus wielded, for that reason alone, abnormal power. Another strain at first was the demand for absolute obedience, the slightest deviation from which brought savage punishments. The prisoner had to ask permission—by no means granted as a matter of course—even to defecate. The power of the SS guard, as the prisoner was hourly reminded, was that of life and death over his body. A more exquisite form of pressure lay in the fact that the prisoner had never a moment of solitude: he no longer had a private existence; it was no longer possible, in any imaginable sense, for him to be an "individual."

Another factor having deep disintegrative effects upon the prisoner was the prospect of a limitless future in the camp. In the immediate sense this meant that he could no longer make plans for the future. But there would eventually be a subtler meaning: it made the break with the outside world a *real* break; in time the "real" life would become the life of the camp, the outside world an abstraction. Had it been a limited detention, whose end could be calculated, one's outside relationships—one's roles, one's very "personality"—might temporarily have been laid aside, to be reclaimed more or less intact at the end of the term. Here, however, the prisoner was faced with the apparent impossibility of his old roles or even his old personality ever having any future at all; it became more and more difficult to imagine himself resuming them. It was this that underlay the "egalitarianism" of the camps; old statuses had lost their meaning. A final strain, which must have been particularly acute for the newcomer, was the omnipresent threat of death and the very unpredictable suddenness with which death might strike. Quite aside from the periodic gas-chamber selections, the guards in their sports and caprices were at liberty to kill any prisoner any time.

In the face of all this, one might suppose that the very notion of an "adjustment" would be grotesque. The majority of those who entered the camps never came out again, but our concern here has to be with those who survived—an estimated 700,000 out of nearly eight million. For them, the regime must be considered not as a system of death but as a way of life. These survivors did make an adjustment of some sort to the system; it is they themselves who report it. After the initial shocks, what was the nature of the "normality" that emerged?

A dramatic species of psychic displacement seems to have occurred at the very outset. This experience, described as a kind of "splitting of personality," has been noted by most of the inmates who later wrote of their imprisonment. The very extremity of the initial tortures produced in the prisoner what actually amounted to a sense of detachment; these brutalities went so beyond his own experience that they became somehow incredible—they seemed to be happening no longer to him but almost to someone else. "[The author] has no doubt," writes Bruno Bettelheim, "that he was able to endure the transportation, and all that followed, because right from the beginning he became convinced that these horrible and degrading experiences somehow did not happen to 'him' as a subject, but only to 'him' as an object." This subject-object "split" appears to have served a double function: not only was it an immediate psychic defense mechanism against shock, but it also acted as the first thrust toward a new adjustment. This splitting-off of a special "self"—a self which endured the tortures but which was not the "real" self—also provided the first glimpse of a new personality which, being not "real," would not need to feel bound by the values which guided the individual in his former life. "The prisoners' feelings," according to Mr. Bettelheim, "could be summed up by the following sentence: 'What I am doing here, or what is happening to me, does not count at all; here everything is permissible as long and insofar as it contributes to helping me survive in the camp.' "

One part of the prisoner's being was thus, under sharp stress, brought to the crude realization that he must thenceforth be governed by an entire new set of standards in order to live. Mrs. Lingens-Reiner puts it bluntly: "Will you survive, or shall I? As soon as one sensed that this was at stake everyone turned egotist." ". . .I think it of primary importance," writes Dr. Cohen, "to take into account that the superego acquired new values in a concentration camp, so much at variance with those which the prisoner bore with him into camp that the latter faded." But then this acquisition of "new values" did not all take place immediately; it was not until some time after the most acute period of stress was over that the new, "unreal" self would become at last the "real" one.

"If you survive the first three months you will survive the next three years." Such was the formula transmitted from the old prisoners to the new ones, and its meaning lay in the fact that the first three months would generally determine a prisoner's capacity for survival and adaptation. "Be inconspicuous": this was the golden rule. The prisoner who called attention to himself, even in such trivial matters as the wearing of glasses, risked doom. Any show of bravado, any heroics, any kind of resistance condemned a man instantly. There were no rewards for martyrdom: not only did the martyr himself suffer, but mass punishments were wrecked upon his fellow inmates. To "be inconspicuous" required a special kind of alertness—almost an animal instinct—against the apathy which tended to follow the initial shocks. To give up the struggle for survival was to commit "passive suicide"; a careless mistake meant death. There were those, however, who did come through this phase and who managed an adjustment to the life of the camp. It was the striking contrasts between this group of two- and three-year veterans and the perpetual stream of newcomers which made it possible for men like Bettelheim and Cohen to speak of the "old prisoner" as a specific type.

The most immediate aspect of the old inmates' behavior which struck these observers was its *childlike* quality. "The prisoners developed types of behavior which are characteristic of infancy or early youth. Some of these behaviors developed slowly, others were immediately imposed on the prisoners and developed only in intensity as time went on." Such infantile behavior took innumerable forms. The inmates' sexual impotency brought about a disappearance of sexuality in their talk; instead, excretory functions occupied them endlessly. They lost many of the customary inhibitions as to soiling their beds and their persons. Their humor was shot with silliness and they giggled like children when one of them would expel wind. Their relationships were highly unstable. "Prisoners would, like early adolescents, fight one another tooth and nail . . . only to become close friends within a few minutes." Dishonesty became chronic. "Now they suddenly appeared to be pathological liars, to be unable to restrain themselves, to be unable to make objective evaluation, etc." "In hundreds of ways," writes Colaco Belmonte, "the soldier, and to an even greater extent the prisoner of war, is given to understand that he is a child. . . . Then dishonesty, mendacity, egotistic actions in order to obtain more food or to get out of scrapes reach full development, and theft becomes a veritable affliction of camp life." This was all true, according to Elie Cohen, in the concentration camp as well. Benedikt Kautsky observed such things in his own behavior: "I myself can declare that often I saw myself as I used to be in my school days, when by sly dodges and clever pretexts we avoided being found out, or could 'organize' something." Bruno Bettelheim remarks on the extravagance of the stories told by the prisoners to one another. "They were boastful, telling tales about what they had accomplished in their former lives, or how they succeeded in cheating foremen or guards, and how they sabotaged the work. Like children they felt not at all set back or ashamed when it became known that they had lied about the prowess."

This development of childlike behavior in the old inmates was the counterpart of something even more striking that was happening to them: *"Only very few of the prisoners escaped a more or less intensive identification with the SS."* As Mr. Bettelheim puts it: "A prisoner had reached the final stage of adjustment to the camp situation when he had changed his personality so as to accept as his own the values of the Gestapo." The Bettelheim study furnishes a catalogue of examples. The old prisoners came to share the attitudes of the SS toward the "unfit" prisoners; newcomers who behaved badly in the labor groups or who could not withstand the strain became a liability for the others, who were often instrumental in getting rid of them. Many old prisoners actually imitated the SS; they would sew and mend their uniforms in such a way as to make them look more like those of the SS—even though they risked punishment for it. "When asked why they did it, they admitted that they loved to look like . . . the guards." Some took great enjoyment in the fact that during roll call "they really had stood well at attention." There were cases of nonsensical rules, made by the guards, which the older prisoners would continue to observe and try to force on the others long after the SS had forgotten them. Even in the most abstract ideals of the SS, such as their intense German nationalism and anti-Semitism, were often absorbed by the old inmates—a phenomenon observed among the politically well-educated and even among the Jews themselves. The final quintessence of all this was seen in the "Kapo"—the prisoner who had been placed in a supervisory position over his fellow inmates. These creatures, many of them professional criminals, not only behaved with slavish servility to the SS, but the way in which they often outdid the SS in sheer brutality became one of the most durable features of the concentration-camp legend.

To all these men, reduced to complete and childish dependence upon their masters, the SS had actually become a father-symbol. "The SS man was all-powerful in the camp, he was the lord and master of the prisoner's life. As a cruel father he could, without fear of punishment, even kill the prisoner and as a gentle father he could scatter largesse and afford the prisoner his protection." The result, admits Dr. Cohen, was that "for all of us the SS was a father image. . . ." The closed system, in short, had become a kind of grotesque patriarchy.

The literature provides us with three remarkable tests of the profundity of the experience which these prisoners had undergone and the thoroughness of the changes which had been brought about in them. One is the fact that few cases of real resistance were ever recorded, even among prisoners going to their death.

With a few altogether insignificant exceptions, the prisoners, no matter in what form they were led to execution, whether singly, in groups, or in masses, never fought back! . . . there were thousands who had by no means relapsed into fatal apathy. Nevertheless, in mass liquidations they went to their death with open eyes, without assaulting the enemy in a final paroxysm, without a sign of fight. Is this not in conflict with human nature, as we know it?

Even upon liberation, when revenge against their tormentors at last became possible, mass uprisings very rarely occurred. "Even when the whole system was overthrown by the Allies," says David Rousset writing of Buchenwald, "nothing happened. . . . The American officer appointed to command of the camp was never called upon to cope with any inclination toward a popular movement. No such disposition existed."

A second test of the system's effectiveness was the relative scarcity of suicides in the camps. Though there were suicides, they tended to occur during the first days of internment, and only one mass suicide is known; it took place among a group of Jews at Mauthausen who leaped into a rock pit three days after their arrival. For the majority of prisoners the simplicity of the urge to survive made suicide, a complex matter of personal initiative and decision, out of the question. Yet they could, when commanded by their masters, go to their death without resistance.

The third test lies in the very absence, among the prisoners, of hatred toward the SS. This is probably the hardest of all to understand. Yet the burning spirit of rebellion which many of their liberators expected to find would have had to be supported by fierce and smoldering emotions; such emotions were not there. "It is remarkable," one observer notes, "how little hatred of their wardens is revealed in their stories." . . .

THREE THEORIES OF PERSONALITY

It is hoped that the very hideousness of a special example of slavery has not disqualified it as a test for certain features of a far milder and more benevolent form of slavery. But it should still be possible to say, with regard to the individuals who lived as slaves within the respective systems, that just as on one level there is every difference between a wretched childhood and a carefree one, there are, for other purposes, limited features which the one may be said to have shared with the other.

Both were closed systems from which all standards based on prior connections had been effectively detached. A working adjustment to either system required a childlike conformity, a limited choice of "significant others." Cruelty per se cannot be considered the primary key to this; of far greater importance was the simple "closedness" of the system, in which all lines of authority descended from the master and in which alternative social bases that might have supported alternative standards were systematically suppressed. The individual, consequently, for his very psychic security, had to picture his master in some way as the "good father," even when, as in the concentration camp, it made no sense at all. But why should it not have made sense for many a simple plantation Negro whose master did exhibit, in all the ways that could be expected, the features of the good father who was really "good"? If the concentration camp could produce in two or three years the results that it did, one wonders how much more pervasive must have been those attitudes, expectations, and values which had, certainly, their benevolent side and which were accepted and transmitted over generations.

For the Negro child, in particular, the plantation offered no really satisfactory father-image other than the master. The "real" father was virtually without authority over his child, since discipline, parental responsibility, and control of rewards and punishments all rested in other hands; the slave father could not even protect the mother of his children except by appealing directly to the master. Indeed, the mother's own role loomed far larger for the slave child than did that of the father. She controlled those few activities—household care, preparation of food, and rearing of children—that were left to the slave family. For that matter, the very etiquette of plantation life removed even the honorific attributes of fatherhood from the Negro male, who was addressed as "boy"—until, when the vigorous years of his prime were past, he was allowed to assume the title of "uncle."

From the master's viewpoint, slaves had been defined in law as property, and the master's power over his property must be absolute. But then this property was still human property. These slaves might never be quite as human as *he* was, but still there were certain standards that could be laid down for their behavior: obedience, fidelity, humility, docility, cheerfulness, and so on. Industry and diligence would of course be demanded, but a final element in the master's situation would undoubtedly qualify that expectation. Absolute power for him meant absolute dependency for the slave—the dependency not of the developing child but of the perpetual child. For the master, the role most aptly fitting such a relationship would naturally be that of the father. As a father he could be either harsh or kind, as he chose, but as a *wise* father he would have, we may suspect, a sense of the limits of his situation. He must be ready to cope with *all* the qualities of the child, exasperating as well as ingratiating. He might conceivably have to expect in this child— besides his loyalty, docility, humility, cheerfulness, and (under supervision) his diligence—such additional qualities as irresponsibility, playfulness, silliness, laziness, and (quite possibly) tendencies to lying and stealing. Should the entire prediction prove accurate, the result would be something resembling "Sambo."

The social and psychological sanctions of role-playing may in the last analysis prove to be the most satisfactory of the several approaches to Sambo, for, without doubt, of all the roles in American life that of Sambo was by far the most pervasive. The outlines of the role might be sketched in by crude necessity, but what of the finer shades? The sanctions against overstepping it were bleak enough, but the rewards— the sweet applause, as it were, for performing it with sincerity and feeling—were something to be appreciated on quite another level. The law, untuned to the deeper harmonies, could command the player to be present for the occasion, and the whip might even warn against his missing the grosser cues, but could those things really insure the performance that melted all hearts? Yet there was many and many a performance, and the audiences (whose standards were high) appear to have been for the most part well pleased. They were actually viewing their own masterpiece. Much labor had been lavished upon this chef d'oeuvre, the most genial resources of Southern society had been available for the work; touch after touch had been applied throughout the years, and the result—embodied not in the unfeeling law but in the richest layers of Southern lore—had been the product of an exquisitely rounded collective creativity. And indeed, in a sense that somehow transcended the merely ironic, it was a labor of love. "I love the simple and unadulterated slave, with his geniality, his mirth, his swagger, and his nonsense," wrote Edward Pollard. "I love to look upon his countenance shining with content and grease; I love to study his affectionate heart; I love to mark that peculiarity in him, which beneath all his buffoonery exhibits him as a creature of the tenderest sensibilities, mingling his joys and his sorrows with those of his master's home." Love, even on those terms, was surely no inconsequential reward.

But what were the terms? The Negro was to be a child forever. "The Negro . . . in his true nature, is always a boy, let him be ever so old. . . ." "He is . . . a dependent upon the white race; dependent for guidance and direction even to the procurement of his most indispensable necessaries. Apart from this protection he has the helplessness of a child —without foresight, without faculty of contrivance, without thrift of any kind." Not only was he a child; he was a happy child. Few Southern writers failed to describe with obvious fondness the bubbling gaiety of a plantation holiday or the perpetual good humor that seemed to mark the Negro character, the good humor of an everlasting childhood.

The role, of course, must have been rather harder for the earliest generations of slaves to learn. "Accommodation," according to John Dollard, "involves the renunciation of protest or aggression against undesirable conditions of life and the organization of the character so that protest does not appear, but acceptance does. It may come to pass in the end that the unwelcome force is idealized, that one identifies with it and takes it into the personality; it sometimes even happens that what is at first resented and feared is finally loved."

Might the process, on the other hand, be reversed? It is hard to imagine its being reversed overnight. The same role might still be played in the years after slavery—we are told that it was—and yet it was played to more vulgar audiences with cruder standards, who paid much less for what they saw. The lines might be repeated more and more mechanically, with less and less conviction; the incentives to perfection could become hazy and blurred, and the excellent old piece could degenerate over time into low farce. There could come a point, conceivably, with the old zest gone, that it was no longer worth the candle. The day might come at last when it dawned on a man's full waking consciousness that he had really grown up, that he was, after all, only playing a part.

CHAPTER 34

ATTITUDES TOWARD
SLAVERY: PRO AND CON

As suggested in the introduction to Chapter 33, Americans have long differed on the subject of slavery. Every student of American history is aware of the opposed views of slavery held by the abolitionists and by the Southern defenders of the institution, although the proslavery argument is often less dramatically and more briefly presented than the abolitionist crusade. Students often are almost wholly unaware of the changing attitudes toward slavery in the United States during the late eighteenth and early nineteenth centuries. Little has been published regarding the Southern liberal opposition to slavery until the 1830's (and its subsequent harsh suppression thereafter); and, likewise, only slight attention is paid to Southern and Northern support of the colonization project, to the debate on whether colonization was a practical or a racist solution to the "Negro problem," to Negro participation in the growing antislavery chorus, and to the hostility in the North to an antislavery offensive both before and after the 1830's.

In this essay Professor Clement Eaton concentrates on the less familiar aspects of American (particularly Southern) attitudes toward slavery, although he outlines the major developments in the abolitionist crusade. He discusses Southern liberal views in the Revolutionary era, Southern support for emancipation and for colonization of slaves, the antislavery activities of Southern Quakers, and the continuing but ineffective opposition to slavery by a small number of Southern liberals. However, Professor Eaton's major contribution is his tracing of the development of the elaborate proslavery argument, which he tags as "one of the great rationalizations that the human mind has conceived." Today, when students demand that people "tell it like it is," the story of how a society succumbed to well-conceived and well-articulated propaganda in a classic example of self-deception is particularly pertinent and relevant.

In reading this selection, students become aware of the dangers of simplistic approaches (for instance, the abolitionist and proslavery arguments) to matters as complex and deeply rooted as American Negro slavery. Specifically, the reader should concentrate on this set of questions: How do you explain the Southern tendency to apologize for slavery and the absence in the North of a strong antislavery movement before the 1830's? What does your answer suggest about the tendency among historians and others to view the North (past and present) as, in Robert Penn Warren's words, the "Treasury of Virtue"? Do you believe that the failure of the American colonization movement and its unpopularity among Negroes have any lessons to teach today, when the relationship between blacks in Africa and in the United States is in the process of definition? Finally, what were the major tenets and the significant effects of the proslavery argument? How does Eaton explain this great victory of "mass propoganda" over the mind of a society?

For an excellent treatment of both the proslavery argument and the antislavery movement, see Alice Felt Tyler, *Freedom's Ferment: Phases of American Social History to 1860** (1944). Louis Filler, *The Crusade Against Slavery** (1960), is a recent scholarly treatment of abolitionism, and Clement Eaton, *The Freedom-of-Thought Struggle in the Old South** (1964), concentrates on the general relationship of the defense of slavery to civil liberties. Avery Craven, *The Growth of Southern Nationalism* (1953), is also especially good on the South. Eric McKitrick's *Slavery Defended** (1963), and John L. Thomas, *Slavery Attacked** (1965), are collections of proslavery and antislavery arguments that are quite valuable.

CHANGING ATTITUDES TOWARD SLAVERY
CLEMENT EATON

The argument that Southerners evolved to justify the institution of slavery is one of the great rationalizations that the human mind has conceived. Like the philosophy of the Scholastics of the Middle Ages, it was a product of many minds, a remarkable intellectual achievement, finely articulated, and based on the far-reaching assumption that Negroes are innately inferior to whites. Before the rise of the proslavery argument large numbers of Southerners, especially in Virginia, did not subscribe to this faith in the rightfulness and permanence of slavery. There was, indeed, a time when Southerners in general apologized for the existence of human bondage in their region—a period extending from the American Revolution to the middle of the decade of the 1830's.

The development of a liberal attitude toward the emancipation of the slaves during this period was explained in part by economic considerations. The exhaustion of tobacco lands and the shift to wheat growing gave to the upper South a surplus of slaves. Slavery was becoming decidedly unprofitable in this region until the invention of the cotton gin in 1793 restored the value of slaves. Washington declared that he had twice as many working Negroes on his estate as could be profitably employed. John Randolph of Roanoke wittily described the economic burden of supporting slavery during this period by remarking that, instead of masters advertising for runaway slaves, the slaves would be advertising for the arrest of fugitive masters.

In addition to economic motives, the natural-rights philosophy of the Revolutionary period predisposed Southerners to a desire for gradual emancipation. One of the earliest persons in America to link the right of Negroes to freedom with the Declaration of Independence was the wealthy South Carolina merchant and planter Henry Laurens, who became president of the Continental Congress in 1777 and 1778. In writing to a son in England, a student of law there, on August 14, 1776, he ex-

SOURCE. Clement Eaton, *A History of the Old South,* New York: The Macmillan Company, 1966 (second edition), pp. 337–356. Copyright 1949, 1966 by The Macmillan Company. Reprinted by permission of The Macmillan Company and the author.

pressed his abhorence of slavery as an institution that was in conflict with the golden rule of Christianity. He was planning, therefore, he declared, to manumit some of slaves and cut off the entail on the remaining servants. But such a bold step, he anticipated, would encounter the opposition of the society in which he had been reared, and might cause his children to reproach him for having deprived them of so much of his estate.

A considerable number of Southerners freed their slaves by will during this period. George Washington set an example by emancipating his slaves by will, so did John Randolph of Roanoke later, and Jefferson was prevented from adopting a similar course by his financial bankruptcy. The wills of emancipation indicate that the liberal planters were disturbed by the inconsistency of holding slaves and subscribing to the equalitarian doctrines of the Declaration of Independence. Most of the prominent Virginia leaders, such as Patrick Henry, George Wythe, and James Madison, condemned slavery as an institution that should be eradicated from a free America. George Mason, the proprietor of beautiful *Gunston Hall* on the Potomac, and the master of 300 slaves, declared slavery to be an infernal school of tyranny for the future leaders of the South, which caused slaveholders to lose sight of "the Dignity of Man which the Hand of Nature had planted in us for great and useful purposes." Furthermore, the most enlightened planters, such as Jefferson, realized that slavery had a pernicious effect on the white population, degrading manual labor, encouraging pride and arrogance, and exposing children to the corrupting influence of licentious slaves.

The grave problem in emancipating slaves was what to do with the freedmen. Practically all Southerners believed that the process of liberation should be gradual and that the freedmen should be colonized. Professor St. George Tucker of William and Mary College proposed in 1796 a plan of gradual emancipation based on liberating all female slaves at birth. Several of the Southern states repealed their colonial laws forbidding the manumission of slaves except for meritorious services, adjudged by the governor and council or the county court, and now permitted emancipation of slaves provided the owner gave guarantees that the freedmen would not become public charges. The experiences of planters who emancipated their slaves, however, were frequently unfortunate. Robert Carter of *Nomini Hall* emancipated in 1791 more than 500 slaves by a plan of gradually freeing groups over a period of 20 years. He tried to rent small patches of land to them, but this practice was not an economic success. The neighbors protested that the freedmen stole and abused their freedom and corrupted the slaves. Ironically, two of Carter's sons, whom he had sent to the Baptist College in Rhode

Island (Brown Univerity) in order that they might escape the immoral influence of slavery, tried to frustrate the noble experiment of their father. When Carter liberated his slaves he was influenced by the teachings of the Baptist and Swedenborgian churches, but also, it is to be noted, the price of slaves had reached the bottom of a 20-year decline in this last decade of the eighteenth century.

The Quakers of the upper South were the principal Southern group that tried to do something practical about removing slavery. Those planters who apologized for slavery, as a rule, made no positive efforts toward eradicating the institution. Since slavery had not originated in their generation, they were willing for its removal to be left to the gradual operation of time. But the Quakers, who loathed the element of force in human relations, actively sought to dissolve the institution. One method they adopted was the use of antislavery propaganda through the press. In 1819 Elihu Embree founded *The Emancipator* at Jonesborough, Tennessee, the first antislavery newspaper in the South. Benjamin Lundy, a saddlemaker who worked in Wheeling, Virginia, established in 1821 the *Genius of Universal Emancipation* at Baltimore, Maryland. In North Carolina flourished the Quaker newspaper the *Greensborough Patriot,* which as late as 1834 championed the cause of freeing the slaves.

To agitate for the removal of slavery, the Quakers organized abolition societies. Since they were close to slavery, they were practical enough to urge the gradual rather than the immediate abolition of the peculiar institution and the amelioration of slavery by repealing the laws against the education of the slaves. Charles Osborn, a Quaker preacher born in Guilford County, North Carolina, was the pioneer organizer of manu-mission societies in Tennessee (1814–1816). After he had emigrated to Mount Pleasant, Ohio, he published an antislavery newspaper as early as 1817. By the year 1827 fifty antislavery societies, with a membership of 3,000, were reported in North Carolina, 25 in Tennessee, and eight in Virginia—a much greater number of antislavery societies than existed in the North. Besides this method of attacking the institution of slavery, the Quakers formed free produce societies, pledged not to use products of slave labor, and became operators in the Underground Railroad. The antislavery sentiment in the South was weakened greatly as many of the Quakers emigrated to free territory beyond the Ohio River in the first three decades of the nineteenth century. In 1834 the last meeting of the North Carolina Manumission Society was held at Marlborough, and in 1860 only about 1,500 Quakers were left in the state.

Most Southerners believed that if the slaves were freed and remained in the South a race conflict would follow and Southern civilization would be destroyed. Jefferson, Clay, Calhoun, and practically all Southern leaders believed that the removal of the freed Negro was indispensable to a scheme of emancipation. In 1817 the American Colonization Society was founded at Washington, D.C., to solve this problem by transporting freed Negroes to Africa. Liberals saw in the movement an encouragement to kindly masters to free their slaves, whereas conservatives supported the colonization society as a means of strengthening slavery by removing the objectionable free Negroes already present in the South. The society, composed largely of Southerners, elected Bushrod Washington, a nephew of the Revolutionary hero, as the first president. In 1819 agents were sent to the west coast of Africa and acquired from the native chiefs large areas for a colony, which was named Liberia, "land of freedom," and its capital, Monrovia, in honor of President Monroe. Not until 1847, however, did Liberia become a republic with a Negro as president.

The American Colonization Society failed miserably in its larger purposes. It was unable to persuade the Federal government to give financial support to its adventure. Sections of the colony were set aside for Negro groups from various Southern states, such as Mississippi in Liberia, Maryland in Liberia, and Kentucky in Liberia. Agents were sent throughout the South to obtain funds and emigrants, and a magazine, the *African Repository,* was published in Washington as a means of propaganda. In Mississippi the society raised approximately $100,000, and the legislature of Maryland pledged its credit to the amount of $200,000 to aid in the colonization of Maryland Negroes. Some benevolent planters provided in their wills for the emancipation of their slaves and transportation to Liberia. Despite the efforts of the American Colonization Society, a relatively small number of Negroes were sent to Africa, 571 from Mississippi, for example, and 1,363 from North Carolina. The Society transported a total of over 15,000 Negroes between 1821, when the first contingent was sent, and 1860. So prodigious was the Negro birth rate that this number was a pitiful fraction of the increase of black babies born in slavery during this period. Thus, colonization proved utterly impractical, not only because of the invincible birth rate of the Negro, but also because of the cost and difficulties of transportation to Africa. The American Colonization Society was branded by the abolitionists as a proslavery device to get rid of the free Negro, but after 1831 slaveholders gave it slight support.

The Southern Negroes themselves had no enthusiasm to return to their ancient home in the Dark Continent. Having become accustomed to American food, climate, and civilization, they dreaded going to a strange land. Many of those who did emigrate to Liberia died from tropical disease. The interior tribes were hostile and dangerous. Some of the Negroes who emigrated wrote discouraging reports to their masters and brethren in the United States—that the Negroes had farms usually no larger than five acres, which they tilled with the hoe without the aid of horses and mules, lived in bamboo houses in a wilderness, and "tell Uncle pleasant that we have snakes here 15 to 20 feet and can Swalow a man, Dear, or a hog with ease." Even to this day Liberia is not an attractive asylum to the American Negro. Sleeping sickness, malaria, hookworm, and dysentery make life precarious. The American Negroes and their descendants have enslaved the interior tribes until as late as 1930. Moreover, they developed the idea that manual labor was degrading and a caste system arose—the descendants of slaves were copying the patterns of the white masters.

In January, 1831, William Lloyd Garrison began the publication in Boston, Massachusetts, of *The Liberator,* the first newspaper in the United States devoted to *immediate* abolition of slavery. This New England printer and journalist was a natural agitator who espoused many other reforms besides the abolition of slavery. Always an enthusiast, Garrison reversed the life process of many men who are liberal in youth but become conservative in middle life; as a young man Garrison was a strong conservative, an ardent Federalist, a scorner of democracy, who was later to become a radical. He had worked for a short time with Benjamin Lundy on the latter's antislavery newspaper in Baltimore, but he knew practically nothing of slavery from observation or experience. Nevertheless, he and his followers indulged in the most bitter attacks against the moral character of the slaveholders in language so extreme that they injured their cause, both in the North and the South. The platform of *The Liberator* was immediate emancipation of the slaves without any compensation to slaveholders. Since the Federal Constitution sanctioned slavery, Garrison condemned it as a compact with Hell and urged his followers not to vote or have anything to do with this iniquitous government. Indeed, he made slavery a great moral issue, upon which he would neither speak with moderation nor accept compromise. In 1857 he and his followers held a Secession Convention at Worcester, Massachusetts, to advocate that the *Northern* states should secede from the union with slaveholders.

The abolition movement in the North was soon organized into very vocal and active societies. The New England Anti-Slavery Society was founded by Garrison in 1832, and during the next year the American Anti-Slavery Society was started in New York City. The New York group of abolitionists until recently has been neglected by historians, but it contained such effective agitators as the wealthy merchants Lewis and Arthur Tappan, William Jay, the son of Chief Justice John Jay, and

Gerrit Smith, the millionaire of Peterboro. The Northern abolitionists were profoundly influenced by the English antislavery crusade, which had led to the abolition of slavery in the British West Indies in 1833. From the reformers across the Atlantic were learned most of the techniques used in advancing the antislavery cause in the United States. The New England and New York societies published tons of lurid and fervid anti-slavery publications which they sent through the mails to leading men in the South. Although the New York group adopted as their slogan "immediate emancipation," they interpreted this term to mean that "measures looking toward ultimate emancipation be immediately begun"—which was a reasonable program that Jefferson might have approved. Southerners made the mistake of thinking of all abolitionists in terms of the extremists. But there were many type of abolitionists, some of them admirable persons. Indeed, there is a reaction today toward a much more favorable view of the abolitionists than was held before the present civil rights struggle developed.

Less spectacular than the eastern abolitionists, but tremendously influential, was the Ohio group, led by Theodore D. Weld. The publication of the correspondence of Weld, the Grimké sisters, and of James G. Birney, as well as modern studies of the abolition movement have called attention to this group. Although Garrison remained in Southern eyes the symbol of the antislavery movement, it is possible that the Midwestern band of abolitionists accomplished more effective work in converting Northerners to the cause than did the Garrisonians. This group arose out of the great religious revivals conducted in the decade of the 1820's by Charles Grandison Finney. These Western abolitionists applied the technique of religious revivals to the abolitionist crusade, emphasizing the point that Southern slavery was a moral sin. Weld compiled a terrible tract called *American Slavery As It Is,* composed of recitals of abnormal and sensational incidents of Southern slavery that he had culled from newspapers and antislavery literature. Oberlin College, Ohio, founded in 1833, became the center of Western abolitionists and also one of the first American colleges to admit Negro students.

The abolitionists started out by attacking the institution of Southern slavery, but soon they began a violent and indiscriminate denunciation of Southerners and their way of life. They built up a stereotype of slavery and of Southern society that modern historians have found difficult to dispel. Ignoring the handicaps of the Negro as a human being and the rural condition of the South, they blamed all the backwardness of the region, the illiteracy of the people, the exhaustion of the soil, and the lack of industrialization on slavery. The abolitionists painted the South as a land where masters made female slaves their concubines and enslaved their mulatto offspring. The whip never ceased to sear the flesh of their trembling bond servants, for Southerners were cruel and coarse in all the relations of life. The slave trade and the separation of families were a constant staple of their exaggeration. The existence of a substantial middle class of yeoman farmers in the South was ignored, and members of the nonslaveholding class were portrayed as debased creatures. In politics the Slave Power was envisaged as always on the aggressive, striving to pollute free soil and exclude honest laborers from the North from settling on the public domain. In short, the abolitionist propaganda was a black-and-white type of ideology. Their libels of Southern civilization naturally aroused the deepest resentment and intolerance below the Mason and Dixon line. Furthermore, with few exceptions, notably the millionaire abolitionist, Gerrit Smith, they did not advocate the only fair and practical step toward accomplishing their objective, namely, the use of Federal funds to aid in compensating the owners of slaves for their loss of property as a result of adopting the abolition program.

The abolition movement led to one of the most violent struggles in the history of the nation to suppress civil liberties. Some of the worst offenses against civil liberties occurred in the Northern border states during the decade of the 1830's. Here abolitionists were mobbed countless times and denied their constitutional rights of free speech and freedom of the press. In 1835 they discovered an effective means of advertising their cause by linking it to the cause of civil liberties. They began the strategy of presenting petitions to Congress to abolish slavery in the District of Columbia. Southern Congressmen maintained that such petitions should not be received, on the ground that Congress had no jurisdiction over domestic slavery. On the other hand, Northern Representatives, as a group, believed that the antislavery petitions should be received, for the freedom of petition, one of the sacred rights of a democracy, was involved in this issue. The chief presenter of the abolitionist petitions, which came in a flood in 1835–1837, was John Quincy Adams, the ex-President, who was now serving as a Congressman from Massachusetts. In this new role as the introducer of antislavery petitions, Adams maintained, perhaps insincerely, that he was not an abolitionist but was fighting for the freedom of petition. This bald-headed, irascible, and satirical New Englander enjoyed taunting the long-haired orators from the South, and his activities in Congress increased the atmosphere of bitter hatred between the sections. The South was not lacking in violent champions, chief of whom was

Henry A. Wise of Virginia, who replied to Adams in kind, and who led a secession of Southern Congressmen from the House of Representatives in 1836 when William Slade of Vermont caustically attacked Southern slavery.

On account of Southern pressure, the lower house of Congress in 1836 adopted the Gag Resolution. Introduced by Henry L. Pinckney of South Carolina, this resolution provided that the House of Representatives should technically receive the abolition petitions, but that such petitions should immediately be laid on the table, without referring them to a committee and without debate. The Gag Rule was continually renewed until it was repealed in December, 1844. The Gag Rule of 1840 read, "That no petition, memorial, resolution or other paper praying the abolition of slavery in the District of Columbia, or any State or Territory, or the slave trade between the States or Territories of the United States in which it now exists, shall be received by the House, or entertained in any way whatever." This rule was finally abandoned when Northern allies withdrew their support and when some Southerners realized that it was doing more harm than good to their cause. Southern chauvinists who insisted on a rigid rejection of abolitionist petitions in Congress did the South a great disservice by alienating the sympathy of many sincere lovers of democracy in the North who were indifferent to the reform of abolishing slavery.

Another flaming issue that involved civil liberties was the right of the abolitionists to use the Federal mails to forward their publications into the Southern states. In the summer of 1835 a mob in Charleston, South Carolina, supported by ex-Governor Robert Y. Hayne, entered the post office and destroyed several sacks of mail containing abolition literature. The whole South was aroused to the menace of the circulation of abolition publications below the Mason and Dixon line. It is an established fact that the abolition societies of the North had adopted a concerted plan in 1835 to flood the South with antislavery pamphlets, newspapers, and periodicals. These publications were addressed to white people to persuade them to abandon slavery, but Southerners believed that the abolitionists designed their publications to foment servile insurrections. A small minority of the slaves could read, some of whom were taught illegally by their masters. It was feared in the South that the lurid antislavery literature would fall into the hands of some brooding Nat Turner who would lead a slave revolt.

In a message to Congress, December, 1835, President Jackson recommended that Congress pass a law prohibiting the circulation through the mails in the Southern states of "incendiary publications intended to insti-

gate the slaves to insurrection." Calhoun was opposed to such a law that
would enhance the power of the Federal government. Instead, he introduced into the Senate early in 1836 a bill that would accomplish the
object of erecting a *cordon sanitaire* against the entry of abolition literature into the South. His bill would have made it illegal for Northern
postmasters to receive and forward abolition publications to those states
whose laws prohibited the circulation of such publications. This bill failed
to pass Congress, but a policy of Federal censorship of the mails, preventing the free circulation of abolition publications in the South, was adopted
unofficially by the Postal Department. With impunity, individual postmasters in the South refused to deliver abolition literature. A series of
Postmasters General, from the days of Amos Kendall in Jackson's cabinet
to Joseph Holt in Buchanan's cabinet, permitted this extralegal censorship
of the mails. No attempt was made to discriminate between literature that
was a rational discussion of the evils of slavery and that which comprised
incendiary appeals to violence. Thus, a genuine blockade was set up that
protected the minds of Southern whites from the contagion of abolitionist
arguments as well as kept the slaves from being inflamed to dissatisfaction
or revolt by emotional antislavery literature.

The development of an elaborate argument justifying slavery began in
the South before the rise of the abolition movement. South Carolina was
the cradle of the proslavery argument, which originated as early as 1789.
In the Palmetto State the economic and social humus was most suited to
the growth of an intellectual defense of slavery. South Carolina had inherited its type of slavery and its attitudes toward the Negro from the
rich sugar island of Barbados. Moreover, rice culture was peculiarly
adapted to the use of slave labor. The Negroes who worked in the rice
fields were blacker and closer to Africa than the slaves of the upper South.
Many of the Gullah Negroes, indeed, had been imported during the
period when the state reopened the African slave trade, and they needed
stricter control than the slaves of the upper South who had been
habituated to the white man's society for a considerable period of time.
Also the prevalence of malaria in the swampy, coastal region of South
Carolina and Georgia caused the wealthy planters to flee from the
miasmic lowlands during the spring and summer seasons, leaving the
blacks and the overseers to the tender mercies of disease-bearing mosquitoes. It was natural that South Carolina should have discarded the apolo-
getic tone of defending slavery, and that, in such leaders as Senator
William Smith, Whitemarsh B. Seabrook, and Doctor Thomas Cooper,
president of South Carolina College during the decade of the 1820's and
early 1830's, should have produced some of the early exponents of slavery

as a positive good. Later, in 1852, the great classic of slavery defense, *The Pro-Slavery Argument,* containing essays by the South Carolinians, William Gilmore Simms, Chancellor William Harper, James H. Hammond, and others, was published at Charleston. Was this elaborate rationalization of a great social evil motivated by the desire to convince nonslaveholders in order to preserve planter control, or was it evoked to quiet the conscience of Southern slaveholders, or was it a recognition of the moral power of world opinion?

In the upper South a pioneer in producing an able argument in defense of slavery was Thomas Roderick Dew. He was a young professor at William and Mary College who had recently returned from study in Germany. In 1832 he published a pamphlet, *Review of the Debates in the Virginia Legislature of 1831 and 1832,* in which he refuted arguments for the emancipation of the slaves made in the Virginia legislature following the Nat Turner revolt. Dew based his polemic partly upon his study of Aristotle, who had justified Greek slavery as a recognition of the natural inequality of man. In addition to deriving a justification of slavery from the order of nature, Dew pointed out that the Bible sanctioned this ancient institution. These philosophical arguments were buttressed by the economic argument, namely, the lucrative profits obtained from the internal slave trade and the immense property loss that emancipation would entail.

One of the most powerful arguments in the proslavery dialectic was the alleged support of the Bible, for the overwhelming majority of Southern people were firmly indoctrinated in a belief in the sacredness of the literal word of the Bible. The apologists of slavery drew their arguments chiefly from the Old Testament, which described a primitive society among the Jews in which the patriarchs held slaves. They also maintained that slavery was ordained by God as a punishment of Canaan, son of Ham, from whom, they affirmed without reliable evidence, the Negroes were descended. In the New Testament the defenders of slavery pointed to the advice that the Apostle Paul had given to a fugitive slave to return to his master as well as Christ's silence in regard to this contemporary institution.

The Baptist, Methodist, and Presbyterian churches in the South, which had condemned slavery in their pioneering period, gradually became proslavery as their congregations grew wealthier and more attached to the vested interests of Negro slavery. Leading Southern ministers, such as J. H. Thornwell, B. H. Palmer, Thornton Stringfellow, H. B. Bascom, and William A. Smith, wrote books and delivered sermons showing that the institution was approved by God. In 1844 the general conference of the Methodist Episcopal Church requested Bishop James O. Andrew of Georgia to cease his episcopal duties until he had disposed of his slaves acquired by a second marriage. This incident led to the separation of the Southern churches from the national organization and the formation at Louisville in 1845 of the Methodist Episcopal Church, South. During the same year, the Southern Baptists, incensed over the refusal of the national missions board to employ a slaveholder as a missionary, organized the "Southern Baptist Convention."

A myriad of arguments were adduced to show that slavery was needed as a social discipline. If the slaves were emancipated, the proslavery argument maintained, they would be uncontrollable, refusing to work, stealing, and committing other crimes. The example of the shiftless free Negro was brought forward as a solemn warning against a wholesale freeing of the blacks. The poor whites and mechanics feared the consequences of competition with hordes of emancipated Negroes. The massacre of the whites in Santo Domingo and the great decline of agriculture in Jamaica after emancipation were cited as proofs of the dangers of emancipation. Religious apologists maintained that the Negro had benefited tremendously from slavery, for he was transported from the barbarism of Africa and was civilized and Christianized in America.

Demagogues raised the bogey of social amalgamation if the slaves were freed and allowed to remain in the country. Deeply rooted in Southern psychology was a fear that the emancipation movement would break down the barriers set up to preserve a pure white race in the South. The census of 1860 clearly indicated that racial antipathy was not enough to prevent considerable miscegenation, for approximately 13 per cent of the Negroes in the United States were mulattoes. The presence of mixed blood among the free Negroes was striking, approximately three fourths of the free Negroes having an admixture of white blood. New Orleans was notorious for the concubinage system by which Creoles maintained mulatto and quadroon mistresses.

The emphasis in the Old South on the biological inferiority of the Negroes bears some resemblance to the Nazi ideology of race. Most Southerners took it for granted that the Negroes constituted a permanently subordinate race, inferior to the white man in intellect, character, and physiology—a childlike people. Dr. Josiah C. Nott, a physician of Mobile, Alabama, strengthened the ethnological argument justifying slavery by his theory of the plural origin of the races. In 1854, with the collaboration of the archaeologist, George R. Gliddon, he published his work *Types of Mankind,* in which he maintained that mankind did not have a common progenitor but that the Negro and the white man were separately created species. This theory, which denied the unity of man-kind, did not win general acceptance in the South, because it conflicted with the Biblical account of the origin of man. Reverend John Bachman of Charleston, South Carolina, confuted the pluralists in his volume *The Doctrine of the Unity of the Human Race* (1850), and Dr. John Wesley Monette of Mississippi wrote a manuscript entitled "The Causes of the Variety of the Complexion and Form of the Human Species," in which he affirmed the primitive unity of the races and explained racial differ-ences as caused by environment and climate. One of the degrading effects of the proslavery argument that has continued into our day is the emphasis on the basic inferiority of the Negro to the white man. Although it is impossible at the present time to determine conclusively whether Negroes as a group are equal in innate intelligence and personality to Caucasians, the advances that have been made within recent years in measuring human intelligence tend to throw doubt on the old allegation of the inherent inferiority of the Negro.

In the last decade of the ante-bellum period the proslavery argument acquired a militant leadership under Henry Hughes of Port Gibson, Mississippi, William J. Grayson, collector of the port of Charleston, and George Fitzhugh, a Virginia lawyer. Hughes wrote a defense of slavery in 1854 entitled *A Treatise on Sociology,* in which the word *sociology* was first used in the title of an American book. It is interesting to note that the proslavery argument led to pioneering efforts, however preju-diced, in developing the science of sociology. Hughes maintained that the advance of civilization in the South had essentially changed Southern slavery, although he produced no valid evidence for his conclusion. He held that slavery had advanced to warranteeism, which gave to the master a trusteeship over the slave and the ownership of the slave's labor only and not of his body. Convinced that slavery was a positive good, he was a strong advocate for reopening the African slave trade under an appren-ticeship system. In 1856 Grayson published a vigorous poem, "The Hireling and the Slave," defending Southern slavery as a paternal institu-tion far more humane than the wage slavery of New England.

Fitzhugh's important contribution was to focus attention on the evils of Northern capitalism, which the abolitionists had ignored in their zeal to reform their Southern brethren. He proclaimed "the failure" of free society, for the condition of the laboring class in the industrial states, he asserted, was worse than that of the Southern slave. Slavery, he main-tained, was a wholesome and natural institution for free *white* workers as well as black slaves. He predicted that the North would experience the diseased symptoms of competitive society prevalent in Europe, strikes, the rise of socialism, and the degradation of the laboring class, whereas the South with its harmonious labor system would become the conservative balance wheel of the nation. In the land of plantations the slaves were cared for during sickness, old age, and in times of economic depression, whereas in the North wages were barely enough to sustain life, child labor of the worst type prevailed, and the workers were ruthlessly exploited by capitalists in a form of wage slavery. These arguments were propagated in *De Bow's Review,* in Southern newspapers, and in two paradoxical books, *Sociology for the South; or, the Failure of Free Society* (1854), and *Cannibals All! or, Slaves Without Masters* (1857). Fitzhugh was not a deep or original thinker, deriving many of his ideas from Carlyle and the English reviews, but he was primarily "a propagandist of the Old South." He did a great deal of harm by exacerbating the relations between the North and the South.

One of the significant phases of the proslavery argument was the repudiation of the philosophy of liberalism. Senator James H. Hammond of South Carolina denounced the Declaration of Independence with its doctrine of the equality of men as a fallacious and glittering generalization. On the contrary, he declared that men were naturally unequal and that Negro slavery furnished "a mudsill" for a white democracy. Calhoun supported this argument in behalf of slavery, contending that the Southern slaves freed the master class from drudgery and allowed them the leisure to cultivate the art of politics and refined living. Thus Southern society was idealized as being a Greek democracy, resting on a base of slave labor. The Whig leader, Abel P. Upshur, and later Fitzhugh, flatly rejected the romantic liberalism of Thomas Jefferson in favor of a thoroughly conservative and aristocratic caste system. But they misrepresented public opinion in the South, which was devoted to a decentralized white democracy. When Fitzhugh proclaimed an irrespressible conflict between the free form of society and the slave system, which would be resolved by the extension of slavery into the North, he represented only a distinct minority of Southerners. By his extreme editorials in the Richmond press he furnished Seward and Lincoln with the ammunition for their famous speeches on "the irrepressible conflict" and "the House Divided" doctrine that alarmed Northern workers and small farmers.

Opposing the overwhelming propaganda of the proslavery argument was a small group of Southern liberals. No one will ever know the strength of the antislavery sentiment in the South during the period 1831–1861, whose finest representatives were persons of tender conscience or critical-minded individuals who were able to free themselves from traditional views. Probably most of the antislavery people were inarticulate because of prudence. The outspoken opponents of slavery, of whom records have been preserved, were chiefly members of the professional class, preachers, college professors, lawyers, and literary men. As regards geographical distribution, they were located principally in the upper South, where Negroes were decidedly less concentrated than in the deep South. . . .

The Southern liberals of the ante-bellum period were lonely individuals, free lances, who were, in general, denied the use of the press or the right of subjecting the Southern social system to sanative criticism. Almost without exception they spurned the epithet *abolitionist,* for they advocated a gradual process of emancipating the Negroes. Some of them were belated Jeffersonians, who believed in the dignity of man even if he wore a black skin. Perhaps the two most powerful impulses that led them to urge the removal of slavery were moral considerations, as evidenced by the considerable proportion of ministers in their ranks, and economic realism. . . .

The conviction of the Southern people in 1860 that slavery was justified (whereas their forefathers had thought it to be wrong) represents a striking victory of mass propaganda—one of the greatest in human history. It may be compared to the absolute victories of the Nazi and Communist propaganda in Germany and Russia. Such conquests over the mind of a society can occur only when the economic and social conditions are ripe for the acceptance of the propaganda. Such was the case of the Old South. These conditions were: (1) a strong economic involvement with the institution of slavery, (2) the fluctuating fear of a servile insurrection incited by the Northern abolition crusade, (3) a power struggle between the sections over the expansion of slavery, and (4) the rise of a fundamentalist type of religion that provided perhaps the strongest support for the preservation of an archaic institution of labor.

CHAPTER 35

THE ANTISLAVERY

MOVEMENT: THE

BLACK ABOLITIONISTS

Although American historians have become, in recent years, extremely interested in Negro history, much of the historical writing about Negroes tells us more about what whites have done to or for the black man than about what blacks themselves have done. In the history books, Negroes have seldom been at the center of historical action. A case in point is the history of the abolitionist movement. The movement clearly concerned Negroes, but most historical treatments emphasize the activities of white abolitionists, such as William Lloyd Garrison, Theodore Dwight Weld, and the Tappan brothers, on behalf of Negroes. Usually ignored, or slighted, is the active and important role that blacks played in the antislavery cause.

In this selection, Leon F. Litwack concentrates on the activities of black antislavery workers, placing them squarely in the mainstream of the abolitionist movement. Negroes not only demonstrated an appreciation of the work of antislavery leaders, but they also provided a black critique of the movement by attacking abolitionist apathy, prejudice, and lack of concern for the Northern Negro. But most important, Negroes participated

525

actively in the movement against slavery. Professor Litwack discusses the part played by Negroes in the post-Revolutionary emancipation movement, the use by Negroes of newspapers, tracts, orations, legislative petitions, and conventions in their antislavery activity, disagreements between white and black abolitionists, internal dissension among Negro leaders over policy and ideology and, finally, the emergence of a new militancy among Negro abolitionists.

A central theme in this selection is the prevalence of disagreement, between blacks and whites, and among Negroes themselves, over the best approach to the slavery problem. Is there a corresponding disagreement today among the leaders of the movement for the uplift of Negroes? On the other hand, despite the differences among black abolitionists, does it appear that their activities had the effect of moving the antislavery crusade toward a more militant approach—one which did not necessarily exclude the use of violence? Has the increased participation of Negroes in the modern movement tended to have the same effect? Finally, to what extent do you see parallels between the attitudes and positions of the black abolitionists and black leaders of the present day? In answering these questions, a perusal of Chapters 38 and 39 in Volume II will be helpful.

In addition to Litwack and Louis Filler, who is cited in the introduction to Chapter 34, the student will find useful Richard Bardolph, *The Negro Vanguard** (1959), Herbert Aptheker, *The Negro in the Abolitionist Movement* (1941), Carter G. Woodson, *The Mind of the Negro as Reflected in Letters Written during the Crisis, 1800-1860* (1926), and Herbert Aptheker, *A Documentary History of the Negro People in the United States** (1951). For use in comparing Negro participation in the abolition movement and in the modern Negro revolt, see Charles E. Silberman, *Crisis in Black and White** (1964).

ABOLITIONISM: WHITE AND BLACK
LEON F. LITWACK

The widely publicized activities of white antislavery workers and the commanding figures of William Lloyd Garrison, Wendell Phillips, and Theodore Weld have tended to obscure the important and active role of the Negro abolitionist. The antislavery movement was not solely a white man's movement. Through their own newspapers, conventions, tracts, orations, and legislative petitions, Negroes agitated for an end to southern bondage and northern repression. The white abolitionist encountered strong and often violent public opposition, but the Negro abolitionist risked even greater hostility, for his very presence on the antislavery platform challenged those popular notions which had stereotyped his people as passive, meek, and docile. As a common laborer, the Negro might be tolerated, even valued, for his services; as an antislavery agitator, he was frequently mobbed.

Negro abolitionism preceded by several years the appearance of Garrison and *The Liberator*. Encouraged by the post-Revolutionary emancipation movement, Negroes worked with sympathetic whites to remove the last traces of slavery in the North and to call for its abolition in the South. As early as 1797, four illegally manumitted North Carolina Negroes, who had fled to the North to escape re-enslavement, petitioned Congress to consider "our relief as a people." Three years later, a group of Philadelphia free Negroes appealed directly to Congress to revise the federal laws concerning the African trade and fugitive slaves and to adopt "such measures as shall in due course emancipate the whole of their brethren from their present situation." In addition to legislative petitions, meetings commemorating the abolition of the African slave trade or the end of slavery in a particular state afforded opportunities for such prominent Negro leaders as Peter Williams, Nathaniel Paul, William Hamilton, and Joseph Sidney to voice their sentiments on public issues. The organization of independent churches, Free African societies, Masonic lodges, and anti-

SOURCE. Leon F. Litwack, *North of Slavery: The Negro in the Free States, 1790-1860,* Chicago: University of Chicago Press, 1961, pp. 230-246. Copyright 1961 by University of Chicago Press. Reprinted by permission of University of Chicago Press and the author.

colonialization meetings further intensified a growing race consciousness and helped to arouse the Negro community in several areas to a more vigorous defense of its civil rights.

Four years before the publication of the first issue of *The Liberator,* two Negro leaders, John Russwurm and Samuel E. Cornish, launched the first Negro newspaper—*Freedom's Journal*—in an effort to disseminate useful ideas and information and to attract public attention to the plight of those still in bondage. In the first issue, the editors announced that Negroes had to plead their own cause: "Too long have others spoken for us. Too long has the publick been deceived by misrepresentations." During its two years of publication, *Freedom's Journal* featured articles on the evils of slavery and intemperance, the importance of education and the progress of Negro schools, literary and historical selections, moral lessons, information on the various Afro-American benevolent societies, and a discussion of colonization. Cornish subsequently withdrew from the partnership and established a short-lived newspaper, *The Rights of All,* and Russwurm abandoned his editorial duties to join the colonizationists.

Negro antislavery agitation took on a more aggressive tone in 1829 as David Walker, a Boston clothing dealer and local agent for *Freedom's Journal,* contributed a powerful tract to abolitionist literature—*Walker's Appeal, in Four Articles.* Addressing his sentiments to the "coloured citizens" of the world, but particularly to those of the United States, Walker described American Negroes as "the most degraded, wretched, and abject set of beings that ever lived since the world began." Indeed, he asked, "Can our condition be any worse?—Can it be more mean and abject? If there are any changes, will they not be for the better, though they may appear for the worst at first? Can they get us any lower? Where can they get us? They are afraid to treat us worse, for they know well, the day they do it they are gone."

In Walker's estimation, four major factors accounted for this wretched state of affairs: slavery, ignorance, "the preachers of Jesus Christ," and the African colonization movement. Consequently, Negroes had to strive for economic and educational improvement and resist the encroachments of the colonizationists. ("America is as much our country, as it is yours.") The southern Negro, on the other hand, faced an even greater challenge, for he had to strike directly and perhaps violently for his freedom as a natural right. Once that thrust for liberty had been made, Walker advised, "make sure work—do not trifle, for they will not trifle with you—they want us for their slaves, and think nothing of murdering us in order to subject us to that wretched condition—therefore, if there is an *attempt* made by us, kill or be killed." To prevent the outbreak of racial war,

Walker warned the white man, recognize the legal rights of Negroes. There can be no mistaking the alternative. "Remember, Americans, that we must and shall be free and enlightened as you are, will you wait until we shall, under God, obtain our liberty by the crushing arm of power? Will it not be dreadful for you? I speak Americans for your good. We must and shall be free I say, in spite of you . . . . And wo, wo, will be to you if we have to obtain our freedom by fighting."

Within a year after its publication, the apparent popularity—or notoriety—of Walker's pamphlet warranted a third edition. The often violent reaction to its contents and the mysterious death of the author in 1830 undoubtedly assisted its circulation. Indeed, it had already caused some consternation in the North, and it understandably created outright alarm in portions of the South. Already beset by a growing fear of slave uprisings, the South could not afford to tolerate the potentially explosive appeal of a Boston clothing dealer. The governor of North Carolina denounced it as "an open appeal to their [the slaves'] natural love of liberty . . . and throughout expressing sentiments totally subversive of all subordination in our slaves"; the mayor of Savannah wrote to the mayor of Boston requesting that Walker be arrested and punished, and Richmond's mayor reported that several copies of *Walker's Appeal* had been found in the possession of local free Negroes; the governors of Georgia and North Carolina submitted the pamphlet to their state legislatures for appropriate action; and the Virginia legislature held secret sessions to consider proper measures to prevent the pamphlet's circulation. Finally, four southern states—Georgia, North Carolina, Mississippi, and Louisiana—seized upon the pamphlet to enact severe restrictions to cope with such "seditious" propaganda.

The South was not alone in its critical reaction. Walker's medicine for the ills of American Negroes was too strong for many white abolitionists. "A more bold, daring, inflammatory publication, perhaps never issued from the press of any country," antislavery publisher Benjamin Lundy declared. "I can do no less than set the broadest seal of condemnation on it." Lundy's disciple, William Lloyd Garrison, had just launched his own career as an aggressive antislavery publicist and was more equivocal in his reaction. The editor of *The Liberator* found it difficult to reconcile his belief in nonresistance with his unconcealed admiration of Walker's courage and forthrightness. While deploring the circulation of this "most injudicious publication" and "its general spirit," Garrison admitted that it contained "many valuable truths and seasonable warnings."

The appearance of *The Liberator* in 1831 and the formation of the American Anti-Slavery Society two years later thus found northern Ne-

groes already engaged in a variety of abolitionist activities. In addition
to publishing a newspaper and several antislavery tracts, Negroes had
taken steps to co-ordinate their actions through annual national conventions. On September 15, 1830, delegates gathered in Philadelphia's Bethel
Church to launch the first in a series of such conventions. Against a background of increasing repressive legislation in the North, the delegates
adopted an address to the free Negro population, pointing out that their
present "forlorn and deplorable situation" demanded immediate action.
Where Negroes were subjected to constant harassment and denied even
the right of residence, the most recent and blatant case being Ohio, such
action would have to take the form of emigration to Canada. There, the
convention advised, Negroes could establish themselves "in a land where
the laws and prejudices of society will have no effect in retarding their
advancement to the summit of civil and religious improvement." Meanwhile, those Negroes who chose to remain in the United States would have
to utilize every legal means to improve their political and economic position. Before adjourning, the delegates called upon Negroes to establish
auxiliary societies and send delegates to the next annual convention.

Convening annually up to 1835 and periodically thereafter, the national
Negro conventions regularly condemned the American Colonization Society, deprecated segregation and "oppressive, unjust and unconstitutional"
legislation, stressed the importance of organization, education, temperance,
and economy, and set aside the Fourth of July as a day of "humiliation,
fasting and prayer" when Negroes would ask for divine intervention to
break "the shackles of slavery." Meanwhile, the formation of auxiliary
state organizations, temperance groups, moral-reform societies, and educational associations created an unprecedented amount of unity and activity among northern Negroes, developed new leadership, and contributed
mightily to the strength of the newly formed white antislavery societies.

While engaged in these independent activities, Negro abolitionists also
hailed the appearance of a new militancy among their white supporters;
they not only welcomed the publication of The Liberator but actually
outnumbered white subscribers in the early years. "It is a remarkable
fact," William Lloyd Garrison wrote in 1834, "that, of the whole number
of subscribers to the Liberator, only about one-fourth are white. The
paper, then, belongs emphatically to the people of color—it is their organ."
In addition to contributing articles and letters to the antislavery press,
Negroes also attended and addressed abolitionist conventions and, notwithstanding some opposition, served as members of the executive committee and board of managers of both the American Anti-Slavery Society
and its later rival, the American and Foreign Anti-Slavery Society.

Negro abolitionists did not confine their activities to the United States. In the 1840's and 1850's, several of them toured the British Isles to promote antislavery sentiment and raise money for abolitionist enterprises. Englishmen crowded into meeting halls to see and hear leading American Negroes tell of the plight of their people and their own experiences as slaves or freemen. Frederick Douglass, for example, described his years of bondage in the South; William G. Allen told of his narrow escape from an enraged northern mob after proposing to marry a white girl; William and Ellen Craft related their flight to freedom and their subsequent exile to avoid prosecution under the Fugitive Slave Act; and Henry Highland Garnet undoubtedly mentioned the mob that ejected him from a Connecticut boys' academy. While arousing their foreign audiences with these tales of slavery and racial violence, Negroes also found much to amaze them. "Here the colored man feels himself among friends, and not among enemies," one Negro "exile" wrote from England, "among a people who, when they treat him well, do it not in the patronizing (and, of course insulting) spirit, even of hundreds of the American abolitionists, but in a spirit rightly appreciative of the doctrine of human equality." For some of these Negro abolitionists, returning home must have been difficult. After extensive travels in England and Europe, for example, William Wells Brown came back to Philadelphia, only to find himself proscribed from the Chestnut Street omnibus on his first day home. "The omnibuses of Paris, Edinburgh, Glasgow, and Liverpool, had stopped to take me up," he recollected, "but what mattered that? My face was not white, my hair was not straight; and, therefore, I must be excluded from a seat in a third-rate American omnibus."

Both Negro and white abolitionists suffered from internal dissension over fundamental questions of policy and ideology. While the white antislavery societies split over the issues of political action, nonresistance, women's rights, disunion, and the nature of the Constitution, Negroes argued the merits of moral suasion and separate conventions. By 1835, the American Moral Reform Society, dominated largely by Philadelphia Negroes, replaced the regular convention movement. Dedicated to "improving the condition of mankind," the new organization urged Negroes to abandon the use of the terms "colored" and "African," to refrain from holding separate colored conventions, to integrate as fully as possible into white society, to support the equality of women, and to adopt the principles of peace, temperance, brotherly love, and nonresistance "under all circumstances." In adopting such a program, the moral reformers obviously allied themselves with the Garrisonians in the growing factional struggle within the antislavery movement.

The American Moral Reform Society found little support outside the Garrisonian strongholds of Philadelphia and Boston. Meanwhile, New York Negro leaders launched a new weekly newspaper, the *Colored American,* which expressed dismay over the growing split in abolitionist ranks and the activities of the moral reformers. Editor Samuel Cornish noted that the delegates to a recent moral-reform convention had impressed him as "vague, wild, indefinite and confused in their views." Only drastic reorganization and the adoption of a more vigorous program of action could possibly salvage the society. As for their efforts to substitute the term "oppressed Americans" for "colored people," Cornish called this sheer nonsense. "Oppressed Americans! *who are they?"* he asked. "Nonsense brethren!! You are COLORED AMERICANS. The indians are RED AMERICANS, and the white people are WHITE AMERICANS and *you are good as they, and they are no better than you."*

While scolding the moral reformers, the *Colored American* also engaged in a controversy with the pro-Garrison *National Anti-Slavery Standard* over the advisability of colored conventions. "We oppose all exclusive action on the part of the colored people," the *Standard* announced in June, 1840, "except where the clearest necessity demands it." As long as Negroes contented themselves with separate churches, schools, and conventions, public sentiment would remain unaltered. Instead, Negroes should join with their white friends to demand equal rights as men, not as colored persons, and thus confirm the abolitionists' contention that racial distinctions had no place in American society. The moral reformers enthusiastically indorsed the position of the *Standard.* Other Negro leaders, however, immediately condemned it and upheld the need for independent action. The abolitionists had done much for the Negro, Samuel R. Ward wrote to the editor of the *Standard,* but too many of them "best love the colored man at a distance" and refuse to admit or eradicate their own prejudices. In the meantime, Negroes had to meet and act for themselves.

Although the American Moral Reform Society had a short life, the split in white abolitionist ranks continued to undermine Negro unity. By 1840, Garrisonians shared the field of agitation with the American and Foreign Anti-Slavery Society and the Liberty party. New England and Philadelphia Negroes generally supported the American Anti-Slavery Society and condemned the critics of Garrison as unworthy of confidence or support. New York Negroes, on the other hand, not only dissociated themselves from the moral reformers but generally indorsed direct political action and contributed to the leadership and campaigns of the Liberty party. At one point, the *Colored American* attempted to restore some semblance of sanity and unity to abolitionists by urging them to avoid peripheral issues and petty bickering and get back to opposing slavery. "Why . . . make governments or anti-governments—resistance or non-resistance—women's rights or men's rights—Sabbaths or anti-Sabbaths, a bone of contention?" the Negro newspaper asked. "None of these should have any thing to do with our Anti-Slavery efforts. *They are neither parts nor parcels of that great and holy cause,* nor should they be intruded into its measures." Rather than promote abolitionist harmony, however, such sentiments, coupled with the editors' indorsement of political action and their refusal to censure Garrison's critics, induced some severe attacks and threats to cut off financial support from the paper. Defending their right to differ with Garrison on any issue and to adopt an independent editorial policy, the editors of the *Colored American* warned Negroes that as long as they permitted white abolitionists to act and think for them, "so long they will outwardly treat us as men, while in their hearts they still hold us as slaves."

In a desperate effort to retain their hold on the antislavery movement, Garrison and his associates made every effort to secure Negro support. In Boston and New Bedford, Negro meetings acclaimed Garrison as a "friend and benefactor" and indorsed his antislavery position. Already abandoned by many of his white followers, Garrison expressed gratification over such reactions. The opposition knew, he wrote, "that, so long as I retain the confidence of my colored friends, all of their machinations against me will prove abortive." Had Garrison known that his most important Negro ally, Frederick Douglass, was about to desert him, he would have had much less cause for optimism.

As late as September 4, 1849, Douglass had insisted that he was a loyal Garrisonian abolitionist, and there was little reason to doubt him. According to the tenets of that faith, he had excoriated the Constitution as "a most foul and bloody conspiracy" against the rights of three million slaves, had supported disunion as the most effective means to remove federal protection from the "peculiar institution," had belittled political action as futile and necessarily compromising, and had advocated moral persuasion rather than violence in attacking slavery. Nevertheless, signs of revolt became increasingly apparent. After founding the *North Star* in 1847 against the advice of his Boston friends and moving from New England to Rochester, Douglass carefully re-evaluated his position and listened to the arguments of various New York abolitionists who had already broken with Garrison. Before long, the Negro leader reached the conclusion that disunion would only place the slaves at the complete mercy of the South, that political action constituted "a legitimate and

powerful means for abolishing slavery," that southern bondage would probably have to expire in violence, and that the Constitution made no guarantees to slavery but in fact implied its eventual extinction. In May, 1851,
Douglass utilized the annual convention of the American Anti-Slavery
Society to proclaim his heresy publicly. "There is roguery somewhere,"
Garrison reputedly declared as he moved to strike the *North Star* from
the list of approved abolitionist publications. Douglass had gone over to
the enemy.

Although he voiced his new position on the lecture platform and in the
North Star, Douglass hoped to avert a complete break with Garrison. "I
stand in relation to him something like that of a child to a parent," he
wrote to Charles Sumner. Nevertheless, Garrisonian anxiety and alarm
soon changed to vigorous denunciation and even personal defamation.
The Liberator now placed Douglass' editorials in the section usually reserved for proslavery sentiments, and it charged that the Negro leader
had betrayed his former friends for the sake of financial gain, that he
possessed ambitions to become the spokesman of the colored race, and
that he had lost much of his moral fervor and influence. When Douglass
reduced the size of his newspaper, one Garrisonian gleefully wrote to an
English friend that the Negro editor "has the confidence of very few, the
respect . . . of none. Do what he may, we shall take no notice of him,
and I think his career—on professedly anti-slavery grounds—will soon
come to an end." Although Garrison generally allowed his followers to
deal editorially with the Negro upstart, he confided to friends that he
regarded Douglass as a malignant enemy, "thoroughly base and selfish,"
"destitute of every principle of honor, ungrateful to the last degree, and
malevolent in spirit," and unworthy of "respect, confidence, or countenance." Such was the thoroughness of the Garrison indictment.

Replying to his critics with equal bitterness, Douglass called them "vigilant enemies" and labeled their Negro followers as "practical enemies of
the colored people" and contemptible tools. The Garrisonians had first
attempted to silence his newspaper, he charged, and now they sought to
expel him from the antislavery fold as a dangerous heretic. "They talk
down there [Boston] just as if the Anti-Slavery Cause belonged to them
—and as if all Anti-Slavery ideas originated with them and that no man
has a right to 'peep or mutter' on the subject, who does not hold letters
patent from them." Douglass also sought to clarify his differences with
Garrison, but these appeared to be lost in the bitter editorial war. Before
long, Negroes in various parts of the country were meeting to discuss the
conflict and to choose sides. Chicago Negroes condemned Garrison's "vile
crusade" against "the voice of the colored people"; a Rhode Island convention hailed Douglass as "our acknowledged leader"; and an Ohio

gathering decisively defeated a proposal calling on Negroes to abstain from voting in those areas where they enjoyed the franchise. Meanwhile, Garrisonian Negro leaders reiterated the charges of *The Liberator* and claimed to speak for "all the true colored men in the country."

Efforts to reconcile the two antislavery leaders met with no success— only time could heal the deep wounds left by this useless and wasteful struggle. To many Negro and white abolitionists, the entire affair presented a rather sordid and dreary spectacle. "Where is this work of excommunication to end?" Harriet Beecher Stowe wrote Garrison. "Is there but one true anti-slavery church and all others infidels?—Who shall declare which it is." While the dispute helped to reduce the effectiveness of the antislavery movement, it also clearly demonstrated some of the weaknesses in Garrison's ideological and tactical position. Nonresistance, the rejection of political action, disunion, and a proslavery interpretation of the Constitution did not strike many abolitionists in the 1840's and 1850's as being either suitable or realistic weapons with which to abolish southern bondage or northern proscription. Indeed, the final triumph of Garrisonian objectives resulted almost entirely from the employment of strictly non-Garrisonian methods—political agitation and armed force.

Internal dissension hampered but did not stifle the independent activities of Negro abolitionists. Despite the Garrisonian antipathy to "complexional conventions," local and state organizations continued to meet in the 1840's, and several national conventions revived interstate co-operation. On August 15, 1843, Negroes from various state met in Buffalo to consider "their moral and political condition as American citizens." After several heated debates—which partly reflected the growing split in abolitionist ranks—the convention adopted a series of resolutions which denounced the American Colonization Society and the proslavery churches, indorsed the Liberty party, stressed the value of temperance, education, the mechanical arts, and agriculture, and attributed the plight of free Negroes—North and South—to the evils of slavery.

Henry Highland Garnet, a New York Negro leader, hoped to secure from the Buffalo delegates a more aggressive stand against slavery. Indicting the cruelties of southern bondage and praising as martyrs those Negroes who had led revolts for freedom, Garnet delivered a powerful plea to the slave population in tones reminiscent of David Walker's *Appeal*. "Brethren arise, arise!" he declared. "Strike for your lives and liberties. Now is the day and the hour. Let every slave throughout the land do this, and the days of slavery are numbered. You cannot be more oppressed than you have been—you cannot suffer greater cruelties than you have already. *Rather die freemen than live to be slaves*. Remember that you are FOUR MILLIONS! . . . Let your motto be resistance! resistance! RESISTANCE!" Although the Garrisonians had suffered a defeat on the issue of political action, they managed to steer the convention away from such a commitment to physical violence in overthrowing slavery. By a vote of nineteen to eighteen, the delegates refused to indorse Garnet's address. Instead, the convention affirmed its faith in the ultimate righteousness of human government and the abolition of slavery through its instrumentality. Relieved at this outcome, one Garrisonian intimated that Garnet, who had also been one of the first Negroes to indorse the Liberty party, had fallen under the influence of bad advisers. "If it has come to this," Garnet replied, "that I must think as you do, because you are an abolitionist, or be exterminated by your thunder, then I do not hesitate to say that your abolitionism is abject slavery."

Although the Buffalo delegates refused to indorse Garnet's address, its contents and the closeness of the convention vote indicated the emergence of a new militancy among Negro abolitionists. Six years later, Garnet's address and Walker's appeal appeared together in a published pamphlet—reportedly at the expense of an obscure New York farmer, John Brown. An Ohio Negro convention immediately ordered five hundred copies to be "gratuitously" circulated. That same year, a New York Negro editor reminded the governor and legislature of Louisiana that their recent expressions of sympathy for Hungarian rebels might be equally applicable to their own bondsmen. "Strike for your freedom now, at the suggestion of your enslavers," the editor wrote. "Make up your minds to die, rather than bequeath a state of slavery to your posterity."

By the end of the 1840's, the appeals of Garnet and Walker—once deemed too radical—received growing support in Negro conventions, newspapers, and antislavery tracts. Even Frederick Douglass, who had bitterly opposed Garnet's address, abandoned his previous conviction that moral persuasion and nonresistance alone could abolish slavery. While still a loyal Garrisonian, he created a "marked sensation" in 1849 when he told a Faneuil Hall audience that he would "welcome the intelligence to-morrow, should it come, that the slaves had risen in the South, and that the sable arms which had been engaged in beautifying and adorning the South were engaged in spreading death and devastation there." Three years later, Douglass told the national Free Soil party convention that the slaveholders had forfeited their right to live. The potential horrors of a slave insurrection should no longer be allowed to obstruct the path of freedom. "The slaveholder has been tried and sentenced," he declared in 1857. "He is training his own executioners." The following year, John Brown visited the Douglass home and remained there for several weeks, devoting most of his time to writing financial appeals for a yet unrevealed plan.

CHAPTER 36

THE GROWTH OF
SECTIONALISM

The development of disparate interests and political controversy among
the several sections of the United States has been one of the central
themes in the nation's history. Joel Silbey, in his pioneering study in
historical quantification, *The Shrine of Party: Congressional Behavior,
1841–1852,* introduces us to the ties that bound the West to the South,
and to the problems that arose from such a marriage. The tensions
probably are of more concern to the historian than are the unifying factors,
since the various points of incompatibility, when coupled with the explosive issue of slavery in the territories, led the West to forsake the
Southern alliance and to join with the North in the 1850's to oppose
proslavery ambitions and, in 1860, to elect Abraham Lincoln.

The factors that united the West and the South in the early period
included a mutual interest in transportation, expansion, and the maintenance of low tariffs on manufactures. In addition, large parts of the two
sections had a common ancestry—much of the Old Northwest, such as
Ohio, Indiana, and Illinois, had originally been settled by Piedmont
Southerners.

There are several factors leading to the later split that are not discussed
here. Probably the most important one was the Polk administration's
delay in acquiring the Oregon country. Influential leaders in the North-

537

west became convinced that the Southern-oriented administration of James K. Polk was dragging its feet in the diplomatic negotiations with Great Britain. This situation was particularly galling after Texas had been annexed in accord with the South's wishes. Later, when the United States compromised on the Oregon boundary but went to war with Mexico rather than compromise on the Texas boundary, the complaints became even more vocal. Acute dissatisfaction also resulted from the Tariff of 1846, which was passed by the votes of the two Senators from Texas. Among other things, it raised rates on Western imports such as coffee, although rates on items of high consumption in the South were kept low. These measures, coupled with Polk's veto of the Rivers and Harbors Bill (important to Great Lakes shippers) and, perhaps more important, with the shift of the transportation routes for Western products from southward down the Mississippi to eastward on the new railroad lines, set the stage for a new alignment of sections. This alignment was quite different from the one that John C. Calhoun had dreamed of and worked for so diligently.

In reading this chapter, students should concentrate on three basic questions. First, what were the factors tending to promote cooperation between South and West? Second, what were the factors operating to disrupt Southern-Western relations? Does the existence of disruptive forces in the 1840's justify the popular conclusion that the American people reacted, in their political activity in that decade, primarily in sectional terms? (It should be noted here that in this excerpt Professor Silbey is summarizing traditional interpretations. His own conclusions, presented elsewhere in his book, suggest that the cohesive power of the political parties was more powerful in the 1840's than were the divisive forces of sectionalism.)

For an early study of the role of sections in our country's history, see Frederick Jackson Turner, *The Significance of Sections in American History** (1932). The overall story of the political realignment of the sections is covered in Avery Craven, *The Coming of the Civil War** (second edition, 1957). For the role of John C. Calhoun in the attempt to bind the West to the South, see the biography by Charles Wiltse, especially the second volume, *John C. Calhoun, Sectionalist, 1840–1850* (1951). Also read C. B. Young's book, *David Wilmot: Free Soiler* (1924), and Eugene McCormac's *James K. Polk* (1922). They are old but still useful. J. C. N. Paul, *Rift in the Democracy** (1961), updates the story.

* Available in a paperback edition.

SECTIONAL CONFLICT IN AMERICAN POLITICS, 1840–1850

JOEL SILBEY

Despite the tumult of political party activity in the middle of the nineteenth century, most American historians have emphasized the overriding influence of sectionalism in American politics in that period. They have stressed the many geographic, economic, cultural, and psychological differences between the sections which, in their view, permitted sectional leaders to forge a unified sectional viewpoint in national affairs, particularly in periods of conflict between the regions of the United States. Several writers have pinpointed the 1840's as one such period of intense internal strain. Then, the Congressional controversy over expansion allegedly stimulated the disintegration of the national political parties into their sectional components. How this happened has been spelled out in some detail.

The South's basic sectional viewpoint apparently stemmed from the implications of its economic system. To understand the South, Professor Ulrich B. Phillips wrote, one must first consider the weather which was "the chief agency in making the South distinctive. It fostered the cultivation of the staple crops, which promoted the plantation system, which brought the importation of negroes, which not only gave rise to chattel slavery but created a lasting race problem. These led to controversy and regional rivalry for power, which produced apprehensive reactions and culminated in a stroke for independence."

The development of a Southern sectional viewpoint in national affairs thus began when men had utilized the existing weather conditions and resources to develop a Southern economic and social system. Sectional leaders then sought ways to maintain what had been built as well as to develop their section further.

SOURCE. Joel Silbey, *The Shrine of Party: Congressional Behavior 1841–1852*, Pittsburgh: The University of Pittsburgh Press, 1967, pp. 35–48. Copyright 1967 by the University of Pittsburgh Press. Reprinted by permission of the University of Pittsburgh Press and the author. Professor Silbey points out that the chapter used in this selection is a marshalling of arguments in favor of a position that the balance of the book finds seriously wanting.

By the 1840's the South was primarily an area of specialized agricultural production. Although there had been a fairly diversified crop system before the 1820's, major Southern production was later concentrated in several staple crops. The leading staple was cotton; tobacco, rice, and sugar were less important. Historians and economists have repeatedly stressed the importance of cotton production because of its major function both in the South and in the nation as a whole. From the 1790's onward, Southerners had devoted more land to the crop and increased their production from 17,500 bales of cotton each year in the 1790's to 1.9 million bales in the 1840's. Several things contributed to this constant expansion: markets, the profitability of cotton investments, the availability of land, the ease of cultivation, and the efficient utilization of a cheap labor force of Negro slaves. Southerners raised cotton on both large plantations and small, nonslave farms. Although many Southerners grew other crops, cotton producing was their most important endeavor. As Paul Gates has pointed out, nothing "was permitted to interfere with producing cotton."

Outside the areas in which cotton could be grown, other farmers also engaged in some form of staple agriculture. Here, too, Negro slaves were the major work force. In the border states commercial farmers produced tobacco; along the Gulf coast they raised sugar; in other areas farmers grew rice and hemp for market. There were, in addition, many varieties of noncommercial agriculture in the South. But in terms of wealth and economic leadership staple agriculture dominated the Southern economy of the 1840's, with cotton production the most important facet of the system. At this time most Southerners showed great antipathy and animosity towards other economic activities, as they exalted their own agricultural way of life. In the South there was an almost complete lack of manufacturing development and only a primitive commercial enterprise. As long as staple agriculture remained profitable, Southern leaders had few incentives or opportunities to break the mold of their section's economic life.

The economic life of the Old Northwest during the same period was both superficially similar to and different from that of the South. The West, like the South, was primarily an agricultural region. Instead of cotton, Northwestern farmers produced mainly wheat, corn, and other provisions. Despite their later development, the various states of the Old Northwest had already outdistanced the leading Eastern centers in wheat and corn production and, in the Ohio Valley, farmers were developing a stock-raising industry. In general, Westerners engaged in a more diversified agriculture than did Southerners, with a work force composed almost exclusively of yeomen farmers. By the 1840's, however, wheat production was becoming predominant in the Ohio Valley. As in the South, moreover, few Westerners engaged in manufacturing and commerce.

Although Western agriculture was more diversified than was Southern, both based their growth on staple crop production. Farmers in both sections shared the idea of producing a marketable surplus and developing a commercial agriculture. Although the farmers needed capital, cheap transportation, and markets for such development, it was their quest for markets which is particularly relevant to the impact of sectional forces on political activity in the 1840's.

At first, in the 1790's, cotton farmers did not have a developed market for their cotton in the United States because of the dearth of textile mills in the country. Their major markets were in England. Although the Northeast had rapidly industrialized in the years after 1790 and had developed a textile manufacturing industry, cotton producers continued to sell most of their raw cotton in England. By the 1840's cotton growers sold 64 per cent of their crop to English manufacturers and only 29 per cent to Northern factories. The English demand for Southern cotton steadily increased, assuring the cotton producer of a large, steady, available market.

The cotton marketing pattern profoundly affected Western development. As Southerners devoted more and more of their energies to cotton production for the expanding English market they had to import foodstuffs from wherever they could. This gave the Western wheat farmers their great opportunity and they supplied the South with the needed provisions. By the 1840's, Western farmers were the main suppliers of food to the South. Western wheat producers thus had a large and expanding home market.

Western wheat production in the Ohio Valley developed so intensively to supply this market that by the 1840's production outstripped consumption. In 1846, Senator Sidney Breese of Illinois called attention to this overproduction when he asserted that ten counties of Illinois could supply the entire home market as it then stood. The West needed and wanted the "market of the world" for its foodstuffs. The Western farmers' needs were especially acute because of the drop in wheat prices during the depression after 1837. Wheat prices fell from an average of $1.92 per bushel in 1838 to $1.05 per bushel in 1840. At the same time, Southern cotton prices fell precipitously, prompting many Southerners to consider growing grain again instead of cotton. Westerners were frightened by their overproduction and their failing markets. Some of them turned towards foreign markets as a means of selling their surplus and keeping domestic prices up. Increasingly, during the 1840's, Westerners, like Southerners, sought markets outside of the United States for their surplus products.

In addition to markets, both Westerners and Southerners were troubled by the lack of adequate and cheap transportation facilities. Americans had always relied upon the country's waterways to meet their transit needs. Whether by the flatboats of the 1820's or the steamboats in their "golden age" in the 1850's, farmers moved their goods primarily on the rivers throughout the ante bellum era. Southern cotton producers were fortunate because their navigable rivers ran to the Atlantic Ocean and the Gulf of Mexico, where their cotton was picked up by waiting sailing ships. In the Old Northwest farmers transported their goods down the Ohio and Mississippi Rivers and their numerous tributaries. Although Americans had tried other means of transportation, rivers and their feeder canals were still the major source of cheap transportation in both the South and West. These transportation patterns profoundly affected sectional relationships during the first half of the nineteenth century.

Thus far we have discussed briefly how Southerners and Westerners utilized the climate and geographic resources of their sections. However, we have to know more before we can understand sectional influences in American life. The two sections' similarities and differences did not create political sectionalism. Rather, it was how men viewed their section's needs, based on its resources, and thus developed sectional programs, that is important for our purposes.

Because of the way each section formed, both Southerners and Westerners developed a series of attitudes, demands, needs, and desires which their leaders brought into the political arena. The Southern grower's pattern of life, for example, obviously conditioned his attitudes. The Southerner believed that cotton and other staple crops were grown best on large-scale economic units, where he could use the cheap labor of Negro slaves. Southerners practiced extensive rather than intensive agriculture. They had plenty of cheap land available for cotton planting and it was easier for them to move to newer lands when their old land was exhausted than to learn more efficient techniques of cultivating land. It was easier for them to move even if the new lands were beyond the borders of the United States. Thus, the Southern planter was little concerned with the scientific aspects of agriculture, so long as there was cheap labor, available land, and a cotton market.

Whether or not the Southerner's approach was actually the best or most efficient is irrelevant. Most Southerners seemed to accept these ideas, even those Southerners who were unable to practice this type of production. Many Southern leaders wanted to protect their agricultural practices from any criticism or interference, especially from non-Southerners. They wished to remain free to grow cotton wherever possible using the labor force they considered best suited to it. Although there was little interference from either government or voluntary reform groups at this time, Southern feeling on this point can be gauged from their hypersensitive reactions to abolitionist literature and agitation.

Moreover, as we have seen, the South had become a specialized economic area by the 1840's. Southern farmers believed cotton was king and little else was important. This placed Southerners in a particular sectional position. As we have already noted, cotton farmers had to import foodstuffs and manufactured goods from outside in order to live. They wanted to pay as low prices as possible for the things they had to purchase and wanted to buy goods wherever they were cheapest. In the 1840's English manufactured goods were cheaper than Northern. Southerners did not want a tariff which protected the manufacturers of New England by raising the price of English manufactured goods sent to the South. To the Southern leaders, such a tariff was an unfair tax on their section.

Northern-Southern differences on the tariff were sharpened during the early 1840's. In the aftermath of the Panic of 1837, cotton prices fell to their lowest levels since the beginning of the nineteenth century. Southern planters found that they had insufficient capital to purchase necessary goods. Yet at the same time prices of Northern manufactured goods, cushioned by the tariff, did not fall as drastically as had cotton. As a result, Southerners found it more difficult to buy the necessities of life.

The economic situation grew worse when the fixed costs of cotton production and trade did not fall in proportion to cotton prices. Southern cotton growers found themselves increasingly in debt to Northern capitalists who controlled the credit and transportation facilities needed to carry on the cotton trade.

The Southern planters' sale of their marketable crops also affected their tariff position. The Northern textile industry absorbed just under one-quarter of the Southern cotton marketed during the 1840's. Southerners still had to rely on English textile manufacturers to buy most of the available Southern cotton. Although there were promises of a future home market for raw cotton, they were still too unsubstantial for the present needs of Southern planters. Therefore they considered it imperative that nothing should interfere with the disposal of their surplus cotton in foreign markets. They demanded a lower tariff on English imports, thinking that if England could sell her goods in the United States, her manufacturers would be both more likely and more able to purchase Southern cotton. If, on the other hand, the tariff discriminated against English goods, Southern cotton planters would be the sufferers. They would neither be able to buy English goods nor sell their crop to England. Southern farmers therefore advocated a nonprotective, nondiscriminatory tariff.

Southern leaders also wanted to reduce the federal government's need for revenue so that customs duties could be lowered without endangering normal government operations. They warned that the federal government should not undertake excessive responsibilities which would raise expenditures. For instance, the federal government should not build or improve internal transportation facilities. To further bolster its revenue, the government should raise, and keep, as much money as it could from other sources such as the sale of federal lands.

The people of the Old Northwest agreed with much of this program in the late 1830's and early 1840's. They wanted to expand the foreign market for their surplus wheat. And, like the South, the Old Northwest was an economically dependent area. Westerners had to import from the East those manufactured and nonagricultural necessities which they did not produce themselves. Therefore, Western farmers were continually in debt to Eastern manufacturers. They could alleviate this by buying cheaper foreign goods. The idea of a low tariff was thus as appealing to Western wheat producers as it was to Southern cotton growers.

Western policy makers also advocated less government spending as part of their low tariff policy. They were basically satisfied with their river transportation, and did not desire federal expenditures in that area. Although their waterways needed some improvement and maintenance, they were content during the 1830's to let the states undertake this work. They felt that such expenditures would not affect the tariff.

Commercial agriculturalists, whether Southern or Western, agreed on another policy during the 1840's. Economists have characterized the agricultural practices of both sections as wasteful and destructive to the soil. The farmers of the era felt that intensive, scientific farming was unnecessary with so much land available. When older land wore out or farmers wanted to expand their holdings, there was still much useful agricultural land available within the United States. Farmers realized that even when they exhausted the available American land, good, undeveloped land remained on the American continent. Although the expansive urge of the mid-nineteenth century had various sources, many

Southern and Western farmers considered the major reason for expansion to be their need for more farm land. Their land desires were to have important consequences as the depression ended and economic expansion began again.

In contrast to the South and Old Northwest, the Northeast was not an export-agriculture area. Rather, the major thrust of that area's economy was in commerce and manufacturing. The manufacturers particularly, according to some historians, were the people who gave the North a different and conflicting sectional outlook from either the South or the West. Since they imported foodstuffs and raw cotton into the region, the New England manufacturers had an interest in keeping the prices of these goods low. More importantly, as we have noted, it was central to their concern to keep foreign manufactured goods out of the United States through the protective tariff.

The slavery-abolition movement also centered in New England in the early 1830's and apparently gained anti-Southern converts during the depression of 1837. Fears of unfair Southern political power directed against the protective tariff also seemed to condition Northeastern minds against territorial expansion in the early 1840's. Sectional psychological factors played a role here as the moral certainty of New England Puritanism gave additional force to the anti-Southern set of mind in the region.

We can infer from all of the above that sectional influences could have shaped public policy demands in the 1840's. We still have to discover, however, how men articulated sectional desires in the political arena. One way could have been through party politics. Sectional leaders may have controlled one of the parties and used it to promote their section's desires. For example, Professor Henry Clyde Hubbart has characterized the Democratic party in this period as responsive to Southern and Western direction. But both parties were strong in each section, an unlikely situation if one party was thought to be the spokesman for just one section.

Perhaps the best way for political leaders to express sectional demands was not through parties but by first unifying their section behind a particular program and then seeking political aid from another section. Southerners and Westerners, it appeared, could operate together due to reciprocal economic interests. The West depended both on Southern markets and Southern waterways and ports for its economic livelihood. The South needed Western foodstuffs. With such an interrelationship it appears logical that the political leaders of the two sections would forge an alliance to secure legislation. As early as 1820 Spencer Roane of Virginia called upon Southerners and Westerners to work together because their two sections had identical interests. Such intersectional co-operation would, he said, make the United States a great nation. Twenty years later S. H. Anderson of Illinois expressed the same idea in a letter to the voters of his Congressional district. Anderson emphasized the common interests of the two sections and suggested that what was best for the South was also best for Illinois. Despite such pronouncements, neither Roane nor Anderson led the movement to forge the two sections together. Most historians have identified John C. Calhoun of South Carolina as the leader of the intersectional movement. Whether his motive was Southern security or personal power, Calhoun's actions during the early 1840's demonstrated his desire to align the policy demands of the two sections.

An astute politician, Calhoun knew that a legislative quid-pro-quo would have to be worked out between the two sections until permanent bonds of friendship were solidified. He noted that occasionally the West and the South differed over public policy. However, he saw several ways to overcome these differences. In the short run, Westerners had to be convinced that they needed a low tariff before all other legislation. At the same time, the South would help the West get certain other legislative needs. In the long run, since the West's transportation dependence upon the South was the best intersectional tie existing, this had to be greatly improved. With this in mind, Calhoun, as the leader of the South, set out to work with the West.

Internal waterways were the main transportation route between South and West, but by the 1840's railroads were a new element in the situation. From the time of the first successful run of the steam locomotive in the United States in the late 1820's over three thousand miles of rails had been laid, most of these in the Eastern states. These rail lines penetrated areas where there were no natural waterways and were built across such barriers as the Appalachian Mountains. Eastern-Western railroads could profoundly affect Southern-Western trade patterns since New York was nearer to Europe than was New Orleans. Southern leaders could counter the East's advantage only if they built their own rail lines, thus strengthening the existing trade routes before the new East-West lines were completed. From the 1830's onward both Southern and Western leaders planned projects to accomplish this aim, including a railroad line between Charleston, South Carolina, and the Mississippi River. Other projects were planned and executed. The most ambitious of these was the Illinois Central Railroad route, which ultimately stretched from Chicago to Mobile, Alabama. Other plans to improve the trade relations between South and West would have connected Cincinnati and Louisville with the South or built North-South lines along rivers.

Southern leaders realized that railroad building and the economic benefits from such lines were long-term undertakings. In the meantime the South and West would be brought closer in other ways. Westerners were concerned about federal land policy. They wanted more liberal legislation to aid Western entrepreneurs. Since the federal government owned the land, only Congress could liberalize land policy. Calhoun, according to both his biographers and historians of land policy, hoped to support Western demands for liberal land laws with Southern votes. Of course, his actions here could bring him into conflict with the Southern tariff position. Many Southerners wanted the public land revenues to be high so that there would be no need to raise customs duties. But Calhoun felt that if the South aided Western land desires, it would gain more than it lost.

Perhaps nothing, however, was potentially more destructive to Southern-Western relations than the issue of internal improvements. As the 1840's opened this matter was taking on new importance. As long as Westerners had settled along navigable rivers, they had had few transportation problems. During the land boom of the 1830's, however, settlers had filled in areas beyond the rivers. By the 1840's these people wanted to send their surplus crops to market but were handicapped by poor transportation facilities. At first, as we have noted, they turned to the state governments for help. Many of the states responded by building canals and improving rivers, but these projects ended with the Panic of 1837 and the chaos of near state bankruptcy. From then on, only the federal government could undertake the needed transportation improvements. The problem was aggravated because even existing river facilities needed improvement for full use.

The Western need for internal improvements embarrassed Southern leaders. Southern cotton planters traditionally had opposed federal expenditures for roads, canals, and rivers. They didn't particularly need internal improvements themselves, and they feared that such federal spending would seriously affect the tariff. Yet Western demands were becoming more insistent in the early 1840's. If the two sections were to maintain relations, the leaders of both would have to work out some sort of accommodation. Spokesmen in both sections called a "commercial convention" of the Southern and Western states to meet at Memphis, Tennessee, in November, 1845. John C. Calhoun presided over the meeting.

The result of this convention was a memorial to Congress calling for the federal government to undertake extensive improvements of the Mississippi River. Unfortunately for the plans and hopes of sectional

leaders, however, too many people opposed the memorial and little resulted from it. Nevertheless, despite its ultimate failure, the Memphis
Convention was important because of the conscious attempts of leaders
to forge permanent Southern-Western sectional ties.

Southerners and Westerners also agreed that the acquisition of new
lands by the United States was mutually beneficial. Furthermore, although it was for different reasons, people in both sections feared foreign
presence on American soil. Both Southerners and Westerners forcefully
asserted their interest in expansion. On the other hand, many Eastern
leaders opposed these aggressively acquisitive desires. As a result, when
expansion became an important issue after 1843, Southerners and Westerners seemed to have found another area in which they could cooperate.

Southern-Western cooperation was not confined to common economic
policy needs. The two sections also united against policies advocated
by Eastern political leaders. Frederick Jackson Turner has shown that
rivalry between East and West was as old as the country. During the
1830's and 1840's, for example, Western leaders violently reacted to
alleged Eastern domination and unfairness to their section in national
politics. One major Western complaint was the large size of new states.
Eastern states were generally quite small in area. The smallest, Rhode
Island, was only 1200 square miles and many of the others were not
much larger. In view of this, Westerners objected when the Eastern-
dominated Congress made new Western states as large as it could. Westerners charged that their Congressional representation and thus their
power in national affairs was deliberately reduced by these Eastern
actions.

Western and Eastern leaders also opposed one another over internal
improvements. Westerners became angry when so many Easterners opposed Western demands. The East, a well-developed society, had had
its share of such improvements when it needed them, but was unwilling to
help the West in the same way. Western leaders sharply attacked Easterners for their opposition to Western interests. This enmity between
East and West brought the South and West closer together. Western
leaders were already quite receptive to Southern overtures, based on
their common interests. Eastern hostility towards Western demands increased this receptiveness.

II

During the 1840's there were some changes in the sectional forces
operating in American life which may also have affected political be-

havior. In fact historians have suggested that these changes resulted in a shifting sectional pattern in the United States and a major political revolution.

The Old Northwest was the fastest growing region in the United States during the 1840's. The completion and utilization of the Erie Canal, and the building of a railroad network towards the Mississippi River, had conquered the Appalachian barrier between East and West. Northeastern settlers, as well as many foreign immigrants, filled in the area around the Great Lakes. This large population was settling a new region and demanding legislative aid from the government. Since they could not use the Mississippi River system effectively, they placed major transportation reliance on Lakes shipping and the railroads. Western goods flowed eastward through the new major trade center of Chicago. By the mid-1840's a major reorientation of interior trade relationships was well under way as traffic through the direct Eastern connection challenged and surpassed the movement through New Orleans. Although trade down the Mississippi River remained a vital factor in the Western economy through 1861, the pattern of Western trade grew more complex from the 1840's onward. As Avery O. Craven and Albert Kohlmeier have pointed out, two Wests were developing in the 1840's: the old Ohio Valley West with its Southern roots; and the Lakes area, looking eastward. And the Lakes area was rapidly growing more populous, stronger, and more important than the Ohio Valley.

The growth of two Wests complicated the sectional influences operating during the era. For example, there was an increased need for more efficient transportation connections to the Lakes, as well as railroad building in newly settled areas. As early as the 1830's sectional leaders planned to build several canals into the Great Lakes which would then lead East through the Erie Canal. But the people of the Lakes region needed much more. As we have already noted, most of the state internal improvement projects collapsed in the aftermath of the Panic of 1837. Since the states had no money to improve transportation routes, the federal government had to build, maintain, and repair the transportation facilities needed by the Lakes' population.

The demands by the people of the Great Lakes for such federal expenditures were not supported by the South or the Ohio Valley West. The river-trade area feared that too much spending would adversely affect the tariff since the government would need additional revenue. As we have seen, the tariff was always the primary policy consideration in the South and the river West. On the other hand, people of the Lakes region were not as vitally concerned about the level of customs duties. The East was rapidly urbanizing and they could sell their grain in that expanding home market. Since the South and the Ohio Valley West differed from the Lakes West in their attitude towards federal expenditures, a potential policy conflict was apparent.

We can see the growing changes in sectional relations in the second of the internal improvements conventions of the 1840's. At the Memphis meeting in 1845 Southerners and Westerners worked together for federal legislation. The convention at Chicago in 1847, however, was Eastern oriented. In fact there was a definite anti-Southern bias to many of the deliberations. Western leaders called this convention after the defeat of the Memphis proposals and the veto of the Rivers and Harbors Bill of 1846 by the Southern President, James K. Polk. The Westerners, who were quite angry at the South, were impatient with constitutional arguments which allegedly limited federal power over internal improvements and pointed out that the Lakes needed aid regardless of any other considerations. In tone and purpose, the Chicago meeting was a long way from the Memphis Convention.

There were other areas of friction between Southerners and people of the Great Lakes. They differed, for example, over the direction of territorial expansion. There were many people in and around the Lakes area who wanted the United States to expand into Canada and to the Pacific, and who militantly advocated such a policy as a means of acquiring more land for Western farmers. However, if the United States expanded into Canada and the Northwest there would be conflict with England which would rupture Southern trade relations. Led by Calhoun, Southern leaders counselled the Western expansionists to follow a more moderate policy.

The disposal of public lands was still another source of potential conflict between the South and the Lakes West. As more and more settlers pressed into new lands they urged the government to lower the price of federal land. They had won a pre-emption policy but they wanted cheap or free land for themselves. The Southern leaders, however, did not want land laws liberalized because it might lead to higher tariffs.

Finally, slavery grew more important as an issue between the South and the Lakes West. Westerners in the Ohio Valley had been tolerant of the institution. But the new Western settlers were not. They condemned slavery on moral grounds. They also realized that Southerners had more national power than they deserved because of the three-fifths clause in the Constitution. An intense political struggle could develop if Southerners used their additional power to thwart Western demands for internal improvements or expansion.

In the 1840's, therefore, it is plain that there were sectional attitudes present in the United States. As a result of these attitudes sectional leaders pressed for certain policies to foster their section's development. But we still have to ascertain whether or not these sectional attitudes and demands led to a strong sectional *influence* on politics, or whether political leaders could ignore purely sectional demands and act in national terms. The two national political parties could have been even more influential than sectional forces if they were able to mute and moderate sectional demands in the interest of achieving a common good. Finally, we should note that sectional influences did not necessarily operate in all matters.

Although many American historians have focused their attention on the idea that sectional influence grew so important during the 1840's that the American people reacted, in their political activity, primarily in sectional terms, however, as we have noted in Chapter One, they have not demonstrated the exact contours of this reaction. In the political situation of the 1840's there were so many different and conflicting factors present that, before we can generalize as to what influenced political behavior, we have to measure and compare the influence of all of the different forces present. To do this, we can begin with the first Congress elected in the decade. It met in May, 1841.

CHAPTER 37

THE ISSUE OF SLAVERY

EXPANSIONISM

We have learned in previous readings that in the 1850's the debate over slavery began to dominate the political scene. Sooner or later in a debate concerning the political merits of any of the great questions of the day, someone was sure to point out the effect that a decision would have on Negro slavery. Questions relating to the acquisition and settlement of new lands were not exceptions. Eugene Genovese, in this chapter from his book, *The Political Economy of Slavery** (1965), discusses Southern attitudes toward expansion. He shows that these attitudes, notwithstanding the opinion of earlier historians, were solidly favorable, at least among the members of the slaveholding aristocracy, which was the element that dominated the South's political life.

As is obvious from this selection, Genovese's view is not the customary historical outlook on slavery. Whereas past writers considered matters such as the profitability of the institution and its relative harshness or mildness, Genovese explores other questions. He argues that one cannot understand the hold that slavery had on the South and on the slaveholder unless he views slavery as the cornerstone of the Southern planters' way of life. This approach has won much acclaim for Genovese's book but has also stirred up considerable controversy.

Genovese's approach to slavery reopens the following questions to historical speculation. Did slavery have to expand to exist? Why? What were

553

the political consequences to the slave system of nonexpansionism? What were the social and economic consequences of nonexpansionism? What were the political, social, and economic consequences of expansionism to the North?

A traditional statement, doubting that slavery was expansionistic, may be found in Avery O. Craven's *The Coming of the Civil War** (original edition, 1942), which is somewhat updated in the same author's *Civil War in the Making** (1959). Harry Jaffa, *Crisis of the House Divided* (1959), insists, in the course of an analysis of the Lincoln-Douglas debates, that slavery was expansionistic. Allan Nevins, in *The Ordeal of the Union,* 2 vols. (1947), and *The Emergence of Lincoln,* 2 vols. (1950), gives a detailed account of events concerning slavery in the territories. Somewhat tighter in compass is J. G. Randall and David Donald, *The Civil War and Reconstruction* (1961). An even briefer treatment, synthesizing recent scholarship, is E. B. Smith, *The Death of Slavery* (1967).

* Available in a paperback edition.

THE ORIGINS OF SLAVERY EXPANSIONISM
EUGENE GENOVESE

Once upon a time in the happy and innocent days of the nineteenth century, men believed that Negro slavery had raised an expansionist slaveocracy to power in the American South. Today we know better. The revisionists have denied that slavery was expansionist and have virtually driven their opponents from the field. Their arguments, as distinct from their faith in the possibilities of resolving antagonisms peacefully, rest on two formidable essays. In 1926, Avery O. Craven published his *Soil Exhaustion As A Factor in the Agricultural History of Maryland and Virginia,* which sought to prove that the slave economy could reform itself, and three years later Charles William Ramsdell published his famous article on "The Natural Limits of Slavery Expansion," which constituted a frontal attack on the "irrepressible conflict" school.

I propose to restate the traditional view, but in such a way as to avoid the simplistic and mechanistic notions of Cairnes and his followers and to account for the data that has emerged from the conscientious and often splendid researches of the revisionist historians. Specifically, I propose to show that economics, politics, social life, ideology, and psychology converged to thrust the system outward and that beneath each factor lay the exigencies of the slaveholding class. Each dictated expansion if the men who made up the ruling class of the South were to continue to rule.

ROOTS AND TAPROOTS

Antebellum Southern economic history reinforces rather than overturns the nineteenth-century notion of an expansionist slaveocracy. That notion undoubtedly suffered from grave defects and considerable crudeness, for it insisted on the lack of versatility of slave labor and the steady deterioration of the soil without appreciating the partially effective attempts to reform the slave economy. Yet the revisionist work of the Craven school, which has contributed so much toward an understanding of the economic complexities, has not added up to a successful refutation.

We may recapitulate briefly the main points of the preceding studies, which lead to the economic root of slavery expansionism. At the beginning we encounter the low productivity of slave labor, defined not according to some absolute or purely economic standard, but according to the political exigencies of the slaveholders. The slaves worked well enough in the cotton and sugar fields, when organized in gangs, but the old criticism of labor given grudgingly retains its force.

Slave labor lacked that degree and kind of versatility which would have permitted general agricultural diversification. Slaves could and did work in a variety of pursuits, including industrial, but under circumstances not easily created within the economy as a whole. Division of labor on the plantations and in society proceeded slowly and under great handicaps. The level of technology, especially on the plantations, was kept low by the quality and size of the labor force. Mules and oxen, for example, replaced faster horses principally because they could more easily withstand rough and perhaps vengeful handling. Negro laborers had been disciplined to sustained agricultural labor before being brought to the Americas. Their low productivity arose from the human and technological conditions under which they worked, and these arose from the slave system.

An analysis of Southern livestock and the attempts to improve it reveals the complex and debilitating interrelationships within the slave economy. The South had more than enough animals to feed its population but had to import meat. A shortage of liquid capital made acquisition of better breeds difficult, and the poor treatment of the animals by the slaves made maintenance of any reasonable standards close to impossible. As a further complication, the lack of urban markets inhibited attention to livestock by depriving planters of outlets for potential surpluses. The South boasted an enormous number of animals but suffered from their wretched quality.

Slavery provided a sufficient although not a necessary cause of soil exhaustion. It dictated one-crop production beyond the limits of commercial advantage and in opposition to the political safety of the slaveholders. Planters could not easily rotate crops under the existing credit structure, with a difficult labor force, and without those markets which could only accompany industrial and urban advance. The sheer size of the plantations discouraged fertilization. Barnyard manure was scarce, commercial fertilizers too expensive, and the care necessary for advantageous application unavailable. The shortage of good implements complicated the operation, for manures are easily wasted when not applied properly.

Craven insists that the existence of a moving frontier, north and south, brought about the same result, but as we have seen, the special force of slavery cannot so easily be brushed aside. The North confronted the devastating effects of soil exhaustion and built a diversified economy in the older areas as the frontier pushed westward. The South, faced with the debilitating effects of slavery long after the frontier had passed, had to struggle against hopeless odds.

These direct effects of slavery received enormous reinforcement from such indirect effects as the shortage of capital and entrepreneurship and the weakness of the market. Capital investments in slaves and a notable tendency toward aristocratic consumption had their economic advantages but inhibited the rise of new industries. The Southern market consisted primarily of the plantations and could not support more than a limited industrial advance. The restricted purchasing power of the rural whites, of the urban lower classes, and indirectly of the slaves hemmed in Southern manufacturers and put them at a severe competitive disadvantage relative to Northerners, who had had a head start and who had much wider markets in the free states to sustain production on an increasing scale. The barriers to industrialization also blocked urbanization and thereby undermined the market for foodstuffs.

Southern industrialization proceeded within the narrow limits set by the social milieu as well as by the market. The slaveholders controlled the state legislatures and the police power; they granted charters, set taxes, and ultimately controlled the lives of regional industries. So long as industry remained within safe limits the slaveholders offered no firm resistance, or at least no united front. Those limits included guarantees against the rise of a hostile and independent bourgeoisie and excessive concentrations of white workers of doubtful loyalty. Since the big slaveholders provided much of the capital for industry and since the plantations provided much of the regional market, the risks remained small, for even the nonslaveholding industrialists necessarily bound themselves to the rural regime and tried to do good business within the established limits. Industry made some progress; industrialization, understood as a self-propelling process, did not.

The South made one form of agricultural adjustment while slavery remained. The great agricultural revival in the Upper South overcame the most serious effects of slavery by reducing the size of slaveholdings, converting surplus slaves into cash, and investing the funds in the supervision, fertilization, and reconversion of smaller estates. This process threatened the economic and ideological solidity of the slaveholders' regime and had other drawbacks, but most important, it broke on an immanent contradiction. The sale of surplus slaves depended on markets further south, which necessarily depended on virgin lands on which to apply the old, wasteful methods of farming. Reform in one region implied exhaustive agriculture in another. Thus, the process of agricultural reform had narrow limits in a closed slave system and had to be reversed when it pressed against them. No solution emerged from within the system, but one beckoned from without. The steady acquisition of new land could alone guarantee the maintenance of that interregional slave trade which held the system together.

This economic root of slavery expansion was only one of several roots, but itself grew strong enough to produce an ugly organism. If we begin with the economic process it is because the external threat to the slaveholders mounted so clearly, objectively and in their consciousness, with each new census report on the material conditions of the contending forces. The slaveholders might, of course, have resigned themselves to Lincoln's victory, accepted the essentials of the Wilmot Proviso, faced the impending crisis of their system, and prepared to convert to some form of free labor. Anything is possible where men retain the power to reason. Such a choice would have spelled their death as a ruling class and would have constituted moral and political suicide. Many contemporaries and many historians ever since have thought that they should have agreed to do themselves in. With this view I do not wish to argue. Neither did they.

The economic process propelling the slave South along expansionist paths had its political and social parallels, the most obvious being the need to re-establish parity in the Senate or at least to guarantee enough voting strength in Washington to protect Southern interests. In an immediate political sense the demand for more slave-state Congressmen was among the important roots of expansionism, but in a deeper sense it was merely a symptom of something more fundamental. Had the South not had a distinct social system to preserve and a distinct and powerful ruling class at its helm, a decline of its political and economic power would have caused no greater alarm than it did in New England.

A second political root was the need to protect slavery where it was profitable by establishing buffer areas where it might not be. Just as the British had to spend money to secure ascendancy in Tibet so that they could make money in India, the South had to establish political control over areas with dubious potentialities as slave states in order to protect existing slave states. The success of the Texas cause removed the fear of Mexican tampering with slaves in Louisiana, much as annexation removed potential British-inspired tampering. "Texas must be a slave country," wrote Stephen F. Austin to his sister. "The interest of Louisiana requires that it should be; a population of fanatical abolitionists in Texas would have a very pernicious and dangerous influence on the overgrown population of the state." In 1835, when a large Mexican force was reported near the Brazos River, the slaves apparently did attempt to rise. One hundred Negroes were severely punished, some executed.

John A. Quitman, former governor of Mississippi, tried to organize a filibustering expedition to Cuba during 1853–1855, particularly because he feared that abolition there would present dangers to the South. Samuel R. Walker and Albert W. Ely, among others, warned that Britain and France would force a weak Spain to sacrifice Cuban slavery and thereby isolate the South as a slaveholding country. Many far-sighted Southerners understood the danger of permitting the isolation of Southern slavery. They desired Cuba in order to secure political control of the Caribbean, as well as for economic reasons.

Beyond Cuba and the Caribbean lay Brazil, the other great slaveholding country. "These two great valleys of the Amazon and the Mississippi," declared the *Richmond Enquirer* in 1854, "are now possessed by two governments of the earth most deeply interested in African slavery— Brazil and the United States . . . The whole intermediate countries between these two great valleys . . . is a region under the plastic hand of a beneficent Providence . . . How is it to be developed?" [*sic*] With black labor and white skill. Cuba and Santo Domingo, it continued, were potentially the bases for the control of the whole Caribbean. Such a political complex would cause the whole world to "fall back upon African labor."

The warning of the Louisville *Daily Courier* in 1860 that Kentucky could afford to remain in the Union but that the Lower South could not touched the central issue. Suppose, it asked, Kentucky sold its slaves south. "And then what? Antislavery will not be content to rest. . . . The war will be transferred to the Cotton States."

The need to push forward in order to ward off concentrations of hostile power arose from the anachronistic nature of the slave regime. By 1850, if not much earlier, world opinion could no longer tolerate chattel slavery, and British opposition in particular was both formidable and implacable. The transformation of the Caribbean into a slaveholders' lake and an alliance or understanding with Brazil held out the only hope of preventing a dangerous and tightening containment.

Slaveholders also sought additional territory to reduce the danger of internal convulsion. Lieutenant Matthew F. Maury, who helped bring about the American exploration of the Amazon Valley in the 1850s, discussed the eventual absorption of much of Latin America by the United States:

I cannot be blind to what I see going on here. It is becoming a matter of *faith*—I use a strong word—yes a matter of faith among leading Southern men, that the time is coming, nay that it is rapidly approaching when in order to prevent this war of the races and all its horrors, they will in self-defense be compelled to conquer parts of Mexico and Central America, and make slave territory of that—and that is now free.

Representative Thomas L. Clingman of North Carolina told the House that Northerners were "too intelligent to believe that humanity, either to the slave or the master, requires that they should be pent up within a territory which after a time will be insufficient for their subsistence, and where they must perish from want, or from collision that would occur between the races." Southerners always kept the West Indian experience in front of them when they discussed the racial proportions of the population.

Probably, steady infusions of new land were also needed to placate the nonslaveholders, but we know little about slaveholder-nonslaveholder relationships as yet and little can be said with certainty.

The psychological dimension of slavery expansionism has been the subject of various essays and has, for example, emerged from interpretations of Southern frustration and resultant aggression. We need not pursue esoteric lines of inquiry, especially with formulas so broad as to be able to encompass almost every society in any age, to appreciate that a psychological dimension did exist. As Southerners came to regard slavery as a positive good and as they came to value the civilization it made possible as the world's finest, they could hardly accept limits on its expansion. To agree to containment meant to agree that slavery constituted an evil, however necessary for the benefit of the savage Africans. That sense of mission so characteristic of the United States as a whole had its Southern manifestation in the mission of slavery. If slavery was making possible the finest society the world had ever known, the objections to its expansion were intolerable. The free-soil argument struck at the foundations of the slaveholder's pride and belief in himself.

It is difficult but unnecessary to assess the relative strength of the roots of slavery expansionism. Each supported and fed the taproot—the exigencies of slaveholder hegemony in a South that fought against comparative disadvantages in the world market and that found itself increasingly isolated morally and politically. From another point of view, each was a manifestation of those exigencies. Although some appear to be objective, or matters of social process, whereas others appear to be subjective, or matters of psychological reaction to possibly imaginary dangers, the difference becomes unimportant when each is related to the fundamental position of the slaveholders in Southern society. The existence of a threatening economic process, such as has been described, would have been enough to generate fear and suspicion, even without the undeniable hostility arising in the North on political and moral grounds. . . .

THE CONTRADICTORY NATURE OF THE "NATURAL LIMITS" THESIS

The "natural limits" thesis is self-contradictory—and, in one important sense, irrevelant—for its simultaneously asserts that slavery was non-expansionist and that it would have perished without room to expand. The only way to avoid judging the thesis to be self-contradictory is to read it so as to state that slavery needed room to expand but that, first, it needed room only in the long run and, second, that it had no room. This reading removes the contradiction but destroys the thesis.

If the slave states would eventually need room to expand, they had to set aside new territory when they could get it or face a disaster in a few years or decades. Hence, wisdom dictated a fight for the right to take slaves into the territories, for ultimately that right would be transformed from an abstraction into a matter of life and death. W. Burwell of Virginia wrote in 1856 that the South needed no more territory at the moment and faced no immediate danger of a redundant slave population. "Yet statesmen," he concluded, "like provident farmers, look to the prospective demands of these who rely upon their forethought for protection and employment. Though, therefore, there may be no need for Southern territory for many years, yet it is important to provide for its acquisition when needed . . ."

To establish that slavery had no room to expand is not to refute the theory of slavery expansionism. If it could be firmly established that slavery needed room to expand but had none, then we should have described a society entering a period of internal convulsion. The decision of most slaveholders to stake everything on a desperate gamble for a political independence that would have freed them to push their system southward emerges as a rational, if dangerous, course of action.

THE TERRITORIAL QUESTION

One of the most puzzling features of Ramsdell's essay is the virtual equation of cotton and slavery. Only occasionally and never carefully does he glance at the prospects for using slave labor outside the cotton fields. To identify any social system with a single commodity is indefensible, and in any case, Southern slavery had much greater flexibility. Ramsdell's essay is puzzling with respect to these general considerations but even more so with respect to his specific contention that contemporary Southerners viewed the territorial question as a cotton question. They did not.

When the more intelligent and informed Southerners demanded the West for slavery they often, perhaps most often, spoke of minerals, not cotton or even hemp. Slavery, from ancient times to modern, had proved itself splendidly adaptable to mining. Mining constituted one of the more important industries of the Negroes of preconquest Africa, and slave labor had a long history there. The Berbers, for example, used Negro slaves in West Africa, where the salt mines provided one of the great impetuses to the development of commercial, as opposed to traditional and patriarchal, forms of slavery. Closer in time and place to the South, Brazil afforded an impressive example of the successful use of slave labor in mining. In the middle of the eighteenth century diamond mining supplemented gold mining in Minas Gerais and accounted for a massive transfer of masters and slaves from the northeastern sugar region. Southern leaders knew a good deal about this experience. "The mines of Brazil," reported *De Bow's Review* in 1848, "are most prolific of iron, gold, and diamonds. . . . The operation is performed by negroes . . . 30,000 negroes have been so employed." The eastern slave states had had experience with gold mining, and although the results were mixed, the potentialities of slave labor had been demonstrated. Planters in the Southwestern states expressed interest in gold mines in Arkansas and hopefully looked further west. "If mines of such temporary value should, as they may, be found in the territories, and slaves could be excluded from these," wrote A. F. Hopkins of Mobile in 1860, "it would present a case of monstrous injustice." . . .

It is one thing to note that Southerners sought to expand slavery into Mexico's mining districts or that they lamented the political barriers to the expansion of slavery into New Mexico's; it is another for us to conclude that their hopes and desires were more than wishful thinking. Allan Nevins has presented a formidable case to suggest that slavery had little room even in the mining districts of the Southwest and Mexico. He shows that even in the Gadsden Purchase the economic exigencies of mining brought about the quick suppression of the enterprising individual by the corporation. Western mining, as well as transportation, lumbering, and some forms of agriculture, required much capital and became fields for big business. High labor costs led to a rising demand for labor-saving machinery, but Nevins does not consider that this very condition might, under certain circumstances, have spurred the introduction of slave labor. . . . On economic grounds Nevins' analysis has much to offer, but his remarks on the competitive struggle in the Southwest and on the inability of Southerners to get national support for Caribbean adventures do not prove nearly so much as he thinks. At most, they suggest that the North was strong enough to block slavery expansionism into the Southwest and frustrate Southern ambitions elsewhere. If so, the case for secession, from the proslavery viewpoint, was unanswerable.

Nevins' remarks illustrate the wisdom of other Southern arguments— that the South had to secure new land politically, not by economic advance, and that the South had to have guarantees of positive federal protection for slavery in the territories. The *Charleston Mercury,* climaxing a decade of Southern complaints, insisted in 1860 that slavery would have triumphed in California's gold-mining areas if Southerners had had assurances of protection for their property. It singled out the mineral wealth of New Mexico as beckoning the South and even saw possibilities for slave-worked mining in Kansas. With fewer exaggerations De Bow, a decade earlier, had pointed to the political aspect of the problem: "Such is the strength and power of the Northern opposition that property, which is ever timid, and will seek no hazards, is excluded from the country in the person of the slave, and Southerners are forced, willingly or not, to remain at home. Emigrants, meanwhile, crowd from the North." During the bitter debate in Congress over the admission of California, Senator Jeremiah Clemens of Alabama replied heatedly to Clay in words similar to those used by De Bow. Free-soil agitation, he said, had kept slavery from the territories. "Property is proverbially timid. The slaveholder would not carry his property there with a threat hanging over him that it was to be taken away by operation of law the moment he landed."

Representative Joseph M. Root of Ohio, Whig and later Republican, commented on such charges by boasting that if the Wilmot Proviso had accomplished nothing more than to create a political climate inimical to slavery expansion, it had accomplished its purpose.

The Southern demand for federal guarantees made sense, but even that did not go far enough. Ultimately, the South needed not equal protection for slave property but complete political control. If a given territory could be organized by a proslavery party, then slaveholders would feel free to migrate. Time would be needed to allow the slave population to catch up; meanwhile, free-soil farmers had to be kept out in favor of men who looked forward to becoming slaveholders. Under such circumstances the territory's population might grow very slowly, and the exploitation of its resources might lag far behind that of the free territories. Nothing essential would be lost to the South by underdevelopment; the South as a whole was underdeveloped. In short, the question of political power necessarily had priority over the strictly economic questions. . . .

Historians like Nevins and Paul W. Gates have expressed confidence that slavery could not have triumphed in Kansas even if it had been allowed a foothold. They may be right, but only if one assumes that the South remained in the Union. Slavery expansionism required fastening proslavery regimes in such territories, but ultimately it required secession to protect the gains. Had Kansas joined a Southern Confederacy as a slave state, its wheat-growing slaveholders could have secured the same internal advantages as the sugar planters of Louisiana, and Union wheat could effectively have been placed at a competitive disadvantage in the Southern market.

Ramsdell's dismissal of Southern interest in Cuba and Central America, however necessary for his argument, does not bear examination. Southern sugar planters, who might have been expected to fear the glutting of the sugar market should Cuba enter the Union, spoke out for annexation. They seem to have been convinced that suspension of the African slave trade to Cuba would raise the cost of production there to American levels and that they would be able to buy Cuban slaves cheaply. Besides, as Basil Rauch points out, Louisiana sugar planters were moving to Cuba during the 1850s and looking forward to extending their fortunes. Southerners, like Northerners, often spoke of annexation in nationalist terms and sometimes went to great lengths to avoid the slavery question. J. J. Ampère heard that Cuba had been detached from the mainland by the Gulf Stream and rightfully belonged to the United States. He recommended that France reclaim Britain on the same grounds. He also heard that Cuba had to be annexed to provide a rest home for American consumptives. J. C. Reynolds, writing in *De Bow's Review* in 1850, described appalling losses in the illegal slave trade to Cuba and urged annexation to bring American law enforcement there and to end the terrible treatment of the Negroes. More sweepingly, some argued that without more territory the Negroes of the United States would be extinguished by overpopulation and attendant famine. All for the poor Negroes! Others, like Soulé and Albert Gallatin Brown, bluntly demanded Cuba and Central America to strengthen and defend slavery.

As for William Walker, he said enough to refute the Scroggs-Ramsdell interpretation. His *War in Nicaragua* makes clear that American politics made it necessary for him to appear to renounce annexation and that he was biding his time. No matter. His purpose there, as he boldly proclaimed, was to expand slavery as a system.

Opposition to territorial expansion by many Southerners has led some historians to deny the existence of an "aggressive slaveocracy" or to assert, with Ramsdell, that Southerners were too individualistic to be mobilized for such political adventures, which were often contrary to their private interests. No conspiracy theory is required. That there were many Southern leaders who sensed the need for more territory and fought for it is indisputable. That individual Southerners were not always willing to move when the interests of their class and system required them to merely indicates one of the ways in which slavery expansionism proved a contradictory process. Southerners opposed expansion for a variety of reasons, but mostly because they feared more free states. Expansion southward had the great advantage of not being cotton expansion, and the economic argument against it was weak. On the other hand, many feared that the annexation of Cuba would provide an excuse for the annexation of Canada or that the annexation of Mexico would repeat the experience of California. This opposition should be understood essentially as a preference for delaying expansion until secession had been effected, although there were, of course, many who opposed both. . . .

INVITATION TO A (SELF INFLICTED) BEHEADING

The South had to expand, and its leaders knew it. "There is not a slaveholder in this House or out of it," Judge Warner of Georgia declared in the House of Representatives in 1856, "but who knows perfectly well that whenever slavery is confined within certain specified limits, its future existence is doomed." The Republican party, said an editorial in *The Plantation* in 1860, denies that it wants to war on slavery, but it admits that it wants to surround it with free states. To do so would be to crush slavery where it now exists. Percy L. Rainwater's study of sentiment in Mississippi in the 1850s shows how firmly convinced slaveholders were that the system had to expand or die. Lincoln made the same point in his own way. He opposed any compromise on slavery expansion in 1860 because he feared new and bolder expansionist schemes and because he wished to contain slavery in order to guarantee its ultimate extinction.

Nevins' discussion of Lincoln's view illuminates one of the most tenacious and dubious assumptions on which many historians have based their interpretations of the origins of the war:

In view of all the trends of nineteenth century civilization, the terrible problem of slavery could be given a final solution only upon the principle . . . of gradual emancipation. . . . The first step was to stop the expansion of slavery, and to confine the institution within the fifteen states it already possessed. Such a decision would be equivalent to a decree that slavery was marked for gradual evolution into a higher labor system. Slavery confined would be a slavery under sentence of slow death. The second step would be the termination of slavery in the border states. Missouri by 1859 stood near the verge of emancipation . . .

The assumption on which these notions rest is that the South, faced with containment, could have accepted its consequences. On the further assumption that men may agree to commit suicide, the assumption is plausible.

If instead of speaking of the South or of the system of slavery, we speak of the slaveholders who ruled both, the assumption is less plausible. The extinction of slavery would have broken the power of the slaveholders in general and the planters in particular. Ideologically, these men had committed themselves to slaveholding and the plantation regime as the proper foundations of civilization. Politically, the preservation of their power depended on the preservation of its economic base. Economically, the plantation system would have tottered under free labor conditions and would have existed under some intermediary form like sharecropping only at the expense of the old ruling class. The "higher" forms depended on the introduction of commercial relations that would have gradually undermined the planters and guaranteed the penetration of outside capital. We have the postbellum experience to cite here, although it took place at a time when the planters had suffered hard blows, but slaveholders saw the dangers before the war and before the blows. "Python," in a series of brilliant articles in De Bow's Review in 1860, warned that emancipation, even with some form of "apprenticeship" for the Negroes, would open the way for Northern capital to command the productive power of the South. Once Negro labor is linked to capital in the open market, he argued, rather than through the patriarchal system of plantation slavery, it will fall prey to a predatory, soulless, Northern capitalism. There will be no place left for the old master class, which will be crushed by the superior force of Northern capital and enterprise or absorbed into them. "Of what advantage is it to the South," he asked, "to be destroyed by Mr. Douglas through territorial sovereignty to the exclusion of Southern institutions, rather than by Mr. Seward through Congressional sovereignty to the same end? What difference is there to the South whether they are forcibly led to immolation by Seward, or accorded, in the alternative, the Roman privilege of selecting their own mode of death, by Douglas? Die they must in either event."

These words demonstrate that the probable effect of a "higher labor system" on the fortunes of the slaveholding class was not beyond the appreciation of its intellectual leaders. We need not try to prove that so specific an appreciation was general. The slaveholders knew their own power and could not help being suspicious of sweeping changes in their way of life, no matter how persuasively advanced. Their slaveholding psychology, habit of command, race pride, rural lordship, aristocratic pretensions, political domination, and economic strength militated in defense of the status quo. Under such circumstances an occasional voice warning that a conversion to tenantry or sharecropping carried serious dangers to their material interests sufficed to stiffen their resistance.

No demagogy or dogmatic speculation produced "Python's" fears. Even modest compensation—paid for by whom?—would have left the planters in a precarious position. At best, it would have extended their life as a class a little while longer than postbellum conditions permitted, but Northern capital could not long be kept from establishing direct relationships with tenants and sharecroppers. The planters would have steadily been reduced to middlemen of doubtful economic value or would have merged imperceptibly into a national business class. The change would have required, and eventually did require under disorderly postbellum conditions, extensive advances to laborers in the form of additional implements, fertilizer, household utensils, even food, and innumerable incidentals. This process guaranteed the disintegration of the old landowning class, however good an adjustment many of its members might have made to the new order.

Those who, like Max Weber, Ramsdell, even Phillips, and countless others, assume that the South could have accepted a peaceful transition to free labor gravely misjudge the character of its ruling class. The question of such a judgment is precisely what is at issue. As noted in the Introduction to this volume, a revisionist historian might accept the empirical

findings reported here and even the specific interpretations of their economic significance and still draw different conclusions on the larger issues.
The final set of conclusions, and the notion of a general crisis itself,
eventually must rest on agreement that the slaveholders constituted a
ruling class and that they displayed an ideology and psychology such as
has merely been suggested in these studies.

The slaveholders, not the South, held the power to accede or resist. To
these men slaves were a source of power, pride, and prestige, a duty and a
responsibility, a privilege and a trust; slavery was the foundation of a
special civilization imprinted with their own character. The defense of
slavery, to them, meant the defense of their honor and dignity, which
they saw as the essence of life. They could never agree to renounce the
foundation of their power and moral sensibility and to undergo a
metamorphosis into a class the nature and values of which were an in-
version of their own. Slavery represented the cornerstone of their way of
life, and life to them meant an honor and dignity associated with the
power of command. When the slaveholders rose in insurrection, they
knew what they were about: in the fullest sense, they were fighting for
their lives.

CHAPTER 38

THE DISRUPTION OF
AMERICAN POLITICS

Perhaps the best way to describe the election of 1860 would be to say that the Democrats lost it rather than that the Republicans won it. In this essay, Roy Nichols describes how some Democrats lost faith in nominating conventions and disrupted the Democratic party, one of the most significant bonds that united the nation. Nichols also shows how relatively minor events can sometimes assume real magnitude. Such an event was the decision (reached at the 1856 Democratic convention in Cincinnati) to hold the 1860 convention in Charleston, South Carolina. In view of the incredibly disruptive issues of 1860, the Democrats would have had trouble reaching compromises anywhere. To meet in the hotbed of secession was to multiply these problems and to make compromise even more difficult. With the aid of historical hindsight, one can easily see that they should have met on neutral ground.

A significant point that Nichols makes by inference is the importance of compromise in making the American political system work. As Herbert Agar states in the preface to the 1966 edition of his great work, *The Price of Union*,* "Once, unhappily, both parties failed at the same time in their assuaging mission, both offered us 'a choice instead of an echo.' The result was Civil War." Agar's judgment should be weighed in the light of two facts: (1) that the Republican party was still extremely young, so that there is no exact comparison between 1860 and the two-party contests of later years, and (2) that, actually, four parties entered the race and, therefore, the voters had the opportunity to choose variety of positions after the conventions.

The Nichols essay also raises the question of whether it was necessary for the South to secede at all. His answer would appear to be "no." Actually, the Democrats controlled the House, Senate, and the Supreme Court. Did this control mean that the voice of the South would be heard and respected? Could Southerners thus hope for a permanent deadlock on the more obnoxious proposals of Lincoln and his party? However, it is possible that, if the South had not made its bid to establish an independent slaveholding Confederacy, it would have continued to decline in economic and industrial importance until, eventually, having lost its political power, it would have been so weak in relation to the North and the West that it could not have seriously contemplated sucession. In short, was it now or never for the disunionists? Perhaps it was even later than they thought. Since the South had already suffered a decline during the fifties, can it be argued that Clay and Webster, by their efforts to achieve the Compromise of 1850, delayed the Civil War in a way that ultimately added to the advantages of the North and that, in fact, they saved the Union (although not peaceably) as they had hoped?

In addition to Agar's work (cited above), the student should study two classics of modern American historical writing. They are Roy Nichols, *The Disruption of the American Democracy** (1948), and Allan Nevins, *The Ordeal of the Union,* 2 vols. (1947) and *The Emergence of Lincoln,* 2 vols. (1950). See E. B. Smith, *The Death of Slavery* (1967), for a recent, concise treatment.

* Available in a paperback edition.

WHY THE DEMOCRATIC PARTY DIVIDED
ROY F. NICHOLS

Like the causes of the Civil War, the reasons for the disintegration of
the Democratic party in 1860 can be and have been elaborated at any
desired length. Rather than repeat the varieties of exegesis involved in
the use of such terms as the morals of slavery, the economic rivalry of
diverse interests, the cultural conflict between the sections, and the eco-
logical and demographic elements among the determinants, it is more
realistic to consider some concepts in group dynamics, in the behavior of
individuals, small groups, and the masses in political association. For the
crux of the matter lay in the fact that complex party machinery collapsed
in a context of human failure. Because the behavior involved in failure
depends on the nature of the stimulation created by individuals and
groups through the senses of sight and hearing for those others in association, an analysis of it becomes a study in communication. In other words,
the analysis involves a consideration of who meets whom, of what is said
and seen during the course of recurrent interchanges, and, what is less
obvious and therefore harder to discover, the kind of reaction countless
nervous systems produce when confronted with the presence and behavior
of other organisms.

An understanding of such complexity requires a close look at the series
of meetings which brought into one train of communication the political
operators who directed the Democratic party's conventions in several
large meeting halls and in auxiliary places of accommodation. Here was
generated the great and devastating explosion of human emotion which in
time rocked the growing nation to its foundations, for the national conventions of the Democratic party were significant bridges of communication

SOURCE. Roy F. Nichols, in George Harmon Knoles, *The Crisis of the Union, 1860–
1861*, Baton Rouge, Louisiana: Louisiana State University Press, 1965, pp. 30–50.
Copyright 1965 by the Louisiana State University Press. Reprinted by permission
of the Louisiana State University Press and the author. Professor Nichols is Professor of History Emeritus, University of Pennsylvania, sometime Vice Provost and
Dean of the Graduate School of the University of Pennsylvania, and was President
of the American Historical Association in 1966.

over which the "great forces" moved to influence the behavior of the nation's political operators.

In Charleston, Richmond, Washington, and Baltimore in April, May, and June of 1860, there were a concentration and dispersion of definable and identifiable human beings through which the forces shaping political behavior operated. It was there that the doctrinaire position of certain Southern Democrats insisting on an endorsement of an impossible idea encountered the overweaning ambitions of Douglas and his followers who were determined to maintain power by demanding a heroic bit of realism. Such a collision produced a fatal impasse. In the almost unbelievable confusion of these meetings it was demonstrated that the Democratic party after thirty years of success was not strong enough, despite its age, its experience, and the skill of its operators, to maintain itself midst the confusion into which the action and interaction of the numerous forces shaping this growing nation had plunged American politics. . . .

For a decade these Democratic national conventions functioned with a reasonable degree of efficiency. But the next ten years told another story. Calhoun's presidential ambitions were not finally completely frustrated in the 1840's and he turned his bitterness on the convention which he charged was an instrument of the spoilsmen. Upon their manipulations he blamed much of his discomfiture. He and his followers wanted to change its rules and upon occasion refused to attend its sessions. Also a new generation, tired of Van Buren and the domination of his henchmen, demanded a "new deal." They were dismayed by the defeat of 1840 and by the rising Whigs; they feared Henry Clay might beat the rather shopworn "Little Van" in 1844. A group of Southern and Western politicos with some help from New England took over the convention in 1844 from the traditional Van Buren managers; the nomination of a "dark horse" was negotiated in the person of James Knox Polk.

Polk's selection was a convention maneuver engineered by a combination of state and congressional managers which eventually was to result in the disruption and disaffection of the New York party. This split in large part occurred because Polk developed no aptitude for party leadership. He was an avowed one-term candidate and thereby abdicated as party leader as soon as he had distributed the patronage. His efforts to heal the breach within New York by distributing offices was a dismal failure; and his foreign policy in Mexico and Oregon, despite its spectacular success, served to break up the New York party for years to come.

This schism destroyed the unity of the leaderless national convention of 1848. Here for the first time a candidate from the Northwest, General Lewis Cass, received the nomination; but the Van Buren half of the New

Yorkers walked out because they were not recognized as *the* Democracy and later joined with certain antislavery groups in forming an enlarged Free-Soil party. This break rather unfairly got the credit for the party's defeat in the fall at the hands of the hero, General Zachary Taylor. The precedent of walking out of a national convention had been set, and the secessionists were given credit for a capacity to defeat which they probably did not deserve.

In the conventions of 1844 and 1848 a new device was being set up for control: the National Committee presumed to give direction to the management of the party conclaves. However, by 1852 it had not achieved full stature; and, in the wake of the defeat of 1848, the party seemed to be drifting, for a second time leaderless, toward 1852. The professionals, by and large attracted by the understandings of 1848 and their status which had been established in that campaign, seemed inclined to renominate Cass now that the schism of 1848 apparently had been healed by a tenuous reunion of the wings of the New York party and by the Compromise of 1850. But such a variety of contestants arose opposing following this ancient trail that confusion began to descend.

The convention of 1852 promised to be a symbol of impotence. It was at this junction that a self-appointed inner group emerged to take over. One of Cass's chief rivals was James Buchanan of Pennsylvania, a candidate since 1844. His Pennsylvania managers joined a Southern bloc from Virginia, North Carolina, Georgia, Alabama, and Mississippi, some of whom had been active in the 1844 coup, to produce another dark horse. A combination of New Englanders and Mexican War generals from the Aztec Club had been pushing as second choice a New Hampshire brigadier general, Franklin Pierce; and he was the one the cabal "put over." They completed the ticket with Buchanan's friend, Senator William R. King of Alabama. The nonentity of this ticket, plus the pacifying influence of the Compromise of 1850 and the absurdity of General Winfield Scott as an opposing candidate, made Pierce's electoral college majority huge although his majority of the popular vote was slim.

Pierce had even less capacity for party leadership than had Polk, and despite his deceptive victory in 1852 the party was soon in difficulties. The New England President not only made similar mistakes in handling party patronage but he had none of Polk's success in foreign policy and in congressional legislation. Most unfortunately he joined Douglas and the other Senators in engineering the castastrophic repeal of the Missouri Compromise, and almost immediately a precocious phoenix arose from the ashes of the Whig party in the form of the young Republican eagle, dedicated to furthering Northern interests. The congressional elections of 1854–55 sounded a sharp warning which at first no one seemed able to heed. Were the days of Democratic power and Southern security numbered?

The maneuverings anticipating the Democratic convention of 1860 really began in 1856. As that fateful presidential year approached, the Democrats found themselves face to face for the first time with their new foe of unknown potential, the Republican party, born in an atmosphere of moral indignation and promotional expectation. Under these circumstances they commenced another chapter in their history. During their first decade they had been led by an efficient group of Jacksonian operators, Van Buren and his Albany Regency and the Richmond Junto associates; and at first Francis P. Blair, Sr., was in charge of the propaganda. In the 1840's the management was seized by a younger group with some senatorial guidance including lower South, Southwestern and Western participation and with old Father Ritchie taking over Blair's pen.

This guidance during the second phase had produced three candidates, Polk, Cass, and Pierce, two of them dark horses and the latter two not fortunate in their leadership. None of these candidates had been of Jacksonian stature. Despite the disasters during the Pierce regime and the threat of the new Republicans, this inept management seemed about to give Pierce the usually available renomination with the blessing of almost the solid South, the popular sovereignty West, and New England Democrats who were emotionally committed to their "first success." Such an invitation to defeat appeared so disturbing that it invited new leadership.

On the eve of the convention of 1856 a few practical operators came to the conclusion that they must intervene. A self-appointed senatorial group therefore decided to try a coup something along the order of the one of 1844. It is significant of the nature of the system of party control that the move originated in the Senate. Four Senators, John Slidell and Judah P. Benjamin of Louisiana, J. D. Bright of Indiana, and James A. Bayard of Delaware, motivated not only by a determination to avert defeat but also by extreme dislike of Douglas and a combination of distrust and contempt for Pierce, set up a headquarters at the convention in the house of a railroad promoter in Cincinnati, a new location for the national conventions. The Democratic National Committee headed by a Maryland chairman had decided that perhaps they had met in Baltimore long enough and that the growth of the Western wing of the party demanded recognition. Therefore they had picked out Cincinnati, the Queen City of the West, for the point of congregation; and it was thither that the Senatorial cabal wended its way.

Its members planned to accomplish their purpose by throwning overboard Pierce, bypassing Douglas, and negotiating the nomination of the veteran James Buchanan. His great assets were his long career and expert knowledge, the fact that he had been out of the country since 1853 and thus had avoided the Kansas malaise, and finally the fact that the hardheaded Senator Slidell of Louisiana thought of him as "his man." These contrivers succeeded. They formed a scattered combination led by Pennsylvania, Virginia, and Louisiana which could and did stop Pierce and Douglas and named Old Buck.

But the nomination of Buchanan was not all that happened at Cincinnati. When the Pierce cause became hopeless his strength was transferred to Douglas. Despite the shift Buchanan soon secured a majority; and at this point instead of fighting it out further and perhaps forcing another dark horse in at the finish, Douglas retired gracefully. Whether to secure this he had been promised a clear field in 1860 or whether he merely hoped he would have it because of his action is anybody's guess. Probably Douglas took encouragement from his situation. At any rate his friend John C. Breckinridge of Kentucky was nominated for the vice-presidency. The disappointed Southern supporters of Pierce would be somewhat placated, it was hoped, by designating Charleston, South Carolina, as the place for the Convention of 1860.

The administration of James Buchanan, the veteran expert, was even more disastrous than that of the novice, Pierce. The new President suffered every disaster from dysentery to John Brown's raid. Douglas likewise had had a trying four years. Buchanan slighted him in distributing patronage. The Supreme Court declared popular sovereignty, his great principle upon which he depended to harmonize Northern and Southern support, to be unconstitutional. The practical working of this provision had blown up in Kansas and had placed him in an almost unbearable dilemma in Congress. He had beaten Lincoln, but he had been compelled to advertise his rival's political skill. His Southern colleagues had taken away his chairmanship of the Senate Committee on Territories, thus depriving him even of office space. His wife had lost their baby through a miscarriage, and he himself had been seriously ill. Despite all this he had been picking up delegates and endorsements.

The climax of calamity came in the form of John Brown's raid in October, 1859, almost on the eve of the Charleston Convention. This disaster set the stage for a third coup, and for a third time its chief operators were in the Senate. When the Congress came together in December, 1859, Brown had just been hanged, certain elements in the South were arming and drilling, and there was no party in certain control of the House though it seemed likely that the Republicans would take over. The Republican management was preparing campaign literature for 1860 which was interpreted as endorsing the idea of slave uprising, and Douglas had appealed from the Supreme Court to history and had published a magazine article proving by historical evidence that the South was without any platform. Also the census of 1860 was being projected, and its figures quite obviously would register the fact that the South was doomed politically to hopeless minority. To the Southern Democracy the prospect was desperate, and to make it unbearable Douglas was the only candidate of prominence. In fact he might easily come to Charleston with a majority of the votes, certainly enough to stop anybody else under the two-thirds rule and to secure an endorsement of the popular sovereignty platform of 1856.

While the House took another frightening two months to organize, thus repeating 1855, the wheels of government were stalled. The Senate had time on its hands and a Southern bloc, reminiscent of those of 1844 and 1856, planned again. What they did has been called a "conspiracy" —this is a somewhat hysterical term, but it is near enough the truth to warrant its use in quotation marks. Certain Senators, and here we find Slidell and his Cincinnati associates working together with Jefferson Davis and a group of other Southern solons, had arrived at a determination. Apprehension had reached such a pitch in their constituencies that their Whig-American opponents were preparing to be 100 per cent Southern and fight them on the ground that they were "soft" on squatter sovereignty which was selling the South down the river. They must have an explicit endorsement of Southern rights in the Charleston platform. Jefferson Davis, in assuming Calhoun's mantle, wrote the formula which was presented to the Senate the day the Republicans at long last organized the House. If this platform was not accepted, the South would leave the convention as the Barnburners had in 1848. As an earnest of this the Alabama state Democratic convention instructed its delegation to Charleston to take the lead in this walkout if the demand was refused.

How far the senatorial managers had gone toward making a firm decision on breaking up the convention at this time is not of record. The indications are that they had, for it should be remembered that there was a code of honor observed in certain Southern political quarters under which it was dishonorable for delegates to refuse to support the program prescribed by a convention in which they had participated. There was a possibility that the Southern platform might be defeated and Douglas nominated. As a significant number of Southern delegates had determined never to support Douglas on a squatter sovereignty platform, honor bound them if they were defeated on platform to leave before he or anyone was nominated on a platform they could not accept.

A further step was also under discussion. What should be done if a Republican were elected in 1860? Here again Alabama serves as an indicator. Her state legislature passed a law requiring her governor, in that event, to summon a state convention to determine whether Alabama should secede. The question of the formation of a confederacy was likewise discussed. How far definite plans were formulated again cannot be categorically stated. It was an age of romantic empiricism so beefed up by hyperbolic rhetoric that it is difficult to discover exactly what some of these extravagant speakers were thinking. Despite the variety of possibilities talked about, it is probable that only one firm decision had been reached. There must be an "honest platform," or the party must be judged to have outlived its usefulness and be scrapped. Such action would clear the stage for new political engineering. Congress might take over. There might be a new Constitutional Convention as Calhoun had proposed. There might be secession and the formation of a new confederacy.

Douglas was living in the midst of this planning and sharing in some of its convivial moments. The practical Eastern operators were fully aware of what was going on; and at least one Republican Senator, William H. Seward, who most observers thought might well be that party's nominee in 1860, was on intimate terms with certain of his Senatorial colleagues from the South. It must not be forgotten that the Senate was a species of social club.

With some general lines of strategy laid out, Slidell, Bright, and Bayard went to Charleston and set up headquarters at the convention city, this time behind an ice cream saloon. From the moment of the opening of the convention shock tactics were employed, an old convention technique. Douglas' strength must be discovered at once and his managers, who after all came in large part from rotten boroughs or from states which could not deliver an electoral vote, must be given unmistakable warning that if the convention didn't damn well take the Southern platform, Douglas and the party could go to hell. This notice was registered in no uncertain terms by shouting, by climbing on tables, by variegated parliamentary disorder, and by threats and certain forms of alcoholic exaggeration.

The Douglas forces were ill-prepared for such a shock. They had come down into this atmosphere, new and strange to them, under close organization and strict discipline. They had hired a hall and set up a dormitory in it where they all slept row on row and where their leaders could keep track of them. They were probably very uncomfortable in the unaccustomed heat and also conscious of their lack of status in aristocratic Charleston. Politically they were as desperate as the Southerners. If they went home with this "honest" platform of Southern rights how could they survive in even the few Northern states left to them after the near disaster of 1856? Douglas was their only chance with some platform that had at least a coincidental resemblance to squatter sovereignty, Douglas' "great brinziple" of "let the people rule." Only this could beat "no more slave states" and "let freedom ring."

But it must not be forgotten that there was a third element in the compound. New York was back in strength though with the usual contest on hand. New York's truculent mayor, Fernando Wood, had tried to capture the management of the party in New York state by strong-arm methods at the state convention. He was in Charleston working up Southern support for his contesting delegation on the ground that his New York City was the only Democratic stronghold left in New York and that he and his "shoulder-hitters," as they were called, were the only outfit which could deliver. Pennsylvania, New Jersey, and the New England states were there likewise looking for the main chance. They had no particular loyalty to Douglas though they recognized his vote-getting power. Their main interest was a negotiated peace; they wanted somehow to trade it out by prestidigious manipulations of words and candidates.

All factions were confronted by statistics. The Southern states had only 120 electoral votes. The victor in the electoral college needed 152. The required 32 votes must come from free states. Southern statisticians figured however that these 32 could probably be acquired only at a semantic price which might cost 34 votes in those Southern states that could go Whig. What a dilemma and besides the weather was hot, the hotels were expensive, bad, and hellishly crowded, and the meeting hall was atrocious. Calhoun's bones rested in a neighboring church yard; perhaps his spirit hovered disapprovingly over the convention which he had always distrusted.

Thirty years of convention experience were drawn upon to discover the way out of this statistical and emotional confusion. The Southerners, who had on occasion shared Calhoun's dislike for conventions, served their violent notice. The Douglasites with their numerical majority sought to change it into a two-thirds endorsement by controlling the committees and the crucial floor votes. The "practical operators" sought to arrange accommodations. But the forces would not budge.

When the Douglas platform, though somewhat modified, was adopted, Alabama began the projected walkout. However the exit was disappointing, only eight of the fifteen slave states responded; and these were only from the lower South. The seceders, despite their disappointment, settled down in an adjacent hall. One of the objects of this secession was to establish possible negotiations which might bring about a compromise nomination or a revised platform or both. Some of the seceders thought that under such circumstances they might still go home not only with a good chance of keeping their local strength but also with some hope of national victory. They would bet on enough support from Northerners who feared Seward's higher law and irrepressible conflict heresies to get the Northern votes necessary. They counted on Seward's enemies within his own party and the distrust of his radicalism in his own section. Let it be remembered that nobody in Charleston then dreamed of Lincoln. Also some of the leading Senators were boon companions of Seward and would have suffered him, not gladly perhaps, but as an alternative to Douglas whose guts they hated. But not only where they not joined by the majority of the South, no one even came to offer overtures for reunion. It was an anticlimax just to sit, despite the fact that they were cheered by the inability of those they called "the rump" to accomplish anything.

The only positive step achieved was the fact that a numerical majority cast their votes for Douglas. The Douglas managers had expected that when the Southerners seceded, two-thirds of the remaining quorum were all that would be necessary to nominate. This was one reason why some of them were in effect anxious to get at least a few of the Southern delegates out. But New York defeated this, holding the door open even wider for negotiation. It would have taken more skill and concession to secure 202 than 168, but since Douglas seemed able to muster only 152½, he would have to make concessions to those who were adept at manipulation.

After balloting fifty-seven times the convention decided on an unprecedented act. On the morning of the tenth day the members recessed until June 18, then to reassemble in Baltimore. Both factions would go home to sound out opinion. The Douglasites hoped that others could be found in the seceders' districts to repudiate them and less intransigent Democrats to fill their places in Baltimore. The seceders could but hope for the endorsement of their stand.

During the ensuing six weeks the hopes of the Douglas managers were in part fulfilled. New delegations were dispatched from Alabama, Arkansas, Georgia, and Louisiana. The original delegates from Mississippi and Texas returned. Those from Florida were in the city but did not attend the sessions as delegates. The controlling facts were probably certain events in the weeks between the two conventions. The Whigs and Americans together with other conservatives had organized a new party called

the Constitutional Union party and had nominated John Bell of Tennessee and Edward Everett of Massachusetts on a simple platform
endorsing the Constitution and the Union. This ticket would be likely to
be strong in the South. Then, too, Abraham Lincoln, not Seward, had
been nominated by the Republicans upon a platform offering generous
subsidies. Lincoln's slate would be more formidable than any headed by
Seward. Facing such developments the Southern wing felt it impossible
to yield on their platform, and the Northern wing on their candidate.

Thus the experienced politicos, who had faced walkouts before and
had composed differences on several occasions, and their less tutored
associates found themselves without any of the familiar materials with
which to work: neither faction would advance concessions on either
principles or candidates. An unprecedented impasse had been reached,
and no accommodation was achieved. The majority nominated Douglas
as they had determined to do from the beginning while the traders from
the middle states sat by helpless and of necessity acquiescent. The
seceders, joined by the rest of the South and a few from Northern
constituencies, chose the Vice-President, John C. Breckinridge, and a
Senator, Joseph Lane of Oregon, to head the ticket on the "honest platform." This was canny. Now that there were four tickets, the contest
might be thrown into Congress. The likelihood that the splintered House
could muster a majority of the states for any of those who might be the
three highest seemed remote. But the safely Democratic Senate would
have no difficulty in choosing their colleague, Joseph Lane. The Democrats might thus save the presidency after all. Some perhaps looked
ahead to another contingency. If there were to be secession, it could be
convenient to have the Vice-President of the United States, Breckinridge,
in a positon to help in their effort. But to most it looked as if the
Democrats had elected Lincoln.

Thus the Democratic party broke up when its national convention
collapsed in 1860. A bloc of Southern delegates shattered the organization deliberately. They had come to Charleston with no candidate to
propose. In the convention they made much of formulae. Though the
majority of the delegates were against them, they sought to control because they had a majority of the states. As they demanded full recognition of the rights of the states, they proclaimed themselves firm supporters
of the Constitution which they maintained was more important than the
Union. They had been suffering in power and prestige ever since 1856.
Then they had failed to renominate Pierce. Twice they had lost control
of the House of Representatives. Now in 1860 they had lost control of
the national convention. Power meant a great deal to them as it naturally

would in an aggregation in which so many were slaveholders. Particularly after the shock of John Brown's raid, power was more than ever necessary for protection and survival. They must have the autonomy with security which Calhoun had prescribed. If they could not find it in the old Union, they would create a new agency to insure it.

So they would destroy the convention and the party as instruments no longer serving their purpose. They were ready to try something new. Douglas and his associates on their part strove desperately to salvage the party mechanism. But they were not strong enough; and besides, they had nothing to take its place. The convention system latterly had been plagued by a weakness which was now proving fatal. The professionals who had invented and operated it had failed to provide real leadership. They had preferred usually to nominate their own kind. They were not favorable to superior talent, to statesmen, or to the nineteenth century equivalent of "eggheads." They chose those who spoke their language and understood their own mores. The Democrats had never in these years of convention practice nominated a man of great talent or commanding reputation. One can go far without finding a more colorless group than Van Buren, Polk, Cass, Pierce, or Buchanan. They were certaintly not much more than representatives of the average man. Van Buren and Buchanan were men of experience and craft but with no capacity to deal with the unusual. Polk had some skill and luck, but he was a man of decided limitations, a statesman incapable of foreseeing or forestalling dangers; even less can be said for Cass and Pierce.

The nation was growing fast in size, wealth, and power. It was also fragmentizing, falling apart because of its own weight. Emotions were getting out of hand, morals were deteriorating, health was bad, and the nature of republican self-government was yielding to temptation and succumbing to corruption. But the leadership necessary to recall men to their duty in maintaining the ideals of democracy could not be summoned by any of the instruments available.

It cannot be said with certainty that in 1860 and in the preceding years a consistently higher grade of leadership would have solved more of the problems and avoided more of the crises, but it can be emphasized that no leadership which could cope with the troubled times became available. Rather the current methods required the choosing of those who patently could not rouse the innate capacities of the people of the United States. A party requires leadership to be effective; one cannot carry any society through trying times by a committee or a conference. There must be a personality, a symbol which can inspire trust and confidence, a personality whom the mass will follow.

It can never be known what might have happened had the Convention of 1860 been able to agree on a platform and on a candidate. With all the confusion stirred up by four tickets, the Democrats were still able to recapture the House in 1860 which they had lost in 1858. Their hold on the Senate was not even threatened. The Supreme Court was safely Democratic. There may be probability, although there can be no certainty, that Lincoln would have been elected in a three-cornered contest. But had he been victorious, with the legislative and the judicial arms against him, could he have done more than the Whig Presidents of a decade and more ago? This is all in the ream of conjecture. But John Brown was dead and the likelihood of other forays exists only in the imagination. Had the nation held together and experienced the ineptitudes of what would have been Lincoln's helpless minority administration, the fears might have been quieted; and the South, with its control of the Congress might have continued to exercise its accustomed rule.

But no, the Democrats destroyed the instrument of accommodation they had used effectively for thirty years rather than exhaust its possibilities, and in so doing they precipitated the catastrophe which was to follow. Their invention was smashed because a large faction, mainly from the South, found it no longer useful. The party must try something else to serve their purposes.

The Douglas wing had nothing else to use so they clung desperately to it. The Southern wing had the ghost of Calhoun and set forth to make use of it. They would keep power in the states by seceding from Charleston and Baltimore. If they were defied by the North they would create a new power—just how they would use it, its engineers hardly knew—but the purpose generally was to insure for themselves, somehow, a position of power, autonomy, and security within a reorganized Union. Unfortunately Calhoun was not alive to lead them; and the steps they took were haphazard, badly planned, and undertaken under circumstances that almost insured failure. Had they been able to enlist their entire strength—fifteen states plus the city of Washington—and had they been able to resist the temptation to assault Sumter, there is a chance they might have won. But Calhoun was dead, and Lincoln very much alive. They had not realized their potential—only seven of the fifteen slave states had seceded. The ratio of manpower and resources was very much against them. They had no navy. They must bear the onus of slavery, and they had fired on the flag. The odds, physical and psychological, were just too heavy. From John Brown's raid to Sumter the course of Southern leadership included an unhappy series of unfortunate decisions. In the name of seeking security and their rights they had temporarily destroyed their own creation. Neither they nor anybody else after this long convention experience of shrinking leadership could have foreseen that the prairie galoot from distant Illinois could in any sense prove to be a messiah.

Had the nation followed its original intent and had no President, the republic would have been governed by the legislative arm in which factions of lawmakers, representing state organizations rather than any nationally organized parties, would have operated. Had these factions been unable to agree and had they developed severe group hostility, if their constituencies had withdrawn from the confederation, there might have been no resistance to this secession as there was no executive to make decisions. However this eventuality might well have destroyed the great republic and put in its place a Balkanized society or something like present-day Africa.

As the turbulent year of 1859 had drawn to its close the New York socialite diarist George Templeton Strong recorded in his voluminous daily commentary: "It's a sick nation, and I fear it must be worse before it's better. The growing, vigorous North must sooner or later assert its right to equality with the stagnant, semi-barbarous South, and that assertion must bring on a struggle and convulsion. It must come. Pity it could not be postponed some twenty years, when Northern preponderance would be overwhelming. If Northern abolitionism precipitate the crisis and force the battle on us *now,* it will be a fearful and doubtful contest."

Had a Southern diarist been commenting at this time he might have written a paraphrase of the above. "This republic has been corrupted and it must be purged of its corruption. The civilized South, cultured in its rural felicity, must maintain its equality with the growing, rapacious North, and that exertion must bring on a struggle and convulsion. It must come. It must come soon before Northern preponderance becomes overwhelming. Northern abolitionism may precipitate the crisis and force the battle on us now; it will be a fearful and doubtful contest."

The Democrats at Charleston and Baltimore had realized that changing conditions were in fact pointing to the emergence of a new establishment governed by a new power based on a new consensus. Despite the demonstration of experience from 1776 to 1860 that Americans possessed the capacity to rule and shape the United States, through the instrumentation of Congress and partisan conventions, in 1860 that capacity failed. It failed because its operators lost faith in its efficiency. Instead of using the convention as an instrument of adjustment and the creation of consensus, they destroyed it. They destroyed it because they did not trust it any longer. They had lost their faith because of fear, conscience, a

sense of honor, bad health, and a complicated series of personal antagonisms built up over years of association in Congress, conventions, and
the peculiar environment of Washington. The Democratic party broke
up because of a complex series of personal failures where, in an intricate
system of group dynamics, people entrusted with responsibility for leadership could not measure up to the demands of the perilous times. The
most spectacular evidence of this failure was the destruction of the
Democratic party by its own managers. Calhoun had always disliked
and distrusted the device employed to destroy him. It was his following
who thirty years later scrapped it.

CHAPTER 39

THE FIRST MODERN WAR

Too often military history is ignored or passed over lightly in American history courses. Too often historians and teachers denigrate military history as fit material for history buffs, genealogists, hero-worshipers, and antiquarians, failing to consider that military history (like other fields of history) can be as meaningless or as significant as historians choose to make it. The following selection is military history—not narrowly conceived, but broadly conceived. Such history can not only tell us a great deal about our past but, in a day of international strife and warfare, can also tell us much about ourselves that will be of value as we confront the problems of today and the future.

In this selection, T. Harry Williams, one of America's foremost military historians, examines the military systems of North and South during the Civil War. Professor Williams views that struggle as basically different from previous wars, and he suggests that the military leadership of both North and South were generally inexperienced in modern warfare and failed to understand the essential nature of the contest. From this point of view Williams discusses the military leadership of the two sections, the development of Northern and Southern strategy, the leadership of the two war presidents, Lincoln and Davis, and the ultimate creation by Lincoln, Halleck, and Grant of a modern command system for the North.

Central to this essay is Professor Williams' view of the Civil War as the first modern war. How does he define modern warfare, and what were the two characteristic features of the Civil War which justify its definition as a modern war? How did the Civil War differ from previous wars, and how did the differences affect demands upon the military leadership of North and South? How does Professor Williams compare Southern and Northern military strategy; how does he compare the war leadership of the two presidents, Lincoln and Davis? Granted the brilliance of Southern tactical maneuvers and battlefield strategy, how does one explain, essentially, the failure of the South to achieve military victory? On the other hand, what role did the 1864 Northern command system play in bringing military victory to the North? Was the development of that command system of importance to Americans of the last half of the twentieth century?

Perhaps more books have been written on the Civil War than any other topic in American history. Of major importance for the specific topic of this selection is Walter Millis' study of the development of the American military system, *Arms and Men** (1956). The writings of Bruce Catton, particularly *This Hallowed Ground** (1956), and *U. S. Grant and the American Military Tradition** (1954), are very valuable. Clement Eaton, *A History of the Southern Confederacy** (1954), is an excellent account of the Confederacy. Charles P. Roland, *The Confederacy** (1960), goes over the same ground and uses more recent material. Frank Vandiver, *Rebel Brass* (1956), touches more directly on Southern martial leadership. T. Harry Williams deals at length with the Northern command system in *Lincoln and His Generals** (1952).

* Available in a paperback edition.

THE MILITARY SYSTEMS OF NORTH AND SOUTH

T. HARRY WILLIAMS

I

Trite it may be to say that the Civil War was the first of the modern wars, but this is a truth that needs to be repeated. If the Civil War was not quite total, it missed totality by only a narrow margin. Instead of ending a military cycle as historians once thought, the war began a new one that has not yet been completed. In two ways the Civil War differed from previous conflicts of the modern era in both America and Europe. First, as a war of ideas on the part of both participants, it was a struggle of unlimited objectives. The policy of the North was to restore the Union by force; the policy of the South was to establish its independence by force. Between these two purposes there could be no compromise, no halfway triumph for either side. One or the other had to achieve a complete and decisive victory.[1] Second, the Civil War was a war of matériel, bringing into full play for the first time the great transforming forces of the Industrial Revolution. Among the techniques and weapons employed—either used for the first time or given their first prominent use—were conscription and mass armies, mass production of weapons, railroads, armored ships, submarines, the telegraph, breech-loading and repeating rifles, various precursors of the machine gun, and an incipient air force in the form of signal balloons. Because of these distinguishing qualities the Civil War was, compared with earlier conflicts, a ruthless, lethal, no-holds-barred war. In the high command arrangements, especially in the North, it witnessed an unprecedented measure of civilian participation in strategic planning and of civilian direction of the war.

[1] The North's objectives could be obtained only by a total military victory. The South, on the other hand, could attain its objectives by preventing the North from winning such a victory. But the South's policy objectives were total; it could accept no result except independence.

SOURCE. T. Harry Williams, *Americans at War: The Development of the American Military System*, Baton Rouge, Louisiana: Louisiana State University Press, 1960, pp. 47-61, 77-81. Copyright 1960 by the Louisiana State University Press. Reprinted by permission of the Louisiana State University Press and the author.

II

At the beginning of the war there were only two officers in the service who had ever commanded troops in numbers large enough to be called an army. One was Winfield Scott, who was seventy-five years of age, and the other was John E. Wool, who was two years older, and both of them had had their active experience in the Mexican War, when the largest field armies numbered about 14,000. Besides Scott and Wool, not an officer on either side had directed as large a unit as a brigade; only a few had commanded a regiment. The largest single army that the younger officers, the men who would become the generals of the war, had ever seen, except for the handful who had visited Europe, was Scott's or Taylor's force in the Mexican War. The 30,000 troops collected by the Federal government at Washington in the spring of 1861 were the largest single American army yet assembled. The photographs of Civil War generals tend to mislead us. We look at those fierce, bearded faces and think of the subjects as being old and hardened warriors. But despite the hirsute adornments, most of them were young men, and none of them, regardless of age, had ever handled troops in numbers before the war. This explains many of the mistakes made by both Northern and Southern generals in the early stages of the conflict. They were simply not prepared to direct the huge armies that were suddenly called into being and thrust upon them. The West Pointers, with the advantage of their technical training, were able to learn their jobs, but sometimes the educational process was painful—for them and their troops.

Both sides at first attempted to raise their armies by the traditional American method of calling for volunteers, and in the first year of the war, when both sections were moved by emotional outbursts of patriotism and optimistic estimates that the war would be of short duration, volunteering served to fill up the armies. But after the initial flush of enthusiasm had flickered out, enlistments dwindled away, and it become evident that the volunteer system would not supply enough men to constitute the huge armies the war was going to require. Both combatants had to resort to conscription, the Confederate States in 1862 and the United States a year later—the first time in the American military experience that national conscription was employed. Because of faulty methods of keeping statistics the total number of men raised by either side can only be estimated. In the Confederacy 1,300,000 enlistments were counted, but this figure includes many short-term enlistments and duplicates. The same qualification must be made of the North's enlistment total of 2,900,000. The best estimates are that 1,500,000 men served in Federal armies for three years and 900,000 in Southern armies for the same period.

The field armies that appeared in the war dwarfed in size any force in previous American wars. Disregarding the many small army units that operated in various theaters, we will concern ourselves here with the maximum forces employed by North and South. In the Eastern theater the Federal Army of the Potomac varied from a minimum of 90,000 to a maximum of 130,000. The highest number attained by its opponent, the Army of Northern Virignia, was 85,000, but the average size of this force was smaller, ranging between 55,000 and 70,000. The largest Federal army in the West comprised 90,000 troops, while the biggest army which the Confederacy placed in the field in this theater numbered 70,000, a total far above average, which ranged between 40,000 and 60,000.

The generals who commanded the large field armies were without exception professional soldiers, graduates of West Point. A large number of citizen soldiers in both armies proved themselves capable of directing divisions and corps, but the few amateurs who were given command of even small independent armies—as Benjamin F. Butler and N. P. Banks —were unequal to the task; N. B. Forrest on the Confederate side was a natural genius who probably could have led an army, but in actual experience he commanded only a cavalry force. It was the professionals, then, who in the area of battle operations fought the war and, for the North, won it. But it would be highly inaccurate to conclude from this that the trained experts demonstrated a consistent level of competence or manifested an immediate and perceptive awareness of the nature of modern war.

On the contrary, most of the Northern generals who came to prominence in the first half of the war were sorry field leaders—were, in fact, unfit for high level command. They exhibited a number of excellent qualities: they knew how—or, more accurately, they readily learned how—to prepare, train, and administer armies. There was only one quality that they lacked, but it was a fatal inadequacy: they did not want to fight their armies. In the first of the modern wars, in a war that both sides were playing for keeps, they were ruled by the military concepts of the eighteenth century. They thought of war as an exercise in bloodless strategy, as a series of maneuvers to checkmate an enemy on a gigantic chessboard. Above all—and here George B. McClellan is the supreme example of the type—they envisioned a leisurely, gentlemanly kind of war; in short, a war of limited objectives: if you don't accomplish your objective this time, all right, try it again later, next month, next year. McClellan always saw the war as a kind of game practiced by himself and other experts off in a private sphere of action that had no connection with the political community. If the public demanded action, if the government might fall because there was no action, such considerations impressed McClellan not at all. Ignorant politicians and other people should not be interfering with the specialists, who would move when the conditions of the game were exactly right and not one minute before.

Generals like McClellan were simply not competent to command in a conflict like the Civil War—a rough, mean war and one in which, whether the military liked it or not, civilians were going to have their say. Instead of recognizing the reality of civilian interference and accommodating himself to it, McClellan wasted his energies by wailing that it should not exist—the same kind of futile protest that his supporters have advanced ever since. Not until 1864 did the North succeed in bringing into the important command posts, in the persons of U. S. Grant, William T. Sherman, Philip H. Sheridan, and George H. Thomas, men who possessed the hard, driving qualities required in modern war and who understood the political nature of the war. Although the South owned its share of fumbling generals, it can be said of most Confederate commanders that, from the beginning, they were at least willing to fight their armies. Doubtless the inferior human and material resources of the South, which compelled her generals to act when they could with what they had, explains their greater aggressiveness.

III

At the outbreak of war neither side had ready at hand a plan of general strategy. The newly formed Confederate government could hardly have been expected to possess a previously devised design, but such a measure of preparation was well within the capacities of the Federal military organization. That no plan existed is, of course, not surprising. Nobody had thought, until the crisis suddenly broke, that the difficulties between the sections would come to war, and—here is the crux of the matter—nobody or any agency in the military system, neither Scott nor the General Staff, was charged with the function of studying strategy or of preparing plans for a possible war. The strategy of the war, then, had to be worked out as the conflict developed in the light of what the planners on each side could learn about the strategic situation. So far as prior preparations were concerned, neither government approached the standards of President Polk and his cabinet, who had outlined a general plan of operations a year before the war with Mexico started.[2]

The policy of the North, or the United States, was to restore the Union by force; hence, Northern strategy had to be offensive. But the strategic objectives of the North were complicated by the fact that this was a civil instead of a foreign war. If it was to win, the North had to do more than occupy the enemy capital or defeat enemy armies. It had to do these things and, in addition, convince the Southern people that their cause was hopeless. In short, to conquer a peace the North had to subdue a population. Northern armies would have to invade the South, seize key points and areas, and occupy large regions of the enemy country—all of which would require a vast expenditure of human and military resources. Northern strategy, as it was finally formulated, set up three principal objectives to be attained: (1) in the Eastern theater to capture Richmond and defeat the defending Confederate army; (2) to seize the line of the Mississippi River, thereby splitting the Confederacy into two parts; and (3) after the second objective had been achieved, to occupy Chattanooga and the Tennessee River line, thereby gaining a base from which an offensive could be launched to divide the South, east of the Mississippi.

The policy of the Confederacy was to establish its independence by force, and to accomplish this purpose the government decided on a defensive strategy. In part, the South had no choice in the matter; its decision was a forced reaction to Northern strategy. But the adoption of a defensive strategy was also in part a deliberate determination by its leaders, particularly by President Davis. For a power that wanted only to be let alone and that harbored no aggressive designs against anybody, a strategy of defense seemed so beautifully logical—and Confederates were always beguiled by logic. But because the South's only purpose was to resist conquest was not sufficient reason to rely on such an inert strategy. With equal logic, and probably with more effect, the South might have achieved its policy of independence by taking the offensive early in the war when its resources were greatest, by demonstrating that it was too strong to be conquered through victories on Northern soil.

---

[2] The several statements in these essays calling attention to the absence of plans at the beginning of wars are not to be taken as a belief in the necessity or feasibility of having a previously drawn up and detailed scheme of operations. Indeed, the possession of a rigid design may handicap a nation, as the experience of Germany with the Schlieffen plan attests. Especially today, when the nature of war is so fluid, it may be advantageous to be able to choose among a number of plans after war begins. What I am saying here is that in some of our wars *no thinking* about what might happen had been done before the advent of hostilities.

Confederate strategy was pervasively and, in a sense, passively defensive. The high command decided to defend every part of the Confederacy, to meet every threatened attack, to hold every threatened point—a policy which dispersed its resources, inferior to those of the North, over a wide strategic circumference and yielded the strategic initiative to the enemy.[3] If the South chose to await attack, it might have adopted an alternative defensive strategy; it could have shortened its lines to inclose the most defensible areas or those containing important resources or possessing a symbolic value. It did not do this, partly for valid reasons. For the new Southern government to abandon any of its territory would have seemed an admission of weakness and would certainly have lost it a measure of popular support. But even without these practical political considerations, President Davis and other civil leaders seemed to think almost instinctively in terms of defending places for their own sake, of holding territory simply because it was their territory.

In general, at the highest command levels the North displayed a greater degree of efficiency and originality than did the South. The Confederates, so brilliant in tactical maneuvers and in battlefield strategy, never succeeded in creating a competent command system or in setting up a unified plan of strategy. The Northern strategy of offense was basically sound; the Southern strategy of defense was fundamentally defective. But it would be inaccurate and unfair to ascribe the differences between the strategic systems to the human beings who operated them, to say that one side had wise leaders and the other had not, to dismiss Davis and his advisers as inept and unintelligent men (as a matter of fact, they were very intelligent) who did not rise to their opportunities. Warfare should always be considered a social institution. As Clausewitz said, a nation's social system or culture will determine the kind of war it will fight. Davis and Lee and other Confederates were the products of their culture, and their culture decided and limited their military thinking. Whereas, the North was a nation of the nineteenth century and looked to the future, the South was a confederation of sovereignties that refused to accept the nineteenth century and looked to the past. The Confederacy was founded on state rights—localism was imbedded in every segment of its system—and it fought a state-rights war and, on the strategic level, a

[3] It is recognized, of course, that on occasion the Confederacy did go over to the offensive, as in Bragg's invasion of Kentucky in 1862 and, most notably, in Lee's thrusts into the North in 1862 and 1863. But these operations were exceptions to the rule. Also, in every case where an offensive was attempted, the size of the Confederate army could have been significantly augmented by adding to it forces that were guarding places at home.

traditional, eighteenth-century type of war. Just as it was difficult for Southern political leaders to envision centralism in government, so it was hard for Confederate military directors to see the war as a whole or to install centralism in its direction.

IV

At the head of the military systems of both countries and of their command organizations were the two presidents, Abraham Lincoln and Jefferson Davis. They form an interesting contrast and offer the materials for an instructive and fascinating study in civil-military relationships and in the higher direction of war. Judging them solely by their backgrounds, one would expect that the Confederate President would be a great war leader, that he would far eclipse his rival. Few civilian war directors have come to their office with Davis' technical advantages. He was a graduate of West Point, he had served in the regular army, he had had battle experience in the Mexican War, and he had been Secretary of War. Lincoln had been a civilian all his life, he had received no military education, and he had had no military experience except briefly as a militia soldier in the Black Hawk War, when, as he liked to recall, he had made some ferocious charges on the wild onions and engaged in bloody struggles with the mosquitoes. And yet the truth is that Lincoln was a great war president and Davis was a mediocre one. The command careers of the two men illustrate perfectly the truth of Clausewitz' dictum that an acquaintance with military affairs is not the principal qualification for a director of war but that "a remarkable, superior mind and strength of character" are more important.

We cannot pause here to measure Davis' defects as a political leader of his people, intriguing though such an analysis of this sincere and tormented man would be. But certainly the weaknesses that he displayed—his excessive pride, his sensitivity to criticism, his impatience of contradiction, his lack of passion for anything, even for the South—detracted from his effectiveness as President and contributed to the final defeat of the Southern cause. We are concerned with his qualities as a war director, and we are obliged to note that in this area he failed as surely as he did in the political sphere.

He failed because he did not seem to realize what his task was or what his proper functions were. He could not grasp the vital fact that the Confederacy was not a going, recognized government but a revolution and that, in order to win, it would have to act with remorseless revolutionary vigor. Always he proceeded on the theory that the Confederacy was a permanent government and could act like older established governments, and always he observed every nicety of legal punctilio and tied himself up in every possible piece of red tape. Because of his military background, he fancied himself a military expert; he would rather have been a general than the head of state. Somebody in our own times has quipped that Davis learned enough about war in a few minutes at Buena Vista in the Mexican War to defeat the South; and during the war Richmond wags, referring to Davis' boasting about a formation he had led at Buena Vista, said that the Confederacy was dying of an inverted V. His image of himself being what it was, he concerned himself overly much with military affairs. The criticism here is not that he interfered with his generals—this point will be discussed later—but that he spent too much time on unimportant routine items, on matters that he should have left to subordinates. Once he even proposed to go through 1,500 documents bearing on promotions high and low. He could not delegate authority to people he knew were not as competent as he. Because he was a capable administrator, he loved to do the administrating himself. He has been an outstanding Secretary of War, but as President he rarely rose above the secretarial level.

Nor can we take time to analyze the qualities that made Lincoln a great war President. They are so well known, perhaps, that they do not need repetition. We may note two factors, however, that reveal something of his concept of the role of commander-in-chief and that help to explain his success as a war director. First, Lincoln was, in a technical sense, a poor administrator. Unlike Davis, who spent much time in his office, Lincoln was rarely in his office. He was often to be found in the offices of other people, generals and secretaries, ostensibly visiting around and telling stories, but really sizing up subordinates and deciding whether he could delegate authority to them. When he found a man whom he could trust to do a job, Lincoln was quite willing to let him handle the details of his office. In short, he was interested in the big administrative picture, and he did not, if he could avoid it, burden himself with petty routine—all of which means that he understood perfectly his function and the proper function of administration (or if he did not understand good administration, he intuitively practiced it). Second, Lincoln realized immediately that the war was a revolution, and he dealt with it on that basis. Whenever he felt that revolutionary methods were necessary to attain the objectives of Union policy, he used them, even to the length of violating law or the Constitution. He was not, he explained, going to see the government and the nation go to smash because of a squeamish regard for legal niceties. It is a curious fact that Lincoln, who headed an established government, acted with more revolutionary zeal than Davis, who led an experimental government.

As a director of war Lincoln displayed, almost from the beginning, a fine strategic sense. He was a better natural strategist than were most of his generals who were trained soldiers. Grasping the importance of economic warfare, he proclaimed a naval blockade of the South. Realizing that numbers were on his side, he called for 400,000 volunteers in 1861. Almost immediately he understood one of the great all-time strategic maxims, which his first generals seem never to have heard of, and applied it to his war: the proper objective of Union armies, he insisted, was the destruction of Confederate armies and not the occupation of Southern territory. Knowing the advantage that superior forces gave the North, he disregarded the traditional Jomini doctrine of concentrating at one point, and showing a startling originality in his strategic thinking, he urged his commanders to keep up a constant pressure on the whole strategic line of the Confederacy until a weak spot was found and a breakthrough could be made. Always, always, he prodded the generals to move, to execute an offensive strategy.

Both Lincoln and Davis have been criticized by historians and military writers for "interfering" with generals and military affairs. Most of these strictures seem misinformed. Judged by modern standards both presidents did some things that a civil director of war should not do. But it must be emphasized that they were operating without benefit of a formal command system, that they executed functions which, in the organization then existing, could have been performed by no other agency. Moreover, if the caliber of many of the generals, the so-called trained experts, is carefully measured, it is evident that the presidents were often justified in the supervision they exerted. Particularly for the Union cause, as will be demonstrated later, it was fortunate that Lincoln called his generals to account. But the vital point about such "interfering" is the purpose for which the war director intervenes—the strategic objective he is trying to accomplish. If the strategy is sound and if the director of war is a man of "a remarkable, superior mind," the results of his intervention will be generally good. Lincoln interfered to make a sound offensive strategy stronger, and Davis interfered to make a defective defensive strategy more defensive. One acted from a valid theory and the other from a faulty one. . . .

VII

Although Lincoln wielded his great powers as war director with a certainty that came from ever growing confidence, he was willing, as he had always indicated, to yield those powers to a general who was competent and willing to exercise them. By 1864 he had found his man—and Congress and the nation ratified the choice—in U. S. Grant, who in the

West had emerged as the greatest Union general of the war. In February Congress created the rank of lieutenant general, expressing a wish that Grant would receive the grade and the position of General-in-Chief, and Lincoln unhesitatingly named Grant to both. At last the United States was about to get a modern command system.

In the system arrived at in 1864, which was the joint product of Lincoln, Grant, and maybe of Halleck, Grant as general-in-chief was charged with the functions of framing over-all Union strategy and directing the movements of all Federal armies. As commanding general, Grant might have been expected to establish his command post in Washington, where he would be near the President and in quick contact with Federal field generals all over the country. But Grant disliked the political atmosphere of the capital, and he set up his headquarters with the Army of the Potomac in the field. He was always close to Washington, which he could reach in a short train trip, and he was in almost instant telegraphic communication with the President. Technically, Grant did not become commander of the Eastern field army—Meade continued to hold that position—but since he traveled with that army, it was subject to his close supervision.

Under the new arrangement Halleck received a new command office, the Chief of Staff. Again, as when we dealt with the nature of the General Staff, we must avoid confusion between nineteenth-century and contemporary usages of the same term. Halleck was not a chief of staff in the modern sense. In the present command system his position would correspond perhaps to the Secretary of the General Staff. Primarily he was a channel of communication between Lincoln and Grant and between Grant and the seventeen departmental commanders under the general-in-chief. Grant sent most of his dispatches for the President to Halleck, who, when necessary, briefed or explained them for Lincoln. Similarly, Halleck transmitted to Grant many of Lincoln's directives or inquiries concerning strategic matters. Because of Halleck's facility in the languages of both soldier and civilian, Lincoln and Grant never misunderstood each other, as Lincoln and McClellan so often had.

Halleck also served as a liaison between Grant and the department and field commanders. If Grant had had to read all the reports from these officers and frame detailed instructions for them, he would not have had much time for strategic planning. At Grant's direction, the subordinate commanders sent their dispatches for Grant to Halleck, who either transmitted them to the general-in-chief or summarized their contents for him. Grant sent most of his orders to subordinates through Halleck. Often he would tell the chief of staff in general terms what he wanted done and ask him to put the objective in a written directive, or he would delegate authority to Halleck to handle a particular situation. Although Halleck professed to think that his role in the command system was insignificant, it was really vitally important. Without such a coordinator of information the system would not have worked as brilliantly as it did.

But the key military man in the system was Grant. As general-in-chief, he proved to be the general for whom Lincoln had been searching. And because the President came to realize Grant's capacities, he gave him more latitude in determining strategy than he had permitted McClellan or Halleck. To a man who asked whether Grant did not have too much freedom of decision, Lincoln said, "Do you hire a man to do your work and then do it yourself?" Grant possessed the rare ability to see the war as a total picture and to devise what in later wars would be called "global" strategy. In fact, he was probably the only general on either side who could envision the war as a whole, the only one who was qualified to act as general-in-chief in a modern war. This is not the place to discuss his plan of grand operations for 1864, but it was a brilliant demonstration of strategic thinking and would do credit to the most finished student of a series of modern staff and command schools. Unhampered by traditional military doctrine Grant was boldly original in innovating new strategic concepts. A young officer once asked him what he thought of Jomini. Grant said he had never read the French-Swiss master, the guiding authority for so many other Civil War generals. He then expressed his own theory of war: "The art of war is simple enough. Find out where your enemy is. Get at him as soon as you can. Strike at him hard as you can, and keep moving on."

It is not true, however, as Grant stated in his memoirs and as many historians have repeated since, that Lincoln gave him an absolutely free hand in deciding strategy and directing operations. According to Grant's account, the President was a military innocent who greeted him with relief when he came to Washington and said, in effect: General, I am not a military man, I don't understand war and don't want to know your plans—go ahead and do exactly as you please. Grant wrote under the influence of his own postwar myth, which cast him in the image of the great soldier who was the architect of victory. Actually, as the evidence in contemporary war documents amply demonstrates, Lincoln, while permitting his general-in-chief wide latitude of action, watched him closely and never hesitated to check him when the need arose. On at least two occasions, as when he forced Grant to come to Washington to supervise personally the launching of the campaign against Jubal Early in the Shenandoah Valley and when he restrained him from removing General George H. Thomas before the battle of Nashville, he saved the general from serious mistakes.

Moreover, as the documents again show, the victorious strategy of the North was the joint product of consultations between Lincoln and Grant. The general submitted to Lincoln the broad outlines of his plans, and the President, approving the objectives and trusting Grant, did not seek to learn the details. Indeed, Grant made his strategy conform to the strategy Lincoln had been advocating since 1862: make enemy armies the objective and move all Federal forces against the enemy line simultaneously so as to bring into play the Federal advantage of superior numbers. An offensive all along the line, violating the Jomini maxim of concentration, was the essence of Grant's strategy. When Grant explained to Lincoln this plan, so eminently sensible for the side with the greater numbers and the superior transportation, he remarked that those forces not fighting could still help the fighting by advancing. Grasping the point and recognizing the application of his own ideas, the President uttered a maxim of his own, one that for modern war was more valid than most of Jomini's dictums: "Those not skinning can hold a leg."

The 1864 command system was a major factor in the final victory of the North. By providing a sound basis for participation by the civil and military branches in the formulating of strategy, it gave the United States a modern command organization for a modern war. With a commander-in-chief to state policy and the general objectives of strategy, a general-in-chief to put the strategy in specific form, and a chief of staff to co-ordinate information, the United States possessed a model system of civil and military relationships and the finest command arrangements of any country in the world. Created in the strain of war, it expressed the national genius to improvise an arrangement to fit the requirements of the moment. The American system was superior to most command organizations then existing in Europe and was at least as good as the Prussian general staff machine. Indeed, it was probably the most efficient system that we have ever had.

CHAPTER 40

THE AMERICAN
CHARACTER

The very title of the next reading—"What then is the American, this new man?"—is significant in a discussion of the American character. From colonial times to the present, both Americans and Europeans have been intrigued about the nature of Americans, but on one thing nearly all commentators have agreed—the American was a new man. He was not a European; neither was he fundamentally a person with regional or local identification. Despite real and persistent differences among themselves Americans were more similar to each other than dissimilar and possessed a distinctive national character.

In this selection, Arthur M. Schlesinger, Sr., suggests that the American character was produced by the interplay of Old World influences and New World conditions. Professor Schlesinger discusses the development of the American character in light of the specific European heritage that was transplanted to America and the ways in which that heritage underwent change. Schlesinger identifies four basic elements, about which are clustered numerous additional attributes, as the bases of American character. It should be noted that in this excerpt the author focuses upon pre-Civil War America; in an omitted section he discusses the changes in the national pattern produced by the rise of urbanization and industrialization after 1860.

In reading this essay the student should concentrate on defining the American character and on identifying the factors most important in shaping this "new man." Do you agree with Schlesinger's suggestion that Americans can explore the American character more deeply and meaningfully than "outsiders" generally can? In view of the unrest and dislocation in American society in recent history, does there still exist a national character? If so, is the national character still distinctive? How does the character of Americans today differ from the American character as defined by Schlesinger? Finally, do the enduring qualities of the national character pinpointed by the author in the last paragraph of this selection still endure?

A great deal of work has been done in this area. A good place to begin is Michael McGiffert, *The Character of Americans: A Book of Readings** (1964). Two indispensable monographs are David M. Potter, *People of Plenty: Economic Abundance and the American Character** (1954), and David Riesman (in collaboration with Reuel Denney and Nathan Glazer), *The Lonely Crowd: A Study of the Changing American Character** (1950). The two volumes of Daniel J. Boorstin's study of the national "personality," *The Americans: The Colonial Experience** (1958), and *The Americans: The National Experience** (1964), are extraordinarily provocative and valuable.

* Available in a paperback edition.

"WHAT THEN IS THE AMERICAN, THIS NEW MAN?"

ARTHUR M. SCHLESINGER, SR.

THE question which forms the title of this essay has never ceased to arouse interest since Crèvecœur posed it in the last years of the Revolution. If we can learn why the American has come to be what he is, how he reacts instinctively to life, wherein he differs from other peoples, we shall have gained a deep insight into the springs of national behavior. Crèvecœur's own answer, the considered opinion of a Frenchman long resident in the New World, may still be read with profit. The American, he said, "is either an European, or the descendant of an European, hence that strange mixture of blood which you will find in no other country. . . . *He* is an American, who leaving behind him all his ancient prejudices and manners, receives new ones from the new mode of life he has embraced, the new government he obeys, and the new rank he holds. . . . From involuntary idleness, servile dependence, penury, and useless labour, he has passed to toils of a very different nature. — This is an American."

I

Crèvecœur, of course, was one of a long procession of Europeans who have tried to describe and appraise the American. Their writings, though of varying merit, possess the common advantage of presenting an outsider's point of view, free from the predilections and prepossessions which blur the American's vision of himself. Viewing the scene from a different background, they are also sensitive to national divergences of which the nativeborn are usually unaware. Though bias may influence the individual observer's judgment, the total number of visitors has been so great as to render far more significant their points of agreement.

The composite portrait that emerges deserves thoughtful consideration. The attributes most frequently noted have been a belief in the universal obligation to work; the urge to move from place to place; a high standard

SOURCE. Arthur M. Schlesinger, Sr., *Paths to the Present*, New York: The Macmillan Company, 1949, pp. 1–21. Copyright 1949 by The Macmillan Company. Reprinted by permission of The Macmillan Company.

of average comfort; faith in progress; the eternal pursuit of material gain; an absence of permanent class barriers; the neglect of abstract thinking and of the aesthetic side of life; boastfulness; a deference for women; the prevalence of spoiled children; the general restlessness and hurry of life, always illustrated by the practice of fast eating; and certain miscellaneous traits such as overheated houses, the vice of spitting and the passion for rocking chairs and ice water.

This inventory, so far as it goes, reveals qualities and attitudes recognizably American. Moreover, the travelers express no doubt as to the existence of a distinctive national character. The native-born looking at their fellow countrymen readily identify them as New Englanders or Middle Westerners or Southerners, as products of old American stock or newcomers of immigrant origin; and they remember that at one period of their history the differences between Northerner and Southerner sharpened into a tragic war. But the detached observer from Europe has always been less impressed by these regional deviations than by the evidences of fundamental kinship, even in slavery times.

James Bryce, most perspicacious of the commentators, goes so far as to say, "Scotchmen and Irishmen are more unlike Englishmen, the native of Normandy more unlike the native of Provence, the Pomeranian more unlike the Wurtemberger, the Piedmontese more unlike the Neapolitan, the Basque more unlike the Andalusian, than the American from any part of the country is to the American from any other part." His conclusion is that "it is rather more difficult to take any assemblage of attributes in any of these European countries and call it the national type than it is to do the like in the United States." The preoccupation of American historians with local and sectional diversities has tended to obscure this underlying reality.

But the particular "assemblage of attributes" recorded by the travelers leaves much to be desired. Not only is the list incomplete, but it carelessly lumps the significant with the trivial. Since the typical European tried to cover as much ground as possible in a short time, his attention was caught by externals, with the result that annoying traits and ways assumed undue importance, much as dust in the eye of a wayfarer distorts the appearance of the landscape. The gospel of work, for example, hardly deserves to be equated with the addiction to spitting. Though the more thoughtful sought to correlate what they noticed with the avowed ideals of the people, they usually lacked sufficient knowledge of the deeper historical trends to grasp either the true import of the ideals or how they manifested themselves in action. Finally, the traveler gave little attention to the crucial problem of why the special combination of qualities and attitudes had become endemic within the borders of the United States.

Hence the judgment of these onlookers, though often clearsighted and frequently valuable as a corrective, leaves ample room for the student of United States history to venture an answer to Crèvecœur's question. If the native-born historian be suspect as a party in interest, he may at least strive to observe that counsel of objectivity which his professional conscience reveres.

II

What then is the American from a historian's point of view? The answer, briefly expressed, is so simple as to be a platitude. This "new man" is the product of the interplay of Old World influences and New World conditions. But just what heritage did the colonists bring with them from Europe, and why and how was it changed? Predominantly it involved that part of Europe's social experience in which they themselves had shared. The great bulk of the settlers, like the immigrants of later times, belonged to the poorer classes. They and their ancestors, whether in England or on the Continent, had been artisans, small tradesmen, farmers, day laborers—the broad foundation which supported the fine super-structure of European civilization. Shut out from a life of wealth, leisure and aesthetic enjoyment, they had tended to regard the ways of their social superiors with misgiving, if not resentment, and by the same token they magnified their own qualities of sobriety, diligence and thrift. Even when many of them, as notably in England, improved their economic position in the sixteenth and seventeenth centuries as a result of the great growth of commerce and industry, they continued to exalt the ancient proprieties.

This attitude found its classic spiritual expression in Calvinism. As Professor Tawney has said, Calvinism was "perhaps the first systematic body of religious teaching which can be said to recognize and applaud the economic virtues." It neatly fitted the glove of divine sanction to the hand of prudential conduct, thereby giving a sense of personal rectitude to the business of getting ahead in the world. But whether in Britain or elsewhere, whether in the religious groups directly concerned or those more remotely affected, Calvinism merely intensified a pre-existing bent. It is similarly true that the stringent code of morals often attributed to Calvinism, and more particularly to the Puritans, represented a lower-middle-class mentality long antedating the Geneva teachings.

This, then, was the type of humanity upon which the untamed New World wielded its influence. It has often been observed that plants and animals undergo modification when removed to America. These mutations arise from differences in climate and geography. But other factors as well affected transplanted people. One was the temperament of the settler, the fact that he was more adventurous, more ambitious or more rebellious against conditions at home than his fellows. It is not necessary to believe with William Stoughton in 1670 that "God sifted a whole Nation that he might send Choice Grain over into this Wilderness," but undoubtedly the act of quitting a familiar existence for a strange and perilous one demanded uncommon attributes of hardihood, self-reliance and imagination. Once the ocean was crossed, sheer distance from the old country and the challenge of new experiences further weakened the bonds of custom, evoked latent capacities and awakened the settler to possibilities of improvement hitherto unsuspected.

The undeveloped continent prescribed the conditions of living the new life, the mold within which the American character took shape. Farming was the primary occupation. At first resorted to to keep from starvation, it quickly became the mainstay of existence. The Revolution was fought by a people of whom nineteen out of twenty tilled the soil. With good land obtainable for more than a century after Independence, agriculture continued, though with gradually diminishing effect, to provide the pervasive atmosphere of American life and thought. "The vast majority of the people of this country live by the land, and carry its quality in their manners and opinions," wrote Ralph Waldo Emerson in 1844. Even when the hosts from Continental Europe began to swell the population after the middle of the nineteenth century, the rural temper of the nation remained pretty much unaltered, for many of the immigrants also turned to farming. This long apprenticeship to the soil made an indelible impress on the developing American character, with results which the modern age of the city has not wholly effaced.

Agriculture in the New World, however, differed from agriculture in the Old. This was the initial lesson which the colonists were compelled to learn. Those who had been farmers in their homelands found many of the traditional methods unsuitable. Those who had worked at urban occupations suffered an even greater handicap. Densely forested land must be cleared; the wildness taken out of the soil; a knowledge gained of indigenous plants and of the best means of growing them. The settlers of Jamestown were barely able to struggle through the early years. "There were never Englishmen left in a forreigne Country in such miserie as wee," wrote one of them. "Unsufferable hunger" caused them to eat horses, dogs, rats and snakes, and instances even of cannibalism are recorded. As is well known, the Plymouth colonists experienced similar trials. Yet in both cases the woods abounded with native fruits, berries, roots and nuts, game was plentiful, and near-by waters teemed with fish.

Had these courageous men been more readily adaptable, they could have enjoyed a gastronomic abundance beyond the dreams of the wealthiest classes at home. But they had never faced such an experience before, and reversion to a stage of civilization which the white man had long since outgrown was not easy. At the very first, all the early settlements actually imported food supplies; the Swedish colony on the Delaware did so for twenty years. A knowledge of self-sufficient farming came slowly and painfully, with untold numbers of men, women and children perishing in the process. In the long run, however, the settlers learned how to master their environment. Utilizing native crops and Indian methods of tillage, they abandoned the intensive cultivation required by the limited land resources of the Old World. It was simpler to move on to new fields when the fertility of the old was exhausted. The typical farm was a small one, worked by the owner and his family. Even when the system of staple production developed in the South, the small independent farmers considerably outnumbered the great slaveholding planters.

Though the colonial agriculturalist owed much to the savage, he had no wish to live like one. Accustomed in the old country to simple comforts and mechanical devices in the home and about the farm, he duplicated them in the wilderness. Every husbandman became a manufacturer and every farmhouse a small factory, producing flour, soap and candles, tanning skins, preparing the winter's meat supply, making nails, harness, hats, shoes and rugs, contriving tools, churns, casks, beds, chairs and tables. Such activities he supplemented with trapping, hunting and fishing. As cold weather closed in, he used his spare time getting out rough timber products, such as shingles and planks, or spent the long evenings before the open fireplace carving gunstocks or making brooms while his womenfolk knitted, spun or wove.

Under pressure of circumstances the farmer thus became a Jack-of-all-trades. As Chancellor Livingston wrote, "being habituated from early life to rely upon himself he acquires a skill in every branch of his profession, which is unknown in countries where labour is more divided." Take the case of a typical New Englander, John Marshall of Braintree, early in the eighteenth century. Besides tending his farm, he bought and sold hogs, was a painter, brickmaker and carpenter, turning out as many as three hundred laths in a day, and served as a precinct constable. The primitive state of society fostered a similar omnicompetence in other walks of life, as the career of Benjamin Franklin so well exemplifies. Lord Cornbury, the governor of New York, characterized Francis Makemie as "a Preacher, a Doctor of Physick, a Merchant, an Attorney, or Counsellor at Law, and," he ruefully added, "which is worse of all, a Disturber of Governments."

The pioneer farmer of later times was the colonial farmer reborn. Up and down the Mississippi Valley he faced the same difficulties and opportunities as his forefathers, and he dealt with them in much the same way. As time went on, to be sure, he managed to buy more and more of his tools and household conveniences. He also took advantage of new inventions like the iron plow and the reaper, while increasingly he raised crops for sale in a general market. Meanwhile along the Atlantic Seaboard similar changes occurred. But whether in the older or newer communities these innovations affected the surface rather than the substance of the traditional mode of life. Nor did the advent of cities at first do much to alter the situation. Mere islands in a sea of forests and farms, they long retained marked rural characteristics and depended for a large part of their growth on continued accessions from the countryside.

III

What elements of the national character are attributable to this long-time agrarian environment? First and foremost is the habit of work. For the colonial farmer ceaseless striving constituted the price of survival; every member of the community must be up and doing. When anyone failed to do his part, the authorities, whether Puritan, Anglican or otherwise, laid a heavy hand upon the culprit. The Virginia Assembly in 1619 ordered the slothful to be bound over to compulsory labor. A few years later the Massachusetts Bay Company instructed Governor John Endecott that "noe idle drone bee permitted to live amongst us," and the General Court followed this up in 1633 with a decree that "noe prson, howse houlder or othr, shall spend his time idlely or unproffitably, under paine of such punishmt as the Court shall thinke meete to inflicte." Such regulations had long existed in England, where it was hoped, vainly, they might combat the unemployment and vagrancy of a surplus laboring class; in America the object was to overcome a labor shortage—that exigent problem of every new country. Of course, most of the settlers, having been inured to toil in the homeland, needed no official prodding.

They were the hardest-working people on earth, their only respite being afforded by strict observance of the Sabbath as demanded by both church and state.

The tradition of toil so begun found new sustenance as settlers opened up the boundless stretches of the interior. "In the free States," wrote Harriet Martineau in 1837, "labour is more really and heartily honoured than, perhaps, in any other part of the civilised world." Alonzo Potter voiced the general opinion of the American people when he asserted a few years later, "Without a definite pursuit, a man is an excrescence on society. . . . In isolating himself from the cares and employments of other men, he forfeits much of their sympathy, and can neither give nor receive great benefit." Even when the usual motives for work did not exist, the social compulsion remained. As William Ellery Channing put it, "The rich man has no more right to repose than the poor," for nobody should so live as to "throw all toil on another class of society."

One source of Northern antagonism to the system of human bondage was the fear that it was jeopardizing this basic tenet of the American creed. "Wherever labor is mainly performed by slaves," Daniel Webster told the United States Senate, "it is regarded as degrading to freemen"; and Kentucky abolitionist David Rice pointed out that in the South "To labour, is to *slave;* to work, is *to work like a Negroe.*" After the Civil War, General W. T. Sherman found public occasion to thank God that now at long last Southern whites would have "to earn an honest living."

Probably no legacy from our farmer forebears has entered more deeply into the national psychology. If an American has no purposeful work on hand, the fever in his blood impels him nevertheless to some visible form of activity. When seated he keeps moving in a rocking chair. A European visitor in the 1890's saw more fact than fancy in a magazine caricature which pictured a foreigner as saying to his American hostess, "It's a defect in your country, that you have no leisured classes." "But we have them," she replied, "only we call them tramps." The traveler's own comment was: "America is the only country in the world, where one is ashamed of having nothing to do."

This worship of work has made it difficult for Americans to learn how to play. As Poor Richard saw it, "Leisure is the Time for doing something useful"; and James Russell Lowell confessed,

> Pleasure doos make us Yankees kind o'winch,
> Ez though 't wuz sunthin' paid for by the inch;
> But yit we du contrive to worry thru,
> Ef Dooty tells us thet the thing's to du.

The first mitigations of the daily grind took the form of hunting, fishing, barn-raisings and logrollings—activities that had no social stigma because they contributed to the basic needs of living. As the years went on, the great Southern planters, imitating the landed gentry in England, developed rural diversions of elaborate sort; but their example, like that of the fashionable circles in the Northern cities, merely made the common man all the more self-conscious when he turned to recreation. Nor did the mid-nineteenth-century German and Irish immigrants, who indulged in spontaneous enjoyments when the day was over, have any other effect upon the native stock than to reinforce suspicions of the newcomers formed on other grounds. "The American," wrote the New Yorker, Henry T. Tuckerman, in 1857, "enters into festivity as if it were a serious business." And a serious business it has in considerable degree continued to be ever since.

Into it goes all the fierce energy that once felled the forests and broke the prairies. Americans play games not for fun but to win. They attend social gatherings grimly determined to have a "good time." Maxim Gorky said of Coney Island, "What an unhappy people it must be that turns for happiness here." The "rich gift of extemporizing pleasures," of taking leisure leisurely, seems alien to the national temper. It is significant that the English *Who's Who* includes the recreations of the notables listed, while the American does not.

The importance attached to useful work had the further effect of helping to make "this new man" indifferent to aesthetic considerations. To the farmer a tree was not a thing of beauty and a joy forever, but an obstacle to be replaced as quickly as possible with a patch of corn. In the words of an eighteenth-century American, "The Plow-man that raiseth Grain is more serviceable to Mankind, than the Painter who draws only to please the Eye. The Carpenter who builds a good House to defend us from the Wind and Weather, is more serviceable than the curious Carver, who employs his Art to please the Fancy." The cult of beauty, in other words, had nothing to contribute to the stern business of living; it wasn't "practical." The bias thus given to the national mentality lasted well into America's urban age. One result has been the architectural monotony and ugliness which have invariably offended travelers used to the picturesque charm of Old World cities.

IV

On the other hand, the complicated nature of the farmer's job, especially during the first two and a half centuries, afforded an unexcelled training in mechanical ingenuity. These ex-Europeans and their descendants became a race of whittlers and tinkers, daily engaged in devising, improving and repairing tools and other utensils until, as Emerson said, they had "the power and habit of invention in their brain." "Would any one but an American," asked one of Emerson's contemporaries, "have ever invented a milking machine? or a machine to beat eggs? or machines to black boots, scour knives, pare apples, and do a hundred things that all other peoples have done with their ten fingers from time immemorial?"

As population increased and manufacturing developed on a commercial scale, men merely turned to new purposes the skills and aptitudes that had become second nature to them. Thus Eli Whitney, who as a Massachusetts farm youth had made nails and hatpins for sale to his neighbors, later contrived the cotton gin and successfully applied the principle of interchangeable parts to the production of muskets; and Theodore T. Woodruff, a New York farm boy, won subsequent fame as the inventor of a sleeping car, a coffee-hulling machine and a steam plow. In this manner another trait became imbedded in the American character.

The farmer's success in coping with his multitudinous tasks aroused a pride of accomplishment that made him scorn the specialist or expert. As a Jack-of-all-trades he was content to be master of none, choosing to do many things well enough rather than anything supremely well. Accordingly, versatility became another outstanding American attribute. In public affairs the common man agreed with President Jackson that any intelligent citizen could discharge the duties of any governmental office. He had an abiding suspicion of the theorist or the "scholar in politics," preferring to trust his own quick perceptions and to deal from day to day with matters as they arose. In his breadwinning pursuits the American flitted freely from job to job in marked contrast to the European custom of following occupations which often descended from father to son.

The most casual scrutiny of the *Dictionary of American Biography* discloses countless instances reminiscent of John Marshall and Francis Makemie in colonial times. Thomas Buchanan Read, born on a Pennsylvania farm, was in turn a tailor's apprentice, grocer's assistant, cigar maker, tombstone carver, sign painter and actor before he became a portrait painter, novelist and poet. Another personage is listed as "ornithologist and wholesale druggist"; another as "preacher, railway president, author"; and still another as "physician, merchant, political leader, magazine editor, poet, and critic." The wonder is that, despite such a squandering of energies, they could yet gain sufficient distinction in any phase of their activities to be recalled by posterity.

Even in his principal occupation of growing food, the farmer encountered harsh criticism from foreign observers because of the way he wore out the land, neglected livestock and destroyed forest resources. But Old World agriculture rested on a ratio of man to land which in the New World was the reverse. It was as logical for the American farmer to "mine" the soil and move on to a virgin tract as it was for the European peasant to husband his few acres in the interest of generations unborn. Not till the opening years of the twentieth century, when the pressure of population dramatized the evils of past misuse, did the conservation of natural resources become a set national policy.

Meanwhile the tradition of wasteful living, bred by an environment of plenty, had fastened itself upon the American character, disposing men to condone extravagence in public as well as in private life. Even governmental corruption could be winked at on the ground that a wealthy country like the United States could afford it. In their daily living, Americans were improvident of riches that another people would have carefully preserved. One newcomer from England in the early nineteenth century wrote that the apples and peaches rotting in Ohio orchards were more "than would sink the British fleet." Another said of her neighbors that she wished "the poor people of England had the leavings of their tables, that goes to their dogs and hogs." A great national emergency like that of the Axis war reveals the extent to which the practice still prevails. People learned that, by responding to the government's appeal to salvage kitchen fats, old iron and other materials usually discarded, they could make a substantial contribution to the war effort.

Toward women the American male early acquired an attitude which sharply distinguished him from his brother in the Old World. As in every new country, women had a high scarcity value, both in the colonies and later in the pioneer West. They were in demand not only as sweethearts and wives, but also because of their economic importance, for they performed the endless work about the house and helped with the heavy farm labor. "The cry is everywhere for girls; girls, and more girls!" wrote a traveler in 1866. He noted that men outnumbered women in thirty-eight of the forty-five states and territories. In California the proportion was three to one; in Colorado, twenty to one. "Guess my husband's got to look after me, and make himself agreeable to me, if he can," a pretty Western girl remarked—"if he don't, there's plenty will." In the circumstances men paid women a deference and accorded them a status unknown in older societies. European observers attributed the high standard of sex morals largely to this fact, and it is significant that the most rapid strides toward equal suffrage took place in those commonwealths whose rural characteristics were strongest.

V

Since the agriculturalist regarded his farm as only a temporary abode
—an investment rather than a home—he soon contracted the habit of
being "permanently transitory." Distances that would have daunted the
stoutest-hearted European deterred "this new man" not at all. Many an
Atlantic Coast family migrated from place to place across the continent
until the second or third generation reached the rim of the Pacific, then
the next one began the journey back. "In no State of the Union," wrote
James Bryce in 1888, "is the bulk of the population so fixed in its
residence as everywhere in Europe; in many it is almost nomadic."

But for this constant mingling of people and ideas the spirit of sectionalism would have opened far deeper fissures in American society than it
did, for the breadth of the land, the regional diversification of economic
interests and the concentration of European immigrants in certain areas
were all factors conducive to disaffection and disunity. Apart from the
crisis of 1861, however, it has always been possible to adjust sectional
differences peaceably. The war between North and South might itself
have been avoided if the system of slave labor had not increasingly
stopped the inflow of persons from other parts of the country as well as
from Europe. Denied such infusions of new blood, the Southerners
lived more and more to themselves, came to exalt their peculiarities over
the traits they had in common with their fellow countrymen and, in the
end, determined to establish an independent state.

As the nation grew older and its institutions took on a more settled
aspect, the locomotive tendencies of the Americans showed no signs of
abatement. . . .

Geographic or horizontal mobility, however, was a less fundamental
aspect of American life than social or vertical mobility, though the two
were not unrelated. The European conception of a graded society, with
each class everlastingly performing its allotted function, vanished quickly
amidst primitive surroundings that invited the humblest to move upward
as well as outward. Instead of everybody being nobody, they found that
anybody might become somebody. In the language of James Russell
Lowell, "Here, on the edge of the forest, where civilized man was
brought face to face again with nature and taught mainly to rely on himself, mere manhood became a fact of prime importance." This emancipation from hoary custom was "no bantling of theory, no fruit of
forethought," but "a gift of the sky and of the forest."

Accordingly, there arose the ingrained belief in equality of opportunity, the right of all men to a free and fair start—a view which in one

of its most significant ramifications led to the establishment of free tax-supported schools. This was far from being a dogma of enforced equality. To benefit from equality of opportunity a man must be equal to his opportunities, with the government serving principally as an umpire to supervise the game with a minimum of rules. The upshot was a conception of democracy rigorously qualified by individualism.

This individualistic bias sometimes assumed forms that defied government. The colonists in their relations with the mother country evaded unwelcome regulations and, prompted by their theologians and lawyers, insisted that acts of Parliament contrary to their "unalienable rights" were void. Within the colonies those who dwelt remote from centers of law and order adopted a like attitude toward the provincial authorities. The Scotch-Irish who illegally occupied Pennsylvania soil in the early eighteenth century contended "it was against the laws of God and nature, that so much land should be idle while so many Christians wanted it to labor on and to raise their bread." As a substitute for constituted authority the settlers sometimes created their own unofficial tribunals, which adjudicated property titles and punished offenders against the public peace. In other instances they resorted to the swifter retribution of individual gunplay, or of mob action and lynch law, for from taking the law into one's hands when it could not function it was but a step to taking the law into one's hands when it did not function as one wanted it to.

The tendency to violence so generated has continued to condition the national mentality to the present time. Thoreau, the great philosopher of individualism, knew of no reason why a citizen should "ever for a moment, or in the least degree, resign his conscience to the legislator," declaring that "we should be men first, and subjects afterward." A similar conviction undoubtedly inspired William H. Seward's flaming declaration to the proslavery Senators in 1850 that "there is a higher law than the Constitution," just as it actuated the thousands of churchgoing Northerners who secretly banded together to violate the Fugitive Slave Act. But generally it has been self-interest or convenience, rather than conscience, that has provided the incentive to lawbreaking, as in the case of the businessman chafing against legislative restrictions or of the motorist disobeying traffic regulations. Sometimes the attitude has paraded under such high-sounding names as states' rights and nullification. This lawless streak in the American character has often been directed to wrong purposes, but it has also served as a check on the abuse of governmental powers and as a safeguard of minority rights.

In still another aspect, the individualism of the pioneer farmer does much to explain the intense cultivation of the acquisitive spirit. In the absence of hereditary distinctions of birth and rank the piling up of wealth constituted the most obvious badge of social superiority, and once the process was begun, the inbred urge to keep on working made it difficult to stop. "The poor struggle to be rich, the rich to be richer," remarked an onlooker in the mid-nineteenth century. Thanks to equality of opportunity with plenty for all, the class struggle in America has consisted in the struggle to climb out of one class into a higher one. The zest of competition frequently led to sharp trading, fraud and chicanery, but in the popular mind guilt attached less to the practices than to being caught at them. Financial success was accepted as the highest success, and not till the twentieth century did a religious leader venture to advance the un-American doctrine that ill-gotten wealth was "tainted money," even when devoted to benevolent uses.

VI

It would be a mistake, however, to think of the American simply as a mechanism set in motion by dropping a coin in the slot. When President Coolidge made his famous remark, "The business of America is business," he quite properly added, "The chief ideal of the American people is idealism. I cannot repeat too often that America is a nation of idealists." This ambivalence puzzled foreign commentators, who found it difficult, for example, to reconcile worship of the Almighty Dollar with the equally universal tendency to spend freely and give money away. In contrast to Europe, America has had practically no misers, and one consequence of the winning of Independence was the abolition of primogeniture and entail. Harriet Martineau was among those who concluded that "the eager pursuit of wealth does not necessarily indicate a love of wealth for its own sake."

The fact is that, for a people who recalled how hungry and oppressed their ancestors had been through long centuries in the Old World, the chance to make money was like the sunlight at the end of a tunnel. It was the means of living a life of human dignity. It was a symbol of idealism rather than materialism. Hence "this new man" had an instinctive sympathy for the underdog, and even persons of moderate substance freely shared it with the less fortunate, helping to endow charities, schools, hospitals and art galleries and to nourish humanitarian undertakings which might otherwise have died a-borning.

The energy that entered into many of these causes was heightened by another national attitude: optimism. It was this quality that sustained the European men and women who with heavy hearts left ancestral homes to try their fortunes in a wild and faroff continent. The same trait animated the pioneer farmers confronted by the hardships, loneliness and terrors of the primeval forest, and served also to spur their successors who, though facing less dire conditions, were constantly pitted against both the uncertainties of the weather and the unpredictable demands of the market. When Thomas Jefferson remarked, "I steer my bark with Hope in the head, leaving Fear astern," he spoke for his compatriots. To doubt the future was to confess oneself a failure since the life history of almost any American documented the opposite view. A belief in progress blossomed spontaneously in such a soil.

If this belief made some men tolerant of present abuses in the confident expectation that time would provide the cure, it fired others with an apostolic zeal to hasten the happy day. As a keen observer in the middle of the last century said of his countrymen, "Americans are sanguine enough to believe that no evil is without a remedy, if they could only find it, and they see no good reason why they should not try to find remedies for all the evils of life." Not even fatalism in religion could long withstand the bracing atmosphere of the New World. This quality of optimism sometimes soared to dizzy heights, impelling men to strive for earthly perfection in communistic societies or to prepare to greet the imminent return of Christ.

It attained its most blatant expression, however, in the national addiction to bragging. At bottom, this habit sprang from pride in a country of vast distances and huge elevations plus an illimitable faith in its possibilities of being great as well as big. The American glorified the future in much the same spirit as the European glorified the past, both tending to exalt what they had the most of. And by a simple transition the American went on to speak of expected events as though they had already happened, being prompted perhaps by an urge to compensate for an inner sense of inferiority. This frame of mind led statesmen to cultivate spread-eagle oratory—a style which the *North American Review* in 1858 defined as "a compound of exaggeration, effrontery, bombast, and extravagance, mixed metaphors, platitudes, defiant threats thrown at the world, and irreverent appeals flung at the Supreme Being."

For the same reason the ordinary citizen resorted to hyperbole. In the thinly settled sections this manner of speech went by the name of tall talk, causing the backwoods to be known as a "paradise of puffers." A Frenchman, however, referred to a national, not a regional, trait when he said Americans seemed loath to admit that Christopher Columbus himself had not been an American, and it was an Easterner writing in an Eastern magazine who soberly averred, "It is easier, say the midwives, to come into this world of America . . . than in any other world extant." In business life this indulgent attitude toward truth lent itself to deliberate attempts to defraud, and made the land speculator with his "lithographed mendacity" the natural forerunner of the dishonest stock promoter of later times. Boastfulness is an attribute of youth which greater national maturity has helped to temper. Still the War Department in its manual of behavior for Yankee soldiers in England during the Axis war thought it prudent to admonish them: "Don't show off or brag or bluster."

This facility for overstatement has lent a distinctive quality to American humor. In the United States humor has never been part of a general gaiety of spirit. It has had to break through a crust of life thick with serious purpose. Hence it has had to be boisterous and bold, delighting in exaggeration, incongruities and farcical effects and reaching a grand climax in the practical joke. Out of a comic mood so induced arose such folk heroes as Mike Fink, Paul Bunyan, Pecos Bill and the myth-embroidered Davy Crockett, whose fabulous exploits flourished in oral tradition long before they were reduced to print. In deference to the national sobriety of temperament the most succesful professional humorists have been those who told their yarns while preserving a decorous gravity of expression. . . .

VIII

Just as the American character has undergone modification in the past, so it will doubtless undergo modincation in the future. Nevertheless, certain of its elements seem so deeply rooted as to withstand the erosion of time and circumstance. Of this order are the qualities that made possible the development of the continent, the building of a democratic society and the continuing concern for the welfare of the underprivileged. These are attributes better suited to peace than to war, yet every great crisis has found the people ready to die for their conception of life so that their children might live it. The American character, whatever its shortcomings, abounds in courage, creative energy and resourcefulness, and is bottomed upon the profound conviction that nothing in the world is beyond its power to accomplish.